International Relations and the European Union

THE NEW EUROPEAN UNION SERIES

Series Editors: John Peterson and Helen Wallace

The European Union is both the most successful experiment in modern international cooperation and a daunting analytical challenge to students of politics, economics, history, law, and the social sciences.

The EU of the twenty-first century continues to respond to expanding membership and new policy challenges—particularly in transnational arenas such as climate change, energy security, and crisis management—as well as political and institutional controversies. The result is a truly new European Union that requires continuous reassessment.

THE NEW EUROPEAN UNION SERIES brings together the expertise of leading scholars writing on major aspects of EU politics for an international readership.

The series offers lively, accessible, reader-friendly, research-based textbooks on:

POLICY-MAKING IN THE
EUROPEAN UNION

INTERNATIONAL RELATIONS AND
THE EUROPEAN UNION

THE MEMBER STATES OF THE
EUROPEAN UNION

THE ORIGINS AND EVOLUTION OF
THE EUROPEAN UNION

THE INSTITUTIONS OF THE
EUROPEAN UNION

THE EUROPEAN UNION: HOW
DOES IT WORK?

International Relations and the European Union

SECOND EDITION

Edited by

Christopher Hill and

Michael Smith

OXFORD
UNIVERSITY PRESS

OXFORD
UNIVERSITY PRESS

Great Clarendon Street, Oxford OX2 6DP

Oxford University Press is a department of the University of Oxford.

It furthers the University's objective of excellence in research, scholarship, and education by publishing worldwide in

Oxford New York

Auckland Cape Town Dar es Salaam Hong Kong Karachi

Kuala Lumpur Madrid Melbourne Mexico City Nairobi

New Delhi Shanghai Taipei Toronto

With offices in
Argentina Austria Brazil Chile Czech Republic France Greece Guatemala Hungary Italy Japan Poland Portugal Singapore South Korea Switzerland Thailand Turkey Ukraine Vietnam

Oxford is a registered trade mark of Oxford University Press in the UK and in certain other countries

Published in the United States
by Oxford University Press Inc., New York

© Oxford University Press, 2011

British Library Cataloguing in Publication Data

Data available

Library of Congress Cataloguing in Publication Data

Data available

Typeset by Laserwords Private Limited, Chennai, India
Printed in Great Britain
on acid-free paper by
Ashford Colour Press Limited, Gosport, Hampshire

ISBN 978–0–19–954480–6

10 9 8 7 6 5

▌ OUTLINE CONTENTS

▌ DETAILED CONTENTS

PART I Frameworks

▋ PREFACE

This book is the second edition of a book first published in 2005 in the New European Union series edited by John Peterson and Helen Wallace and inspired by Helen and William Wallace's original *Policy-Making in the European Union* (now in a sixth edition).

The subject is a still a relatively neglected one, even if there has been a greater acknowledgement in recent years of the need for specialists in International Relations (IR) to incorporate EU external relations, and not just the integration process, into their theoretical schemes and empirical pictures of the world. The EU's global presence, economic, political, cultural, and now also military, can no longer be dismissed as a paper tiger. For its part the smaller group of experts on the EU's external relations used rarely to reach out to the wider field, rooting itself in the institutions of European foreign policy making and/or the relevance of foreign policy to the historical enterprise of integration. But it has gradually emerged from its European Studies fortress to overlap with mainstream political science and International Relations. Our aim was from the outset to contribute to this process of opening out, by explicitly bringing the discussion of the EU's world role(s) into a conversation with mainstream IR debates. We attempted to do this by conceptualizing the issues ourselves, as editors, in terms that are as much informed by our experience as teachers of International Relations as by our special knowledge of European affairs. But we have also chosen contributors, for both editions, who are in a position to bridge the two areas of expertise. Contributors were asked to use IR theory and to show how it is always potentially relevant to the EU's international experience. Conversely, all on the team took great care to marry their specialist expertise to the broader theme of the EU as a factor, and a player, in the international system.

As was the case with the first edition, this is a research-led text, aimed at advanced students and scholars, and we hope that readers will find that it contains creative thinking and new, up to date, empirical material, as well as a clear analysis of the central problems at stake. We are immensely grateful to all our colleagues for their insights, hard work, and amiability in what from time to time are the inevitably trying circumstances of putting together a large collective book under significant time pressures.

All the chapters in this second edition have been thoroughly revised, and some are wholly new. Having decided to include chapters on the environment and on the newly emerging powers, we are most grateful to John Vogler, to Stephan Keukeleire, and to Hans Bruyninckx for having risen so effectively to the challenge. We are also particularly grateful to Carmen Gebhard, Amy Verdun, and Maurizio Carbone, who faced the not easy task of following in the footsteps of Simon Nuttall,

Loukas Tsoukalis, and James Mayall in writing chapters on coherence, political economy, and development respectively.

We have received much help from outside as well as from within the team. Our thanks are particularly due to our editors at OUP, Catherine Page and Joanna Hardern, for their wholly efficient support, and to our truly eagle-eyed proofreader, Cathryn Primrose-Mathisen. A huge vote of thanks must also go to Martin Mik of Loughborough University, without whose outstanding work in getting the final manuscript together we should not have made our final deadline—and this despite his being in the last stages of his own doctoral work. Finally, our greatest debt is owed to our families, both of which have been unfailingly supportive despite their own pressing concerns.

▌ LIST OF FIGURES

▌ LIST OF BOXES

▮ LIST OF TABLES

■ LIST OF ABBREVIATIONS

AASM	Associated African States and Madagascar
ACPs	African, Caribbean, and Pacific Countries (of the Lomé/Cotonou system)
AFET	Committee on Foreign Affairs (European Parliament)
AFSJ	Area of Freedom, Security, and Justice
AIDCO	EuropeAid Cooperation Office
ARENA	Advanced Research on the Europeanization of the Nation-State
APEC	Asia–Pacific Economic Cooperation
ASEAN	Association of South East Asian Nations
ASEAN+3	Association of South East Asian Nations + Japan, Korea, China
ASEM	Asia–Europe Meeting
ATTAC	Association for the Taxation of Financial Transactions for the Aid of Citizens
AWG-KP	ad hoc working group (Kyoto Protocol)
AWG-LCA	ad hoc working group on long-term cooperative action
BASIC	Brazil, South Africa, India, and China
BiH	Bosnia Herzegovina
BP	British Petroleum
BRIC	Brazil, Russia, India, and China
CAP	Common Agricultural Policy
CAR	Central African Republic
CARICOM	Caribbean Community
CCAMLR	Convention on the Conservation of Antarctic Marine Living Resources
CCP	Common Commercial Policy
CDM	Clean Development Mechanism
CDU	Christian Democratic Union
CEE	Central and Eastern Europe
CEECs	Central and Eastern European Country
CELAD	Comité Européen de la Lutte Anti-Drogue
CEO	chief executive officer
CEPS	Centre for European Policy Studies (in Brussels)
CESDP	Common European Security and Defence Policy
CET	Common External Tariff
CFCs	chlorofluorocarbons
CFP	Common Fisheries Policy
CFSP	Common Foreign and Security Policy
CGS	Council General Secretariat

CHODs	Chiefs of Defence
CIS	Commonwealth of Independent States
CISA	China, India, and South Africa
CITES	Convention on International Trade in Endangered Species
CivCom	Civilian Crisis Management Committee
CJTFs	Combined Joint Task Forces
CMCO	Civil–Military Coordination
CMEA	Council for Mutual Economic Assistance
CMPD	Crisis Management Planning Department
COD	co-decision
COMECON	Council for Mutual Economic Assistance
COP	Conference of the Parties
COPS	Political and Security Committee
Coreper	Committee of Permanent Representatives
COREU	Correspondant Européen (EPC communications network)
CPA	Cotonou Partnership Agreement
CPCC	Civilian Planning and Conduct Capability
CSCE	Commission on Security and Cooperation in Europe
CSD	Commission on Sustainable Development
CSDP	Common Security and Defence Policy
CSPs	Country Strategy Papers
DAC	Development Assistance Committee
DCAF	Centre for the Democratic Control of Armed Forces (Geneva)
DDR	German Democratic Republic
DEVE	Development Committee (European Parliament)
DG	Directorate-General
DG CLIMA	DG Climate Action
DG DEV	DG Development
DG E	Directorate General of the Council Secretariat (External Relations)
DG E VIII	Directorate for Defence Aspects
DG E IX	Directorate for Civilian Crisis Management
DG ELARG	DG Enlargement
DG RELEX	DG External Relations
DG TREN	DG Transport and Energy
DRC	Democratic Republic of Congo
EAC	European Affairs Committee
EaP	Eastern partnership
EAS	East Asian Summit
EBA	Everything But Arms
EC	European Community

ECB	European Central Bank
ECD	European Consensus on Development
ECHO	The Humanitarian Aid department of the European Commission
ECJ	European Court of Justice
Ecofin	Economic and Financial Affairs Council
ECOWAS	Economic Community of West African States
ECSC	European Coal and Steel Community
ECU	European Currency Unit
EDA	European Defence Agency
EDC	European Defence Community
EDF	European Development Fund
EDTIB	European defence technological and industrial base
EEA	European Economic Area
EEAS	European External Action Service
EEC	European Economic Community
EFP	European foreign policy
EFTA	European Free Trade Association
EMCDAA	European Monitoring Centre for Drugs and Drug Addiction
EMS	European Monetary System
EMU	Economic and Monetary Union
ENP	European Neighbourhood Policy
ENPI	European Neighbourhood and Partnership Instrument
EP	European Parliament
EPAs	Economic Partnership Agreements
EPC	European Political Cooperation
ERM	Exchange Rate Mechanism
ESDI	European Security and Defence Identity
ESDP	European Security and Defence Policy
ESS	European Security Strategy
ETS	Emissions Trading Scheme/System
EU	European Union
EU3	Euro-3 (United Kingdom, France, and Germany)
EUBAM	European Union Border Assistance Mission
EUFOR	European Union Force
EUISS	European Union Institute for Security Studies
EULEX	European Union rule of law mission in Kosovo
EUMC	European Union Military Committee
EUMS	European Union Military Staff
EU NAVFOR	European Union naval force Somalia
EUPM	European Union Police Mission

EURATOM	European Atomic Energy Community
Eurocorps	Strasbourg-based force for the EU and the Atlantic Alliance
Eurodac	European Dactyloscopy (a database of fingerprints of applicants for asylum and Ilegal immigrants found within the EU)
Eurojust	European Judicial Office (European network of judicial authorities)
Europol	European Police Office
EUSRs	EU Special Representatives
FAC	Foreign Affairs Council
FAO	Food and Agriculture Organization
FDI	Foreign Direct Investment
FORNET	European Foreign Policy Research Network
FP	foreign policy
FPA	foreign policy analysis
FRIDE	Fundación para las Relaciones Internacionales y el Diálogo Exterior
Frontex	European Agency for the Management of Operational Cooperation at the External Borders of the Member States of the European Union
FSC	Foreign Sales Corporation
FYROM	Former Yugoslav Republic of Macedonia
G2	USA and China
G7	Group of Seven (Canada, France, Germany, Italy, Japan, UK, USA)
G8	Group of Seven plus Russia
G8+5/G13	Group of Eight plus China, India, Brazil, Mexico, and South Africa
G20	Argentina, Australia, Brazil, Canada, China, France, Germany, India, Indonesia, Italy, Japan, Mexico, Russia, Saudi Arabia, South Africa, South Korea, Turkey, UK, USA, plus the EU as 20th member
G22	a group of developing countries
G77	Group of 77
GAERC	General Affairs and External Relations Council
GARNET	Network of Excellence on Global Governance, Regionalisation, and Regulation
GATS	General Agreement on Trade in Services
GATT	General Agreement on Tariffs and Trade
GCC	Gulf Cooperation Council
GDP	gross domestic product
GHG	greenhouse gas
GMO	genetically modified organism
GNI	gross national income
GPE	global political economy
GSP	generalized system of preferences
HG 2010	headline goal 2010
HHG	Helsinki headline goal

HR-CFSP	High Representative for the Common Foreign and Security Policy
HR/HRFASP	High Representative of the European Union for Foreign Affairs and Security Policy (under the Lisbon Treaty)
HR-[/SG]	High Representative Secretary General (of the Council)
HR/VP	High Representative/Vice President
IAEA	International Atomic Energy Agency
IBSA	India, Brazil, South Africa
ICTY	International Criminal Tribunal for the former Yugoslavia
IFRI	French Institute for International Relations
IGC	intergovernmental conference
IISS	International Institute for Strategic Studies
IMF	International Monetary Fund
INTA	Committee on International Trade (European Parliament)
IO	international organization
IPCC	Intergovernmental Panel on Climate Change
IPE	international political economy
IR	International Relations
ISIS	International Security Information Service
ISO	International Organization for Standardization
JHA	Justice and Home Affairs
JI	joint implementation
JLS	Justice, Freedom, and Security
KFOR	Kosovo Forces (NATO)
LAC	Latin America and the Caribbean countries
LDCs	least developed countries
LRTAP	Convention on Long-Range Trans-boundary Air Pollution
MDGs	millennium development goals
ME	Middle East
MEP	Member of the European Parliament
Mercosur	Common Market of the Southern Cone (Argentina, Brazil, Paraguay, and Uruguay)
MERCURY	academic consortium on EU's contribution to multilateralism
MILREPS	military representatives
MRA	mutual recognition agreement
NATO	North Atlantic Treaty Organization
NAFTA	North American Free Trade Agreement
NEPAD	New Economic Partnership for Africa's Development
NGO	non-governmental organization
NICs	newly industrialized countries
NIEO	new international economic order
NIPs	National Indicative Programmes

NSAs	non-state actors
NTA	New Transatlantic Agenda
OAS	Organization of American States
OCT	Overseas Countries and Territories
ODA	official development assistance
OECD	Organisation for Economic Co-operation and Development
OHQ	operational headquarters
OpCen	European Union Operations Centre
OPEC	Organization of Petroleum Exporting Countries
OSCE	Organization for Security and Cooperation in Europe
PCA	Partnership and Cooperation Agreement
PCD	Policy Coherence for Development
Phare	Pologne–Hongrie aide à la reconstruction économique
PIC	prior informed consent
PJHQ	Permanent Joint Headquarters
PNR	Passenger Name Record
PoCo	(European) political cooperation (EPC)
POPs	persistent organic pollutants
PPP	purchasing power parity
PSC	Political and Security Committee
PU	Policy Unit
QMV	qualified majority voting
R&D	research and development
REDD	(United Nations Collaborative Programme on) Reducing Emissions from Deforestation and Forest Degradation in Developing Countries
REIO	Regional Economic Integration Organization
Relex	external relations
RIC	Russia, India, and China
SAA	stabilization and association agreements
SAARC	South Asian Association for Regional Cooperation
SADC	Southern African Development Community
SAP	stabilization and association process (in the Balkans)
SCO	Shanghai Cooperation Organization
SCR	Common Service for External Relations
SEA	Single European Act
SIS	Schengen Information System
SIS II	Schengen Information System II
SitCen	Joint Situation Centre (in the European Council Secretariat)
SMP	single market programme
SWIFT	Society for Worldwide Interbank Financial Telecommunication

TACIS	Technical Assistance for the CIS
TAD	Transatlantic Declaration
TBR	Trade Barriers Regulation
TCA	Trade and Cooperation Agreement
TDI	Trade Defence Instruments
TEC	Transatlantic Economic Council
TEP	Transatlantic Economic Partnership
TEPSA	Trans European Policy Studies Association
TEU	Treaty on European Union
TFEU	Treaty on the Functioning of the European Union
ToA	Treaty of Amsterdam
TREVI	Terrorisme, Radicalisme, Extrémisme et Violence Internationale (EPC working group)
TRIPS	trade-related aspects of intellectual property rights
TRNC	Turkish Republic of Northern Cyprus
UHRFA	Union High Representative for Foreign Affairs and Security Policy
UK	United Kingdom
UN	United Nations
UNCED	United Nations Conference on Environment and Development
UNCHE	United Nations Conference on the Human Environment
UNEP	United Nations Environment Programme
UNESCO	United Nations Educational, Scientific, and Cultural Organization
UNFCCC	United Nations Framework Convention on Climate Change
UNSC	United Nations Security Council
US/USA	United States of America
USSR	Union of Soviet Socialist Republics
USTR	United States Trade Representative
UV	unanimous voting
VAT	value added tax
VIS	Visa Information System
WB	World Bank
WEU	Western European Union
WMD	weapons of mass destruction
WSSD	World Summit on Sustainable Development
WTO	World Trade Organization

▌ LIST OF CONTRIBUTORS

FILIPPO ANDREATTA	Università degli Studi di Parma
HANS BRUYNINCKX	Katholieke Universiteit Leuven
MAURIZIO CARBONE	University of Glasgow
GEOFFREY EDWARDS	University of Cambridge
CARMEN GEBHARD	Institute of Advanced Studies, Vienna, Department of Political Science
CHRISTOPHER HILL	University of Cambridge
JOLYON HOWORTH	Yale University
STEPHAN KEUKELEIRE	Katholieke Universiteit Leuven
ANDREW LINKLATER	University of Wales, Aberystwyth
CHRISTOPHER LORD	ARENA, University of Oslo
SOPHIE MEUNIER	Princeton University
KALYPSO NICOLAÏDIS	University of Oxford
WYN REES	University of Nottingham
KAREN E. SMITH	London School of Economics and Political Science
MICHAEL E. SMITH	University of St. Andrews
MICHAEL SMITH	Loughborough University
REBECCA STEFFENSON	DePaul University, Chicago
SOPHIE VANHOONACKER	University of Maastricht
AMY VERDUN	University of Victoria, British Columbia
JOHN VOGLER	Keele University
REUBEN WONG	National University of Singapore

▌ EDITORS' NOTE

Readers should note that most references in the text are to the consolidated list of References at the end of the book. There are, however, a few which refer to the Further Reading sections at the end of each chapter.

It may also be worth pointing out that International Relations (uppercase) refers to the academic subject, and to its literature, whereas international relations (lower case) refers to the actual world of interaction between states, peoples, organizations and individuals.

New to this Edition:

- A chapter offeringa detailed examination of the EU's relationship with 'The New Emerging Powers' including China, India, and Russia.

- A chapter on 'Energy and the Environment' exploring the possibility for EU leadership in these important policy areas.

- All chapters have been revised to take in the latest developments affecting the EU's external relations including the ratification of the Lisbon Treaty and the consequences of the global financial crisis.

PART I

Frameworks

CHAPTER 1

International Relations and the European Union: Themes and Issues

Christopher Hill and Michael Smith

▌ Summary

The European Union has increasingly been studied as an international actor, but it is important to make the linkage between the Union's internal processes of integration and policy making and the development of international relations more generally. This means that established concepts and frameworks in international relations can be brought together with the approaches from comparative politics and public policy that have characterized study of the EU. In this way, the development of the EU as a system of international relations in itself can be related analytically to the place it occupies in the processes of international relations, and to its position as a 'power' in the international arena. Such an analysis facilitates an understanding both of the ways in which the EU produces international action and of the ways in which the international dimension enters into EU policy making, and can help in the identification of key elements of change in the EU's international position.

Introduction

The EU has increasingly been studied as a particular kind of international actor, and during the years since the end of the Cold War there has been a substantial growth of attention to the ways in which the EU's international policies are made and pursued (Allen and Smith 1990; Allen 1998; Bretherton and Vogler 1999, 2006; Ginsberg 2001, 2007; White 2001; H. Smith 2002; M.E. Smith 2003; K. Smith, 2004, 2008; Keukeleire and MacNaughtan, 2008; Telò, 2007, 2009). Such a sustained and substantial interest reflects both the empirical importance of the EU in the international arena and the analytical challenge of dealing with what is a distinctive if not unique type of internationally acting body. Empirically, the EU can be seen as one of the world's two economic 'superpowers', and increasingly a significant influence in the realms of international diplomacy, 'soft security', and broader world order. Analytically, the Union poses major challenges by virtue of its status as something more than an intergovernmental organization but less than a fully fledged European 'state' (Wallace 1983, 2005). Not surprisingly, much of the attention paid to the EU in the international arena has thus consisted of charting the development of this 'partial superpower' and evaluating the ways in which it does or does not perform important 'state functions' in the changing world order (see the references cited above, plus Carlsnaes, Sjursen and White 2004; Elgström and Smith, 2006).

Such a focus raises a number of important issues, most of which are touched upon later in this chapter. Yet this volume widens the agent-centred perspective of 'the EU as a global actor' to the more systemic 'international relations and the EU'. What does this mean? In part it refers to the fact that member states do still conduct residual foreign relations among themselves, as with Greek–German tensions in 2010 over Greek debts and German history, or various difficulties involving Hungary, Romania, and Slovakia over ethnic minorities. This, however, is not our principal concern. We are mainly interested in the number of respects in which the EU constitutes part of the international/global system, and in which it can be studied through the lenses of academic International Relations (IR). This does not rule out consideration of the EU's credentials as an international/global actor; rather it connects the issue of 'actorness' to the broader study of IR and of international policy making. What we are explicitly concerned to do is to counter the tendency to assume that the EU's external behaviour can be understood through a combination of understanding the EU's *sui generis* qualities and a reliance on the tools of comparative politics. Both are important, with the latter providing an indispensable opening to the internal dynamics of the Union and its member states; but without an understanding of the international, and its distinctive features, the analysis is bound to be superficial.

Looking at the EU's place in international relations, seen from the outside as it were, involves a new take on a number of established international relations concepts. Ideas such as those of balance of power, multipolarity, world system, and globalization are relevant to understanding the contexts in which the European Union has reflected and affected major forces and changes in international relations. The EU may be interpreted in very different ways according to which dominant concept—or indeed, underlying paradigm—we employ. It may be seen as a power, a centre of gravity, a model, a magnet, a regime, and a mere arena, or various combinations of these. But whichever interpretation is favoured, this volume argues that we need to combine an understanding of the EU's internal character with an analysis of its international situation. The very conception of international 'actorness' depends on bringing 'inside' and 'outside' into a relationship with each other, just as agents and structures are mutually dependent (Wendt 1987, 1992, 1999; Hill 2003). Thus *International Relations and the European Union* is about both the place of Europe in the world and the way the world contributes to the shaping of Europe. At the same time, it is about the place—actual and appropriate—of the EU in the academic subject of International Relations.

An integrated focus of this kind has not been easy for the two 'camps' that have been interested in the European integration project. On the one hand, as we have noted, the study of European integration has tended to emphasize the distinctive nature of the project, and thus inevitably to play down the ways in which it has been part of the broader development of international order, subject to analysis in terms of IR theory and method. On the other hand, the literature of IR has not found it easy to accommodate the EU fully in its study of the international system, its processes, and its evolution, although there have been notable efforts in the area of foreign policy analysis (White 2001; Carlsnaes, Sjursen and White 2004) and in analyses of identity and order (Kelstrup and Williams 2000). Some of the most sustained study has come from those interested in regionalization and regionalism (Telò 2007), but this has tended to neglect the ways in which the EU reaches the parts that other forms of regionalism do not—in particular through the developing capacity to formulate and implement a 'European foreign policy'. Perhaps inevitably in the aftermath of the Cold War, the EU has been studied as a particular form of 'security community' or a zone of peace (Kelstrup and Williams 2000: Schimmelfennig 2003); whilst this captures some of the ways in which European integration has shifted expectations among its member states and societies, it does not fully address the ways in which the EU is more than simply an arena for the shaping of national expectations and policies. Alongside this, there has also been renewed attention to the ways in which the EU plays into the broader European order (Croft *et al.* 1999; Gärtner, Hyde-Price, and Reiter 2001; Niblett and Wallace 2001), but this is only slowly being extended into the study of the EU's power to shape processes and outcomes in the IR sense within the 'new Europe' (works beginning to change this are Schimmelfennig and Seidelmeier 2005, Zielonka 2006, and M. Smith 2007). Whilst we do not claim to have remedied all of these shortcomings or areas of underdevelopment, the attempt to address them is central to the focus of this volume.

Assumptions

In pursuing the analytical focus outlined above, we make a number of initial assumptions, three of them substantive and three methodological. At this point they are merely asserted, so as to help render the huge universe of data and approaches more comprehensible. We will return to them in Chapter 19 when we present our overview of the findings in this volume.

Substantive assumptions

Our first set of assumptions is substantive, in the sense that it deals with the forces affecting the development and the impact of the EU's international relations. The assumptions are as follows:

1. *The EU matters in the world and the world matters to it.* The political simplicities by which some scorn the total ineffectiveness of Europe, and a smaller number advocate a form of Euro-isolationism, are set aside. The interplay between the EU and the international system as a whole is one of the big issues of modern international relations, given that the former represents the collective weight of 27 of the richest countries on the planet and creates an extensive demand for its foreign policy actions. Accordingly, international outcomes involving the EU are shaped by both global and domestic structures, even if the latter refer ambiguously both to trans-European and intra-state factors.

2. *EU positions, decisions, and actions in the world are produced as the result of often complex interactions in a multilevel system,* involving the member states singly and collectively, as well as the common institutions. The 'three pillars' of the Treaty on European Union (pillar 1: the European (economic) Community; pillar 2: Common Foreign and Security Policy; pillar 3: justice and home affairs) in principle were merged as a result of the Treaty of Lisbon's conferral of legal personality on the Union (as opposed to the European Community) but there are still important differences between the supranational aspects of the Union's functioning and the intergovernmental dimension, which is still dominant in foreign and security policy. In consequence there still exists in practice what was termed for two decades after Maastricht 'cross-pillar activity', viz. activities that required harmonization not just between the different institutions of the EU but also between different modes of decision making. Yet even the pillars metaphor did not provide a complete representation of what may be termed the 'European foreign policy system', since it did not allow for the persistence of independent national foreign policies, which are a critical part of the web of activity that entangles 27 member states, the Commission, the Council Secretariat, the Parliament, and

occasionally the Court. Some would characterize this regular pattern of inter-action as 'multilevel *governance*', but we doubt that it is yet dense or homoge-neous enough to deserve such an encomium.

3. *The process of EU action and reflection internationally is dynamic, and often reflexive, but not always progressive or cumulative.* There has been a self-con-scious attempt to develop a European foreign policy since the early 1970s, while the 'ratchet' mechanism—whereby each codification or treaty revi-sion provides for further revision at a not-too-distant interval—has ensured constant movement. The progressive enlargement of the EC/EU has also brought new subjects regularly onto the foreign policy agenda and widened its geographical scope, and the widening scope of the 'internal' integration process has produced new areas of international engagement, for example in monetary or environmental policy. When combined with the dynamic but often ambiguous development of processes such as globalization or region-alization in the world arena, or with the shifting balance of global power, it is clear that the movement of 'European foreign policy' and the broader inter-national relations of the EU can only be understood as part of a broader set of changes.

Methodological assumptions

Our second set of assumptions is methodological: that is to say, assumptions that we make about the components of an effective analysis of the EU's international relations, and about the aspects of IR theory that are relevant to such an analysis. They are as follows:

1. *An historical understanding of the origins of EU international relations is essen-tial,* as they have highly particular characteristics and are still affected by readings of the past. What is more, given that this is a highly dynamic set of processes (see above), it is even less susceptible to synchronic generalization than other areas of international politics. Since there are different and com-peting narratives of the ways in which the EU's international relations have been developed and understood, it is important for analysis to reflect this plu-rality of 'histories'.

2. *Both ideas and material factors have shaped the development of the EU's interna-tional relations, and will continue to shape them in the future.* From the outset, there has been a dynamic relationship between processes of practical policy formation and interaction and those of identity formation and role develop-ment. Few commentators would fully align themselves with either a mate-rialist or an ideational set of assumptions. Thus both need to be taken into account by attempts to explain and understand the subject, as indeed do his-torical, even historicist, approaches.

3. *It follows that a methodological pluralism is required when seeking to explain and understand the EU's international relations.* No one approach, whether broad-brush as in realist, rationalist, and constructivist, or more specific, as in geo-politics, intergovernmentalism, or 'expectations', comes near being adequate by itself. The usual problems then arise of how to relate diverse, and possibly incommensurable, middle-range theories to each other, but these are inevitable in any attempt to do justice to complexity.

As can be seen from the two sets of assumptions outlined above, we are committed to a view of the EU's international relations that is essentially problem-focused, deploying an eclectic mix of evidence and methods in an attempt to produce a rounded understanding of what is going on and how it might develop. This does not mean, however, that we do not have a point of view. Our standpoint can be summarized in terms of three complementary perspectives on the EU's international relations, outlined in the following section. We contend that together they provide a rounded picture of the EU's place in the international system.

Three perspectives on international relations and the EU

The three key perspectives that we identify are:

- the EU as a *subsystem* of international relations, by which we mean the way in which it has dealt with its internal 'foreign' relations, but also its capacity to generate external collective action;
- the EU as part of the wider *processes* of international relations, a term that refers to the legal, institutional, and political mechanisms through which the problems of international conflict and/or political economy are addressed;
- and the EU as a major *power* impacting upon contemporary international relations, in which category we want to be able to assess the extent to which the EU shapes its external environment, is perceived by other actors as so doing, and occupies a certain position in the international hierarchy of power.

In the terms we have already used, these perspectives are both substantive (i.e. they enable us to describe key areas of the EU's international relations) and methodological (i.e. they enable us to think more clearly about the approaches in IR that most help us to analyse and evaluate the EU's international relations). The chapters in this volume focus on these three perspectives, albeit in varying combinations of emphasis and detail. They define the EU's international existence and impact, and they help us to think about its role in a variety of global contexts. Each is explained further below.

The EU as a subsystem of international relations

Under this heading, we are interested in three distinct issues. The first is the way in which the EU has dealt with *its own international relations* internally. This is not a contradiction in terms. Notwithstanding the view that the EC was initially and primarily a set of economic bargains, we hold to the position that it arose out of the need to resolve the war problem in Europe, and in particular the age-old Franco-German antagonism. It was thus, at least in one key respect, an inward-looking foreign policy device. What is more, relations between member states did not suddenly become like those between provinces overnight—and may not be so even now. French suspicion of Germany endured up to the point where Mitterrand (as well as Thatcher) attempted to prevent unification in 1989–90, while Italy pursued a hostile diplomatic campaign against the German wish in the 1990s to get a permanent seat on the UN Security Council. Tensions remain in both Berlin and Rome as a result of the ensuing stalemate.

Nonetheless, there is no denying that there are much stricter limits on the tactics that member states are prepared to use against each other than on those between any random pairing of states in international relations. The Franco-German relationship has become a miracle of pacification and institutionalization, almost at the level of the special Benelux arrangements. Britain and Ireland, likewise, have been helped to advance their difficult relationship by their common membership of the EU. These are among the most advanced 'democratic dyads' in the terms made familiar by the literature on the 'democratic peace', and it might be argued that this reflects the benign influence of treaty-based 'civilizing processes' (see Linklater's arguments in Chapter 18 below). 'Europeanization' is not the only process at work here, however: the USA has been a key player in Anglo-Irish cooperation, and relations between the Scandinavian countries have become regularized independently of EU involvement. The broader impact of the 'democratic peace', and of geopolitical settlements, may thus be just as powerful as explanations of the stable, civil diplomacy on view as is the impact of the treaties. Yet the desire of the brittle states of the ex-Warsaw Pact to join the EU, on political as well as economic grounds, shows how the latter is seen as a 'safe harbour'—a distinctive stable region where the most dangerous elements of international relationships appear to have been suspended for the duration. In this sense the 'domestic' international relations of the Union remain critical to its own destiny and to its functions as a subsystem of the wider international order (Hurrell 2007, 249–54; M. Smith 2007).

Second, we are interested in the way in which the EU can be considered as a set of international institutions and arrangements within which *the interests and preferences of member states and other actors can be coordinated for international purposes*. This is the problem of collective action and policy formation in relation to the outside world. It is an essential part of our framework because it draws attention to the linkages between internal dynamics and external activity. External demands can stimulate internal cohesion as well as complicate it. Conversely, internal socialization can produce increased international actorness over time, just as unpredictable upheavals inside key states can disrupt existing patterns of joint action. Key to this area is the ways in which the preferences of EU member states are articulated and the ways in which they interact, but outcomes are not only determined by procedures. The process of collective external policy formation is not an insulated one; it is penetrated or perforated by the broader activities and institutional development of the EU, and it is embedded within a variety of international/global frameworks. It is thus important not only to identify the characteristic processes of decision making and implementation, but also to address the wider questions of legitimacy and identity. Where are the boundaries of actual and appropriate inclusion and exclusion? Turkey poses this very question at the moment in the sharpest form in relation to its potential membership of the Union. Lastly, there is a convergence–divergence problem to be addressed in that the differing preferences and 'weights' of the component parts of the EU's system of IR make common action often unpredictable and not straightforwardly progressive.

There is a level-of-analysis issue to be explored here, since it might be argued that the EU—and thus its subsystem of IR—is part of an emerging system of multilevel governance in the global arena. How does EU external policy making fit in with that of other institutions in which member states may also participate, such as the UN, the WTO, or the G8? Is European cooperation central to the effective workings of multilateralism more generally? This issue is central to the chapters in Part III of this volume, dealing with the activities and impact of the EU in relation to other actors.

Third, we are interested in *the ideas that bind the EU member states together.* Not only is there a justifiable pride in the EU's achievement in having solved the centuries-old problem of war in Western Europe, but there is also a strong emphasis on the EU's evolving approach to IR on the ideational quality of the EU's international role. This involves the development of the EU's principles and a view of its contribution to 'international society'. As Ian Manners has argued, what the EU is matters as least as much as what it does, in terms of the impact on others (Manners 2002, 2006; Lucarelli and Manners 2006). Through both action and example, the EU can help to influence what is regarded as 'normal' and acceptable in international relations (Whitman 2010). In terms of political practice, the point of entry into this set of issues is the extent to which the EU might promulgate an 'ethical foreign policy' (Aggestam 2008). There is a need to link the EU's system of IR into broader debates about issues such as intervention and human rights within the IR literature, whilst not forgetting the distinctive aspects of the EU, viz. intense trans-governmentalism, 'civilian power', the legalization of EU structures and processes, and responsibility for the post-Cold War European security order (Sjursen 2007). The European heritage, beyond the EU itself, is also relevant here: the impact of history; the ambivalent relations between Europe and the developing world; the temptation to fall back on a civilizational view of European identity in the face of external (and internal) challenges; the continuing role of national foreign and development policies. What is more, there is a 'second image reversed' factor to take into account: the extent to which participation in international relations feeds back to effect changes in the EU's own political system—fostering or hindering integration, constituting common identity, and determining the distribution of resources. Various kinds of interference, intervention, complication, or mere noise may occur in the internal affairs of the EU and member states as a consequence of international relations. For the most part this will affect the capacity to generate collective action, but it may also act directly on the complex political, social, and intellectual processes by which 'Europe' comes to decide on what in the world it does stand for.

The EU and the processes of international relations

From the outset, the European project has been intimately related to the processes of international relations, by which we mean the common mechanisms, formal and informal, through which international problems are confronted. During the Cold War, European integration can be seen as performing a vital role in the stabilization of the West, and in forming the basis for a 'Europe between the superpowers', a conception of the continent that emphasizes its dual role both as a stake and as a participant in the superpower confrontation (DePorte 1987). This duality of status was not simply a matter of high politics and security, although that was not absent: the EEC played a vital role in the evolution of the political economy of the Western Alliance. The process of détente during the 1960s and 1970s created a new context for the European project, one in which it continued to play a central shaping role; in the 'Helsinki' process after 1975, the position of the EEC and the evolution of European Political Cooperation were of increasing significance, and the ways in which the development of the European political economy took place during the 1970s and 1980s had a strong shaping influence both on the Atlantic Alliance and on emerging East–West relations in Europe (a matter of some concern to successive Washington administrations) (Nuttall 1992; Sjursen 2003, 135–46).

From the mid 1980s onwards, it became part of conventional wisdom that the EC and then the EU were an emerging 'economic superpower' and that this had implications for the roles played by the Europeans (both nationally and collectively) within the changing international order. Arguably, the success of the EC helped to undermine the faith of the population of Eastern Europe in the welfare and security provided by COMECON and the Warsaw Pact, making possible the reunification of Europe in 1989. During the current period, it is clear that the EU is intimately related to the co-existing and intersecting processes of globalization and regionalization, that it plays a key role in a variety of inter-regional contexts, and that it is increasingly (and literally) a force to be reckoned with in the matter of international security relations, despite its continuing limitations.

It is clear that the EU's international activity reflects a consistent search for settled frameworks within which to define and pursue international relationships. The EU (as noted in respect of other issues) has been a relentless generator of strategies and proposals for framework agreements, both in terms of political economy and in terms (more recently) of political/security issues. Some might link at least part of this to the EU's character as a 'trading state', seeking a stable and predictable environment in which to pursue its civilian activities (and thus not developing to a high degree the capacity to deal with the unexpected and the fluid). The EU can be seen as expressing a fundamentally conservative bias in its approach to international relations, and as having a profound desire to systematize or pigeonhole its growing set of relationships (M. Smith 2004a).

This rough sketch naturally raises as many questions as it answers. If the EU is increasingly prominent, central, and influential, exactly *how* has that come about and why are there still evident gaps in its capacity to shape its external environment? We shall address some of the issues arising from these questions in the third part of this chapter, but here the key focus is on the nature of the EU's activities and their links to the major global issues of the contemporary era. We are interested in four issues arising from a focus on the EU's involvement in the process of international relations.

First, we ask how the EU comes into contact with these issues, how it contributes (differentially) to their pursuit, treatment, and resolution, and how it projects 'European' interests as defined by the EU's system of international relations in interaction with the international environment. In light of what has already been said about the complexity of the EU's internal processes, we expect an answer to this question to depend on the specific issue area in which the EU was engaged, and on the fluctuating constellation of preferences among the Union's member states and other institutions.

Second, we explore the nature of the EU's capabilities when participating in and shaping contemporary international processes. Here the questions to be asked overlap with those we shall address when considering the EU as a 'power' (see below), but they relate sharply to its capacity to enter into the process of international relations as well as to its attainment of a particular international position or impact. In particular, how does the EU muster 'hard' and 'soft' power, the 'capacity to act' in specific and diverse issue areas, and the ability to regulate or to set common standards? There has been considerable discussion in both the European integration and the IR literature about exactly what the EU brings to the international table, and studies of its resources have identified a number of problems relating to the EU's negotiating capacity and its 'mobilization capacity' relative to the resources available to and used by its member states. There is, though, significant evidence that the EU's institutional resources and its ability to act within key international organizations, especially in the global political economy, have strengthened and broadened over time.

Third, we enquire into the problems of status and legitimacy confronted by the EU when participating in the processes of international relations. What is the EU's status within international organizations and institutions, how are its roles affected by participation in the various forms of global governance, and how can EU collective action be sustained in the face of external resistance or temptation? Because of the multilayered nature of EU policy making, and its engagement in processes of multilevel governance within the global arena, it is clear that the potential for member state defections or deviations, or for the emergence of shifting coalitions within the Union itself, can be a key issue, affecting its capacity to maintain common positions or convey a consistent message. It has also produced what the international lawyers call 'mixity', or agreements with third parties that contain—confusingly—elements of both the Community method and intergovernmentalism. This inevitably links with issues of credibility and the ability to match external expectations.

Finally, we explore what is (and what should be) the extent of EU involvement relative to other actors. This is a matter of intense interest and debate within the EU, but also more broadly in the international arena and international institutions. How much can the EU hope to aggregate the interests of its members, to express the 'European interest' and also to displace the activities of other international bodies such as the OSCE, NATO and the like? Is it possible to identify the EU's distinctive (inter)'national interests'? The Union exists in a 'multi-institutional' context, where there are always alternative channels for the pursuit of national or 'European' policies. Indeed, it is itself the embodiment of the principle of multilateralism, which it has come close to turning into a foreign policy doctrine (Lazarou *et al.* 2010). This creates dilemmas in terms of the choices between self-regarding EU regionalism and the willingness to embrace other partners and fora. Furthermore, the EU has powerful competitors for international influence and status, most obviously the USA at the global level but others in specific regions or sectors of activity. Most analysts would describe the EU–USA contest as balanced in some areas (political economy in particular) but massively unbalanced in others (especially matters of 'hard security'). Equally, however, we need to be alert to the constantly evolving terms and conditions of the polyhedric competition between the EU, the USA, and the other key competitors, notably the BRICs (Brazil, Russia, India, and China, discussed in Chapter 16).

The focus here is thus very directly on the EU as an international actor—and interactor—within the current international arena, and on the attempt to evaluate its effectiveness, not only in taking action but also in participating in, or competing with, other available international structures. We should be able to arrive at some broad estimate of the extent to which the EU achieves effectiveness or participation, but we must also be aware of the ways in which this feeds through into perceptions of the EU as a 'power' in international relations (see below) and into problems of world order more broadly defined. We should also be sensitive to the ways in which effectiveness is inevitably uneven, patchy, and unpredictable, given the conditional legitimacy and the underdeveloped policy instruments in a number of key areas of the EU's makeup.

The EU as a power in international relations

The notion of the EU as a 'power' is particularly related to the impact of the EU on the international arena and on other actors. We have already discussed the notion of the EU's power resources and the issues that arise from their mobilization or targeting. Now we need to explore the way in which the EU impacts on the 'shape' of the global arena, on specific targets in terms of external groupings or actors, and on the substance of key issues. We take the basic position that in international relations the impact of particular structures or groupings is conditioned by a number of critical variables, many of which have been touched upon already. They include: the establishment of collective preferences and understandings; the pursuit of international status and legitimacy; the development of regional and inter-regional frameworks for the pursuit of international aims; the deployment of appropriate instruments within this set of conditions; the external perception of policies and positions; the historical and geopolitical setting; and the 'distance' and intensity of international relationships. In respect of the EU and its international relations, a number of key features stand out, and will need to be explored or measured.

There is a persistent tension between the desire to systematize and work within settled multilateral frameworks on the one hand, and the growing expectations of EU intervention on the other—both complicated by the persisting fluidity of inter-national order. This tension puts increased pressure on the EU and underlines the problems of attention and resource allocation pointed to earlier. It is of course pos-sible to resolve this tension in the direction of increased EU collective capacity but it is also quite possible that it will be resolved in favour of withdrawal from chal-lenging areas of international relations in the wake of traumatic failures.

The issues noted above also relate strongly to issues of 'European identity' and the understandings that the EU and its member states have of its international role (Elgström and Smith 2006). Is it an inward-looking and self-referential security community, constructed not only by its institutions but also by the interactions and discourses within them? Or is it the prototype of a new form of international order founded on the management of large-scale complex systems both in the political/ economic and the political/security domains?

These factors say something about the orientation of EU collective action (as well as raising questions about the extent to which the EU can or should capture the international preferences and actions of its member states and other groupings or actors). They also raise issues about impact—that is to say, about the ways in which the EU wishes to impress itself on regional and world order, the extent to which it then gets its own way, and thus the extent to which it is a force for change or consolidation.

When it comes to impact, the following issues can be identified. First, how does the EU's impact relate to the resources deployed, to its stated preferences, and to the required levels of collective action and solidarity? In principle, given the EU's propensity for explicit statements of strategy noted above, these elements can be measured and a comparison made between expected and actual performance in specific theatres of operation (for example, the Asia-Pacific, or global environmental issues). Second, how is the impact of the EU viewed by the 'recipients' of EU actions? One of the paradoxes of the EU's international role is that often it appears very much more impressive to the outsider than to the insider (or perhaps to the relatively distant rather than the intimately involved, since it is not always apparent that the USA is impressed). The actual or potential gap between understandings about the EU's international performance and impact is likely to be implicated in more general estimates of the EU's success or failure in international relations.

This links with a further question: How can we deal with variable impact across a number of different dimensions of activity? We have already seen that the EU's participation and effectiveness are uneven and patchy, and this clearly implies that impact will also be uneven and patchy. We do need to remember, though, that the impact of 'absence' can be as important as the impact of 'presence' (US foreign policy in the 20th century, with its fluctuating balance between isolationism and internationalism, shows ample evidence of this).

Finally, how far is the EU's conception of world order, and in particular the relationship between order in the near neighbourhood and order more broadly defined, beginning to have a real impact? The picture is complicated, given that there are several European versions of international order available: a 'stabilization of the near neighbourhood' model, an 'inter-regional' model involving competition as well as collaboration, a 'global values' model involving the elevation of global institutions and norms, and the 'conservative trading state' model noted above. The impact of the EU's changing membership is felt here, for example in the influence of Polish accession on relations with both Russia and the USA. A more theoretical way of looking at the EU's wavering in approach to international order is to see it pulled between a rational 'costs and risks' approach, a more reflexive concern with 'self-actualization', and a third emphasis on exporting the EU 'model'.

It is thus far from clear that the EU has a unified view of the model of world order it would wish to bring about, despite the 2003 European Security Strategy adding a specification of security goals to its established economic interests. This is one of the most serious problems of the EU's international relations. Moreover, the complexities of the post-Cold War period have made it genuinely uncertain as to whether the EU should aim to be itself a major world power, or will have to settle for being a constellation of like-minded nation states, acting in broadly the same direction, and perhaps representing a pole of attraction in an emerging multipolar system. The elements of 'can' and 'should' in this discussion are difficult to disentangle, as will be evident in all the specialized chapters that follow.

Structure of this volume

As noted above, in constructing this volume we have invited contributions from those who broadly share the substantive and methodological assumptions we have made—as outlined above. We have also asked contributors to take into account the three perspectives we have delineated as being important for an understanding of the EU's role in international relations (the EU as a subsystem of international relations, the EU and processes of international relations, and the EU as a 'power' in international relations). We hold that between them, these three ways of approaching the subject help us to account for the multiple roles of the EU in the world, and their continual evolution. None of the three has become less important since our first edition in 2005. Furthermore, we have not imposed a straitjacket on individual contributors: the balance between substantive and methodological issues, and the extent to which the three perspectives are employed, have been for each of them to decide individually, reflecting the fundamental pluralism of our approach.

The organization of the book as a whole has changed to the extent necessary to reflect changes in the agenda of world politics in recent years. Accordingly, we have substituted a chapter on relations with the BRICs for an overview of inter-regional relations, and we have added a new chapter on the EU and environmental issues. All remaining chapters have been significantly updated and rewritten, in some cases by different authors, as personal commitments have changed. In particular, the chapter on enlargement has had to take account of important developments in 'neighbourhood policy', while that on the EU and development has moved from a broadly historical to a more contemporary focus. The significant developments in the ESDP have attracted attention in various places, especially in Chapter 9, while the significance (or otherwise) of the foreign policy innovations of the Treaty of Lisbon forms a thread that runs throughout the book.

The 19 chapters are grouped into four parts. Part I, including this chapter, deals with the broad framework for understanding the EU's international relations. In this chapter, we have set out a broad framework for analysis, inevitably generating more questions than answers. In Chapter 2, Filippo Andreatta focuses explicitly on theory and methodology, asking how International Relations theory can inform our study of the EU's international relations, and indicating some of the key ways in which that theory has to be adapted for the study of this area. Chapter 3, by Geoffrey Edwards, focuses on the substance of the EU's international relations, drawing attention to the key patterns of international activity and engagement, geographical and functional, and forming a foundation for the more detailed studies of later chapters.

Part II of the volume addresses the institutions and processes that surround the EU's international relations and that give rise to the EU's international policies. Here the focus is inevitably more on the 'internal' characteristics and policy-making processes than on the international context, although in all cases the chapters draw attention to the ways in which the 'internal' and the 'external' are intimately linked. In Chapter 4, Sophie Vanhoonacker deals with the institutional framework for EU international policies and explores the significance of institutional change (especially that created by the Lisbon Treaty) for the character and substance of policy. Chapter 5, by Carmen Gebhard, addresses a persistent and important problem in EU international policy making, that of consistency and coherence within a complex policy-making process, organized for two decades around three distinct 'pillars', which the Treaty of Lisbon has changed in form but not necessarily in substance. In Chapter 6, Christopher Lord explores an emerging issue for all international actors, that of legitimacy and democracy, showing how it takes on a specific meaning within the EU's international relations. Chapter 7, by Reuben Wong, investigates the extent to which the international activities and policies of EU member states have become 'Europeanized' through a process of convergence around distinct European positions and procedures, whilst in Chapter 8, Michael E. Smith deals with the problem of translating aspiration into practice, showing how implementation poses a particularly difficult challenge for a multi-agent actor like the EU.

Part III of the volume concentrates on key areas of policy substance and has the general aim of exploring the ways in which EU policies are pursued and have effects within the international arena. Chapter 9, by Jolyon Howorth, describes and analyses the dramatic ways in which the EU has moved from a generalized foreign and security policy towards a common defence policy during the late 1990s and 2000s, disappointing some but surprising others with its ability to put troops on the ground in over 20 overseas missions. In Chapter 10, Wyn Rees investigates the other face of security policy, by focusing on the linkages between internal and external security in the EU—a matter of great significance in the era of the 'war on terror' and the novel discourse of 'homeland security'. The next two chapters address the ways in which the EU relates to the global political economy: in Chapter 11, Amy Verdun deals with the relationship between the regional integration process and key areas of international interdependence in a globalizing world, whilst in Chapter 12, Sophie Meunier and Kalypso Nicolaïdis take this further by exploring the conception of the EU as a 'trade power' in the global arena. There follow two chapters dealing with international order, regional and global: Karen E. Smith, in Chapter 13, deals with the ways in which the enlargement of the EU has contributed to the development of a new 'European order', extending beyond the Union's frontiers, whilst Maurizio Carbone, in Chapter 14, addresses the relations between the EU and the developing world that began with the process of decolonization and has evolved into one of the most substantial aspects of its external relations. He examines the key tension that exists between development goals and the foreign policy dimension that has increasingly intruded into the area. Finally, three chapters focus on specific types of relationships within the EU's international relations: in Chapter 15, John Vogler investigates how the EU has developed an environmental policy, to some degree acting as a global leader, while in Chapter 16, Stephan Keukeleire and Hans Bruyninckx analyse the challenges posed to Europe by the emergence of the BRICs, both as a group and as major individual players in world politics. Michael Smith and Rebecca Steffenson complete Part III in Chapter 17 by exploring the single most important bilateral relationship in the EU's international relations, that with the USA.

Part IV brings the volume to a close with two 'overview' chapters, each with a different focus. In Chapter 18, Andrew Linklater looks closely at the ways in which the EU's international relations reflect a dominant set of normative assumptions, in particular those connected with 'civilizing' processes, whilst in Chapter 19, the editors return to the initial framework set out here, reassessing its propositions and extracting a number of themes from the evidence provided by the intervening contributions.

Conclusion

The European Union is not just an important geographical area but also a crucial dimension of modern international life. It has internalized and domesticated a significant amount of previously 'foreign', and dangerous, interstate relations. It has been drawn ineluctably into wider processes through its successes as a customs union and a commercial actor, to the point where it has now put in place much of the scaffolding for a common defence and foreign policy. The USA remains the world's only superpower, but the EU has certainly come to represent the other major pole of the Western world, and perhaps a significant one in the global system.

Whether this new phase of international activity reflects only the perceived need of Europeans to do more to ensure their own security, or whether it implies the willingness to risk more through taking on responsibilities for international order, remains to be seen. One of the important tasks for academic observers and for students both of IR and of the EU now is to conduct an audit of how much has been achieved, in what areas and what it amounts to. How far are the achievements cumulative and how far variable according to issue area? This should enable us to make judgements both on particular enterprises like the CESDP and the dynamics of the overall project. Where is the EU going in international relations? What kind of entity is it, might it be, and in our judgement will it be? In this context the normative agenda must not be neglected; that is, those principles or discourses that have been historically or are currently dominant in Europe's relations with the outside world and those that represent possible futures (Rogers 2009a; Manners 2010). We hope that by using this book, both students and those with a more general interest in the subject will be able to answer—or at least define more sharply—the questions of who and what the EU is for, in its international relations. What should it be trying to achieve and how might this be done?

Perceptions of European foreign policy—in the broadest sense—are important entry points both for charting actual progress and for understanding the reasons for disagreement over the EU's role. Domestic opinion, national and transnational, as well as the views held by outsiders, generates regular gaps between expectations of what the EU can do in the world and its actual capabilities: gaps which may or may not then narrow on the principle of homeostasis, i.e. that systems tend towards equilibrium. How the EU looks from beyond its borders is a particularly important area to investigate. As noted above, this involves the images held by non-EU citizens both of the EU in general and of its various roles, differentiated by region and issue area. By focusing on the latter we aim to provide the basis for more detailed appreciation of the extent to which the EU has the capacity to have a significant impact on the world.

We hope that the questions and general framework, as well as the more specialist contributions, provided in this book will encourage others to pursue the issues raised in greater depth. In particular the aim is to make possible a conversation between comparativists and European Studies scholars on the one hand, and those working within IR on the other. In the past this was prevented by a lofty disregard on both sides, but we are now pushing at a rapidly opening door. The EU's international role is in constant flux as the result of both Europe's internal politics and the changing demands from the international system. To understand this process of change, we need all the intellectual tools at our disposal.

 FURTHER READING

The following list provides an initial set of perspectives on international relations and the European Union. Thus, it contains the key 'standard' introductions to the international relations of the European Union (Bretherton and Vogler 2006; Ginsberg 2001, 2007; H. Smith 2002; K. Smith 2004, 2008; White 2001), together with selected works taking further some of the key issues: foreign policy analysis (Carlsnaes, Sjursen and White 2004), security and order (Kelstrup and Williams 2000, Schimmelfennig 2003, Zielonka 2006), the EU's international role (Elgström and Smith 2006), and regionalism (Telò 2006, 2007). Nuttall 1992 and 2000 provide an indispensable history of foreign policy cooperation, while Hill and Smith 2000 provide a commentary on the key documents of the first 40 years. Many of the issues touched on in this chapter are taken up in more detail and fully referenced in later chapters.

Bretherton, C., and Vogler, J. (2006), *The European Union as a Global Actor,* 2nd edition (London: Routledge).

Carlsnaes, W., Sjursen, H., and White, B. (eds) (2004), *Contemporary European Foreign Policy* (London: Sage).

Elgström, O., and Smith, M. (eds) (2006), *The European Union's Roles in International Politics: concepts and analysis* (London: Routledge/ECPR).

Ginsberg, R. (2001), *The European Union in International Politics: Baptism by Fire* (Lanham, MD: Rowman and Littlefield).

Hill, C., and Smith, K. E. (eds) (2000), *European Foreign Policy: Key Documents* (London: Routledge).

Kelstrup, M., and Williams, M. (eds) (2000), *International Relations Theory and the Politics of European Integration: Power, Security and Community* (London: Routledge).

Keukeleire, S., and MacNaughtan, J., (2008), *The Foreign Policy of the European Union* (Basingstoke: Palgrave/Macmillan).

Schimmelfennig, F. (2003), *The EU, NATO and the Integration of Europe: Rules and Rhetoric* (Cambridge: Cambridge University Press).

Schimmelfennig, F., and Sedelmeier, U. (eds) (2005), *The Politics of European Union Enlargement: Theoretical Approaches* (London: Routledge).

Smith, H. (2002), *European Union Foreign Policy: What it is and What it Does* (London: Pluto Press).

Smith, K. (2004), *The Making of EU Foreign Policy: The Case of Eastern Europe*, 2nd edition (Basingstoke: Palgrave/Macmillan).

Smith, K. (2008), *European Union Foreign Policy in a Changing World*, 2nd edition (Cambridge: Polity).

Smith, M. E. (2003), *Europe's Foreign and Security Policy: the institutionalization of cooperation* (Cambridge: Cambridge University Press).

Telò, M. (2006), *Europe: A Civilian Power? The European Union, Global Governance, World Order* (Basingstoke: Palgrave/Macmillan).

Telò, M. (ed.) (2007), *European Union and New Regionalism: Regional Actors and Global Governance in a Post-Hegemonic Era*, 2nd edition (Aldershot: Ashgate).

White, B. (2001), *Understanding European Foreign Policy* (Basingstoke: Palgrave Macmillan).

Zielonka, J. (2006), *Europe as Empire: the Nature of the Enlarged European Union* (Oxford: Oxford University Press).

 WEB LINKS

Basic information on the international activities of the EU can be found on the Commission website: **http://europa.eu**, where there are pages for all of the many international involvements of the Union, especially those dealing with external relations generally, with foreign and security policy, and with external trade and development. For more detailed or specific information on various aspects of European foreign policy, see especially the FORNET website, **http://www.fornet/info**, and the Online Resource Guide *Exploring EU Foreign Policy*—**http://www.exploring-europe.eu/foreignpolicy**— compiled by the Jean Monnet Centre of Excellence on 'The EU, Foreign Policy and Global Governance' of the University of Leuven. On the development of a European 'diplomatic system', see the website of the Jean Monnet Network 'The Diplomatic System of the EU' hosted at Loughborough University: **http://dseu.lboro.ac.uk**. Academic research projects funded by the European Commission, such as CONSENT, GARNET and MERCURY, are all also rich sources. See:

http://www.eu-consent.net/

http://www.garnet-eu.org/Home.192.0.html

http://www.mercury-fp7.net/

CHAPTER 2

The European Union's International Relations: A Theoretical View

Filippo Andreatta

▌ Summary

This chapter[1] analyses theoretical answers to two key questions arising from the emergence of the European Union on the world stage. Firstly, what have been the causes of European integration in general and in the foreign policy field in particular? Given that prevailing models of international politics assume that states do not easily give up their sovereignty, classical and recent theoretical approaches to IR (realism, liberalism, and constructivism) have struggled to find the motives for integration and integrate them in their overall frameworks. Secondly, the chapter investigates theoretical interpretations of the consequences of European integration for international relations in Europe and in the wider world. The chapter concludes by focusing on the possible future development of a European foreign policy.

Introduction

Theoretical work on international relations is characterized by a high degree of heterogeneity. It has come to be divided along paradigmatic lines, primarily between realism, which is pessimistic about progress in political relationships, liberalism, which is more optimistic about the possibility of avoiding conflict, and constructivist approaches, which reject traditional views about both the centrality of states in international affairs and the importance of material factors.

Despite this diversity, there is a paradox in the relationship between the theoretical study of international politics and the development of a common European foreign policy, defined broadly as the attempt of the European Union and its member states to ensure that their many and various external relations present as coherent a face as possible to the outside world. On the one hand, the study of international relations has always been considerably Eurocentric, as it developed strongly in Europe after the First World War, and even when, after the Second World War, it mainly shifted to the USA, the Cold War kept the focus on the problem of European order. On the other hand, the development of a common European foreign policy has been largely ignored by international relations theorists, or treated as a purely empirical event (Rosamond 2000a). Somewhat surprisingly, even when Europe is dealt with, it is treated mainly from a general integration point of view rather than in terms of foreign policy. For this reason, the study of European institutions is more easily found in international political economy (IPE) syllabi, because of the more advanced integration that has taken place in the trade and monetary fields, than in traditional international politics courses.

The reasons for this paradox are threefold. Firstly, whereas most mainstream theories of international politics deal with states and relations between them, the European Union is neither a state nor a traditional alliance, and it therefore represents a heterodox unit of analysis. Secondly, since IR theory has a bias towards the explanation of broad phenomena, it tends towards generalizations, while the European Union is, at least so far, a unique example of international cooperation and integration (Wallace 1994). As will later be argued, the precise nature of European foreign policy and the attempt to view its explanations in a general, rather than specific, framework are the questions at the heart of the theoretical debate on the subject. Thirdly, the achievements of integration in domestic policies, whether in trade, agriculture, or money, seem more substantial than those in the area of the Common Foreign and Security Policy, which appears to many critics as little more than wishful thinking, especially after the recent deep divisions in major crises (Hill 2004). On top of these reasons stand the major changes in the global system, such as the fall of the Berlin Wall, which have radically changed the background for an important but regional phenomenon like European integration (Calleo 2001).

This chapter will firstly review the main schools of thought that have advanced an explanation for the emergence of European institutions in general and a common

European foreign policy in particular. It will begin with an account of the two classic accounts of European integration—federalism and neo-functionalism—and then move on to discuss the views of the main traditions in IR theory: realism, liberalism, and constructivism. The analysis of the causes of the emergence of a European foreign policy will be followed by a discussion of its consequences, with a review of the most important suggestions about the role and impact of European foreign policy with respect to the global international system. A final section will deal with the likely future developments and the light cast on them by theory. It should be borne in mind that different theories highlight different aspects of the EU's international role and capabilities. Federalism and realism, for instance, tend to focus on high politics, while neo-functionalism and liberalism inherently cast the net wider, to include the cultural and political economy aspects of external activity.

Classical explanations: federalism and neo-functionalism

The classic account of European integration derives from federalism, which inspired its first proponents before, during, and after the Second World War. For this school of thought, the main problem in international relations is international anarchy, because the independence of multiple nation states brings mistrust, reciprocal threats, rivalry, and violence. Federalists were concerned about events in the first half of the 20th century, which had brought about two world wars, and thought that the decentralization of sovereignty had been the root cause of conflict. They were therefore sceptical about traditional remedies for interstate anarchy, such as diplomacy or the balance of power, and suggested a truly revolutionary solution that tackled the very essence of the international system: the abolition of national independence and the fusion of different political entities into one. According to Altiero Spinelli (1972, 68; see also Lodge 1984; Pinder 1991) 'the national states have lost their property rights since they cannot guarantee the political and economic safety of their citizens'. Federalists therefore built on the tradition dating back to the Enlightenment's schemes for perpetual peace (Hinsley 1963), as well as on the US example, in which the Union allowed the 13 colonies to defend each other, but also to avoid mutual attacks (Deudney 1995; see also Eilstrup-Sangiovanni and Verdier 2005).

Federalists believed that a union would bring Europe to solve conflict among different groups by an institutional deus ex machina, since no group would any longer enjoy the liberty to resort unilaterally to arms. The autonomous use of force, or even the liberty to raise independent armies, would be legally forbidden. A supranational form of government, according to a domestic analogy, would regulate relations among states as governments do internally among citizens (Suganami 1989).

The reasons for unification, according to federalists, are ultimately political and have to do with the objective of tackling international anarchy and the conflicts it tends to produce. According to the classical distinction between 'high politics', which concerns life-and-death issues of political order and violence, and 'low politics', which revolves around economic and social questions, federalism is situated firmly on the first side.

Federalism typically sets up two tiers of government, the parts and the whole, and distributes specific functions to each (Friedrich 1968). However, a federation must enjoy ultimate control of the instruments of violence, otherwise there is the risk that the parties fight with each other or with the central, supranational power. The achievement of a common defence and foreign policy is therefore the main aim of the federalist project. However, the federalist approach to the question is more normative than analytic in nature, as could be expected from a tradition firmly rooted in political philosophy. It is more a discussion of why states should form a union rather than an explanation of why they would willingly surrender their sovereignty, despite the fact that such a voluntary transfer has been extremely rare in history, and even in the European case is still far from certain. It nonetheless remains true that one of the strongest arguments for federalism, theoretical and practical, is the perceived need to have an effective European foreign policy.

The other classical approach to European integration derives from the functionalist school. Functionalists believed that modern society was increasingly dominated by matters of 'low politics' such as the welfare of citizens and economic growth and criticized federalists because of their neglect of such issues. The fundamental motive for integration would not therefore concern the legal relationships between political communities but would stem from the inability of nation states to provide essential services to their citizens. While the first school deals with political groups, the latter stresses the importance of individuals and their societies. According to functionalism, political functions must be performed at the most efficient level, and its logic ultimately leads to the whole world being unified. Mitrany therefore criticized European federalists for their narrow geographical focus. 'Between the conception of continental unions and that of a universal league there is a difference not merely of degree but of essence. The one would proceed in the old way by a definition of territory, the other by definition of functions; and while the unions would define their territory as a means of differentiating between members and outsiders, a league would select and define functions for the contrary purpose of integrating with regard to the interests of all' (Mitrany 1933, 116; see also Mitrany 1943, 1975).

The neo-functionalists, who became a significant factor in political science in the 1960s, utilized Mitrany's framework of analysis and its emphasis on 'low politics', but agreed with federalists, in contrast with Mitrany, on the desirability and feasibility of a continental union becoming a superstate, eventually with its own foreign and defence policy. For the most prominent neo-functionalist, Ernest Haas (1958, 16; see also 1964; Nye 1971), integration brings 'loyalties, expectations and political activities toward a new centre, whose institutions possess or demand jurisdiction over the pre-existing national states. The end result of a process of political integration is a new political community, superimposed over the pre-existing ones'. Neo-functionalists believed that the process of integration is endogenous, meaning that the current level of integration determines—by facilitating and amplifying them—future levels. The expectation is therefore of an 'ever closer Union' based on original intentions as well as on the integration already reached. The mechanism behind unification is radically different from that identified by federalists. There is in fact no conscious and explicit attempt to introduce a new federal constitution, as, according to Haas, '[a] new central authority may emerge as an unintended consequence of incremental earlier steps'. Neo-functionalist integration evolves spontaneously by a process of spillover. Integration—even in a secondary and technical area—creates pressures to integrate contiguous areas for which the original area is crucial and which, therefore, can no longer be controlled at the national level. Functional spillover, from one area to the next, generates a technical spillover, which enlarges at the supranational level the dimension fit to deal with the issue. Technical spillovers—in turn—can create a political spillover, meaning that formal control is necessarily transferred from the national level, and political loyalties and attentions are shifted to the supranational level.

The increasing difficulty in dealing with technical issues at the national level, and the tendency of integration to generate spillovers, can be exploited by supranational agencies, which could therefore promote a strategy for further integration 'from above'. Just as a rock can provoke an avalanche, integration in a specific and technical area, such as coal and steel, can eventually lead, by a series of small and gradual steps, to integration in a very wide area crucial for national sovereignty. The process follows an incremental path, in the sense that there is no single moment, unlike the introduction of a federalist constitution, that can be identified as the point of no return. The functionalist framework even allows for non-linear paths of integration. According to Schmitter (1974), integration could happen in wider areas but without institutional deepening (spill around), or with institutional deepening but without involving other areas (build-up). In certain extreme circumstances, integration could even recede by reducing the institutional deepening in a certain area due to national resistance (retrenchment) or by returning authority in an area to the national level (spill back).

In the neo-functionalist framework, because of its emphasis on 'low politics' and its traditional distaste for power politics, foreign policy is relegated to an ancillary position, and it is generally expected that political spillovers will follow economic and social integration. The failures of the EDC and the Fouchet Plans, of 1952–4 and 1961–2 respectively, could be ascribed to a failure to wait for natural spillovers. However, there remains one possibility for integrating foreign policy even before the completion of the process in other fields, as is demonstrated by the arrival of European Political Cooperation (EPC) in the 1970s, well before the main thrust of integration in the 1980s and 1990s. That is, other states outside the integration process can provide a stimulus for integration in the foreign policy field, a process known as 'externalization', due to non-members' pressures to negotiate with a single partner rather than with all member states individually (Schmitter 1969). In this case also then, a functional demand could lead to a decision on the part of European states to pool their resources for maximizing efficacy, facilitated by the fact that foreign policy rests more on political decisions than on legislation.

European integration and IR theory

The two classic approaches have been criticized mainly on two counts. On the one hand, their emphasis was too Eurocentric. Both schools were in fact formulated in general terms, but they highlighted characteristics of the process of European integration that were not to be found in other regions of the world. Federalism and neofunctionalism appeared to be more specific 'local' theories apt to explain events in Western Europe rather than general models of behaviour in international politics. On the other hand, they employed a teleological approach, taking eventual full integration for granted, underestimating the 'obstinate rather than obsolete' potential resistance of the nation state as well as the possibility of forms of integration that could stop short of the creation of a superstate (Hoffmann 1966). For these reasons, the theoretical debate in the 1970s shifted towards accounts more in tune with the broader paradigms in international relations theory, which gave more importance than did the classical theories to the role of states in the international system and which utilized variables having a broader empirical base of application. In particular, most of these accounts specify exogenous causes for integration, pointing out that each further step in integration must rest on actors' interests rather than on an inertial and teleological process leading to a predefined—and superstate—result. It followed that these approaches could also take into account the possibility that integration could lead to various possible outcomes, observable in other regions as well.

The beginning of EPC in the 1970s—as well as the resilience of the wider process of European integration—constituted a turning point in the conceptualization of the foreign policy of European institutions. These first timid attempts contradicted expectations, as for example those of the Tindemans Report, that a common European foreign policy could happen only when basic integration had been achieved. EPC demonstrated that there was indeed a foreign policy dimension to the EEC, and it therefore forced those theorists who had hitherto ignored the issue to consider the subject. On the other hand, the limits of EPC also forced the enthusiasts for integration to reconsider their position as it became clear that European institutions would not soon acquire the cohesiveness of a superstate. These reasons induced the two main schools of thought in international relations theory, realism and liberalism, belatedly to come to terms with European integration in general and with the role of European institutions in the world in particular.

Realism was based on three main assumptions:

1. The state is the dominant actor on the international scene, and is capable of acting as a coherent, unitary, and rational unit.

2. Since states recognize no authority above them, international relations are in a state of anarchy, or lack of hierarchy, which forces states to self-help.

3. In anarchy, politics is dominated by military considerations and by the fragility of trust and cooperation. War is therefore always a possibility.

Realism is therefore concentrated—like federalism—on 'high politics' and shares much of its analysis on the conflictual consequences of anarchy, although it is not as optimistic on the ability of states to develop sufficient trust to enter into a federation.

Liberals responded with different assumptions, which allowed for a more flexible, and positive, view of the world:

1. States are not the only actors in world politics. Other types of actors are important at the supranational level (international organizations, such as the EEC), transnational level (for example, multinational corporations or religious organizations), or subnational level (for instance, interest groups or political parties).

2. Interstate anarchy can therefore be tamed by a network of relations between states, between states and other types of actors, and between other types of actors themselves.

3. International politics is not fully determined by the distribution of military power. Other issues, namely of an economic nature, can be crucial. There is therefore more room for choice than in realist accounts, allowing for cooperation and the development of international institutions.

Liberals envisaged a more complex model of international politics, which could more easily account for the role of European institutions in world politics. In particular, liberals tended to share neo-functionalist assumptions about the importance of 'low politics' and the necessity of interstate cooperation, although they also shared realist scepticism about the ultimate abandonment of national sovereignty (Ruggie *et al.* 2005).

It is therefore possible to sketch a typology of the main theories of European integration according to two variables (see Table 2.1). On the one hand, while realists and federalists concentrate on high politics, liberals and neo-functionalists give more emphasis to the importance of low politics. On the other hand, while federalists and neo-functionalists believe that the end result of the process of integration will be a fully fledged Union, realists and liberals argue that integration could well stop short of the creation of a superstate. According to Karl Deutsch (Deutsch *et al.* 1957, cf. also Deutsch 1968, Adler and Barnett 1998), integration brings states into

TABLE 2.1	Main approaches to integration		
		Motive for integration	
		'High politics'	**'Low politics'**
End result of integration	Pluralistic security community	Realism	Liberalism
	Amalgamated security community	Federalism	Neo-functionalism

a 'security community', which is a group of states among which war is so improbable as to become unthinkable. If integration brings about a unified state, it leads to an 'amalgamated' security community, while it is termed a 'pluralistic' security community if it maintains the independence of members.

Realist views of European foreign policy

Realists are in general sceptical about the possibility of international cooperation, given the constraints of anarchy. In particular, realist theories assume that 'the most basic motive driving states is survival. States want to maintain their sovereignty' (Mearsheimer 1994–5, 10). For these reasons, 'realism [is not] well designed to explain the political integration of Western Europe' (Wayman and Diehl 1994, 17). Yet the success of European integration and the beginning of a 'European' foreign policy have somehow forced realists to give an explanation of these phenomena, even at the cost of adapting their main theories. According to Grieco: 'the interest displayed by the European countries in the EU creates a problem for realist theory' (Grieco 1997b, 184; see also 1995, 1996).

The founder of neorealism, the most influential contemporary version of realism, Kenneth Waltz, has advanced a 'local' solution to the question of European integration. For Waltz, integration is an exceptional event:

Although the integration of nations is often talked about, it seldom takes place. Nations could mutually enrich themselves by further dividing not just the labor that goes into the production of goods, but also some of the other tasks they perform, such as political management and military defence. Why does their integration not take place?

(Waltz 1979, 105)

There are exceptions to this rule, as there is 'the fact that some states may persistently seek goals that they value more highly than survival; they may, for example, prefer amalgamation with other states' (Waltz 1979, 92). However, even if it eventually took place, integration could only alter the distribution of power among different units (for example, the United States of Europe could become a world superpower), but it could not alter the basic characteristics of the international system, as the fusion of several states into one does not alter the anarchic relationship between the new unit and all the other ones which have not participated in the union (Waltz 1979). When asked to comment on the future of international politics after the end of the Cold War, Waltz states that 'the emerging world will nevertheless be one of four or five great powers, whether the European one is called Germany or the United States of Europe' (Waltz 1993, 70). In a 2000 article, Waltz suggests that Europe will not become a great power 'in the absence of radical change' (essentially Europe becoming a state). He is dubious about the prospects of this and therefore predicts that a European great power is unlikely (Waltz 2000, 31–2; cf. also Gordon 1997, 81).

Although Waltz's attempt to conceptualize the EU may help to save the general propositions of the neorealist model, it does not account for the causes that may have brought integration about. Other realist theories have thus provided hypotheses in this respect, which are consistent with the realist framework in general and in particular with its emphasis on rational state strategies and the constraints imposed by the international system. In other words, integration may be seen as a rational response to the peculiar systemic position, and the consequent war exhaustion, in which European countries have found themselves after 1945. While one group of theories concentrates on the position of Europe within the wider international system, another group analyses the systemic conditions within Europe itself. Of these, the first is the role of American hegemony within the Western camp. According to Robert Gilpin (1981), international cooperation is possible only when a state is capable of imposing order in the international system by virtue of its superior power. When there is a clear hierarchy of power, there are few or no clashes of interests, as the stronger state can impose its will and the weaker ones have to comply. The USA during the Cold War wanted to increase the power of the Western coalition against the Soviet Union and wished Western Europe to contribute to its own defence, and therefore favoured measures—such as integration—that reduced inter-allied conflicts and increased collective economic and military efficiency. Following a similar perspective, but from a starting point that combines realism with liberalism, Ikenberry has argued that American leadership has been crucial for the development of European integration (Ikenberry 2004).

Other theories emphasize the role of the post-war bipolar structure of the international system. According to Joanne Gowa (1989) and Hyde-Price (2006), in bipolar systems agreements between states are stable and durable because alignments are structurally determined, allowing for a higher degree of cooperation and trust. By contrast, alignments in multipolar systems are the result of choice among multiple options and can therefore change over time. Cooperation is therefore inhibited by the risk that today's friends will become tomorrow's adversaries. The main point of the theories linking European integration to the Cold War international system is that, with the end of bipolarity, the structural conditions for the emergence of European cooperation will be altered.

This could have ambivalent effects on European cohesion. In John Mearsheimer's pessimistic view, even the established achievements of integration may be subject to revision: 'Without the Soviet threat or an American night watchman, Western European states will do what they did for centuries before the onset of the Cold War, look upon one another with suspicion ... Cooperation in this new order will be more difficult than it was during the Cold War. Conflict will be more likely' (Mearsheimer 1990, 46). However, the end of bipolarity might also be seen as a stimulus for deeper European cooperation in the foreign policy sphere. With the end of the Soviet threat, the Western alliance that was created to counter it would also lose its rationale. Kenneth Waltz (1993) has suggested that NATO, like all other alliances, will not eventually survive the loss of the threat that gave rise to it in the first place. The end—or the weakening—of transatlantic ties could spur Europe to a more active role in the world, or even to an attempt to 'balance' US power, which after the demise of the Soviet Union has become preponderant and may have inaugurated a 'unipolar' world awaiting challengers. In the view of realists, a stronger Europe would anyway contribute to the weakening of the relationship with the USA. For example, according to Henry Kissinger (1965, 232), 'European unity is not a major cure-all for Atlantic disagreements. In many respects it may magnify rather than reduce differences. As Europe gains structure, it will be in a better position to insist on differences whose ultimate cause is structural rather than personal.' More recently, Lawrence Kaplan (1996, 29) has argued that 'If the European movement ultimately embraces a military component, it could be the final act in NATO's history.'

Some have indeed argued that closer European cooperation may be precisely the result of attempts to 'balance' the overwhelming power of the USA after the bipolar era. For example, Posen argues that the main motive behind a European foreign policy might be the belief that the USA will pursue its unilateral interests now that the Soviet threat is gone. Europeans might therefore be tempted to influence world events collectively now that the distribution of power has shifted in favour of Asia (Posen 2006). Others maintain that closer European cooperation, and a more independent foreign policy with ties to other powers like Russia and China, could be the result of 'soft' balancing aiming to curb US tendencies to unilateralism (Paul 2005, 57–8). Still others suggest that the development of a common European foreign policy is the 'neorealist' attempt to manage the Eastern European transition from a position of strength (Hyde-Price 2006).

The other group of realist theories concentrates on international relations within Western Europe itself, and is therefore less dependent on broader systemic conditions. In particular, Joseph Grieco, elaborating on an earlier insight by Hans Morgenthau (1973, 509), suggests that European integration may be the result of the attempts of other member states to constrain Germany, especially after it has emerged potentially stronger after unification. According to Grieco, 'if states share a common interest and undertake negotiations on rules constituting a collaborative arrangement, then the weaker but still influential partners will seek to ensure that the rules so constructed will provide sufficient opportunities for them to voice their concerns and interests and thereby prevent or at least ameliorate their domination by stronger partners' (Grieco 1995, 34; see also 1996, 1997a). Robert Art agrees on the fact that 'the desire for security vis-à-vis one another has played a role in the Western European states' second great push for closer union in the 1990s, just as it did during their first great push in the late 1940s and early 1950s' (Art 1996, 2). Agreement was therefore possible because 'if other nations did not completely trust Germany, neither did Germans completely trust themselves [and this is why they chose] a strategy of voluntary self-entanglement' (Art 1996, 24).

More generally, the efforts to create a common European foreign policy could be conceptualized as a strong and permanent form of alliance. Paul Schroeder (1976; see also Gelpi 1999) has suggested that alliances are formed for two main purposes: 'capability aggregation and the control of allies'. In order to gain on these two fronts, states are willing to limit their own autonomy and follow the prescriptions of alliances and other international agreements (Snyder 1997). Integration could represent a more dramatic loss of autonomy justified by an equally dramatic increase in common capabilities and in the capacity for mutual control. After all, as Stephen Krasner (1999; see also Caporaso 1996 and Lake 2007) argues, absolute 'Westphalian' sovereignty is an abstract concept that has in history tolerated many exceptions. Given the drastic changes in Europe's international position after the Second World War, and in particular the realization that continental anarchy could have near-suicidal consequences and that European states had no longer the critical mass to compete with the superpowers, the decision to begin integration became logical. Where this realization was clearer, such as in the defeated Axis countries (Italy and Germany), the propensity to integrate was higher than in the victorious continental powers—such as France and the Benelux countries, which had been subject to German occupation but emerged victorious—and higher still than in the United Kingdom, which had not even been successfully invaded.

The importance given by realists to security considerations as a key motive for integration seems substantiated by historical experience. On the one hand, Goertz and Diehl (1992, 54) have shown that integration is indeed a rare phenomenon. Of all territorial changes, only 5 per cent have happened by political unification, while 72.4 per cent have happened by the more traditional means of conquest, annexation, and secession. On the other hand, in his study of federalism, William Riker (1964, 1975, 1996) has analysed all the 35 successful cases of political unification up to 1975, finding that in all cases there was an internal or external military threat.

Liberal views

The liberal paradigm is more easily adapted to explain European integration and the emergence of a European common foreign policy for two reasons. On the one hand, liberals adopt a more flexible approach than realists on the question of the actors in international politics, allowing also for the role of international, or supranational, organizations. On the other hand, liberals are generally more optimistic on the prospects of interstate cooperation, and are therefore more willing to acknowledge the successes of the European Community and the European Union. There are three main liberal groups of theories that can be applied to the subject in question: republican, commercial, and institutional.

The first group of theories is based on the importance of domestic regimes in the formulation of foreign policy. Democracies (or republics, in Kantian language) behave differently from non-democracies in the international scene because they are forced to take the electorate's view into account, because they are governed by a complex institutional mechanism, and because they are based on norms prescribing peaceful conflict resolution (Doyle 1983; Russett *et al.* 1993; Lynn-Jones and Miller 1996; Russett and Oneal 2001; Lipson 2003). In particular, democracies tend, for these reasons, not to go to war with each other, forming a democratic security community in which a 'separate peace' rules. European integration would therefore be a result of the democratization that has taken place after the Second World War in the Western half of the continent.

One interesting work that employs a similar line of thought is Mancur Olson's *The Rise and Decline of Nations* (1982), which emphasizes that, in democratic politics, younger regimes are more capable of engaging in policies that favour general interests, while older regimes are more prone to be influenced by particular interests, and which have had more time to organize their collective action. In the case of European integration, it would follow that the timing of the process would be influenced by its proximity to the end of the Second World War, given that most European countries had to rebuild their political systems after the conflict. This would also help to explain the different propensities of the various countries (Koenig-Archibugi 2004a), with the most recent democracies—Italy and Germany—more enthusiastic than the older ones, and with the oldest, the United Kingdom, least eager of all. History thus plays an important role in explaining integration. Those countries which suffered defeat in 1945 were able to establish new democratic institutions as well as European cooperation, while in other areas of the world democratization has been either not as fast or not contemporaneous.

Olson's more general theory of public goods is also useful to highlight the limits of Europe's common policies. When a collaborative arrangement produces a public good, each party to the agreement has an interest in free riding; that is, in enjoying the benefits without paying the costs. Given that all parties are subject to this incentive, however, there is a tendency to underproduce public goods as most or all will defect, producing a suboptimal result. With respect to Europe's common foreign policy, this means that even if all members agreed on a basic policy and found it desirable to implement it, it could still fail since each would prefer that others shoulder the cost of its implementation. Christopher Hill (1996, 7) suggests that European states, even when they are willing to envisage common strategies, find it genuinely difficult 'to hold to these strategies once agreements are reached'.

The theory of public goods could also help to explain why European integration has advanced much further in the economic sphere than in the field of foreign policy. On the one hand, the latter area is less divisible and is therefore more prone to collective action failures than economic development, which provides incentives for everyone to participate. On the other hand, US military preponderance in the Western alliance, which was necessary (and sufficient) to deter the Soviet Union, gave no real incentives to Europeans to spend intensively on defence, because their security was already guaranteed, and led to the frequent debates about burden sharing within NATO, as the USA was contributing a disproportionate amount of resources to the collective defence effort (Oneal 1990; Lepgold 1998). Liberals, unlike realists, believe that NATO is based on common values and ideologies, and that it can therefore survive both the end of the Cold War and a stronger European profile. According to Olson and Zeckhauser (1966, 279), 'a union of smaller members of NATO, for example, could be helpful, and be in the interest of the United States. Such a union would give the people involved an incentive to contribute more toward the goals they shared with their then more nearly equal partners. Whatever the disadvantages on other grounds of these policy possibilities, they at least have the merit that they help to make the national interest of individual nations more nearly compatible with the efficient attainment of the goals which groups of nations hold in common'.

The emphasis on domestic structures has also produced the so-called intergovernmentalist school. Building on the model of two-level games first developed by Robert Putnam (1988; see also Evans, Jacobson, and Putnam 1993; Milner 1997), this tradition envisages a world in which governments act on two arenas simultaneously: the domestic and the international. Andrew Moravcsik, who more than any other scholar can be associated with intergovernmentalism, argues that—on the one hand—governments negotiate at the supranational level only on those issues that are favoured by their domestic constituencies, since their primary interest is in being re-elected. Indeed, in these models the government is designated as 'agent' of a 'principal', which is the social coalition supporting them. On the other hand, Moravcsik suggests that: 'international negotiations and institutions change the domestic context in which policy is made by redistributing ... political resources ... The reallocation of control over domestic political resources ... generally favours those who directly oversee national involvement in international negotiations and institutions, generally executives ... This shift in domestic power resources feeds back into international agreements, often facilitating international cooperation' (Moravcsik 1998, 3). In other words, by delegating certain policies to a supranational level, governments can increase, rather than decrease, their power because they gain extra resources against their domestic adversaries. Integration is therefore a process under strict governmental planning, and proceeds only when governments judge it in their interest to resort to supranational strategies and to reinforce their control over a certain issue. In this view, foreign policy would remain outside the 'community' integrated framework that characterizes monetary or commercial policy, and could remain rigidly separated from integration in general. Conversely, once major commitments are made, they are difficult to back out of, which makes a genuinely collective foreign policy an important Rubicon to cross.

This line of thought is substantiated by the historical enquiry of Alan Milward, who has argued that European integration—far from eroding national sovereignty—has helped to reinforce European states in the reconstruction era. Regarding the origins of the EC, Milward (1992, 12; see also 1984) writes that 'nation states have played the dominant role in its formation and retained firm control over their new creation'. In this view, foreign policy has undergone less integration than other areas, such as monetary or agricultural affairs, because governments already enjoy a high degree of autonomy in that particular field. This position also explains the emergence of a so-called 'democratic deficit', according to which decisions at the European level are not subject to the same controls as decisions at the national level (Kaiser 1971; Moravcsik 1999; Scharpf 1999; Koenig-Archibugi 2002; Koenig-Archibugi 2004b).

The second group of liberal theories is based on the commercial tradition and stresses the importance of economic processes (Rosecrance 1986). According to this school of thought, the recent growth in transnational flows has created interdependent modern societies that have altered the traditional conception of 'national interest' (Keohane and Nye 1977). In particular, security matters have lost their preeminence vis-à-vis economic considerations, and the latter force governments to unprecedented levels of collaboration. The difficulty in controlling transnational interdependence with the scale of the nation state has even created an incentive to pool political resources together by building institutions with a sufficient critical mass to deal with the new issues. European integration would then be a byproduct of this more general process of governance under globalization (Weiss 1999; Zurn 2000), given Europe's tighter web of transnational relations and the relatively small dimensions of its states, for example compared with the USA, and other regions could be following a similar path (Mansfield and Milner 1999; Choi and Caporaso 2002). The interdependence school borrows from functionalist logic, although it does not share its teleological conclusions, and its insights regarding foreign policy depend on the extent that contemporary interdependence creates a demand for a common and unified European role in world affairs. For example, this approach could help to account for the different levels of success in developing a common position in the various fields, with a higher propensity to integrate foreign economic policy than military capabilities, for which, given Europe's relative sense of security, there is a less intense feeling of urgency. Relations on security matters with the USA have also mainly remained close (with the exception of 'out of area' problems), whereas more frequent conflict has arisen in trade issues, given Europe's wider and deeper capabilities in economic affairs.

The last group of liberal theories concerns the development of international institutions. According to neo-liberal institutionalists, conflict in the international system is an effect of the lack of trust between states in a condition of anarchy. Although this places them close to realists, cooperation is still presumed to be possible. Using simple game-theoretic reasoning, this school of thought shows that negotiations can lead to suboptimal outcomes, even when there exists a common interest in cooperation. However, it is possible to reinforce the prospect of cooperation by enhancing the commonality of interests among players, by reducing the number of uncertain variables, and by reiterating the interaction in a more structured setting (Keohane 1984; Axelrod and Keohane 1985; Hasenclever *et al.* 1997; for an application to the European Community, see Martin 1992). These conditions can be created by establishing international institutions, aimed at reducing uncertainty and mistrust in interstate relations. When transaction costs are prohibitive, and ad hoc institutions are not economical, states may even resort to integration (Lake 1996; Weber 1997; Koenig-Archibugi 2000). Given its focus on bargaining and procedures, institutional analysis has been applied to the decision-making processes of the Union (Tsebelis and Garrett 2003; König and Slapin 2006; Slapin 2008). The institutionalist model has also been applied to European common security policy by Carsten Tams (1999), who argues that European institutions serve the purpose of ameliorating collective action problems emerging from cooperation in the military field. In particular, while France and Germany wish for stronger European institutions because the more ambitious the project the more acute are the collective action problems, the United Kingdom prefers weaker institutions because it wants a more limited role for European foreign policy. Finally, it must be remembered that there have been recent attempts to combine the three strands of liberalism in a coherent framework, with the democratic peace school suggesting that the 'separate peace' among democracies is especially effective when there are also high degrees of institutionalization and interdependence, as in the European case (Hasenclever and Weiffen 2006; Pevehouse and Russett 2006; Haftel 2007).

Constructivist and critical approaches

A number of critiques have been developed over the years against the mainstream debate between realists and liberals, which has been considered by some too rigid to capture the essence of international politics. In particular, in the last two decades a number of alternative approaches has emerged emphasizing the importance of cognitive factors in the elaboration of foreign policy, which had been ignored by the more 'scientific' and 'positivist' methodology of both realists and liberals. On the one hand, while the traditional theories assume the rationality of actors, some middle-range theories based on the foreign policy analysis tradition employ notions of 'bounded rationality', which take into account the cognitive constraints facing decision makers. The limited amount of time to gather information, its possible bias, and the limited capacity to process it, lead to decisions based on less than full rationality. On the other hand, other theories question the ability to observe social events objectively, opting for a more 'reflective' approach based on the fact that even theories are an inextricable part of social reality. More than the explanation 'from the outside' of international events, scholars should therefore concentrate on the understanding 'from the inside' of the point of view of decision makers, reconstructing the objective as well as the subjective milieu in which they operated (Hollis and Smith 1991). Both groups of theories—in short—agree that the emphasis placed by realists and liberals alike on 'exogenous' objective interests is misplaced and that it is better to consider actors' motives as an 'endogenous' variable dependent on certain cognitive conditions. This would allow us to overcome a rigid agent–structure divide and to conceptualize agents and structures as 'mutually constitutive' (Wendt 1987).

These approaches tend to consider European institutions as more than a simple set of rules, and can be organized into three groups, all of which might be seen as loosely associated with the constructivist approach, in that they ascribe importance to the social origins of behaviour and to the power of ideational variables (Bretherton and Vogler 1999, 28–36; Adler 2002). Firstly, although states do not transfer sovereignty to institutions and retain, in theory, ultimate control over their policies, in practice states tend to conform to the institutional rules and 'scripts' to which they have subscribed (Hall and Taylor 1996). In other words, states adopt the logic of 'appropriateness', according to which they follow institutional rules, unless this explicitly infringes one of their vital interests, because they fear being considered untrustworthy or 'inappropriate' (March and Olsen 1998). Institutions can therefore penetrate into a foreign policy 'standard operating procedure' and influence decisions by, for example, fostering common platforms, which are then followed by national policies in the absence of better alternatives. A process of 'Europeanization' could follow, which, like a coordinated reflex, could progressively draw national positions closer. Furthermore, policy networks and epistemic communities can influence decision making in an institutional context (Haas 1992). Belief systems can also be viewed from a post-positivist viewpoint as a means of identifying 'general lines in a country's foreign policy', as for example in the form of national attitudes and discourses on European integration (Larsen 1997, 10).

Secondly, other approaches emphasize that states do not seek only material objectives, but are also inspired by ideological motivations. European institutions are therefore to be considered in this light as a normative entity (Parsons 2002) or a normative power (Manners 2002). At a minimum, the fact that the EU exists creates pressures to preserve its unity, and develops a consistent bias toward common, rather than national, positions. At a maximum, the existence of the EU as an institution that embodies certain principles—democracy, the rule of law, human rights, free markets—creates an incentive for states to sustain those same objectives and constitute a 'European' identity. States that are part of the process become socialized with institutional aims and with those of other members (Smith 2004a). According to Wayne Sandholtz (1996, 406), institutions 'allow … governments to become intimately acquainted with the goals, aversions, tastes and domestic constraints of each other'. In other words, identities and roles are not constant, and can vary in a process in which agents and structures are 'mutually constitutive' (Risse *et al.* 1999; Biersteker 2002; Legro 2009). In time, national loyalties could give way to a true European identity (Cederman 2001). Having provided a normative and ethical framework for relations within Western Europe, the EU could then project these same instincts externally, constituting an 'ethical power' on the world stage.

Thirdly, institutions and norms can be seen as part of the international environment facing states. In particular, the presence of a tight network of rules in Western Europe can approximate the traditional conception—introduced by the English school of international relations—of an international society. Unlike in an international system, in which interactions between states occur in a normative vacuum, in international society there are conventions that guide foreign policy and limit eventual conflict. Western Europe, also due to its institutions, could be considered as the most developed example of an international society. A more radical view sees the international system itself, and its characteristic anarchical condition, as a 'social construction' that can be altered or transformed by finding an alternative lens through which to conceptualize international relations (Wendt 1992). Seen in this light, European integration could represent an experiment in the construction of a different type of international order, in which conflict is replaced by cooperation and suspicion by mutual trust. For example, Robert Cooper sees the Treaty of Rome as the pillar of 'postmodern Europe'. According to Cooper (2003, 27): 'the postmodern system does not rely on balance; nor does it emphasize sovereignty or the separation of domestic and foreign affairs. The European Union is a highly developed system for interference in each other's domestic affairs, right down to beer and sausages.'

In studying a subject like the EU, whose procedures are based on rules and which experiments with altering members' identities and roles, the reflectivist analysis has such obvious strengths that a number of calls have been made for integrating it with more rationalist approaches (Jupille *et al.* 2003; Sorensen 2008). The constructivist challenge has also led to a reconsideration within the realist camp, with a strand of 'neoclassical' realism revisiting the original emphasis on ideologies and domestic structures as corollaries of power (Rose 1998). International outcomes would not be solely determined by the distribution of material capabilities, as in neorealist theory, but would also be influenced by the attitudes of elites. Such hybrid approaches clearly show that the theoretical debate is far from over and that in the future theoretically oriented research will be able to advance new interpretations for the origin and development of European integration. Let us now move to its consequences.

The last approach that may be considered 'alternative' is that of neo-Marxism, which is different from the paradigms of mainstream international relations because it believes that political institutions are governed by economic interests. In particular, states and international organizations are part of a superstructure governed by and in the interest of capitalist elites, which establish a Gramscian type of hegemony over the rest of the world. On this view the origin and development of European integration followed the logic of capitalism, including US support at its inception to expand global markets, and its important role in the last phase of globalization. The European Union is therefore seen—in a centre–periphery model—as yet another instrument by which the former is capable of exploiting the latter, and of maintaining its subordinate status (Galtung 1971; Wallerstein 1979; Holland, S. 1980; Chase-Dunn 1999; cf. also Arrighi 2005). Particularly interesting from this point of view would be the attempts to develop a common development aid policy via the Lomé Conventions, as well as the suggestions for a higher European profile in global financial organizations such as the International Monetary Fund (IMF) and the World Bank.

The role of Europe in the world

Having reviewed the most important causes suggested by theoretical accounts for the emergence of European integration and a common foreign policy, attention should now shift to the effects of these phenomena on the international system. For this purpose, it is useful to introduce two key distinctions. On the one hand, one should distinguish between the role of the European Union inside its own borders and its impact on the outside world as a power or as a participant in the general processes of international relations. On the other, one should distinguish between those theories which analyse Europe's role as an actor in its own right and those which conceptualize the Union as an institution whose influence is mainly felt through the foreign policies of member states (Wolfers 1962, 21; see also White 2001). The current status quo is in fact quite unsatisfactory. According to Christopher Hill (1993a, 316) 'the cartoon which once showed 12 Prime Ministers voting on whether or not to press the nuclear button pithily summarized the impossibility of having a genuinely intergovernmental defence community'. It is therefore clear that Europe has to choose one of two paths: either it strengthens the institutional backbone behind a common policy, or it decides to value flexibility, informality, and subsidiarity instead.

The theories that envisage Europe as an independent actor are quite sceptical about the possibility of projecting power abroad without the characteristics of statehood. In particular, they tend to emphasize the two special factors that set international politics apart from other policies and require a 'communitarian' and integrated approach. Firstly, the rhythm of decision making cannot be set by cumbersome intergovernmental processes because the pace of action is determined by outside events demanding urgent responses. Secondly, since foreign policy can—ultimately—lead to the use of force, no real foreign policy can be worthy of the name unless it has a military component, which in Europe's case cannot be guaranteed until there is a transfer of democratic legitimacy and of sovereignty to the European level. For example, according to David Allen (1998, 42), there must be a level—national or common—that is ultimately responsible: 'the determination to preserve national foreign policies is ultimately at odds with the ambition to create a European foreign policy'.

On the contrary, the proponents of the 'Europe as an institution' approach believe that significant levels of cooperation can be attained even without transforming the EU into a state. Sovereignty in the field of foreign policy can therefore be shared between the national and the community level as other policies, including for example commercial or agricultural policies, have been in the past. According to this position, while speaking of a European superstate is either unrealistic or undesirable, it is possible instead to imagine a 'foreign policy system' in which a European common policy and national foreign policies converge and combine in their impact on international events and which represents, in Hill's view, 'the sum of what the EU *and* its member states do in international relations' (Hill 1998a, 18, emphasis added). As a corollary, while the first position would prefer the full institutionalization of European foreign policy, this view values the flexibility of an intergovernmental arrangement and the possibility of resting on ad hoc coalitions, directories, and variable geometries in the conduct of international affairs.

From these distinctions it is possible to construct the typology in Table 2.2, which identifies four possible ways to reason about Europe's international role.

The first way is to emphasize the internal effects of integration in the foreign policy field as a necessary step toward the creation of a supranational—or statal—actor. This would be the way preferred by federalist and neo-functionalist theories, or by those realist theories that imagine the European Union becoming a fully fledged superstate. Particular attention is devoted to the transfer of sovereignty from member states to the Union level, with the analogy in mind of what has happened to another traditional area of state control, monetary affairs. Particularly relevant for

TABLE 2.2   Europe's international role

	Significance for members	Significance for wider world
Europe as independent actor	EU taking on the characteristics of a state	'Superpower in the making'
Europe as institution of national actors	Security community	International alliance or 'civilian power'

this view is integration in the field of defence, with the creation of a common European industry, the strengthening of the European Defence Agency, the establishment of a military headquarters and even some concertation of armed forces.

The second way to conceptualize Europe's impact on the international stage is to concentrate on its reflexive effects but without necessarily imagining the creation of a superstate. While the previous conception concentrates on the relationship between member states and the Union, this focuses on the states' relationships with each other. Such a view—which builds on the 'democratic peace' tradition—stresses the importance of European integration on the pacification of the continent, with the creation of a 'pluralistic security community' among Western European countries (Hassner 1968, 21; Keohane *et al.* 1993; Hoffmann 1995). In this view, the most important global consequence of European integration is the exemplar model that it offers to other regions to overcome their tensions, rather than any direct impact (Cooper 2003). In Manners's words (2002), Europe's role would not be shaped by 'what it does or what it says, but by what it is' (cf. also Sjursen 2006, and Linklater's chapter in this volume).

A third position highlights Europe's role in the outside world and considers its impact as if it were a power endowed with its own autonomous resources—in Johan Galtung's phrase, a 'superpower in the making' (Galtung 1973; Buchan 1993). This view generally concentrates on Europe's potential aggregate capabilities, which are indeed considerable both in economic and even in military terms. For example, the EU comprises the largest single market in the global economy, it has the largest gross national product and is the biggest commercial power and aid donor in the world. Even the combined military resources of European states are, on paper, impressive, with about a quarter of global military expenditures being spent by EU members, a higher proportion than the Soviet Union during the Cold War (see Howorth's chapter in this volume). Even now, the European military presence abroad is not insignificant (Giegerich and Wallace 2004; their data is updated by the International Institute for Strategic Studies in *European Military Capabilities: Building Armed Forces for Modern Operations* (2008), (London: IISS Strategic Dossier).

Finally, a fourth position imagines Europe's impact on the wider international system not as an autonomous actor but as an institution capable of influencing the various foreign policies of member states. Although the most classical instance would be that of an international alliance, less traditional solutions are also possible. The idea is that of a European 'presence' or a European 'identity' (Allen and Smith 1990; Whitman 1998) borne out by a 'civilizing process' (see Linklater's chapter in this volume). The most influential definition is that of Europe as a 'civilian power' that utilizes non-military means to uphold civilian ends such as the defence of human rights and the support for the consolidation of democracy or of an open global economy (Duchêne 1972; Bull 1982; Hill 1990 for a critical view; see also Aron 1966, Chapter 10, section 3). A prototypical example is that of Europe's sanctions against South African apartheid, which employed economic means to further a human rights goal (Holland 1995). Clearly, such an approach depends on a non-realist view of the world, in which non-military means and goals have a significant impact on international outcomes.

Given the Union's quite formidable limits in terms of military power, which have so far not allowed the development of common capabilities, at least for high-intensity conflicts, most of the attention has been devoted to the last approach. In particular, a useful distinction has been introduced (Nye 1990) between the 'hard' military power of coercion and the 'soft' power of persuasion, which rests more on political and economic instruments. Since the European comparative advantage is less military and more economic, being in this field almost as strong as the USA, the possibility of influencing events by 'soft' power is crucial for Europe's role in the world.

Conclusion: the future of European foreign policy

There is one area in which the application of soft power has an impact second only to that of military conquest, and that is the enlargement of the EU. Europe's neighbours, far from being threatened by integration or the extension of its borders, have in general been willing either to propose their own membership, or to cooperate with the Union (Rosecrance 1998). The entry of new members into the EU changes the geopolitical context of the continent and has a profound impact on political equilibria and outcomes, as it relegates the Iron Curtain to the past, and ensures the consolidation of transition, so important in order to avoid other collapses into violence like the one experienced in former Yugoslavia. Even if it has rarely been conceptualized as such, enlargement is therefore first and foremost a foreign policy action, as it permanently changes the international environment. However, it is atypical because it is reached mainly by the extension of domestic policies rather than with traditional foreign policy instruments. Enlargement also modifies the traditional concept of foreign policy because it creates porous borders; today's neighbours could become tomorrow's members and any rigid distinction between outside and inside collapses. A debate has therefore begun on the eventual 'final' borders of the EU.

But there are two reasons why Europe is pushed to assume a more traditional role if it wants to exert influence beyond the continent. Firstly, Europe's atypical policy of enlargement and civilian power could emerge only because US protection during the Cold War guaranteed continental order even without a European contribution. Where this order is wanting, as for example in the Middle East or in the Caucasus, more traditional means—such as the ability to use force—are necessary. Secondly, while Europe's importance as a strategic theatre has diminished in recent decades,[2] Europe must now concentrate on global issues because some of the risks it faces, such as terrorism or the proliferation of weapons of mass destruction, originate in extra-European regions and therefore require a power-projection capability (Piening 1997). This has been noted through the elaboration of a European security strategy (European Council 2003b).

Much will depend, as during the Cold War, on the transatlantic relationship. Robert Kagan (2003) predicts that the differences between the USA and Europe will grow, due to the weakness of a 'European' foreign policy. The USA will therefore be forced to use its power globally to preserve international order, while Europe will retrench itself behind its prosperity and relative security after enlargement. Charles Kupchan (2003) takes the opposite view and believes that Europe will acquire the instruments of hard power which it still lacks, not least because the world is becoming multipolar, and the foreign policy of the USA will become more parochial and unilateralist. It will therefore no longer seem attractive in terms of protecting European interests. John Ikenberry (2002), finally, takes a middle position by arguing that—unless the traditional US multilateralism is abandoned—the transatlantic relationship and NATO could prosper for some time to come. Accordingly Europe will continue its incremental steps toward integration without being affected by— or provoking—sea changes in global alignments.

If Europe wants to develop a foreign policy based on both hard and soft power, this will ultimately and intimately be linked to the more general process of integration. European democratic institutions cannot in practice withstand the possibility of war being declared by common institutions without full democratic legitimacy, while the EU would be incapable of fighting a high-intensity conflict unless control is transferred to the collective European level. It is difficult to imagine a war being conducted through the cumbersome decision-making procedures of intergovernmentalism, with 25 veto powers and/or with rotating presidencies. Ultimately, only the establishment of a federation can approximate the foreign policy of a state (Hill 1993a, 316).

Notes

1 I am indebted to Mathias Koenig-Archibugi for many of the ideas here presented. I am also grateful to Christopher Hill for his patience in waiting for, and improving, the various drafts of this chapter.

2 According to Hinsley (1963, 8), European integration was possible only because of Europe's decline. 'The [eventual] success of [European integration] will have taken place in a changed situation which renders it irrelevant to a solution of the international problem, and will have taken place because of that changed situation.'

FURTHER READING

The most orthodox theoretical treatment, from a realist standpoint, of European integration and EU foreign policy is Grieco (1996, 1997a), while for a liberal view, one should take note of Moravcsik (1998). Hill (1993b) explains the conditions for an effective single European foreign policy. White (2001) and Whitman (1998) are broad analytical discussions of the way in which it operates. Kagan (2003) and Cooper (2003) discuss contemporary international politics with a special emphasis on Europe: while the first is critical of European attitudes, the second believes the EU to be a model for other parts of the world.

Cooper, R. (2003), *The Breaking of Nations: Order and Chaos in the Twenty-First Century* (New York: Atlantic Monthly Press, London: Atlantic Books).

Grieco, J. (1996), 'State Interests and International Rule Trajectories: A Neo-Realist Interpretation of the Maastricht Treaty and European Economic and Monetary Union', *Security Studies*, 5/3.

Grieco, J. (1997a), 'Systemic Sources of Variation in Regional Institutionalization in Western Europe, East Asia and the Americas', in Mansfield and Milner (eds), *The Political Economy of Regionalism* (New York: Columbia University Press).

Hill, C. (1993b), 'Shaping a federal foreign policy for Europe', in Hocking (ed.), *Foreign Relations and Federal States* (Leicester: Leicester University Press), 268–83.

Kagan, R. (2003), *Paradise and Power: America and Europe in the New World Order* (London: Atlantic Books).

Moravcsik, A. (1998), *The Choice for Europe: Social Purpose and State Power from Messina to Maastricht* (Ithaca, NY: Cornell University Press and London: UCC Press).

White, B. (2001), *Understanding European Foreign Policy* (Basingstoke: Palgrave Macmillan).

Whitman, R. (1998), *From Civilian Power to Superpower? The International Identity of the European Union* (London: Macmillan).

WEB LINKS

The most useful website for initial exploration of thinking about the international relations of the European Union are those of the FORNET network (**http://www.fornet. info/**). Each of these presents current debates about the nature of the EU's international relations and has links to additional academic resources. More generally on international relations theory and foreign policy analysis, see the following: **http://www.isanet.org** (the International Studies Association), **http://www.bisa.ac.uk** (the British International Studies Association) and **http://www.essex.ac.uk/ECPR/standinggroups/ir/index. htm** (the Standing Group on International Relations of the European Consortium for Political Research).

CHAPTER 3

The Pattern of the EU's Global Activity

Geoffrey Edwards

▌ Summary

This chapter provides a broad survey of the activities of the European Communities, now the Union, since their beginning in 1958. The EU has recently been most active in its own region, but its first historical priority was the far-flung ex-colonies of France and Belgium, to which those of Britain were later to be added. From the mid 1970s the Mediterranean had a high profile until overshadowed by the newly independent countries of Eastern Europe while, for a multitude of reasons, the Atlantic has also proved of persistent importance. Functionally, the chapter identifies the main elements that have pushed forward the EU's international role and those that have held it back. These often turn out to have been the same. Some are institutions, such as the European Commission and European Council; others are processes such as the Community method or political cooperation. The most important of all, both pushing and pulling, have been the member states. Their wavering, combined with external complications such as the actions of a distinctly ambivalent USA, present the contemporary EU with a difficult set of tensions, and accompanying choices.

Introduction

So far in this volume the analysis has focused on the inherent problems of thinking about the place of the EU in international relations (Chapter 1), and what may be usefully taken from the academic subject of International Relations in approaching this task (Chapter 2). Here we begin to survey the empirical reality of EU actions in the world. The current chapter covers the pattern and scope of the EU's global activity, providing an overview of what the European Communities/Union have done, where, and when. It serves as a backcloth to the more specialized accounts of institutions and processes and particular issue areas that make up Parts II and III of the book.

The chapter begins with a narrative of the historical evolution of the interaction of an evolving European Union with the rest of the world. It begins in the 1950s with the emergence of common policies on trade and development aid, follows the growing cooperation on foreign policy through European Political Cooperation (EPC) in the 1970s and 1980s and its 'pillarization' under Maastricht with the creation of the Common Foreign and Security Policy (CFSP) in 1993. The chapter then tracks the expanding scope of contacts through the widening range of policy instruments, including the (limited) use of armed forces and further institutional reforms, to the Lisbon Treaty of 2009.

The central part of the chapter is divided in two. Firstly, it focuses on the main geographical areas in which Europe has been active, namely Africa and other ex-colonial theatres, Europe's own regional environment, and to a lesser extent Asia, and the North Atlantic region. History, traditional trading links and security have been obvious motivating factors, but the EC/EU from early on has also sought to project the idea of itself as a model of regional organization and signed up to a wide range of agreements with other regional groupings of states. The chapter then goes on to examine further the main 'drivers' of Europe's external relations, whether common institutions, procedures, or particular member states, taking into account that, at the same time, these drivers can also at times act as brakes on any developments. This is the complex and dialectical nature of European cooperation, not only in the external area, whereby change is rarely ever linear, but also in terms of evoking contradictory political instincts within the various actors involved.

The final part of the chapter then identifies the major tensions that arise from these dialectics. They are fivefold, between rhetoric and achievement, Europeanization and national foreign policy, big and small member states, old and new Europe, and finally the concept of civilian Europe and the growing military dimension of the EU. The considerable variety and scope of Europe's international relations, especially in an era of continuing enlargement and internal disputes over treaty changes have made for a particularly patchy record of EU activity in a global system that appears subject to ever greater complexity and deepening suspicion.

Historical evolution

A Belgian minister's remark that the EU in the global system added up to little more than 'an economic giant, political dwarf and military worm' has long haunted the EU. The scope and pattern of the EU's international role were determined by the initial decision that the Economic Community should be a customs union with a common external tariff rather than an industrial free trade area. A common commercial policy thereby became inevitable. The fact, too, that several of the member states still had colonies meant that trade concessions had to be made to enable them to have continued access, while Community aid was also regarded, especially by France, as a condition of membership. Not only did these two elements provide the bases for EC/EU external relations, but their expansion has been rapid.

The economic weight of the EU meant greater opportunities for the exercise of political influence or 'structural power' (Keukeleire 2003), with, frequently, the aim of regime development if not regime change over the longer term. The EU has, after all, particular values to promote such as economic liberalism, international law (particularly the sanctity of contracts and freedom from arbitrary change) as well as its own legal order in the protection of the *acquis communautaire*. Effective multilateralism (to use the language of the EU's 2003 security strategy), whether in the UN or the WTO, has long been a cornerstone of the EC/EU's foreign external relations—whether to protect or promote its interests. So, too, has been the proactive approach towards other regional groupings—in Africa, the Americas, South East Asia, Southern Asia, or the Gulf, whether these have been based on the European model or not—in the interests of promoting common political as well as economic values within an inter-regional framework and, possibly, extending them more globally. That is not to say that Europe has not often used its weight reactively against increased competition—whether from the newly industrialized countries (NICs) in the 1960s or from the USA and Japan in the 1970s and 1980s—or in reaction to increased migratory flows and international crime in the 1990s and 2000s. But whether reacting to or attempting to shape the issues bound up with globalization, adapting to change in an increasingly interdependent system has been critical: forcing the pace of completing the internal market, bringing treaty reform or establishing new patterns of relationships. Foreign economic policies, broadly defined, are in a very significant sense at the 'core of EU "foreign policy"'; to ignore them excludes possibly less dramatic but certainly no less consequential developments (M. Smith 1998b).

And yet the idea that the 'flag follows trade' does not capture the full concept of the European construct held by many within the member states. From the outset there were plans for Europe to become a political entity, beginning with the proposal in 1950 for the establishment of a European defence community. That initiative, and the Political Community proposal that accompanied it, may have been killed off by the French National Assembly in 1954, but the idea lived on, not simply among small groups of Euro-federalists but in a number of European parties in and out of government, not least the Christian Democrats in Germany and in Italy. It took on a new lease with the creation of EPC in 1970. Even though EPC was very clearly limited to a procedure for coordinating foreign policy based on intergovernmental cooperation rather than supranational decision making, the rhetoric accompanying it saw it as the first step towards political union.

If the EC's external policies gradually widened in scope with the transfer of competences to the European level through successive treaty revision, EPC also developed, although at a rather different pace. While the former often led to a proactive change in the EC's relationships with third countries, EPC was frequently criticized for its limitations and its reactive and declaratory characteristics (Edwards 1997). The need to react to international events, especially crises, frequently caused immobilism and failure even if it then led to new efforts to deepen commitments and refine procedures and policy instruments. There were some successes—in the sense of the EC/EU six or nine acting together—as at the Conference on Security and Cooperation in Europe (CSCE, later OSCE) in 1975, or in the Middle East (as in the Euro–Arab dialogue of 1974, or in drawing up the Venice declaration in 1980). But what unity there was tended to be underpinned by economic considerations and therefore required the involvement of the European Commission. Conceptualizing Europe's nascent foreign policy as a single system was therefore difficult even when attempted (by, for example, Ginsberg 1989). This remained the case with EPC's transformation into the Common Foreign and Security Policy (CFSP) within the second pillar of the Treaty on European Union (TEU) signed at Maastricht, though the treaty also called for a 'single institutional framework'. Clarity in terms of the EC/EU's 'foreign policy' was further complicated by the increasing pressures to complement, externally, moves to promote the EU's internal security within Maastricht's third pillar on justice and home affairs. Even under EPC in the 1970s, issues such as terrorism had been increasingly dealt with—on an intergovernmental basis—within the so-called TREVI group (Terrorisme, Radicalisme, Extrémisme et Violence Internationale) on internal security cooperation. TREVI and other groups dealing with the management of borders, asylum, and immigration were incorporated within pillar III. But bringing in interior ministers did little to enhance the coherence of EU foreign policy. It did, however, reinforce the role of the European Council as the only body capable of overseeing all aspects of the EU.

Subsequent treaty reforms at Amsterdam and Nice saw a greater emphasis on the single decision-making framework and new instruments of policy such as common strategies—and this has been extended further in the Lisbon Treaty. Member states as well as the EU institutions themselves have clearly recognized the need both for greater efficiency in decision making and more effectiveness in implementing policy, even though they have not always worked in quite the same direction. Member states have sought to retain an intergovernmental base for the CFSP and for the European Security and Defence Policy agreed at Nice in December 2000, thereby ensuring that they can still take autonomous action in the event of a lack of common agreement. At the same time, they agreed to the creation of a High Representative to express the EU's unified position, a post first taken by Javier Solana, a former Spanish Foreign Minister and Secretary General of NATO. He was given a small but increasingly effective infrastructure in support and allowed considerable discretion in his dealings with other states and actors. Lisbon has enlarged the High Representative's role, even while maintaining a largely intergovernmental basis for decision making.

The conceptual problems of consistency, coherence, and continuity that have bedevilled Europe's foreign policy thus continue. Nuttall usefully distinguished three dimensions of consistency: 'horizontal' (between the different policies of the EU, whether across the Maastricht pillars, or even within pillar I between foreign economic policy, aid, and development); 'institutional' consistency (between the intergovernmental and Community bureaucratic structures); and 'vertical' consistency between EU and national policies (Nuttall 2005). To expect such coherence at the European level is doubtless unrealistic when at the national level there are frequently interdepartmental rivalries between ministries of foreign affairs, trade, development, defence, and finance. Not all member states have effective governmental coordination mechanisms, thereby compounding problems at the European level when there are already pressures within different Councils to reach agreement on the merits of each case according to their own *acquis*. Nonetheless, frequent ringing declarations by heads of state and government—on the need for greater European unity and coherence—do tend to raise expectations. This has a particular resonance in periods of crisis when 'joined-up' decision making may be at a premium. In the aftermath of 11 September 2001, for example, European efforts in the fight against terrorism extended across all three pillars and beyond in that there was agreement on policies such as better coordination through Europol and Eurojust, the introduction of anti-terrorist clauses in agreements with third countries, and better targeted assistance with the declared emphasis on preventative measures and diplomacy. The aim of strengthening the relationship with the USA, however, proved more problematic, with participation in the US-led anti-terrorist forces in Afghanistan and then Iraq only on the basis of coalitions of the willing.

The Lisbon Treaty goes some way in meeting such issues. A more permanent President of the European Council (appointed for a term of two and a half years, renewable once) may be able to focus greater attention on the need for greater consistency across policy sectors and pillars. Similarly, a strengthened High Representative may be able to extend consistency in all the Nuttall senses as well as providing for a greater continuity (even though it could also bring about competition with the European Council President). It had long been a complaint about CFSP as of EPC before it that leaving the organization and representation of the EU on foreign policy matters to a Presidency of the Council that rotated every six months undermined the EU's weight and credibility in the world. It was not until the Amsterdam

IGC of 1996 that it was finally agreed that there should be a senior figure able to speak for the EU on foreign policy issues, and then only alongside the Presidency and the Commission. However respected Javier Solana became as the Council's High Representative in bringing some continuity, the EU remained susceptible to counter pressures especially from the member states, particularly when holding the Presidency. The Lisbon Treaty seeks to bring greater authority to the EU's centre by taking up the responsibilities and dual role of the High Representative/Commission Vice President proposed in the ill-fated Constitutional Treaty (though Lisbon, as a concession to the British, retains the title of High Representative rather than that of an EU Minister of Foreign Affairs).

Geographical scope

Africa, the Caribbean, and the Pacific

From the beginning, the colonies and overseas territories of the member states were incorporated into a close network of relationships, strongly institutionalized and covering not only trade but also aid and technical assistance. The French, indeed, had been insistent on such a relationship in the negotiations establishing the EEC. The result was the beginnings of what has been described as a 'pyramid of privilege' in terms of preferential relationships with third countries (Mishilani *et al.* 1981).

If, initially, the colonies and former colonies were largely French and Belgian possessions in Africa, with the accession of the UK former British colonies in the Caribbean and Pacific as well as Africa were included, grouped after 1975 within an institutionalized framework governed by successive Lomé Conventions. Despite their disparate nature and discrepancies in size, the African, Caribbean, and Pacific countries (ACPs) have proved to be an enduring group even if subject to strong centrifugal pressures as the different regions became themselves more institutionalized. But in 1975, at the height of the New International Economic Order, the Lomé Convention placed considerable emphasis on ideas of partnership notwithstanding the inequality of dependence, non-reciprocity of trade concessions, and need for aid and assistance (Twitchett 1981; Ravenhill 1985; Grilli 1993). The asymmetries were only too obvious insofar as the EC development policies determined access to the largest market in the world and the largest source of assistance. They were apparent, too, in the widening scope of successive Lomé Conventions, which gradually took into account growing European concerns about abuses of human rights and the lack of respect for democratic principles and the rule of law, especially in Africa. The influence of the 'Washington institutions' (the IMF and World Bank) was also important in bringing about the shift that found expression in Lomé IV (1995–2000) (Holland 2002). Although there have been criticisms of a lack of even-handedness in dealing with developing states and others—raising questions about the EU's unequivocal commitment to upholding human rights norms (Ward 1998; Youngs 2001)—Lomé provided for the possibility of dialogue on non-compliance. An increased focus on political conditionality was extended in the Cotonou Agreement, which replaced Lomé in 2000 (K. Smith 2003). The agreement, signed so far by 78 states (including South Africa, though not all Cotonou provisions apply in its case), continues the trend of politicizing the aid relationship by emphasizing good governance, the role of civil society and the private sector, and conflict prevention (Hilpold 2002; Hill 2001).

The neighbourhood

A similar pattern of politicization is discernible in the EC/EU's relationship with the countries of the Mediterranean and, as the EU's enlargement continued to Central and Eastern Europe, with the remaining countries of Eastern Europe and the Southern Caucuses.

To take the Mediterranean first, its strategic importance was obvious from the outset of the Communities. Member states were keen to ensure stability in the region, only too well aware of the tensions generated by the Arab–Israeli conflict, the need to ensure oil and gas supplies and supply routes, and the size of the Mediterranean market. There were growing pressures, too, created by migration from North Africa. At the same time, several member states, led by France, while seeking to 'Europeanize' their relationship with the countries of the southern Mediterranean, were also keen to retain close relations with individual North African states (Algeria had, after all, been a part of metropolitan France until 1957) (Edwards and Phillipart 1997). If the ACP countries had initially been at the top of the pyramid of privilege, the countries of the Mediterranean sought to exploit their geographical proximity. In practice the result was a mosaic of different types of agreement that gradually encompassed all the countries of the Mediterranean, first through a complex series of individual agreements that ranged from association with the prospect of a customs union and presumed future membership with Greece and then Turkey (1961 and 1963) to preferential trade agreements (as with Israel in 1964) to association agreements with the countries of the Maghreb. From 1972 onwards, the mosaic was always subject to European attempts to impose more global principles of free trade between the EC/EU and individual Mediterranean states—beginning with free access for industrial goods (with exceptions for more sensitive goods such as refined petroleum products, as well as agricultural produce).

While the end of the Cold War meant that EC/EU attention shifted increasingly towards the countries of Central and Eastern Europe, there was also an acute sense of insecurity engendered by continued instability in the Mediterranean region and an ever growing rate of migration, legal and illegal, from and through North Africa. The first Gulf War of 1990–1 increased the intensity of that concern. Thus, while other member states were preoccupied with similar migration flows via the Balkans and through Eastern Europe, as well as increasing aid and investment flows,

France, joined by Italy and Spain, determined on the need for a more holistic approach to the Mediterranean region. Their efforts culminated in 1995 in the so-called Barcelona Process, with its three 'baskets' that mirrored those of the Helsinki Final Act of the CSCE some 20 years earlier, and which covered security, economic relations, and humanitarian and cultural relations. It clearly reflected a multidimensional view of security in which migration, terrorism, and drug-trafficking took precedence (Barbé and Izquierdo 1997, 122) and which required cross-pillar coordination. It was, for one EC/EU veteran:

... reduced to its elementary political substance ... nothing but a political deal with Europe offering its advice, its moral presence, its vast political and economic experience and, of course, sizeable financial cooperation to those determined to tackle their problems effectively.

(Rhein 1996, 83)

The Barcelona Process has not, however, been regarded as a particularly successful deal. While the economic dimension has usually been foremost, it has not provided the expected leverage in other fields. The regional security dimension, for example, has made little headway with the Arab–Israeli conflict rarely separable and frequently to the fore in the Process, preventing meetings in Arab countries or emptying them of much significance (Vasconcelos and Joffe 2000).

In addition, while migration pressures continued to mount, they became inextricably linked with growing concerns over terrorist attacks. This was the case especially in France through much of the 1990s and in Spain in March 2004 when an al-Qaeda-linked group claimed responsibility for the bombings at Madrid railway station. The need for stronger counter-terrorism measures became a dominant factor in Mediterranean relations, sometimes even at the cost of maintaining the more normative promotion of democratization and liberalization, particularly as the hoped-for dynamism in economic development and direct investment had not been achieved (Joffe 2008). Indeed, one of the few new elements agreed at the celebration of the tenth anniversary of the Barcelona declaration was a new code of conduct on countering terrorism.

However, by 2005, the Mediterranean region was, again, having to compete for attention with countries in Eastern Europe and the Southern Caucuses. The prospect of the enlargement of the Union to include the countries of Central and Eastern Europe led to discussions from 2002 on a new European neighbourhood policy (ENP) that was to include all the countries of Eastern Europe and the Southern Caucuses as well as of the Mediterranean. Together they would form, according to the then Commission President, Romano Prodi, a 'ring of friends' around the enlarged EU, with the Union offering 'more than partnership and less than membership' (Prodi 2002). It was to be a new strategic framework that took policy instruments from across the three pillars of the Maastricht Treaty and looked to strengthening human rights, creating greater institutional capacity as well as incentives for economic liberalization and development.

The policy was geared to those countries that were not regarded as likely members of the European Union. It thereby excluded Turkey, already an EU applicant. Russia excluded itself, seeing itself as a strategic partner rather than simply part of the neighbourhood. The neighbourhood policy was immediately subject to criticism for its lack of coherence and political vision—much as the EC/EU had been criticized in the period immediately after the Cold War for its lack of a coherent policy towards the countries of Central and Eastern Europe (CEECs) that were looking both 'to return to Europe' by acceding to the EU and to join NATO for fear of the uncertainties further east. Then, policies had tended to emerge by default rather than by design, in part because the EU and its member states had no conception of 'Europe', and, as Zielonka argues, in the absence of any vision, EU policies towards the CEECs were dominated by the internal agenda (Zielonka 1998c). Given the other events of the 1990s, with the move towards economic and monetary union and the single currency, Yugoslavia's collapse into conflict, the implosion of the Soviet Union and the uncertainties surrounding the prospects of democracy in Russia, it was not surprising that domestic interests had successfully asserted themselves in the policy-making processes (Tewes 2002).

In 2003–4, even while domestic concerns, most notably anxiety over the absorption capacity of the EU or 'enlargement fatigue' and the question of treaty reform, still tended to dominate debates over the wider neighbourhood, there appeared to be a clearer sense of purpose. The aim of the ENP was to ignore questions of membership but, nonetheless, to bring about the convergence of neighbouring states on EU norms and practices using conditionality, an instrument that had been successfully employed in the accession negotiations that had led to the enlargements of 2004 and 2007 (Del Sarto and Schumacher 2005; Cremona and Hillion 2006; Edwards 2008). The problem, expressed clearly by the newer member states, as well as Ukraine, Georgia, and others, was that these policies of conditionality were now being applied to countries that had not been given the incentive of future EU membership. The Polish, Lithuanian, and other governments were consistent in pushing for a membership 'perspective' in order to maintain any reform momentum among those still outside the Union who wished to 'return to Europe'.

While the East Europeans were important in bringing about proposals to improve the ENP, it was in the Mediterranean that the first serious steps were taken to complement or supplement the ENP. This was the proposal for a Mediterranean Union put forward by the French President, Nicolas Sarkozy, initially in his election campaign in 2007, and then with the support of the Spanish and Italian governments. The actual outcome was somewhat less than a body made up only of Mediterranean states that would be complementary to the EU, but a Union for the Mediterranean that, under pressure from, particularly, the German Chancellor, Angela Merkel, was open to all EU member states. It was also designed more to build on the 1995 Barcelona declaration than to replace it. Nonetheless, the Union for the Mediterranean was launched with great ceremony in Paris in July 2008 under joint French and Egyptian chairmanship.

Reinvigorated, the Poles, together with the Swedes, proposed a new partnership with the countries of Eastern Europe and the Southern Caucasus to include further incentives to bring about further convergence on European norms even if without any significantly increased financial assistance. The Prague declaration of May 2009 on a new eastern partnership held out the prospect of a more ambitious relationship accelerating political association and further economic integration. However, relations with individual countries within the partnership were to continue to be based on principles of differentiation and conditionality.

In contrast to the treatment of the countries of Eastern Europe and the Southern Caucasus, the prospect of membership has been an integral part in the reconstruction objectives in the Balkans. The collapse of Yugoslavia had presented the EC/EU with an existential challenge as much as a strategic one, for the destruction and bloodshed seemed 'the antithesis of everything the EU stood for' (Pentland 2003, 145). Strategically, it was a serious defeat made worse by an initial certainty that 'This was the hour of Europe, not of America,' as the then Luxembourg Foreign Minister was reported as saying (Edwards 1997, 176). The lack of coherence among the member states and the inability of the EC/EU to resolve the conflict meant that it was left to the USA to bring about the temporary peace with Slobodan Milosevic at Dayton in 1995. Dependence on the USA was again only too clear during the Kosovo crisis of 1998–9, when it was left to the USA and NATO to take the lead. However, the outcome was not only a gradual consolidation of various plans and programmes into a coherent policy towards the Balkans as a whole but also the move towards a European security and defence policy. The initially reactive Regional Approach gave way in 1999 to the more proactive stabilization and association process (SAP) that has included recognition of the Balkan states' vocation as possible EU members. If the emphasis was initially on economic reconstruction, it became more highly politicized and interventionist in order to ensure that political norms compatible with those of the EU were introduced and maintained (Pippan 2004). Such has been the relative success of the SAP that Croatia and Macedonia have been accepted as candidates for membership while Montenegro and Serbia have applied for membership. All remain a part of the stabilization process, as, since 2008, has Bosnia Herzegovina.

The Balkans also saw the beginnings of the EU's security and defence policy in practice. EU military forces were present in Macedonia in 2003 as part of Operation Concordia and police forces as part of EUPOL Proxima to help ensure the implementation of the 2001 Ohrid framework agreement between the Macedonian Slavs and the Albanians. EU forces still remain—now in limited numbers—in Bosnia in Operation Althea along with a police mission. The EU launched its largest civilian mission in Kosovo in December 2008.

The need to bring Russia into a more inclusive relationship with the EU had long been a goal of member states, not least of Germany. Both the EU's continued integration through treaty reform and its further enlargement have demanded a more comprehensive relationship. But at the same time, the consequence of that enlargement (and that of NATO) has been to create deep divisions among the member states over how to deal with Russia—while intensifying Moscow's own ambivalence towards the EU (Leonard and Popescu 2007; Hughes 2007). The Soviet Union had proved particularly equivocal towards Western European integration, seeking to ignore and bypass it as much as possible. Russian Presidents from Yeltsin and Putin to Medvedev have not appeared much more enthusiastic. Successive governments have, for example, been anxious to prevent Ukraine and Belarus from following others too closely on the track towards EU membership, particularly Ukraine. For the EU's part, there were not only sensitive trade issues to negotiate in the PCA, but, after 1995, there were also increased concerns over, for example, Russia's policies in Chechnya. The EU imposed some delays in implementing the Partnership and Cooperation Agreement (PCA), but for the most part preferred to maintain channels of communication rather than to foreclose them, especially after 11 September 2001, when Russian governments sought to identify dissident Chechens with terrorism in general. But if the focus after 2005 was on exploring the four 'common spaces' (the economy and environment; freedom, security and justice; external security; and research and education), it was against a background of growing concern within many EU members over declining respect for human rights and democratic norms in Russia, which then had to be set against increasing anxiety over energy security and Russia's energy policies. The new negotiations launched in 2008 were again put on hold after the Georgian–Russian conflict. For its part, Russia has often appeared to prefer to negotiate bilateral agreements with individual member states, especially on energy, thereby making agreement among the 25/27 member states even more difficult to secure.

The Atlantic

Although the USA has been the EC/EU's most important trading partner and ally, no formal relationship was established between the EC and the USA until the declaration of 1990. Against a background of particularly dense non-governmental links, as well as NATO, successive US administrations have run with both an integrating Europe and with its member governments (particularly those of the UK and Germany—at least until divisions over the invasion of Iraq in 2003). But US support for European integration had frequently been tempered by alarm over the consequences that integration might bring. There have been spats, for example, over trade, less often resolved within the General Agreement on Tariffs and Trade (GATT) than in the WTO. Burden sharing in terms of security has been a continuous concern. Uncertainties over the role, purpose, and strategy of a post-Cold War NATO have been both cause and effect, creating American ambivalence towards European efforts to create a security and defence policy after 1998.

For much of the past, the EC/EU's relationship with the USA had been successfully compartmentalized—though with occasional efforts such as that of Dr Kissinger in 1973 in his 'Year of Europe' to bring them together within one 'ball of wax'

(M. Smith 1984). From an economic and commercial perspective, the 1990 declaration was succeeded by the New Transatlantic Agenda signed in Madrid in 1995, which included what was termed a confidence-building process on the resolution of bilateral trade issues, together with a wide-ranging agreement on promoting global peace and stability, working towards common responses to global challenges and expanding world trade. A transatlantic economic partnership agreement followed in 1998 although it was only in 2007 that the economic relationship was 'upgraded' with the Transatlantic Economic Council.

Moves towards deepening and widening European integration and establishing a distinctive European identity have frequently led to US demands for compensation (altruism has its limits even for a hegemon), while US involvement in resolving conflicts in the Balkans has invariably shown up European weaknesses and continued US dominance. But concern over the USA's reluctance to continue its involvement in European security issues as in the past, as well as a more unilateralist approach in general, led the incoming government of Tony Blair to make a radical shift in British policy, with the build-up of the Kosovo crisis proving decisive (Hoffmann 2000; Shearer 2000; Howorth 2001). The outcome, the Franco-British declaration at Saint-Malo in December 1998, which presaged the European Security and Defence Policy, wrong-footed the Clinton administration, whose Secretary of State, Madeleine Albright, demanded 'no duplication, no decoupling and no discrimination' on the EU's part against NATO and its non-EU allies (Edwards 2000, 9). That ambiguity and a mixture of concern, scorn, and scepticism towards the venture continued, despite the EU's willingness to cooperate closely with US authorities on counter-terrorism measures in the aftermath of the events of 11 September 2001 (Rees 2006). While many within the EU supported the USA in their invasion of Afghanistan (even if through a coalition of the willing within NATO), the invasion of Iraq threatened to divide the enlarging EU. In such circumstances, the unanimous agreement on the European Security Strategy in December 2003 proved an important marker of a European determination to regroup. With the growing unpopularity of the Bush administration (opinion being alienated by its hostility, for example, to the Kyoto agreement on climate change and its opposition to the International Criminal Court, as well as by Iraq), there was a tendency in Europe to wait for change in America's leadership. There was considerable relief and high expectations of a changed US position on a raft of policies with the election of Barack Obama in 2008.

Asia

If, institutionally, the EU's relationship with the USA was relatively limited, this was in part because the two sides met in a multitude of other multilateral fora, notably NATO and the G7/8. But the density of the EU–US relationship has still been in marked contrast to the relative weakness of EU–Asia links. Intentions such as those of the Asia–Pacific Economic Cooperation group of some 21 states to move to free trade by 2020 created a strong incentive on the part of the EU to take a more proactive role, which met with an interested Asian response (Forster 1999). Biannual Asia–Europe meetings were launched in 1996 under the telling slogan of 'Towards a new Asia–Europe partnership for greater growth' (Wiessala 2002, 76). Trade issues have invariably been the catalyst for EC/EU involvement, whether in meeting the competitive challenge of the NICs and Japan in the 1960s and 1970s, or inspiring hopes of new markets in Japan (disappointed, especially since the financial difficulties of the late 1990s). More recently, China's phenomenal growth figures became a particular focus of EU efforts leading, *inter alia*, to EU support for Chinese accession to the GATT/WTO (achieved in 2001). However, the arms embargo imposed on China in the aftermath of the suppression of the Tiananmen Square protests, together with European concerns over human rights in Tibet and elsewhere, have inhibited closer relations, as have differences over climate change.

Even in the EC–ASEAN relationship, which dates back to 1978, economic interests have usually complemented any political interests reinforcing what Dent has called 'value system friction' (Nuttall 1992; Dent 1999, 51). The relationship with ASEAN became subject to increased difficulty after 1991 over the issue of East Timor because of Portuguese concerns, and over Burma/Myanmar's membership of ASEAN. The active pursuit of human rights concerns by the European Parliament as well as by individual member states has also provoked antagonism in the region. Nonetheless, the EU was seen to play a more positive political role when it contributed to the re-establishment of stability in Aceh by sending a small monitoring mission in 2005–6.

Group-to-group relations

The EU's relationship with groups such as ASEAN and the ACP countries reflects strong historical, geopolitical, and strategic ties between member states and the 'developing world', but indicates, too, a deep interest on the part of Europe in other groupings of states. Inevitably the EU has frequently had to react to events, whether coups, civil wars, state failures, natural disasters, or other conflicts that threaten to spill over to challenge EU interests. Relationships have been further affected by both the EC's own enlargement whether to the south to include Greece, Spain, and Portugal, or towards Eastern Europe. But there has been an underlying trend on the part of the EC/EU to link and reinforce political and economic dialogues with the growing range of other regional groupings that emerged in the last decades of the 20th century.

These dialogues have been based on varying foundations, reflecting the very different types of regional groups that have been established, some being largely trade driven and others more security driven, and with varying degrees of institutionalization. The resulting somewhat hybrid links have ranged from those with ASEAN, via the Gulf Cooperation Council (GCC), through the Economic Community of West African States (ECOWAS) to the Common Market of the Southern Cone

(Mercosur), with many others in between (Edwards and Regelsberger 1990; Monar 1997b; Alecu de Flers and Regelsberger 2005).

What has made for greater complexity in such dialogues has been the fact that, much as the EC/EU itself has been in a constant state of flux, both geographically and functionally, so, too, have many of the other groups. Groups have ebbed and flowed in terms of the extent of their integration and/or cooperation and have been amoeba-like in their membership or the extent to which they or some of their participating states have become part of a larger grouping, sometimes with overlapping, sometimes complementary, interests. ASEAN has grown from five to ten members since 1967 and the subjects discussed have evolved from trade to financial cooperation to security. It now also functions within the wider framework of the Asia–EU Meeting (ASEM) launched in 1996 (Forster 2000; Stokhof *et al.* 2004; Gilson 2005). In South America, the EU has relations with Mercosur, the Andean Community, the Central American Community, and CARICOM (in the Caribbean) as well as with the wider Rio group, a strategic partnership with the Latin American and Caribbean countries (LAC), and even holds observer status (along with the EU's member states) at the Organization of American States (OAS) (Santander 2005; Hardacre and Smith 2009). In Africa, EU relations with regional groups such as ECOWAS or the Southern African Development Community (SADC) have been complemented by its increasingly comprehensive relationship with the African Union, whose structure was itself based heavily on that of the EU.

A vital factor in the EC/EU's enthusiasm for such inter-regional dialogues has been its own sense of purpose as a model for reconciling regional differences and bringing about the peaceful settlement of disputes, that might lead to economically and politically liberal democratic unions. The Commission and some member states have welcomed the sense of regionality that complements and enhances that of Europe. Regardless of the potential paradox, the EC/EU has also seen itself as an example of regional economic integration that creates a consequent strength in the global system (Farrell 2005).

But the complexity of such interactions of motives and relationships has been further reinforced by another somewhat contradictory trend: if, on the one hand, the EU has encouraged a sense of regional identity and closer integration among its regional partners, on the other, it and its member states frequently have sought bilateral agreements with particular states, not least Brazil, India, or South Africa, and other strategic partners. Moreover, in part in response to meet pressures within WTO, the EU has negotiated free trade areas with the ACP on the basis of (more limited) regional groupings through Economic Partnership Agreements (EPAs). There has, in other words, been continuous tension between multilateral approaches and regionality, as well as between regionalism and differentiated bilateralism.

Drivers and brakes

The development of so many varied relationships across widely diverging geo-graphical areas has inevitably been subject to a range of forces and players. Many have sought to drive forward integration in Europe's external relations, both for its own sake and as a means of exerting international influence. Others have been con-cerned, sometimes in conjunction with interested non-EU parties, about the impli-cations for existing national foreign policies, or for other international institutions. This section analyses the main elements that have pushed for cooperation in the external field, while showing how almost every positive initiative has had an equal and opposite reaction. The focus here is on the intra-European forces at work, even though they are clearly in continuous interaction with outsiders, notably the USA.

The general EC framework

If, until 1992, Europe's 'foreign policy' was of somewhat dubious legal and political standing, the Treaty of Maastricht both established CFSP and, in many respects, codified the tensions between the EU's foreign economic and foreign policies by separating them into distinct but interrelated pillars. Chris Patten, when looking back over his period as Commissioner for External Relations (2000–4) and his rela-tionship with Javier Solana, the EU's High Representative, wrote:

... Solana occupied the front office and I was in charge of the back office of European foreign policy... But at least in the back office, the levers are connected to machinery; pull them and something normally happened, if somewhat too slowly.

(Patten 2005: 155–6)

Patten points to the core importance of the general EC framework as the princi-pal driver of a more coherent, integrated foreign policy. The basic structure of the EC's international relations was determined by the establishment not simply of a customs union, but also a common market with four freedoms relating to factors of production, and certain common policies, particularly agriculture and competi-tion. It necessitated not only the negotiation of bilateral trade agreements but also almost continuous negotiation within the framework of the GATT and later the WTO. Moreover, as the EC became an increasingly genuine single market, so it led to the creation of a regulatory regime with few parallels elsewhere (Majone 1996). The consequence of this has been the promotion of the *acquis* beyond the EU's bor-ders in agreements and in a host of multilateral fora, which has led to innumer-able disputes bilaterally and multilaterally (Mayes 1993; Weiler 2000; Hocking and Smith 1997; Young 2002).

As the EC has agreed to common policies, so it has sought also to protect them. Pre-eminent among the common policies since the 1960s have been the Common

Commercial Policy (CCP) and the Common Agricultural Policy (CAP). While mutual interests, notably among the USA, Europe, and Japan, kept agriculture off the GATT agenda until the 1990s, the CAP has frequently been a complicating factor in relations with the USA and other temperate producers, and developing producers—with the example of bananas suggesting the complexities of the negotiations in that the EU had to modify its banana regime at the behest of the WTO in favour of Latin American producers supported by the USA against its traditional (ACP) suppliers. As other policies, such as competition policy, industrial, R&D, immigration, and environmental policies were developed so they, too, were gradually added to the EC/EU agenda. Even in areas where Community competence is limited, as in culture and education, there has been increasing coordination among member states, whether through 'television without frontiers' directives or the so-called 'Bologna process' relating to education. Such coordination has been both to protect European cultures and to enhance Europe's global competitiveness—with, as a result, the extension of the EU's international policies, further rationalized by the belief that when Europe speaks with one voice it carries considerably greater weight than any individual member state.

However, even while they have agreed to the unsteady and sometimes difficult expansion of the Community's competences, member states have at the same time been loath to allow the Community a single voice, simply because they do not believe that their interests are being adequately protected. This has been particularly the case in the area of services, especially culture and intellectual property where differences among the member states (notably on the part of France) have left the EC's position unclear. The Community's exclusive competence in trade matters was established early, thus allowing the Commission to negotiate on behalf of the EC/EU as a whole. But the position on services has been much less obvious and the Lisbon Treaty has not wholly resolved any ambiguity. However, the European Court of Justice in a number of cases has held that member states have a 'duty to cooperate' where such issues of mixed competence were involved, especially in a WTO context. Member states retain a veto in policy making but if unanimity cannot be achieved, there remains concern that an individual member state as well as the Union could then, in effect, be left without a voice.

This kind of blockage occurred from the outset of the EC, even within those areas ostensibly always within the competence of the EC, such as trade policy (Hayes 1993, 123). As Hayes points out, even on trade, member states have taken full advantage of treaty provisions (originally Article 113; later, under Maastricht, 133; now 207 under Lisbon), which lay down that the Commission will undertake trade negotiations within the framework of directives agreed by the Council. However, while the role of the committee of (senior national) officials has frequently been critical in terms of oversight or management (Johnson 1998), it has often proved inadequate. The Commission has appeared to be beyond control insofar as negotiation invariably implies compromise. French ministers have been far from reticent about complaining at subsequent meetings of the Council about a process once described as 'the mushroom treatment': ministers 'are kept in the dark, and every so often the door is opened and a bucket of manure is thrown over them' (Hayes 1993, 125). French hostility to successive—especially British or other too liberal—Trade Commissioners and, more seriously, to the extension and development of Community competences, as in the case of culture and intellectual property, has frequently been the result of this kind of behaviour.

The Commission and foreign policy

This suspicion of the Community framework and the role of the Commission was particularly apparent in the beginnings of cooperation on foreign policy, i.e. EPC in 1970. This soon became the focal point for aspirations for a common foreign policy even though de Gaulle's legacy necessitated a separate intergovernmental procedure that excluded the Community institutions. As a result, EPC had perforce to rely on the commitment of the member states: EPC procedures were designed for them, maintained by them, and developed by them. The role of the Presidency was critical. It was, indeed, gradually that a secretariat was established in support of the Presidency. This was enlarged under Maastricht to service the CFSP, and brought within the general Council Secretariat to become the alternative, albeit limited, institutional infrastructure to that of the Commission. The changes brought about by the Amsterdam Treaty, in creating the High Representative and his Policy Unit, enormously strengthened the Council Secretariat's role and inevitably created suspicion within the Commission.

Member states' determination to keep EPC and then CFSP intergovernmental in terms of structure and procedures and therefore formally separate from the EC and the Commission continued despite a common awareness that the division was artificial and that policy outcomes were often limited as a result. But it did gradually break down, with the Commission an active if wary partisan on the side of a more coherent foreign policy. As a driver of foreign policy integration, it had the advantage, at least from the mid 1980s, of being able to bring the economic and political aspects of policy together. It alone could initiate Community action over the widening range of policy instruments within the EC framework, not least sanctions and aid programmes—and this even though ministries of foreign affairs might have wished to retain the distinction between high and low politics. Moreover, under the Single European Act (SEA) as reaffirmed by Maastricht, the Commission shared with the Presidency of the Council the responsibility for ensuring consistency between EC external policies and those agreed under EPC. To quote Nuttall: 'It would be misleading ... to give the impression that EPC has been purely intergovernmental, as the emphasis on coordination of policies might have led one to expect' (1994, 85). Ultimately, indeed, the Commission came to enjoy a formal shared right of initiative in the CFSP, although this was not a power it found possible to exploit.

The Commission's role expanded both because of its presence under the treaties and the growing scope and scale of the EU's activity and the concomitant growth in the EU's overseas representation. This was in marked contrast to the experience of the member states where cutbacks have been rather more common (Hocking and Spence 2002). The representation of the Commission has been steadily expanding so that by 2005, for example, it was accredited to 121 countries and organizations (Hocking and Spence 2005). Its delegations have diplomatic functions and their political reports have been of increasing significance. The Commission, in other words, has long had its own sources of information, sometimes rather more exten-sive than the sources available to many of the smaller member states. At the same time, the Commission has the capability to implement external policy and some of the external elements of EU internal policies, as well as negotiating on behalf of member governments in the GATT/WTO, etc. As Pollack has pointed out, fol-lowing Putnam, this places the Commission at both the internal and international negotiating tables, providing it 'with the possibility of using external pressure to strengthen its negotiating position internally, and vice versa' (Pollack 2003, 270). Institutionally, the spillover effect from foreign economic to foreign policy mak-ing has been significant—as can be seen in the Commission's participation together with the original and the reformed troika of EU representation. Even when not par-ticularly visible, the Commission's role as a policy entrepreneur and policy driver should not be underestimated.

Those roles could become even more significant as the Commission's delegations begin to provide the basis for the External Action Service under the Lisbon Trea-ty—which explains why member states have taken such an interest in the proposed Service and the Commission has been trying to guard its achievements. The details of the Service have been subject to sporadic discussion since the proposal was first mooted in the Constitutional Treaty but are likely to see the advent of Council offi-cials and seconded national officials, working to the High Representative/Commis-sion Vice President, and taking on the responsibilities of the (formerly rotating) Presidency of the Council. Such a Service could be central in bringing about coher-ence and effectiveness to the EU's future foreign policy, even while severely testing the willingness of member governments to forgo some of the prerogatives that they have held particularly dear.

Member states

It became commonplace to criticize EPC and CFSP as intergovernmental processes for coordinating foreign policy that were invariably if not inevitably too reactive to events and too declaratory in terms of any outcome. This was particularly the case in crises when, despite their treaty commitment, member governments would resort to unilateral action either before discussions were completed at the European level, or even—in some cases—afterwards.

And yet, just as often, member governments committed themselves to developing foreign policy cooperation further. In this sense they have been both a driver and a brake, with no given country falling neatly into one category or the other. Balancing the EC/EU's economic strength with political clout has remained a constant in the EU's development—whether in the interests of more effective external/foreign policy or of deepening European integration. With every setback, from the 1973 Yom Kippur War, to the first Gulf War and the collapse of Yugoslavia from 1991, to the second Gulf War, member governments have sought to bring about reform, whether through successive reports within EPC, Presidency conclusions after meetings of the European Council, or treaty reform as in Maastricht, Amsterdam, Nice, or Lisbon. If the Maastricht Treaty introduced CFSP, it was at the Nice European Council in December 2000 that heads of government agreed to the establishment of a European Security and Defence Policy (ESDP), which, as the Common Security and Defence Policy, became treaty-based in Lisbon.

The key states in this long process towards a security and defence policy have been France, Germany, and the UK. Peterson saw the Franco-German alliance as key to the development of European foreign policy: when the two were in harmony, advances were possible (Peterson 1998); or, as Wolfgang Schäuble (long a leading figure in Germany's CDU) declared in 1997, when they cannot agree, 'things will go wrong in Europe' (Aggestam in Manners and Whitman 2000, 77). Franco-German initiatives had frequently provided the motor both in terms of integration in general and foreign policy in particular, not least in their joint initiative for an IGC on political union in April 1990, even if the CFSP was, in part, the result of the need to mend the rift that reunification had caused in their relationship: 'To Paris and Bonn, the CFSP was more important as symbol than as substance' (Nuttall 2000, 271).

During the 1990s, France had to come to terms with a 'new' Europe that included a reunified Germany (and, indeed, three new smaller and neutral member states) even while believing that 'their position and status had been devalued while those of Germany had been enhanced' (Szukala and Wessels 1997, 78). The search for alternative allies temporarily led France to look to other Mediterranean states and to Europe and the initiation of the Barcelona Process, albeit without tremendous enthusiasm, and they soon reverted to a more bilateral relationship with individual Mediterranean states. There was also a minuet with NATO, with France coming closer to but ultimately shying away from full reintegration until President Sarkozy returned France to the integrated command structure in 2009.

Even on CFSP, there appeared to be differences, with Germany, for example, generally keener on reducing the distinctions between the Maastricht pillars. While efforts continued to be made, not least through bilaterals under the rubric of the Elysée Treaty of 1963, to steer European Council meetings, little of substance often seemed to emerge. Yet reports of the demise of the Franco-German tandem proved either premature or exaggerated. In the autumn of 2002 the British and others appeared surprised by the reassertion of Franco-German pressure within the Convention on the Future of Europe, even though mutual support in opposition to the US-led invasion of Iraq had been increasingly evident. France and Germany (together with Belgium) also pressed for a new security and defence headquarters to be set up in the Brussels suburb of Tervuren in their mini-summit in April 2003, creating pressure for a planning, command, and control structure for European actions that could be autonomous, if not wholly separate, from that of NATO. Again, after a period of relative distance, President Sarkozy and Chancellor Merkel also agreed on a variety of proposals for closer collaboration and leadership in Europe in February 2010, including improving the EU's relationship with Russia.

The British cannot always be excluded from those driving towards a more effective and coherent EU foreign policy, despite the frequency with which they have sought to apply a brake, especially where NATO seemed to be under threat. As Hill (1996) and Forster (2000) have noted, the UK has been a strong supporter of both EPC and CFSP, even if for the most part as a supplement or complement to its national foreign policy positions, while Dover (2007) has discussed the 'uploading' of British defence preferences within a process of Europeanization. A core British position has been the continued coordination of policy on an intergovernmental basis—even while calling for greater coherence and effectiveness. In October 2000, for example, Tony Blair called for Europe to have not only a 'more' coherent foreign policy but even 'the military capability we require without which common defence policy is a chimera'. Europe, however, was to become 'a superpower but not a superstate' (Leonard 2000, 26–7).

Setting the EU's agenda has invariably been seized on by member states, and not only the Franco-German tandem, to try to drive the process forward. Most states, including the UK, have sought to ensure that particular issues appear on the agenda, whether a region of special concern or some aspects of the promotion of human rights. Pre-Lisbon, this tendency had been especially pronounced during a member state's Presidency, even if the outcome was not always that intended. While smaller member states, for example, may have relished the opportunities provided by holding the Presidency to represent the EU in the world and to move the agenda on, the effect has sometimes been only to reinforce the tendency towards closer relations among the big three. The Lisbon reforms, however, mean that there is a semi-permanent President of the European Council and a High Representative who chairs the Foreign Affairs Council. That will not prevent individual member states raising particular concerns, especially the rotating Presidency, which still chairs the General Affairs Council and which will continue to deal with issues such as development assistance closely linked to foreign policy. The opportunities for confusion rather than coherence remain legion.

Despite the reforms, the member states will continue to try to drive EU foreign policy in their own directions because they continue to have special relationships with particular countries or regions. Bridge building has often been a significant element in the way the new member states, in particular, have conceived their value to the EC/EU, but it has also been used to try to set a particular path for coordinated action by the EU. Perhaps the most obvious example has been that of the UK in its 'special relationship' with the USA—even if others, too, including Ireland, Italy, or pre-Schröder Germany, have had their own special relationships. The idea that particular member states could be *interlocuteurs valables* has a long history, even if it has sometimes lacked credibility or has eventually been counter productive if a government is seen as too *parti pris*.

Member states have also sought to project their own political culture onto the EU. For example, there has long been an element of reasserting a sense of *grandeur* for the French (and British), via Europe. The French initially tended to emphasize ideas of *défense européenne* and the higher end of the Western European Union-agreed Petersberg tasks, of peace making rather than simply humanitarian assistance. But others have emphasized very different concerns. With the 1995 enlargement the non-aligned countries Sweden and Finland, together with neutral Austria, became members of the Union. While not opposed to the EU taking on the Petersberg tasks, nor, indeed, to the proposals for a security and defence policy, they had a particular attachment to the civilian dimension of subsequent actions. The Swedes during their Presidency of 2001, for example, launched an EU programme for improving the EU's capacity for conflict prevention as well as civilian crisis management, while in 2006 the Finns sought to improve civil–military coordination.

Such initiatives have been important simply because the moves from 1998 onwards towards the creation of an ESDP raised serious questions about civilian power Europe, which had considerable resonance among a number of member states. Denmark, for example, with an opt-out on all defence-related issues granted at Maastricht, and Ireland with its repeated efforts to ensure recognition of its (military) neutrality, have tended to hold that such moves weaken the EU's distinct profile both inside the EU and in relation to other states (Sangiovanni 2003). The result may have been a certain ambiguity about the ends and objectives of ESDP enough to create uncertainty and some anxiety and even irritation in the USA. But that ambiguity has also been constructive in that it has allowed governments to accept ESDP as part of a balanced parallel development of military and civilian capabilities that can bolster their and Europe's role in crisis management. Significantly, under Lisbon, the High Representative was given responsibility for coordinating the civil and military aspects of tasks under the newly labelled Common Security and Defence Policy, rather than simply the member states in the Political and Security Committee (Quille 2008, 6).

The European Council

Inevitably, problems inherent in cross-pillar coordination have enhanced the role of the European Council. For many leaders, since the EU's legitimacy derives from the member states, it is proper for heads of government to take the major, strategic decisions. Thus the Council became increasingly important in shaping and voicing the EU's international position from the 1980s on. The development of CFSP and moves towards ESDP necessarily involved heads of governments—whether the proposals came via foreign, trade, or interior ministers prepared by the Commission within an EC framework, or were drawn up by the High Representative in pillar II as with the appointment of an EU counter-terrorism coordinator in March 2004 within the Council Secretariat. With the development of the European Council's role, so the inadequacies of the system of rotating Presidents became more apparent and the move towards a more permanent elected chair irresistible (despite some anxiety on the part of smaller member states and/or the more federalist governments). The Constitutional Treaty's provisions for a more permanent Presidency continued into the Lisbon Treaty, and to the appointment of Herman Van Rompuy, the then Belgian Prime Minister, as the first President. His appointment, together with that of Baroness Ashton as the first double-hatted High Representative/Commission Vice President, with an integrated external service eventually at her disposal, may reflect a further step in the evolution of a more coherent European foreign policy. But the European Council arguably epitomizes the paradox of European foreign policy cooperation: it may take place at ever higher levels with potentially greater impact on the ground, without necessarily raising the EU's actual profile within Europe itself.

The European Parliament

The double-hatting of Baroness Ashton means that the role of the European Parliament (EP) in the Union's international relations is enhanced. In some respects, Lisbon merely reinforced the EP's right only to be informed and consulted on foreign, security, and defence policies. Such a consultative role had been first granted within the EC framework, extended by the SEA of 1986 to allow the EP to assent to accession and association agreements. Yet where these have budgetary implications, the role of the EP is significantly enhanced and it has used its position to halt or delay financial protocols, etc. It has been using these budgetary powers since Lisbon to try to leverage a broader foreign policy role through the funding of the External Service. Otherwise, since the SEA, the EP has only had to be regularly informed by the Presidency on specifically foreign policy issues—or at least 'on the main aspects and basic choices' of policy. Parliamentary efforts to exploit such vague language did not always garner success—much depended on the attitudes of individual Presidencies—but the right to have its views taken into consideration has been important. Despite these limited formal powers, the EP has sometimes managed to exercise significant influence through providing a 'grand forum' for debate and inviting leaders to address it. Its emphasis on human rights has made it a particular focal point for non-governmental organizations (NGOs) and others, and a voice that has often had to be taken seriously even when it challenges the coherence and consistency of the EU's position.

Enduring tensions

The growing number of civilian and military operations being carried out by the EU suggests a certain coming of age. There remain, however, a number of not wholly resolved tensions.

First is the tension between rhetoric and achievement. Despite the continuous reiteration of the aims of speaking with one voice in a common foreign policy, commensurate with the possession of economic 'superpower', the EU continues to lack credibility, both domestically and on the international scene. On the one hand, there has been the agreement on a security strategy (2003), and the establishment of more than 20 ESDP missions in Europe, the Middle East, Africa, and even South East Asia (Aceh). On the other hand, awareness of these modest successes—a vital precursor to acceptance and legitimacy—remains limited. Differences among or within member states tend still to grab the headlines, particularly when refusing to take common action or when governments have not carried popular opinion. Inaction has often appeared preferable, reinforced by a more widespread aversion to taking risks (Coker 2009). There is, too, the continuing temptation to fall back on more familiar traditions of bilateral action. As in the past, the repetition of lofty aims has done little to promote common actions—the split over Iraq being the most glaring example. A capability-expectation gap remains, and remains to be exploited by others, thereby ensuring that the EU's credibility as a strategic international actor is continuously in question.

Secondly, there remains a tension between the processes of Europeanization and national foreign policies. This involves different dimensions and levels. One of the fundamental drivers of integration, for example, was 'the German question', which became again a vital issue on Germany's reunification in 1989. Since Maastricht, Germany's competing discourses on responsibility have maintained a sense of ambiguity: one tends to see Germany as a 'normal' state, emphasizing its national interests, pragmatic even if generally still committed to multilateral solutions and playing to a large domestic audience, which Chancellor Schroeder exploited in 2002; a second tends to emphasize responsibility to partners and allies, even if it now leads to military intervention, as in Kosovo and Afghanistan, which still creates anxiety within Germany. The continuing war in Afghanistan has deepened that concern—as witnessed by Chancellor Merkel's reluctance in 2010 to commit more forces there. But if the German question has taken on a new dimension, it has to be seen, too, against the wider background that, for other countries as well, Afghanistan and Iraq have created problems in heightening public opposition to the projection of force overseas in support of a presumed 'responsibility to protect', whether under the institutional umbrella of NATO or the EU.

In terms of different levels, policy making by heads of state and government reveals clearly the tensions between the logic of common policy making and that of national distinctiveness. Heads of state and government have not always proved as predictable as might have been expected from their ever growing familiarity through European Councils, informal Council meetings, other summit meetings, and the growing number of bilaterals. On the one hand, they have frequently confirmed if not set Europe's agenda, becoming more formally institutionalized in the interests of collective leadership. And yet they necessarily have to look back to their national constituencies if they wish to retain their position, especially when elections are imminent. Whatever the potential for more efficient or at least consistent preparation for European Council by the new President, heads of government still have limited time and many other distractions, whether political, financial, media, or personal to inhibit common action.

Meanwhile at the level of foreign ministers, a Europeanization process has taken a rather different path, if only through overloading them with responsibilities. Not only did foreign ministers have to cope with collective foreign policy making, they were also responsible for the coordination of the expanding work of the EC/EU as a whole in the General Affairs Council—with the result that they were regarded as inefficient and ineffectual (Gomez and Peterson 2001). Various reforms have been suggested to divide up their labour more efficiently, as at Seville in 2002. The Lisbon Treaty's division of labour between the External Relations Council chaired by the High Representative, and the General Council, still to be chaired by the rotating Presidency, creates a new dynamic—one that creates the potential for a lengthy period of 'turf-fighting' before consolidation can occur.

Closely interrelated has been the process of socialization within CFSP and ESDP. Even in the EPC period, foreign ministry officials enjoyed the flexibility of the process and the new opportunities for diplomats (Nuttall 2000). The blurring of the distinctions between the Maastricht pillars created some bureaucratic in-fighting which left 'victory' with the Committee of Permanent Representatives (Coreper) as the final negotiating forum at official level. On the other hand, the Political and Security Committee, with its extended responsibilities for ESDP and crisis management, challenged the status quo but now faces the complications introduced under Lisbon. While the numbers of those involved in ESDP missions, the Military Committee, and EUMS has gradually expanded, EU socialization faces continuing competition not simply from national cultural forces but from those emanating from NATO, which itself has been in a constant state of adaptation (Cornish and Edwards 2001, 2005; Meyer 2006).

A third area of tension, long lurking in the background but which became particularly explicit during the Convention on Europe's Future (2001–3) is that between the small and the big member states. It is not simply a question of the big having more global interests or, rather, the conceit of being a global power against the more limited and parochial interests of the small. Small states have frequently shown that they have particular interests in and knowledge of regions outside Europe (whether through past colonial links, trade, or aid). Moreover, despite the burdens of the Presidency, they have frequently enjoyed the 'political tourism' of representing the EC/EU, whether on the steps of the White House or in the UN (Rummel 1990). This has often been to the irritation of the big states, not least since the smalls have often regarded EPC/CFSP as a way of exercising at least some restraint on the big.

The latter have become more restless now that the number of smalls has increased through successive rounds of enlargement. It has posed a challenge, perhaps especially to France and the UK, both of which have tended to regard EPC/CFSP as an instrument of their own national foreign policies. While London and Paris have often been made aware that their global credibility rests heavily on their membership of the EU, that appears only rarely to influence their foreign policy discourse, at least as articulated through their national media.

Given the circumstances, it is not surprising that the big three have not only found the pressure to work together irresistible, but have often positively sought such a *directoire*. This self-characterization as a triumvirate of the willing and able has not been easily accepted by the Italians—who have frequently sought determinedly to be a participant, as in the so-called Quint (i.e. with the USA as the fifth member) on the Balkans (Gegout 2002)—by the Spanish and Poles (both of whose interior ministers joined with others to create a G6 on justice and home affairs and internal security issues), or by the smaller member states. Meetings among the big three in October and November 2001 to discuss the intervention in Afghanistan descended into near farce when Tony Blair invited French and German leaders to Downing Street only to find himself entertaining the Belgian President of the Council, the Italian and Dutch Prime Ministers, and the High Representative, all of whom gatecrashed the party. There were, however, rather fewer complaints over the role of the so-called EU3 (the UK, France, and Germany) in the negotiations with Teheran over Iran's proposed nuclear programme, particularly with the gradual involvement of first the High Representative and then the Commission.

A fourth set of tensions derives from characterizations of 'old' and 'new' Europe. Donald Rumsfeld, the US Defense Secretary, may have been slightly inaccurate in his critique of those opposing US action in Iraq in 2003 as 'old Europe' insofar as a number of 'older' European states including Denmark and the UK became a part of the US-led coalition, but there have been increased tensions with enlargement to Central and Eastern Europe. Many of the new member states, retaining vivid memories of Soviet domination, looked for and found strong American support in their search for security. Although their preoccupation with territorial defence may have been challenged by the way in which, since 2001, the USA has come to regard NATO as having a global mission, they still do not see the EU as a realistic alternative in terms of any possible defence against Russia. That is not to say that the new member states have not been involved in, or supportive of, present EU missions and the ESDP in general, but they retain a distinguishable sense of gratitude towards the USA and NATO and, arguably, tend to see support for ESDP as a means of retaining US interest in Europe as a partner. They have, too, pressed hard for a 'membership perspective' for the other countries of Eastern Europe and the Southern Caucasus—with the support of only some but not all the other member states—a position strengthened after the Georgia–Russia conflict of 2008.

A fifth set of tensions revolves around the question of the continued relevance of the concept of civilian power Europe and the scope and nature of the EU's ESDP. So far, the EU's growing participation in policing/peacekeeping missions, particularly at the behest of the UN, has been viewed with satisfaction. The search for balance in the security strategy of 2003 between civilian and military means of responding to threats, risks, and crises won significant support. But there remain elements of constructive ambiguity and tension even as ambitions may have become more limited. As the divisions over Iraq fade, and the Obama era replaces that of George W. Bush, so some of the differences between Europe and the USA dwelt on by Robert Kagan in his widely debated article in 2002 seem exaggerated (Kagan 2002). His critique of Europe's weaknesses and his characterization of Europe as from Venus (and the USA as from Mars) were widely resented, not least because they were believed to be commonplace in Washington. The concept of 'soft power' was generally regarded in Europe as a European strength, while 'smart power', the ability to bring the most appropriate means of influence to bear, has seen as better characterizing the EU than NATO. On the other hand, President Sarkozy's call for a new initiative in terms of the European Security Strategy during France's EU Presidency in 2008 ended up as no more than a Report on Implementation with a few more threats added (including cyber security) rather than anything more ringingly ambitious.

The relationship with the USA remains of particular salience in the continuing development of the CFSP and ESDP. The issue of how to live with a hyperpower in an economically multipolar world continues to tax the member states. France, for example, has frequently emphasized the need for Europe to operate on the basis of a multipolar world, although rejoining the military command of NATO has, perhaps, allayed US concerns. While Chancellor Schroeder's opposition to the war in Iraq engendered further German questioning of the value of NATO, Chancellor Merkel has sought a more ameliorative position, even eventually over Germany's commitment in Afghanistan. The UK government has appeared determined to prove its loyalty as an ally, seemingly regarding it as inconceivable that the UK would fight a war without the USA—though allowing, at Saint-Malo and subsequently, for an ESDP and its greater operational effectiveness, despite US suspicions. Insofar as the USA has been wary of a European caucus on security and defence matters in the past and looks to NATO either to accept a more global role in the future or at least to provide a coalition of the willing, the EU will continue to be subject to strain as a foreign policy actor.

Finally, and in part as a response to such differences, provisions for greater flexibility or enhanced cooperation are developed further in the Lisbon Treaty. Member states willing and able to fulfil higher criteria and make more binding commitments to one another with a view to undertaking the more demanding missions are allowed to establish permanent structured cooperation 'within the Union framework'. Insofar as the EU has had varying elements of such flexibility in the defence field since it was created (with the WEU, NATO, Eurocorps, etc. on the one hand, and the Danish opt-out or Irish military neutrality on the other), this creates little that is new. However, it can also be seen as both opportunity and danger: it provides an opportunity for the EU to act even if not all the member states are wholly in agreement—increasingly important in an EU of 27. Yet it also creates dangers, at least in relation to the orthodox view (and treaty provision) that the declared aim of the EU remains the development of 'mutual political solidarity … and the achievement of an ever increasing degree of convergence of Member States' actions'. (Article 24.2).

Conclusions

While it has become commonplace to agree with the characterization of the EU as economic giant, political dwarf, and military worm, this underestimates, as this survey suggests, the scope and variety of the EU's international relations. Both remain patchy insofar as the EU's concerns have been determined not simply by its own volition, difficult to achieve though that has often been, but by its need to react to change, whether over the longer term or to short-term crises. And the tensions that have accompanied the evolution and development of the present toolbox of policy instruments—including a military capacity—are likely to remain, both external and internal. Both the USA and Russia, for example, are likely to remain ambivalent about working with the EU rather than through individual member states. Internally, although the ratification of the Lisbon Treaty may mean the end of a long period of constitutional introspection, member governments have manifested different levels of enthusiasm for the changes involved, while their publics are even less predictable. In terms of implementing a more coherent external policy, governments are likely to retain an element of schizophrenia—well aware of the advantages of a politics of scale, but nonetheless reluctant to give up all pretence of individual weight and importance, especially in areas where they have traditionally been strong or with a particular contribution to make. The growing number of EU foreign policy interventions may create a familiarity and gradually, if they continue to be successful, a wider acceptance. But the fundamental tensions remain. The historical process has been in continual movement, and the scope has ever widened. But the strains have grown in parallel, with the result that incrementalism and inconsistency are likely to remain the order of the day in Europe's external activity.

FURTHER READING

The substantive geographical and functional patterns of the EU's international relations are generally well covered in the standard texts. See, for example, Bretherton and Vogler (2nd edition 2006) and K. E. Smith (2nd edition 2008). The problem of 'drivers and brakes' and of the roles played both by member states and EU institutions can be approached from a number of different angles. See, for example, Peterson and Sjursen (1998) and Nuttall (2000) on the contending forces in the evolution of the CFSP, and Hill (1996) and Manners and Whitman (2000) on the influence of member states. More specific studies of policy issues demonstrating the different patterns of EU activity include Keukeleire and MacNaughtan (2008), K. E. Smith (2004), M. Smith (2004), and Holland (2002).

Bretherton, C., and Vogler, J. (2006), *The European Union as a Global Actor* (London: Routledge).

Carlsnaes, W., Sjursen, H., and White, B. (eds) (2004), *Contemporary European Foreign Policy* (London: Sage).

Casarini, N., and Musu, C. (eds) (2006), *The EU's Foreign Policy in an Evolving International System: the road to convergence* (Palgrave).

Christiansen, T., and Tonra, B. (eds) (2004), *Rethinking EU Foreign Policy* (Manchester: Manchester University Press).

Ginsberg, R. (2001), *The European Union in International Politics: Baptism by Fire* (Lanham, MD: Rowman and Littlefield).

Hill, C. (ed.) (1996), *The Actors in Europe's Foreign Policy* (London: Routledge).

Jones, E., and van Genugten, S. (eds) (2009), *The Future of European Foreign Policy* (Routledge).

Keukeleire, S., and MacNaughtan, J. (2008), *The Foreign Policy of the European Union* (Basingstoke: Palgrave Macmillan).

Manners, I., and Whitman, R. (eds) (2000), *The Foreign Policies of European Union Member States* (Manchester: Manchester University Press).

Nuttall, S. (2000), *European Foreign Policy* (Oxford: Oxford University Press).

Peterson, J., and Sjursen, H. (1998), *A Common Foreign Policy for Europe? Competing Visions of the CFSP* (London: Routledge).

Smith, H. (2002), *European Union Foreign Policy: What it is and What it does* (London: Pluto Press).

Smith, K. E. (2008), *European Union Foreign Policy in a Changing World*, 2nd edition (Cambridge: Polity).

Smith, K. E. (2004), *The Making of EU Foreign Policy: the Case of Eastern Europe*, 2nd edition (Basingstoke: Palgrave Macmillan).

 WEB LINKS

For general information on the patterns of the EU's international activities, the best sources are the websites of EU institutions and delegations, especially the Europa web site, **http://www.europa.eu.int/** and the website of the EU delegation in Washington DC: **http://www.eurunion.org/**. On the foreign policies and priorities of the member states, the best sources are the national government websites and especially those of foreign offices, for example: **http://www.fco.gov.uk/** (Britain) and **http://www. foreignministry.se/** (Sweden). Among think tanks, the European Union Institute for Security Studies, **http://www.iss.europa.eu/**, covers ESDP issues (and has also published a series of core documents on the ESDP), as does ISIS Europe (**http://www.isis-europe.org/**). The Centre for European Policy Studies (CEPS), (**http://www.ceps.be/**), covers a wide range of foreign policy issues including some of the external dimensions of internal policy in 'Challenge: Liberty and Security', otherwise at **http://www.libertysecurity.org/**.

Other institutes include Egmont (IRRI-KIIB): **http://www.egmontinstitute.be/**, SWP in Berlin (**http://www.swp-berlin.org**), ARENA in Oslo (**http://www.arena.uio.no/**), and Real Instituto Elcano (**http://www.realinstitutoelcano.org/wps/portal/**) and FRIDE (**http://www.fride.org/**), both in Madrid. Via the TEPSA link (**http://www.tepsa.be**), access can be gained to various national institutes, some of which, especially the Scandinavian think tanks, publish a great deal on foreign and security policy (see, for example, the Danish Institute of International Studies, **www.diis.dk**). ETH Zurich also hosts the website that points to a multitude of relevant sources sorted by subject and region (**http://www.isn.ethz.ch**), as does the Institute for International and European policy at Leuven (**http://soc.kuleuven.be/iieb/eufp/**) and the Archive of European Integration at Pittsburgh (**http://aei.pitt.edu/**). Other academic analyses include the websites of FORNET, **http://www.fornet.info/** and MERCURY, **http://www.mercury-fp7.net/**.

PART II

Institutions and Processes

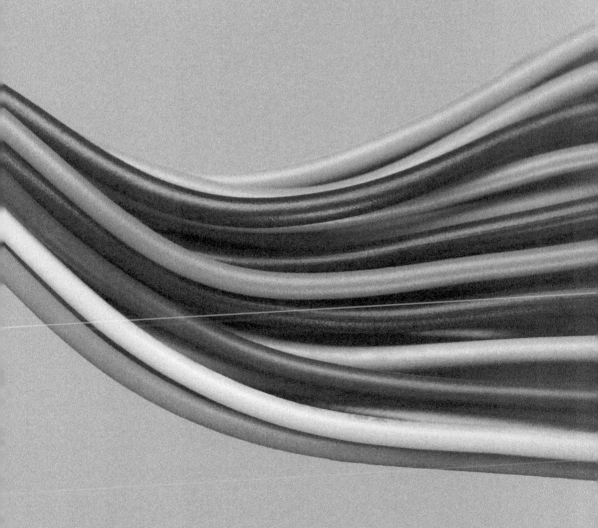

CHAPTER 4

The Institutional Framework

Sophie Vanhoonacker

▌Summary

Despite the abolition of the so-called pillar structure and the introduction of a new general heading on the guiding principles of EU external action under the Lisbon Treaty, there continues to be a complex institutional context for the evolution of the EU's external relations, within which the roles of the Council, Commission, European Parliament, and European Court of Justice in various areas and on different policy issues differ considerably. Such marked variations reflect differing paths of evolution and the different degrees of integration in different areas of external policy. This chapter focuses on the institutional basis of the international policy role of the EU, asking initially how we should think about the roles of institutions, and reviewing some of the key ideas about the ways in which the EU's institutions work. The chapter then reviews three key areas of EU international policy with particular reference to the changes introduced by the Lisbon Treaty, and finally returns to ideas about institutions and their effects on policy.

Introduction: institutions and why they matter

The European Union manifests itself on the international scene in many different ways: through its trade policy, development cooperation and humanitarian aid, as well as through the Common Foreign and Security Policy (CFSP), including the Common Security and Defence Policy (formerly ESDP or the European security and defence policy). Being the logical consequence of the establishment of the customs union and the Common External Tariff (CET), the Common Commercial Policy (CCP) is one of the Union's oldest and most integrated policies. Decision making in the area of trade is organized according to the supranational Community method, whereby the Commission has the exclusive right of initiative and the Council decides by qualified majority voting (QMV). Since the entering into force of the Lisbon Treaty, the Council shares its legislative power with the European Parliament (EP). The Community method also applies to development cooperation, although in contrast to the Common Commercial Policy, development is not a truly common policy but an area where individual member states have maintained a high level of sovereignty. The Treaty on the Functioning of the EU (TFEU) stipulates that although the Union can conduct a common policy in the area of development and humanitarian aid, this should not prevent the member states from carrying out their own activities (Article 4, TFEU). Cooperation in the area of foreign policy started from the 1970s onwards, but only took off after the end of the Cold War when the Union started to tackle the sensitive question of security. The level of institutionalization in the foreign policy area has historically been lower than in trade but since the development of an EU crisis management role the number of permanent bodies has grown considerably. The creation under Lisbon of the position of the High Representative of the Union for Foreign Affairs and Security Policy (HR) and the European External Action Service (EEAS) are further illustrations of how the centre of gravity is gradually moving from the national capitals to Brussels.

This chapter focuses on an institutional analysis of the international relations of the Union. It looks not only at formal constitutional entities and decision rules as defined in the Treaty on European Union (TEU), but also examines political practices and forms of informal interaction—in other words, institutions in the broadest sense. As the institutional frameworks of the above-mentioned policies (trade, development, foreign policy, security) came about at different periods and developed along various tracks with their own integration logic, each policy will initially be treated separately. Even if the institutions are to some extent the same, the rules of the game between the various policy areas of external relations vary considerably, and the Lisbon Treaty does not change this fundamentally. But it must be remembered that although there are apparently separate institutional tracks for the handling of the EU's international relations, some of the key issues in external policy making are concerned with the interactions and the tensions between the different tracks. The questions of 'consistency' to which this coexistence of institutional frameworks gives rise are dealt with specifically in Chapter 5 of this volume.

Why and how do institutions matter, both within the process of European integration more generally and more specifically in relation to the EU's international relations? The role(s) of institutions both broadly and narrowly defined has been a continuing preoccupation of scholars dealing with the integration process in its 'internal' aspects (Stone Sweet, Sandholtz, and Fligstein 2001; Pollack 2003, 2004; Peterson and Shackleton 2006), and this has been extended by others into the field of international policy making (Elsig 2002; M. E. Smith 2003, 2004a). From this work, and from what has been said already in this chapter, it can be seen that institutions can matter in a number of significant ways to the international relations of the EU:

- First, institutions in their most formal sense reflect the prevailing conceptions and levels of agreement among member states and other significant bodies about the scope and nature of the EU's international relations as well as about the division of tasks between the domestic and the European level (Wagner 2003). In order to increase efficiency or to deal with compliance problems, member states can decide to delegate certain responsibilities to supranational bodies providing expertise or fulfilling certain organizational functions (Pollack 2003; Beach 2005). Most formally of all, the successive institutional bargains at the intergovernmental level are encapsulated in the successive treaties. In this form, institutions can be said to reflect the power and preferences of the member states and to be the product of interstate bargaining within a broadly rationalist framework (Moravcsik 1993, 1998, etc.).

- Second, institutions, as indicated above, say something important about the history of the European integration process and about where the international relations of the EU have been as well as where they might be going (Juncos 2007; McNamara and Meunier 2007). Analysts who emphasize 'historical institutionalist' approaches have drawn attention not only to the impact of successive institutional bargains but also to the ways in which prior bargains and institutional arrangements shape what is seen to be possible or appropriate at a given time. This analysis has given rise to ideas of 'path dependency' in which the evolution of EU policies can be read off from the institutional bargains concluded often years beforehand (Pierson 1996; Thelen 1999).

- Third, institutions and institutional changes can reflect the changing political complexion of the EU and of its engagement with the outside world through a process of 'multilevel governance' (Kohler-Koch 1996; Marks *et al.* 1996; Jachtenfuchs 2001). In other words, the institutions through which—in this case—the EU frames and conducts its international relations are partly a response to the changing internal makeup of the Union and partly a response to external demands and opportunities (M. E. Smith 2004b; Vanhoonacker,

Dijkstra, and Maurer 2010, forthcoming). Thus, some of the changes that have taken place in the EU's institutional framework as it relates to international relations have reflected the growth of the Union itself and the needs or assets of new member states. Equally, some of the external demands and opportunities themselves emerge from the institutional frameworks that surround the EU, in the shape of organizations and rules associated with (for example) international trade, the global environment and global security issues (Joergensen 2006).

- Fourth, institutions are not inert, 'neutral' mechanisms that simply obey orders. Rather, they can profoundly shape the ways in which EU policy makers develop their preferences, their priorities, and their understanding of what is possible for the Union in the international arena. The proponents of 'sociological institutionalism' have thus assessed the institutions of the EU's international relations in terms of the ways in which they shape and respond to expectations, the ways in which they reflect 'social learning' on the part of those engaged in them, and the ways in which they shape the framing ideas of EU external policies (Tonra 2003; Bretherton and Vogler 2006). Here, the definition of an 'institution' is clearly a long way from the idea noted above that institutions are what is formally laid down in the treaties or other treaty-like arrangements: the nature of institutions broadly defined can include informal norms and conventions as well as formal institutional frameworks or rules that can be written down and are subject to judicial interpretation (Risse-Kappen 1996; Checkel 1999; Risse 2009).

Not surprisingly, therefore, there has been a continuing tendency, which has become especially marked in the past decade, to analyse and evaluate the development of the EU's international relations in terms of institutionalist approaches (M. E. Smith 2003, 2004a; Joergensen 2006). Seen in this light, and with admittedly considerable variation among adherents of different schools of thought, the growth of the Common Commercial Policy, the development and humanitarian assistance policies, and of the Common Foreign and Security and Common Security and Defence Policies are reflections of the ways in which institutions emerge, expand, and shape or reshape the activities of those operating with them or within them. The rest of this chapter will deal successively with the broad institutional frameworks for the three central strands of the EU's international relations and will then return to the issues raised here in terms of the impact and implications of institutions.

Institutions and their impact in three policy areas

In this part of the chapter, the key concern is to analyse and evaluate institutional trends in three main areas of the EU's international relations. Key to this analysis is the fact that within the three areas at issue—the common commercial policy, development and humanitarian aid policy, and CFSP/CSDP—institutional change has occurred to different degrees, in different directions, and with different impacts. To put it simply, the origins, the trajectory, and the implications of the institutional developments that have taken place in the three areas are markedly different, suggesting that the insights from different areas of institutionalist analysis will be a fertile source of comparative analysis. As can be seen from other chapters in this volume, however, the institutional environment is not the only variable explaining the variety of policy outcomes in the field of EU external relations, but it deserves close attention and analysis because it creates certain possibilities and constraints, as well as facilitating comparative analysis and evaluation. The final part of this chapter will return explicitly to evaluation of the impact of institutions on the Union's external policies.

The Common Commercial Policy

The CCP is one of the oldest EC policies as well as a policy with a high level of integration; it has often been argued that the inevitable institutional consequence of the establishment of a customs union was the need for a common commercial policy with the delegation of authority over trade negotiations to the Community and more particularly the Commission. In the early years of European integration, it was primarily tariff issues, subsidies, and anti-dumping duties that dominated the agenda, reflecting the predominance of trade in goods in the international economy. The creation of a customs union implied the establishment of a common external tariff (CET) and required that the member states spoke with one voice in international trade rounds. From the 1970s onwards the focus of the debate and of international trade negotiations shifted from tariff issues to non-tariff barriers (such as quotas or technical barriers to trade), and in the 1980s it was broadened to trade in services, intellectual property rights, and foreign direct investment (Woolcock 2000, 374). In contrast to trade in goods, which is an exclusive EU competence, these areas were initially of mixed EU and national competence and only certain aspects fell under the CCP (Nicoll and Salmon 2001, 213). Trying to adapt to the new realities of a globalizing world and the pressure to speak with one voice at the international scene, the successive Amsterdam, Nice, and Lisbon treaties, however, gradually expanded the scope. Today also trade in services, the commercial aspects of intellectual property rights, and Foreign Direct Investment (FDI) are exclusive EU competences.

Traditionally the two main institutional actors in the CCP decision-making process were the Council and the Commission but since the Lisbon Treaty the role of the European Parliament has been considerably strengthened (Article 207, TFEU). Having the exclusive right of initiative, the role of the European Commission has always been pivotal. With regard to anti-dumping measures, it even has decision-making powers: it determines whether to start an investigation following a complaint and decides whether or not anti-dumping duties will be imposed. It also plays a crucial role in the conclusion of international trade agreements. The portfolio of the Commissioner for trade is therefore an important one.[1] The Trade Commissioner gives guidance to the Directorate General for Trade (DG Trade). The latter distils the overall Commission position and works in close cooperation with other DGs such as DG Development, Agriculture, Consumer Protection, Environment, etc. As these DGs have their own priorities and concerns, this coordination process is often difficult and time consuming. Since Lisbon, the Commissioner for Trade and his staff also have to coordinate with the High Representative and the European External Action Service, responsible for the consistency between the different dimensions of EU external action (Article 18, TEU) (see Chapter 5).

Within the Council it is the Foreign Affairs Council (FAC) composed of the Ministers of Foreign Affairs that deals with the trade-related dossiers. There is no formal Council of Trade Ministers, but they can attend the FAC if trade matters are on the agenda. Although the Lisbon Treaty stipulates that the FAC is chaired by the High Representative, it has been agreed that when trade issues are on the agenda, the High Representative will ask the rotating Presidency to take over (Council Rules of Procedure, December 2009).[2] This decision may seem somewhat surprising given the central coordinating role of the HR in EU external policy. From the point of view of vertical coordination, however, it is understandable. Both Coreper II as well as the special trade policy committee in charge of preparing the trade dossiers for the FAC are also chaired by the rotating Presidency (see below). This implies that there is one single Presidency for all three levels from the working groups up to the Council.

The two main supporting bodies of the FAC are the trade policy committee and Coreper II, the meeting of the Permanent Representatives of the member states to the EU. The trade policy committee, previously known as the 113 (Treaty of Rome) and the 133 (Amsterdam Treaty) committee is composed of high-level officials specialized in trade matters. It has responsibility for monitoring the progress of trade negotiations and other activities in the trade area. It normally meets once a week, usually on Fridays. It plays a key role in shaping EU trade policy as many of its decisions are merely rubber stamped at a higher level. Coreper II prepares the trade and development issues on the FAC agenda. At all levels the member states and the rotating Presidency are assisted by the staff of DG E (External Relations) of the Council General Secretariat.

Until recently the role of the European Parliament and its committee on international trade (INTA) was purely consultative, leading to repeated criticisms that the CCP was lacking legitimacy. Since the Lisbon Treaty, however, co-decision or the so-called 'ordinary legislative procedure' has become the general rule (Article 294, TFEU), implying that it has become a co-legislator on equal footing with the Council.

The role of the European Court of Justice (ECJ) often goes unnoticed but is crucial. Through a series of judgements it has extended the scope of the CCP and it can also act in accordance with the 'doctrine of implied powers', meaning that where

Community institutions have the power to regulate a matter internally, they may also act externally (Young 2000, 102). This has been a major factor, for example, in negotiations on air transport or trade policy aspects of the environment.

As one of the central aspects of the EU's trade policy is the conclusion of agreements with third countries or international organizations such as the World Trade Organization (WTO), it is important to describe in more detail how the different EU institutions interact in this process (Meunier 2005; Dür and Zimmermann 2007). The legal basis for such negotiations is to be found in the Treaty on the Functioning of the EU: Article 207, TFEU (trade) and Article 218, TFEU (agreements with a broader scope than trade, such as association and international agreements). The European Commission proposes to open negotiations, makes recommendations to the Council, and represents the member states. It does not act autonomously but on the basis of a mandate adopted by the Council which formally authorizes the opening of the negotiations. During the negotiations there is a continuous dialogue between Council and Commission through specialized committees (the trade policy committee when it concerns trade). When the negotiations take place in Geneva, the delegations of the member states to the WTO are consulted. This allows member states to monitor the process and if necessary to adjust the mandate. In principle, international agreements are adopted by the Council deciding by QMV (Articles 207 and 218, TFEU) but there are several exceptions. When concluding agreements in trade in cultural and audiovisual services risking endangering the EU's cultural and linguistic diversity, or agreements disturbing the national organization of social, education, and health services, the unanimity rule applies. This is also the case for areas where unanimous agreement is required for the adoption of internal rules, for association agreements, for economic, financial, and technical cooperation with accession candidates, and when acceding to the European Convention for the Protection of Human Rights and Fundamental Freedoms.

As a result of strong pressures to reduce the lack of legitimacy and transparency in EU trade policy, the role of the European Parliament has over the years gradually been strengthened. It is still not involved in the definition of the negotiation directives prepared by the Council but it has become customary to inform the EP *post facto* about the negotiation mandate and the negotiation process (Nicoll and Salmon 2001, 195). With Lisbon this practice of reporting about the progress of the negotiations has been formalized. A further incentive for the Commission and the Council to take the views of the Parliament seriously is that in an increasing number of cases agreements are subject to the EP's consent.[3] The shadow of a possible rejection gives the EP an important leverage over the negotiation process. In addition to association agreements and agreements with important institutional or budgetary implications (such as the outcome of the Uruguay round), the EP now also has to give its consent over trade agreements.

Since the early years of European integration, trade has been one of the most integrated policy fields, with the European Commission playing a central role as the body conducting international trade negotiations on behalf of the member states. At the same time, however, the national capitals have not hesitated to use the changing nature of international trade relations to regain a grip on this important policy area. In addition, the Council has been extremely reluctant to allow the European Parliament into its bilateral game with the European Commission. The need to act more forcefully in a globalizing world and increasing criticism of the lack of transparency and accountability have, however, gradually turned the tide. Today the CCP, covering also trade in services, intellectual property rights, and FDI, has become much more of a common policy in the true sense of the word. Furthermore, the Lisbon Treaty has fully opened the door for the EP. Whether these changes will be sufficient to make the EU a more powerful international trade actor able to compete with other rising powers remains, however, to be seen (see Chapters 12 and 16).

Development cooperation policy and humanitarian aid

Although the provisions on development cooperation (Articles 208–11, TFEU) were only introduced into the core treaties of the EU with the adoption of the Treaty on European Union in Maastricht, formal relations between the EC and the developing world are almost as old as the Community itself. Due to their colonial past, several member states had historical links with the developing world and they therefore had significant interests in using the EC as a vehicle for their continuing relationships with their previous colonies as well as more generally supporting these countries in their further development. Today the Treaty of Lisbon defines the reduction and eradication of poverty as the primary objective of EU development cooperation (Article 208, TFEU). Other policy areas taking action that affects developing countries should also respect this goal.

The EU and its member states are important actors on the international development scene. Together they provide more than half of official development assistance (ODA) and two-thirds of global humanitarian aid. As regards development aid, the member states provide the bulk of the funds (90 per cent), whereas for humanitarian aid, the partition is more equal (Orbie and Versluys 2008; Versluys 2008a).

One of the most important instruments of EU development policy is the cooperation and association agreements that have been concluded with countries and regional groupings all over the world. While the EEC initially focused on the (sub-Saharan) African, Caribbean, and Pacific (ACP) countries, today EU development policy is global in scope with, since 2002, an important redirection of aid towards the near abroad and the Mediterranean (Orbie and Versluys 2008). Nonetheless, the Cotonou Partnership Agreement with the ACP countries continues to be the most elaborate and institutionalized form of cooperation.[4] Building on the *acquis* of the Lomé Conventions (1975–2000), this 20-year agreement (2000–20) provides the basis for political dialogue, development cooperation, and closer economic and trade cooperation. In contrast to Lomé, Cotonou also imposes political conditionality, emphasizing respect for human rights, democratic principles, the rule of law, and good governance.

> **BOX 4.1** **Institutional framework for the Cotonou Partnership Agreement**
>
> - ACP–EU Council of Ministers: composed of one minister of each of the participating countries as well as a representative of the Commission. It meets once a year and is chaired alternately by an EU and an ACP country. It is responsible for the implementation of the agreement and its decisions are binding. The Council is assisted by committees and ad hoc working parties.
> - Committee of Ambassadors: composed of a representative of each EU and ACP state and a representative of the Commission. It meets at least every six months and assists the Council with its implementing tasks.
> - ACP–EU Joint Parliamentary Assembly: composed of an equal number of members of the EP and ACP parliamentarians and meets twice a year alternately in the EU and in an ACP country. Its role is purely consultative.

The cooperation between the EU and the ACP countries is supported by a number of joint institutions, which have been seen by many as unique in the global political economy (see Box 4.1). Some have argued that this high level of institutionalization contributes to the stability and the effectiveness of the relationship (Holland 2002, 49).[5] Others have made the case that what matters in the stability of these arrangements is the power of the EU and its capacity to sustain commitment to the kinds of partnership that have developed. If this view is accepted, then the institutions become the symptom of this power, rather than the generators of stability in an independent sense.

As with the case of the CCP, it can be seen from this brief sketch that the significant institutions for the EU's international relations with respect to development assistance are not all to be found within the EU itself; it is the interaction of the EU's institutions with those of the broader global arena that makes for important complexities and tensions.

Unlike the CCP, development cooperation is not an area where the Union has exclusive competence, and bilateral aid programmes of the member states continue to occupy an important place. The treaty clearly states that the EU competencies in the area of development cooperation and humanitarian aid shall not prevent the member states from exercising their own competencies (Article 4, TFEU). EU development cooperation and that of the member states should complement and reinforce each other (Article 208, TFEU), and both levels are supposed to consult and coordinate their policies (Article 210, TFEU). In practice, however, it has proven not to be simple to implement this principle (Carbone 2009; see also Chapter 14). Lack of political will and diversity in traditions and working methods are important obstacles. But in addition, and with particular relevance to the focus of this chapter, the weaknesses of the internal EU institutional structure are a significant explanatory factor.

As in the area of trade, the two principal institutional players in development policy are the Council and the European Commission. At the level of the Council, it was for many years the Development Council that dealt with development cooperation. As from 2000 onwards, development policy was discussed within the framework of the General Affairs and External Relations Council (GAERC) and since Lisbon it is handled by the Foreign Affairs Council, under the chairmanship of the HR. Decisions in the area of development are prepared by Coreper II and by the working groups, both chaired by the rotating Presidency. This difference in chairmanship, whereby the Council is presided over by the HR and the underlying levels by the rotating Presidency, raises new coordination questions.

The European Commission has a wide range of responsibilities in the area of development policy. On behalf of the member states, it negotiates cooperation and association agreements with Third World countries, it manages the EU aid budget and the European Development Fund (EDF) (see Chapter 8), and it can undertake initiatives to coordinate the policies of the EU and the member states. Nonetheless, its role is much weaker than in the area of trade. Partly this has to do with the reluctance of the member states to cede sovereignty, and partly it can be explained by the Commission's hybrid organizational structure. The Commission responsibilities for development cooperation are shared out by geographical region and supervised by different Commissioners and DGs, including the HR and the EEAS. The division of work is as follows:

- ACP and Overseas Countries and Territories (OCT): Commissioner for Development and Humanitarian Aid supported by DG Development (DG DEV);
- Pre-accession aid to the candidate countries and countries of the former Soviet Union: Commissioner for Enlargement and European Neighbourhood Policy supported by DG Enlargement (DG ELARG);
- North Africa, Latin America, most of Asia, the Middle East: the HR supported by the EEAS;
- Macro-financial assistance such as debt relief: DG Economic and Financial Affairs.

One of the most important initiatives to address the fragmentation in EU development policy has been the decision to try to reunify the project cycle (from programming to evaluation) of the largely project-based funding mechanisms for EU development policy.[6] In 2001, under the Prodi Commission (1999–2004), the newly established EuropeAid Cooperation Office (also known as AIDCO) was made responsible for all the phases of the project cycle (from identification to evaluation) except for the programming phase that stayed with DG DEV and DG RELEX (see Box 4.2). The plea to go even further and create one single DG, under a development Commissioner responsible for both policy and programming functions, was not heard. Following the establishment of the EEAS, the first three

---

BOX 4.2   **The EuropeAid Cooperation Office (AIDCO)**

- Established in January 2001.
- Successor of the Common Service for External Relations (SCR) (1998–2000).
- Responsible for the final two phases of the project cycle (implementation and evaluation).
- Consists of seven directorates (of which four are responsible for geographical programmes).
- Does not deal with pre-accession aid, humanitarian aid, macro-financial assistance, actions under CFSP, and the rapid reaction mechanism. (The pre-accession instruments are managed by a single administrative structure, namely DG ELARG.)
- Operates under the guidance of the Commissioner for Development.

---

phases of the project cycle (programming, identification, formulation) have now been allocated to the HR and the EEAS, leaving the European Commission with an implementing and more technical role. Given her central role in the conduct of EU foreign policy and in supervising the coherence between the different areas of EU external action, it was considered crucial that the political and strategic choices on development projects—involving huge budgets—would be taken by the HR rather than by the Commission (Council Decision 11507/10, 2010).

Another important element of institutional reform under the Prodi Commission was the decision to devolve more responsibilities to the Commission delegations to third countries and international organizations. Being based on the spot, their staff are generally better placed to manage aid projects, to take into account the needs of the partner countries, and to coordinate aid with other areas of policy. The transformation of the Commission delegations to Union delegations under the Lisbon Treaty has further strengthened their position; they now also deal with foreign policy issues more broadly. This responsibility for the full spectrum of external action should positively affect the coherence of the EU's international performance. The integration of seconded national diplomats into the delegations should furthermore boost the coordination between EU and national initiatives (Koeb 2009).

The role of the EP and its Development Committee (DEVE) is weak. The EP's budgetary powers are limited to the aid that is funded from the EU budget. The European Development Fund (EDF) providing aid to the ACP countries consists of national contributions and escapes control by the EP. This may change in the future since under Lisbon the TEU no longer contains a declaration stipulating that the EDF should remain outside the EU budget. This means that the member states can now integrate the EDF into the EU budget without having to amend the treaties. Development cooperation falls under the co-decision procedure and since Lisbon this so-called 'ordinary legislative procedure' also applies to the trade agreements concluded with developing countries (see above). In the case of association agreements, the EP has the power of consent.

Finally, a few words should also be said about EU humanitarian aid, which in the Lisbon Treaty for the first time receives a specific legal basis (Article 214, TFEU). The funds provided by the EU are managed through the European Commission and more particularly by the Humanitarian Aid department of the European Commission (ECHO—see Box 4.3). ECHO is a separate agency because it has to respond rapidly and effectively to humanitarian crises. It is primarily a financing body and has to limit itself to providing emergency aid. It relies on funds of the general EU budget, the European Development Fund and the Emergency Aid Reserve, which provides allocations for unforeseen circumstances (Versluys 2008a). Contrary to AIDCO, it is responsible for the management of the full project cycle (from programming to evaluation). A lot of the management functions are devolved to staff in the field. These field offices operate independently from the Union delegations and are staffed by independent experts and local staff (Versluys 2008a).

Despite the earlier mentioned reforms of the Prodi Commission and the new division of tasks since Lisbon, today's institutional picture in the area of development is still one of fragmentation: between Brussels and the member states; among various Commissioners; and more recently between the Commission and the HR/EEAS. In policy terms the result is that the EU, instead of taking the lead, tends to respond to the changing international development agenda (Orbie and Versluys 2008). It is doubtful whether the Lisbon Treaty will turn the tide. From a political perspective the allocation of the programming function to the EEAS certainly makes sense but it raises new coordination challenges with the other administrative players involved in the rest of the policy cycle. The emphasis on policy coherence and the need to better streamline development cooperation with the general principles and objectives guiding EU external action is a positive development. However, it further strengthens the trend whereby development policy is increasingly overshadowed by foreign policy and security considerations.

BOX 4.3	**Humanitarian Aid department of the European Commission (ECHO)**

- Established in 1992.
- Provides humanitarian assistance to populations of third countries affected by disasters or conflicts (see Council Regulation (EC) No. 1257/96 of 20 June 1996, *Official Journal L 163*, 2 July 1996).
- Funds are mainly drawn from the Commission budget and from the EDF in the case of the ACP countries.
- Implementation is done through third parties: humanitarian organizations (NGOs and international organizations such as UN agencies).

European foreign policy and security cooperation

The third leg of EU external relations is that of cooperation in the field of foreign policy and security. Foreign policy, security, and defence are issues that reach to the core of the sovereignty of the nation state, and as a result the member states were for many years extremely reluctant to integrate (as opposed to cooperating) in this area. It was only from 1970 onwards that they first started to formally exchange information and coordinate positions in the framework of European Political Cooperation (EPC) (1970–93).[7] In contrast to the area of trade where the basic institutional structure has been in place since the treaties of Rome, the institutional architecture of European foreign policy cooperation has developed much more incrementally. The main decision-making body in EPC (1970–93) was the 'conference' of foreign ministers supported by the Political Committee composed of the political directors and the thematic and geographical working groups. Since the Commission had no right of initiative, a key role was played by the rotating Presidency.

After the fall of the Berlin wall, uncertainty about the future of NATO and instability in the Balkans relaunched the debate on a European foreign policy and opened up the institutional as well as the political field of play. At Maastricht (1991) the member states agreed on the creation of a Common Foreign and Security Policy (CFSP) and from the late 1990s onwards also security was put high on the agenda, with the EU starting to play an active role in the field of crisis management from 2003 onwards. This section successively examines the institutional underpinnings of CFSP and CSDP in more detail, taking into account the changes introduced by Lisbon.

Towards a common foreign and security policy

The post-1989 ambition to move beyond a merely declaratory foreign policy was gradually given shape during a series of intergovernmental bargains reflected in the successive treaties of Maastricht (November 1993),[8] Amsterdam (May 1999), Nice (February 2003), and Lisbon (December 2009). The debate on the institutional architecture of the Common Foreign and Security Policy, first discussed in Maastricht, occupied a central place because it was seen as an important building stone for the EU's development into a coherent and effective international actor. The two main questions on the agenda were the decision-making method in CFSP in general as well as the institutional underpinning of an EU crisis-management role. We start by examining the role and the interaction among the main players in the EU foreign policy process more broadly, also taking into account the changes introduced by the Lisbon Treaty (Duke 2008; Blockmans and Wessel 2009; Whitman and Juncos 2009). The wide range of bodies underpinning the EU's military and civilian crisis management role is dealt with separately in the next section.

At the core of the debate on the decision-making rules in European foreign policy is the age-old discussion between intergovernmentalists and supranationalists

---

BOX 4.4   **CFSP decision-making rules (Article 31, TFEU)**

- Decisions in the area of CFSP are taken by the European Council and the Council (FAC) acting unanimously.

- Constructive abstention: a member state abstaining in a vote is not obliged to apply the decision but will refrain from any action that conflicts with or impedes Union action on the decision in question. Those abstaining should not represent more than one-third of the member states comprising at least one-third of the EU population.

- The Council can act by qualified majority voting (QMV) when adopting implementing decisions (i.e. all four decisions mentioned under Box 4.5) and when appointing a special representative. However, in the case of 'vital and stated reasons of national interest' a member state can oppose a decision by QMV. If the HR does not find an acceptable solution, the Council (by QMV) may refer the question to the European Council for a decision by unanimity.

- The European Council can decide by unanimity to extend the areas covered by QMV.

BOX 4.5   **Decisions in the area of CFSP since Lisbon (Article 25, TFEU)**

- Decisions defining the general guidelines (before Lisbon: the common strategies).

- Decisions defining the actions to be undertaken by the Union (before Lisbon: the joint actions).

- Decisions defining the positions to be taken by the Union (before Lisbon: the common positions).

- Decisions implementing the actions and positions of the Union.

---

and the question whether in this sensitive policy area there is a place for supranational bodies and decision making by qualified majority voting (QMV). Despite the introduction of a single institutional framework, the Maastricht Treaty continued to underline the intergovernmental character of foreign policy cooperation by placing the CFSP provisions in a separate, so-called second pillar falling outside the scope of the supranational Community method.[9] Even if the Lisbon Treaty provides the EU with legal personality and abolishes the pillar structure, today CFSP continues to be subject to specific rules. The Amsterdam Treaty introduced the possibility for constructive abstention and QMV for implementing decisions, but unanimity is still maintained as the general rule (see Box 4.4).

Acting under the general guidelines and strategic guidance of the European Council,[10] the Council meeting as ministers of foreign affairs is the central decision-making body in CFSP. Prior to Lisbon, foreign affairs fell under the scope of the General Affairs and External Relations Council (GAERC), dealing both with external relations and general policy questions and chaired by the rotating Presidency.

Since Lisbon, however, the General Affairs Council meets as a separate configuration and external relations is covered by the Foreign Affairs Council (FAC), chaired by the High Representative of the Union for Foreign Affairs and Security Policy (see Box 4.6).[11] The decision to appoint a Brussels-based European foreign policy chief who is also Vice President of the European Commission is an important break with the past and a reflection of the (reluctant) acceptance that in an enlarged EU the fragmented system whereby each member state in turn provided direction was no longer feasible. The first occupant of the new position, Baroness Catherine Ashton, is *de facto* fulfilling tasks previously carried out by three different persons: the rotating Presidency, the former High Representative for CFSP based at the Council General Secretariat (Solana 1999–2009) and the Commissioner for External Relations (Benita Ferrero-Waldner 2004–9). The appointment of a permanent chair of the Foreign Affairs Council (five years) who has the co-right of initiative has been triggered by the triple ambition to bring more continuity, coherence, as well as leadership in EU external relations. The new position, however, also brings new challenges. The double-hatting as Vice President of the European Commission and chair of the Council places the HR in a vulnerable and sometimes even impossible position, as she is subject to opposing pressures from both institutions. Furthermore, the position also brings its own coordination requirements, not only with the other members of the European Commission and permanent chair of the European Council, who externally represents the Union at his level, but also with the rotating Presidency—which still plays a crucial role in the areas of trade and development.

Before reaching the Council, decisions in CFSP are successively discussed at working group level, in the Political and Security Committee and in Coreper II (see Figures 4.1 and 4.2). At the lowest level, the work of the foreign affairs ministers is prepared by thematic and geographical working parties,[12] drafting and negotiating the various CFSP decisions (see Box 4.5). Since 2000, they report to the Political and Security Committee (PSC), also known by its French acronym COPS.[13] The PSC has replaced the Political Committee (see above) and was a response to the need

---

BOX 4.6	**The HR of the Union for Foreign Affairs and Security Policy**

- Appointed by the European Council acting by QMV, with the agreement of the President of the Commission and subject to a vote of consent by the EP on the incoming Commission.
- Double-hatted as chair of the FAC and Vice President of the Commission.
- Responsible for the conduct of CFSP and the consistency between the different areas of EU external action.
- Has the right of initiative with the Commission's support.
- Supported by the EEAS (i.e. a central administration based in Brussels, plus Union delegations to third countries and international organizations).

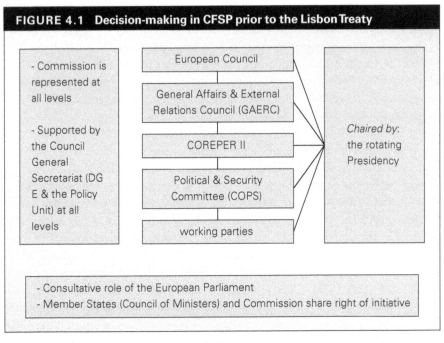

FIGURE 4.1 Decision-making in CFSP prior to the Lisbon Treaty

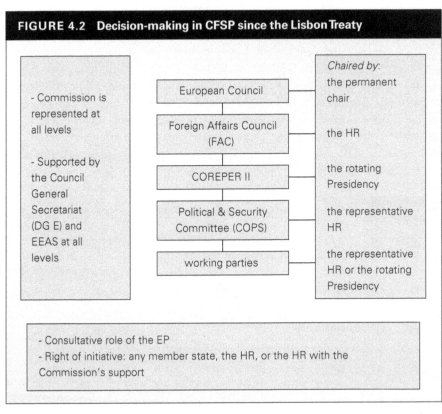

FIGURE 4.2 Decision-making in CFSP since the Lisbon Treaty

for a more permanent body dealing with foreign policy on a day-to-day basis. It consists of representatives of the member states at (junior) ambassadorial level, and since Lisbon, it is chaired by a representative of the HR. It normally meets twice a week and is seen as the linchpin of CFSP. It discusses ongoing international events, deals with the day-to-day management of CFSP, prepares the meetings of the Council and monitors the implementation of European foreign policy decisions, including in the area of crisis management (see below, next section) (Juncos and Reynolds 2007). In this multiplicity of tasks it is assisted by the so-called Nicolaidis group dealing with procedural issues and signalling possible problems and national sensitivities (Duke and Vanhoonacker 2006). Since Maastricht, Coreper II, which is formally in charge of preparing the Council agenda, also plays a role in CFSP. While the PSC focuses on substance, Coreper II primarily looks at the institutional, legal, financial, and Community aspects of the draft decisions and is assisted by the CFSP or Relex counsellors. Present at both the meetings of Coreper and the Political Committee, the Relex counsellors fulfil an important role in establishing consistency between the pillars (see Chapter 5).

The role of the European Parliament in CFSP is still consultative. It can ask questions and adopt recommendations but depends to a large extent on the goodwill of the HR and the member states to take its views into account. Still, with the support of its Committee on Foreign Affairs (AFET) and thanks to its power of the purse, it has managed to carve out a role for itself, especially in questions related to human rights, promotion of democracy, and political conditionality—all questions on which the EP is relatively united (Bickerton 2010). The Court of Justice has no jurisdiction in CFSP (Article 24, TFEU) but that does not necessarily mean that it is entirely powerless. In the famous ECOWAS (Economic Community of West African States) case for example, it condemned the Council for encroaching upon the EC competencies by using a CFSP decision, rather than an act based on the EC treaty for the support of this regional organization in the fight against small arms and light weapons. By doing so it played a crucial role in clarifying the role of CFSP in the broader Union structure (Hillion and Wessel 2009).

The day-to-day running of CFSP is supported by a whole range of Brussels-based administrative bodies. Prior to Lisbon, these players were mainly based in the Council General Secretariat and to a lesser extent in the Commission (DG RELEX). The Council Secretariat first started to play a role after the entering into force of the Maastricht Treaty when the member states established a CFSP unit within DG E (external relations). It was composed of a mixture of civil servants of the Council Secretariat, a Commission official and seconded national diplomats (Christiansen and Vanhoonacker 2008; Dijkstra 2008, 2010). With the appointment of Xavier Solana as Secretary General of the Council and HR for CFSP (1999–2009) and with the development of an EU crisis-management role, the Secretariat moved beyond its purely supportive role and also started to participate in the formulation and implementation of CFSP. A special Policy and Early Warning Unit, better known as the Policy Unit and reporting directly to Solana, was made responsible for monitoring and analysing international developments.

BOX 4.7   The European External Action Service (EEAS)

- Established by Council decision 11507/10.

- Consisting of a Brussels-based central administration and the Union delegations to third countries and international organizations.

- Secretary-General in charge of the day-to-day management of the six Directorates General.

- Two Deputy Generals able to replace the HR at internal EU meetings or certain international events.

- CMPD, CPCC, EUMS, SitCen are under direct authority of the HR (see next section).

- Selection based on merit and on the broadest possible geographical basis in conformity with the staff regulations and the conditions of employment of other servants of the other EU institutions.

Since the advent of the new HR, however, the CFSP role of the secretariat has largely been taken over by the EEAS, foreseen by the Lisbon Treaty to assist the HR in her daily work (Article 27, TEU). This functionally autonomous body brings together for the first time the expertise of civil servants and diplomats previously scattered across the Commission (mainly DG RELEX), the Council Secretariat, and the national capitals (see Box 4.7). As the stakes were high, the establishment of the service in 2010 has been accompanied by fierce turf battles, while national considerations about power and influence have been at least as important as criteria of quality and efficiency (Keukeleire, Smith, and Vanhoonacker 2010). It is well known, however, that once institutions are in place they develop their own rules and practices and they grow into more than mere translators of the original wishes of their creators. In line with the neo-institutionalist argument that institutions matter, it may be expected that in the long term the EEAS will develop into a body with its own identity, becoming a central and influential player in the European foreign policy process.

Besides the Brussels-based central administration, the EEAS also comprises the 136 Union delegations to third countries and international organizations. Under the authority of the HR, the staff of these former Commission delegations has been extended with national diplomats, and its scope of action is no longer confined to trade and development but also includes CFSP. A further difference with the pre-Lisbon period is that the Union delegations are also replacing the rotating Presidency as chair of the meetings among the embassies of the different EU member states.[14]

A final important supportive instrument of the HR is the Special Representatives (EUSRs). Nominated by the Council, they function as the face and voice of the Union in third countries or regions and also fulfil an information-gathering role (Grevi 2007). In mid 2010, there were 11 EUSRs in office covering Afghanistan, the African Great Lakes Region, the African Union, Bosnia Herzegovina, Central Asia, the Former Yugoslav Republic of Macedonia, Georgia, Kosovo, the Middle East, Moldova, the South Caucasus, and Sudan. The role and importance of EUSRs differs depending on the ambitions of the EU in a particular region. While some have a permanent basis in the third country or region in question, others operate from Brussels.

The EU as a crisis manager

The second theme that has been present at every single IGC since Maastricht is that of the development of a European security identity (see also Chapter 9). The Maastricht Treaty explicitly included security into the scope of CFSP but it was only in June 1999 that the Cologne European Council formally adopted the goal to establish a European Security and Defence Policy (ESDP). The ambition to carry out the full range of conflict-prevention and crisis-management tasks—also known as the Petersberg tasks (see Box 4.8)—required a new type of expertise and professional supporting structures able to react promptly to international crisis situations with the timely delivery of human and material resources.

While at the political level the decision-making structures remained the same as those for CFSP more broadly (see Figures 4.1 and 4.2), at the administrative level the impact was huge. Both in the area of military and civilian crisis management, a whole range of new Brussels-based bodies was established. A first group is the *permanent committees*. Besides the earlier-mentioned PSC, key players are the EU Military Committee (EUMC)[15] and the Civilian Crisis Management Committee (CivCom).[16] The EUMC, composed of the Chiefs of Defence (CHODs) of the member states—normally represented by their military representatives (MilReps)—provides military advice.[17] They are supported by the EUMC working group. The role of CivCom, composed of member-state and EEAS representatives, is to make recommendations on the civilian aspects of crisis management. It is also actively involved in the planning and monitoring of civilian missions. Both the EUMS and CivCom report to the PSC. Since the MilReps hold the rank of a three-star general or admiral and the permanent chair (three years) of the EUMC is a four-star

---

| **BOX 4.8** | **The Petersberg tasks** |

- List of security tasks first adopted by the WEU in June 1992 and referring to 'humanitarian and rescue tasks, peacekeeping tasks, and tasks of combat forces in crisis management, including peacekeeping' (*Europe Documents*, No. 1787, 23 June 1992).
- Integrated into the TEU under the Amsterdam Treaty.
- Further extended under the Lisbon Treaty (Article 43, TEU): 'joint disarmament operations, humanitarian and rescue tasks, military advice and assistance tasks, conflict prevention and peacekeeping tasks, tasks of combat forces in crisis management, including peacemaking and post-conflict stabilization.'

officer, the members of the EUMC have more seniority than the officials attending the CivCom meetings who generally are junior diplomats. In both cases, however, the PSC generally follows their advice, which makes them relatively influential players (Cross 2010a). In addition to the above-mentioned intergovernmental committees, the member states have also delegated a number of tasks to the *Brussels-based supranational administrations*. Before Lisbon it was primarily the Council Secretariat and the European Commission that were providing policy advice and some of the organizational functions and technical expertise but it is to be expected that their roles will increasingly be taken over by the EEAS. The structures supporting the military operations were originally all based in the Council Secretariat and were staffed by a mixture of seconded national officials and permanent staff. DG E was extended with a new Directorate for Defence Aspects (DG E VIII) and played a key role in providing political strategic input and the elaboration of the crisis-management concept of operations. As a result, it cooperated closely with the earlier-mentioned EUMC as well as the EU Military Staff (EUMS). The latter, composed of about 200 military staff seconded from the member states, provides military expertise for the planning and implementation of operations and fulfils an early-warning function.[18] Another player previously based in the Council General Secretariat and now transferred to the EEAS is the Joint Situation Centre (SitCen) providing analysis and risk assessments. For the conduct of military operations the member states have so far relied on the Operational Headquarters of NATO and on those made available by the member states. Since 2007, however, there is also the EU Operations Centre (OpCen) within the EUMS, meant primarily for small-scale operations requiring a civil–military response. It is not a permanent fully manned headquarter but can be activated when the two other options are not available.

The structures for *civilian* crisis management (police, rule of law, civil administration, civil protection mission) were initially weaker than those in the military area. The original focus of ESDP was on the development of a military role and the experience among member states with civilian crisis management was in many cases rather limited. This meant that procedures were to a large extent developed as needs were arising (Grevi *et al.* 2009). As in addition there was no civilian equivalent to the EUMS, much of the burden was on the Directorate for Civilian Crisis Management (DG E IX), which was initially responsible for planning, command, and follow-up of the civilian missions. It was not until 2007 that a separate Civilian Planning and Conduct Capability (CPCC) was established, serving as the civilian equivalent of both the EUMS and the military Operational Headquarters, leaving it to DG E IX to do the political and strategic work. In 2009, with the aim to better coordinate the civilian and military dimensions, DGE VIII and IX as well as parts of the EUMS were merged in to the Crisis Management Planning Department (CMPD), now also based within the EEAS.

Last but not least, one should not forget to mention the impact of CSDP on national structures of decision making. The timely delivery of soldiers, police, judges, and other capabilities by the member states requires the involvement of a wide range of national ministries including defence, interior, justice, and finance. This operational dimension means that much more than in the past European foreign policy has the potential to trigger processes of domestic institutional change both in terms of competence allocation as well as coordination, placing the Europeanization debate in European foreign policy in a new perspective (see Chapter 7) (Vanhoonacker and Jacobs 2009).

Conclusion: how and how much do institutions matter?

Having given an overview of the institutional foundations of EU external policy and of the key developments in three core areas, the argument now returns to the more theoretical question posed at the beginning of this chapter: how and to what extent do institutions matter? It was proposed earlier that institutions mattered in four key ways:

- First, they expressed the limits of intergovernmental agreement and successive 'bargains' encapsulated in the various treaties (the intergovernmentalist position).
- Second, they embedded historical bargains and in that way could constrain or shape subsequent institutional developments in the EU's international relations (the 'historical institutionalist' position).
- Third, they reflected the changing nature of demands and opportunities within the EU itself, especially, for example, through the process of enlargement and at the same time the interaction between the institutional developments taking place within the EU and the influence of broader institutional frameworks in the global arena (the 'governance' position).
- Fourth, they provided a context for 'social learning' and the development of expectations and understandings through the interaction of the various groups engaged in the international relations of the EU, from NGOs through to national governments and the European institutions (the 'sociological institutionalist' or the social constructivist position).

What can we say about these four propositions, in light of the evidence gathered together in this chapter? First, in general it is clear that be it in the fields of trade, development, foreign policy, or defence, EU external relations go beyond interaction among member states and their foreign counterparts. Supranational players such as the European Commission, the EP and the ECJ play an important role, and the way they are structured undeniably has an impact on the political debate, on the expectations of significant actors, and on policy outcomes. It is, for example, impossible to understand the sometimes rigid EU position in the WTO without any knowledge of the central role of the Commission and its interaction with the Council and the trade policy committee (see Chapter 12).

As would be expected by historical institutionalist analysis, the high degree of institutional complexity and diversity in EU external relations can to a large extent be explained by the ways in which the different policies developed (McNamara and Meunier 2007). As one of the oldest and most integrated policies, the CCP is highly institutionalized so that even if some member states would like to recapture some of their powers, the traditionally strong position of the Commission makes it difficult to realize this goal. The institutional framework is not only embedded in a series of treaties; it has been strengthened by practise and by the evidence that, especially in global trade negotiations, the member states are stronger acting collectively than they ever could be acting apart. The bargains made in the 1950s have been cemented not only by the evidence of policy effectiveness but also, sometimes with some reluctance, in the face of change at the level of the global political economy expressed in the WTO and other multilateral institutional frameworks. Historical institutionalists would also point to the evidence provided by the development and humanitarian aid policy area, to indicate that the relative weakness of the historical bargains among member states has made it difficult to overcome the essentially mixed nature of the policies adopted (see also Chapter 14). To a degree, the same goes for foreign policy cooperation. Having embarked upon the intergovernmental path, successive IGCs have not been able to communitarize this policy (Juncos 2007). This said, however, it has been pointed out by a number of analysts that the development of powerful informal norms and working practices has also enabled cooperation in the foreign and security policy area to be consolidated, and by others that the foreign policies of member states have been increasingly 'Europeanized' and 'Brusselized' (Allen 1998; Nuttall 2000).

The chapter also provides evidence that change in the composition of the EU itself and in the institutional arrangements surrounding the EU within the global arena has important implications for the development of the EU's 'internal' institutions. EU activities in all three of the areas discussed here have been affected by the enlargement of the EU, through which new constellations of member states with new preferences and priorities have been introduced into the development of external policies (Michalski 2006). The introduction of Britain in the 1970s created new directions in the framing of trade policy, aid policy, and foreign policy because of the powerful influence wielded by the historical experiences and international connections of the 'awkward partner'. In perhaps a more subtle way, the introduction of Sweden, Finland, and Austria during the mid 1990s gave greater salience to institutional arrangements in the area of human rights, development policies, and the broadening nature of security policies. But neither of these sets of developments can be taken in isolation from other areas of institutional development within the EU or from the changing international scene itself (Maull 2005). In particular, the post-Cold War era and the changing nature of 'global governance' has given new salience to attempts to institutionalize EU policies in areas such as asylum and immigration (see Chapter 10), security policy (see Chapter 9), and the management of the global political economy (see Chapter 11). For some observers this means that in a host of new and old policy areas, the EU should be seen increasingly as part of a global system of 'multilevel governance'.

The strong degree of path dependency noted above does not imply that institutions in the field of external relations are static—or that formal institutions tell the whole story. Adjustments take place but they have to be negotiated both formally and informally, and rarely reflect an entirely novel institutional design. The reforms in the management of external assistance under the Prodi Commission after 1999 are a case in point, and the increasing trend to Brusselsization in the area of CFSP shows that adjustments are possible, even if they are slow. Very often, these adjustments in formal institutional processes actually lag behind the development of new degrees of mutual understanding and 'social learning' that would be emphasized by the adherents of sociological institutionalism and its near relative, social constructivism (Tonra 2003; Bretherton and Vogler 2006). This means that there has to be an emphasis not only on the formal rules and institutions in examining the international relations of the EU but also on the informal games and interactions that take place.

Looking at the way formal institutions interact and informal institutions have evolved in the EU's international relations, we see that for a long time the game has been primarily played by the Council and the Commission. In the CCP, the initiative is often said to lie very much with the Commission, especially in areas where the prevailing need is for technocratic types of policy formulation. However, in a number of instances the increasing politicization of trade-related issues such as human rights and environmental concerns has modified the picture, and with the new right of co-decision we may see that the EP will increasingly try to assert its role in the trade area. In development policy and humanitarian assistance, the picture is essentially one of mixed institutional roles, with key significance attaching to the interaction between preferences, institutions, and resources both of the member states and of the relevant EU institutions. In the case of CFSP and ESDP, it is still very much the Council deciding by unanimity that sets the tone, but the significant institutional innovation in recent years and the creation of the HR/EEAS may create new dynamics that will make it difficult to describe European foreign policy as merely intergovernmental (Mérand *et al.* 2010). The role of the EP has traditionally been weak in EU external relations but here also things may be changing. Its strengthened role in the area of trade opens new prospects and it may be expected that under the Lisbon Treaty the Parliament will try to fully exploit its new powers. In the field of CFSP, however, there is still a long way to go. The argument that the sensitive character of foreign policy and the need for rapid reaction justify different standards and working methods in terms of democratic decision-making procedures has been criticized from various corners but so far the debate has been mainly conducted at the academic level (Barbé 2004; Wagner 2006a; Stie 2010). A further challenge is that of consistency (see Chapter 5), reflecting the uncertain boundaries between the EU institutions, the interests and actions of member states, and the wide range of international contexts in which EU actions can now be taken. The institutional framework for the EU's international relations is complex, reflecting a variety of histories, trajectories, and innovations, but the questions it generates remain central to a full understanding of its implications.

Notes

1 In the second Barrosso Commission (2010–14), the trade portfolio has been attributed to Commissioner Karel de Gucht.

2 'When the Foreign Affairs Council is convened to discuss common commercial policy issues, its President will ask to be replaced by the six-monthly Presidency.' See 'Council Decision of 1 December 2009 adopting the Council's Rules of Procedure, 2009/938/EU', *Official Journal L 325*, Vol.52, 11 December 2009, 35–61.

3 The consent procedure (Treaty of Lisbon) is the successor of the assent procedure.

4 The text of the Cotonou Partnership Agreement is available at: http://europa. eu.int/comm/ development/body/cotonou/ overview_en.htm.

5 On the instruments of the EU development policy, see Chapter 8 by Michael E. Smith and Chapter 14 by Maurizio Carbone.

6 The different steps of the project cycle are: programming, identification, formulation, implementation, and evaluation.

7 On EPC, see: S.J. Nuttall (1992) *European Political Cooperation* (Oxford: Clarendon Press); E. Regelsberger, P. de Schoutheete de Tervarent, and W. Wessels (eds) (1997) *Foreign Policy of the European Union. From EPC to CFSP and Beyond* (Boulder, CO: Lynne Rienner); M. Holland (ed.) (1991) *The Future of European Political Cooperation. Essays on Theory and Practice* (London: Macmillan).

8 The dates in brackets refer to the entering into force of the respective treaties.

9 For an overview of the Maastricht negotiations on foreign policy, see S.J. Nuttall (2000).

10 Since the Treaty of Lisbon, the ministers of foreign affairs are no longer present at the European Council.

11 The General Affairs Council is responsible for the consistency of the work of the different Council configurations, it prepares and ensures the follow-up of the meetings of the European Council, is responsible for the overall coordination of policies, institutional, and administrative questions, and deals with horizontal dossiers. The FAC deals with CFSP, CSDP, CCP, development policy, and humanitarian aid.

12 'List of Council Preparatory Bodies', 11301/08, Brussels 8 July 2008.

13 Comité politique et de sécurité.

14 At the time of writing, the change in chairmanship has only been implemented for the smaller EU delegations.

15 'Council Decision 2001/79/CFSP of 22 January 2001 setting up the Military
Committee of the European Union', *Official Journal* L 27, 30 January 2001.

16 'Council Decision of 22 May setting up a Committee for civilian aspects of
crisis management', Doc. 2000/354/CFSP, Brussels, 2001.

17 With the exception of Belgium, France, Luxembourg, and the non-NATO
members, all military representatives are double-hatted, also representing
their country at NATO.

18 'Council Decision 2003/479/EC of 16 June 2003 concerning the rules applicable to national experts and military staff on secondment to the General Secretariat of the Council', *Official Journal L 160*, 28 June 2003.

FURTHER READING

For general approaches to and analysis of the EU's institutions, see especially Peterson
and Shackleton (2006); for analysis of EU policy making in areas including trade, development, and CFSP, see the relevant chapters in Wallace, Pollack, and Youngh (2010). On
the Common Commercial Policy, see Saunders and Triggs (2002), Elsig (2002), Meunier
(2005). The last focuses on the EU role in international trade negotiations.

On development cooperation, see Holland (2002), Carbone (2007), Orbie and Versluys
(2008). The development of EPC and CFSP is comprehensively covered by Nuttall (1992,
2000), Keukeleire and McNaughtan (2008), and M. E. Smith (2003); the last focuses
especially on institutional approaches and developments. For a collection of relevant
documents on CFSP, see Hill and Smith (2000). On ESDP/CSDP, see Howorth (2007),
Mérand (2008), Grevi, Helly, and Keohane (2009). For a legal approach towards EU foreign relations, see Cremona and De Witte (2008).

Carbone, M. (2007), *The European Union and International Development: the politics of
foreign aid* (London: Routledge).

Cremona, M., and De Witte, B. (2008), *EU Foreign Relations Law: constitutional fundamentals* (Oxford and Portland: Hart).

Elsig, M. (2002), *The EU's Common Commercial Policy. Institutions, Interests and Ideas*
(Hampshire: Ashgate).

Grevi, G., Helly, D., and Keohane, D. (2009), *European Security and Defence Policy. The
First 10 years (1999–2009)* (Paris: European Union Institute for Security Studies).

Hill, C., and Smith, K. E. (eds) (2000), *European Foreign Policy: Key Documents* (London:
Routledge).

Holland, M. (2002), *The European Union and the Third World* (Basingstoke: Palgrave).

Mérand, F. (2008), *European Defence Policy: Beyond the Nation State* (Oxford: Oxford University Press).

Meunier, S. (2005), *Trading Voices: the European Union in International Commercial Negotiations* (Princeton, NJ: Princeton University Press).

Nuttall, S. (1992), *European Political Cooperation* (Oxford: Clarendon Press).

Nuttall, S. (2000), *European Foreign Policy* (Oxford: Oxford University Press).

Orbie, J., and Versluys, H. (2008), 'The European Union's international development policy: leading and benevolent?', in J. Orbie (2008), *Europe's Global Role External Policies of the European Union* (Aldershot; Ashgate), 67–90.

Peterson, J., and Shackleton, M. (eds) (2006), *The Institutions of the European Union* (Oxford: Oxford University Press).

Saunders, C., and Triggs, G. (eds) (2002), *Trade and Cooperation with the European Union in the New Millennium* (Alphen aan den Rijn: Kluwer Law International).

Smith, M. E. (2003) *Europe's Foreign and Security Policy: the institutionalization of cooperation* (Cambridge: Cambridge University Press).

Wallace, H., Pollack, M., and Young, A. (eds) (2010) *Policy-Making in the European Union*, 6th edition (Oxford: Oxford University Press).

WEB LINKS

For an overview of the internal organization of the different EU institutions and their role in the external policy process, see: **http://ec.europa.eu/world/index_en.htm** (European Commission); **http://www.consilium.europa.eu/** (Council) and **http://www.europarl.europa.eu/** (European Parliament).

A useful broad-based website on European foreign policy is **http://www.fornet.** FORNET is an academic network focused on research and teaching, and the website includes a bulletin, documentation, and news items. For data and documents on development assistance, see especially **http://www.ec.europa.eu**. See also (especially for defence issues) **http://www.iss-eu.org**, the website of the European Union Institute for Security Studies, which includes text of policy papers and documentation. On the emerging EU diplomatic system, see: **http://dseu.lboro.ac.uk**.

CHAPTER 5

Coherence

Carmen Gebhard

Summary

The EU as it presents itself today is made up of a vertically and horizontally multilayered, and hence highly complex, system of institutional structures. This chapter deals with one of the most fervently discussed implications of this complexity: coherence, or the challenge and ambition to coordinate the multiple parts of the EU's international relations in order to increase both strategic convergence and procedural efficiency across several strands of EU external action. After a brief historical review, the chapter discusses different conceptual dimensions of coherence, which should help to structure the immense range of issues that come up in its context. It then proceeds to discuss the various faces the notion of 'coherence' can assume in the course of internal debates—that is, neutral, benign, or malign. The various legal and institutional measures that have been taken to facilitate coherence are discussed against this background. The chapter then moves on to discuss the potential impact of the Lisbon Treaty provisions on the management of coherence, which leads into the conclusions and outlook.

Introduction

Coherence has been a recurrent concern in EU matters, and not only in foreign policy.[1] In fact, coherence—or rather, the lack of it—constitutes one of the most frequently bemoaned aspects of the EU's political and bureaucratic performance. The concern as such, however, is not unique to the EU. Almost any governance system is faced with the challenge of having to reconcile concurrent policy spheres, and of managing the very implications of structural complexity, which are, essentially, an enhanced need for coordination and the necessity of closing ranks across a growing range of functional areas. What exacerbates this challenge in the case of the EU, however, is its specific structural character as a multilevel actor. Unlike a nation state, the EU is vertically and horizontally multilayered, and hence a highly complex system of institutional structures. Furthermore, the realm of foreign policy is faced with particularly intricate circumstances. Contrary to the aim of 'speaking with one voice', the EU has no built-in institutional framework that would allow for sound and concerted external action. It does not just have to bring together an increasing number of national positions. As a result of its own history as an organization, the governance of the EU's external relations is also spread across pillars and thus divided into two different procedural channels governing decision-making, financing, and implementation—a supranational channel primarily governed by the European Commission, and an intergovernmental one centred on the Council.

Confusingly, complaints about a lack of coherence in the EU's policy making and implementation often arise in fairly disparate contexts, ranging from instances of procedural disjuncture to cases where member states merely failed to agree on a common position. Generally, the more diversified and developed the EU's institutional structures, the more common it was to ascribe all sorts of political failures to a lack of coherence (Nuttall 2005). Therefore, this chapter seeks to clarify the various meanings 'coherence' can have in the realm of EU foreign policy, particularly against the background of how it affects the present and future performance of the EU as an international player. With the global strategic environment growing ever more complex and unpredictable, and the expectations held of the EU in such areas as international conflict resolution, stabilization, and development rising exponentially, managing its vast range of policy instruments in a coherent way has become an ever more pressing challenge. Although European leaders frequently stress the comparative advantage of the EU as a multi-sectoral international actor that has both operational and structural instruments at its disposal (political, diplomatic, and economic), in practice the functional fragmentation of the EU's institutional structures (still) keeps it from performing unitarily on the global scene. And this is what places the issue of coherence at the centre of any assessment of the EU's foreign policy. In a way, the overall success of the EU in the world stands or falls on its political and administrative capacity to cope with the very core features of its distinctiveness as an international actor: its versatility and holistic predisposition, which in turn are based on its multifaceted structural character and thus its institutional complexity.

The chapter begins with a short historical review of the developing debate on coherence in EU foreign policy as European integration has evolved. This will serve to contextualize current discussions about the issue, and to explain the reasons why incoherence persists despite all the political and academic awareness of it. The proliferation of concerns over 'coherence' and 'consistency' in the political debate has not exactly helped to clarify the actual meaning of the concept and its political implications. The second part of this chapter therefore presents a set of answers as to how the complex of issues commonly related to the topic can be structured analytically. What types of coherence can be identified, and what is the political meaning of the quest for enhanced coordination commonly related to the issue? After discussing these questions, the chapter moves on to review various legal and institutional steps that have been taken so far in order to enhance coherence in different respects. Particular attention will be paid to the specific context of crisis management, given the significant impact of the dynamic evolution of ESDP on the overall institutional balance in EU external relations. The chapter closes with an early evaluation of the implications of the Treaty of Lisbon for the management of coherence, leading to more general conclusions and a look to the future.

Historical background of coherence

The basic conception of, and perceived need for, political and institutional coherence has been an issue since the early days of the European integration process and more specifically since the Merger Treaty (1965) established a single Council and a single Commission for the European Communities, and thus a 'single set of institutions' to exercise the powers conferred on them by the treaties. However, up to the 1970s, 'coherence' as such was mainly used along with the notion of 'cohesion' to refer to the benefits states could have if they decided to team up on certain foreign political matters.[2] After the creation of European Political Cooperation (EPC) in 1970, however, the term was increasingly used in the way that is most common today—and as it is mainly addressed in this chapter, that is, referring to the necessity of bringing together different strands of political action both strategically and procedurally.[3] When EPC was eventually adopted and formalized in the framework of the Single European Act (SEA) in 1987 as an intergovernmental attempt to ensure that the internal market was balanced by a foreign policy dimension, the question arose as to how this new 'political Europe' could be functionally reconciled with the then established supranational framework of the Community. The SEA introduced the so-called coherence/consistency requirement, which stipulated that the external policies of the EC and the policies agreed in EPC ought to be in line with each other:

The external policies of the EC and the policies agreed in EPC must be consistent. The Presidency and the Commission, each within its own sphere of competence, shall have special responsibility for ensuring that such consistency is sought and maintained.

(SEA, Title III, Article 30)

In the overall arrangement of the act, however, a strict line was drawn between the two policy realms. Nuttall (2001) has a point when stating that today's bifurcation of the EU's external profile originated in this very context, when 'at the insistence of France, EPC and the Community were kept as far as possible in hermetically sealed compartments'. In the years to follow, the lack of consensus over further integration was compensated by mere interaction, and coherence or consistency became 'the art of managing the interface' (Nuttall 2001). In any case, it soon became clear that keeping up this dysfunctional division between economic and political diplomacy was highly problematic in many ways.

The following intergovernmental conference (IGC) did not find any solution for the EPC–Community divide. Although the Treaty of Maastricht reiterated the above coherence/consistency requirement with only slight alterations,[4] and referred to a 'single set of institutions' to manage the implementation of the new structure, the concurrent establishment of the Common Foreign and Security Policy (CFSP) as a self-contained pillar complicated the picture more than it improved anything. The institutional background the treaty provided for political cooperation among the Member States *reinforced* the pre-established dualism between supranational integration and intergovernmental cooperation instead of removing it. What is more, the basic choice for a pillar structure and for the establishment of a 'Union' to back the 'Community' politically, generally determined the course of institutional developments for the years to come.

At both consecutive treaty revisions in 1997 and 2000, member states equally failed to do more than provide partial solutions to the problem. The Treaty of Amsterdam brought no substantial changes to the coherence/consistency requirement,[5] and as such, again, provided no lasting solution to the structural disconnect between the EC and the CFSP. The creation of a High Representative (HR) for the CFSP in turn actually exacerbated the internal conflict between the two realms of external action. As the post was conferred on the Secretary General of the Council, the Commission saw its overall position considerably weakened. In view of the political power at stake, the amendment that the Commission 'shall be fully associated' with the work carried out in the framework of the CFSP (Article J.17), was no more than a stock phrase.

The Treaty of Nice also largely left the management of the persisting institutional bifurcation to political practice. The issues of coherence and how the functional and legal relationship with the EU's external economic policies could be improved were not a priority at the time the treaty was drafted. The member states rather focused on a set of 'Amsterdam leftovers' that needed to be dealt with before enlargement. The fact that even the Treaty of Nice preserved the dualist logic was especially unfavourable for the institutional development of the newly created ESDP and crisis management respectively. What is more, the legal formalization of the structures for the fledgling ESDP marked the beginning of a new wave of conflicts between the Council and the Commission. The establishment of ESDP, and its further development as a particularly dynamic and functionally expansive new policy field, exacerbated the tension between the pillars even further. The treaties kept providing a very weak base for the settlement of these newly arising conflicts. However, the importance attached to the issue in the framework of the European Convention, and later on in the context of the formulation of what became the Treaty of Lisbon, ratified in December 2009, at least shows the respective awareness among member states. After the failure of the initial attempt to create a Constitution, the issue continued to be high on the agenda. As the chapter will come to show, the Treaty of Lisbon put very strong emphasis on the management of coherence and in fact brought about a set of significant changes to the institutional set-up underlying EU external action. European leaders and law experts alike were hoping for a factual dissolution of the pillars. A closer look at the treaty text, however, shows that while 'depillarization' has been attempted, it has not in fact taken place at the deeper levels.

Before discussing the most recent debate on coherence in EU external action, the chapter now turns to the question of how 'coherence' can be conceptualized, and to what extent the nuances of the concept matter for a deeper understanding of the EU's external relations.

Conceptualizing coherence

'Coherence' and 'consistency'

Although 'coherence' has been a recurrent concern for more than four decades, the notion has remained inherently ambiguous to this day. Confusingly, in EU legislation, the terms 'coherence' and 'consistency' are often used interchangeably although their meaning is in fact considerably different. The problem possibly comes from the way the term has been translated into other Community languages in the first place: the French *cohérence* has commonly been turned into the English 'consistency' (instead of 'coherence') while it remained *Kohärenz* in German, *coherencia* in Spanish, and *coerenza* in Italian.[6] There are conflicting views in the literature about whether the conceptual difference between 'coherence' and 'consistency' really matters or not. While some see the risk of 'linguistic pedantry' (Nuttall 2005) in any attempt at distinguishing between the two, others consider the distinction an analytical necessity. As this chapter aims at clarifying the concept rather than reproducing the arbitrariness with which it is commonly employed in political practice and public debate, a terminological discussion is considered useful in this context.

The ambiguities in official translations make it very difficult to grasp the conceptual distinction that some legal theorists draw between the two terms. Even though there is no general agreement on the legally defining features of 'coherence' and 'consistency', there is a broad consensus in the literature about their conceptual differentiation (Tietje 1997; Cremona 1999; Missiroli 2001; Bertea 2005). 'Coherence' is commonly considered as superordinate to the notion of 'consistency'. It is seen as a high stage of structural harmonization, which presupposes a set of 'more primitive' secondary conditions or requirements such as comprehensiveness, completeness, continuity—and consistency (Bertea 2005). Along these lines, 'consistency' is thought of as a 'minimal requirement' that mainly involves the 'absence of contradictions'. 'Coherence' in turn is about increased systemic synergy and is hence to be seen as more of a 'desirable plus' that involves 'positive connections' between several factors (Missiroli 2001). Gauttier (2004) suggests a similar interpretation for the specific context of EU external action, inferring that 'coherence encompasses both the absence of contradictions within the external activity in different areas of foreign policy (consistency), and the establishment of a synergy between these aspects'. What this comes down to is that each term essentially refers to a different ontological context. While 'consistency' mainly refers to the character of an outcome or state, which is logically compatible with another or not, 'coherence' rather specifies the quality of a process, in which ideally the single entities involved join together in a synergetic procedural whole.[7] This implies that the two notions also differ in the way they relate to time and space. One can be (in)consistent over a period of time, and as such, provide continuity (or not), but coherence remains a matter of quality of interaction between organizational entities.

In both treaty language and in political practice, this sort of conceptual clarification appears to be of only marginal relevance. However, for analytical purposes, it remains important to differentiate between the meanings and implied specifications of the two. Declining the broader notion of 'coherence' into its separate conceptual components helps to untangle the complex set of issues that past and current debates are raising. What can be concluded from the above in the first place is that 'coherence' is the more accurate notion for what is being discussed in this chapter. Consistency is part of the challenge but as a term it falls short of implications that are crucial to obtaining a clear understanding of the issue. Generally, there are two dimensions to 'coherence': one *strategic* or *policy related* (as referring to conflicting objectives or clashing political agendas) and one *technical* or *procedural* (as referring to the administrative implications of having to reconcile two different channels of policy making, including their respective bureaucratic machineries). Awareness of these two dimensions of coherence is also fundamental for grasping the following typology.

Types of coherence

While in this chapter the focus lies on the relationship between the intergovernmental and the supranational domain of EU external action, i.e. on so-called 'horizontal coherence', generally the concept of coherence can be said to be relevant in four very specific contexts of EU external relations (see Box 5.1):[8]

- *Vertical coherence* means the concertation of member-state positions and policies with and in respect of the overall consensus or common position at the Community or Union level. This includes general compliance with political commitments laid down in the treaties but also the technical compatibility of specific national policies with common policies. It thus concerns issues of solidarity, reconcilability of single policies, bottom-up commitment to integration, and a readiness to comply with the *acquis* as well as matters of top-down harmonization and regulation, which stand for the reverse side of the aforementioned issues.[9]

- *Horizontal coherence* in EU foreign policy in turn is concerned with concertation at Community and Union level, i.e. with the coordination between the supranational and the intergovernmental sphere of external action, and thereby also between the main institutional entities governing them, meaning the European Commission and the Council of the EU, including their associated bureaucratic machineries. Horizontal coherence is equivalent to the notion of 'inter-pillar coherence' as it challenges the relationship between the first and the second pillar of the EU in two ways (see two dimensions above): (a) in terms of converging or compatible policy contents, which implies strategic consent or dissent on the broad objectives of external action, or (b) in terms of procedural and technical soundness, which points at the problems caused by the distinct approaches to decision-making and implementation traditionally present in each realm. The fact that the governance of EU foreign policy is spread across two pillars places 'horizontal coherence' at the centre of any investigation of the EU's external profile. This view differs from those readings which distinguish between 'horizontal coherence' as referring to the cohesiveness or compatibility of various EU policies (even between purely Community policies), and 'institutional coherence', which essentially

---

BOX 5.1   Types of coherence

- Vertical: between the member states and the Union level.
- Horizontal: between the CFSP and the external policies of the Community.
- Internal: within each of these two foreign policy domains.
- External: between the EU and third actors.

denotes the procedural aspects of the former in both an inter-pillar and intra-pillar context (Missiroli 2001; Nuttall 2001, 2005). Yet such a classification only confuses the picture. Coherence across various policy strands of the *Community* realm (intra-pillar) is certainly crucial to the overall quality of the EU's external performance. However, lumping it together with the analytically distinct *inter-pillar* issue is not conducive to any deeper understanding. Thus, in the classification adopted in this chapter, coordination within the Commission's domain is termed 'internal coherence'.

- *Internal coherence* is concerned with the sound management within each of the above domains, hence with the intra-pillar functioning of the CFSP/ESDP on the one hand, and of the external domain of the Community on the other.[10] As a matter of logic, internal coherence is a matter of technical and procedural development rather than of conflicting or converging policy content. The challenge lies in integrating a compound bureaucratic machinery into a specific policy- and decision-making system and for the purpose of established policy objectives. Where strategic politics comes in, however, (and where vertical coherence interferes with internal coherence) is in the way member states might try to influence internal procedural coordination, which is essentially a technical matter.[11]

In the case of ESDP, the challenge was exacerbated by the fact that the Council had to optimize and adapt its procedures to a fast-moving and expansive range of operational challenges and, at the same time, had to accommodate a set of new organizational entities within the given procedural framework. While formally part of the CFSP, the ESDP soon took on the quality and functional range of a fourth pillar. The inception of ESDP and the resulting reorganization of the Council structures have in turn also pushed forward reforms inside the Commission. This is not to say that any attempt to optimize the internal functioning of one of the two realms is necessarily inspired by structural developments in the other. In many instances, however, awareness of the importance of enhanced internal coherence has arisen within one pillar whenever the other appeared to be performing particularly well, or at least to be developing new functional competencies in a specific area of foreign policy. That in turn has frequently affected the inter-pillar relationship and balance between the EU's supranational and intergovernmental policies. For this reason, any analysis of horizontal coherence also has to look at the internal dynamics and coordination efforts on each side.

- *Inter-organizational* or *external coherence* is related to the way the EC/EU presents itself to third parties or within a multilateral system, thus having major importance for the Union's relationship with the UN, OSCE, and NATO or with key partners such as the USA. Apart from having decisive impact at the operational level, external coherence is basically determined by a range of internal coordination processes. Recent debates about the establishment of a

European External Action Service (EEAS) are an important case in point: finding the right balance between Commission delegations, national embassies, and Special Representatives is a matter of both vertical and horizontal coherence. Any failure to coordinate positions within the EU—be it among member states or between the Council and the Commission—has a significant impact on the EU's ability to perform towards other major actors. What is more, external coherence is primarily concerned with functionality and credibility rather than with specific foreign policy contents. Establishing technical interoperability with other international actors is thus crucial for the EU's ability to act unitarily.

In general, these four different aspects of coherence in EU external action are inherently interlinked with each other, and to some degree mutually reinforcing. Vertical coherence lies at the heart of CFSP in particular. It determines the ability of the EU to 'speak with one voice', most importantly when a rapid 'common' response is required. However, attaining it is more a political question than a matter of institutional or structural improvement. As long as member states retain their national sovereignty in some areas of EU external action, vertical coherence will basically remain a matter of case-by-case balancing. Horizontal coherence by contrast is very much an institutional issue—both in respect of its policy/content dimension and its procedural/administrative dimension. Internal/intra-pillar coherence is important here, too, to the extent that the degree of concertation within each of the domains has an impact on the quality of and potential for horizontal coherence. What is more, problems arising in the context of internal coherence are often voiced against the background of concerns about horizontal coherence and inter-pillar balance respectively. In any case, achieving horizontal coherence is inherently connected with the compatibility, interoperability, and credibility of the EU as a bilateral or multilateral partner, hence also with the interorganizational and external dimensions. This is what makes the enhancement of horizontal coherence such a pressing challenge: despite all the internal struggles for reform and convergence, and despite the inherent challenge of having to cope with institutional complexity, the EU is increasingly perceived as—and is expected to act like—a coordinated, if not unitary, actor.

The three faces of coherence

What might be drawn from the above specification of different *types* of coherence is that achieving coherence necessarily involves making a positive effort—although the controversies about the issue lead straight to the question of whether coherence is always and necessarily something to be striven for. Still, there is a variety of phrases and notions commonly employed in the context of coherence that convey its desirability. Expressions like 'acting as a whole', 'speaking with one voice', 'consonance', 'unity', 'continuity', and 'consistency' all express the core idea of striving for unified cohesion and an ultimate structural integratedness, seen as a constructive process. Such Euro-talk conceals the various *faces* that the fostering of 'coherence' can take on in political practice. In a way, however, it simply reflects the iconic meaning that coherence tends to have in most official documents. As the following extract from the TEU Nice shows, the coherence/consistency requirement appearing in the treaties carries a strong normative connotation:

The Union shall be served by a single institutional framework which shall ensure the consistency and the continuity of the activities carried out in order to attain its objectives ...

(Article 3, TEU Nice)

The notion conveys the general aspiration of acting with ever more unity, of becoming more cohesive, and thus of moving closer to an optimum level of integration. Hence, it is positively loaded in the sense that it directly appeals to the very core objectives of integration. The normative charge becomes even more evident when the treaty turns to external action and the EU's 'activities as a whole', when 'to this end':

The Union shall in particular ensure the consistency of its external activities as a whole in the context of its external relations, security, economic and development policies. The Council and the Commission shall be responsible for ensuring such consistency and shall cooperate to this end.

(Article 3, TEU Nice)

The positive expectation lying behind this quest for coherence (between the Council and the Commission, the member states and the Union, and the Union and the Community) clearly builds on the intuitive hope that more coherent internal structures necessarily translate into more successful and more efficient external action (Missiroli 2001, 2003). In fact, apart from the treaties, most key documents[12] on the issue argue on the hopeful assumption that enhanced coherence will result in more effective actorness and ultimately in a different quality of 'union'—which will effect a 'unity of action':

The assumption is of course that, by acting unitarily and with a common purpose, the EU (i.e. the 15 plus 1 Community/Union) also becomes ipso facto more efficient and effective: an assumption that is more intuitive than well founded, given that European foreign policy has often achieved unanimity at the expense of effectiveness and that, in general, a policy can be effective without necessarily being consistent (as the 'carrot-and-stick' metaphor and the 'good cop-bad cop' example epitomize).

(Missiroli 2001, 182)

Practice has indeed shown that reaching coherence, e.g. in the form of a consistent common position or policy (i.e. in the vertical sense), often comes at the expense of functional depth. One case in point has been the development of a strategic framework for the EU's relationship with Russia. The resulting strategic partnership constitutes a common policy but its substance has remained limited. As the lowest common denominator on which the member states were able to agree, the policy is sound and in that sense 'coherent'; its functional value, however, has been marginal. Another example is the European Security Strategy, which at first—and particularly against the background of the controversy over the Iraq war—seemed to be a remarkable achievement in terms of the EU's ability to speak with one voice. In substance, however, the document remained vague on a number of crucial issues, such as common interests and the way the member states were going to pursue them. What is more, in official contexts coherence is commonly promoted as a guiding principle that even *legitimizes* EU external action, which amounts, paradoxically, to the means justifying the end. In the same vein, EU external action is said to be determined by a (benign) pursuit of common interests and core values. Even the realist interest in acquiring power and influence in the world is thus linked with the normative aim of establishing unity for a common purpose.

Another aspect that needs to be taken into account, particularly with respect to procedural and technical coherence between the two major foreign policy realms but also within each one of them, is that establishing coherence often implies a necessity for coordination. This in turn raises the delicate question about which actors are coordinated and which indeed do the coordinating. Pointing at an instance of *incoherence* hence often suggests the necessity of some coordinating hierarchy or institutional prioritization among the actors involved (Nuttall 2000), which then raises some critical questions about *finalité* and the merits of the different ways to achieve objectives, which are usually politicized. Against the background of these essential nuances of the term, Nuttall (2001, 2005) identified three levels of understanding of 'coherence': *banal*, *malign*, and *benign* (see Box 5.2).

- The *banal* or neutral meaning is equivalent to the technical quest for an 'absence of contradictions', which is—in line with the above specifications—synonymous with 'consistency'. This reading of the term is fairly devoid of any normative or critical connotation and instead is closely determined by practical necessity and the imperative of functionality. It also falls short of grasping the various political implications of attaining this 'absence of contradictions'.

- The *malign* take on, and the power-related subtext of, the concept of coherence relates to the internal struggles between institutions, which commonly arise whenever 'coherent' procedures are being established and respective

BOX 5.2	The three faces of coherence

- Banal: coherence as the absence of contradictions.
- Malign: coherence as a function of internal power struggles ('turf battles').
- Benign: coherence as a desirable way of interacting.

reforms are taking place within a compound and inherently polycentric bureaucratic apparatus like the EU (Bertea 2005). The malign understanding also refers to conflicts at the strategic level of competing policy objectives. What is most present in the literature in this context, however, is the issue of fierce 'turf battles' between rivalrous institutions, 'pillarized' bureaucratic cultures, and the multiple instances of perceived overlap and duplication. At the root of all this understanding is a pragmatic and problem-oriented approach, stressing the need for compromise, while avoiding an idealized notion of unity.

- The *benign* meaning, in contrast, takes coherence as a positive type of interaction between institutional entities bound 'to the service of a common purpose'. This notion also implies a constructive element as the continuous joint pursuance of this common purpose is expected first to generate a different, more integrative quality of interaction, and then, in the long run, to create a condition of unity and enhanced systemic integrity.

The broad meaning of this tripartite distinction is most significant with respect to horizontal and internal coherence in the EU's foreign policy and thus more in an institutional than a political context. On the face of it, vertical coherence as a matter of aligning member states with EU policies hardly gets to take on a malign aspect in the above sense since the distribution of power and hierarchy seems to be more or less clear. This is not to say that establishing vertical coherence is essentially less controversial—quite the contrary. However, given that unanimous voting is still dominant in the most vital areas of foreign and security policy, there is no *immediate* room for turf battles as we experience them between institutional actors. This is also a central aspect when it comes to analysing the legal and institutional measures taken so far to enhance coherence in its various contexts (see section below).

External coherence in its turn also mainly carries a banal meaning in as far as it concerns the EU's technical ability to present itself as a unitary actor and to develop a certain extent of maturity as an organization to make for a credible and reliable partner. The question about how this level of maturity and interoperability with other global actors is to be achieved, however, is a very contentious issue indeed, which may involve malign instances of vertical, horizontal, and internal power struggles.

This leads us to the question of how these categories are linked to the above typology of vertical, horizontal, internal, and external coherence. Although in practice each type of coherence may take on benign, malign, and neutral aspects, there is an underlying pattern that links the two sets of categories. As the third, 'benign', interpretation is more normative than the other two ('the common purpose'); it certainly comes closest to the schematic notion of (horizontal) coherence predominant in the treaties. In official EU practice, this normatively charged quest for coherence is recurrently employed in declarations and legal provisions. The aim is to indicate *finalité* in the sense of the direction that institutional integration should follow. Needless to say, in official documents, as opposed to inter-institutional communication and practice, the 'malign' aspect of horizontal coherence hardly ever appears in explicit terms. On the same lines, most of the concrete institutional measures intended to tackle the problem of incoherence, that is, to make institutional realities move closer to the aspired state of 'acting as a whole', adhere to the neutral reading as laid out above. Hence, they usually focus on ensuring the ad hoc and banal 'absence of contradictions' in technical terms, until more extensive measures can be agreed by the member states, or on an inter-institutional basis.

Means of enhancing coherence

All four types of coherence—vertical, horizontal, institutional, and external—have received recurrent attention in both political and academic debate, and have been referred to in the treaties at different levels of stricture. Specific measures towards enhancing coherence have most particularly concerned the institutional and technical implications of 'speaking with one voice' and thus instances of horizontal and internal coherence. Certainly vertical coherence has never ceased to be an issue of debate, and most of the major institutional changes in EU foreign policy making have claimed to be steps towards improving it. However, it is the structural causes of horizontal and internal coherence that make them particularly fruitful objects of study when it comes to the *means* of enhancing coherence. Thus, this section mainly focuses on horizontal coherence—including both its political and procedural dimension—and on internal coherence, while issues of vertical coherence are discussed only where relevant to the main theme.

Looking at the past two decades of discussions about horizontal coherence, there have hardly been any occasions where incoherence has actually been addressed as a problem to be solved. Both the treaties and respective political initiatives rather speak of coherence as an ideal or desirable quality of interaction, while the implications of establishing it remain blurred by the normative charge attached to the concept as such. Hence, when it comes to enhancing coherence it is often tried to solve problems without actually naming them.

Generally, one can distinguish three types of measures employed for enhancing coherence: legal remedies, institutional reforms, and political initiatives (see Box 5.3).

BOX 5.3	**Enhancing coherence**

- Legal remedies: legal requirements to interact, combination of separate instruments.
- Institutional reforms: fostering bureaucratic capacity to coordinate across pillars.
- Political initiatives: raising awareness about a 'culture of coordination'.

Legal remedies

The issue of legal remedies is inherently ambiguous since much of the problem derives from the treaties and thus has legal root causes. As pointed out earlier in this chapter, the problem of functional fragmentation that lies at the heart of horizontal incoherence is mainly a result of the way member states have decided to manage the EU's external relations. The problem originated in the SEA, which established the EPC as a subject of international law detached from the EC. However, what is more decisive for the management of incoherence today is the fact that this essential dysfunctionality was retained and reproduced when the EU was created by the Treaty of Maastricht, with the CFSP established as a distinct pillar with its own decision-making procedures. The Treaty of Lisbon, 16 years later, entails some changes in this respect, to be discussed in the last section of this chapter.

The coherence/consistency requirement (Article 3, TEU Nice) is the principal legal provision that points explicitly at the issue of horizontal coherence. In the Treaty of Maastricht, the responsibility to ensure such coherence across the EU's external activities was jointly assigned to the Council and the Commission (Article C, TEU Maastricht). The Treaty of Amsterdam added the requirement that they should also 'cooperate to this end' (Article 3, TEU Amsterdam) but did not strengthen the provision as such. It was retained in the Treaty of Nice, including the final line that the Council and the Commission should fulfil this responsibility 'each in accordance with its respective powers'—thus indicating the source of possible incoherence. In order to manage coherence in the stipulated way, the treaties would have needed to confer such responsibility on one coordinating entity instead of splitting it along the very line of conflict. What is more, the way the 'requirement' has so far been framed in the treaties determines that while it is legally binding it is not legally enforceable. It has the character of a normative objective that ought to be considered by both sides. In essence, however, the shared responsibility of the Council and the Commission cannot be enforced when it comes to single cases of coordination. In terms of political theory, this is the problem of divided sovereignty which Thomas Hobbes warned the world against in *The Leviathan* and which the project of European integration has struggled valiantly to transcend since its inception.

The Maastricht Treaty created one major obstacle, which affects the EU's external actorness to this day. The member states have not been able to clarify the functional relationship between the EC and the EU's legal framework. Through several revisions, the treaties have remained inherently ambiguous about whether the external aspects of the Community were strategically and politically superior to the CFSP or even how the two domains actually related to each other. According to Article 1, TEU (Nice), the Union was to be '*founded on* the European Communities, *supplemented* by the policies and forms of cooperation established by this treaty.' This formulation clearly provided for the Community framework, including the external action elements of the respective policies, to remain superordinate to the intergovernmental dimension of external action as contained in the Union's CFSP. Furthermore, Article 47, TEU stipulates that nothing in the EU Treaty 'shall affect the treaties establishing the European Communities'. Yet Title V, TEU (Nice), in the way it defines the scope of CFSP, explicitly includes and covers *all areas* of foreign and security policy, in which the role of the Commission remains limited.

As the treaties have generally not been clear about the delimitation of powers between the pillars, one might look for provisions that enhance coherence by stipulating a dual involvement of both pillars for one and the same external action. However, the treaties have little to offer in this regard: so far, only economic sanctions have explicitly required both a joint action in the framework of CFSP and an EC Council Regulation. Articles 301 and 60, TEC are so far the only ones that require inter-pillar cooperation in foreign policy.[13] Another case in point of a cross-pillar (and thus a structurally coherent) decision was that taken in 1994 over the handling of exports of dual-use goods. Unlike the category of economic sanctions, however, this procedural choice has never been formalized legally. It did not even persist in political practice. In 2000, when the dual-use regime was revised, the CFSP framework was not involved, and a simple EC Council Regulation was adopted to finalize the issue (Nuttall 2005). However, there is another legal instrument providing the involvement of both the supranational framework and the member states, which has been employed more frequently and successfully. Through so-called 'mixed agreements', i.e. agreements in which—besides third states and/or international organizations—the EC and one or more of the member states are parties to an international agreement, the EU/EC has found a way to get around the pillar problem in relation to third parties. Important examples are the United Nations Convention on the Law of the Sea and most association agreements as well as the WTO agreements (Leal-Arcas 2001). In principle, mixed agreements should die with the pillar system after the Treaty of Lisbon, but the fundamental issue of different decision-making pathways remains.

One kind of solution might exist in the legal basis of CFSP as the *supplementing* domain of EU external relations. When the CFSP was established in the Treaty of Maastricht, several observers expected its legal instruments—joint actions and common positions—to become the appropriate tools of a coherent foreign policy, to ensure compatibility with the EC domain of external action. Yet rather than providing a remedy over time, the legal instruments that CFSP was provided with in the treaties actually exacerbated conflict in certain contexts. Debates about the CFSP's early joint actions were dominated by the question of how their content would or could affect the competences of the Community. Although Article 47, TEU stipulated that nothing in the new pillar could 'affect' the EC framework, there was not enough clarity in the treaties about the scope of application of joint actions. Similar conflicts developed in view of common positions, which according to the treaties should serve to determine the overall approach of the EU to a wider geographical or thematic issue. The pervasive use of this instrument often led to fierce conflicts with the European Commission, as in many cases these positions included objectives that seemed to be in the domain of the Community, such as the consolidation of democracies through development cooperation and social and economic reconstruction (see Gauttier 2004 for examples). When the Amsterdam Treaty then introduced common strategies as a third legal instrument for the CFSP, these turf battles continued, despite the fact that they were evidently intended to provide overarching guidance. Although the instrument was placed in the CFSP chapter, the treaty text as such was inherently ambiguous, stipulating that common strategies should 'set out ... the means to be made available by the EU'. There was no reference to any limitation of scope or to the protection of the EC *acquis* in the event of overriding political considerations. As it happened, common strategies hardly got off the ground, falling into disuse in the face of the scorn of High Representative Javier Solana and his colleagues, who regarded them as at best bland statements of the obvious.

Yet while none of the consecutive treaty revisions brought much more clarity into the issue of CFSP instruments and their functional relationship with the Community framework, inter-pillar debates have increasingly taken on a more pragmatic style. The enhanced (self-)involvement of the Commission in the early phases of drafting the document nowadays often prevents the emergence of any major grey zones, which could lead to clashing competencies at the level of implementation.[14]

In terms of the legal remedies for *vertical* incoherence, one might say the treaties so far have had even less to offer than with respect to inter-pillar coordination. When it comes to the compatibility of member-state policies with the EU level, it seems that the respective legal approach has not been directly aimed at enhancing 'vertical coherence' as such. The focus was rather on how to extend the range of possibilities for the member states to avoid being disruptive by taking a conflictual stance in a key policy matter. By offering an increasing variety of so-called opt-outs, including Constructive Abstention after Amsterdam in 1997, the treaties gradually diluted the formal requirements for mutual consent, which confirms the above contention that vertical coherence and establishing it are hardly an institutional matter. This system builds on the assumption that in terms of efficiency and the ability to 'speak with one voice', it is less relevant whether a certain action is *actively* supported by all member states as long as there is a common line agreed.

Institutional reforms

Institutional reforms can be thought of as one of the most direct ways of enhancing coherence. In the EU's foreign policy apparatus, however, they have very rarely focused on horizontal coherence as such, largely being guided by operational requirements. In fact, in its early institutional development, CFSP (later including ESDP) created problems for the management of coherence, rather than enabling particular cross-pillar synergies. From the late 1990s onwards, the CFSP machinery—and in particular its ESDP offshoot—was confronted with an ever growing functional agenda and rising political expectations, which placed matters of *internal* functioning at the centre of most reform efforts. The most challenged entity in this regard has been the General Secretariat of the Council, most particularly after the appointment of Javier Solana as High Representative in 1999. The primary aim in all this was to establish internal bureaucratic and organizational capacities, and in a next step, to enhance procedural coherence along internal channels of interaction. Some of these dynamics within the realm of CFSP were also reflected on the Commission side, again, however, not entailing any major improvements for inter-pillar coordination.

From an institutional perspective, the creation of these new Council structures strengthened the position of the member states and the Council in an area where the Commission had a weak standing anyway. Soon after the ESDP was introduced as a new framework for the operational side of CFSP in the area of crisis management, intense debates started about a fundamental reform of the Commission structures. Many of the restructuring efforts were directed at the harmonization and streamlining of internal procedures, with efficiency, transparency, and account-ability as guiding principles. However, given the preceding crisis (in the context of the surprising resignation of the College in March 1999) it was clear that more was at stake than mere issues of efficacy. The situation was seen as a decisive point for the Commission to re-establish its status within the institutional triangle, and in this context also to stress its central role for the overall 'functioning of the EU and its standing in the world' (European Commission 2000b). This aim was given a boost by enlargement, on which the Commission led, enabling it to expand its functional responsibilities.

Looking at the overall picture, the institutional development of the two pillars has been balanced, at least in the sense that the divide has not been exacerbated further over time. The key point to note is that where changes have been possible, they have still not been able to step out of the shadow of the treaties, which remain the superordinate framework and continue to dictate the scope and effect of institutional reform.

Political initiatives

Many of the above institutional reforms have been preceded by extensive debates, which in turn were often sparked off by political initiatives. One worth mentioning in this regard is the so-called 'Patten Initiative', which largely coincided with the reactive restructuring of the Commission described above. Shortly before the IGC in 2000, while experts were fervently discussing the 'Amsterdam leftovers', Chris Patten, then Commissioner for External Relations, initiated a general debate about the division of competences and responsibilities in EU external action. In the framework of a series of public speeches about the 'EU's evolving foreign policy dimension' he put some contentious questions on the table about the Union's external political actorness and its role in the world (Patten 2000a, b, c). While he did not directly address any security-specific issues, Patten was certainly inspired by the most recent developments in the field of external action, which indeed involved ground-breaking and decisive changes for the overall complexion of the EU as a global actor. The inception of a European security and defence policy at the Cologne European Council in June 1999 offered abundant ground for discussions about efficiency and unity of action. His initiative also had to be seen against the background of the Helsinki Council Conclusions in December 1999. In view of the appointment of Javier Solana as the first High Representative for the CFSP, the European Council had emphasized the importance of 'taking the necessary steps to ensure that optimum use is made of all the various means at the Union's disposal for more effective and comprehensive external action' (European Council 1999a).

In his speech at the French Institute for International Relations (IFRI) in June 2000, Patten stated that 'mere intergovernmentalism' was a 'recipe for weakness and mediocrity: for a European foreign policy of the lowest common denominator'. He therefore advocated the strengthening of the role and position of the European Commission in the EU's external relations, arguing:

The important point is that—however awkward they may be—the new structures, procedures and instruments of CFSP recognize the need to harness the strengths of the European Community in the service of European foreign policy. That is why the treaty 'fully associates' the European Commission with CFSP ... It would be absurd to divorce European foreign policy from the institutions, which have been given responsibility for most of the instruments for its accomplishment: for external trade questions, including sanctions; for European external assistance; for many of the external aspects of Justice and Home Affairs'.

(Patten 2000b)

Most issues he raised boiled down to a more fundamental question, about the overall *finalité* of EU external action. He also thereby took up a clear position on the structures and procedures evolving in the framework of ESDP. He not only repeatedly pointed to the policy's institutional infancy; he was also fairly outspoken about the role the Community should take on in this evolving field. Patten's speeches hence ultimately revolved around the scope of European *security* political actorness, and the extent to which the Council and the member states should be administering the respective policies by themselves and without the Commission having its traditional role as the EU's executive arm. The debate reflected the inherent tension between the integrationist and the intergovernmental approach to external action, which coexist in the form of two distinct pillars.

In the same year, a political initiative was launched under the label of 'Enhancing the coherence and effectiveness of European Union external action'. This 'Evian Process' was named after an informal meeting of the General Affairs Council held in the French town of Evian in September 2000, where it was decided to take a set of practical and concrete measures to strengthen the EU's visibility in the world by way of improving internal coordination and streamlining inter-institutional procedures (Council of the European Union 2000b). These considerations built on the assumption that even though the EU was already a leading actor in world affairs, about to strengthen both its geopolitical dimension—through enlargement—and its security political capacities, the question remained whether the Union was actually making the best possible use of its resources, whether it exerted an influence on the world scene commensurate with the external instruments and resources already at its disposal, and whether it was and is being perceived as a unitary actor.[15]

Since its inception in 2000, the Evian Process has put forward a set of annual progress reports. Despite the broad framing initially put forward, these reports have so far focused largely if not exclusively on the internal coordination of the Community policies, mainly development cooperation, humanitarian assistance, trade, environment, and the promotion of human rights. Commissioner Patten had an understanding of the indivisibility of foreign policy as a task, but the issue of the functional role of ESDP in this respect remained largely neglected. The documentation of the Evian Process has also generated very few cross references to the parallel process of establishing coherence in EU security policy and, most importantly, in EU crisis management. The early days of ESDP were dominated by concerns about coherence, which, however, were mainly related to the rising external expectations. In November 2000, the Council Secretariat published a 'reference framework' for the coherence and effective management of 'any crisis the Union might have to face', stating that:

A coherent framework needs to be defined within which instruments coming under the various pillars and the competence of different institutions and bodies are implemented in synergy. This is a complex task [which] is due to the existence of decision-making mechanisms peculiar to each pillar, and to the fact that the institutions and their various subordinate bodies have distinct (and occasionally exclusive) powers and prerogatives under the treaties.

(Secretary-General/High Representative 2000)

In January 2001, the Council Secretariat launched a catalogue of 'Suggestions for procedures for coherent, comprehensive EU crisis management', which provided possible procedural solutions for each specific phase of the conflict cycle, including both Community and Council instruments. This was remarkable in so far as functional necessities were taken as the reference point instead of putting the onus for the comprehensive task of crisis management onto the fragmented institutions themselves. This problem-oriented approach, however, was no guarantee of success. Once the ESDP was operational, the working concept of comprehensive crisis management was dropped in favour of less ambitious initiatives. In September 2002, the Council Secretariat and the Commission delivered a joint note about 'Civil–Military Coordination' (CMCO)—which then essentially became the label for any debate about coherence in EU crisis management (Council Secretariat and European Commission 2002).[16] The scope of the initiative was again broad:

Civil–Military Coordination (CMCO) in EU crisis management is understood to encompass both civil–civil and civil–military coordination as well as 'internal' (intra- and inter-pillar) and 'external' (between the EU and other actors). It is understood to be required at all levels of EU crisis management, i.e. in Brussels, between Brussels and the field, and in the field.

The way the concept was arranged at this point, however, was highly symptomatic of the very problem addressed. The core part of the document did not provide much more than a mere description of the institutional status quo, while the Commission's and the Council Secretariat's roles even appeared in different sections, and with no cross references whatsoever. In the following years, CMCO continued to be an issue within the Council—albeit mostly in terms of its operational aspects. Acknowledging the importance of the issue, Solana appeared to push forward a CMCO implementation process. The Commission in turn never followed up on the concept when addressing coherence in its own realm. Hence, over time, the two pillars each cultivated their own working concepts for enhancing coherence both internally *and* between the pillars. Many observers regard the CMCO process as a major failure given the lack of concrete cross-pillar outcomes. When some later CMCO documents suggested the establishment of a 'culture of coordination' to compensate any given structural division, the criticism seemed appropriate. The two sides obviously did not succeed in developing their relationship through any 'ties that bind'. From a more pragmatic point of view, however, the way the initiative had evolved merely reflected the practical deadlock that these two entities were facing. CMCO was neither expected nor probably intended to *remove* the inter-pillar conflicts in this specific context. Looking at the way CMCO was framed in the joint note (see above), it becomes clear that coherence was in fact intended to be achieved *despite* the actual gap between the pillars. Bearing this in mind, it should not be either a surprise or a source of frustration that nothing more tangible or binding was introduced than the objective of a 'culture of coordination' to be incorporated by all institutional actors involved—cross-pillar or internally.

The course of development this initiative has taken is in fact characteristic of most measures and tools that have been employed to enhance coherence in EU external action. The solutions are informal, pragmatic, and ultimately incremental by nature. As a matter of fact, the Council and the Commission, including their bureaucratic machineries, have to a very large extent developed a *modus operandi* that ensures cross-pillar synergies as far as are needed to be functioning technically. While this mode of interaction is far from achieving the normative ideal of coherence, it does more or less exhaust the legal possibilities. In other words, incoherence continues to persist to the extent that it is systemically induced by the treaties.

The Treaty of Lisbon introduces a range of provisions that hold the potential to enhance coherence in the long run but it has still not brought about the breakthrough many observers have hoped for.

Implications of the Lisbon Treaty

The aim of enhancing coherence in EU external action played a major role in the course of the European Convention, and after the failure of the Constitutional Treaty it remained high on the agenda. Many of the provisions of the latter in the realm of external action have been retained by the Treaty of Lisbon. In institutional terms, the treaty brought about three major novelties, already heralded in the Constitutional Treaty: the High Representative of the EU for Foreign Affairs and Security Policy (HRFASP), the appointed Presidency of the European Council, and the European External Action Service (EEAS).

BOX 5.4	Impact of the Lisbon Treaty compared with the Treaty of Nice	
A. Indicators	**B. Treaty of Nice**	**C. Lisbon Treaty**
Unity in decision taking	Yes European/General Affairs Council	Yes European/Foreign Affairs Council
Unity of decision-making process	No Pillar I and II methods	No Distinct methods retained
Unity of bureaucratic cultures	No CFSP and Community	Yes European External Action Service
Unity in external representation	No Presidency, HR, Commission President, Commissioner	Yes? President, Commission President, but Union High Representative for Foreign Affairs and Security Policy is also Vice President of Commission

A. Indicators of enhanced horizontal coherence
B. Conditions under the Treaty of Nice
C. Conditions under the Lisbon Treaty

The new High Representative

Although in the Treaty of Lisbon the post no longer claims to be that of a 'foreign minister' for the EU, its responsibilities are practically identical to those outlined in the Constitutional Treaty. From the point of view of coherence, the most important innovation lies in the double-hatting of this new HR as both chief of the CFSP and one of the Vice Presidents of the Commission. This places the HRFASP at the very interface between the supranational and the intergovernmental domain of EU external action. In contrast to previous treaties, the task of ensuring coherence across the various strands of external action is no longer shared between the Council and the Commission, but is now the sole responsibility of the new HR (Article 18.4, TEU Lisbon). While the creation of such a coordinating post could be seen as an achievement in itself, it remains to be seen to what extent Catherine Ashton, as the first appointed candidate, will really be able to bridge the pillar divide (which remains) and at the same time to maintain the balance within the Commission and the Council. In terms of vertical coherence and the ability of the EU to speak with one voice, the creation of the post certainly has significant potential. In theory the new HR will represent the EU in all foreign policy issues, no matter whether the respective competencies eventually lie with the Commission or the Council. However, here again, the mere existence of such a representative for the EU does not ensure enhanced coherence given the member states' freedom to pursue their own national foreign policies. In the first few years Ashton faces an extremely difficult balancing act, which might not produce any immediate synergies.

The President of the European Council

The creation of a permanent President of the European Council to supplant the existing rotating presidency constitutes another decisive novelty that the Treaty of Lisbon has brought about for the management of coherence and consistency. More generally, the treaty has for the first time formalized and acknowledged the role of the European Council as a self-contained institutional actor (Article 13.1, TEU Lisbon). Over the years it has taken on a key role in the formulation and implementation of EU external action. The respective legal provisions define the role of the European Council very broadly, i.e. stipulating its right to identify the strategic interests and objectives for both CFSP and the external portfolios of the Community. The existence of a permanent President to chair this newly reinforced body is meant to enhance continuity in the EU's external action, and at the same time to ensure greater vertical coherence among the heads of state of the EU member states. In terms of horizontal coherence, the new president is obliged to cooperate closely with the European Commission, which places Herman van Rompuy, as the first appointed candidate, with Catherine Ashton at the very interface between the pillars. Here too it remains to be seen to what extent this cross-pillar link will lead to enhanced coherence in the EU's external action. It is not encouraging that in the first few months of the new arrangements the (Spanish) presidency behaved as if nothing had changed by convening a number of important international meetings without reference to Mr van Rompuy. In so doing it managed to irritate President Obama, who let it be known that he did not have time to meet multiple EU presidents.

European External Action Service

From the point of view of coherence, the establishment of a joint diplomatic service for the EU is among the most significant innovations of the new treaty. According to the respective legal provisions, the so-called European External Action Service (EEAS) will be working to support the new HR, assisting her in fulfilling both her representative and her internal functions in the different domains of EU external action. The service will cooperate closely with the diplomatic services of the member states and consist of officials from relevant departments of the General Secretariat of the Council and of the Commission as well as of seconded staff from the national services of the member states (Article 27.3, TEU Lisbon). The significance of the EEAS for the enhancement of coherence lies in its specificity as a common bureaucratic machinery. Up to this point legal and institutional reforms have mostly concerned the highest levels of interaction between the pillars, while the appended bureaucratic communities—the Council bodies on the one side, and the Commission structure on the other—have remained largely compartmentalized and detached from each other. For the first time, the EEAS suggests an organizational merger of the lower levels of day-to-day administrative work in EU external action, and as such its potential for creating synergetic effects is very high. However, at the time this chapter was finalized, the member states had not yet agreed on how this service will eventually be structured, and (symptomatically for the whole debate) on whether it will build on an intergovernmental or a supranational model of organization. There are also a number of outstanding practical problems relating to staffing, pensions, and the lines of managerial authority.

Conclusions and outlook

Despite its overuse in the literature and in political debate, the notion of coherence is among the most frequently misinterpreted and misused concepts in EU foreign policy. Coherence is neither a specific solution to any political, strategic, or technical problem of coordination nor a universal remedy for complex governance systems. What is more, despite its significance, incoherence is not the sole or even the most frequent source of failure in EU foreign policy. In political practice the major divide in EU foreign policy runs still through the lines of CFSP itself as the member states continue to retain their sovereign rights in key areas of external action—that is, the vertical form of (in)coherence. The so-called 'inter-pillar divide' has certainly had a negative impact on the overall capacity of the EU to perform more efficiently, let alone on the ability to act more *unitarily*. However, the EU's structural character is conditioned by its very specific historical background, which makes the bifurcation of EU external relations as much a political reality as the structural fragmentation inherent in any governance system, national or collective. In practical terms, coherence is—*stricto sensu*—an unattainable state, which does not imply that it is inappropriate as a guiding principle. What can be achieved in practice, however, is to compensate structural deficiencies by way of informal modes of interaction—be they closer to mere day-to day functioning or to a 'culture of coordination' proper. Instances such as the management of CMCO have shown that the institutional protagonists in EU external action have learned quite well to deliver operational solutions *despite* institutionally compartmentalized channels of interaction. It is too soon to judge whether the Treaty of Lisbon can turn the EU external action machinery into a neatly functioning structure. Nevertheless, the EU has proven historically to be able to develop its foreign policy capabilities even without a satisfactory legal basis or governance system.

Notes

1 While differing in some ways from his argument, this chapter has greatly benefited from that written for the first edition of this book by Simon Nuttall, and draws on some of his ideas.

2 As will be explained later in the chapter, this sort of coherence has been defined in the literature as 'vertical', i.e. as coherence between the national level of the member states and the Union/Community level.

3 At that time, English texts mainly referred to 'consistency', while in other languages 'coherence' prevailed. But even these terms were not employed in a consistent manner, which makes it difficult to really identify the first occurrence of the word 'coherence'. As is still the case, 'coherence' was also used to refer to very different sets of problems, such as a perceived need for political solidarity or a quest for more responsiveness in view of certain common interests.

4 'The Union shall in particular ensure the consistency of its external activities as a whole in the context of its external relations, security, economic and development policies. The Council and the Commission shall be responsible for ensuring such consistency. They shall ensure the implementation of these policies, each in accordance with its respective powers.' Article C, TEU Maastricht.

5 The Treaty of Amsterdam just added 'and shall cooperate to this end' (after 'ensuring such consistency'), which essentially expressed the willingness of

the member states to work towards a more cooperative working relationship with the Commission but did not change the basic tenets of Maastricht.

6 See for instance Articles 1, 3, and 13(3), TEU Nice. For a related discussion on previous treaties, see Tietje (1997, 211–13). What complicates the matter even further is that the English term 'consistency' has been translated into the Dutch, Swedish, and Danish equivalents of 'continuity'.

7 Missiroli (2001) additionally emphasizes the difference between the two terms, stating 'it is quite conceivable that something is *more or less* coherent, while something cannot be *more or less* consistent—it is or it is not' (original emphases).

8 'Coherence must be sought at several levels: between the instruments and capabilities available within each pillar of the Union, between the pillars themselves, between Member State and Community activities, between the Union and its international partners, and in the political commitment of policy elites' (Tonra 2001b, 31).

9 In the treaties, this reading of coherence as a 'vertical' issue is most prominently expressed in Article 24(3), TEU Lisbon (former Art. 11(2), TEU Nice): 'The Member States shall support the Union's external and security policy actively and unreservedly in a spirit of loyalty and mutual solidarity and shall comply with the Union's action in this area. The Member States shall work together to enhance and develop their mutual political solidarity. They shall refrain from any action, which is contrary to the interests of the Union or likely to impair its effectiveness as a cohesive force in international relations.'

10 Nuttall (2005) identifies matters of intra-Community coherence (e.g. between agriculture and development) also as 'horizontal' concerns, which is logically correct but not very helpful for enhancing the understanding of inter-pillar and trans-pillar horizontality.

11 An important example in this respect is the way member states have tried to influence the structural development of the ESDP planning machinery. While France, Belgium, and Germany pushed for the establishment of an autonomous command-and-control structure for the planning and conduct of ESDP missions, Britain and the Netherlands advocated a more rudimentary structure to complement existing arrangements with NATO. This *vertical* conflict had a decisive impact on the overall ability of the ESDP machinery to coordinate inter-institutional actions *internally*.

12 A prominent example in this context is the Commission document on 'Greater Coherence, Effectiveness and Visibility' (European Commission 2006e).

13 Nuttall (2005) points out that the main reason for this dual procedure being formalized and adopted in the treaties was that the tension between those favouring an intergovernmental and those favouring an integrationist approach was too great to allow any compromise. What is more, when Article 301 was established, deciding on economic sanctions through a cross-pillar process had already become common political practice, employed for instance

in the cases of the Soviet Union and Argentina in 1982, and in the case of apartheid in South Africa.

14 Based on private interviews with Council officials conducted in 2009.

15 The main points brought up at the Evian meeting were incorporated at the European Council in Nice in December 2000; the focus, however, was moved away from the broader issue of coherence in external action to the specific area of external assistance and the way the Community procedures could be streamlined in the service of increased effectiveness and flexibility.

16 In contrast to what the term would suggest, Civil–Military Coordination (CMCO) is neither exclusively concerned with managing the relationship between the civilian and military components of crisis management nor restricted to the ESDP domain. In fact, given its broad focus, it is also concerned with all thematic and geographical policies, external cooperation programmes and activities directed by the Community that have potential relevance for comprehensive crisis response, crisis management, and preventive action. In the CMCO framework, inter-pillar coherence is referred to as a matter of 'civil–civil coordination', which alludes to the multiple functional overlaps between some Commission policies and civilian ESDP.

FURTHER READING

Nuttall (2000) offers an excellent historical introduction to the problem of coherence and the way it has evolved over time. Gauttier (2004), Hoffmeister (2008), and Bertea (2005) provide a legal perspective, Missiroli (2001), Duke (2006), and Nuttall (2004) discuss the topic with a focus on policy, while M. E. Smith (2001) presents a distinctively institutional analysis.

Bertea, S. (2005), 'Looking for Coherence Within the European Community', *European Law Journal*, 11(2), 154–72.

Duke, S. (2006), 'Areas of Grey: Tensions in EU External Relations Competences', *EIPA-SCOPE*, 2006(1), 21–7.

Gauttier, P. (2004), 'Horizontal Coherence and the External Competences of the European Union', *European Law Journal*, 10(1), 23-41.

Hoffmeister, F. (2008), 'Inter-Pillar Coherence in the European Union's Civilian Crisis Management' in Blockmans, S. (ed.) *The European Union and Crisis Management. Policy and Legal Aspects*, 157–180 (The Hague: T.M.C. Asser Institute).

Missiroli, A. (2001), 'European Security Policy: The Challenge of Coherence', *European Foreign Affairs Review*, 6, 177-96.

Nuttall, S. (2000), *European Foreign Policy* (Oxford: Oxford University Press).

Nuttall, S. (2004), 'On fuzzy pillars: criteria for the continued existence of pillars in the draft constitution', *CFSP Forum*, 2/3, http://www.fornet.info.

Smith, M .E. (2001), 'The quest for coherence: institutional dilemmas of external action from Maastricht to Amsterdam' in Stone Sweet, A., Sandholtz, W., and Fligstein, N. (eds) *The Institutionalization of Europe*, 171–93 (Oxford: Oxford University Press).

 WEB LINKS

The most useful online source for the issue of coherence are: the website of the European Foreign Policy Unit at the London School of Economics and Political Science: (**http://www2.lse.ac.uk/internationalRelations/centresandunits/EFPU/ EFPUhome.aspx/**); the website of ISIS Europe (**http://www.isis-europe.org/**); and the CFSP Forum (**http://www.fornet.info/CFSPforum.html**).

CHAPTER 6

Legitimate and Democratic? The EU's International Role

Christopher Lord

█ Summary

This chapter considers the legitimacy and democratic control of the European Union's international policies. It makes a point of trying to relate some of the more philosophical issues posed by the Union's legitimacy to concrete institutional arrangements for democratic control via the European Parliament and national parliaments. However, it notes that even democratic control may not satisfy a need to justify the EU's international role to outside audiences in addition to the member states and citizens of the Union itself.

Introduction

From those who fear it might be a superpower in the making to those who argue that the Union's international 'policies' are only camouflage for the evasion of international responsibility, many views are possible on what kind of an international actor the Union is, can, or ought to be. My purpose here is not to repeat those debates. Rather, it is to demonstrate that if we are to say anything sensible at all about the EU's international role we need to do more than, for example, assess the resources and institutional capacities that are available to the Union. We also need to consider what might be needed to legitimate the various international roles the Union could adopt. We need to do that, moreover, in a way that does not use the word 'legitimacy' loosely as a synonym for acceptance, support, and all things nice, but with an awareness of the precise meaning of the term in political theory. Only then will we be able to grasp just how far legitimacy shapes, constrains, and enables the ways in which political power can be institutionalized and employed; and only then will we, in turn, be able to formulate satisfactory theories of how and how far the Union can exercise power internationally, participate in the different processes defining of the contemporary world order, and adopt a more or less active/passive role as a 'shaper' or a 'taker' of the international system.

I will fill out my terms as I go along. But, broadly, I assume that institutions are legitimate where their *right* to exercise political power is acknowledged by others. Within polities the most obvious question to ask is whether that right is acknowledged by their own citizens. Outside polities the most obvious question to ask is whether it is acknowledged by other participants in the international system. Crucial, though, to an understanding of legitimacy is the manner in which it constrains *all* actors. A particular polity may encounter higher enforcement costs—and even resistance—if it attempts to exercise political power in ways its own citizens or its international counterparts do not accept as right. Yet those inside and outside actors may themselves be constrained—by their own moral and political beliefs and by their own dependence on various norms for powers and rights they themselves claim—to accept that a particular policy has every right even to make those decisions they otherwise bitterly oppose. In sum, then, a polity that enjoys legitimacy can exercise power in a very different way to one that does not. It can do so knowing that others have political obligations to let it use its powers effectively; though only, of course, as long it does that in a way that respects the limits of its own legitimacy.

To demonstrate the relevance of all this to the Union, I begin the chapter by disputing the claim that the Union's international role does not require much legitimation. To the contrary, I suggest that the Union's international role presents a novel and complex challenge of legitimation with at least the following elements:

- To some degree, the Union resembles single liberal democratic states in so far as it has been unable to develop even its present international role without raising questions about the internal public control of its international policies.

- Since, though, democracy implies both *kratos* and *demos*—both an effective form of public control and agreement on which group of people should have a right to exercise that control in ways that are collectively on binding—it is often less than obvious how any powers that are thought necessary for the democratic control of the Union's international role should be distributed between its own arena and those of its member states.

- Indeed, the Union faces a further legitimation challenge that is peculiar to its composite form: namely, one of finding some external justification for why its member states and societies should mediate some imprecisely defined proportion of their relationship with the outside world through an institutional configuration that has no exact analogue in the ways other participants in the international system organize themselves.

The next two sections of the chapter set out these difficulties in greater detail. The ensuing section illustrates them through the example of a 'nuts and bolts' problem of institutional design: namely, that of adapting parliamentary procedures—at the European and national levels—to the development of the Union's international policies. The final section concludes.

Legitimacy and the EU's international role

Perhaps the best way of clarifying why we should care about the legitimacy of the Union's international policies is to identify possible answers to the contrary point of view: namely, that the legitimacy of the Union's external actions is a 'non-problem'. One such argument might be as follows: the Union's international role is well supported by public opinion. Therefore its legitimacy can be assumed. As set out in Table 6.1, there would, indeed, seem to be a high level of support for the notion that the European Union should operate as an international actor.

However, the data need to be interpreted with care. They indicates room for disagreement on exactly what form the Union's international role should take. Higher support for a common foreign policy in general (column 1) than for Union involvement in defence in particular (column 2) might suggest that public opinion is more comfortable with a civilian rather than a military model of European power. Even then, civilian instruments may enjoy less appeal where they have financial costs (column 3). Above all, differences are evident across member states. Whilst a defence role has little support in the UK, Denmark, and Ireland, even a role in guaranteeing human rights is less enthusiastically supported in the Czech Republic and Slovakia than in the rest of the Union (column 4).

The main objection, though, to attempting to infer legitimacy from opinion poll data is more philosophical than methodological. Not only is support for the Union's different international roles more ambiguous and varied once we read the figures

TABLE 6.1	Public support for the European Union's international role, arranged in descending order of member states			

% of those in favour of a common foreign policy towards other countries; Eurobarometer 70, 2008		% of those agreeing that decisions about European defence should be taken by the Europan Union (as opposed to national governments or NATO); Eurobarometer 66, 2006		% of those agreeing that the European Union provides financial help to deal with internal conflicts of its neighbours (adjusted to exclude Don't knows and those replying 'It depends'); Special Eurobarometer 67.3, 2007		% of those agreeing that 'the EU should work to guarantee human rights around the world, even if this is contrary to the wishes of some other countries'; Eurobarometer 63, 2005	
Slovakia	82	Cyprus	74	Cyprus	83	Cyprus	97
Germany	79	Luxembourg	66	Malta	79	Belgium	91
Greece	79	Greece	61	Bulgaria	72	Greece	91
Slovenia	79	Belgium	60	Greece	71	France	88
Poland	77	France	59	Spain	71	Luxembourg	87
Belgium	76	Bulgaria	59	Romania	70	Denmark	85
Cyprus	75	Germany	57	Latvia	66	Hungary	85
Estonia	75	Italy	54	Denmark	65	Austria	84
Hungary	74	Slovenia	54	Slovakia	61	Netherlands	84
Lithuania	74	Slovakia	54	Poland	59	Sweden	84
Spain	73	Finland	52	Estonia	59	Finland	82
Netherlands	72	Estonia	51	Czech Republic	59	Slovenia	82
Bulgaria	72	Netherlands	50	Lithuania	56	Ireland	81
Luxembourg	70	Portugal	50	Slovenia	56	Italy	81
Austria	70	**EU average**	**49**	Portugal	53	Spain	81
Latvia	70	Czech Republic	48	Sweden	52	**EU average**	**81**
EU average	**68**	Hungary	48	Netherlands	51	Germany	80
France	68	Malta	48	Finland	46	Poland	80
Czech Republic	68	Romania	48	**EU average**	**46**	Malta	79
Romania	68	Latvia	47	Germany	44	Portugal	79
Denmark	64	Sweden	47	Hungary	44	Bulgaria	78
Italy	62	Lithuania	46	Luxembourg	41	Latvia	77
Finland	61	Austria	43	Ireland	40	Lithuania	77
Ireland	56	Poland	43	Belgium	34	UK	76
Sweden	56	Spain	42	UK	33	Romania	74
Malta	56	UK	33	Austria	33	Estonia	71
Portugal	51	Ireland	31	France	32	Czech Republic	66
UK	49	Denmark	20	Italy	32	Slovakia	64

carefully, but it may in any case be a mistake to take support as an indicator of legitimacy at all. As Jean-Jacques Rousseau pointed out long ago, legitimacy consists of an obligation to comply even with those policies we do not support (Rousseau 1973 [1762], 250). We may, in other words, be committed to acknowledge the rightfulness of the procedures by which policies are made even when we don't like those policies very much. Those procedures may correspond to our moral beliefs about ways in which people should live and decide matters together; and we may rely heavily upon them—and the rights they secure—in other instances where outcomes are more to our liking. It is not hard then to understand why Jürgen Habermas defines legitimacy as those 'political obligations' actors 'put themselves under' through the force of their own 'moral' beliefs (Habermas 1996, 67).

However, there is another possible reason for doubting how far we should concern ourselves with the legitimacy of the Union's international policy. It might be thought that any policy whose impact is external to a polity is likely to be easier to legitimate than one that reallocates values within it. Yet such a position is, in turn, open to the fairly obvious counter argument that external issues of war and peace, and of democracy and human rights in the international system, may also be internal values. We do not need to assume that citizens are saints to anticipate that they may feel committed—by their own moral beliefs—to at least some 'dos' and 'don'ts' in how their governing institutions behave towards the outside world. Indeed, the international behaviour of their governing institutions may be their responsibility, as well as their business, in so far as a moral case can be made that in those political systems where individuals can control institutions of government they have a duty not to endorse harms to outsiders that conflict with those obligations they believe they owe to all persons (Miller 2007).

Far, then, from international policy always operating as a politics-free zone of 'executive discretion' and 'permissive consensus'—in which governing institutions are given free rein—foreign policy questions are often divisive and not just because they involve danger, frustration, and the expenditure of scarce resources outside the polity itself but also because they affect the judgements publics make of the normative standards of their own political systems. Bearing in mind, moreover, that the legitimacy of a polity may only be fully tested when it faces crisis or policy failure, the history of states contains a cautionary tale for all would-be international actors, the EU included: domestic legitimation crises derive as often as not from the international system (Bobbitt 2002), its peculiar configuration of risk, and mistakes (of omission and commission) in designing policies and institutions to deal with those risks. In sum, then, there is a double blurring—of value and of performance—between the legitimacy of power deployed internationally and the legitimacy of power exercised domestically.

Indeed, there is one sense in which the legitimation of international policy is more demanding than that of internal policy: it faces the added complication of needing to be justified to outsiders and not only to domestic audiences. This challenge, arguably, takes an unusual form in the case of the EU. One problem is that international legitimacy has often been distinguished from that internal to polities on the grounds that it is acknowledged, if at all, by other states, rather than by individuals. Moreover, states are thought to accord one another legitimacy on the basis of 'isomorphism', or, in other words, classification of other entities as 'one of us' because they too have the characteristics of a state and thus an entitlement to be treated as part of the society of states (Bull 1977, 82).

So how might states accustomed to according one another legitimacy—on the grounds that they too are states—accommodate the claims of a seemingly non-state entity such as the European Union to play an international role? Different responses are possible. One might be to view any international role assumed by the Union as little more than a novel way of dressing up—and coordinating—the international policies of its component member states. This would require little adjustment to any received view that states are the legitimate actors in the international system. However, even a Union that is very much controlled by its member states could structure their cooperation in such a novel and thorough-going way as to raise questions in the minds of outsiders. The integration of any one group of states is likely to involve a mix of negative as well as positive externalities for different outsiders and from different points of view.

More challenging of received views of international legitimacy, however, would be a perception that European integration is not so much a coordination of states as an implied criticism of international relations as they have been previously structured and practised. If in the past acquiring the characteristics of stateness was key to being recognized as a legitimate player in a world of states, the Union's expressed preferences for international relations based on multilateral frameworks can be understood as an attempt to set a new standard by which it is not the bare fact of 'stateness' that confers legitimacy but the willingness of states to develop their policies through multilateral frameworks, to justify themselves through open and critical debates in those frameworks, and to submit themselves to the monitoring and scrutiny of the latter. How legitimate the Union is to outsiders as an international actor may then depend on how far they are also willing to accept as legitimate the broader pattern of international relations it would appear to promote and exemplify.

That said, the question of just how far the Union is likely to call upon outsiders to acknowledge the legitimacy of a new form of international actor, and of new norms of international behaviour, is beset by uncertainty. Not only is it unclear just how far actors within the Union are themselves committed to its international actorness, or agreed on what form it should take, but international norms are changeable in who they imply are the legitimate units of the international system and what they imply are the legitimate behaviours within it. As Ian Clark observes, there is nothing new about participants in the international system attempting to build 'normative constraints into legitimacy' additional to those required by 'order and co-existence between states' (2007). Whether, then, the Union leads or lags— whether it challenges outsiders to revise international norms more than they are inclined to agree, goes with the grain of change that is occurring for other reasons, or even ends up by being a somewhat 'conservative' force in the international system—is like all legitimacy questions a relational one to be decided between the body in need of legitimation (the Union) and those in a position to confer it (its interlocutors in the international system).

Still, there is one final reason why the legitimacy of the Union's international policies might be considered a non-problem. As Rodney Barker reminds us, there can only be a problem of legitimacy where there is an exercise of political power. Even in relation to its internal policies it is questionable just how far the Union exercises significant power of its own. As Barker continues:

> [L]egitimacy is a concept which can usefully be applied to rule or challenges to rule. It cannot usefully be applied where rule is absent, hypothetical or so indirect as to be invisible to the ruled … the EU may govern but it does not follow that it has subjects in the same way a state has.
>
> (2003, 159–60)

Such doubts as to whether there is much to legitimate—beyond, as suggested above, a novel way of coordinating the actions of states—apply with even greater force to those of the Union's international policies, such as CFSP and ESDP, where the member states seemingly retain especially high levels of control. If, indeed, the Union's external policies seemingly involve a light and controlled set of obligations in relation to its own member states, they can likewise be interpreted as far from coercive externally. The Union may act towards the world, but it is doubtful that it exercises any 'rule' over it, except, perhaps, under conditions where it is reasonable to assume at least some consent of outsiders themselves, for example to peacekeeping missions or to the adoption of aspects of the Union's *acquis communautaire* for reasons of mutual advantage.

Yet it seems to me that such arguments rest on an inadequate understanding of political power. Consider the following initiatives in the area of security cooperation: a European rapid reaction force; an arms procurement agency aimed at promoting the compatibility and interoperability of European militaries; the pooling of certain capabilities such as the collection of intelligence; and structured cooperation between member states who want to integrate their forces still more closely than the rest.

Now in so far as each of these things requires the consent of each member state, none involves an exercise of power by the Union in the classic sense of A compelling B to do something B would rather not do. But note something further about the various options for security cooperation. Each can be expected to involve a heavy dose of path dependence (Pierson 2000). Each is likely to involve high start-up costs. Yet, once initiated, each may yield increasing returns to scale. Capabilities—such as rapid reaction forces or more specialized security missions—may develop with use. Experience gained and skills developed in one mission will be available to subsequent ones. Each component of any specialized division of labour in force structures or in arms procurement can be expected to have positive externalities for all others.

The downside, though, of any increasing returns is that European security cooperation may involve limited exit options for its participants. The more national forces are integrated into a specialized division of labour, the more difficult it may be even to attempt to revert to self-sufficiency in security provision: the more force structures may be based on the assumption that, if they are to be used at all, they are to be used with partners, and a specific and fixed group of partners. It may therefore be possible for security cooperation to develop through a succession of completely uncoerced decisions—to which each member state has willingly and even enthusiastically given its consent—and, yet, for the whole structure to be very much constraining of participating societies. Whilst, indeed, the power to decide whether to participate in any one security mission may formally rest with each member state, there may be some instances where some may hesitate to say no for fear of damaging the credibility of the process or of reducing the chances of partners reciprocating when another security mission of greater importance to the member state in question is proposed.

If, then, we define power not just as A compelling B to make a certain choice but also as actions that constrain the choices that are available to B in the first place (Lukes 2005), it is not hard to imagine how security cooperation can at one and the same time rest on the formal agreement of each member state and yet amount to an exercise of power over it. In so far as member states are limited in how effectively they can act internationally without forms of coordination at the European level, then even those quite routine decisions to structure the agenda of choice in one way rather than another that follow from the limited capacities of institutions to mobilize attention and resources at any one time around more than a restricted number of priorities and a handful of shared definitions of the problem at hand (March and Olsen 1995) will amount to an exercise of power, quite regardless of whether each member state retains a veto or not over final decisions.

This section, then, has suggested that the Union's international role involves the exercise of political power to make decisions that reallocate values and affect individual life chances. These are precisely the conditions where democratic control is often considered a necessary condition for legitimation. Yet it can hardly be a sufficient condition in so far as the Union's international policies may also need to be legitimate with outside actors—notably third states—who cannot be party to any internal democratic control. I will return to the latter problem after I have dealt with the first by distinguishing the dimensions of legitimation in a democratic polity and demonstrating the relevance of each to any discussion of the Union's international role.

Dimensions of legitimacy

Of its nature, legitimacy is a complex phenomenon. In societies with liberal democratic values it has at least three dimensions: the performance of the political system, popular identification with the system, and the acquisition and exercise of power according to democratic values (Beetham 1991). These dimensions are cumulative and interactive: where each is present, it reinforces the others in producing legitimacy; where any is lacking, it cannot entirely be compensated for by a superabundance of either of the other two. What, then, are the possibilities of legitimating the international policies of the Union along the three dimensions of performance, identity, and democracy?

Beginning with performance, or output legitimacy, there are at least three reasons for believing Union policies might be able to achieve things internationally that uncoordinated national policies cannot. First, a decision to make international policy through the Union may offer benefits of scale, notably where high fixed costs mean that individual member states struggle even to cross minimum resource thresholds for effective foreign or security policy provision.

Second, there may be gains from removing inconsistencies between national policies. This may be a simple housekeeping act of avoiding duplication. But it can also be a matter of safety and stability. Successful coordination can reduce risks of member states constructing inconsistent notions of what it is to be secure such that one can only feel more at its ease at the price of another feeling less so: security dilemmas (Jervis 1976, 66). It can also anticipate relationships with outsiders that risk entangling member states in third-party disputes in a manner that only aggravates the latter while provoking spill-back frictions in the Union itself.

Third, 'positive externalities' may be involved in pouring different kinds of international policy (security, economic, humanitarian, and so on) through the Union, even if different institutional means are used in each case. Each aspect of policy might, in other words, have spin-off benefits for the others. Thus part of the thinking behind the development of the CFSP was that access to the single market—and even EC membership itself—could be used as foreign policy leverage in the resolution of security problems with third states. Security thus conceived is not just a matter of accumulating military capabilities. Rather it requires 'joined-up' government across all policy instruments (commercial, environment, judicial, and so on) if the complex causes of security problems are to be tackled (M. Smith 1996b, 249). In so far as those 'other policy instruments' have been vested in EU institutions, 'joined-up security governance', in turn, presupposes discussion of security issues at Union level. In addition, third-party incentives to cooperate with the EU's distinctive non-state political system may be sufficiently different from those associated with dealings with any of its component states to open up new sources of foreign policy leverage. For example, a treaty agreed with the EU can only be changed or set aside with the unanimous approval of EU member states and the assent of the European Parliament, as opposed, for example, to a simple majority of a single national parliament. This allows member states to 'increase the credibility of their promises' by structuring relationships with third countries through EU treaties. It also allows third countries to benefit from more entrenched agreements.

Whether the Union can turn the foregoing into 'output legitimation' through superior performance depends in practice on institutional effectiveness. It is often argued that transaction costs associated with the complex character of Union institutions cancel out at least some of the gains from using them to solve collective action problems in international policy. The CFSP has been charged with losing credibility by raising expectations beyond its capabilities to deliver (Hill 1993a). The coherence of the EU's contribution to the World Trade Organization (WTO) has been criticized on account of the multiple veto points and complex interest politics of the Union's internal political system (Van Oudenaren 2001, quoted in Keohane 2002, 749). The EU's potential as the world's biggest single donor of development aid has, in the view of many, been stymied by poor institutional capacity on the ground, with the result that only a small proportion of the aid has reached those it is supposed to benefit. Indeed, perceptions of effectiveness, rather than objective measures, may be the ultimate arbiter of the Union's capacity to secure output legitimacy for its international role.

Turning to the question of identity, any policy is more likely to be seen as legitimate where it is underpinned by a 'we' feeling: by a feeling among a group that it is 'we' who are agreeing to act together, rather than 'they' who are imposing some unwanted policy on us. Whilst this clearly overlaps with the more general challenge of agreeing the terms of a collectively binding political community—or *demos*—at the Union level, the challenge of agreeing a specific 'foreign policy identity' poses problems of its own. We have already discussed difficulties that might follow from attempting to externalize any identity politics and institutional structures internal to the Union which are aimed at changing the very nature of statehood, territory, and boundaries (Keohane 2002; Manners and Whitman 2003). But what of the somewhat different possibility of attempting to form a European foreign policy identity that operates as the external counterpart to an internal identity based on 'constitutional patriotism' (Habermas 2003); or, in other words, shared attachment to democracy, rights, and the rule of law? Now a common objection to any notion of a 'normative power Europe' (Manners and Whitman 2002) is that it would be more presumptuous than virtuous in failing to understand the deliberate normative minimalism of international norms, which are framed precisely to allow each political community to choose for itself which norms it wants to live by (Miller 2007). Such an objection would, however, have less force against attempts merely to define the limits of what the Union's internal values will allow it to do externally. But that, in turn, raises the question of whether an external identity can be based purely on self-delimitation. It would also increase the urgency of aligning the Union's external identity with its internal standards of legitimation. It is therefore to the question of the democratic control of the Union's international policies that I now turn.

Democratic legitimacy

In discussing issues of democratic legitimacy, I take an unashamedly procedural approach that corresponds to my view argued elsewhere (Lord 2004 and 2008): that democracy is not primarily a matter of producing those policy outputs which amount to 'doing what the people want'. Before it is that, it is a procedural right citizens enjoy as equals to exercise public control over those who make collective decisions binding upon them.

As shown in Table 6.2, there is great variety in the procedures by which the Union decides. Only some retain member-state vetoes. Only some allow the European Parliament (EP) agenda-setting or veto powers (co-decision and assent). Only some allow the Commission to 'gate keep' choice by giving it an exclusive right of initiative. Only some allow the European Court of Justice jurisdiction. It follows that different international policies of the Union tap into different conceptions of input legitimacy. They vary in how far they draw on indirect legitimation through the unanimous agreement of member states; on parliamentary legitimation through the scrutinizing and controlling powers of a representative body; on technocratic legitimation through a role for 'independent experts' (the Commission); or on judicial legitimation by a court able to ensure legality and the protection of rights in the pursuit of the Union's international policy (Lord and Magnette 2004).

Yet, this complexity notwithstanding, member states have adopted the mantra that decisions taken at the Union level are ultimately justified by one principle of legitimation delivered through two channels. Thus the Lisbon Treaty asserts that the 'European Union shall be founded on representative democracy' before going on to assert that a) 'Citizens are directly elected at Union level in the European Parliament', and b) 'Member States are represented in the European Council by their heads of government and in the Council by their governments, themselves democratically accountable either to their national parliaments or to their citizens' (Article 8A). If, then, we are to assess those who exercise the powers of Union institutions against their own legitimation claims, the question we need to ask is whether the European Parliament and national parliaments, taken together, exercise adequate controlling powers over the Union's international policies. Needless to say, this is a difficult question, which is open to many different judgements. However, the next two sections can at least flag some of the issues that might be involved in considering it.

The European Parliament

Directly elected every five years by all adult citizens of the Union, organized into transnational party groups, specialized for the accumulation of expertise needed to scrutinize Union policies, and endowed by the treaties with powers over the

TABLE 6.2   Procedures for selected international policies of the EU

	Treaty articles	Power of initiative	Council decision rule	Obligations to consult	Powers of the European Parliament (EP)	European Court of Justice (ECJ) jurisdiction
Common commercial policy Legislation to implement	Treaty on functions of the European Union (TFEU) 206–7	Commission	Qualified majority vote (QMV)		Co-decision (COD)	Yes
Development cooperation	TFEU 208–11	Commission	QMV	Union and member states shall consult one another on their aid programmes	COD	Yes
International agreements with third countries and international organizations (Note: slightly different arrangements in Articles 206–7 for commercial agreements)	TFEU 216–8	Commission or the High Representative (where a CFSP matter) makes a recommendation to the Council to authorize the opening of negotiations	Normally QMV; however, unanimous vote (UV) is needed where the agreement associates a third country or involves matter where UV required for internal legislation	The 'negotiator' (i.e. Commission or High Representative) must consult a special committee appointed by the Council and follow any directives issued by the Council	Assent of the European Parliament where the agreement involves a) an institutional framework for cooperation, c) budgetary implications, d) matters covered by ordinary legislative procedure	Yes

TABLE 6.2   (Continued)

Common foreign and security policy decisions	Treaty on European Union (TEU) 30–1	Initiatives can be proposed by a) any member state, b) the High Representative, or c) the High Representative with the Commission's support	Agreed by the European Council or Council of Ministers acting unanimously, but a) with allowance for up to one-third of member states to abstain and b) for QMV for CFSP decisions that adopt a guideline previously agreed unanimously by the European Council	EP informed by the High Representative about the evolution of the CFSP	No, except A40
Common security and defence policy missions	TEU 42	Proposal of a) any member state or b) High Representative	Unanimous vote of Council. But, note, the Council can entrust implementation to a group of member states		No

Union's legislation, finance, and the European Commission, the EP would seem to be in a favourable position to exercise some controlling powers over the Union's international policies. Even the much discussed 'second-order' pattern of European elections—they are seemingly contested on domestic rather than European issues (Reif and Schmitt 1980)—need not be altogether fatal to the Parliament's claims to represent European publics. As Herman Schmitt and Jacques Thomassen (2000) demonstrate, the preferences of Members of the European Parliaments and of their voters would even seem under present arrangements to correlate along key main dimensions of choices (left–right and pro–anti integration). Indeed, from another point of view there is a certain serendipity in the Union's second-order elections. National parliaments are unable to give a full-time focus to the scrutiny and control of Union issues. Yet by in effect delegating that task to a European Parliament whose elections remain largely second order and thus structured by national parties, they achieve two things: first, the election of national party delegations to the European Parliament whose loyalties and preferences are likely to remain close to the same national parties that exercise the powers of national parliaments; and second, a strong representation of national parties of opposition in a European Parliament whose powers of legislative and budgetary co-decision allow it to check and balance the monopoly access of national parties of government to the Council of Ministers. Whilst the Schmitt and Thomassen argument implies that a Parliament elected in second-order contests may still have value as a representative body in its own right, the delegated democracy argument implies it may also have some value as a proxy for national parliaments.

Assuming, then, that its claim to act on behalf of voters is not altogether empty, the following sub-sections analyse the EP's controlling powers over the Union's international policies.

A veto power over commercial treaties and enlargements

The assent procedure (see Box 6.1) gives the European Parliament a veto over commercial treaties, whether concluded bilaterally with non-member states or in multilateral frameworks such as the WTO. Although the procedure is a 'take it or leave

---

BOX 6.1   The assent procedure

The assent of the European Parliament is needed for:

- Treaties that admit new states to the EU.

- Association agreements with other states or organizations that create 'reciprocal rights and obligations'.

- Other international agreements that 'establish a specific institutional framework', have 'budgetary implications for the Community', or 'entail amendment to an act' adopted under co-decision.

it' vote that does not allow the EP to propose amendments of its own, the risk of the Parliament rejecting international treaties means that it is in practice consulted throughout the course of their negotiation (Corbett *et al.* 2007).

The EP also has to give its assent to treaties enlarging the Union to include new member states. Since this requires a majority of the EP's membership (and not just of those voting) an oversized majority of around 55 to 60 per cent may in practice be required, given normal rates of participation in parliamentary votes (Hix *et al.* 2007). This high hurdle adds to the incentive to take the views of the EP into account in developing Union policies towards countries that might one day become members. A possible justification for the high hurdle is that an accession amounts to an agreement to terminate a foreign policy relationship and admit a state to the EU's own internal system of shared rules. It is thus a kind of end game and virtually irrevocable. In contrast, international agreements and protocols short of accession frequently need revision and renewal. This gives the EP repeat opportunities to use its powers of assent (Corbett *et al.* 2007), so softening the impact of the rule that it has no powers of amendment in relation to any one use of the procedure.

Whether used to exert parliamentary control over enlargement or other international policies such as trade and aid, assent is most likely to be an effective instrument of parliamentary accountability and control where international dealings fall 'within the shadow of any veto' that the EP might one day exercise on attempts to formalize external relationships into a treaty. Up to a point, the Council has scope to call the Parliament's bluff knowing that it would not lightly veto a treaty that it itself values. On the other hand, there are some questions on which a threat of a parliamentary veto carries special credibility, notably human rights and democracy in third countries, either of which can emerge as conditions for EP ratification of commercial or accession treaties. It is also worth mentioning that the EP has developed signalling techniques, designed to encourage the Commission and Council to justify third-country relationships and adjust them to future threats of failed assent procedures on an almost continuous basis. Apart from procedures for consulting the EP during the negotiation of treaties that require assent, the Parliament drafts annual reports on accession states. The appraisals reached, the amendments tabled, and the size and composition of majorities for and against those amendments in both committee and plenary are all clues to how the Parliament could decide an assent vote.

Budgetary and legislative co-decision as a mixed veto/agenda-setting power

The example of international aid treaties such as the Cotonou Agreement which regulates relations between the EU and various developing countries are covered by what has just been said about the assent procedure. In addition, the EP has co-decision with the Council on ordinary legislation covering development aid, and, of course, it can use its powers to amend or veto the annual budget of the Union to gain a measure of control of the various kinds of financial aid offered by the Union to third countries. It is important to understand what is and is not possible here. The EP's powers over any one annual budget are tightly constrained by multi-year framework agreements between the member states. These set a limit to how far the Parliament can vary expenditure overall or between individual categories. Still, the EP can make a difference by targeting just one or two international priorities in successive annual budgets (Corbett *et al.* 2007). Thus the 1999–2004 Parliament repeatedly increased funding for stabilization programmes in the Balkans. Moreover, by adding so-called 'remarks' to international budget lines the EP can shape the procedural and substantive conditions under which allocations can be spent on international policies. This can be a powerful weapon of accountability. First, because the Parliament can vote to keep funds in reserve until the Commission satisfies it further on how it is proposed money should be spent. Second, because the approval of the EP is needed to discharge the Commission's accounts, or, in other words, to certify that all money has been spent as intended and authorized. The EP has made it clear that criticism of how programmes have been managed in the past is grounds for scaling them back in the future (European Parliament 2001b).

Scrutiny and control of CFSP/ESDP

When the Treaty on European Union (1992) established the CFSP it merely required the Council to take the views of the European Parliament into consideration. Moreover, that obligation to consult amounted to less than in relation to European Community policies. Only the latter were covered by the ECJ ruling that the Council must allow reasonable time for the EP to submit a written opinion, which the member states are then obliged to consider actively in their own deliberations (Dehousse 1998, 98). Yet the Parliament has gradually strengthened its control over CFSP and even ESDP (Bono 2006). Even the right to be consulted as it was originally formulated in the TEU failed conveniently, from the EP's point of view, to specify whether the Parliament should be consulted before or after the event, a gap the EP has exploited in subsequent dealings with the Council, going so far on at least one occasion as to threaten to refer this question to the ECJ. As Esther Barbé and Anna Herranz Surrallés explain, inter-institutional agreements now allow for the disclosure of sensitive information about CFSP/ESDP to a special committee of five MEPs and for 'Joint Consultation' meetings which cover both implementation and budgetary implications (2008, 81).

Indeed, it is above all the partial funding of the CFSP out of the Union's budget that has allowed the EP to assert an element of control, even if it has sometimes had to play hardball and deploy an element of institutional cunning in order to get its way. When, for example, the Council proposed to fund CFSP peacekeeping envoys from its own budget the EP threatened to terminate the 'gentleman's agreement' by which the Council and Parliament have each abstained from intervening in the other's budget since 1970 (European Parliament 2000a, 26). On another occasion, it threatened to halve the CFSP budget (Barbé and Herranz Surraillés, 2008, 81).

From early on in the development of the EDSP, the EP noted that the ambition of the member states to draw if necessary on the 'entire spectrum of civilian and military instruments available to the Union' (European Parliament 2000a) created a case for it to exercise *ex ante* scrutiny of military missions that could, in an emergency, have implications for other Union policies. Whilst, perhaps unsurprisingly, the Council has not conceded the EP's 'maximalist' demand that ESDP missions should be approved by an absolute majority of MEPs, the EP has on occasions adopted the unilateral practice of passing resolutions stating the terms on which it would have approved ESDP missions had it the formal power to do so (Barbé and Herranz Surrallés, 2008, 81). This could conceivably develop into a source of influence in the future in so far as member governments conclude that it is better to discuss the terms of missions with the Parliament than leave themselves exposed, if things subsequently go wrong, to the charge that they did not take all risks into account at the time of deployment.

New possibilities of parliamentary control are also opened up by innovations in the Lisbon Treaty. To recall, these create a new High Representative of the Union for Foreign Affairs and Security Policy, who will head up an External Action Service, which, at the time of writing, is expected to consist of around 3,000 personnel. Given her dual role as chair of the Foreign Affairs Council and as a Vice President of the Commission with responsibility for its external relations, the new High Representative is subject to the veto of the Parliament on the designation of each new College of Commissioners. Her actions—and presumably those of officials within the External Action Service—will also be covered by the power of the Parliament to dismiss the College. Although the Parliament can only use its powers of appointment and dismissal to confirm or remove the entire College of Commissioners, it has, in the recent past, successfully used those powers in response to complaints about individuals.

Still, the dual responsibility of the High Representative to both the Council and the Parliament could lead to little accountability in so far as there is uncertainty as to which principal the High Representative should primarily be answerable to or has some scope to use the demands of one principal as a pretext for evading accountability to the other. It could, conversely, lead to a perverse form of accountability—a 'rough justice' in which the High Representative has responsibility without power—to the extent she finds herself having to answer to the European Parliament for policies and actions she cannot fully control in her role as agent of the member states.

Needless to say, the appointment of the first High Representative has also been accompanied by attempts by the EP to define procedures that would give it a maximum of control over the External Action Service. So far the Council would seem to have resisted the EP's demand—corresponding to a long-standing complaint that CFSP has tended in the past to result in delegations of powers without clear lines of responsibility—to subject each special representative appointed under joint actions to a parliamentary vote of approval. On the other hand, the Commission has agreed to arrangements that would allow representatives of EP committees to be present in international negotiations for which it is responsible.

National parliaments

Even where qualified majority voting (QMV) is possible, the Council often attempts to decide by a consensus of member states, or even without voting at all (Mattila and Lane 2001). Thus even those of the Union's international policies which are covered by QMV—such as trade and aid—are, in principle, open to being scrutinized and controlled by national parliaments through their relationship with their own governments. Then, of course, there are other international policies—conspicuously the CFSP and ESDP—where possibilities of national parliamentary control are not even inhibited by the absence of formal national vetoes on individual decisions. Yet national parliaments are quite different in how far they control what their governments do in the Council of Ministers.

First, they vary in the resources and attention they devote to following Union matters. Whilst all now have European affairs committees (EACs), the latter vary in the frequency of their meetings and the thoroughness of their scrutiny. Second, national parliaments vary in the formal powers they enjoy on Union questions. Whilst some can exercise a legally binding mandate on what their governments can accept in the Council of Ministers, others can only ask their governments to enter a 'scrutiny reserve' to allow more time for the national parliament to consider its position. Third, national parliaments vary in the autonomy with which they can exercise those powers they do enjoy. National political systems vary in how far the would-be controller (the national parliament) is itself controlled by the very body (the national government) whose behaviour in the Council of Ministers it might seek to control. Indeed, there is an important connection between the second and third of these points. The Danish Folketing, which is often held up as an exemplar of national parliamentary control on account of its power to issue legally binding mandates, is only autonomous in its exercise of that power in so far as it almost always has minority governments, with the consequence that it is the parliamentary majority that controls the government and not the governing majority which controls the parliament. In contrast, the Austrian parliament, which can also issue legally binding mandates, is none the less constrained by governing majorities from exercising the same level of control.

Cutting across these differences are some constraints common to all national parliaments. One difficulty is posed by the Union's extended policy cycle. Whilst CFSP as well as European Community policies with external implications would seem to be covered by the treaty protocol that requires all documents to be forwarded to national parliaments before they are decided in the Council, national parliaments might in practice want to be able to exercise control both 'upstream' and 'downstream' of that single intervention point. By the time a proposal is sent to the full Council, many options may have been foreclosed. On the other hand, much may be left to be decided during the implementation of the decision. Indeed, a further structural difficulty is that any one national parliament can only control the behaviour of its own government in the Council. To the extent that—short of doing more to coordinate their actions with one another—national parliaments cannot be in a position to exercise collective control, some of their number often complain of being confronted by *faits accomplis*: decisions their own governments tell them can only be reopened at some cost to the reputation of the member state as a reliable and efficient negotiator or to the credibility of the overall policy framework at the European level.

This last problem has become acute with the involvement of the Union in security questions. Of national parliaments included in a study by Wolfgang Wagner (2006b, 11), six are classified as having a high level of control over military deployments (Denmark, Finland, Germany, Ireland, Slovakia, and Sweden), five as having a medium level of control (Austria, the Czech Republic, Italy, Luxembourg, and the Netherlands), and seven as having little control (Belgium, France, Greece, Hungary, Poland, Portugal, and the UK). Of course, control in practice can be greater or less than that set out in formal specifications of powers. Thus the Geneva Centre for the Democratic Control of Armed Forces (DCAF) has also carried out a survey of how far national parliaments were actually involved in authorizing or scrutinizing plans for selected ESDP missions. The results are set out in Table 6.3. A number of problems emerge from these studies. First, any prospect of national parliaments with strong scrutiny powers acting as 'proxies' for those with fewer powers is offset by the possibility that security missions could conceivably be formed almost entirely from those member states whose national parliaments have fewer controlling powers. Second, there may even be a trend towards making it easier for governments to commit troops without national parliamentary scrutiny. Three member states—Bulgaria,

TABLE 6.3	Level of national parliamentary involvement in selected ESDP missions; DCAF study; all references from Anghel *et al.* 2008
EUFOR Althea (Bosnia Herzogovina)	Approved by 12 national parliaments. In the case of four Member States that committed personnel, there was no parliamentary debate or hearing.
EUFOR DRC (Democratic Republic of Congo)	Approved by ten national parliaments and discussed in committee in a further five.
EUPM BiH (Bosnia Herzogovina)	Approved by ten national parliaments. Those that held no hearing or debate included at least five member states that committed personnel.
EU BAM (Palestinian Territories)	Approved by six national parliaments. Those that were not consulted included at least four national parliaments from member states that committed personnel.

the Czech Republic, and Romania—have recently even relaxed those controls (Anghel *et al.* 2008, 56ff). Third, it is not always clear how far national parliamentary controls over troop deployments also cover the deployment of gendarmes under policing missions, which thus far account for the majority of ESDP actions.

Now that we have analysed the participation of both the European and national parliaments in the Union's international policies, we can return to my earlier claim that the problem of parliamentary control illustrates difficulties in legitimating the Union's external role simultaneously at the national, European, and international levels. Whilst national parliaments may be constrained in how easily they can develop capabilities in relation to the Union level (notably expertise specific to the Union's policies and institutions) and in how far they can exercise collective as opposed to individual control, the European Parliament would seem to be constrained by low levels of political competition and political community in the Union arena. Its second-order elections may allow some indirect representation of national arenas, but they also imply that the exercise of the Parliament's powers—those on international questions included—are not directly linked subject to electoral choice, competition, and debate. Even, however, if national parliaments and the European Parliament were in combination able to provide adequate democratic control of the Union's international policies, that would not ensure their full legitimacy. The problem here, of course, is that of legitimating the Union's international role externally and not just internally. To the extent that democratically controlled institutions are in general less likely to be arbitrary, and more likely to be constrained (Pettit 1997), even outsiders may take some comfort from them. To the extent, though, that those affected by democratic polities do not correspond to those with formal voting rights within them, democratic polities may even have a structural incentive to reach internal agreement at the expense of outsiders (Grant and Keohane 2005).

Conclusions

Polities with high internal legitimacy find it easier to ask for sacrifices, to extract resources, to use more majoritarian decision rules, and to concentrate powers of leadership and policy initiative. In the jargon, they face fewer barriers to political and administrative centre formation. Polities with low internal legitimacy have to work with the consent of their parts. Thus the question of legitimation is likely to be crucial to how the Union can develop as an international actor and with what implications for the international system. The less the Union's international role can establish some legitimacy of its own, and the more that role has to rely on the indirect legitimation of member states for each decision, the more the Union will be constrained to operate as little more than a mechanism for the coordination of 27 national foreign policies. Such an outcome would probably make few demands on the external legitimation of the Union's international role, since it would only require outsiders to accept established practices of regional and international organization. Yet it would, conversely, mean that the responsibilities the Union can assume in the international system—its contribution to the provision of international public goods ranging from international order to the stabilization of complex economic and ecological systems—will be more or less constrained to what can be achieved with the concurrent consent of however many member states are legally or practically necessary for action by the Union.

FURTHER READING

Whilst little has been directly written on the legitimacy and democracy of the Union's international policies, much has been written on the legitimacy of the Union in general. Lord and Beetham (2001) extend the idea that legitimacy will be a product of performance, democratic control, and identity to the case of the Union. Scharpf (1999) applies the distinction between input and output legitimacy to the EU.

Lord, C., and Beetham, D. (2001), 'Legitimizing the EU: Is there a "Post-Parliamentary Basis" for its Legitimation?', *Journal of Common Market Studies* 39/3: 443–62.
Scharpf, F. (1999), *Governing in Europe: Effective and Democratic?* (Oxford: Oxford University Press).

WEB LINKS

The European Parliament website, **http://www.europarl.eu.int/**, provides for committee reports on its scrutiny and control of various of the EU's international policies.

CHAPTER 7

The Europeanization of Foreign Policy

Reuben Wong

Summary

The first half of this chapter reviews five meanings of 'Europeanization', then proposes an operational definition of the phenomenon, linking and contrasting it with the paradigmatic European integration theories—neo-functionalism and intergovernmentalism. It goes on to ask if 'Europeanization'—so often understood as a process of transformation in domestic politics and institutions—can be identified in EU member states' *foreign* policies and proposes three dimensions of the process: top-down policy convergence, bottom-up national projection, and socialization.

The second half of the chapter evaluates the utility of the concept in understanding the European foreign policy-making regime—how policies result and why they change—from the interactions between member states' capitals and the EU institutions (chiefly the Commission, the Council, the Parliament, and the European External Action Service).

Introduction

'Europeanization' is no longer a new concept in the European Studies and International Relations literature, but it remains fashionable if ill-defined. Like globalization theory, there is much debate over the nature, causes, and effects of Europeanization and precious little agreement on what exactly Europeanization is (Harmsen and Wilson 2000; Cowles *et al.* 2001; Olsen 2002; Wong 2005; Vink and Graziano 2006; Moumoutzis forthcoming, 2011). The term often refers to the political and policy *changes* caused by the impact of membership in the European Union on the member states. Europeanization theorists draw on ideas found in institutionalism as well as in rationalization and globalization theories. Some see Europeanization as an 'institutionally thick form of rationalization within the global economy' (Rosamond 2000b, 179–180). Borrowing from institutionalist theory's hypothesis that international institutions have 'persistent and connected sets of rules that prescribe behavioural roles, constrain activity, and shape expectations' (Keohane 1989, 161), various Europeanization scholars argue that sustained membership and participation in the EU leads to the convergence of national policy making, both in style and content (Cole and Drake 2000; Hanf and Soetendorp 1998; Ladrech 1994).

As Hill and Smith argue in Chapter 1 of this volume, established concepts in International Relations are increasingly being brought together with approaches from Comparative Politics and Public Policy. This cross-disciplinary trend is evident in the 'Europeanization' approaches in European Studies, even in studies of the European Union's international relations. This chapter proposes Europeanization as an alternative approach to understanding EU member states' foreign policy. It seeks to develop an operational theory of Europeanization in order to better understand the extent of the influence, opportunities, and constraints on member states' choices afforded by the European Union. The key proposition of 'Europeanization' is that membership in the European Union has an important impact on each state's foreign policy. States joining the EU have to adapt to pressures for changes in their foreign policies. *Foreign policy Europeanization* is thus a dynamic and increasingly dense interplay between national policies through a complex process of negotiating and coordinating through EU institutions.

Exploring Europeanization

The meanings of Europeanization

The concept of 'Europeanization' contains an intrinsically schizophrenic understanding of the EU as both an independent and a dependent variable. In an oft-quoted article, Olsen suggested that there were 'five faces' of Europeanization in usage: changes in external boundaries; developing institutions at the European level; central penetration of national systems of governance; exporting forms of political governance; and a political unification project (Olsen 2002). In my chapter in the first edition of this volume, I grouped these different usages and varied meanings of the concept 'Europeanization' into a taxonomy of five categories: national adaptation, national projection, identity reconstruction, modernization, and policy isomorphism (Wong 2005, 135–140).

Although the concept of Europeanization is beset by different uses of the term, I contend that the central focus of the concept, common to practically all authors, is the penetration of the EU into the politics, institutions, and policy making of member states. This provokes and stimulates adaptation in national capitals to the demands of EU membership. Hence, Robert Ladrech's 1994 definition of Europeanization as a process of national adaptation to EU membership remains salient today (Ladrech 1994, 69):

... an incremental process reorienting the direction and shape of politics to the degree that EC political and economic dynamics become part of the organizational logic of national politics and policy making.

This reorientation or *national adaptation* sense of Europeanization championed by Ladrech suggests that Europeanization is a top-down process translating change from the supranational/European level to the national level in decision-making politics. In an idealized form, there would be 'a clear, vertical chain of command, in which EU policy descends from Brussels into the member states' (Bulmer and Radaelli 2004, 61). It is a process in which 'Europe, and especially the EU, becomes an increasingly more relevant and important point of political reference for the actors at the level of the member states' (Hanf and Soetendorp 1998, 1), and one can observe 'domestic adaptation to European regional integration' (Vink and Graziano 2006, 7). It is *not*, however, a Haasian process (to use neo-functionalist language on integration and convergence) that follows a self-perpetuating integrationist logic, where political actors in Europe 'shift their loyalties, expectations and political activities toward a new centre, whose institutions possess or demand jurisdiction over the pre-existing national states' (Haas 1961, Tranholm-Mikkelsen 1991), and where the end result is a supranational state. In other words, Europeanization as understood by Ladrech is a reactive process, where the state adapts and makes adjustments in its domestic politics and policy in compliance with the constraints and requirements of European institutions.

Lequesne and others have used the lenses of Comparative Politics in suggesting an incremental 'iterative process' of Europeanization in the national administrations as governments adapt their mechanisms and practices of policy making in politics, administration, and law. Incrementalism and 'muddling through' are the main processes in this model of Europeanization. Adaptations are ad hoc and there is no thought-out, coherent plan. Moreover, the extent and nature of the EU influence depend on endogenous factors in the member states that affect their capacity to adapt. National institutions may clash with, or conform to, European integration; in particular, their capacity to accommodate, refract, or resist pressures for change are key to understanding the distinctive national and sectoral trajectories of Europeanization (Lequesne 1993; Hanf and Soetendorp 1998, 188; Kassim *et al.* 2000; Goetz and Hix 2001; Guyomarch 2001; Kassim 2003).

In addition to the dominant 'national adaptation' school that characterized most of the first-generation theorizing on Europeanization, a bottom-up understanding of this concept is also common currency. In this conception, which I will call the '*national projection*' school, nation states are the primary actors and agents of change and the EU is the object of their activity. Ideas and practices are 'uploaded' from 'pace-setting' member states that seek to promote their national preferences to the EU level (Börzel 2002). The construction of the European Union is viewed as a means and vehicle for the achievement of nationally defined goals. In the place of a reactive state being constrained to change its policy-making processes, this notion of Europeanization sees the state as being proactive in projecting its preferences, policy ideas, and models to the European Union (Guyomarch *et al.* 1998; Bulmer and Burch 1999; Milward 1992, 2000; Laffan and Stubb 2003). This 'national projection' perspective shares many similarities with rational-choice, interest-based accounts of national preferences and national elites using the EU as an instrument to further national interests. They argue that by exporting their preferences and models into EU institutions, member states in effect generalize previously national policies onto a larger European stage.

Some scholars have noted that even small states within the European Union may pursue integration as a way of 'formalizing, regulating and perhaps limiting the consequences of interdependence' (Milward 2000, 19). At any rate, a strong European presence in the world is potentially beneficial to all in increasing individual member states' international influence. In the same vein, scholars have argued that Germany 'Europeanized' its low-deficit, fiscally disciplined macroeconomic policies into the EMU convergence criteria, and that France projected its institutions into the early EC and its predecessor, the High Authority of the European Coal and Steel Community (Regelsberger *et al.* 1997). These examples suggest that foreign policy making is as susceptible to Europeanization as domestic policy, politics, and processes. Yet beyond this instrumental perspective of using the EU for selfish ends, there are attempts by member states, either individually or in groups, to push the EU in certain general directions. An example would be the tendency, analysed by Manners and others, to carve out a 'normative power' role for the EU (Manners 2002).

A third meaning of Europeanization, predominantly informed by social constructivist lenses, refers to *elite socialization* in contemporary Europe (Aggestam 2004; Rieker 2006). Studies of this type of Europeanization have focused on the redefinition and negotiation of identities among European foreign policy elites. The identity reconstruction thesis finds echoes in the old Deutschian idea of political communities. Europeanization here is a way of blending the national and federal

impulses to create a transnational and culturally integrated Europe. Elite socialization is a phenomenon frequently associated with national officials attached to
the Commission and other EU institutions in Brussels. Most scholars agree that
intense and repeated contacts have socialized not only EU officials, but also national officials working in EU institutions. Even national diplomacies are becoming
more 'European' and displaying a 'coordination reflex' in foreign policy making
(Øhrgaard 1997; Glarbo 1999; Hill 1996, 6). In their study of the impact of the EU
on Irish officials, Laffan and Tannam note that 'public officials are no longer just
agents of the Irish state; they are participants in an evolving polity which provides
opportunities for political action but also imposes constraints on their freedom of
action' (Hanf and Soetendorp 1998, 69; Tonra 2001a). Research in this school suggests convergence as prolonged participation in the Common Foreign and Security
Policy feeds back into EU member states and reorients their foreign policy cultures
along similar lines. The main agents for convergence include elite socialization,
bureaucratic reorganization, and an institutionalized 'imperative of concertation'
(Glarbo 1999, 650; M. E. Smith 2000).

A fourth sense of Europeanization is the political, economic, and social *modernization* set in motion by prospective membership in the European Union. The term
is often applied to economically less developed states on the geographical periphery
of Western Europe as they are being brought into the core of West European institutions through EU membership. This modernization meaning of Europeanization
is common in works on Ireland, Greece, Spain, and Portugal (Morata 1998; Corkill
1999; Featherstone and Papadimitriou 2008). Similarly, the term is also taken
to mean 'joining Europe' and applied to the 2004 Central and Eastern European
accession countries in the context of EU enlargement (Ágh 1999). This applies to
the adoption of a West European state model and involves the firm anchoring of
democratic institutions and market economies. Ágh has suggested a variation of
the concept of Europeanization as describing a successfully completed process of
transition in which some or all of the candidate countries become fully integrated
into the entire range of West European and transatlantic cooperative institutions.
Studies of the EU's effects on national foreign policy in the enlargements of 1986
and 1995 have also demonstrated how new member states 'modernize' their foreign
policies upon accession by jettisoning outmoded national policies, so as to align
themselves with established European norms.

Policy isomorphism, the fifth and final meaning of Europeanization surveyed in
the first edition of this volume, is again a variant of national adaptation. It is concerned with the degree of convergence in substantive policy areas. Claudio Radaelli
has suggested that the Europeanization of policy has two dimensions. On one hand
there is the 'direct' Europeanization of various areas of public policy to the extent
that regulatory competence has passed from the member states to the European
Union. On the other hand, there has been an 'indirect' Europeanization of policy
learning where member states begin to emulate one another regarding particular
policy choices or policy frameworks. Advocates of this school of Europeanization

as isomorphism draw on the work of Dimaggio and Powell from the 1980s, arguing that over time, particular organizational forms or policy choices come to be perceived as 'legitimate' by the actors concerned, to the exclusion of other choices. They argue that in the present context, the type of intensive transnational cooperation fostered by European integration may lead to the emergence of such shared senses of legitimate (and illegitimate) choices (Radaelli 1997, 2000; Lodge 2000; Knill 2005).

These five meanings of Europeanization are summarized in Table 7.1.

The fourth and fifth senses of Europeanization (modernization and policy isomorphism) are not really relevant to foreign policy, so only the first three meanings are used to apply the concept in this study.

Operationalizing the concept of Europeanization

European foreign policy as a subject of enquiry up until the end of the 1990s tended to be either dismissed out of hand by realists as nonexistent, or idealized teleologically

TABLE 7.1   Five schools of thought on Europeanization

	Direction of change/ related processes	Major proponents
A. National adaptation	Top-down; globalization; policy convergence	Ladrech (1994); Kassim, Peters and Wright (2000); Kassim (2003); Cole and Drake (2000); Lequesne (1993); Goetz and Hix (2001); Vink and Graziano (2006)
B. National projection	Bottom-up and sideways; policy projection; policy learning; policy transfer	Börzel (2002); Bulmer and Burch (1999); Moravcsik (1993, 1998); Guyomarch et al. (1998); Laffan and Stubb (2003)
C. Identity reconstruction	Top-down; elite socialization	Aggestam (2004); Rieker (2006); M. E. Smith (2000); Hill and Wallace (1996); Nuttall (1992, 2000); Øhrgaard (1997); Zielonka (1998a); de Schoutheete (1986)
D. Modernization	Top-down; democratization; economic development; 'Westernization'	Ágh (1998, 1999); Corkill (1999); Featherstone (1998); Featherstone and Papadimitriou (2008)
E. Policy isomorphism	Top-down and sideways; policy learning; emulation and transfer	Radaelli (1997, 2000); Lodge (2000); Knill (2005)

as an inevitable end product of European integration, quite divorced from the realities of persistent (and often divergent) national foreign policies. Within European foreign policy studies, one camp sees member states as the principal actors while another emphasizes the role of supranational institutions (e.g. the Commission) and the emergence of a 'European interest'—a kind of pan-European national interest. Neither side developed good causal theories of EU foreign policy because they tend to be highly normative and to advocate positions on what the EU should be rather than what the EU is actually doing in world politics.

The study of the foreign policy of EU member states is thus split into two rival camps. In one camp is the traditional approach, focusing on the foreign policy of individual member states as utility maximizing, selfish, and purposive actors—let us call this the 'state-centric' school. The 'hard' position in this tradition claims that states are the only essential and salient actors. Any study of EU foreign policy is thus unproductive as the 'real' Europe is the one of state governments. As Hedley Bull claimed, 'Europe is not an actor in international affairs, and does not seem likely to become one' (Bull 1982). Bull felt that only an independent European nuclear deterrent and military power (represented by a West European military alliance led by France and Britain) would give Europe a real capability in foreign affairs. Of course, Bull's assessment was coloured by the escalating Cold War tensions of the 1980s between the USSR and Reagan's USA, but his prognosis for a European military capability independent of the USA/NATO finds vindication today in the aftermath of Bosnia, Kosovo, and Iraq (Gordon 1997; Howorth 2005).

Not all scholars in the state-centric tradition dismiss the EU as a serious international actor because of its lack of state-like qualities, nor do they agree with Bull's military-security conclusion. Neorealist intergovernmentalists privilege the centrality of the state while acknowledging the EU's influence, albeit only as a forum in which governments meet periodically to negotiate new contracts that enhance their interests and power. They view the EU as merely representing an advanced forum for negotiations at intergovernmental conferences (IGCs). The 'Harvard approach' of liberal intergovernmentalism, represented by Andrew Moravcsik, believes that the member states can raise the common interest in EU policy making. It has a materialist and rationalist bias in its stress on 'interstate bargain' deals and side payments between member states' governments who at certain times come to common agreements when their preferences converge. In this conception, decisions at the European level are viewed as 'conventional statecraft' between sovereign states— the key actors in all EU activities (Moravcsik 1991).

In the other camp—which I will call 'Europeanist'[1]—is the perspective that treats European Foreign Policy (EFP) as a given, i.e. as a foreign policy that already exists, has a consistent personality that makes an impact on world politics, and is taken seriously by other actors (Carlsnaes and Smith 1994; Zielonka 1998b; Nuttall 2000; White 2001; H. Smith 2002; K. E. Smith 2005). While this approach does not deny the continued importance of individual member states' foreign policies and accepts that EFP will not supplant national foreign policies any time soon—especially in defence and security matters—it often presumes that EFP's scope will expand eventually to subsume national policies in almost all other functional areas (M. E. Smith 2000). Walter Carlsnaes and Steve Smith in 1994 made the bold prediction that the essentially 'multilayered character' of the new Europe would mean that 'differentiated as to function, and maybe implicitly acknowledging suzerainty-like hierarchies, they will develop kinds of diplomatic relations and foreign policies that we best anticipate by reading about "proto diplomacy" in Der Derian's *On Diplomacy* (1987) and by searching even further away in time and space—among the empires of antiquity, the Chinese and Indian diplomatic traditions' (Carlsnaes and Smith 1994, 271).

The Europeanist perspective downplays the realist emphasis on state power and national interests, and privileges instead the role of supranational European institutions in building a common 'European' identity and a distinctive moral presence in world politics. François Duchêne, the first major spokesman in this school, envisaged the EU as a 'civilian power', a kind of 'soft power' that wields civilian instruments on behalf of a collectivity that has renounced the use of force among its members and encourages others to do likewise (Duchêne 1973). Taking as their starting point Duchêne's premise that the EU should and can become a 'civilian power' and a model of reconciliation and peace for other regions in the world, European idealists posit that EU foreign policy should focus on the promotion of democracy, human rights, and security cooperation. Many have advocated the German model of using economic leverage focusing on issues such as environmental concerns and open trading rather than military power as the way forward for the EU after the Cold War. Karen Smith lists propaganda, diplomacy, and economic instruments as three of the four instruments (excluding military) that the EU could and should exploit as a civilian power (K. E. Smith 1998). Acknowledging that the European Union may never possess a common defence policy, others have suggested that the EU has unparalleled foreign policy strengths as an 'attractive power' at the pivotal point between overlapping international clubs (Rosecrance 1998). Meanwhile, neo-functional accounts of convergence have been given a new lease of life in the study of European foreign policy by social constructivist accounts of the interaction of foreign policy elites under the regimes of European Political Cooperation (EPC) (1970), Common Foreign and Security Policy (CFSP) (1991) and European Security and Defence Policy (ESDP) in the 2000s. Enmeshed in such a context of policy making where national elites interact with Commission, Council, and other EU member states' national diplomacies, a *réflexe communautaire* becomes the norm rather than the exception (Øhrgaard 1997; M. E. Smith 2000; Tonra 2001; Carlsnaes *et al.* 2004).

Since the early 1980s, Europeanist studies of member states' foreign policies have focused almost entirely on comparing individual member states' foreign policies, albeit *within* the framework of the EPC/CFSP (Hill 1993a, 1996; Manners and Whitman 2000; Tonra 2001). Scholarship along this vein argues that there is something 'distinctive' about the foreign policies of EU member states. These states' foreign policies are made under opportunities and constraints qualitatively different from those of the USA, hence a distinctive foreign policy analysis method to study EU member states' foreign policies is necessary (Carlsnaes and Smith 1994; Manners and Whitman 2000). It clearly matters if a state is a member of the EU or not; relations between that state and the EU (and its policies, e.g. the Common Agricultural Policy) can pass overnight from being 'foreign' to domestic policy.

The Europeanization approach attempts to bridge these two rival approaches to the study of EU member states' foreign policies. On the mechanisms and scope of foreign policy Europeanization, some scholars have found that foreign policy convergence is to be expected over the long term (Wong 2006, looking at France). Others have argued that only the most superficial convergence—usually in procedure rather than substance—is taking place, and that national foreign policies retain their essential independence (Tsardanidis and Stavridis 2005, looking at Greece). There is general agreement, however, that three distinct dimensions (downloading, uploading, and crossloading) of the Europeanization process are evident in the relationship between a member state's foreign policy and the EU (summarized in Table 7.2).

We could measure the degree to which a state's foreign policy has been Europeanized over time according to three criteria (cf. the first three meanings of Europeanization in Table 7.1).

National adaptation and policy convergence. Has convergence and/or adaptation of national policy to EU norms and directives taken place? Have national institutional structures and policy-making processes been adapted in response to European integration?

Projection of national policy onto EU structures ('national projection'). Has the state pushed for its national foreign policy goals to be adopted as EU goals/policy? Has the state benefited from the 'cover' of the EU? How indispensable is the EU to the achievement of national foreign policy goals?

Internalization of 'Europe' in national identities ('identity reconstruction'). Has there been a reshaping or hybridization of identities, which privileges a European identity over the national? What kinds of European norms have arisen among national officials and how do they apply to foreign policy?

The first dimension of Europeanization is used predominantly in the literature to explain the top-down adaptation of national structures and processes in response to the demands of the EU. This concept predicts cross-national policy convergence between EU states after a sustained period of structural and procedural adaptation. The second Europeanization dimension refers to the bottom-up projection of national ideas, preferences, and models from the national to the supranational level. Third, Europeanization in its broadest sense means a process of identity and interest convergence so that 'European' interests and a European identity begin to take root alongside national identities and interests, indeed to inform and shape them.

TABLE 7.2   Three dimensions of Europeanization in national foreign policy

ASPECTS OF EUROPEANIZATION	NATIONAL FOREIGN POLICY (FP) INDICATORS
Adaptation and policy convergence • Harmonization and transformation of a member state to the needs and requirements of EU membership ('downloading'). • For various reasons: historical, instrumental, integrationist.	• Increasing salience of European political agenda. • Adherence to common objectives. • Common policy obligations taking priority over national *domaines réservés*. • Internalization of EU membership and its integration process ('EU-ization'). • Procedural change in national bureaucracies.
National projection • National foreign policy of a member state affects, and contributes to, the development of a common European FP ('uploading').	• State attempts to increase national influence in the world. • State attempts to influence foreign policies of other member states. • State uses the EU as a cover/umbrella. • National FP uses the EU level as an influence multiplier.
Identity reconstruction • Result of the above two dimensions. Harmonization process tending towards middle position; common EU interests are promoted ('crossloading').	• Emergence of shared norms/values among policy-making elites in relation to international politics, i.e. 'socialization'. • Shared definitions of European and national interests. • Coordination reflex and 'pendulum effect' where 'extreme' national and EU positions are reconciled over time.

Adapted from Tsardanidis and Stavridis 2005; Wong 2005, 142; Major and Pomorska 2005; Wong 2006, 236

Evaluating Europeanization

Europeanization theory privileges the roles played by European institutions in shaping the interests, politics, and policy making of its member states over time into a more convergent whole. Even attempts by member states eager to upload their national preferences and set the agenda for EU actions are mediated by reactions and responses by other member states and EU institutions that privilege convergent decisions (Börzel 2002). In this sense, the concept of Europeanization shares insights and assumptions with sociological institutionalism, which suggests that the EU's common policies, or *acquis politiques*, have encouraged new conceptions of interest and identity among its member states. Sociological institutionalists believe that institutions play more than a cost-minimizing, information, and utility-maximizing coordinating role in ensuring reciprocal cooperation for the collective good. The 'sociological institutions' in EFP are found in the form of *unwritten* rules, norms, and practices, found in both pillar I and CFSP, and include the 'Gymnich formula' (foreign ministers' informal retreats held every six months or so by each Presidency), and the premium placed on consultation and consensus. Sociological studies from the late 1990s indicate that EPC/CFSP institutions have a strong 'socialization' effect; elites involved even in the intergovernmental bargaining process of EPC/CFSP show surprising signs of internalizing supranational norms and interests, feeding these back to their national capitals (Øhrgaard 1997; M. E. Smith 2000, Bellier 2000, 147–150). CFSP is today an essential component of member states' foreign policy formulation. Between 1974 and 1999, over 74 'Gymnich' meetings were held at foreign minister level, i.e. an average rate of three times yearly. At the official level, the intense activity of some 30 CFSP Working Groups in Brussels had become an integral part of each member state's foreign policy. The *process* of formulating CFSP—if not always the results—is clearly becoming Europeanized.

How far does Europeanization explain member states' recent foreign policies? We are thus faced with a dichotomy. The Europeanization perspective portrays the individual state as subject to the strains, constraints, opportunities, and influences of EU 'club' membership and obliged to behave and play a certain role in the EFP regime. In contrast, the intergovernmental perspective (with its realist and liberal variants) views the member state as an independent power driven by its national interests, a state that shapes, influences, and sets the pace of European foreign policy and determines its level of cooperation according to its interests in the issue at hand. The two paradigms and their major characteristics are summarized in Table 7.3.

Of course, Table 7.3 exaggerates the differences between the two perspectives. The supranational–intergovernmental divide has narrowed considerably today as

TABLE 7.3	Europeanization versus intergovernmentalism in the study of national foreign policy		
	Europeanization theory	**Intergovernmentalism**	
		Realist variant	Liberal variant
Central variables	Knowledge/learning/roles	Power	Domestic interests
Role of Institutions	Strong (top-down); medium to weak (bottom-up)	Weak	Weak
Meta-theoretical orientation	Sociological (top-down); rationalistic (bottom-up)	Rationalistic	Rationalistic
Behavioural model	Role player	Concerned with relative gains	Concerned with absolute gains
Main actors	European elites, member states (bottom-up), institutions, international organizations, interest groups	State	Government elites, domestic interests
Actors' preferences	Socialized and negotiated	Exogenously given and fixed	Dynamic, rising from processes in national polities

member states adjust to the increasing Brusselsization of foreign policy making. Britain and France, the two most 'independent' member states in the EU, increasingly accept that they can no longer assure their own national defence nor pursue an independent global role today. Even Britain, the member state traditionally most opposed to European supranational integration and in favour of intergovernmental decision making in the EU, shows some signs of moving towards foreign policy decision making at the European level (White 2001; Allen and Oliver 2006).

How have scholars used the lens of Europeanization to study EU member states' foreign policy, and how valid are their findings? The increasingly dense interplay of national foreign policies within the framework of 'Europe' has led some to conclude that Europeanization is synonymous with foreign policy convergence.

Those who expect convergence to be the dominant tendency over the long term list geopolitical, institutional, and socialization factors. They argue that European states have become relatively less powerful in the 20th and 21st centuries with the rise of competing centres of power such as the USA, Japan, China, and India. Smaller member states, such as the Netherlands, Ireland, Portugal, and Denmark, have been forced to adapt to the changing world environment by aligning themselves with EU positions so as to amplify their voices in international trade and politics. This does not mean that the EU always smothers the smaller states' foreign policies—it sometimes gives small states the necessary institutional resources to profile themselves in 'new' regions, or to project their own interests as European interests.

Thus Portugal found that the Mediterranean, especially North Africa, became part of its foreign policy agenda, and that it was able to draw effective attention to East Timor through the EU (Vasconcelos 1996; Miles 2000; Phinnemore 2000; Tonra 2000, 2001). The 'post-neutral' member states Austria, Sweden, Denmark, and Finland have had to redefine their defence policies in response to the CFSP in 1991 and the Common European Security and Defence Policy in 1999, while even the largest member states have had to adapt to developments in security policy (Rieker 2006; Gross 2009).

Many scholars argue that EU foreign policy is not an independent variable, but a variable dependent on the roles played by member states themselves—especially the larger and more powerful ones—in fashioning EU structures and policies. These states, in 'projecting' their national policies and policy styles onto the larger European structure, 'Europeanize' their previously national priorities and strategies and create a dialectical relationship (cf. Table 7.2). By exporting their preferences and models onto EU institutions, they in effect generalize previously national policies onto a larger European stage. This has several benefits. First, the state increases its international influence. Second, the state potentially reduces the risks and costs of pursuing a controversial or negative policy (e.g. sanctions) against an extra-European power. At any rate, a strong European presence in the world is potentially beneficial to all in increasing individual member states' international influence. In the same vein, scholars have argued that the UK Europeanized its sanctions on Argentina during the Falklands/Malvinas conflict in 1982 (Regelsberger *et al.* 1997; White 2001). However one may conceptualize Europeanization—whether as a cause, effect, or process in national foreign policies—we would argue that these examples suggest that foreign policy is not a special case immune to Europeanization pressures on member states.

Elite socialization is a phenomenon frequently associated with national officials attached to the Commission and other EU institutions in Brussels. Research undertaken in recent years by Aggestam, Øhrgaard, M. E. Smith, and Glarbo suggests that officials are increasingly thinking in 'European' rather than 'national' terms. Anthropological studies of European Commission officials indicate that these officials were exhibiting traits of cultural 'hybridization' whereby their 'national being' was becoming a 'European being' (Harmsen and Wilson 2000, 149–50). Most scholars agree that intense and repeated contacts have socialized not only EU officials, but also national employees seconded to EU institutions. Even national diplomacies are becoming more 'European' and displaying a 'coordination reflex' in foreign policy making (Øhrgaard 1997; Glarbo 1999, 2001). In 1996, Hill and Wallace pointed out the potential transformational effects of elite socialization within this complex network (Hill and Wallace 1996, 6):

From the perspective of a diplomat in the foreign ministry of a member state, styles of operating and communication have been transformed. The [EPC communications] telex network, EPC working groups, joint declarations, joint reporting, even the beginning of staff exchanges among foreign ministries and shared embassies: all these have moved the conduct of foreign policy away from the old nation-state sovereignty model towards a collective endeavour, a form of high-level networking with transformationalist effects and even more potential.

Research challenges

Not yet communitarized despite the Lisbon Treaty, CFSP follows an intergovernmental decision-making process. Unlike commercial, competition, or monetary policy, there is no supranational entity above the national governments (in spite of Baroness Ashton's responsibility for the External Action Service) that can authoritatively state what CFSP should be. While the Europeanization approach was originally applied to the domestic impact of the EU on national polities (policies and politics in first-pillar issues where the direction of change was primarily top-down), applying the concept to CFSP, where decision making is dominated by a bottom-up process, was certain to cause confusion about actors, structures, cause, and effect.

Defining Europeanization as multidimensional and as 'a matter of reciprocity between moving features' (Bulmer and Radaelli 2004) is also epistemologically problematic as it blurs the *boundaries between cause and effect*, between dependent and independent variables. Considering Europeanization as a process suggests that the result will be (more) Europeanized national foreign policies. But how can EU foreign policy—so often defined as the cause of change at the national level—itself be generated at the national level by member states (Bulmer and Radaelli 2004)? There are elements of circularity here. Unlike major schools of integration theory such as neo-functionalism or intergovernmentalism, Europeanization does not put forward a series of interrelated hypotheses concerning either the dynamic or the end state of the European integration process. Europeanization is a concept that can thus be criticized as lacking 'core tenets, common to all or most usages of the term, which might serve as the basis for constructing a common paradigmatically defined research agenda' (Harmsen and Wilson 2000; Olsen 2002, 2003; Moumoutzis forthcoming, 2011). At best it identifies a process of mutual entanglement and some degree of increased orientation towards common points of reference.

Another research challenge is delineating the impact of 'Europe' from that of other possible causes. If most of the case studies involve EU member states, *how do we control for other causal variables*? The methodological problem here is what Peters characterizes as 'a collection of cases without variance in the dependent variable' (Peters 1998, 72). Most studies of foreign policy Europeanization assume *a priori* that European integration has an important effect on national foreign policies. But variables at the global, European, national, and sub-national levels interact in intricate ways, so that to claim pressures from European integration as *the* deterministic, or dominant, causal variable would be overstating the case (Wong 2005, 151; see also Haverland 2007). It is genuinely difficult to separate out the European factor (not, of course, that this problem is unique to this particular area of political science).

Perhaps that has been why each study claiming that a member state's foreign policy has been Europeanized is challenged by another claiming that it has *not*. Interestingly, a lively debate has focused on a particular member state—Greece—with some studies claiming that a previously obstructionist, uncooperative national foreign policy has come to conform with EU norms (Keridis 2003; Economides 2005; Terzi 2005), and others arguing that conformity has occurred only in form and not in substance (Tsardanidis and Stavridis 2005).

There is thus a need to account more systematically for foreign policy changes, and to allow for alternative explanations, rather than simply ascribing causation to the EU. The use of *counterfactual analysis*, in other words consciously posing the hypothetical question 'What if the EU did not exist?', which is almost inherent in any Europeanization study, would be very relevant here. Counterfactuals are not substitutes for field research, but they are useful to help one arrive at more accurate conclusions after the range of real available cases has been exhausted. When even non-EU states (notably Norway, Switzerland, and Turkey) formulate foreign policies that seem to respond to Europeanization pressures (Major 2005, 178–9; Terzi 2005) researchers should be careful to control for the impact of other variables that might cause the same kinds of effects otherwise ascribed to the impact of the European Union. Equally, one can argue that the effects of EU foreign policy cooperation are sufficiently powerful as to ripple out beyond the EU's actual borders.

Convergence or diversification?

Within EFP studies, an enduring cleavage has been between one school that views member states as the principal actors, and another that emphasizes the role of supranational institutions (especially the Commission) and the emergence of a pan-European identity and 'common interest'. Neither school has developed good causal theories of EU foreign policy because they tended to be highly normative and to advocate positions on what the EU should be rather than what the EU is actually doing in world politics. The Europeanization approach attempts to strike a middle path as it accepts that member states adapt to CFSP decision-making structures and norms, while at the same time recognizing that these same member states are actively involved in creating/shaping these structures and norms. The growing currency of Europeanization in foreign policy studies in recent years could be attributed to the concept's utility in capturing, more accurately than the paradigmatic European integration or International Relations theories, the significant changes that are taking place at the national level, fostering at the same time both convergence and diversification at various levels of European polities (Miskimmon and Paterson 2003; Hill and Smith 2005, 393–4; Wong 2006).

As a top-down process, Europeanization is the process of policy convergence caused by participation over time in foreign policy making at the European level. This produces shared norms and rules that are gradually accumulated (Øhrgaard 1997; Sjursen 2001, 199–200). As a bottom-up process, it is the projection of national preferences, ideas, and policy models into Europe. Europeanization is thus a bi-directional process that leads to a negotiated and non-linear convergence in terms of policy goals, preferences, and even identity between the national and the supranational levels (M. E. Smith 2000; Aggestam 2004). The supranational–intergovernmental divide has become considerably blurred as member states adjust to the increasing pressures of foreign policy Europeanization. Even Britain and France, the two member states traditionally most opposed to European supranational integration and in favour of intergovernmental decision making in the EU, have gradually come to make foreign policies much of the time in conjunction with their European partners (White 2001; Allen and Oliver 2006; Wong 2006).

Foreign policy studies that find evidence for increasing foreign policy convergence point out that the EU provides even the larger states (especially those with colonial histories), with a means to re-engage in areas of former colonial influence in Africa and Asia. Britain reinforced ties with its former Southeast Asian colonies through the ASEAN–EU dialogue from 1980. France was able to re-engage with all the countries in the East Asia region through the vehicle of the Asia–Europe Meeting, launched in 1996 and effectively a summit meeting of EU and East Asian leaders. The EU offers a means or cover in affording a 'politics of scale' to support member states' interests (Ginsberg 1989). By acting as an agent of European foreign policy, Britain, France, Belgium, Portugal, and the Netherlands could claim more credit for their dual national/European roles in troubled areas in the African Great Lakes regions, Southeast Asia, and even discussions on North Korea. Moreover, many large operations in the Balkans, Asia, and Africa are not confined to CFSP, but require Community resources and member states' contributions, e.g. peacekeeping forces.

In seeking to Europeanize their national approaches, these key states needed support from allies in the EU, as seen in French and German efforts in 2004–5 to upgrade political dialogue with China and to end the arms embargo imposed since 1989. On the side of those who argue for convergence are foreign policy studies in the enlargements of 1986, 1995, and 2004, where new member states 'modernized' their foreign policies upon accession by jettisoning outmoded national policies, to align themselves with established European norms. Thus Spain changed its position on the Western Sahara and recognized Israel, and Austria revised its neutrality policy (Barbé 1996; Luif 1998; Grabbe 2001). Poland, after its first few years of self-assertion, is now showing enthusiasm for common foreign policy positions.

Of course, while such convergence *pressures* exist, the actual *processes* are neither predetermined nor irreversible. Member states continue to resist being locked into a fixed path of identity and policy convergence. French and British policies are often contrasted with those of Germany, supposedly the model of a 'Europeanized' state, with a European identity. Yet even Germany took a distinctly unilateralist posture against agreed EU policy in its recognition of Slovenia and Croatia in December 1991 (Rummel 1996; Marcussen *et al.* 1999). National interests, as defined by incumbent national elites, still play a decisive role in national foreign policy making, and the CFSP has no enforcement mechanisms against defectors. But while national elites may resist the institutionalization of EU practices and a reflex of working for the collective interest, changes in the international context and venues of decision making that are increasingly oriented towards Brussels have incrementally altered even the definition of what constitutes the 'European' or the 'national' interest.

Commercial policy is a prime example of this shift. The Commission's 1991 car deal with Japan undertook to dismantle, over ten years, quotas for Japanese car imports in the protected markets of France, Italy, and Spain. States share the same interest in improving access to world markets and habitually entrust the Commission to take the lead in multilateral negotiations with strong economic powers such as the USA, Japan, and China, especially at the WTO (Devuyst 1995; M. Smith 1998b). Economic convergence is not limited to top-down processes proceeding from the Commission. The successful national policies of other member states are often copied. British and Dutch successes in attracting Japanese foreign direct investment in the 1980s and Germany's export success in China in the 1990s are two examples of policies emulated by other (more protectionist) EU governments (Lehmann 1992; Nuttall 1996; Wong 2008, 61–6). The Lisbon Agenda of benchmarking good practice was a natural development. In the modern world such issues are closely connected to traditional 'foreign policy'.

The Union's pre-Lisbon human rights policy throws up an even more complex picture of convergence and divergence. The EU typically suffered from conflicting interests and coordination problems between the member states, the General Affairs and External Relations Council (GAERC), the Commission, and the European Parliament (EP) when dealing with human rights situations from Chad to China. While the formal locus of effective decision-making on human rights issues was the Council—empowered by the Maastricht Treaty to ensure the 'unity, consistency and effectiveness of action by the Union'—deliberations on human rights action in practice impinged on other policies across the three-pillar structure (affecting, *inter alia*, development assistance, trade and cooperation agreements, enlargement, justice, and immigration), and thus involved a multiplicity of intra-EU actors, not to mention interactions with the USA, UN, Council of Europe, and human rights NGOs (Clapham 1999; K. E. Smith 2001).

If Europeanization is a dependent variable or effect, what is/are the independent variable(s) driving the process? I would argue that we have to cast the net wider for explanatory variables than the current Europeanization literature, into Comparative Politics and Public Policy, and deeper into time, for an answer. One 'push' factor is the historical process of European integration, which itself can be traced to the underlying political and economic imperatives for highly coordinated cooperation between member states that early integration theorists identified (Haas 1958).

On the 'pull' side are the demands of other states in the international system for coordinated European positions and the need for some means of associating with the USA without being dominated by it (Shapiro and Witney 2009).

The significance of Europeanization in the foreign policy arena is that foreign and security policy is one of the last remaining bastions of national sovereignty, and thus the ultimate hard case. Treaties, not legislation, govern CFSP. Foreign policy Europeanization is much more a process of socialization than forced, formal adaptation. Yet in this policy area originally designed to avoid supranational integration, socialization and learning processes have taken place and actually fostered integration—albeit in a distinctive form (Tonra 2001; Glarbo 2001; Aggestam 2004). Perhaps the primary contribution of the Europeanization concept to foreign policy analysis is its attempts to account for the unexpected results of intergovernmental deal making and intense foreign policy coordination within the EU.

Conclusions

The five major meanings of Europeanization are: a top-down process of national adaptation (school A), a bottom-up and sideways process of national projection (B), the multidirectional processes of socialization (C) and modernization (D), and policy isomorphism (E). The five schools are not mutually exclusive but share many overlapping assumptions about causes, effects, and processes. For example, the top-down school of national adaptation (school A) would accept that member states play critical roles in forging 'European' policies (school B) in the first place.

Unlike major schools of integration theory such as neo-functionalism or intergovernmentalism, the Europeanization concept lacks paradigmatic consistency. Europeanization does not put forward a series of interrelated premises concerning the dynamic or the end state of the European integration process. The growing currency of Europeanization in recent years could be attributed to the concept's utility in two areas. First, it evokes parallel and interconnected processes of change at both the national and European levels. The concept recognizes and captures more accurately than the paradigmatic theories the significant changes that are taking place at the national level, fostering at the same time convergence and diversification at various levels of European polities and societies. Second, the concept has a strong focus on the interrelationship of institutions and identities. It shows how institutional change and development may affect identities and interests, as well as how changing identities may create pressures for new institutional forms and modes of behaviour.

The wide range of usages of the term Europeanization in the literature touches on most aspects of political, societal, and economic change in Europe today and can be applied to foreign policy analysis. This chapter proposed that three of the five schools of the Europeanization concept outlined in the literature survey could be useful in explaining the changes taking place in foreign policy making in an EU member state. Under the CFSP, 'Europeanization' can be understood as a process of intense foreign policy coordination under pressures for convergence. It is a *dependent* variable contingent on the ideas and directives emanating from actors (EU institutions, statesmen, etc.) in Brussels, as well as policy ideas and actions from member-state capitals (national statesmen). Europeanization is thus identifiable as a process of change manifested as policy *convergence* (both top-down and sideways) as well as national policies amplified via EU policy (bottom-up projection). Identity reconstruction (towards a 'European' identity) is a closely related effect observable over time.

As a top-down process, Europeanization is the process of policy change caused by participation over time in foreign policy making at the European level. This produces shared norms and rules that are gradually accumulated (Sjursen 2001, 199–200, Øhrgaard 1997). For scholars such as Ladrech, Kassim, and Cowles *et al.*, Europeanization is national adaptation to pressures arising from European integration. For Harmsen and Wilson, it has itself an *effect* on national institutions, identities, and citizenship. The primary usage of the Europeanization concept—that of capturing the top-down adaptation of national structures and processes in response to the demands of the EU—is critical in testing if national policy making has indeed been affected by EU membership, and in what ways. Europeanization scholars may debate the institutional forms and distinctive national responses to EU pressures. Some may note that Europeanization as adaptation has actually increased divergence within the EU (Mazey and Richardson 1996). Over the longer term, however, a sustained period of structural and procedural adaptation would necessarily result in cross-national policy convergence between EU states. Convergence in policy style and content is expected as EU institutions prescribe roles and constrain activities. Coupled with the second and third processes of national projection and identity reconstruction, the overall picture expected is one of converging rather than diverging policy outputs, whatever the differences between national structures, preferences, and policy inputs.

The second process, that of the projection of national ideas, preferences, and models from the national to the supranational level, can be expected of states that command more resources or have a dogged commitment to forge a certain EU policy, perhaps driven by strong domestic pressures. National preferences are expected to be projected onto the European structure by member states that seek to structure EU institutions and policies according to their interests. This was the case for France in the EU's trade privileges and development assistance for former colonies in Africa, the Caribbean, and the Pacific (see Chapter 14 by Maurizio Carbone), and for Germany in pushing for détente in the 1970s, and the Stability Pact in Central and Eastern Europe after the Cold War.

Third, Europeanization in its broadest sense of identity and interest convergence—so that 'European' interests and a European identity begin to take root—does not mean that the European will simply supplant the national over time.

National identities and interests in Europe have evolved and grown over centuries and will not go away after just a few decades of European integration. However, European identity shapes and is increasingly incorporated into national identities.

The Europeanization of foreign policy thus leads to a negotiated convergence between the national and the supranational levels. When there is convergence between member states and EU institutions, this could result in a raising of the common interest, e.g. encouraging the development and consolidation of democracy and human rights abroad by trading and having full political/diplomatic relations with governments that respect minimum human rights standards. At other times, it is the lowest common denominator decision/preference that prevails and becomes EU policy. This could be the case in legitimizing one member state's interests by raising EU protectionist barriers against other trading countries/groups of states.

Unlike intergovernmentalism, Europeanization theory acknowledges the important roles played by non-state actors and Europeanized elites in formulating national and European foreign policy. For example, it takes note of the proliferation of pan-European NGOs and interest groups that lobby the Commission and European Parliament on European foreign policy issues. These groups effectively act as agents promoting a common foreign policy. The arrival of ESDP has also created a whole array of new stakeholders (including national armies and defence industries) with vested interests in a more coherent and coordinated European foreign policy.

Europeanization theory, in contrast to integration theory, does not foresee a supranational centre eclipsing the national capitals. The key proposition of Europeanization is that membership in the European Union has an important impact on each member state's foreign policy. States that join the European Union have to and do adapt to pressures for changes in their foreign policies—frequently even *before* formal membership. The overlapping and interrelated forces of Europeanization (policy convergence, national projection, and identity reconstruction) interact with often surprising results. The ensuing foreign policy of each member state is the end product of a complex series of negotiations between governments, EU institutions (Commission, Council, and Parliament), officials, and member state representatives, as well as a process of policy learning and emulation between individual member states. With the added resources accorded to the External Action Service under Lisbon, and its staffing (merging staff from the Commission, the Council Secretariat, *and* the member states' diplomatic services), the impact of the EU on member states' foreign policies is likely to increase.

Notes

1 Here I am using 'Europeanist' in the sense of believing in, arguing for, and advocating a coherent and powerful European actor in international politics, as opposed to nation-state-based foreign policies within a Europe of nation states.

FURTHER READING

Some of the best literature surveys of the uses of the concept 'Europeanization' are found in Harmsen and Wilson (2000), Olsen (2002, 2003) and Graziano and Vink (2006). To better understand how Europeanization relates to earlier debates between neo-functional intregrationists and intergovernmentalists, refer to extracts of two classic texts on European integration and intergovernmentalism: Haas (1958) and Hoffmann (1966) in Nelsen and Stubb (2004), Chapters 16 and 18 respectively. For assessments of the impact of EU integration on the *domestic* politics and policies of member states, see Ladrech's (1994) article on France; Mény, Muller and Quermonne (1996); Goetz and Hix (2001; also published as a special issue in *West European Politics*, 24/3, 2000); and Cowles, Caporaso, and Risse (2001). Also see Hanf and Soetendorp (1998), which discusses the impact on smaller member states. Books dealing with the European Union's impact on member states' *foreign* policies (and vice versa) include Hill (1996), Manners and Whitman (2000), and Wong and Hill (forthcoming 2011).

Cowles, M. G., Caporaso, J., and Risse, T. (2001), *Transforming Europe: Europeanization and Domestic Change* (Ithaca and London: Cornell University Press).

Goetz, K., and Hix, S. (eds) (2001), *Europeanised Politics? European Integration and National Political Systems* (London: Frank Cass).

Graziano, P., and Vink, M. P. (eds) (2006), *Europeanization: New Research Agendas* (Basingstoke and New York: Palgrave Macmillan), 3–20.

Hanf, K., and Soetendorp, B. (1998), *Adapting to European Integration* (London: Longman).

Harmsen, R., and Wilson, T. (eds) (2000), 'Introduction', *Europeanisation: Institutions, Identities and Citizenship* (Amsterdam: Rodopi).

Hill, C. (ed.) (1996), *The Actors in Europe's Foreign Policy* (London: Routledge).

Ladrech, R. (1994), 'Europeanization of Domestic Politics and Institutions: The Case of France', *Journal of Common Market Studies*, 32(1), 69–88.

Manners, I., and Whitman, R. (eds) (2000), *The Foreign Policies of European Union Member States* (Manchester: Manchester University Press).

Mény, Y., Muller, P., and Quermonne, J.-L. (eds) (1996), *Adjusting to Europe: The Impact of the European Union on National Institutions and Policies* (London: Routledge).

Nelsen, B., and Stubb, A. (eds) (2004), *The European Union: Readings on the Theory and Practice of European Integration*, 3rd edition (Boulder, CO: Lynne Rienner).

Olsen, J. P. (2002), 'The Many Faces of Europeanisation', *Journal of Common Market Studies* 40(5), 921–52.

Olsen, J. P. (2003), 'Europeanization', in Cini, M. (ed.), *European Union Politics* (Oxford: Oxford University Press).

Wong, R., and Hill, C. (eds) (forthcoming 2011), *National and European Foreign Policies Towards Europeanization*.

WEB LINKS

The online journal *European Integration Online Papers* (EIoP) has published many of the seminal articles on Europeanization: **http://eiop.or.at/eiop/index.php/eiop/index**. Conferences on the 'Europeanisation of national foreign policies' (2002) and 'European Foreign Policy' (2004) yielded many useful research papers on foreign policy Europeanization. They are available on the European Foreign Policy Unit (EFPU) website of the London School of Economics and Political Science: **http://www.lse.ac.uk/Depts/intrel/EuroFPUnit.html**. The website of Advanced Research on the Europeanization of the Nation State (ARENA) at the University of Oslo includes relevant papers on Europeanization: www.arena.uio.no. See also the materials and links at **http://www.fornet.info/**, the FORNET website.

CHAPTER 8

Implementation: Making the EU's International Relations Work

Michael E. Smith

▌ Summary

The EU has developed a wide variety of policy instruments to translate its common interests into collective action in the international system. It also possesses its own financial resources to help fund those policy instruments, an important attribute not found in any other regional organization. While there is wide variation across different types of policy instruments in terms of their sophistication and external influence, the EU now enjoys a capability for global action—including military operations—that was nearly unthinkable during the 1990s. However, this unique capacity for policy implementation can be very erratic, and with every major policy decision the EU must balance the competing incentives for cooperation among its member states with their inherent desire to act unilaterally in world affairs.

Introduction: the problem of implementation in foreign policy

Foreign policy, which includes security and defence policy for the purposes of this chapter, involves many problems that set it apart from most domestic-oriented policy domains, such as social welfare policy. This is true whether speaking of national foreign policy making or foreign policy cooperation among nation states and can be seen whether considering the EU as a regional subsystem of international relations, as a leading participant in international processes/politics, or as a unique power or actor in international relations.

Most importantly, the stakes are perceived to be much higher in the realm of foreign policy, up to and including the very survival of the state itself; in this sense the EU and its member states, like all other global actors, are subject to the broader political dynamics, and competitive pressures, of international relations. These factors can easily encourage EU member states to act unilaterally and thus undermine the search for a common EU foreign policy. Compared with domestic policy, foreign policy also is not easily regulated through the use of forward-looking and detailed legislative instruments owing to the limited availability of information about global affairs and the need to preserve flexibility in the face of changing circumstances. This often results in the delegation of wide-ranging authority to executive bodies and may make it difficult for opposition parties or other actors to criticize certain decisions (Pollack 1997). Foreign policy also involves a mix of policy tools and institutional procedures that can undermine the coherent behaviour of any global actor, whether a state or a regional institution like the EU (see Chapter 5). Similarly, it is often very difficult to assess and distribute the gains, if any, from foreign policy actions. All of these problems in turn also present challenges to the democratic oversight of foreign policy, where the watchdog role of legislators and the media is often undermined by the strict controls on information maintained by foreign policy makers.

The EU's persistent attempts to manage these kinds of problems in the hopes of transforming itself into a global political actor—and one with a highly distinctive set of power resources—represent a unique experiment in world politics. However, if we conceive of the EU as a regional subsystem of international relations, there are strong reasons to expect such cooperation. The Western European states which founded the EU in the 1950s share powerful historical memories, cultural values and norms, and even a vision, however shadowy, of a common destiny (Haas 1958). The EU's position, geographic and ideological, between the USA to the west and numerous states to the east and south also contributes to perceptions of a base of common interests to promote joint action. European hopes of rejecting balance-of-power politics on the continent after 1945, and of promoting reconciliation among former enemies, also represent a fundamental break with a centuries-old pattern of competitive international relations in this region (Deutsch et al. 1957). Finally, high levels of social, economic, and political interdependence also contribute to the idea that common European problems can be solved effectively only through common European policies.

Yet this pool of common values and interests is embedded within a larger system of international relations subject to its own dynamics of action. Fundamentally, the EU is still a system of sovereign states bound in a treaty-based regional institution, as confirmed most recently with the Treaty of Lisbon. Although EU member states may have delegated certain aspects of their foreign policies to the EU, they still reserve the right to act unilaterally in foreign policy and they often do so. A demand for action based on common interests does not automatically lead to the supply of collective action in world politics (Keohane 1983); in many cases, EU states still must be convinced of the need to act together. This propensity to cooperate can also vary between economic issues (such as trade or aid), 'soft' political issues (such as human rights and civilian security), and 'hard' political issues (such as military defence). Cooperation in economic affairs represents a clear goal—such as the elimination of trade barriers—that can be explicitly measured according to agreed timetables. Many economic issues also involve a fairly high degree of consensual knowledge about the effects of economic conditions on national welfare, such as the relationship between inflation and economic activity. A common foreign policy, however, does not share these characteristics; it can mean only a constant process of policy coordination on a case-by-case basis, sometimes at the expense of existing national foreign policy positions.

Even when states may agree on general common goals, such as the promotion of human rights or democracy, they may fundamentally disagree on the specific tactics or means to achieve those goals. This is especially true among the larger EU member states, and in areas where EU states claim a 'special relationship' or unique national interest (such as relations with former colonies). Although the EU has gradually managed to diminish the influence of many of these '*domaines réservés*' in its conduct of external relations, and although the Lisbon Treaty has created a more sophisticated infrastructure for developing European foreign/security policy (see Chapter 4), some EU member states still resist delegating their foreign policies to the EU. Moreover, coordination among all foreign policy missions, once chosen, must be managed and paid for. If it is to be sustained and monitored in any coherent fashion, it must also be institutionalized. This results in a constant process of negotiation for most foreign policy decisions taken by the EU, even in fields like trade policy where EU organizations (chiefly the Commission) possess a fairly high degree of authority. And in cases where the details of policy implementation are left to EU member states, compliance may become an issue since those states vary widely in their ability to uphold common policy decisions in a timely and efficient manner. As outright opposition to commonly agreed foreign policies is actually quite rare in the EU, compliance is more frequently undermined by commonplace domestic political issues such as election campaigns, parliamentary rules, budgetary limits, party competition, and bureaucratic disputes (M. E. Smith 2004b).

Even so, the EU still manages to act coherently in world politics through the use of various policy instruments. Although most EU policies involve some external component, directly or indirectly, the objective in this chapter is to explore how the EU executes its key foreign policy decisions through the use of common resources and policy tools. Before turning to this question in detail, we should note several other general features of the EU's ability to implement common policies.

First and most obviously, this ability varies widely across the EU's major policy tools, ranging from diplomatic to economic to military/police instruments. Each of these instruments, with representative examples, will be explored below. Second, the EU's capacity for action has not developed according to a grand institutional blueprint, although all of its major policy sectors have become more institutionalized since the Treaty of Rome in 1957 (Stone Sweet and Sandholtz 1998). Instead, processes of trial-by-error learning, incremental capacity building, and crisis-induced decision-making have strongly influenced specific EU actions in world politics. The EU's institutional arrangements for external action reinforce this somewhat ad hoc approach to policy initiation/execution, as various competencies in EU foreign policy still involve different decision-making processes and policy tools, even under the Treaty of Lisbon. These competencies may be grouped as the European Community (EC), the Common Foreign and Security Policy (CFSP), and the Area of Freedom, Security and Justice (AFSJ). Further, the CFSP itself involves its own major sub-category of policy, the European Security and Defence Policy (ESDP); under Lisbon, the ESDP will be known as the Common Security and Defence Policy (CSDP) (see Table 8.1).

This persistence of what used to be known as the 'tri-pillar' system of EU policy leads to our third general point: the EU's repertoire of policy tools cannot be understood fully by examining treaty articles and formal institutional arrangements alone; the EU has managed in many cases to do more than we might otherwise expect by a reading of EU treaty documents. This often involves creative coordination across various policy competencies, moving funds across different budgetary lines, arranging national contributions to common policies on a case-by-case basis,

TABLE 8.1	EU foreign policy competencies and external policy instruments		
	Diplomatic tools	**Economic tools**	**Military/police tools**
I. EC	Yes	Yes, including a very large budget	No
II. CFSP	Yes	Yes, including a limited budget	Yes (through the ESDP/CSDP)
III. AFSJ	Yes	Yes, including a limited budget	Limited to police/customs cooperation

creating common-pool resources to fund policies outside the EU budget, and even the creation of new informal rules to handle situations where a breakdown occurs between deciding a policy and implementing it (i.e. the 'slippage problem'). While instances of deliberate national defection are fairly rare in the EU, other cases of involuntary defection do occur (most often due to domestic political procedures) and can interfere with effective implementation.

Fourth and finally, all of these dynamics must be understood in light of the changing domestic politics of EU member states, whose foreign policy machinery and national political processes both contribute to and complicate the EU's own efforts in world politics. These processes, which result from the EU's inherent structure as an organization of sovereign states, include not only governmental decision-making inputs at the EU level, but even domestic ratification processes in certain areas of EU policy not subject to supranational procedures. While these complex dynamics make it difficult to measure the EU's true capacities as a global actor, they also make the EU a fascinating laboratory for exploring the dynamics between comparative domestic politics, European integration, and international relations, the primary theme of this volume.

The EU's own resources in external relations/third countries

Why is the EU such a unique actor in world politics? One of its most important attributes involves a capacity to finance its own policy decisions. In fact, the EU possesses a larger pool of independent legal/institutional, technical, and financial resources than any other regional organization on the planet. This capacity, known as the EU's 'own resources', has gradually expanded over a period of four decades. Under the 1957 Treaty of Rome, national contributions at first provided the bulk of financial resources to the nascent EC, but with a view to giving the EC its own budgetary resources. Article 201 was a key provision of this treaty; it stated that: 'Without prejudice to other revenue, the budget shall be financed wholly from own resources.' Such resources are understood to be a source of operational funds separate from and independent of EU member states, such as tax revenue assigned to the EC to fund its budget without the need for any subsequent decision by the national authorities. EU member states would be required to make these payments available to the EC for its operational budget.

This process took longer than expected to achieve as some EU states (particularly France) adamantly resisted the requirements of the treaty. As the EU has always been, and still is, a treaty-based system under international law rather than a confederation or federal union, it is to a large degree subject to the good faith of its member states and to broader political dynamics in international relations, which can complicate EU decision-making over resources and policies. Thus, it was not until the Hague summit in 1969 that EU member states, in the face of the first-ever EU enlargement, finally took the decision to fully implement Article 201. This inaugurated a system of independent financing based on 'traditional' own resources (customs duties and agricultural levies) and an additional resource based on the value added tax (VAT) applied across EU member states. These two traditional own resources are considered the 'natural' own resources of the EU, since they are revenue collected by virtue of Community policies rather than revenue obtained from the member states as national contributions.

However, these traditional resources were not enough to balance the EU's budget, so a new source of revenue, VAT own resources, came into use in 1980. In 1988 the Council decided to add a fourth own resource, based on a gross national income (GNI) scale, which now accounts for the majority (around 76 per cent) of the EU's total revenue. All of these instruments were consolidated into a new own resources system following a report by the Commission in 1998. Inaugurated in 2002, this new system set a cap of own resources at 1.27 per cent of the EU's GNI and reduced dependence on the VAT as a source of revenue. It also provided that no new own resource would be introduced despite the financial pressures of the major EU enlargements to the east/southeast in 2004–7. This cap on funding, which is reinforced through a multiannual financial framework agreed by the Commission, the Council, and the European Parliament (EP), has resulted in a general decline in EU expenditures (as a percentage of EU GNI) from about 1.21 per cent during the 1990s to around 0.98 per cent for the 2007–13 budgetary period. And although the EU endured some difficulties in managing the budgetary procedures of its CFSP and Justice and Home Affairs (now AFSJ) pillars in the 1990s (Monar 1997a), today there is more effective coordination between the EU organizations and member state financing procedures in most areas of external relations. This effort now includes a new 'Instrument for Stability' EU budget line to speed up the disbursement of funds controlled by the Commission in situations involving crisis management, conflict resolution, and peacebuilding.

To summarize, the EU at present controls a total budget of €141.5 billion a year (or nearly $200 billion), making it one of the most powerful (in financial terms) international organizations in the world. In comparison, the budget of the United Nations is about $2 billion a year, plus another $2.5 billion a year for peacekeeping operations. Moreover, the main source of UN funds is the contributions of its member states; it does not possess its own resources. However, although only a portion of the EU's large budget is explicitly devoted to external policies (see below), the EU's ability to finance its projects, and the ability of the Commission and the EP to help implement the budget, give the EU a source of influence far beyond any other regional economic organization. Now that financing for the EU is relatively secure, the more recent challenge for the EU has been to find a way to marshal its financial and other resources in service of common foreign policy goals.

National resources and EU external relations

Beyond its own budgetary authority based on the revenue sources noted above, the EU is also able to draw upon the experience and resources of its individual member states. Bilateral and multilateral special relationships based on colonial or cultural connections are still important for EU states, especially the large ones (i.e. the British Commonwealth and France's Organisation Internationale de la Francophonie). Britain and France also enjoy unique responsibilities as permanent members of the UN Security Council, while other EU member states rely on close interest-based ties by virtue of their geographic locations (the Nordic countries, the Mediterranean countries, etc.). These relationships will not disappear with the pursuit of the EU's global ambitions and they have the capacity to both frustrate and inspire action at the EU level (Hill 1996; Manners and Whitman 2000). For example, Britain's special relationship with the USA certainly complicated the EU's search for a common policy on Iraq, while Sweden and Finland successfully pressed for a new 'Northern dimension' to EU foreign policy after their accession to the EU in 1995.

However, EU member states still must pursue these relationships in the context of EU norms and structures, which make them an indirect source of power for the EU in three ways. First, EU norms require member states to consult on all major questions of foreign policy before forming their own policies. All EU member states recognize, though to varying degrees, that they will have more impact on world affairs if they act in common, and the EU foreign policy system attempts to reinforce this understanding by ensuring regular communications on all major subjects of foreign policy (the so-called 'consultation reflex') through various channels such as working groups, inter-institutional meetings, and secure communications. The common foreign policy positions developed through this process, or the EU's *communauté de vue* (de Schoutheete de Tervarent 1980), may then inspire joint actions (or policy coordination) to handle specific issues. These positions and actions must be respected by all EU member states, even if they choose to 'opt out' of certain policies (such as those involving security affairs). Moreover, wholly unilateral foreign policy actions taken without any consultation are generally disdained by other EU states and usually do not gain much internal support. As former British foreign minister Douglas Hurd once noted (1981, 389) 'Perhaps one reason why these unilateral efforts now usually come to nothing is precisely that they are unilateral.'

Second, the EU has produced additional rules for areas where national and EU competencies overlap. These are especially prominent in cases of economic policy, where the notion of 'mixed agreements' was developed to unite the competencies of the Commission and those of EU member states in areas not governed by EU treaties. For example, all of the 'Europe agreements' negotiated with the Central and Eastern European countries in the 1980s were mixed agreements as they involved both economic aspects (governed by the Commission) and political aspects (governed by EU member states and the Commission). A similar approach has been applied to the European Neighbourhood Policy (ENP), which applies to 15 states bordering the EU to its south and east, plus the Palestinian Authority (see Chapter 13). Thanks to this type of arrangement, the EU can always draw upon the diplomatic and intelligence resources of all of its member states and the Commission, even where formal treaty authority for implementing collective action is lacking or incomplete. Such agreements may also include a financial component contributed by EU member states, depending on the question at hand. The EU's administration of the Balkan city of Mostar, for example, relied on special contributions by EU member states calculated according to a GNI scale. Yet the complicated logistics of organizing such contributions (a key example of slippage between policy making and policy implementation) ultimately resulted in greater use of the EU budget, as a normal rule, for such mixed agreement policies. As EU member states delegate more of their economic policies to the EC, such as trade in services and trade-related aspects of intellectual property rights, then European foreign policy actions will have to rely on EU budgetary resources even more.

Third, the EU's most recent ambitions to field an independent military force are promoting new experiments in permitting states to contribute to operations on a case-by-case basis. The commitments from 30 European states inside and outside the EU amount to about 100,000 ground troops, 400 aircraft, and 100 ships in line with the so-called 'headline goals' agreed at a commitment conference on 20 November 2000, reinforced by a series of follow-up meetings over the next decade. These commitments have clearly enhanced the EU's military capabilities in a number of areas (see Chapter 9). All six European NATO members outside the EU at the time (the Czech Republic, Hungary, Iceland, Norway, Poland, and Turkey) also contributed to the EU's 'force catalogue' (Salmon and Shepherd 2003), and now the Czech Republic, Hungary, and Poland are full members of both NATO and the EU. Note, however, that these force commitments do not involve the raising of new troops; they are existing forces already committed to national and/or NATO operation plans. They are now 'separable' from NATO for the ESDP (or since Lisbon, the CSDP) on a temporary basis but are not quite 'separate' from the alliance.

Beyond these specific military contributions, the EU has also devised an intergovernmental mechanism to improve the rapid financing of military tasks as the EU budget cannot be used to fund military operations. This is the 'Athena' facility, which provides for a common pool of financial and other resources supplied by, and drawn upon, EU member states when setting up an ESDP/CSDP military operation. Similar to the Instrument for Stability funded under the EU's normal budget (which cannot be used for military operations), the Athena facility speeds up the disbursement of funds and, critically, allows for contracts to be signed with subcontractors and other suppliers of mission resources. In addition, the EU has gradually improved European arms cooperation through the creation of a formal European Defence Agency in 2004, as well as many joint procurement projects among various EU member states (see Chapter 9). Although these efforts are more modest in comparison to NATO's resources (much of which are supplied by the USA), they do represent a considerable expansion of the EU's policy toolkit compared to the situation during the 1990s, when the idea of an independent EU military force was unthinkable for some of its member states.

The instruments of EU foreign policy

With the transition from the ESDP to the CSDP under the Lisbon Treaty, as well as the creation of the EU's own diplomatic service (the European External Action Service) and its own international legal personality, the EU today possesses many of the major foreign policy instruments of a state. In fact, the EU's main problem in foreign policy implementation is not so much the lack of effective instruments, but in the difficulties involved in finding the will to use those instruments in a strategic, coherent fashion. Part of this problem is political: finding a consensus among 27 EU member states can be difficult, especially in areas involving security or defence where decisions cannot be taken by any form of majority voting. Another part of the problem is institutional: the effective implementation of EU foreign policy often requires various decision-making procedures and implementing authorities, which invites turf battles or other disputes among EU member states and between EU states and EU organizations, such as the Commission and EP (see below). In addition to these dilemmas, economic/financial sanctions are also problematic, as they require decision-making by both the Commission and EU member states acting through the EC and CFSP respectively. These various instruments of policy coordination can be grouped under three general capabilities: diplomatic, economic, and military/policing.

Diplomatic capability

The question of diplomatic capability can be examined in terms of who speaks for the EU, on what subjects, and with what authority and resources. Finding specific answers to these questions has taken much time and energy in the EU, and this capability is still in development despite the Lisbon Treaty reforms. Yet there is little doubt that the EU is perfectly able, though not always willing, to speak with a single voice on an expanding array of subjects relevant to international politics.

General diplomacy

The 1957 Treaty of Rome did not provide for common diplomacy on foreign policy issues, although it did include a minor provision for consultation on problems, such as war, that might impact the functioning of the EC. At the time, EU member states were preoccupied with a debate over whether to include a defence component to European integration. This idea was eventually abandoned in favour of a weak intergovernmental system, European Political Cooperation (EPC). EPC was created in 1970 to facilitate discussions, and if possible joint action, in matters of foreign policy (Nuttall 1992). Later provisions under EPC allowed for a system of joint representation (the 'Troika') involving the immediate past, current, and immediate following holders of the sixth-month rotating EU presidency. By the 1980s, the Commission was a full participant in EPC and could help implement EPC's two main policy tools: declarations and *démarches*. Declarations merely express to the world the EU's opinion on an issue, while *démarches* are formal presentations of the EU's position made to specific representatives of third states and international organizations. Diplomats representing the Commissions or EU member states make dozens if not hundreds of such *démarches* every year to non-EU member states and international organizations, on an increasingly wide range of subjects. The number of EPC declarations made each year has expanded as well since the 1970s to well over 100 by the late 1990s. A final general point is that the EU has the capacity to impose diplomatic sanctions, such as recalling its diplomats or preventing officials from third countries from travelling to the EU. Although the impact of such diplomatic sanctions on outsiders is likely very minimal, they do provide a low-cost way for the EU to signal displeasure in cases where more robust measures cannot be agreed.

While the original EPC framework did not specify any topics for discussion, EPC participants in member states (and eventually in the Commission) gradually defined a number of areas suitable for diplomatic cooperation, such as the Arab–Israeli conflict and relations with the Soviet bloc through what became the Organization for Security and Cooperation in Europe (OSCE). EPC also helped the Community enhance its reputation as a defender of human rights by facilitating its collective condemnation of South Africa's system of apartheid. By the time of the Maastricht Treaty on European Union, EPC was replaced by the CFSP and two new policy instruments were institutionalized in addition to the declarations and *démarches*: CFSP common positions and joint actions. In principle, common positions were to be implemented through the use of coordinated national action, and joint actions were to be implemented through the use of EC instruments, such as aid and sanctions (see below). In practice, however, this distinction was lost as it became more effective to rely on EC procedures and resources rather than intergovernmental coordination among EU member states. One important example of a successful joint action involved the large network of agreements under the single heading of a 'Stability Pact' to stabilize borders in Central and Eastern Europe. Several positions and actions involved security issues as well (see below).

Between the Amsterdam Treaty of 1997 and the Lisbon Treaty of 2009 the EU has bolstered its general diplomatic capability in several ways. First, there is much greater use of EC resources and policy tools in areas beyond traditional foreign economic/ trade policy. Second, there is more coherent and even strategic planning across various EU foreign policy competencies regarding specific problems, such as a certain state/region or policy problem (such as weapons proliferation). This activity takes the form of general plans (such as the European Security Strategy of 2003) and specific policy tools (such as the ENP). Third, the Lisbon Treaty has enhanced the position of High Representative for the CFSP into more of an EU foreign minister role (the High Representative of the Union for Foreign Affairs and Security Policy) to help give the EU/CFSP a single prominent voice. Former NATO Secretary General Javier Solana of Spain was appointed to this position in 1999; he was superseded in December 2009 by Catherine Ashton. Although Solana built the office into a very prominent part of the EU's foreign policy machinery, it is too early to tell whether Ashton will maintain his level of achievement. In early 2010 the signs were not promising. For example, even though the EU now has a new President of the European Council (Herman Van Rompuy) and 'foreign minister' (Ashton), these officials still must compete with the Commission President (José Manuel Barroso) and the head of the state holding of the six-month rotating Presidency of the Council of the EU, which has been retained by the Lisbon Treaty. Finally, the EU also appoints special representatives for areas of important interest, such as the Great Lakes region of Africa, the Middle East, Central/Eastern Europe, the Former Yugoslav Republic of Macedonia, Ethiopia/Eritrea, and Afghanistan.

A related point regarding the general diplomatic activity of the EU, which largely involves the CFSP, is that the CFSP budget is fairly small relative to spending in other areas of external relations: about €281 million for 2010 (up from €63 million for 2004). However, many of the decisions taken in the context of the CFSP, particularly during its early years, have instead been funded through other EU budgetary resources, such as those for development cooperation, human rights, and even agriculture. This trend has continued and it is therefore quite incorrect to examine the CFSP budget alone to judge the EU's overall diplomatic resources and activities.

Cultural diplomacy

Among other foreign policy innovations, the 1991 Maastricht Treaty created a new EC competency for culture in order to both respect the cultural diversity among EU states and promote cross-cultural projects among them. Although most of this activity is inward directed, the cultural competency does include an external relations component. Indirectly, culture-related actors are encouraged to participate in every EU contract competition that involves external relations. Participants have included Southeast Europe; countries of the former Soviet Union; countries of the Mediterranean, South America, and Asia; the African/Caribbean/Pacific (ACP) countries; Canada; Mongolia; and the USA. The EU also participates fully in the cultural activities of the UN Educational, Scientific, and Cultural Organization (UNESCO) and the Council of Europe.

The most prominent policy tool directly involving European cultures is the Culture 2000 programme, which was established for 2000–4 with a total budget of €167 million, followed by a programme for 2007–13 with an even larger budget of €400 million. Unlike previous EU cultural projects, these programmes provide grants to cultural cooperation projects in all artistic and cultural fields. Among other things, a key objective here is to promote the dissemination of art and culture, intercultural dialogue, and knowledge of the history of the European peoples; a secondary goal is to invest culture with a social integration and socio-economic development role. So far, participants from 30 European countries have taken part in these programmes. Of course, just as with foreign policy in general, many EU states retain their own influential mechanisms for promoting their own cultures abroad. Yet here again the EU is a unique regional actor in light of its legally based authority to promote cultural cooperation as part of its broader efforts in global diplomacy.

Economic capability

Although the EU's diplomatic capability has expanded considerably since the creation of EPC, its real strength lies in the economic tools found primarily in the EC. Through the development of this policy domain, and its formal links to the CFSP and other EU activities, the EU has managed to evolve from a relatively inward-focused regional economic organization to a more outward-focused global political actor. Although the EU is still sometimes accused of being an 'economic giant' but a 'political dwarf', its foreign policy capabilities still range far beyond what might be expected of an organization primarily devoted to regional economic integration. In fact, the EU not only regularly asserts its economic interests against other major players, such as the USA, it increasingly attempts to reshape international economic affairs (and thus the international system itself) according to its own standards. This can be seen with EU foreign economic policies regarding issues such as genetically modified foods, privacy rights, competitiveness (or antitrust) policy, intellectual property rights, and others, all of which have provoked transatlantic disputes. In a number of these cases, the EU has been able to act as an economic power in international relations and force the USA (and other actors) to adjust their own policies.

Regarding how the EU implements specific foreign economic policies, this capability involves both 'carrots' and 'sticks', or positive and negative policy tools. Before examining these tools individually, an overview of all EU spending in external relations might be useful. According to official EU sources, the EU's external relations budget seeks to support the objectives of the EU external policy by means of development aid, conflict prevention, human rights programmes, and the CFSP. As Table 8.2 reveals, total EU spending on its major external relations programmes (not including pre-accession aid, trade, or relations with the ACP countries) amounts to over €4 billion a year.

Development aid

The EU's first and perhaps most prominent economic carrot for foreign policy involves its devotion to development aid, particularly among former colonies of EU member states. Africa was the recipient of its first such aid programme, beginning in 1963 in the form of the Yaoundé Convention between the EC and 18 African

TABLE 8.2	The EU's external relations (Title 19) budget appropriations (rounded up to the nearest € million)	

Activity	2010 commitments € million	2008 commitments € million
Administrative expenditures	435	387
Asylum/migration cooperation	53	52
CFSP	281	289
European instrument for democracy and human rights	154	143
Cooperation with industrialized non-member countries	24	24
Crisis response and global threats to security	296	247
European neighbourhood policy and relations with Russia	1,723	1,735
Relations with Latin America	356	348
Relations with Asia, Central Asia, and the Middle East (Iraq, Iran, Yemen)	856	840
Policy strategy and coordination	32	25
TOTAL	€4.2 billion	€4.1 billion

Source: European Commission, *General Budget of the European Union* (Luxembourg: Office for Official Publications of the European Communities 2010)

states. This programme was replaced in 1975 by the Lomé Convention, which also expanded the programme to a total of 46 ACP states. Today Lomé (or, since June 2000, the 'Cotonou Agreement') covers 78 ACP states, making it the largest coherent aid programme for non-members of the EU. It is funded directly by EU states by national contributions to a 'European Development Fund' (EDF) and is not part of the EU budget, so the figures in Table 8.2 do not fully reflect the EU's resources in this area. The most recent financial commitments (covering the period 2008–13) amount to about €22.7 billion in EDF aid for developing countries; this represents a 65 per cent increase over the previous funding cycle. The overall goal for development aid is to reduce and eventually eradicate poverty by supporting sustainable economic, social, and environmental development in all developing countries and regions in a consistent manner. This programme includes their gradual integration into the world economy.

The Organisation for Economic Co-operation and Development (OECD) tracks the aid spending of its Development Assistance Committee (DAC) member states, which include 15 EU member states and the EC itself. As Table 8.3 shows, spending by the EU, including the EC budget and the combined aid of 15 EU member states on the DAC, represents over 60 per cent of all official development assistance (ODA). This proportion has remained above 50 per cent for well over a decade now. The ODA spending by the USA is less than a third of what the EU provides, and the USA's aid as a percentage of GNI—at 0.19 per cent—is one of the lowest of all DAC members. Individually, four of the 15 EU member states on the DAC even manage to exceed the UN target of providing 0.70 per cent of their GNI in development assistance: Denmark, Luxembourg, the Netherlands, and Sweden, which leads the EU in providing 0.98 per cent of its GNI in ODA (2008 figures). In addition, much US foreign aid requires the purchase of US goods or services (such as surplus grain), which may be more costly than local supplies.

In terms of aid recipients, Community ODA is spread across a number of regions, as shown in Table 8.4.

Although these commitments are admirable as a potential source of 'normative power' for the EU (Manners 2002), it must be noted that implementation problems frequently delay or even prevent the delivery of aid. Domestic political circumstances within EU member states and within target countries often complicate the disbursement of funds, especially when national budgets of EU member states are strained. To be fair, however, this problem is not unique to the EU; the entire system of aid delivery from the North to the South, through the OECD, the G7/8, and the UN system itself, can be criticized for lacking sensitivity to the problems of developing countries. Yet the EU does consciously attempt to improve

TABLE 8.3   Official development assistance 2008: OECD DAC members

	US $	as % of GNI
Australia	2.954 billion	0.32
Canada	4.785 billion	0.32
Japan	9.579 billion	0.19
New Zealand	348 million	0.30
Norway	3.963 billion	0.88
Switzerland	2.038 billion	0.42
USA	26.842 billion	0.19
(15) DAC EU member states	70.974 billion	0.43
EC budget	14.757 billion	
TOTAL	136.240 billion	

Source: OECD figures for DAC members 2008

TABLE 8.4	Regional distribution of EC development aid	
		US $
1	Sub-Saharan Africa	4.649 billion
2	Europe	2.254 billion
3	Middle East/North Africa	2.033 billion
4	Latin America/Caribbean	1.099 billion
5	South/Central Asia	1.045 billion
6	Other Asia/Oceania	603 million
7	Unspecified	1.424 billion

Source: OECD *Aid at a Glance* charts for DAC members 2008

its aid delivery through the use of institutionalized frameworks such as Cotonou (Holland 2002).

Humanitarian aid

The EU also spends hundreds of millions of euros a year on general humanitarian aid, primarily through the Humanitarian Aid department of the European Commission (ECHO) within the Commission. This amount of financing, totalling €937 million in 2008 alone, makes the EU the world's largest donor of such aid. ECHO is especially concerned with handling 'forgotten crises' neglected by other donors, as well as unstable post-crisis situations where other donors may be reluctant to get involved. Key examples include aid for crisis management in the Great Lakes region of Africa and in Afghanistan following the US-led war on that country in 2001. In fact, the EU was the largest reconstruction and humanitarian aid donor to Afghanistan, spending about €800 million in the year after the war began and committing a further €1.9 billion for 2002–6 at the January 2002 donor conference in Tokyo. This represented nearly half (44 per cent) of all aid pledges to that country. And, like most other EU foreign policy tools, ECHO spending is also intended to mesh with the EU's broader normative or political goals, such as democracy and human rights.

Trade policy

Finally, a note about trade policy, which is covered in more detail in Chapter 12. Although most efforts here involve breaking down internal barriers to trade and coordinating a common external tariff toward non-member states, the EU also manages to incorporate free trade pacts into many of its most important external relationships. Today the EU, largely through the Commission, increasingly tends to structure its most important foreign policies into broad dialogues or framework agreements, which involve economic, political, and even security dimensions.

These cooperation agreements are made with regions (such as the 'Europe agreements' with Central/Eastern Europe and the 'Euro–Arab Dialogue' in the Middle East) or individual countries (such as the 16 ENP partners, South Africa, Russia, Mexico, and the USA) (see, for example, Allen 1978; Holland 1995; H. Smith 1995; K. Smith 1999; Weber, Smith, and Baun 2007). Trade agreements often form the centrepiece of these dialogues, and this incentive encourages non-EU states to accept other political goals important to Europe, particularly democracy, respect for the rule of law, and human rights (Szymanski and Smith 2005). These arrangements also enable the EU to promote regional integration in other key areas of the world, such as the Middle East, Latin America, and Asia. This capacity to 'package' all EU external policies towards an important outside actor into single comprehensive deals may be far more important for the EU's global power than the implementation of any single policy area alone, although the EU has yet to fully exploit this capability.

In addition, each of these positive measures (financial aid or favourable trade agreements) involves a negative component as well: the EU's ability to stop aid or suspend trade negotiations (at a minimum) or impose diplomatic or economic sanctions, including weapons embargoes (at a maximum). The EU's willingness to use this negative power developed gradually; during the first two decades after the Treaty of Rome economic sanctions were imposed in only two cases: against Rhodesia (1965) and Greece (1967). Following the creation of EPC in 1970, the EU began to impose various sanctions and/or suspend trade negotiations against a number of other countries: Iran, the Soviet Union, Argentina, Poland, Libya, South Africa, Yugoslavia, Iraq, and even one of its own members (Austria). In May 1995 the EU decided to institutionalize the principle of political conditionality with a standard clause incorporated as Article 1 of every framework agreement signed by the EU; it is thus compulsory. Such agreements can be suspended if either side violates this clause, which reads in part: 'Respect for democratic principles and fundamental human rights, as proclaimed by the Universal Declaration of Human Rights, underpins the domestic and external policies of both Parties and constitutes an essential element of this agreement.' The greatly expanded use of sanctions since the 1970s clearly demonstrates the EU's ability to use its formidable economic power for political ends.

Military/policing capability

The question of whether the EU requires its own military force is one of the longest-running, and most divisive, debates in the history of European integration. An initial attempt for a defence capability, the European Defence Community (EDC), failed in 1954, as did subsequent efforts to revive such a plan in the 1960s. Until the Maastricht Treaty, most of Europe's defence capability was coordinated in NATO and, to a much lesser extent, the Western European Union (WEU) and various loose arrangements among smaller groups of EU states (such as the 'Eurocorps').

Following the revolutions in Eastern Europe, the Persian Gulf War, and the disintegration of Yugoslavia, the negotiators of the Maastricht Treaty made the first successful attempt to mention the possibility of an EU defence capability (through a weak link to the WEU). This decision did not lead to any concrete EU–WEU policies through the 1990s, although the WEU did participate in the EU's administration of Mostar. However, a number of CFSP decisions did touch upon security matters, including both common positions (on blinding laser weapons, biological and toxic weapons, the creation of an emergency travel document for EU nationals, and plans for the rescue of EU diplomatic missions) and joint actions (renewal of the Nuclear Non-proliferation Treaty, action against anti-personnel landmines, the Korean Peninsula Energy Development Organization, and controls on dual-use technology).

Following the 1997 Amsterdam Treaty, which mentioned the possibility of an ESDP, the NATO attack on Kosovo, which was largely dominated by US forces, prompted another intra-European debate about the necessity for a military capability independent of NATO. Even before the military action in Kosovo, in 1998 the 'Saint-Malo agreement' between the UK and France paved the way for concrete plans for the ESDP and a merger between the EU and the WEU, long a point of contention for the EU's neutral states (Austria, Ireland, and Sweden). A major focus of the ESDP/CSDP has been the so-called 'Petersberg tasks': humanitarian and rescue missions, peacekeeping, and crisis management, including peacemaking. To support these operations, the ESDP/CSDP comprises three major elements: military, civilian, and crisis management/conflict prevention. These elements are discussed in more detail in Chapter 9; the key point here is that the ESDP/CSDP can now project both military and civilian resources (including land/air/naval forces and policing/judicial officials) to help manage a range of security-related tasks.

Implementation of the ESDP proved difficult during its initial phase (1999–2002) despite several opportunities at the time: Macedonia, Afghanistan, and Iraq. In each case, several EU states suggested sending EU forces to the conflict, yet other EU states opposed joint EU action in favour of national contributions. However, since the 2001 Nice Treaty, which further codified the ESDP plan, the EU has managed to mount a number of ESDP operations. The first official ESDP action involved a contribution to civilian police forces in Bosnia starting in January 2003, taking over from the UN's International Police Task Force. This was soon followed by an ESDP takeover of NATO's military operation in Macedonia; here, 'Operation Concordia' was requested by the government of Macedonia to help implement an internal peace agreement. A third major ESDP deployment was 'Operation Artemis' in the Democratic Republic of Congo (DRC) in 2003; since then the EU has launched an additional 24 ESDP missions for a grand total of 27, involving around 70,000 personnel. However, the question remains whether the ESDP/CSDP will lead to greater EU *defence* cooperation and thus take over some of NATO's basic functions, although the Lisbon Treaty does take the EU further down this path than ever before (see below and also Chapter 9).

Credibility and capability gaps

Does EU foreign policy really matter? Before answering this question, we should first reiterate the highly distinctive nature of the EU's role in world politics. What began as a weak system to manage common coal and iron resources has grown into a stable, highly complex, supranational policy-making system with its own governing institutions, financial resources, diplomatic network, monetary system, and military/police forces. No other regional economic organization has achieved such success in expanding its functions and in linking its foreign economic policies with cooperation in related fields of external relations, such as development policy, human rights, humanitarian aid, environmental policy, security affairs, and defence cooperation. In addition, the EU's growing ability to target these policies toward a single goal in a coherent fashion represents a unique accomplishment in world politics. This achievement alone should lead one to view the EU as an unqualified success in the history of international cooperation, and every assessment of the EU's 'performance' in world politics should acknowledge that fact.

However, we might also ask whether the lofty international ideals expressed by the EU are in fact matched by solid policy successes in the real world of diplomacy. In other words, does the EU's substantial policy cooperation actually produce effective results? Here we must be more critical, and the truth is that numerous gaps between capability and expectations do persist in the EU's conduct of foreign policy (Hill 1993a, 1998a), although these vary across different policy domains and specific initiatives. In terms of policy implementation, the key divide is between the 'low politics' of economic affairs, where the EU is able to wield considerable influence, and the 'high politics' of security/defence affairs, where the EU is still finding its way. In economic affairs, policies over trade in goods and development cooperation are handled almost exclusively at the EU level and national inputs to this process are often decided by various forms of majority voting, not consensus. Trade policy in particular is the foundation of regional economic integration, and here the EU's supranational approach has succeeded far beyond other experiments with regional common markets. If the EU manages to reform its Common Agricultural Policy to make it more compatible with free trade in general and the promotion of economic growth in the developing world in particular, the EU could reap a huge amount of goodwill in the poorer countries of the world, and perhaps even gain a major edge, in both rhetorical and material terms, over the USA.

The area of high politics is more problematic. As security/defence affairs still largely involve consensual decision-making among EU states and a limited role for the Commission (compared with economic policy), common policy initiatives can be limited or even blocked by the actions of just one EU member state. This often happens because of lingering divisions between EU member states over the basic rationale for an EU military force (i.e. whether for defence or humanitarian/peace-keeping tasks), and because of more specific opposition to giving EU institutions an operational role in any security/defence policies. Both of these disputes are further complicated by a need to specify the division of labour between the ESDP/CSDP, NATO, the UN, and other arrangements with non-EU member states (such as 'Contact Groups'). Yet the EU is perfectly aware of its shortcomings in this area, and it continues to take steps to close this gap through the various institutional measures discussed in this chapter and throughout this volume. The EU does attempt to learn from its mistakes and has never rolled back its foreign policy ambitions in the face of a perceived policy failure. As with all previous EU treaty reforms, this process continues with the Lisbon Treaty, which is likely to require several years of struggle within and among EU institutions, officials, and member states before we can fully assess the extent to which this document actually represents real progress—or merely 'business as usual'—in this area.

Despite this ongoing uncertainty regarding the Lisbon reforms, foreign policy cooperation in the EU is now so entrenched that the EU seems to receive more attention when it fails to cooperate than when it acts collectively. We might also recall that even during EPC's early years, when foreign policy cooperation was expressed only in the form of declarations and *démarches*, non-EU states (particularly in the developing world) took note of Europe's attitude toward various global issues. And as EPC/CFSP developed its policy tools in the form of economic aid and sanctions, its influence has broadened (for a detailed examination, see Ginsberg 2001). This has been demonstrated in crisis situations (such as the Falklands

---

BOX 8.1   **Operation Atalanta: the EU as a maritime power?**

The EU's potential to combine military/policing forces with its many other policy tools (i.e. the 'comprehensive approach') could become a unique trademark of its foreign policy. This capacity was recently demonstrated in Operation Atalanta (or EU NAVFOR), an EU-led naval mission to fight piracy off the coast of Somalia. In using military force under a UN mandate to protect the maritime interests of both European and non-European vessels, Atalanta is the first ESDP mission that clearly goes beyond the Petersberg-type humanitarian tasks noted above and makes a direct contribution to EU security interests. Moreover, Atalanta involved coordination between the Commission and the EU Military Staff for the purpose of not just capturing the pirates but also bringing them to justice. While NATO was criticized for having to release the pirates it had captured, the Commission used its financial influence (through the new instrument for stability) to encourage the government of Kenya (and later, that of the Seychelles) to accept and prosecute the pirates captured by EU forces. Given NATO's negative reputation in sub-Saharan Africa and in other less developed parts of the world, it simply could not have achieved such a high degree of voluntary cooperation, under a clear legal mandate, with local authorities. Operation Atalanta is also embedded within a larger EU strategy, the integrated maritime policy of 2007, which deals with a wide range of seaborne or sea-based EU economic and security interests, such as environmental protection, fishing, shipping, illegal immigration, trafficking, terrorism, and now piracy (Germond and Smith 2009).

War), long-range security issues (such as the OSCE process), and in areas where the EU has attempted to institutionalize a long-range policy into a dialogue (such as the Middle East, Eastern/Central Europe, South Africa, and Central America). Moreover, these efforts are also important for cohesion within the EU, in terms of helping to prevent foreign policy disputes from interfering with European economic integration over the past four decades. In this sense EU foreign policy has an important confidence-building function within Europe, while outside the EU it symbolizes Europe's identity in the international system, and (possibly) represents a major alternative to the hegemony of US foreign policy.

The capability-expectations gap is widest in the area of military/defence affairs. The Kosovo operation in particular, where a NATO air force dominated by the USA coerced Yugoslavian President Slobodan Milošević to halt his attacks on ethnic Albanians in that province, helped instigate more detailed plans for the ESDP and EU military forces. Similarly, the EU's highly public split over the Iraq war in 2003 encouraged its member states to push for a formal security strategy statement similar to those produced by the USA. Even with its disunity over Iraq, the EU's internal deliberations challenged the USA to articulate its case for war in the UN and at home. The EU's military operations in Macedonia, the Democratic Republic of the Congo, and beyond also demonstrate that virtually no policy tool is completely off limits in achieving its ambitions. Still, it is questionable whether the new CSDP will ever include the key elements of a true defence pact; although Lisbon does include a 'solidarity clause' to encourage EU states to assist each other against threats, it still lacks a formal security guarantee, a unified command-and-control structure, and a policy on nuclear weapons (see Chapter 9). Lacking these elements, the EU might find it difficult to deter, compel, and defend against major threats in a coherent fashion, although it is clearly starting to cope with some of these issues on a small-scale basis. In the meantime, the EU will continue developing its strengths in the area of long-term conflict prevention with mostly economic tools rather than short-term crisis management with military means.

Conclusion: what kind of power does the EU possess?

The EU's foreign policy capabilities are as complex and varied as those of its 27 member states. Despite its trappings of a supranational superpower, and despite the Lisbon reforms, the EU remains a treaty-based regional organization designed to promote international cooperation primarily through the use of 'soft' power. This means it is subject to the domestic political imperatives of its member states and to broader pressures in international relations, whether at the regional or global level. In the EU, these 'bottom-up' and 'top-down' priorities can easily lead, whether alone or in combination, to incoherence at best and impotence at worst when dealing with a major international problem.

However, when its member states do manage to cooperate the EU's power can be quite formidable, and it can have a clear impact on large international problems and on specific competing actors who might become the 'targets' of EU foreign policy (Ginsberg 2001). It certainly has the power to defend its economic interests through the use of economic instruments such as trade and aid and through negotiations on major global issues with other leading players. This power can be seen most clearly in forums such as the World Trade Organization or in policy areas such as competition (or antitrust), where the Commission has challenged major US firms such as General Electric, Google, and Microsoft. By presenting itself as an alternative to US hegemony, the EU builds upon and reinforces its social democratic normative goals. Here there are considerable risks for the EU, but also potential benefits as well, especially in light of the 2007–9 global economic crisis. In fact, the EU has shown increasing willingness, even before the war with Iraq, to confront the USA on a number of contentious foreign policy issues: national missile defence, the Kyoto Protocol on global warming, the international campaign to ban landmines, the International Criminal Court, the sale of genetically modified foods, the regulation of the financial industry, and many others. This US–EU opposition even extends to domestic policy issues, such as the use of the death penalty and the war on drugs in the USA (Manners 2002).

All of these issues present multiple opportunities for the EU to articulate its own set of global political goals. The EU's capacity to defend these political interests, such as democracy and human rights, has also grown in recent years, especially through the use of specialized framework agreements with key regions. These experiments could go a long way towards the creation of zones of democracy, or at least stability, in many troubled areas of the world. Here again the EU is at odds with the US approach to free trade pacts, which tend to avoid the inclusion of important political elements such as the development of civil society. The next challenge for the EU is to bolster its economic and political goals with an effective military capability, and even here the EU has made considerable progress in just the past few years. The operations in Bosnia, Macedonia, the coast of Somalia, and elsewhere, although small in scale, have proceeded without major complications, and they should help build confidence in the EU's ability to implement the CSDP.

Yet the EU's efforts to speak with a single voice in world politics will continue to face major stresses. The international role of the euro, the ongoing campaign against terrorism, and, most importantly, questions about the next expansion of the EU will provide Europeans with numerous opportunities for either cooperation or discord. These factors inspired the EU's first-ever constitutional convention and the difficult negotiations surrounding the Lisbon Treaty, where foreign policy was just one of many difficult items on a complex agenda. The many institutional reforms devised under this treaty provoked a great deal of controversy and not just in the realm of foreign/security policy, and it is still unclear whether Lisbon represents true progress or merely exchanges one set of problems for another. If past experience is any guide, the true impact of these reforms will remain a mystery until the EU attempts to utilize them on a case-by-case basis. As always, the EU will thus 'learn by doing' and then institutionalize these lessons into its existing system for foreign policy. In doing so, the EU will continue its erratic though progressive development as a unique global actor, helping to shape not only the regional future of Europe but also the international environment on which that future depends.

FURTHER READING

Many of the arguments in this chapter are drawn from M. E. Smith (2003). For general overviews of EU foreign policy-making processes, see Cameron (1999), White (2001), and H. Smith (2002). In addition to the references above, specific EU foreign policy actions are covered in Ginsberg (1989 and 2001), Monar (1998), Youngs (2002), and Wiessala (2002). For a more critical analysis of the EU's foreign policy capabilities, see Zielonka (1998a).

Cameron, F. (1999), *The Foreign and Security Policy of the European Union: Past, Present and Future* (Sheffield: Sheffield Academic Press).

Ginsberg, R. (1989), *Foreign Policy Actions of the European Community: the Politics of Scale* (Boulder, CO: Lynne Rienner).

Ginsberg, R. (2001), *The European Union in International Politics: Baptism by Fire* (Lanham, MD: Rowman & Littlefield).

Monar, J. (ed.) (1998), *The New Transatlantic Agenda and the Future of EU–US Relations* (The Hague: Kluwer).

Smith, H. (2002), *European Union Foreign Policy: What it is and What it does* (London: Pluto Press).

Smith, M. E. (2003), *Europe's Foreign and Security Policy: the Institutionalization of Cooperation* (Cambridge: Cambridge University Press).

Weber, K., Smith, M. E., and Baun, M. (eds) (2007), *Governing Europe's Neighbourhood: Partners or Periphery?* (Manchester: Manchester University Press).

White, B. (2001), *Understanding European Foreign Policy* (Basingstoke: Palgrave Macmillan).

Wiessala, G. (2002), *The European Union and Asian Countries* (London: Sheffield Ac. Press/Continuum).

Youngs, R. (2002), *The European Union and the Promotion of Democracy: Europe's Mediterranean and Asian policies* (Oxford: Oxford University Press).

Zielonka, J. (1998a), *Explaining Euro-Paralysis: Why Europe is Unable to Act in International Politics* (Basingstoke: Palgrave Macmillan).

WEB LINKS

Details of all EU programmes can be found at **http://europa.eu/**, which has links to the international activities of all of the main EU institutions and agencies. Analysis and links to academic materials can be found at **http://www.fornet.info/.** Links listed for other chapters in this volume will in many cases carry information about the implementation of EU activities in specific areas.

PART III

Activities and Impact

CHAPTER 9

The EU's Security and Defence Policy: Towards a Strategic Approach

Jolyon Howorth

▌ Summary

This chapter is concerned with the ways in which, between the late 1990s and the late 2000s, the EU emerged as an increasingly autonomous security and defence actor, albeit one that focused overwhelmingly on overseas missions connected not with expeditionary warfare but with crisis management, conflict prevention, and nation building. It begins by reviewing the theoretical approaches to the emergence of this new policy area, before addressing the factors which drove the Union to tackle new and significant security challenges. It then examines the significance of the EU's overseas interventions, both as a military and as a civilian crisis management entrepreneur. Finally, it assesses the implications of the Lisbon Treaty for the further development of Europe's security and defence policy.

Introduction: EU security and defence in the IR context

The Union's competence in matters of common foreign and security policy shall cover all areas of foreign policy and all questions relating to the Union's security, including the progressive framing of a common defence policy that might lead to a common defence.

(Article 11/1, Lisbon Treaty)

On paper, the terms of the Lisbon Treaty, which entered into force on 1 December 2009, seem clear cut. Foreign policy, security policy, and, eventually, defence policy are to be progressively coordinated and even integrated. Of the 62 amendments to the existing treaties that were introduced by Lisbon, no fewer than 25 concern the Common Foreign and Security Policy (CFSP) and the European Security and Defence Policy (ESDP). All of them are designed to strengthen EU coordination. Indeed under Lisbon, ESDP is rebranded as the Common Security and Defence Policy (CSDP), further underscoring the objective of commonality in the EU's approach to international relations. The major innovations of Lisbon were the creation of two senior EU positions: President of the European Council and High Representative for Foreign Affairs and Security Policy, the latter post doubling up as Vice President of the European Commission. On 19 November 2009, the long-awaited appointments to these positions were announced. The entire world reacted with bewilderment when two virtually unknown politicians, former Belgian Prime Minister Herman Van Rompuy and former Trade Commissioner Catherine Ashton were appointed. Whatever the personal qualities and political competence of these two officials, it seemed that the member states had conspired to select appointees who would present no challenges to the continued exercise of national preferences in foreign and security policy. This ongoing tension between the collective interests of the EU on the international stage and the specific interests of a handful of (essentially large) member states constitutes the great puzzle behind the CFSP and the CSDP. Why did the member states go to the trouble of creating high-profile European positions and pursuing commonality of objectives if they remain determined to exercise their sovereign rights over foreign and security policy?

The notion of a CFSP was first floated in February 1990. The EU, since the early 1970s, had been attempting to generate a common foreign policy—mainly in the guise of European Political Cooperation (EPC) (Nuttall 1992). However, there was not, in the early 1990s, any serious attempt among the then EU12 to coordinate security policy. At the time, defence was considered a zero-sum game against a hostile adversary. Notions of security, a positive sum value whereby one state's security depended on that of its neighbours, were in their infancy. The Western European Union (WEU), which, since its creation in 1955, had lain almost dormant, had been 'reactivated' in the 1980s (Deighton 1997). Its Ministerial Council asserted in October 1987 that 'the construction of an integrated Europe will be incomplete as long as it does not include security and defence'. The main institutions of WEU (the Council and the Secretariat) were relocated in 1992 from London to Brussels to enhance coordination with NATO. Some European states—through the WEU— sought to create a European Security and Defence Identity (ESDI) from inside NATO, but any notion of an autonomous EU role in the field of security (let alone defence) was virtually unthinkable for most of the 1990s.

And yet, beginning in 1999, after the ground-breaking Franco–British summit in Saint-Malo,[1] the EU progressively sought to develop an autonomous capacity in security and even—at least on paper—defence policy. This involved the creation of an entirely new set of Brussels-based institutions and an intensive political quest for greater and more usable EU military and civilian capacity for deployment in over- seas crisis-management missions. Between 2003 and early 2010, the EU engaged in 27 overseas missions (see below). This seemed to portend a revolution in the tra- jectory of CFSP. The aim of this chapter is to place this set of developments not only in the context of changes within the EU and the international arena, but also in the context of thinking about security and defence policies in International Relations more generally. It begins with a review of the ways in which International Rela- tions theory might approach the reality of and the questions raised by ESDP. Next, it explores the continuing tensions in EU security and defence policies in terms of resources and institutions, particularly in the context of tensions between Brussels and the national capitals. It also explores the prospects for operational implementa- tion of an EU security and defence policy. Finally, the chapter turns its attention to the longer term, and to the elaboration of a strategic vision for the EU.

European security and defence in theoretical perspective

The role of the European Union as an international actor on the global stage over the past ten years has arguably become the most widely analysed of all the EU's policy areas. From a situation in the early decades of European integration in which foreign policy was regarded as the poor relation of European studies, we have wit- nessed the burgeoning of a vast international laboratory of research and writing that seeks to shed light on this important policy area (Bickerton *et al.* 2010). Scholars of International Relations on both sides of the Atlantic have begun to focus more closely on what is perceived as a unique type of international actor and behaviour.

Traditional academic theories, of both international relations and Euro- pean integration, have had difficulty in explaining the existence of ESDP (see Chapter 2). Most theorists, from most schools, have long suggested that, whatever other policy areas might one day come under the aegis of European integration, security and defence would not be among them. Indeed, what most theorists over the years have focused on and 'explained' is the *absence* of ESDP (Ojanen 2006, 58–60). In the case of International Relations theory, none of the existing schools seems to come close to explaining the 'ESDP effect'. Structural realism, so long the dominant force in US International Relations theory (Waltz 1979, Mears-heimer 2001), has no convincing explanation for the phenomenon whereby sovereign state actors pool their sovereignty and, apparently ignoring the rules of the Westphalian system, elect to intervene in the internal affairs of neighbouring—or even in some cases quite distant—sovereign countries. For structural realists, state actors alone can engage in security and defence—that is, military—activities, either individually or as part of a military alliance. A body such as the European Union, in this conception, is theoretically incapable of engaging in security and defence policy. Indeed, Mearsheimer (2001, 392–6), gives little credence to European integration and tends to assume, on the contrary, that the EU, as a result of the end of the Cold War, will go 'back to the future' and revert to the type of nationalist rivalry we saw in the 19th and early 20th centuries. ESDP is, in any case, little studied by neorealists for the simple reason that it does not fit into their vision of things. The principal explanation offered for the EU's behaviour—that it is 'balancing' against US dominance (Walt 2005; Posen 2006)—is not hard to refute (Howorth and Menon 2009).

Other scholars from within the realist family tend to see European integration as a standard process of interstate bargaining with a view to furthering the national interests of member states. This school, among scholars of European integration, is known as intergovernmentalism. Stanley Hoffmann argued 40 years ago that integration could only take place in policy areas where state gains constantly outweighed losses. This, he predicted, would not and could not be the case in the area of 'high politics', of which defence was the ultimate example (Hoffmann 1966). This approach was taken to its ultimate theoretical conclusion by Andrew Moravc-sik (1998), who argued that although actors other than just states—social actors of many types—can bargain at the international level for more rational policy coordination, ultimately, key decisions will always be taken by states. Once again, foreign, security, and defence policy is regarded as the prime policy area where coordination (let alone integration) will not happen. That received wisdom also concurred with the findings of the other main school of European integration theory, neo-function-alism, which excluded from its key processes of spillover the entire field of foreign and security policy—considered as the last bastions of sovereignty (Haas 1958). Hanna Ojanen has recently suggested that all these theorists were so focused on finding a reason for the empirical absence of integration in security and defence that they failed to realize that their own theories could in fact explain a phenomenon such as ESDP if they simply jettisoned the distinction between high and low politics (Ojanen 2006, 61). We must therefore look elsewhere than to the realists for an explanation of ESDP.

Neo-liberalism, with its emphasis on trade and economics as the twin pillars of interdependence and soft power (Keohane and Nye 1972, 1977), while offering useful interpretations of the purely civilian actor the EU used to be, has its work cut out trying to explain why the EU has now chosen to don the accoutrements of military power. Neo-liberal approaches are, at one level, geared to explaining the absence of war and the presence of peace in complex multilateral settings. Their focus on soft power is informed by a belief that military instruments have been over-analysed in IR and that the significant aspects of the present are the features of attractiveness and exemplarity of which the EU is a model (Nye 2004). These approaches appear to lend themselves awkwardly to the analysis of ESDP that at first glance seems to run against the grain of neo-liberal theory. On the other hand, supranationalists are also hard put to come to terms with a European reality in which the main actor in their integrationist system—the European Commission—has little more than a bit part to play in ESDP (Stone Sweet *et al.* 2001). As with the realists, neo-liberals and supranationalists have tended to neglect or eschew analysis of this key policy area, whose very existence poses a challenge to the bases of their theoretical approach.

To the extent to which the recent wave of constructivism has addressed these issues, it has been to suggest that international relations can be understood in more value-based or normative terms (rather than as a simple clash of interests), and that in this sense EU security integration is theoretically unproblematic. Where neorealists and neo-liberals insist that states have more or less fixed preferences dictated by unchanging factors such as the international system or national interests, constructivists have insisted that those preferences are in fact socially constructed through forces such as identity, ideas, normative beliefs, and socialization—which are in a state of constant evolution. Initially, constructivists seemed, for the most part, somewhat ill at ease with the EU. Two of the major tomes of constructivist theory (Katzenstein 1996; Wendt 1999) fail even to look at the European Union as such. Constructivism has, since the mid 1990s, succeeded in broadening national concepts of security (Buzan et al. 1998), with the result that there has been some measure of convergence between neorealist and neo-liberal approaches on the one hand and the newer, sociologically derived theories of international relations on the other (S. Smith 2000). The past decade has seen a veritable outpouring of constructivist scholarship on ESDP which has finally begun to offer valuable theoretical insights into this dynamic policy area (Croft 2000; Risse 2002; Keating 2004; Berenskoetter 2005; Tofte 2005; Giegerich 2006; Meyer 2006; Mérand 2008; Cross 2010b).

Two other approaches must be mentioned, even though they relate more to foreign policy than to security and defence policy. The first is the approach that sees a central role for political leaders. There is no question that, at key moments in history, no matter how seemingly compelling may be the constraints of path dependency or systemic forces, individual leaders can make a significant difference. To underestimate the role of Tony Blair in breaking, at Saint-Malo, with 50 years of traditional British refusal to countenance a security and defence role for the EU would be to miss a fundamental element behind ESDP.

The second of these remaining theoretical approaches, one that builds on leader narratives but goes beyond it, is that of foreign policy analysis. This approach concentrates on the wider policy-making and institutional context of decision-making. The domestic and international political contexts within which decision makers function constitute a central element in this approach, as do the complexities and inter-agency tensions behind ultimate security and defence policy making. While this approach has been largely confined to foreign policy (White 2001; Hill 2003), it offers considerable potential for application to security and defence policy (Irondelle 2003; Duke and Ojanen 2006).

In one of the earliest studies of ESDP, I coined the concept of 'supranational intergovernmentalism' (Howorth 2000, 36 and 84). By that I meant the phenomenon whereby a profusion of agencies of intergovernmentalism take root in Brussels and, through dialogue and socialization processes, reaction to 'events', and a host of other dynamics, gradually create a tendency for policy to be influenced, formulated, and even driven, from within that city. This is close to the idea of 'Brusselsization' used by other commentators (Nuttall 2000; Allen 2004). Governments, often against their wishes, are constantly being forced in directions they had not anticipated. European statesmen, even the most powerful, have demonstrated repeatedly that national institutions are inadequate to the task of driving forward a coherent European response to the external environment. New European institutions and agencies have recently popped up like mushrooms to fill the gap (Cross 2010a; Howorth 2010). Policy legacies and preferences—the extent to which long-standing approaches remain valid—are likewise factors to which even the most powerful statesmen have been forced to submit. Above all, discourse—the ability to change preferences by altering actors' perceptions and articulation of the available options—has proven to be an immensely powerful factor in driving forward the ESDP process (Howorth 2004; Schmidt 2008, 2010). Policy preferences which, only a few years previously, would have seemed unimaginable to many a leading actor have in recent years and in this crucial policy area rapidly been embraced, developed, and integrated into the mainstream.

However, the specific trajectory taken by ESDP has been overwhelmingly attributable to 'events'. When, in 1958, the UK Prime Minister was asked by a young journalist what had been the most difficult problem to cope with in his first year in Downing Street, Harold Macmillan replied: 'Events, dear boy! Events!' Since November 1989, and especially since 11 September 2001, 'events' have run ahead of the capacity of politicians and statesmen—even strong ones—to determine their precise course. In the area of security and defence, events have also ridden roughshod over most of the established theories of European integration.

From foreign policy coordination to a European security and defence policy

By the turn of the 21st century, the EU had begun to ride roughshod not only over IR theory, but—more importantly—over its own previous diffidence in the field of security and defence. It now sought to generate a European security and defence policy, which, as it arose from the Saint-Malo declaration of December 1998, explicitly called for the 'capacity for autonomous action, backed up by credible military forces'. The story of ESDP's gestation has often been told (Howorth 2000; Hunter 2002; Quinlan 2002). Two important explanatory sets of variables underlie the EU's move towards assuming a security and defence remit. The first set—exogenous factors—derives from the shifting tectonic plates of the international system in the aftermath of the Cold War. The second set—endogenous factors—derives from the internal dynamics of the European project.

When the Berlin Wall fell on 9 November 1989, it brought down with it a Eurocentric reading of international relations that had been unquestioned since the Treaty of Westphalia in 1648. Europe had been the fulcrum of world history since the 16th century as its internal wars and external expansion dictated the fates of countries and peoples around the globe. The very discipline of IR was built around analysis of European conflicts. All of that came to an end in 1989. For the USA and for much of the rest of the world, the 'dawn of peace in Europe' (Mandelbaum 1996) shifted the continent to the margins of the international radar screen where it featured as little more than a blip. In particular, the focus of policy makers and military planners in Washington DC switched to Asia, to the Gulf, to the Middle East. Europe was simply no longer a problem.

The corollary to this realization was that tens of thousands of US troops were not optimally employed sitting around in bases in Germany preparing for a war that would never happen. The security of the European continent should logically be delivered through Europe's own resources. This was the earliest affirmation of ESDP as a subset of the international system. Why was this so problematic? The biggest difference between US forces and European forces as they emerged from the Cold War derived from geography. The Europeans, dug in along the Iron Curtain, were configured for static line defences, based on mass mobilization of conscripts and reliance on artillery and tanks. The Americans, coming from across the ocean, were configured for distant force projection involving strategic transport facilities, rapid mobility, sophisticated logistics, and 'stand-off' weaponry: in short, for 'force projection'.

The new crisis management missions of the 21st century required specific kinds of assets, especially force projection. The USA possessed them; the Europeans did not. Europe suffered from a 'capabilities gap' (Hill 1993a). While the Europeans discussed ways to convert their lumbering militaries into useful—projectable—instruments, it seemed sensible that they should seek access, through NATO, to available US assets that would allow them—temporarily—to plug the capabilities gaps between their past and their future. This would take the pressure off US forces more urgently needed elsewhere, and would allow EU forces, pending their professionalization and modernization, to take over peacekeeping missions in areas such as the Balkans where the USA had no identifiable interests. Two powerful exogenous forces then combined to galvanize that seriousness of EU purpose: the prospect of US military disengagement from Europe and the re-emergence of insecurity and instability on the EU's periphery.

The second set of explanatory variables behind ESDP stems from the dynamic processes unleashed within the EU itself by the developments of the late 1980s and early 1990s. However long delayed may have been the Union's embrace of 'actorness', there was never any doubt that the European project was a political project. Its fundamental objective was the resolution of a double conundrum: how to bind together the fates of Europe's core nations in a way that would both render intra-European war unthinkable and maximize European influence in the outside world. Indeed, the European project began with this same defence conundrum. The treaties of Dunkirk (1947) and Brussels (1948), and the debates over the European Defence Community (1950–54) all aimed to provide solutions. Failure in those endeavours produced NATO—which removed the issue of European security autonomy from the agenda for almost 40 years. Yet the notion that the European states might one day look to their own interests predated the fall of the Berlin Wall, as nervous European leaders pondered the security dilemmas posed by a US president who, in 1981, first appeared to be contemplating nuclear war and then, in 1986, seemed to have converted to unilateral nuclear disarmament.[2] As European integration gathered speed in the late 1980s, impelled by the Single Market project, by plans for a single currency, and by the Schengen process, the domestic forces behind foreign policy convergence meshed with those suggesting the need for greater security policy autonomy. These dynamics were intensified after the fall of the Berlin Wall by the growing awareness of the strategic challenges posed by enlargement to the countries of Central and Eastern Europe (CEE).

The immediate European security challenge in the 1990s was twofold. Institutionally, it involved rethinking the complex relationship between the European Union itself (which several member states, led by the UK, wished to deny any active involvement in security or defence discussions), the WEU (which was too small and increasingly too diverse in membership to be effective), and NATO (which many analysts were declaring moribund if not obsolete). Militarily, it involved developing a serious EU military capacity that would allow the Union to assume responsibility for crisis management tasks. At a meeting in Petersberg, near Bonn, in June 1992, the WEU had defined three such tasks: 'humanitarian and rescue tasks; peacekeeping tasks; tasks of combat forces in crisis management, including peacemaking'. The latter might even include war fighting such as the Kosovo operation of 1999—that is, 'high-end Petersberg tasks'. The EU's initial attempt to meet these challenges involved using the good offices of the WEU to work with NATO in generating European Combined Joint Task Forces (CJTFs; Terriff 2003, 39–59) drawing on earmarked NATO troops (Howorth and Keeler 2003). This involved the so-called 'Berlin Plus' arrangements (see Box 9.1) whereby the EU could enjoy 'assured access to NATO planning', 'presumed access to NATO assets and capabilities', and a pre-designated Europeans-only chain of command. This awkward process proved unsatisfactory in several ways. First, the WEU was too insignificant a body to be entrusted with the major political responsibility for oversight of European military operations. Second, the unresolved nature of the political relationship between the EU and WEU failed to demonstrate who owned the process. Third, the mechanics of Berlin Plus proved extremely difficult to nail down.

By the spring of 1998 (as Kosovo began to erupt), Tony Blair, whose first year in office had been dominated by domestic politics, began to look seriously into security issues. A group of senior officials in Whitehall, liaising with their opposite numbers in Paris, had come up with a solution to the EU–WEU–NATO 'trilemma' (Howorth 2004). Since the inadequacies of WEU were clearly a large part of the problem, they suggested that that organization, whose 50-year treaty base was up for renewal in 1998, should be scrapped. The EU should take on direct political responsibility for deciding on and overseeing military operations. And, in the hypothesis (which the experience of Kosovo rendered increasingly likely) of an EU-only operation in which the USA wanted no part, it should develop autonomous forces in order to escape dependence on complex borrowing arrangements such as Berlin Plus. That was the Rubicon crossed by Tony Blair at the historic summit meeting with Jacques Chirac in Saint-Malo in December 1998. ESDP was emerging as an increasingly autonomous subset of the international system.

Saint-Malo raised a number of challenges with which the EU collectively and the member states individually have been grappling ever since. The institutional implications were rapidly resolved and the EU successfully implanted in Brussels a raft of new bodies—the High Representative for the CFSP (HR-CFSP: Javier Solana)

BOX 9.1   Berlin Plus

Deriving from a NATO summit in Berlin in June 1996, the 'Berlin Plus' procedures referred to the mechanisms whereby the EU would be able to borrow assets from the USA in order to carry out regional crisis-management missions. They include 'assured access' to NATO operational planning capabilities (essentially the services of SHAPE at Mons); 'presumption of availability' to the EU of NATO capabilities and common assets; and NATO European command options for EU-led operations. It took over four years to reach formal agreement on the details of these arrangements, which remain tightly classified. The resolution of this issue allowed the EU and NATO to make a landmark 'Declaration on ESDP' (16 December 2002), providing a formal basis for a strategic partnership between the two organizations in the area of crisis management and conflict prevention.

and his advisory Policy Unit (PU);[3] the Political and Security Committee comprising ambassadors from each member state's permanent representation in Brussels; the European Union Military Committee (EUMC) formally made up of the Chiefs of the Defence Staff of all member states; and the EU Military Staff (EUMS) comprising some 150 senior officers from across the Union. This institutional nexus, modelled largely on NATO, rapidly demonstrated its ability to work and to work well. In 2010, it was considerably enhanced by the dispositions of the Lisbon Treaty (see below).

More problematic was the resolution of the EU's working relationship with NATO. This involved two interlocking issues. The first was the implementation of the Berlin Plus arrangements for transfer to and from the EU of NATO (meaning US) military assets (see Box 9.1). The second was the involvement in ESDP of non-EU NATO members such as Turkey and Norway. Turkey was particularly disturbed by the ESDP project for two main reasons. First, while Turkey had been fully involved in intra-European security discussions as an associate member of the WEU from 1992, under ESDP it was abruptly excluded. Second, this was all the more unpalatable for the Turks in that most scenarios for armed conflict and crisis management in the European theatre were situated in the south-eastern parts of the continent, which Turkey regarded as its own backyard. In particular, Ankara feared the use of ESDP military assets to intervene in Cyprus in support of Greece. Turkey therefore decided, in spring 2000, to block the entire Berlin Plus process by threatening to veto the transfer to the EU of those indispensable NATO assets without which the EU could hardly embark on any military operation. It took almost three years of high-level negotiations to reach an agreement acceptable both to Ankara and to Athens (Tofte 2003; Haine 2003, 136–40). On 16 December 2002, the EU and NATO issued a 'declaration on ESDP', announcing their strategic partnership and asserting that, while the EU would ensure 'the fullest possible involvement of non-EU European members of NATO within ESDP', NATO, for its part, would guarantee the EU 'assured access to NATO's planning capabilities'. However, in practice, these arrangements have never been made to work and relations between ESDP and NATO remain essentially dysfunctional (Howorth 2009). This did not prevent the EU from embarking on its first military missions in 2003, when ESDP came of age.

European military operations and capacity: the rhetoric and the reality

2003: The EU becomes a 'military' actor

On 31 March 2003, the EU launched its first military operation—a peacekeeping mission in the Former Yugoslav Republic of Macedonia (FYROM). 'Operation

Concordia' deployed 357 troops (from all EU states except Ireland and Denmark, and from 14 additional nations—an average of 13 troops per participating member state) into a small mountainous country and successfully kept the peace between bands of lightly armed irregulars and the Macedonian 'army', which boasts a defence budget less than half that of Luxembourg. This was an operation high in political symbolism and modest in terms of military footprint. By 2010, however, the EU had embarked on a total of 27 missions in 16 countries on three continents (see Table 9.1).[4] It is important to note that, of the 27 missions, only six have involved military force. In the early days of ESDP, when minds were focused on the recent conflict in Kosovo, many analysts assumed that most EU missions would be essentially military in nature. The EU has demonstrated that it can deploy military forces in a variety of guises. The 7,000 peacekeeping troops sent to Bosnia Herzegovina in 2004 constituted the largest force yet deployed, on a major stabilization mission initially undertaken by NATO. The 2,000 combat troops deployed in the Democratic Republic of the Congo (DRC) in 2003, without any NATO backup, demonstrated the EU's ability to fight high-intensity battles against sizeable insurgent forces. The 3,700 troops deployed to protect refugee camps in Chad and the Central African Republic in 2008 demonstrated the EU's ability to overcome major logistical and environmental challenges. The anti-piracy mission off the coast of Somalia has seen the EU take the lead in a major naval operation in which many other countries' warships (including those of NATO) are coordinated from an EU headquarters. But the military 'footprint' of the EU is not the main ESDP narrative.

TABLE 9.1 ESDP missions		
Type of mission	**Number**	**Countries involved**
Police	7	Bosnia Herzegovina (BiH), FYROM/Macedonia (2), Democratic Republic of Congo (2), Palestinian Territories, Afghanistan
Military	6	FYROM, DRC (2), BiH, Chad/CAR, Somalia
Border control	3	Georgia, Gaza, Ukraine/Moldova
Rule of law	3	Georgia, Iraq, Kosovo
Monitoring	3	Yugoslavia, Aceh/Indonesia, Georgia
Security sector reform	2	DRC, Guinea-Bissau
Assistance	2	Sudan, Somalia
Planning	1	Kosovo

Source: ISIS-Europe: http://www.csdpmap.eu/mission.html

The EU and civilian crisis management

The EU's 'mission profile' has emerged as overwhelmingly civilian in nature, with a somewhat rhetorical emphasis on synergies between civilian and military instruments (the 'comprehensive approach'). The typical 'mission' involves the deployment of small numbers of EU personnel—from a handful to around 100—involved in various types of stabilization, reconstruction, and 'nation-building' exercises (Nowak 2006). Missions generally last less than one year. Throughout the 2000s, the EU progressively defined a complex set of objectives in terms of civilian crisis management, seeking to identify and deliver key civilian enablers: planning assumptions and illustrative scenarios for stabilization and reconstruction missions; capabilities inventory; assessment of national contributions and identification of shortfalls. In November 2007, these procedures were refined via a 'civilian headline goal 2010' which set itself ambitious objectives in terms of improving quality, enhancing availability, developing instruments, and achieving synergies with other actors, as well as drawing up a strategic inventory of available personnel—possibly concentrating on recent retirees from the civilian sector who can rapidly be retrained in the appropriate nation-building skills. Moreover, in August 2007, a new structure was established in Brussels, the Civilian Planning and Conduct Capability (CPCC) with 60 staff seconded from the Council and the member states with overall responsibility for the planning and conduct of civilian missions, under a civilian operations commander, the Dutch diplomat Kees Klompenhouwer. The CPCC has been in overall charge of the 15 or so essentially civilian missions undertaken since its inception (ESDP Newsletter 2008).

It took several years before analysts began to assess the reality and the lessons of these civilian missions. When they did, the verdicts varied widely. The most systematic and comprehensive assessment concluded gloomily that 'ten years after the creation of ESDP, most EU missions remain small, lacking in ambition and strategically irrelevant' and that such missions are 'woefully ill prepared to deal with threats to their own security' (Korski and Gowan 2009, 11). The disparities between member-state capacity and willingness to recruit civilian experts (judges, accountants, auditors, customs officials, penitentiary officers, etc.) is enormous and the EU suffers from chaotically divergent recruitment practices. Turf wars between the EU Council and the Commission and cumbersome bureaucratic procedures in Brussels have all exacerbated the problem. However, another comprehensive analysis concluded that 'the EU has managed to make valuable civilian contributions in conflict and post-conflict environments, especially when they are close to Europe. Although the EU has often fallen short of its own goals, especially when it comes to staffing, and has encountered frequent logistical and planning problems, the general trend is positive. Provided that European states continue to invest in developing civilian capabilities, the EU can be expected to make a growing contribution in the years ahead' (Chivvis 2010). These are the key processes to which the editors refer in Chapter 1.

Is the glass half empty or half full? There is little doubt that the general field of 'nation building' is set to expand over the coming decades and that the EU has its work cut out to rationalize and streamline its civilian capacity to meet the growing demand for this type of international expertise (Dobbins 2008). But the challenges are significant. It is far more difficult to deploy overseas policemen, judges, tax lawyers, auditors, customs officers, and the like, all of whom are invariably volunteers. And yet, as the Council fully recognizes, 'there is a continuous need to develop a body of crisis management capabilities and to ensure that the EU uses all available means to respond coherently to the whole spectrum of crisis management tasks, including in a substitution scenario'. General David Leakey noted that, as commander of the EUFOR Althea mission in Bosnia in 2005, 200 auditors were of more use to him in stemming state corruption than 2,000 soldiers.

Spending patterns, defence budgets, and deployability

It should be borne in mind that none of the activities subsumed under 'crisis management intervention' has anything to do with European defence per se. Collective defence remains, in all official discourse, the responsibility of NATO. The EU27, in 2008, nevertheless spent US $301 billion on 'defence', less than half the US defence budget for that year of $696 billion (see Table 9.2). But the EU includes eight of the top 20 national defence budgets in the world, and currently contains the world's number two and three spenders (France and the UK) (see Table 9.3). The collective EU spend is equivalent to the combined defence budgets of the eight next biggest defence spenders (China, Japan, Russia, Saudi Arabia, India, Brazil, South Korea, and Australia: $289,108), which include all the 'rising powers'. And yet the EU gets very little bang for its euros. Out of that colossal overall 'defence' outlay, the EU27 have been attempting to fund 27 separate armies, 23 air forces and 19 navies. Furthermore, just three countries in the EU (France, the UK, and Germany) together account for 60 per cent of the combined EU27 defence budgets; and if Italy is added to the trio, the four nations alone contribute over 70 per cent of the total EU defence expenditure. The only one of the new accession states with any significant military clout is Poland, which has doubled its defence budget in the past five years and ranks (at $10,176 million) in seventh place out of the EU27. Many member states (and not just the smallest ones) are simply free riders. The average 'defence' expenditure of the 15 lowest-spending EU member states (who collectively account for 7.7 per cent of the 'EU budget') comes to just $1,495 million. That is half the defence budget of Vietnam. One might ask exactly what those nation states believe they are buying with their money. In the view of one leading expert, much of the money the EU spends each year on defence 'is simply wasted' (Witney 2008). The case for rationalization is overwhelming and long overdue.

Yet some progress has been made. Emerging out of the Cold War, the first practical necessity for most EU member states was to abolish conscription and organize

TABLE 9.2	EU member states' defence expenditure 2008			
	US $ million	US $ per capita	% of GDP	Forces (000)
USA	696,268	2,290	4.88	1,580
1. France	67,185	1,049	2.35	353
2. UK	60,794	998	2.28	175
3. Germany	46,943	570	1.28	251
4. Italy	30,934	532	1.34	293
5. Spain	19,263	476	1.20	128
6. Netherlands	12,276	738	1.41	47
7. Poland	10,176	264	1.94	100
8. Greece	10,141	946	2.85	157
9. Sweden	6,659	736	1.39	13
10. Belgium	5,551	534	1.10	38
11. Denmark	4,468	815	1.31	27
12. Portugal	3,729	349	1.53	43
13. Finland	3,632	693	1.33	23
14. Austria	3,193	389	0.77	27
15. Czech Republic	3,165	310	1.46	18
16. Romania	3,005	135	1.53	73
17. Hungary	1,869	188	1.22	29
18. Ireland	1,588	382	0.60	10
19. Slovakia	1,477	271	1.55	17
20. Bulgaria	1,315	181	2.62	35
21. Slovenia	834	415	1.53	7
22. Lithuania	547	153	1.16	9
23. Latvia	542	241	1.60	6
24. Cyprus	537	503	2.16	10
25. Estonia	450	344	1.94	5
26. Luxembourg	232	478	0.43	1
27. Malta	49	122	0.60	2
EU27 Total	300,554			
EU27 Average	11,132	475	1.50	70

Source: The Military Balance 2010, 462–8

TABLE 9.3   World military expenditure 2008

	US $ million	US $ per capita	% of GDP
1. USA	696,268	2,290	4.88
2. France	67,185	1,049	2.35
3. UK	60,794	998	2.28
4. China	60,187	45	1.36
5. Germany	46,943	570	1.28
6. Japan	46,044	362	0.93
7. Russia	40,484	288	2.41
8. Saudi Arabia	38,223	1,357	8.15
9. India	31,540	28	2.58
10. Italy	30,934	532	1.34
11. Brazil	26,254	134	1.66
12. South Korea	24,182	500	2.60
13. Australia	22,194	1,056	2.24
14. Canada	19,836	597	1.31
15. Spain	19,263	476	1.20
16. Israel	14,772	2,077	7.41
17. UAE	13,733	2,972	5.09
18. Turkey	13,531	179	1.85
19. Netherlands	12,276	738	1.41
20. Taiwan	10,495	458	2.76
21. Poland	10,176	264	1.94
22. Greece	10,141	946	2.85
NATO	1,021,746	1,149	3.01
NATO Europe	305,642	556	1.65
EU27	290,378	475	1.48
M. E. & N. Africa	110,498	306	4.71
C. & S. Asia	41,167	26	2.42
E. Asia & Australia	191,400	88	1.44
Caribbean & Central/South America	58,048	101	1.35
Sub-Saharan Africa	12,113	15	1.24
Global total	1,547,801	232	2.56

Source: The Military Balance 2010, 462–8

US expenditure ($696,268 million) is more than the combined totals of the remaining 21 powers on this list ($619,187 million) and is not much lower than the rest of the entire world combined ($851,533 million)

professional military forces capable of being usefully deployed (Gilroy and Williams 2007). In 2005, when the first edition of this book was published, of the armed forces of the EU27, only seven were fully professionalized, the others relying to varying extents on conscripts. Since 2005, that picture has changed significantly, albeit through a process of uncoordinated policy transfer. While certain EU member states (Cyprus, Finland, Germany, Greece, Sweden, etc.) continue to retain conscription for specific political-cultural or geostrategic reasons, a further eight have, in recent years, joined the ranks of professional militaries (the Czech Republic, Hungary, Italy, Latvia, Poland, Portugal, Slovakia, and Slovenia). One key objective is *usability*. There are almost 1.9 million European troops 'in uniform' (see Table 9.4). Of that number, about 10 per cent (190,000) are adequately trained for serious peacekeeping missions, and of those probably a maximum of 50,000 could be used for the type of peace*making* operation needed in a conflict such as that in Iraq. Factoring in the requirements of rotation, the number falls to a maximum of 20,000 who, at any given moment, are genuinely usable in serious military missions (Venusberg 2004, 27). In 2007, only 64,134 military personnel from the EU's 27 member states were deployed on missions—a total of 3 per cent of the available manpower (Giegerich and Nicoll 2008). What are the remaining 97 per cent actually *doing*?

In the context of these revealing figures, it seems paradoxical that, as the EU has progressively mounted a range of overseas missions, the need for greater diversity in the Petersberg tasks has been recognized. The Lisbon Treaty, under Article 28B, sees the ESDP missions as henceforth covering: *'joint disarmament operations*, humanitarian and rescue tasks, *military advice and assistance tasks*, *conflict prevention* and peacekeeping tasks, [and] tasks of combat forces undertaken for crisis management, including peacemaking *and post-conflict stabilization'* (expanded Petersberg tasks in italics). While the overall thrust of the EU's intentions with regard to the deployment of forces remains firmly rooted in international crisis management missions, its determination to maintain the ability to engage in high-intensity combat (driven, naturally, by the UK and France, in association with Sweden, the Netherlands, and one or two others) has implications for the future. The European Council's 'Declaration on strengthening capabilities' of 11 December 2008 stated that the EU should develop the capability of mounting a number of missions simultaneously: two major stabilization and reconstruction operations; two rapid response operations of limited duration; an emergency operation for the evacuation of European nationals; a maritime or air surveillance/interdiction mission; a civilian–military humanitarian assistance operation lasting up to 90 days; plus about a dozen ESDP civilian missions of varying formats. The EU has a very long way to go before it can deliver on that ambition, since there are inherent limits to the number and type of missions that can be pursued simultaneously. But the potential certainly exists, even if the political will is often lacking.

TABLE 9.4   European armed forces 2008

	Professional/ Conscript	Army	Navy	Air force	Total	Reserves
Austria	conscript	13,600	–	2,300	27,300*	195,000
Belgium	professional	14,013	1,605	7,203	38,452	2,040
Bulgaria	professional	16,268	3,471	6,706	34,975	302,500
Cyprus	conscript	10,050	[numbers	sub-sumed]	10,050	50,000
Czech Republic	professional	12,656	–	5,276	17,932	–
Denmark	conscript	10,570	3,498	3,446	26,585	53,507
Estonia	conscript	4,200	300	250	4,750	25,000
Finland	conscript	16,000	3,800	2,750	22,600	350,000
France	professional	134,000	43,995	57,600	352,771**	70,300
Germany	conscript	163,962	24,407	62,244	250,613	161,812
Greece	conscript	93,500	20,000	31,500	156,600	237,500
Hungary	professional	10,936	–	5,664	29,450	44,000
Ireland	professional	8,500	1,100	850	10,460	14,875
Italy	professional	108,300	34,000	42,935	293,202***	41,867
Latvia	professional	1,058	587	319	5,745	10,866
Lithuania	professional	7,190	470	950	8,850	6,700
Luxembourg	professional	900	–	[sub-sumed]	900	–
Malta	professional	1,954	[numbers	sub-sumed]	1,954	167
Netherlands	professional	21,825	9,420	9,559	46,882	3,339
Poland	professional	46,400	8,000	17,500	100,000	210,000
Portugal	professional	26,700	10,540	7,100	43,330	210,900
Romania	professional	43,000	7,150	9,700	73,350	45,000
Slovakia	professional	7,322	–	4,190	16,530	–
Slovenia	professional	7,200	–	[sub-sumed]	7,200	–
Spain	professional	79,736	17,943	21,606	128,013	319,000
Sweden	conscript	5,900	2,850	4,300	13,050	200,000
UK	professional	100,290	35,650	39,750	175,690	199,280
EU total					1,897,234	2,753,653
Norway	conscript	7,900	3,550	2,500	24,025	45,250
Turkey	conscript	402,000	48,600	60,000	510,000	378,700
Grand total					2,431,259	3,177,603

Source: The Military Balance 2010, 462–8

*   Austrian 'support forces': 11,400
**   Gendarmerie: 103,376
*** Carabinieri: 107,967

Note: The totals in the penultimate column include various ancillary personnel as well as the three main armed services listed here.

The generation of European military capacity

The Helsinki headline goal (HHG), established at the European Council in Helsinki in December 1999, was conceived as a broad 'force catalogue' from which would be drawn appropriate resources for a range of hypothetical European missions, including the original three levels of Petersberg tasks. The force catalogue (made up entirely of voluntary contributions from the member states) envisaged 60,000 troops, 100 ships, and 400 aircraft, deployable within 60 days and sustainable for one year under the EU flag. Via a series of 'pledging conferences', this pool of resources was intended to be continually refined, deficiencies identified, and remedies discovered. However, while key decisions were taken on certain 'strategic enablers' such as the 'heavy lift' transport aircraft A400-M (itself to become a long-drawn-out and unsatisfactory saga: International Institute for Strategic Studies 2010), many important procurement targets went unfilled. Thus, in the view of the first CEO of the European Defence Agency, ten years after Helsinki, 'procrastination, weak coordination and persistent absenteeism by some member states have hobbled the Union's ability to tackle the real threats to its citizens' security and to make a significant contribution to maintaining international peace' (Witney 2008).

By 2004, it was clear to EU defence chiefs that the Helsinki headline goal was simply not being met. At the European Council on 17 June 2004, a new target—headline goal 2010 (HG 2010)—was adopted. Building on the HHG, the HG 2010 committed the Union 'to be able by 2010 to respond to a crisis with rapid and decisive action applying a fully coherent approach to the whole spectrum of crisis-management operations covered by the Treaty on the European Union'. Interoperability, deployability, and sustainability were at the heart of the project and the member states identified an indicative list of specific milestones within the 2010 horizon, including: the establishment of the European Defence Agency (EDA) by the end of 2004; the implementation of an EU strategic lift joint coordination by 2005; the ability by 2007 to deploy force packages at high readiness broadly based on the EU 'battle-groups' concept; the availability of an EU aircraft carrier group by 2008; and 'appropriate compatibility and network linkage of all communications equipment and assets' by 2010. HG 2010, by focusing on small, rapidly deployable 'battle-group' units of around 2,000 soldiers, capable of high-intensity warfare in desert, jungle, or mountain environments, shifted the objective from quantity to quality (Lindstrom 2007). Although the battle-group formations (many of them multinational) have been drawn up and have since 2007 been on standby for their six-month stint, to date none has been deployed on a single mission. This reflects a serious inability among the EU's member states to agree on sending soldiers into combat missions (Henrion 2010). Most of the HG 2010 targets were met, by and large, but it was clear to analysts that progress was largely being dictated by the slowest ship in the convoy. France determined, under its Presidency of the Union in the second half of 2008, to accelerate matters.

One of the top priorities for the French Presidency was to give a significant boost to European capacity building. Yet, as global financial markets approached meltdown and as entire nations began to face bankruptcy, the time was hardly ideal to persuade EU member states to release any significant additional resources for ESDP. France nevertheless devoted considerable energy to the delivery, by the European Council meeting in December 2008, of a package of agreements on new military and civilian capacity. Several key meetings of the EU defence ministers and several high-level expert seminars were organized, leading to a 'Declaration on strengthening capabilities' adopted by the December 2008 Council. While many of these agreements remained cast in 'letter of intent' mode, clear progress was made towards identifying specific member states' involvement in specific capacity-generating projects. In particular, agreements were reached on improvements in operational force projection, strengthening information gathering and space-based intelligence, increased force protection assets, and strengthening interoperability.

Several new developments were also announced in the defence industrial sector, including support for the EDA's strategy for a 'robust and competitive European defence technological and industrial base (EDTIB)', leading to 'the emergence of world-class transnational European groups' organized around key technologies. While recognizing that this process must be industry led, the December 2008 declaration insisted that member states must facilitate its progression, in particular through the 'preservation of key industrial capabilities in Europe', so as to lessen European dependence on the USA. The Council also proved supportive of the European Commission's so-called 'defence package', promoting intra-Community transfers of defence-related products and the coordination of fully transparent procedures for public defence and security contracts. Particular attention was paid to research and technology, where Europe lags lamentably behind the USA.

One can criticize many aspects of the package of measures, not least on the grounds of wishful thinking (Menon 2009). There are, nevertheless, two reasons for cautious optimism. The first is that the methodology of capacity generation is now generally accepted. All member states, including the large ones, accept the necessity of rationalization, pooling, sharing, and specialization (Maulny and Liberti 2008). Paradoxically, the financial crisis helped drive home this stark reality. Secondly, there is growing recognition in EU capitals of the need to shift from a purely reactive ESDP to a more proactive, strategic vision. The December 2008 Council recognized that over the preceding five years, the threats facing the EU had become 'increasingly complex', that 'we must be ready to shape events [by] becoming more strategic in our thinking', and that this will involve being 'more effective and visible around the world'.[5] The ratification of the Lisbon Treaty in late 2009 introduced a number of potentially significant 'enablers' of an effective CSDP.

Cooperation, planning, and intelligence

Permanent structured cooperation

One important innovation introduced by the Lisbon Treaty will be permanent structured cooperation, a new procedure designed to encourage member states to

---

> **BOX 9.2**   **Permanent structured cooperation**
>
> Under these procedures, member states will:
>
> - cooperate, as from the entry into force of the Treaty of Lisbon, with a view to achieving approved objectives concerning the level of investment expenditure on defence equipment, and regularly review these objectives, in the light of the security environment and of the Union's international responsibilities;
> - bring their defence apparatus into line with each other as far as possible, particularly by harmonizing the identification of their military needs, by pooling, and, where appropriate, specializing their defence means and capabilities, and by encouraging cooperation in the fields of training and logistics;
> - take concrete measures to enhance the availability, interoperability, flexibility, and deployability of their forces, in particular by identifying common objectives regarding the commitment of forces, including possibly reviewing their national decision-making procedures.

---

coordinate their military capacity in a variety of ways. Article 28A/6 calls for the following:

Those Member States whose military capabilities fulfil higher criteria and which have made more binding commitments to one another in this area with a view to the most demanding missions shall establish permanent structured cooperation within the Union framework.

The procedures whereby member states may enter into permanent structured cooperation are laid out in detail both in the main body of the treaty and in a protocol (see Box 9.2).

The most important feature is that the dynamics of this procedure must be as inclusive as possible (Biscop 2008). The bar for membership should not be set impossibly high, for the aim must be to mobilize the maximum capacity of which the EU is capable, drawing on whatever instruments are available from whatever source. But neither must it be set so low that there is no value added. This will be a difficult calculation. ESDP cannot and will not work if it relies massively on a few contributors, with the others as free riders or paymasters. If permanent structured cooperation works as intended, it could have a significant effect on the generation of EU military capacity.

Solidarity clause and mutual assistance clause

Proposals to institute some kind of mutual assistance clause among EU member states have a long and distinguished pedigree, going back to the Brussels Treaty of 1948. The Treaty on European Union (Maastricht) had raised the prospect of 'a common defence policy which might in time lead to a common defence'. During the preparatory work prior to the 2004 constitutional treaty, it was recommended that the treaty introduce both a solidarity clause outlining procedures in the event of a terrorist attack and an 'opt-in' facility whereby those member states who wished to take over the mutual assistance commitments of the WEU Treaty be authorized to do so within the framework of the Union. These measures have been incorporated into the Lisbon Treaty. The 'solidarity clause' (Article 188 R) is in reality little more than a common-sense statement of the obvious: that if a member state is the victim of a terrorist attack or a natural or man-made disaster, the other member states will rally round with whatever means they can muster. Nevertheless, the fact that it is formally included in the treaty is yet further recognition of the extent to which the member states increasingly see their fate as being indivisible.

This is even more significantly stated in the clause on mutual assistance, which goes further than the EU has ever gone before in suggesting that some time, at the end of the road, collective defence is written in the logic of CSDP:

The common security and defence policy shall include the progressive framing of a common Union defence policy. This will lead to a common defence, when the European Council, acting unanimously, so decides. It shall in that case recommend to the Member States the adoption of such a decision in accordance with their respective constitutional requirements.

(Article 28A b/i)

The use of the words 'shall include' and 'will lead' is significant. The EU, at least at discursive level, is explicitly pulling ever more closely together, even in these areas that were once the last (and indeed the first) bastion of sovereignty. But several long-standing problems still need to be resolved.

Operational planning

The absence of any significant EU planning capability and in particular of a dedicated Operational Headquarters (OHQ) has long been seen as a major handicap to the development of ESDP (Biava 2008). France has consistently sought to promote such a facility (in the name of empowering and autonomizing ESDP) and the UK has equally consistently opposed it (arguing that this would 'duplicate' existing planning facilities at NATO, and that ESDP should prioritize civilian planning where it can add value). Germany has hidden behind this stand-off to avoid taking any decision, conscious that it has misgivings about France's military ambitions for the EU and, for its own different reasons, not unsupportive of the UK's somewhat disingenuous support of civilian planning (Simon 2010). The UK, throughout the debate on EU planning arrangements, had always prioritized national headquarters as the most appropriate facility for EU-only operations almost certain to be led by a 'framework' nation, as was the case with the French-led mission in Congo. The model here is the UK's Permanent Joint Headquarters (PJHQ) at Northwood in Middlesex, which has been the OHQ for the anti-piracy operation in the Indian Ocean. French operational planning has always assumed rather more ambitious objectives, explicitly presented as only being achievable at EU level. Most other member states, while supportive of France's logic, are suspicious of her motives and have no wish to confront the UK.

The arrangements agreed upon at the European Council in December 2003 involved a compromise between these approaches that has its own distinctive flavour. An EU cell was established inside NATO ensuring transparency between the two entities in preparation for operations taking place under the Berlin Plus procedures. NATO also established liaison arrangements alongside the EU Military Staff. In addition, an autonomous EU 'civ–mil' planning cell was established within the EUMS, and attached to that cell was a new Operations Centre, 'a sort of embryo of an OHQ that could be activated at the request of the Council on a case-by-case basis' (Simon 2010). However, these arrangements are temporary and voices have continued to be raised for the establishment of a significantly sized OHQ. Luis Simon, in early 2010, put forward a pragmatic compromise between a fully fledged OHQ (SHAPE, for example, has a permanent staff of 3,000) and the embryonic and inadequate cell currently on offer within the EUMS (Simon 2010). Without some progress on this issue, the prospects for further development of CSDP missions look bleak.

Intelligence

Intelligence is a domain that goes to the very core of state sovereignty. Attempts to develop some formal EU intelligence-sharing agency (or even procedures) have been bedevilled with suspicion and mistrust (Muller-Wille 2004). Small states with no intelligence-gathering facilities of their own resent their dependence on the large states. Large EU states that do gather their own national intelligence are reluctant to share it fully either with one another or (still less) with smaller states. The result is that the EU has to make do with whatever scraps of intelligence its member states are prepared to give it. There are two main intelligence operations in the EU, the Situation Centre and the EUMS Intelligence Division. The former involves about 100 analysts from all member states, working 24/7. It feeds intelligence, garnered from agencies around the world, to the Council, via the Political and Security Committee. The Intelligence Division, which is the largest single component of the EUMS, involves several dozen senior officers working in three main branches: Policy, Requirements, and Production, supplying focused intelligence reports for the purposes of operational planning and early warning (Antunes 2007). Smaller units in the Council Secretariat (Policy Unit) and the Commission also carry out limited situation assessment. All these agencies liaise with and receive data from the EU's Satellite Centre in Torrejon, Spain.

In February 2010, it was announced that these activities will progressively be merged into a single unit operating under the aegis of the External Action Service. This is a bold step forward, but for the EU to generate a serious intelligence-gathering facility of its own would require two major developments, neither of which seems likely in the foreseeable future. The first would be for the large member states that enjoy their own intelligence-gathering facilities to agree to pool the results in a comprehensive and transparent way. The second would be for the United Kingdom radically to revise its intimate relationship with US intelligence—the price of which is a US-imposed prohibition from sharing most data with EU partners. For the moment, the EU's intelligence arrangements are relatively satisfactory for the limited purposes of overseas crisis management. But if the EU were to aspire to become a major actor on the world stage, a qualitative leap towards an entirely new intelligence framework and practice would be essential. This leads logically to the question: What are the political ambitions of the EU under CSDP? To what extent, and in what ways, does the EU aspire to the third of our editors' perspectives: the attributes of power?

Political developments and dilemmas

The 2003 European Security Strategy and its sequel

The European Security Strategy (ESS), approved by the European Council on 12 December 2003 (European Council, 2003b), was an initial attempt to think through the broader political objectives behind ESDP. It aimed to harmonize the different views of the member states without falling into lowest-common-denominator rhetoric. The document, entitled 'A secure Europe in a better world', identifies five key threats: terrorism, weapons of mass destruction (WMD), failed states, organized crime, and regional conflicts. It draws attention to the root causes of world poverty and global suffering, and stresses the 'complex' causes behind contemporary international terrorism. It recalls the destabilizing effects of regional conflicts such as Kashmir, the Great Lakes, and the Korean peninsula, all of which feed into the cycle of terrorism, WMD, state failure, and even international criminality. The very complexity of these issues, the document asserts, calls for 'an effective multilateral system leading to a fairer, safer and more united world' (Biscop 2005; Dannreuther and Peterson 2006; Biscop and Andersson 2008).

However, the 2003 document was hardly a statement of the EU's strategic purpose. It focused on responding to security challenges posed by 'new' threats and saw the EU response overwhelmingly in terms of crisis management, international institutions, multilateralism, improved governance, and development aid. It did not attempt to analyse the emerging centres of strategic power in the 21st century world, or to probe the shifting dynamics of an embryonic multipolar system. It made no effort to apprehend the shifts in strategic ambition that were already becoming apparent among a new range of global players (China, India, Brazil, Russia, South Africa), instead comforting itself with the reassuring notion of multiple partnerships.

It failed to ask questions about the essential collective interests of the EU's member states, particularly in terms of their ongoing access to the vital arteries of global trade: sea lanes, strategic choke points, energy pipelines (Rogers 2009b). Although the ESS did note that the EU had become a global player, its gaze rarely rose above its near neighbourhood and hinterland. Above all, in asserting its need for military power, the Union cautiously framed this in terms of regional crisis management and humanitarian intervention rather than in terms of strategic need or direction. The development of crisis management instruments is essential and urgent. But it does not constitute a strategy.

The Lisbon Treaty and its sequel

The squabbling and backbiting between member states, Union agencies, and leading individuals that followed rapidly in the wake of the implementation of Lisbon in early 2010 was a stark reminder that Lisbon as such solved nothing and that, henceforth, the EU's ability to make use of the Lisbon provisions in order to enhance and render effective both CFSP and CSDP would depend on a great deal of give and take between all players, but particularly on a willingness on the part of the member states genuinely to seek out common approaches to international affairs (Menon 2010). This will require bold and imaginative leadership for the following key challenges.

Institutional coherence

The central challenge facing the EU is that of resolving the political/institutional tensions between the Union itself and its member states. The new positions of Council President and HR/VP were intended to help unify CFSP/CSDP discourse and execution. Yet the reality seemed to generate even greater confusion, the two new positions sharing the international limelight not only with the President of the Commission but also with the rotating Presidency, which was maintained for policy areas other than foreign and security policy (Castle 2010; Wielaard 2010; Witney 2010). There had always been a risk that the two new posts would vie with one another for preponderance, given the ambiguities of their respective terms of reference under the treaty. A sensible and effective division of labour must be devised to maximize both the coherence and the specific impact of each of the major agencies. Irrespective of the specific qualifications and performance of the initial incumbents, the position of HR/VP should be considered to be the central forum for policy initiative, that of President of the Council one of coordination and chairmanship, and that of Commission President one of execution and implementation. The development of policy commonality between the 27 member states is unlikely to become total any time soon. But sensible management of the Lisbon instruments can assist significantly in minimizing friction.

External Action Service

Another major challenge is to create a dynamic and effective EU diplomatic service (Avery *et al.* 2007; Crowe 2008). Persuading the member states to commit to this service both high-quality personnel and politico-diplomatic seriousness of purpose will require deft handling of existing foreign policy empires. All players must recognize the crucial significance and high stakes of this new venture and help generate a framework that will prove attractive and indispensable to high-flying young career diplomats from all member states. The early 2010 scramble on the part of the larger member states for leading positions in the new service, as well as the tug of war between the Commission and the Council for preponderance was an unedifying spectacle. Having decided, for perfectly obvious reasons, to establish this service, all parties should strive to make it work. Otherwise, the EU, far from being effective on the world stage, will merely look ridiculous.

Foreign policy coordination

The third challenge will be progressively to use the Lisbon instruments to help the EU acquire genuine leverage over the main security issues of the next five years: Middle East, South Asia, Russia, Africa, climate, development, proliferation. This is not impossible. Member states often claim divergence of interest. But the differences are more of nuance than of real substance. The first task is to break free from an exaggerated concern not to offend the USA. While coordination with Washington is desirable, European interests and values should be *the only criteria* for the elaboration of EU foreign policy (Shapiro and Witney 2009). All member states broadly agree on the shape of an eventual settlement in the Middle East. All member states know that a strategic partnership with Russia requires a tightly unified discourse. European public opinion is supportive of ever greater Europeanization of foreign policy (Eurobarometer 2007). The member states cannot continue to fiddle while Brussels burns.

Development of strategic vision

To date, ESDP has essentially reacted to global events. Policy responses have been largely tactical. In future, the absence of a clear strategic approach will condemn the EU to increasing marginality in international affairs. The Union suffers from major handicaps in the emerging international pecking order: lack of political unity, demographic decline, limited natural resources, geographical exiguity, energy dependency, and colonial baggage. To compensate for these deficiencies, a strategic approach combining means and large ends will be crucial. A number of substantive studies have outlined the institutional, political, and procedural requirements of an EU 'grand strategy' (Biscop 2009; Biscop, Howorth, and Giegerich 2009). Until the Union has a much clearer sense of overall strategic vision, it cannot properly assess the respective value of the many different strategic partnerships it is currently pursuing (USA, Canada, Brazil, China, India, Japan, Mexico, Russia, South Africa). Concrete proposals exist as to how best to achieve this (Grevi and Vasconcelos 2008; Peral 2009; Renard 2009).

Towards a global grand bargain?

In this brave new emerging world, there are really only three likely scenarios for relations between the major actors. Throughout history, power transitions have usually led to war. This is unlikely, though not impossible. The elements of complex interdependence linking the major players are such that the advantages of cooperation over conflict are clear cut. The second scenario, promoted by US liberals, involves an attempt to force the rising powers to slot into the existing international liberal order (Ikenberry 2008). Many Europeans, with their emphasis on 'universal values' and human rights, sympathize with this approach. The problem is that the rising powers will refuse to be co-opted. The third scenario takes full account of the multiplicity of preferences, the diversity of cultural realities and governance systems, the asymmetries and imbalances that still persist between east and west, north and south, rising and declining powers, rich and poor. It calls for a global grand bargain (Hutchings 2009). The global grand bargain will involve a necessary series of trade-offs, some bilateral, some multilateral, between the rising and the declining powers. These trade-offs will be necessary in all major policy areas—governance, security, finance, trade, agriculture, energy, climate, development, proliferation, cultural exchanges, and intellectual property. The EU will need to bargain hard around its key strategic interests, but be prepared to compromise where necessary in order to avoid international collapse. The EU has many assets in this multilateral process. The price of failure will be a return to the jungle—a jungle in which European assets will count for very little.

Conclusion

ESDP/CSDP is a strange political phenomenon. Traditional International Relations theorists have difficulty understanding the acquisition, by a grouping of sovereign nation states in an international subsystem, of the accoutrements of collective decision-making over security and defence policy. Constructivist scholarship helps explain the phenomenon in terms of identity, ideas, and discourse, but it fails to pay due account to the powerful historical forces that have driven the new policy area since the end of the Cold War. Those forces derive from a new strategic focus on the part of the USA and from the internal dynamics issuing from the European integration project itself. They also stem from a new globalized international order in which failed states are more problematic than powerful ones, human security is as significant as state security, underdevelopment in the global south is a source of direct concern for the well-being of the industrialized north, the deployment of naked military power is increasingly perceived as being of limited usefulness, and in which the major challenges concern environmental harmony, regional stabilization, crisis management, conflict prevention, and counter-proliferation. The most appropriate instruments with which to address these challenges are of the 'softer' type—multilateral bargaining, institutional capacity, the forces of international law, civilian nation-building assets, humanitarian relief. The EU possesses these attributes in abundance and, once it begins to think strategically (as opposed to reactively) about its long-term objectives in an emerging multipolar world and the way in which it can deploy its considerable assets to help meet those objectives, it will be able to bring much to the collective table.

The greatest weakness of this new policy area is the tendency of some of the EU's (mainly larger) nation states to believe that they can still make more impact in the 21st century through traditional national assets. Old habits die hard and the sense of national interest is deeply rooted. Yet even the most powerful EU states recognize that the Union is an actor that can multiply their own global influence. They have, sometimes grudgingly but always lucidly, presided over the emergence of a collective security ambition that has seen ever greater importance and impact accrue to 'Brussels'. There is little reason to believe, given the powerful forces of history and 'events', and given the fact that the existing and rising powers are all clear-sighted long-term strategic actors, that the EU member states will reverse the trends of the past quarter century. CSDP is a policy area with a vibrant future.

Notes

1 This summit constitutes the birthplace of ESDP. The text of the Saint-Malo declaration of 4 December 1998 is published, along with other *Core Documents* of ESDP, in Rutten 2001, 8–9.

2 In October 1981, Ronald Reagan, in response to a journalist's question about NATO's plan to deploy a new range of nuclear missiles in Europe, stated that he could imagine fighting a nuclear war in Europe without it spreading to the territories of the superpowers. In 1986, at Reykjavík, he informally agreed with Mikhail Gorbachev to scrap all nuclear weapons from the face of the earth.

3 In fact, the decision to introduce these features was taken at the European Council in Amsterdam (1997).

4 For the most complete analysis of the 21 main ESDP missions, see Grevi, Helly, and Keohane, 2009 (Chapters 4 to 24).

5 Report on the Implementation of the European Security Strategy, Brussels 11 December 2008: http://www.eu-un.europa.eu/documents/en/081211_EU per cent20Security per cent20Strategy.pdf.

FURTHER READING

There has been a huge literature on ESDP/CSDP since the first edition of this book appeared in 2005. The annual volumes of *Core Documents* produced by the EU-ISS, as part of their Chaillot Papers series, are an invaluable source. Eight volumes have been produced to date, the most recent being Chaillot 117 (2009). In addition, in 2009, the EU-ISS produced two major books to mark the tenth anniversary of ESDP: Grevi *et al.* and de Vasconcelos.

Three major overviews, offering quite different perspectives, are to be found in Howorth (2007), Jones (2007) and Mérand (2008). On the European Security Strategy, see Biscop (2005) and Biscop and Andersson (2008). Good constructivist accounts, offering insights into both security culture and institutions are Meyer (2006), Giegerich (2006) and Cross (forthcoming, 2011). On the development of military capacity, see Giegerich and Nicoll (2008).

On the changing international role of the EU as a security actor, see Gänzle and Sens (2007), Tardy (2009), and Gross (2009). A volume of theoretical articles was published as a special issue of the *Journal of Common Market Studies* (Bickerton *et al.* 2010).

Bickerton, C., Irondelle, B., and Menon, A. (2010 forthcoming), 'Introduction: the European Union in International Security', *Journal of Common Market Studies*, 48/4.

Biscop, S. (2005), *The European Security Strategy: a Global Agenda for Positive Power* (Aldershot: Ashgate).

Biscop, S., and Andersson, J. J. (eds) (2008), *The EU and the European Security Strategy* (London: Routledge).

Cross, Mai'a (2011 forthcoming), *Security Integration in the European Union* (Ann Arbor: University of Michigan Press).

De Vasconcelos, A. (ed.) (2009), *What Ambitions for European Defence in 2020?*, 2nd edition (Paris; EU-ISS).

Gänzle, S., and Sens, A. G. (eds) (2007), *The Changing Politics of European Security: Europe Alone* (London: Palgrave).

Giegerich, B. (2006), *European Security and Strategic Culture* (Baden Baden: Nomos).

Giegerich, B., and Nicoll, A. (2008), *European Military Capabilities: Building Armed Forces for Modern Operations* (London: IISS).

Grevi, G., Helly, D., and Keohane, D. (2009), *European Security and Defence Policy: The First Ten Years (1999–2009)* (Paris: EU-ISS).

Gross, E. (2009), *The Europeanization of National Foreign Policy: Continuity and Change in European Crisis Management* (Basingstoke: Palgrave Macmillan).

Howorth, J. (2007; 2nd edition forthcoming in 2011), *Security and Defence Policy in the European Union* (Basingstoke: Palgrave Macmillan).

Jones, S. G. (2007), *The Rise of European Security Cooperation* (Cambridge: Cambridge University Press).

Mérand, F. (2008), *European Defence Policy: Beyond the Nation State* (Oxford: Oxford University Press).

Meyer, C. O. (2006), *The Quest for a European Strategic Culture: Changing Norms on Security and Defence in the European Union* (London: Palgrave).

Tardy, T. (ed.) (2009), *European Security in a Global Context* (London: Routledge).

WEB LINKS

Two key websites give wide access to most aspects of CFSP/CSDP. The European Council site at **http://www.consilium.europa.eu/showPage.aspx?id=1&lang=en** offers links to CSDP itself (**http://www.consilium.europa.eu/showPage.aspx?id=261&lang=en**), to the offices of Herman Van Rompuy (**http://www.european-council.europa.eu/the-president.aspx**) and of Catherine Ashton (**http://www.consilium.europa.eu/show-Page.aspx?id=1847&lang=en**), as well as to the various overseas operations of CSDP.

The website of the European Union Institute for Security Studies is an unparalleled source of analytical materials: **http://www.iss.europa.eu/**.

CHAPTER 10

The External Face of Internal Security

Wyn Rees

▌ Summary

This chapter examines how the development of EU internal security has resulted in implications for external policy. The EU has identified growing security challenges from outside the territory of the member states, in the form of international crime and drug trafficking, terrorism, and illegal immigration. The responses that the EU has made to these challenges, through judicial and police cooperation as well as the creation of common frontiers, has highlighted the interconnectedness between internal and external security. This aspect of security policy is an exemplar of the themes running through this book: namely, the EU as a subsystem of international relations, as part of the processes of international relations, and as a 'power' within the international system.

Introduction

The fact that the EU's internal security policy has developed an external dimension should come as no surprise. All the EU's internal policies have external policy considerations. For example, European Community activities in the areas of agriculture and trade policy were acknowledged to have external ramifications in terms of relationships with third countries. The external aspects of internal security have been slower to emerge than in agriculture or in trade because this domain was not added to the EU's remit until after 1992.

A related factor was its political sensitivity due to the determination by national governments to retain control over this area of sovereignty. Operational powers still reside with nationally based police and domestic security agencies and it has been necessary for the Union to demonstrate that it can 'add value' above the level of its member states in order to justify an increase in its competences. The EU has witnessed the emergence of an internal security regime to which all its countries have subscribed to varying extents. The development of such a regime has had important implications for the rest of Europe. The fact that 'the 27' act in concert in internal security matters serves as a powerful model for the rest of the continent and as a source of attraction.

Two factors have driven the external dimension of the EU's internal security policy. First, the changing perceptions of security among the member states and how these translate into internal security challenges. As the EU has assumed new responsibilities, it has needed to respond to its members' insecurities. The traditional preoccupation with interstate, military security issues has diminished, as has the division between internal and external security. State borders have become more porous in the face of sub-state threats, such as crime and drug trafficking. Terrorism has become de-territorialized and global in nature, as exemplified by groups espousing the ideology of al-Qaeda conducting mass-casualty attacks across Europe, North Africa, and Turkey. The environment of post-Cold War Europe has amplified the risks arising from these new threats. The collapse of former socialist states; the economic turbulence and corresponding social dislocation surrounding the transition to market economies in the east; the opening up of borders and the emergence of inter-ethnic conflicts all served to increase the sense of vulnerability in Western Europe. The dark side of globalization has meant that illegal activities are increasingly being conducted across borders rather than just in the territories of vulnerable states.

EU member states have recognized that just as the threats are transnational, then so must be the responses. Countering illegal immigration, drug trafficking, and cross-border crime requires members to work closely together. This acceptance of interdependence has been reinforced by the contemporary experience of international terrorism. The EU's European Security Strategy (ESS) of 2003 noted that in the face of terrorism, 'no single country is able to tackle today's complex problems on its own' (European Council 2003b). The way of dealing with these threats also presents novel challenges. Internal security agencies must be mobilized to work with other countries, and law-enforcement agencies must find ways to share crucial information.

The second factor has been the exigencies of the EU enlargement process. As the EU has expanded its membership, and as its borders have come up against new neighbours, the Union has recognized the need to externalize its security policy to these other countries. The EU has sought to export its internal security *acquis communautaire* as a cost-effective way of enhancing its own safety. It has sought to achieve this through employing a range of its own instruments and seeking to influence the domestic priorities of states in close proximity to its borders. The extent to which it has been successful has been influenced by 'power' and reputation within its region.

It can be seen from this brief outline that the linkages between internal and external security considerations are strongly related to the key themes of this book. In the first place, the need to reconcile the interests and perceptions of member states and to work though European institutions underlines the notion that the EU remains in many respects a distinct system of international relations in itself. Secondly, the growth and the changing nature of EU security policies intersects with important changes in the broader processes of international relations and in the structure of international law and institutions. Finally, as pointed out above, the EU in extending its influence to neighbouring countries and regions is often to be seen using its significant power resources to create an accommodating European and international order, and can thus be seen as a growing 'power' in the governance of security issues.

This chapter begins by exploring the range of security threats that the EU is seeking to counteract. It proceeds to assess the instruments that the Union has created to combat these threats and the countries with whom the EU has been engaged in order to export its policies. The chapter concludes by analysing some of the obstacles that have stood in the way of the Union externalizing its internal security policies.

Evolving internal security threats

Immigration and refugees

Large-scale immigration has presented a global problem due to the growing ease of cross-border movement. But immigration has presented a particular problem in Europe due to the Schengen agreement that was signed in 1990. The founding members of Schengen—Germany, France, Belgium, the Netherlands, and Luxembourg—agreed to remove their internal borders, in order to facilitate the free movement of goods and people, and replace them with a common external frontier.

Measures to control immigration were agreed in the Dublin Convention of 1990 that laid down common standards for processing asylum applications across the territory of the member states. Each member had the obligation to test the eligibility of an asylum seeker if they were the first territory on which the applicant arrived.

Concern over immigration into Europe is not a new phenomenon. Spain and Italy, for example, have long experienced migration pressures from the poor states of North Africa. Migrants have been attracted by high Western standards of living but have generated anxiety among the recipient states due to the potential imbalances caused to their labour markets. The problem was compounded by the policy of European governments since the 1970s of refusing to accept migrants for reasons other than family unity. The end of the Cold War raised fears that mass migration pressures would shift from the south to the east and that waves of economic migrants would emerge from Eastern Europe. In the face of these fears the EU has struggled to find mechanisms by which to share the burden of immigration among the member states.

In recent years illegal immigration has presented a particular problem from the shores of the Mediterranean. Two of the principal migrant routes have led to boats full of illegal immigrants arriving in the islands of the Canaries and into Lampedusa and Malta from North and West Africa (Boyes 2010, 52–3). Once a route into the EU is policed more assiduously, the migrants shift to other, more hazardous, routes in order to obtain entry. Keukeleire and MacNaughton estimate that the numbers of African migrants landing in the Canaries increased sixfold between 2005 and 2006 (Keukeleire and MacNaughton 2008, 231). People either enter illegally into the Schengen space or overstay visas that have expired. The European Security Strategy went so far as to identify illegal immigration as one of the foremost threats to the EU (European Council 2003a).

Asylum applications to West European countries grew rapidly in the 1990s and contributed to a perception of a crisis. Germany, for example, bore the main brunt of the refugee flows from conflicts in Bosnia and Kosovo in the mid and late 1990s. Legitimate asylum applications increased as people sought to flee countries in turmoil, such as Afghanistan, Iraq, and Sri Lanka. But there was a corresponding increase in illegitimate asylum applications as people claimed they were fleeing from persecution when in fact their motivation was to improve their economic circumstances. In 2008, the EU accepted 74,360 asylum applications but rejected 204,800 (Boyes 2010, 53). Returning failed asylum seekers to their home countries has been difficult because of the lengthy appeals processes in European countries and the risk that individuals will abscond before the orders of the courts can be carried out.

In addition to the intra-European trafficking that takes place, human beings are trafficked from outside the territories of the member states. These tend to be people seeking to escape from lives of extreme poverty and deprivation elsewhere in the world, and who place themselves in the hands of gangs that will smuggle them into Western Europe. Sometimes women and children are trafficked against their will

and sold into prostitution or forced labour—a form of modern-day slavery. An esti-
mated 100,000 women are the victims of trafficking into the EU each year (Council
of the European Union 2005a). Europol identifies Bulgarian, Romanian, and Nigen-
ian organized crime groups as particularly active in this form of activity (Europol
2009, 21).

Transnational organized crime

One of the foremost post-Cold War European security concerns has been the
increase in crime carried out by organized gangs, some of whom are based outside the continent. Schengen has provided an added incentive as once the common
external frontier is breached, then there are no other obstacles to prevent criminal
groups from moving throughout the European space. Europol divides the Union
into five predominant criminal hubs. The first is the north-west Europe hub centred on the Netherlands and Belgium but extending its activities into Germany, the
UK, and France. This area draws on criminal activity from the Middle East region
among others. The second is the north-east hub, which draws upon criminal activity permeating the EU from the Russian Federation and Kaliningrad. The third
is the southern hub that is focused on Italian organized crime. The fourth is the
south-west hub based upon Spain and Portugal that draws on criminal activity from
North and West Africa. Finally, there is the south-east hub, with links to Romania,
Bulgaria, and the Balkans (Europol 2009, 13–14).

The types of interstate crimes that are conducted are diverse in nature. They
include commodity crimes, such as those involving cars or cigarettes, which are
frequently stolen in the West and then smuggled to neighbouring regions to be sold
on the black market, or smuggled weapons or sensitive materials. Certain crimes
are associated with organized groups due to the scale of the activity and the infrastructure and sophistication required to execute them. Crime groups may conduct
several types of criminal activity: for example, drug running and people trafficking, whilst the large profits generated are likely to result in involvement in money-
laundering operations. Those countries at the eastern edge of the EU have felt most
vulnerable to the rise of organized crime groups penetrating from Central and Eastern Europe as well as the disintegration of the states of the former Yugoslavia. It
has been difficult to determine how much of the perceived rise in organized crime
activity has resulted from groups extending their activities from east to west compared with domestically grown groups in Europe operating beyond their borders.

Drug trafficking is the foremost activity of cross-border crime groups. Heroin is
smuggled to the EU from the principal producer states of Afghanistan, Myanmar,
Pakistan, and Laos. It follows two main routes into Western cities: one through the
Balkans, via Pakistan, Iran, and Turkey, and the second through the Russian Federation and on to central and northern European countries (European Monitoring Centre for Drugs and Drug Addiction 2009, 71). Cocaine is derived from the
Andean states of Colombia, Bolivia, and Peru, and is trafficked into Europe by a

variety of routes. The European Monitoring Centre reports that seizures of cocaine have risen significantly since 2003 and use of the drug is particularly prevalent in the UK and Spain (European Monitoring Centre for Drugs and Drug Addiction 2009, 61). Cannabis is cultivated in many European countries but the bulk of it is smuggled into Europe from Morocco, South Africa, Nigeria, and India (Picarelli 2008, 457). Most synthetic drugs, such as amphetamines and ecstacy, are produced indigenously within EU countries but the bulk of methamphetamines are smuggled in from South-east Asia and North America.

The EU has responded energetically to the problem posed by drug trafficking, not least because it still accounts for the majority of information requests submitted to the European Police Office (Europol). Not only has the EU created cooperative structures, such as the Mutual Assistance Group and the Comité Européen de la Lutte Anti-Drogue (CELAD), it has also undertaken regular four-year action plans, starting in 1990, in order to establish EU-wide priorities in combating the problem.

Money laundering is a major form of criminality that results from the activities of organized crime groups and drug traffickers. Laundering is a process by which criminally derived funds are passed through the international financial system in order to render them as legitimate. Money can be invested in high-value items, in businesses and property as well as in financial markets. The unpredictable flows of money can present real difficulties for legitimate businesses and for regulatory oversight. The size and complexity of the EU Single Market have made it vulnerable to infiltration by large amounts of illegitimately derived money.

International terrorism

Europe has been no stranger to the problem of terrorism in the post-war period. But the terrorism that it experienced in the past was predominantly ethno-nationalist or radical left in nature. These movements concentrated their activities within the boundaries of states and their attacks were usually limited in nature, inflicting small numbers of casualties and seeking maximum public attention. Terrorist groups were eager to avoid alienating the political support of those who sympathized with their cause. As a result, there was relatively little need for cooperation between European governments and what sharing of information did occur was orchestrated through the intergovernmental TREVI forum (Terrorisme, Radicalisme, Extrémisme et Violence Internationale), founded in 1976, that served as a bi-annual meeting for interior ministers.

The 9/11 attacks by al-Qaeda on New York and Washington shattered these relatively comfortable assumptions and ushered in a wave of terrorism that appeared far more dangerous (*The 9/11 Commission Report* 2004). This 'new' terrorism, fuelled by religious extremism, is dedicated to simultaneous mass-casualty attacks (Hoffman 1998; Lesser *et al.* 1999). The terrorist attack on Madrid in March 2004 in which over 200 people died confirmed that Europe was equally vulnerable to the contemporary wave of atrocities. The US government emphasized the linkages that such groups could have to anti-Western states that were seeking to develop weapons of mass destruction (WMD). This raised the nightmare scenario of catastrophic terrorism in which a group might be able to use some form of WMD against a Western country.

The new terrorism also blurred the boundary between domestic and international threats. One fear that emerged was that illegal residents in European countries could perpetrate acts of violence, thereby creating a linkage between immigration and terrorism (Huysmans 2006, 64). The other fear was that resident Muslim populations in European countries could become the focus of radicalization. The primary danger was perceived to derive from second and third generations of young people, alienated within their host societies, willing to use acts of terror to strike back at them. The two bomb plots in London in July 2005 illustrated this phenomenon. Yet the radicalization of such individuals can be conducted over the internet by groups in countries such as Pakistan, Yemen, and Iraq. With the al-Qaeda ideology being franchised to groups all over the world, it has become harder to draw a distinction between internal and external sources of threat.

The 9/11 attacks brought home to Europe the virulence of the threat from Islamist extremism. There have been regular trials in member states of individuals under national terrorism legislation (see Table 10.1). The immediate response from

TABLE 10.1	Number of individuals tried between 2006 and 2008 for terrorism charges in EU member states		
	2006	**2007**	**2008**
Belgium	24	5	12
Denmark	0	11	16
France	21	54	75
Germany	16	7	10
Greece	0	17	0
Ireland	0	6	9
Italy	0	47	25
Spain	154	231	141
Sweden	3	0	1
Netherlands	20	8	12
UK	3	33	59
Total	241	419	360

Source: TE-SAT 2009 EU Terrorism Situation Report, Europol, The Hague; http://www.europol.europa.eu/publications/EU_Terrorism_Situation_and_Trend_TE-SAT/TESAT2009.pdf

the EU took the form of a European action plan with over 200 counter-terrorism measures. In the light of the bombings in Europe in 2004 and 2005, the action plan was revised and then subsequently replaced by a counter-terrorism strategy. In this strategy, the EU focused on four principal areas: protecting citizens from the threat of attack; disrupting terrorist networks; minimizing the damage from attacks; and preventing people being recruited by extremist organizations (Nilsson 2006, 75). The strategy has helped to set a framework in which counter-terrorism cooperation has grown. It has also been successful in shaping particular policy priorities, for example in countering radicalization and in protecting European critical infrastructure that falls outside the remit of national governments.

The instruments for combating security challenges

Nation states are poorly equipped to counter the sorts of transnational security threats posed by organized criminals and terrorist organizations. Sovereign powers over a specified territory, national legal frameworks and domestic security agencies act as powerful constraints in the face of security challenges that move fluidly across state borders. Securing prosecutions, when criminal activity may have been carried out across several legal jurisdictions, demands the admissibility of evidence between national judicial systems as well as the willingness of courts to respect judicial decisions from neighbouring countries. Police forces and domestic security agencies need to learn new patterns of sharing information across boundaries and must build up trust in the practices of their neighbours. In contrast to transnational criminals, states are relatively inflexible agents that must engineer cooperation and remain constrained by legal processes. States are limited by the means that police forces can employ to obtain evidence and have to draft special legislation to counter organized forms of criminal activity.

These assumptions have underpinned efforts to use the European Union to coordinate the internal security efforts of its members. National and EU-level responses have developed in concert, with member states weighing up what additional benefit the Union can provide. The development of a common internal security regime is unparalleled among states within the international system. No other group of countries treats its own domestic security arrangements as interdependent and allows the encroachment of an external actor upon core areas of sovereign control. This regime is one of the EU's contributions to the creation of a European order that acts as a model to third countries within its region. The influence that the EU wields means that other countries must interact with it and are drawn into a web of cooperative relationships.

This is not to suggest that the emergence of the Union as an internal security actor has been a straightforward process. Some areas are more integrated than others and the process of granting additional competencies to the Union has waxed and waned. Whilst a common set of policies has developed in the field of immigration and asylum, counter-terrorism policy remains the preserve of member states. For instance, the creation of the Group of Six countries in counter-terrorism—the UK, France, Spain, Germany, Italy, and Poland—was indicative of the desire to preserve intergovernmental cooperation among the leading European states rather than allow the EU to become intimately involved.

The Justice and Home Affairs (JHA; subsequently changed to Justice, Liberty and Security) portfolio, or 'third pillar' of the Treaty on European Union (TEU), has been one of the fastest growth areas of EU activity. In the first part of the 1990s, relatively little development was evident in the JHA domain and the external dimension was barely acknowledged. But two major changes occurred that altered the situation fundamentally. The first was the Treaty of Amsterdam (ToA), which transformed the relationship between the member states and the EU in relation to internal security. The ToA 'communitarized' key aspects of the JHA portfolio that had hitherto been intergovernmental in nature. Matters relating to asylum, immigration, and external border controls were removed from former Title VI, TEU and placed in the first pillar, under a new Title IV. This meant that Community instruments could be employed after a transitional period of five years. Certain intergovernmental features were retained in Title IV, such as a shared right of initiative between the European Commission and the member states as well as limited powers for the European Parliament. Policing and judicial cooperation issues were not communitarized in the treaty, as they were considered too sensitive, and they were kept within Title VI, TEU. The Amsterdam Treaty left the EU with a mixed intergovernmental and communitarized internal security regime, but one in which there was momentum towards closer integration.

The ToA incorporated the Schengen Convention into the European Union. At a stroke this simplified the framework for EU internal security by ending the artificial split between matters relating to immigration, asylum, and visas from the vital issue of the control of borders. Three states, the UK, Ireland, and Denmark, chose to remain outside the Schengen provisions. Nevertheless, Schengen brought a vital ingredient in the Union's relationship with neighbouring countries inside the EU *acquis*. For example, Norway and Iceland had previously negotiated special border arrangements with the Schengen members in order to ensure that their citizens did not need to apply for visas to visit the EU. With the signing of the ToA, both of these countries had to draw up an agreement with the EU to preserve their special status.

The ToA also made it possible for the Union to conclude agreements with third countries on policing and judicial issues. In the TEU, provision had not been made for the EU to make treaty agreements with other countries on JHA matters (Neuwahl 1998). Changing this enabled the EU to play a full part in the drawing up of such agreements as the December 2000 UN Convention on Transnational Organized Crime. This enhancement of the EU's capabilities made it even more important that the EU ensure coherence in its policy responses. With the instruments for countering internal security challenges ranging across all of its three pillars, it became imperative for the EU to coordinate its actions more effectively. These concerns were echoed in the Hague Programme that sought to elaborate an agenda for EU internal security in the period 2005–10. It declared the need to pursue 'the coordination and coherence between the internal and the external (security) dimensions' (Council of the European Union 2005a).

The other major change was the special European Council meeting at Tampere in October 1999. This was designed to translate the ideas in the Amsterdam Treaty on JHA into an operational programme. Significant steps forward were achieved in relation to the commitment, in Section D, to build 'Stronger External Relations in the Field of JHA' (European Council 1999c). This was an important acknowledgement that an external dimension existed in relation to internal security. Working closely with third countries to tackle international terrorism, transnational organized crime, and drug trafficking would be a 'key element for ... success' (European Council 1999c). The Treaty of Amsterdam created an 'Area of Freedom, Security and Justice' (AFSJ) and asserted the aim of 'provid[ing] citizens with a high level of safety' (Title VI, Article 29, Treaty on European Union). Henceforth, it would be necessary to reconcile the contending objectives of maintaining a secure internal environment with the principle of assuring the free movement of people. This raised important issues concerning the potential linkage between crime and immigration and led the EU to focus its attention on controlling illegal immigration from the states acceding to the Union as well as from the Balkans.

The Amsterdam Treaty and the Special European Council at Tampere provided the bases for the enhancement of the EU's internal security efforts. Four organizations have provided the cutting edge of these activities: Europol, the European Judicial Office (Eurojust), the European Monitoring Centre for Drugs and Drug Addiction (EMCDAA), and the European Agency for the Management of Operational Cooperation at the External Borders of the Member States of the European Union (Frontex). These organizations have taken a lead in internal security policy and they have been at the forefront of the EU's efforts to develop cooperation with a range of third countries through the sharing of information and the adoption by neighbours of EU best practice (See Box 10.1.).

In addition to its dedicated security organizations, the EU has sought to construct interoperable databases that can assist the workings of national law enforcement and immigration agencies. For example, Eurodac has been developed as a database of fingerprints of asylum seekers; the Visa Information System (VIS) keeps records of visa applications; whilst the Schengen Information System (SIS) and SIS II keep records on stolen vehicles and other types of commodity crime. The linking together of these issues has resulted in the conflating and amplifying of threat perceptions. In numerous EU documents, problems as diverse as terrorism and bogus asylum applications are grouped together as part of the new security challenges. Illegal immigration is put together with transnational crime even though they are self-evidently dissimilar problems. In this way, security challenges and their

---

BOX 10.1 **Key European institutions in justice and home affairs**

Europol

Europol was created under Article K1.9 of the Treaty on European Union (1992) as the European Drugs Unit and became operational in 1994. Based in The Hague, it comprises liaison officers from the EU member states who are seconded to the organization. It evolved into Europol in July 1999 and its remit was extended to include the sharing of law enforcement information relating to all forms of organized criminal activity. The willingness of states to share information with Europol has varied and it has no operational power to conduct arrests, relying instead upon national law enforcement agencies. In 2006 it was agreed to replace Europol's situation reports with annual threat analyses. In 2010 Europol became an EU agency, with direct funding, and its personnel rose to 620.

Source: http://www.europol.europa.eu

Eurojust

Eurojust is a body of magistrates and judges from the member states that specialize in complex, cross-border prosecutions cases such as terrorism, drugs, and people trafficking. It was set up in February 2002 under Council Decision 2002/187/JHA after having existed in temporary form as pro-Eurojust since 2000. Eurojust has developed liaison arrangements with third countries and assists in cases of extradition or where multi-state criminal cases are involved. In July 2008 its operational capabilities were enhanced in a 'New Council Decision on Strengthening Eurojust'.

Source: http://www.eurojust.europa.eu

The European Monitoring Centre for Drugs and Drug Addiction

The European Monitoring Centre for Drugs and Drug Addiction (EMCDDA), located in Lisbon, has been operational since 1995. It has taken the form of a decentralized agency of the European Union. It draws up annual reports on the problem of illegal drugs within the European Union and relies on inputs from some 30 national monitoring centres. EMCDDA shares information with third countries on drug issues and seeks to develop patterns of cooperation on counteracting the problem of drug misuse.

Source: http://www.emcdda.europa.eu

Frontex

The European Agency for the Management of Operational Cooperation at the External Borders of the Member States of the European Union (Frontex) was proposed in 2001 at the Laeken European Council and became operational in October 2005. Located in Warsaw, its purpose has been to provide an operational capability to manage the Union's external borders and to work with countries adjacent to the EU. Frontex has developed patterns of cooperation with other countries, including the sharing of information, technology, and the training of personnel. It has conducted a monitoring mission on the Ukrainian–Moldovan border and it has undertaken patrols in the Mediterranean and the Atlantic. Sea patrols have been designed to assist countries that have been suffering an influx of illegal migrants, both to manage the flow of human beings and to assist with their welfare.

Source: http://www.frontex.europa.eu

responses become interwoven in EU thinking. The result has been the actuation of an all-embracing security discourse that fails to differentiate between problems and tends to justify blanket responses.

EU policies towards third countries

Central and East European countries

The EU has recognized that its own security interests are best served if it is surrounded by democratic and well-governed states. If it can promote the transfer of its own rules and norms to its neighbours, and interdict and disrupt criminal activity before it reaches the territory of the Union, then the EU can use them to ensure its own internal security. Rather than attempt to protect a 'fortress Europe' from a set of external threats, the EU has sought to co-opt its neighbours into implementing its own security agenda.

The Union has been eager to communicate its intentions to third countries through a policy of active and sustained engagement. The EU developed a range of positive and negative inducements in order to encourage third countries to comply and the Council made explicit that its relationship with them would be 'positively affected' by their attitude towards cooperation in JHA matters (Council of the European Union 2005a). Lavenex has described this as 'a form of external governance in which internal and foreign policy goals come together' (Lavenex 2004, 681). The main mechanism that the EU has been able to use to secure compliance from Central and East European countries (CEECs) and states in the western Balkans has been through its process of enlargement. The EU has linked overtly the implementation of its *acquis communautaire* with the prospect of accession. This practice of conditionality has enabled the EU to impose its model of internal security upon countries seeking membership and subject them to regular monitoring. Schimmelfennig and Sedelmeier see this occurring either through a rational actor model of compliance improving the prospects of accession, or 'models of appropriateness' in which candidate states seek to emulate the policy norms of the EU (Schimmelfennig and Sedelmeier 2004, 671).

The CEECs have been of particular importance in the process of constructing the JHA regime. As states situated on the eastern border of the EU, they occupy zones through which organized criminals, illegal drugs, and economic migrants would be expected to pass en route to the territory of member states. The EU feared that it would import the crime and immigration problems not only from the CEECs when they become members, but also their eastern neighbours, such as Belarus, Ukraine, the Russian enclave of Kaliningrad, and the Balkans. Once the applicant states became members, they would serve as the EU's 'front line'. Prior to joining the EU in May 2004, Central and East European countries were expected to implement the Union's pre-accession pact on organized crime. This aimed to provide the accession states with specialized knowledge that had been amassed within the EU, to assist with training and equipment, and to draw the newcomers into a cooperative relationship with Europol. Furthermore, the Pact agreed to draw up an annual strategy document, reached between the existing and future members that would be focused on combating the threat from transnational crime. This linked the accession states with the EU's own action plan on organized crime that had been endorsed by the June 1997 Amsterdam European Council and its regular action plans on drugs.

The challenge for the CEECs of adopting the EU *acquis* in JHA, including the Schengen provisions, was considerable. The law enforcement and judicial officers in these countries experienced low salaries and relatively low social status, due to the hangover of their association in the public mind with unpopular former regimes. There were shortages of experienced judges and senior officials because of the dismissal of figures linked to the old regimes. Since the end of the Cold War, the countries had been subjected to a process of rapid transformation whilst simultaneously suffering grave financial pressures. Raising their internal security standards to those of the rich Western democracies resulted in considerable burdens. The CEECs were expected to amend their domestic legislation, create new administrative organs, judicial structures, and liaison bodies to interface with EU agencies, retrain their police and border guards, and adopt new practices in relation to judicial and customs services. They had to purchase sophisticated equipment, such as heat sensors and database management systems for border areas that squeezed limited budgets (Storbeck 2003, 287). The added burden for the CEECs was that the JHA *acquis* presented a moving target.

In order to assist the applicant states in adopting the JHA *acquis*, the EU brought to bear all its pre-accession instruments: the Structured Dialogue, the Europe agreements and the funding of technical assistance through the Phare (Pologne-Hongrie aide à la reconstruction économique), Grotius, Oisin and Falcone programmes (Mitsilegas, Monar, and Rees 2003, 150). Both the European Commission and the EU member states expressed concerns over the ability of the CEECs to attain the necessary standards. Two evaluation processes were initiated: the 'collective evaluation' in 1998 by the Council and the other by the Commission. Even after accession, the EU imposed transition arrangements on the new members that led to resentment of perceived second-class status. As in the earlier cases of Greece and Italy, the new members had to wait before they were regarded as 'Schengen mature'.

In relation to the western Balkans, the EU's focus of attention has been twofold. One has been to counter the problem of illegal migration because of the region's role as a trafficking route. The other has been to act against the threat of transnational organized crime, especially the smuggling of various commodities, ranging from contraband cigarettes to drugs and small arms. The conflicts in Bosnia and Kosovo in the mid and late 1990s, and the accompanying instability in Albania and Macedonia, resulted in wide-scale dislocation that criminal gangs have been quick to exploit. The Union has carried forward its security priorities into the post-conflict peacekeeping and reconstruction efforts in which it has been engaged in the region. For example, the EUFOR Althea mission in Bosnia Herzegovina contained an explicit component to combat organized criminal activities.

In terms of broader strategic-level policies towards the western Balkans, the EU has enjoyed the leverage that has derived from its source of attraction and the prospect of future membership. The EU's stabilization and association process (SAP), initiated in 1999, opened an 'accession perspective' for states in the region and prescribed for them a variety of measures. These included the drafting of appropriate legislation by the countries concerned, the instigation of anti-money-laundering measures, and the reform of policing services and policies to root out corruption in the judiciary (Hanggi and Tanner 2005, 37). The EU member states have been aware that once aspirant states have been granted membership, the Union's influence and power to shape the internal security policies of those states would diminish considerably.

The European Neighbourhood Policy

Among other countries, where there has not been the possibility of membership, such as in Eastern Europe and the Mediterranean, the EU has needed to find other ways of steering them towards contributing to its internal security objectives. It has feared the security problems that originate from these neighbours, especially the flow of migrants and soft drugs from North Africa. In turn, these neighbouring countries have regarded the EU as inward looking and preoccupied with the pursuit of its own selfish security interests. They have viewed the EU as concerned with threats to its own internal security and not with their difficulties, such as rapidly rising birth rates and poor employment records. European Neighbourhood Policy (ENP) countries have not seen in the Union's internal security regime measures that address their own security needs.

The Union has adopted a mixture of incentives and sanctions towards such neighbours. In return for countries negotiating action plans that tighten their border controls and strengthen their police and judicial capacities, the European Commission has offered a range of benefits. These include aid programmes and financial help, as well as the secondment of officials to advise with the drafting of appropriate legislation. In its 2006 Communication on ENP the European Commission proposed enhancing the incentives for countries to align themselves with the Union's *acquis* on migration (European Commission 2006a, 3). The EU has offered trade agreements to states that support its policies on migration, and the Commission has approved measures to speed up the supply of visas for entry into Europe for nationals from compliant states (*Agence Press* 2007b). Visa facilitation has come to be regarded as an important inducement for countries to work with the EU. The Union's JHA Commissioner noted that it was impossible to expect countries like Libya, Morocco, and Algeria to take on the role of border guards for the EU unless they were offered more substantial benefits than just economic aid (*Agence Presse* 2007a). Lavenex and Wichmann argue that the EU has also employed more informal strategies towards these countries, utilizing transgovernmental networks of information sharing, consultation, expert assistance, and twinning projects (Lavenex and Wichmann 2009, 92).

To its credit, the EU has tried to tackle some of the underlying structural causes of the problems, such as poor governance and the neglect of human rights, through its Common Foreign and Security Policy (Council of the European Union 2005a). It has accepted that poverty and deprivation can contribute to the preconditions for both migration and terrorism (Boswell 2003, 624) and that political instability can enable organized crime to take root. The Union has pursued a comprehensive approach to security challenges that supports the internal capacities of states with development assistance, and has integrated its engagement with North African countries into a 'global approach to migration' (European Council 2007). By doing so it has acknowledged that transnational security challenges will not be defeated just by the externalization of its own security measures and that enhancing the stability and good governance of its neighbours serves its own long-term interests.

Yet the EU has also resorted to a range of sanctions in order to pressure states to comply with its internal security provisions. It has sought to prompt its neighbours into initiating their own policies that will materially assist the security of the EU. For instance, ENP countries have been urged to tighten their emigration controls through better document security, the improvement of border management, and cracking down on the smuggling of people. 'Readmission agreements' have been imposed under which countries accept the return of their own migrants or people who have transited across their territory (Lavenex 2006, 341). Action plans have been drawn up with countries as diverse as Ukraine, Armenia, and Azerbaijan, and Egypt, Jordan, and Morocco, and the European Commission has monitored their compliance, accompanied by threats of pressure if they fail to meet their obligations.

The EU has linked aid to matters of asylum. Since the June 2002 Seville European Council, which focused on the issue of illegal immigration, every agreement that the Union has concluded with third countries has contained a clause on managing migration and on the readmission of illegal immigrants (European Council 2002b, 10). Similarly, since 2004, counter-terrorism clauses have been inserted into agreements with all third countries requiring a commitment to share information and the acceptance of training. The EU has designated certain countries as safe from persecution, with the result that asylum seekers from these states are immediately determined to have an unfounded claim for sanctuary. States designated as safe third countries are those whose human rights records are considered to be free from large-scale abuse.

The proclivity of the EU to use coercion towards its neighbours has been the subject of criticism. Pastore has decried the list of tools the EU has used to externalize its migration controls, 'rang[ing] from an enormous increase in the use of visas

... sanctions on carriers, seconding immigration liaison officers ... and readmission agreements' (Pastore 2006). ENP countries, although far from a homogeneous group, are overwhelmingly poorer than the member states of the Union and it has been unfair that the EU has transferred some of its economic burdens to them. Punitive EU policies tend to impact disproportionately on the poor and vulnerable within neighbouring societies and this has reflected badly on the Union's claims to be an ethical foreign policy actor.

Recourse to punitive policies has illustrated the limited power of the EU. In the absence of the prospect of accession, the Union has possessed relatively little influence over ENP countries. The same sort of weakness, albeit for different reasons, has been mirrored in the EU's relationship with the Russian Federation. The EU has been concerned by the threat from organized crime, drug trafficking, and money laundering originating from the Russian Federation. The Union drew up a common strategy for Russia and situated a Europol liaison office in Moscow (European Commission 2006a). Nevertheless, the Russian government has been reluctant to comply with the EU's agenda: it has not viewed the Union as an actor of sufficient import to alter its behaviour.

European Union cooperation with the USA

In light of the inequitable relationship between the EU and ENP countries, it is ironic to find that in the USA–EU relationship the tables are turned (see Chapter 17). Here, in the Union's most important bilateral security relationship, it is the EU that has found itself the weaker actor for several reasons. One reason is that it is composed of many states and it has found it difficult to act in the purposeful manner of a single state. Another is that its split competences and the relative novelty of its powers in internal security matters have placed it at a disadvantage in the face of US experience. A third reason is that the EU has been confronted by a USA that has been galvanized by the horror of the 9/11 attacks. In their aftermath, the USA has demanded cooperation from its allies and the EU has found the political pressure to be irresistible.

In the 1990s, the pattern was one of the USA pressing for cooperation with the EU against the threats of organized crime and drug trafficking, and the Union reacting negatively to these advances. It was testament to the significance and sophistication of the Union in internal security matters that the USA was approaching it asking for cooperation. The USA looked upon the EU as the most viable partner for working alongside it in countering growing security challenges. The more ambitious frameworks for post-Cold War cooperation that the USA sought to instigate received little support from the EU. The New Transatlantic Agenda (NTA) of 1995 attempted to refocus transatlantic energies on to a range of US global concerns that included transnational crime, drug trafficking, and international terrorism. But for much of the 1990s the EU was preoccupied with building its own internal security structures through the treaties on European union and Amsterdam. The EU was being invited to cooperate but its own internal structures were not ready to respond (Winer 2005, 107).

It was the issue of counter-terrorism that led to a step-level change in USA–EU internal security cooperation. After 9/11, the USA initiated a homeland security strategy that focused on protecting its borders and air travel, overhauling its intelligence and bureaucratic structures, and enhancing the powers of its law enforcement agencies (White House 2002). These decisions were taken unilaterally but had significant ramifications for its European allies. In effect, the USA was putting in doubt the privileged access to its territory by EU countries. This was driven partly by a fear in the USA that the threats to its own territory could originate in Europe. The result was that the EU found itself reacting to a US-inspired agenda: scrambling to put in place security policies that ensured conformity with new US laws and according it a privileged relationship that no other state enjoyed.

The implications of US policies led to the threat of the withdrawal of visa-waiver status for EU countries if they did not introduce biometric identifiers into passports. Member states have complied with the US VISIT programme and allowed their nationals to be fingerprinted and have their irises scanned on entry into the USA. There was also the risk that European airlines would lose landing rights at US airports if the data on their travellers, Passenger Name Records (PNR), were withheld from the US Department of Homeland Security. A PNR agreement was reached between the USA and the EU in May 2004 but it was successfully challenged by the European Parliament through the European Court of Justice. The European Commission responded with the unusual step of redrafting the agreement in 2006 under third-pillar provisions that excluded the involvement of the European Parliament (Rees 2009, 116).

As a consequence, a new framework of counter-terrorism cooperation has emerged. One aspect of this cooperation has been a growth in the volume of intelligence information that has been shared across the Atlantic. Second, authority was granted to the EU Presidency to negotiate a multilateral judicial agreement between the USA and the EU that would supplement the existing bilateral arrangements. This 'Agreement on Extradition and Mutual Legal Assistance' was eventually signed at the EU–USA summit in Washington in June 2003. It makes clear the evidence that can be shared for criminal prosecution and speeds up the process of extradition. Third, there has been significant new transatlantic cooperation to combat various forms of money laundering. Fourth, there has also been the opening up to cooperation and participation of US representatives in working groups of the Council as well as in Eurojust and Europol. A long-standing deadlock in sharing information with US authorities was overcome with the signing of an agreement in December 2001 by the Director of Europol, Jurgen Storbeck. Differences between Europol and the US government over data protection had prevented any previous cooperation but these were overcome after significant concessions from the side of the Union.

The USA and EU have been at the forefront of efforts to encourage counter-terrorism cooperation in the wider international community. Both sides have been active in fulfilling the aims of UN Security Council Resolution 1373 that encouraged states to criminalize the financing of terrorist activities and established a counter-terrorism committee to monitor compliance. Both sides of the Atlantic have also directed their efforts through the Group of Eight leading industrial states to target money laundering, seize assets, and prevent the use of the international financial system to further terrorist activities. The USA and the EU have shown through their own cooperation that new patterns of collaborative international action can be generated to address some of the risks caused by terrorism.

Nevertheless, tensions remain in the transatlantic internal security relationship. Data sharing remains a prickly issue because of differences between the two sides in how data are stored and shared with third parties. The US policy of the extra-judicial transfer between countries of people held on suspicion of terrorist crimes— 'extraordinary rendition'—caused deep-seated differences with European countries. It was compounded by the holding of detainees at US military installations, such as Guantanamo Bay and Bagram airbase. These tensions and differences of approach have been assuaged to an extent by the administration of Barack Obama, who has made a deliberate effort to change the tenor of the USA's War on Terror and address the concerns of its allies.

Conclusion

The post-Cold War period has witnessed a growing recognition of the need to build Justice, Freedom, and Security (JLS) objectives into the external action of the EU. This has arisen from two sorts of pressures. First, the need to react to perceptions of increasing threats from organized crime and drug trafficking, illegal immigration, and transnational terrorism. EU member states have recognized the important role that the Union can play in coordinating their responses. This trend has been accelerating as European interior ministers have come to the view that only through concerted action can they have an effective response to these threats.

The drift of internal security competences to the EU is testament to its perceived value. Member states have recognized that the nature of the challenges that they face, particularly in areas like illegal immigration and terrorism, demand concerted action in order to be effective. The EU's internal security system has come to resemble an emerging regime that is available for the rest of the continent to emulate and adopt. But the extent to which this regime is being adopted has depended upon the relations of third countries with the EU and, more precisely, what the Union has to offer them. The limitations of the EU have meant that those states ineligible to be offered membership have resisted the Union's internal security provisions.

Countries within the ENP as well as the Russian Federation have proved resistant to being drawn into the EU's internal security regime.

Second, EU external relations and the enlargement process have increased the priority attached to protecting internal security. The EU has sought to improve its cooperation with other states by making internal security an explicit element in its foreign relations. This has been pursued in various trade and other agreements with states in Central Europe as well as beyond. Countries that are regarded as sources of danger to the EU, such as through migration, transnational crime, or terrorism, are particular targets of the EU's approach. Developments in the international environment have also played an important role in shaping this agenda. The aftermath of 9/11 dramatically increased the attention accorded to international terrorism and provided a major stimulus to developing cooperation with the USA.

EU policies have generated resentment as well as cooperation among its neighbours. The EU has prioritized its own security interests and has been accused of using too many sticks and not enough carrots towards its neighbours. Countries bordering the Union have been treated as buffer zones and have been obligated to sign readmission agreements and accept returning migrants. The EU has placed an increased burden on countries less able than its own members to bear the strain of repatriating migrants. It has exported some of its problems to less affluent states. For an organization that claims to act ethically, based upon human rights considerations, this appears to be in conflict with its stated values. Only with the start of the Stockholm Programme in 2010 has the Union committed itself to finding a better balance between the objectives of freedom and justice for third countries.

Thus, the Union's attempt to export its internal security regime has not been an unqualified success. The EU has used its economic power and influence to insist that those countries that wish to interact and trade with it, as well as enjoy its aid, must comply with its strictures on JLS. As a major economic actor this has accorded it significant leverage. Yet it has also exposed some of the limits of the EU as an international actor. Countries at greater distance from the Union, with no prospect of membership, have not been swayed by economic incentives. They have concluded that the benefits of complying with the EU's priorities in JLS are outweighed by the costs that they would incur.

This decidedly mixed picture takes us back to the key themes in this book. One of the major reasons why the transfer of internal security responsibilities from member states to the EU has been uneven is precisely the fact that in this area the EU remains an international system of cooperation rather than a unified superstate. At the same time, in order to pursue its aims in matters of internal security, the Union has had to enter into broader processes of international cooperation and institutionalization that raise questions about its status and effectiveness. And finally, the ways in which the EU has sought to exercise leverage over neighbouring countries and regions, but has also had to recognize the strict limits on such power, highlight important questions about the extent to which it can take a full role in creating international order as a 'power' in the world arena.

FURTHER READING

For changing threat perceptions in the European Union see Kirchner and Sperling (2007). For analysis of the securitization of migration within the EU see Huysmans (2006), and for terrorism see Spence (2007). For an overview of developments in the field of Justice, Freedom and Security see Zwaan and Goudappel (2006) and for EU–USA internal security cooperation see Dalgaard-Nielsen and Hamilton (2005). For EU efforts to export its internal security policies to its neighbours see Lavenex and Wichmann (2009).

Dalgaard-Nielsen, A., and Hamilton, D. (eds) (2005), *Transatlantic Homeland Security: Protecting Society in the Age of Catastrophic Terrorism* (London: Routledge).

Huysmans, J. (2006), *The Politics of Insecurity: Fear, Migration and Asylum in the EU* (London: Routledge).

Kirchner, E., and Sperling, J. (2007), *EU Security Governance* (Manchester: Manchester University Press).

Lavenex, S., and Wichmann, N. (2009), 'The External Governance of EU Internal Security', *European Integration*, 31/1, January, 83–102.

Spence, D. (ed) (2007), *The European Union and Terrorism* (London: John Harper Publishing).

de Zwaan, J., and Goudappel, R. (eds) (2006), *Freedom, Security and Justice in the European Union: implementation of the Hague programme*, (The Hague: T. M. C. Asser Press).

WEB LINKS

Relevant documentation on EU activities in this field can be found on the Europa website (**http://europa.eu/pol/justice/index_en.htm**), and the website of the European Commission Directorate General for Justice, Freedom and Security (**http://europa. eu/dgs/justice_home/index_en.htm**).   **www.consilium.europa.eu/showPage.aspx? id=249&lang=en**). The websites of Europol (**http://www.europol.europa.eu**), Eurojust (**http://www.eurojust.europa.eu),**   Frontex   (**http://www.frontex.europa.eu**),   and the European Monitoring Centre for Drugs and Drug Addiction (**http://www.emcdda. europa.eu**) are worth investigation. The website of the Centre for European Policy Studies (**http://www.ceps.be**) has a wide range of analysis on EU internal security issues.

CHAPTER 11

The EU and the Global Political Economy

Amy Verdun

Summary

This chapter charts the position of the European Union (EU) in the global political economy (GPE), identifies key dimensions of change and development, and evaluates the EU's impact on the operation of the contemporary GPE. It does so by outlining key ideas in international political economy (IPE), by relating these to the growth of the EU, and by assessing the EU's role in the GPE in three areas: European integration itself, the EU's engagement in the GPE, and the EU's claims to be a major economic power. The final part of the chapter brings these together in an examination of global economic governance—in particular, the EU's role in the financial and economic crisis of 2007–10.

Introduction

The EU occupies a special position in the GPE—indeed, it could be argued that this is the area in which the distinctive characteristics and resources of the EU have most shaped the contemporary world, and in which it is most possible to discern the impact of the EU on the global arena. But what do we mean when we refer to the GPE? In recent years, the term 'global political economy' has gained ground compared with the more established term 'international political economy' (cf. Ravenhill 2008) in the analysis and evaluation of the political dimension of international economic structures and processes. Essentially, the term GPE is preferred by many analysts as it covers more precisely the content and phenomena to be evaluated; interactions are not only 'international' (i.e. initiated by national governments or occurring between nations) but rather 'global', (i.e. transcending national boundaries and involving a wide range of other potential actors). The term 'global' implies that these interactions encompass the activities of multinational companies, non-governmental organizations, traders on financial markets, and so on. It is not simply a question of actors, however: the challenges the world faces more often than not are global rather than international, such as those relating to climate change and environmental degradation, stability of the financial system, benefits and costs of free trade, migration, uneven economic growth, development and prosperity, and distribution of wealth among peoples and regions.

Despite the increasing focus on globalization and its manifestations, the academic literature that studies these matters is still referred to broadly as international political economy (IPE). The IPE literature, first developed in the 1970s in response to turbulences in macroeconomic developments in the world economy and the growth of financial markets, has since become a well-developed field (cf. Kindleberger 1970; Strange 1970, 1971, 1976; Krasner 1976; Cohen 1977, 1998; Keohane and Nye 1977; Cox 1987; Gilpin 1987; 2001). This literature asks questions about how domestic economic and political factors as well as the structure of national economies affect their relative prosperity and their relationship with the GPE, and also explores the role of socio-economic actors and institutions in influencing countries' stances towards the outside world (Frieden and Martin 2002). IPE scholars have pointed to the fact that many of the possible stresses on a country could come from the international system rather than from purely domestic sources. They found that international or global economic factors may affect a country more than would be expected on the basis of the country's macroeconomic fundamentals, which is particularly the case with currencies and internationally traded assets (Helleiner 1994; Gilbert and Helleiner 1999). The areas most studied by IPE scholars are international trade and finance, monetary and exchange rate policies, and the role of international institutions and norms (often referred to in terms of international regimes) in determining how countries position themselves in the GPE.

One of the key concerns of the IPE literature is the relationship between states and markets: the degree of autonomy states have in pursuing national economic goals and in shaping the regimes for trade, exchange rates, capital controls, and other key international economic processes. It also increasingly reviews developments that are captured under the broad heading of 'globalization'—indeed, the IPE literature dealt with globalization before the term became mainstream from the late 1980s onwards. The globalization literature reviews a wide range of economic, political, social, cultural, administrative, and legal developments, with a focus on the growth of interconnectedness between societies and the issues of management, stability, and (in)security that can emerge from this intensification of exchange. It often also offers a normative assessment, assessing whether or not these exchanges can be considered a 'good' or a 'bad' thing (Hirst and Thompson 1999; Scholte 2005). Such blanket judgements are likely to conceal wide variations in specific sectors or regions of the GPE: the more sophisticated answer is usually that the results are mixed, with winners and losers within, between, and across national societies (Stiglitz 2002). This situation is very much a political one, with the resulting insecurities and demands for protection or redress making themselves felt on national governments everywhere.

Where does the EU 'fit' in this broad concern for the study of IPE? As an entity, the EU is neither a state nor an international organization. It has features of both, and also reflects the growth and increasing integration of one of the world's largest 'domestic' markets. As noted earlier in this book, its hybrid form of governance reflects a peculiar institutional architecture that includes representatives of member states as well as supranational decision makers, and which also responds to pressures from civil society groups at the European level. Decision-making on an increasing range of economic and commercial issues is channelled through the institutions of the European Union, but this has not eliminated the national level—indeed, it might be argued that for many member states, their national economic resources have been enhanced by membership of the EU. At the same time, the EU is inevitably and increasingly entangled with mechanisms of global economic governance. It is also noteworthy that the EU[1] has experienced deepened integration in the very areas studied most by IPE scholars (see Jones and Verdun 2005): trade (both in goods and in services), monetary policies, and a wide range of regulatory policies.

As a result, the EU has developed a distinctive relationship with the GPE (see Ravenhill 2008; Laursen 2009). From its early days European integration was a process that aimed at removing barriers to trade and exchange within the entity even if it was not quite so liberal in its outward orientation. European integration also sought to reduce the role of government protection of industries or sectors and reduce or dismantle monopolies. Both the creation of the customs union on which the EU's external commercial policies are founded, and the elaboration of internal policies with significant external effects, implied the need for a 'foreign economic policy' in key areas from the outset of the European integration project.

As an example, we can point to antitrust and competition policy: at one and the same time, this is a driver of internal European integration and a building block of the EU's external regulatory influence. Through this policy, the EU has come to exercise considerable influence not only over major European corporations but also over non-European world leading multinational companies, such as Microsoft, and over the development of competition policies at the global level.

As this implies, the EU, first in the form of the European Communities, was a significant international economic actor as early as the 1960s, especially after it completed the Customs Union in 1968. It increased its influence in the 1970s and 1980s when through various rounds of enlargement and expansion of policies, it was able to respond to external challenges and maintain the integration process (even if not without international scepticism about its success). But at this time the EC was a minor partner to the USA in a profoundly polarized world: the Americans had been instrumental in establishing the key post-Second World War regimes for trade and monetary relations, and continued to dominate their development. The fragmentation of US international economic dominance in the 1970s and 1980s was thus a key element in the growing assertiveness of the European Community, for example in trade policy and development assistance (see Chapters 12 and 14). The Community and then the EU experienced a further surge of influence (and expectations) once the Cold War ended and the Maastricht Treaty entered into force in November 1993; one key aspect of the treaty was the initiation of moves towards a single European currency, the euro. Although the end of the Cold War is often presented purely as a process in diplomacy and security policy, it can equally be argued that it was a key stage in the development of the GPE and within that of the EU as a major actor.

Within this broad context of change, the EU has sought to strike a balance between regionalism and globalization. Regionalism in the EU has different meanings. The first meaning focuses on the development of regions within the EU; the second on integration of the larger integrated area as a region within the world economy. In part the EU has focused on using European-level policies to reduce the gap between the rich and the poor sub-national regions within its boundaries—a gap given additional force during the early 21st century by the accession of 12 new member states, many of them with problems of economic as well as political development. The second meaning is its role in creating an integrated region on which to base action in the GPE, which has been quite successful according to numerous indicators (see below). However, there are questions to be asked about the extent to which the EU has succeeded in transforming its economic expansion into a position in the global political arena proportional to its economic power. These questions are as much political as they are economic, since they reflect the fact that except in certain areas of policy the EU is not an integrated economic actor, lacks the ability to pursue a coherent European interest, and is deficient in the legitimacy that it might claim as a state actor. Although the EU has significant 'state powers' and performs important 'state functions', at the end of the day it is not a state. This situation raises important questions not only for EU policy making but also for IPE.

In light of these reflections on the position of the EU in the global political economy, this chapter addresses a number of key questions: how does the process of EU integration 'fit' in the GPE, and how does it challenge approaches to IPE? How does the growing presence of the EU in the GPE affect key processes of exchange and issues of growth, development, and crisis? Can the EU be considered as a 'power' in the GPE, and what is the effect of the peculiar characteristics of EU power? How does the EU contribute to the governance of the GPE and what does this tell us about the linkages between EU integration, EU presence in the GPE, and the EU as a power? The structure of the chapter broadly follows this set of questions. The first section examines integration in the EU and its implications for the GPE. The second section reviews the EU presence in the GPE, whilst the subsequent section examines the EU as a power in the GPE. The penultimate section looks at the EU's role in global economic governance, and particularly at the Union's role in pursuing international competitiveness and in responding to the international economic and financial crisis of 2007–10. The final section concludes by reassessing the position and roles of the EU in the GPE.

Integration in the EU and the global political economy

The creation of the European Communities (EC) in the 1950s took place in a different international economic world from that which characterizes the era of globalization. The prevalent mode of governance was hierarchical, with the government playing a central role in society (see Tömmel and Verdun 2009). Pervasive controls existed on international movements of capital as well as those of traded goods. As already noted, the integration process in the EU aimed at adopting a more liberal stance internally by reducing barriers to trade and enhancing market principles. At the same time, throughout the 1950s and 1960s more attention was paid to the creation and expansion of the welfare state. In many countries, government was also a large stakeholder in various industrial sectors, either through direct nationalization or through partnerships with private corporations. In terms of the language of IPE a number of policies were Keynesian (the member-state government looking after its own issues by taxing and spending, often running a deficit, and in this manner enhancing growth and prosperity, particularly in areas such as welfare state development and industrial policy). Yet in other areas policies were liberal, in particular those that related to market integration—and those in which the European Communities came to play a major role.

That the EC started with integration of production and regulation of coal and steel was part of the *zeitgeist* of the immediate post-war period (see Chapter 3)—the underlying aim was to create such mutual entanglement of national enterprises in heavy industry that mobilization for war became costly and in effect unthinkable. Similar reasoning dictated that a key initial area of policy integration at the European level was agricultural policy. Food security was one reason to choose this policy as a matter of common concern; another was that this sector still represented a fairly large proportion of society: 23 per cent of the population in the original six EC member states was involved in agriculture just after the Second World War, versus 4 per cent in the early 2000s (Tsoukalis 2005). The choice of a centralized policy for agriculture was in part also inspired by a federalist ideal, which in the case of some of the founding fathers lay at the heart of the creation of the EC (see Skogstad and Verdun 2009). Both the focus on coal and steel and the focus on agriculture were to have major implications for the EC's international economic involvement, since they related to key areas of international trade and competition.

Although coal, steel, and agriculture were at the centre of the initial integration process, other EC policies were not quite as top-down or centralized. At first the EC sought market integration and rules harmonization by agreeing to common standards—for example, in transportation or public procurement. It quickly became clear that harmonization was very time consuming and often politically difficult. The European Court of Justice offered the solution to this conundrum. Following the famous 1979 Cassis de Dijon case, the principle of 'mutual recognition' was adopted to allow goods from different countries to be sold in other member states (Schmidt 2007). This was one of the key foundations of the programme to 'complete the internal market', which became a key driver of European integration in the late 1980s and early 1990s (see below).

Another area of policy that had major implications for the political economy of the EC was its regional policy. Here we see some elements of fiscal federalism: the principle of collecting tax revenues centrally and then disbursing them to areas in the federation that need them most according to agreed indicators. In the case of regional policy the EC managed to define areas that were weaker and thus deserving of so-called structural funds or regional funds to enhance their development and make them more capable of benefiting from the opportunities offered by the integration process. The issue with this policy was that there was always the risk that national authorities would no longer invest in these areas unless the EU had paid up as well. In terms of the IPE model this policy was one that kept a strong role for the EC and later the EU as a centralized actor that taxes and spends (albeit on a scale that is dwarfed by the governments of EU member states)—it also had important effects on the incentives to invest in certain regions and, by implication, for the movement of capital and other resources in the global arena.

However, by the mid 1980s these policies with centralized components had not always secured the growth and the internal integration that had been envisaged. Together with difficulties in the international context caused by turbulence on the money markets and by shifting patterns of international competitiveness, these elements of internal stagnation gave rise to a new impetus for internal reform of the EC's political economy. As a result, the European integration process was given new life by a plan to 'complete the single market'—a plan that was put in place in the mid 1980s with a view to being completed at the end of 1992. In terms of the regime adopted, the adoption of the Single European Act (1987) that facilitated the adoption of rules to complete the single market by qualified majority vote and which was buttressed by the 'mutual recognition' system noted above, marked the turning point. Until that time, member-state governments in the EU were more focused on centralized intervention and steering than having economic policies that let the market do the work. This does not mean the EU since the single market programme (SMP) has been completely liberal with no state intervention—although perhaps significantly, the government of Margaret Thatcher in the UK was a strong supporter of the SMP. Quite the contrary; there are complex rules and regulations for many aspects of economic activity. What it did mean, however, was that the overall driving force behind the integration process became one that sought to ensure that market forces should be able to do their work. One of the key policies that was exploited for this purpose was competition policy. This policy had been in place since the 1960s but was now used more explicitly in order to 'complete the internal market'.

Another area in which the single market programme had important implications was international trade. EC actors were dealing with others in the international arena via the General Agreement on Tariffs and Trade (GATT, since 1995 part of the World Trade Organization (WTO)). Since the EC was a customs union, EC supranational actors (primarily the Commission acting on a mandate from the Council of Ministers) had the authority to negotiate international trade agreements. Although often cumbersome and tedious, the EC managed to participate as one actor on behalf of its member states. A traditionally difficult area was the clash between the international trade regime that increasingly sought to move towards more free trade (a liberal regime) and the area of agriculture the EU (but also leading counterparts such as Australia, Canada, Japan, and the USA) which kept a more protectionist stance (see Chapter 12). The single market programme, on the other hand, gave the EC a direct interest in international liberalization in areas where it was expected that the Community would be best placed to compete, such as trade in services or a number of areas of regulatory policy. The resulting tensions between 'fortress Europe' and 'world partner Europe' during the late 1980s and mid 1990s were a key policy problem for EC decision makers.

Last but not least, in the area of monetary and exchange rate policy the EC started off with an informal system. In the early years the EC member states were part of the Bretton Woods system of fixed but adjustable exchange rates in which national currencies were pegged to the dollar, which in turn was pegged to gold. This system meant that the EC did not need to set up its own system of fixed exchange rates. Even if there was not much need for coordination, the EC countries still coordinated short- and long-term economic policy objectives through an informal set of EC committees (see Verdun 2000). As the 1960s proceeded, the US dollar peg to gold became less credible, as the USA was issuing more dollars to pay for the cost of the Vietnam War. Towards the late 1960s the broader international monetary system showed cracks, and a number of major asymmetries became apparent—for example, the weakness of the pound sterling and the strength of the German Deutschmark, as well as the instability of the US dollar. Therefore the EC countries became keen to create their own system, partly as a measure of integration and partly as a means of insulating themselves at least to some extent from the fluctuations of other major currencies.

During the monetary crises of the late 1960s and early 1970s that led to the effective demise of the Bretton Woods system of fixed exchange rates in 1971, the EC countries sought to deepen economic integration. A first blueprint for Economic and Monetary Union (EMU) was created through the Werner Plan in 1970, but insufficient agreement could be reached on the degree of transfer of sovereignty over economic and monetary policy to a centralized authority and on what would be the appropriate policy mix between monetary and fiscal policies. The so-called 'snake' (later the 'snake in the tunnel') was set up to keep exchange rates stable within narrow limits but not all EC countries participated, whilst others who did participate were forced out by the pressures of international financial flows. The 1970s thus was a period when some countries were experiencing fairly high inflation and exchange rate volatility, whilst the broad asymmetries persisted and were exacerbated by such factors as the impact of successive oil price crises. In 1979 the European Monetary System (EMS) was set up to seek to keep exchange rates stable. It met with mixed success, but can be seen as a key foundation stone for later progression towards the euro.

In terms of IPE, during the 1960s and 1970s European policy makers can be characterized as having been of one mindset, namely to see a strong role for state intervention in the economy and a limited role for the market. On monetary policy there was a divergence in views as to what were appropriate targets and what was an appropriate policy-making regime within the EC.

With hindsight, however, one can trace back to the early 1980s a change in paradigm regarding two main economic concerns that were at the core both of European integration and of the broader emerging GPE. The first of these was the relationship between state and market. From the early 1980s, the tendency at national and European levels was to give a larger role to the market and a smaller role to the state (the latter becoming more of a regulator, less a stakeholder/investor). The other shift related to the role of monetary policy. Neoclassical economists such as Milton Friedman suggested that economic growth would benefit from cheap money—meaning low inflation and stable money—and thus that the key role of government was to control the money supply. Added to these points was the view that fixed exchange rates were important in a system in which the constituent parts were increasingly trading with one another. The result was a shift towards low inflation and currency stability, giving an increasing role to market principles and reducing the role of the state intervention in industry (Hall 1986). This paradigm shift, which took hold of Europe but also the USA and elsewhere, took some years to sink in completely, and led to considerable instability in international money markets during the 1980s. Eventually it became a key driving force behind the push to complete the single market and in its wake to muse about economic and monetary union once again. The slogan 'One market, one money' became a central part of the drive to move beyond the single market programme and into a more unified macroeconomic policy for the EC.

EMU was put on the agenda in 1987 and a blueprint was in place by April 1989. The project gained further political momentum with the fall of the Berlin Wall in autumn 1989, and became one of the two central pillars in the plan to revamp the EC treaties, through the intergovernmental conference that was established in 1990. EMU was incorporated as a goal in the Treaty on European Union with a view to being created before the turn of the century. However, the model of EMU was different from the currency regimes of national states. The EU plan would transfer sovereignty over monetary policy to a European system of central banks with a European Central Bank (ECB) at its core. But there would not be a centralized budget to spend beyond that contributed by member states to existing Community policies, nor a unified system of taxation; thus in turn there were few stabilizing mechanisms to counter the kinds of asymmetries a single monetary policy might produce or to balance against major external shocks to the European system (Verdun 1996). Throughout this time there was a cap on the EU budget of 1.27 per cent of EU GDP. Thus, in the terms used earlier in this chapter, there was no fiscal federalism of any significance to accompany EMU.

The movement to the single currency and to monetary union entailed major domestic reforms for those EU member states that committed themselves to entering the system at its inception. After intense efforts on the part of the member states, most met (or came close to) the so-called convergence criteria that stipulated the rules on the extent of member state budgetary deficits, public debt, inflation, and exchange rates. Aspiring members of the euro also had to commit themselves to major institutional changes, and especially to ensuring that their national central banks were independent. Eventually, this meant that 11 were ready to join the third stage of EMU on 1 January 1999 (see Box 11.1). Banknotes and coins circulated in 2002 and at the time of writing 16 member states are members of the euro area. It can readily be seen that the creation of an integrated monetary zone including a number of the world's more powerful national economies could have important effects on the GPE; indeed, the creation of the euro was accompanied by predictions that the global monetary system would become 'bipolar' between the dollar and the euro, and that the eurozone might become a more important focus of investment than the USA. Not only this, but the EU member states that remained outside the eurozone could not avoid being profoundly influenced by what went on within it. As such, the eurozone was a potentially fundamental change to the global monetary regime.

What does this review of the IPE of European integration tell us about the ways in which the EC and then the EU processes have changed the landscape of the

BOX 11.1	The path to the euro
October 1970	Werner Plan (report): three-stage approach to EMU is presented; it fails a few years later due to the difficult economic situation of the 1970s
1972	European system of fixed but adjustable exchange rates ('snake') set up; experiences mixed results throughout the 1970s
March 1979	Launch of the European Monetary System, which consisted of Exchange Rate Mechanism (ERM) and the European Currency Unit (ECU)
February 1986	Single European Act signed in 1986 in Luxembourg with an objective of establishing the single European market by the end of 1992
April 1989	Presentation of Delors report, which provided a blueprint for the establishment of economic and monetary union in three stages
July 1990	First stage of EMU launched
February 1992	Maastricht Treaty signed, laying down the convergence criteria and the timetable for EMU
January 1994	Second stage of EMU launched; European Monetary Institute created
December 1995	Naming the single currency 'euro' at the Madrid summit
June 1997	Amsterdam summit and agreeing on the stability and growth pact; European Council also agreed on ERM-2
May 1998	European Council agrees to launch of the third stage of EMU on 1 January 1999; 11 member states fulfil the convergence criteria
June 1998	European Central Bank starts operating
31 December 1998	Exchange rates of the 11 member states adopting the euro will be irrevocably fixed between their currencies and the euro
1 January 1999	Third stage begins: launch of the euro as the currency for 11 member states; the euro is still only a virtual currency
1 January 2001	Greece meets the convergence criteria and joins the euro area
1 January 2002	Introduction of the euro banknotes and coins in 12 member states
1 January 2007	Slovenia joins the euro area
1 January 2008	Cyprus and Malta join the euro area
1 January 2009	Slovakia joins the euro area
1 January 2009	Euro celebrates its ten-year anniversary

Source: Verdun (2000) and European Commission Directorate-General for Economic and Financial Affairs (2010), Economic and Monetary Union: A Timeline. Checked online May 23, 2010. Available online at: http://ec.europa.eu/economy_finance/emu10/timeline_en.pdf

GPE? In line with the discussion earlier in the chapter, we can conclude that the process of integration in the EC/EU has led to a mix of winners and losers. Especially after the initiation of the single market programme in the late 1980s, the winners were and are those who could do well in an increasingly integrated market; in other words, those who would thrive in a competitive environment. A number of state monopolies were broken up and new entrants were allowed into the market. It meant that consumers benefited from a reduction in prices for utilities, as these companies increasingly needed to compete with one another, which led to a downward pressure on prices. Also, the cost of other goods that used to be dominated by one or a few suppliers was affected by increased competition: for example, the cost of telecommunications and transportation (air travel in particular) came down dramatically in the EU.[2] Workers who were mobile, or who had international appeal, benefited from the single market. The market for financial services increased and workers and investors in that sector for the most part prospered.

The losers in this integration process were those that had been dependent on government support or other forms of protection. As the decades progressed, national governments were unable to protect ailing industries from decline. So the automobile and airline industries needed to find partners to survive; others such as those in the textiles industry more often than not shut up shop or relocated outside the EU borders (or to Central and Eastern Europe as part of the consequences of the 2004/2007 enlargement). As the labour market liberalized, workers faced a different set of support structures. In many EC member states in the 1960s, 1970s, and 1980s employees had life-long employment and would not change jobs much in their lifetime; generous unemployment benefits were handed out to the unemployed without too many demands being made on them. By the 2000s these benefits had been reduced and more demands were placed on them. Increasing numbers of workers in the EU in the 21st century were working on a contract basis without a clear guarantee of employment or long-term benefits, and they would change jobs many times in their lifetimes. These were trends in the EU, but they are by no means exclusive to the EU; they can also be found throughout the rest of the world. Indeed, one conclusion from this discussion is that the EU has become in some ways a microcosm of globalization trends, with increased interconnectedness and volatility and resulting problems of 'societal security' in the face of rapid economic change.

In terms of EMU, those in the euro area benefited from cheap money, (low interest rates and easy access to credit for government, consumers, and investors), and a reputation built on that which had its origins in the policies of Germany. But there were also costs associated with EMU. Specifically, in order to reap the fruits of the single currency, member-state governments had to keep their budgetary house in order and ensure that they met the convergence criteria even when in EMU. This reflected the fact, noted above, that there was no central EU government (or 'economic government', an idea supported by the French) that could bail out a country if it were deemed to be borrowing too much (which would be necessary if its debt-to-GDP ratio or budgetary deficit was high). Given that there was no such EU-level economic government, the EU Treaty, backed up by the Stability and Growth Pact strongly supported by Germany, stipulated a no-bailout clause: no country was to be given EU funds if it was unable to pay off its debt. Being in EMU, with irrevocably fixed exchange rates and a single currency, also meant that if a country was uncompetitive it could not use devaluation as an instrument. Instead, it would have to improve competitiveness either by reducing the cost of labour and prices or by increasing productivity. In a GPE where intensification of competition (and the emergence of new competitors) could almost be taken as a given, the potential for major economic shocks and dislocations was built into European monetary integration.

The EU's presence in the global political economy

The status of a country in the GPE is often measured by its economic size and wealth. In the early days of European integration, when only a few member states made up the EC, it could not yet claim a strong position in the GPE. Over time as the EC and then the EU expanded, and with the falling apart of the Soviet Union and the Warsaw Pact, the USA was the only remaining superpower in political and security terms, but was increasingly challenged in the GPE, both because of its internal economic weaknesses and because of the rise of new competitors. As we have seen, the EU came onto the stage more seriously for two key reasons: first, because of the increasing size and resources brought by successive enlargements, and second, because of the increasing freeing up of the single market, which had beneficial effects on competitiveness. From an early stage, as noted above, the EU was also an important actor because it united within itself a number of the largest economies in the world. This was reflected in the EC's and then the EU's relationship to key international economic institutions; in the late 1990s when the G8 was meeting, the countries around the table were the USA, Japan, Germany, France, Italy, the UK, Canada, and Russia. In other words, four of the eight were EU members. In the meetings of the G20, which has in some respects replaced the G8 as a global economic forum since the 2007 financial crisis broke, besides these eight and various other industrialized and emerging market countries, the European Union also takes its place as a separate entity. In some international economic organizations, the EU constitutes a majority of the membership—for example, the Organisation for Economic Co-operation and Development is dominated numerically by EU member states since the 2004/2007 enlargement.

With the growth of the size and scope of the EU, it thus has also increased its presence in the GPE. Today it has the largest internal market in the world and represents an area of 500 million people (compared to just over 300 million in the USA). The EU of 27 member states (EU27) is a power similar to the USA in terms of its gross domestic product (GDP) based on purchasing power parity (PPP) share of world total GDP (per cent). As can be seen from Figure 11.1, the EU and the USA in the latter half of the first decade of the 21st century each commanded between 25 and 30 percent of the world GDP. For the 27 current members of the EU, in fact, this represents a relative decline in the 1990s and the new millennium. In the 1980s those countries still commanded 30 per cent of world GDP in PPP terms (although data from countries then in the Soviet bloc are difficult to assess). In comparison, the USA's share of total world GDP measured in PPP stayed roughly the same over the same 30 years.

If we look at what this means in the case of individual countries we find a number of other phenomena. In particular, we find that there have been 'winners and losers' in relative terms within the EU itself and that the benefits of integration are often unevenly distributed. Thus, many of the larger EU member states have experienced a recent decline in GDP per capita if one compares it against an index of the EU27. Table 11.1 shows that the EU15 (the countries that made up the EU of 15 member states between 1995 and 2004) on average saw their GDP per capita decrease slightly over that period. At the same time, their GDP per capita remained well ahead of the less developed new members of the EU27, whose entry in 2004–7 had the effect of marginally reducing the GDP per capita for the Union as a whole. Within this general picture, there were significant variations: for example, the Netherlands and Luxembourg did better than the average; Germany, France, and Italy did worse; whereas the UK stayed at approximately the same level. In

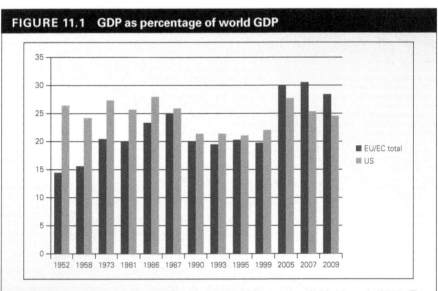

FIGURE 11.1 GDP as percentage of world GDP

Source: Personal calculations from OECD data, viz. (1) OECD website; (2) Maddison, A. (2001), 'The World Economy: A Millennial Perspective', Paris, OECD; (3) IMF Economic Outlook 2010, http://www.imf.org/external/data.htm; (4) United Nations (1993), 'Trends in International Distribution of Gross World Product', New York.

TABLE 11.1   GDP per capita in purchasing power standards (EU27 = 100)

	1997	1998	1999	2000	2001	2002	2003	2004
EU27	100	100	100	100	100	100	100	100
EU15	115.5	115.4	115.3	115.3	114.9	114.3	113.8	113.1
Euro area (16)	113.0	113.1	112.9	112.5	112.1	111.3	110.6	109.4
USA	160.9	160.7	162.6	160.9	156.5	154.2	156.3	157.3
Japan	127.9	120.9	117.7	116.9	113.6	111.9	112.2	113.0

Source: Own compilation from Eurostat data

comparison, over this same period the USA experienced a gradual slight decline, whilst Japan declined more substantially, reflecting its lengthy period of economic stagnation. To put this in perspective, the USA remained significantly ahead of the EU15 and the EU27 on this measure throughout the period. It is also important to remember that a number of large emerging economies such as China, India, and Brazil achieved spectacular growth rates throughout this period, with significant increases in wealth for large parts of their populations—a fact that has had important implications for the EU's position in the GPE (see Chapter 16).

Another indicator of success that enabled the EC and later the EU to command authority is its growth rates. During the 1960s the countries that made up the EC showed spectacular growth rates of 4 or 5 per cent annually (see Table 11.2). Most EC countries maintained similarly strong growth rates in the 1970s (if one excludes

TABLE 11.2   Annual percentage change in GDP (denominated in national currencies), selected countries and years

	1963	1973	1983	1993	2003
Germany	2.8	4.8	1.6	−0.8	−0.2
France	6.3	6.6	1.2	−0.9	1.1
Italy	5.6	3.7	1.2	−0.9	0.0
UK	4.3	7.2	3.6	2.2	2.8
USA	4.4	5.9	4.5	2.9	2.5
Japan	8.8	8.0	3.1	0.2	1.4
Canada	5.1	7.0	2.7	2.3	1.9

Source: Own compilation from data supplied by European Commission Services 2010

the recession years of 1974–5). In the 1980s, 1990s, and the first decennium of the 21st century, growth slowed somewhat (especially because of the 2008 financial crisis and its aftermath).

Though spectacular in the 1960s and 1970s, the pattern of growth in the 1980s and 1990s in EC countries was somewhat similar to that experienced by other advanced industrialized societies (such as Canada, Japan, and the USA). In other words, the EU could not really claim an exceptional overall economic performance in terms of annual growth rates over the long term, except in the early years of the post-Second World War 'economic miracle'. This reflects the 'maturing' of economies and is in many ways an inevitable process. Yet, the EU still could command authority as it had among its members some of the largest economies in the world; and collectively the area commanded attention from other countries in the GPE—not least because, as we have noted, it also controlled one of the largest and most sophisticated markets in the GPE, encompassing 500 million people by 2010.

In terms of the EU's presence in the GPE, its role is particularly noteworthy in the area of trade (see Chapter 12). Another area in which the EU dominates is in setting international standards. Because the EU has a competition policy and other regulatory policies that seek to ensure that there is a level playing field for all those who wish to enter the market, but also to discourage those who would take advantage of differences between national standards, the EU formulates international standards for its market. Given the size of its market, others who want to enter the large EU market find themselves in a position where they have to adapt even where EU standards are not favourable to them. As a result, the EU is potentially in a position not only to create standards for its own market but also to 'encourage' the adoption of EU standards as international standards.

The picture, however, is not uniform. As we noted earlier, the EU has different levels of competence and resources in different areas of policy, and this inevitably feeds through into its impact on the GPE. In areas closely related to the Single Market and to common policies such as those in steel and agriculture, there is a strong basis for the EU to pursue global influence—or at least to resist attempts to limit its influence. In other areas it is much less clear how the EU operates as a collective actor, mostly because the EU member states are often involved as the main actors or there is a sharing of competence between the Union and its member states. Such areas include external development assistance (see Chapter 14) and environmental policy (see Chapter 15).

This raises a key question: how much does the EU manage to 'capture' or to encompass the collective action of its member states in the GPE? From an IPE perspective, this links to a fundamental issue: why do governments transfer sovereignty to international institutions? Scholars such as Moravcsik (1998), following Hoffmann (1966), have emphasized that states really only want to cooperate at the supranational level when there is a clear and immediate trade-off that will secure returns in the short run. In the 1980s and 1990s it became apparent that the composite parts of the EU (its member states) were willing to give up some sovereignty, or to be more precise, 'pool sovereignty' (cf. Keohane and Hoffmann 1990) so as to create a better order that would benefit most of the sum of its parts most of the time. As such the EU has been for some time on track to becoming more deeply integrated and in practice en route to increased federalization; on this basis, it would be possible to argue that it is a 'quasi-federal state' even if falling well short of being a fully fledged federation. But this means that in terms of its participation in the GPE, the EU remains an uneasy hybrid, with the capacity for comprehensive collective action in only a few sectors such as trade and broader commercial policy.

The events of the late 1990s and 2000s, in particular the extended and troubled treaty negotiations over the Constitutional Treaty and the Lisbon Treaty, and their ratification processes, as well as the responses to the financial crisis of 2007–8 and the subsequent 2009 economic crisis, have led to a renewed examination of this quasi-federalist view of the EU. The assumption that the EU is deepening as well as widening (and by implication that this adds to its international status) may be hard to sustain, as there have been so many clear challenges to deeper integration in recent years—not only this, but the increased number of member states may make it more difficult to make efficient decisions. The EU has, of course, made major progress in various areas of policy making, but it is a far cry from becoming an entity that resembles a federal state (even if there are some areas in which developments have led to the EU taking on a more federal-like form). The post-2007 financial crisis in particular has brought to the fore not only divergent responses by member-state governments but also the struggle to find the right balance between collective decision-making and maintaining state sovereignty. Recent developments in the EU surrounding difficult issues, such as the question of what to do about Greece's financial troubles and the risk of contagion to other weaker euro area countries, confirm the general conclusion that the EU is struggling to find the balance between collective action and maintaining state sovereignty. Given this fluctuating struggle within the EU, there is a strong possibility that uncertainty will be transmitted to the broader GPE, in key areas such as economic and financial management.

The EU as a power in the global political economy

As we have seen in the previous sections, the EU27 has jurisdiction over a great number of policy-making areas, ranging from trade, monetary policy, competition, state aids, and agricultural policies—areas in which it has extensive or exclusive powers—to areas in which member states and the EU share competences such as social policy, health, environment, transportation, and more recently education. In political economy terms, this reflects the varying degrees to which member states have been willing to transfer control over specific policy sectors to the Community and now the Union, and to provide the Union with the resources to undertake collective policy making and implementation in key areas of economic activity. The question is: how do these 'internal' powers created by the integration process translate into the EU's role as a 'power' in the GPE?

Looking back at the 1950s and 1960s, it is clear that most of the European integration process focused on cooperation in the area of economics rather than deeper political integration. Economic cooperation, as opposed to, let us say, defence cooperation was less politically controversial and promised to create recognizable returns in the form of economies of scale and scope over the medium term. Economic integration in this context was a way to divert attention away from the whole notion of nation building and the question of who has the power—or as it was once put, 'sneaking up on sovereignty'. Economic cooperation also focused on mid-range results from which all could reap the benefits. This choice to focus in the first instance on issues that could be considered low politics (technical and professional issues) rather than high politics (foreign policy matters, issues that are politicized and considered at the core of national sovereignty), was at the heart of the so-called 'Monnet method', a strategy developed by Jean Monnet to avoid drawing too much attention to who has the power, who is giving it up, and who is controlling the rules of the game. Monnet himself may have been inspired by the experience in the New World (Canada, for instance) where he observed the importance of the integration of people from different backgrounds and the value of economic integration (Ugland 2011) as a step towards deeper political integration.

Thus EC power initially was in the area of low politics, market integration, and technocratic issues. High politics remained with member states; in particular, any security or defence matters remained with member-state governments. They were unwilling to hand over power to the supranational level in these areas (although they also collaborated on an intergovernmental level through organizations such as NATO). As a result the EC was powerful only in being a market maker: an entity focused on setting standards and norms for market integration. This situation inexorably shaped the extent to which the Community could assert itself as a power in the global arena. Whilst from the early 1960s onwards it was an increasingly influential participant in trade negotiations under the GATT, and influenced patterns of international development assistance through the Lomé Conventions from 1975 onwards, it was not yet a real economic power to reckon with, especially given its lack of control over macroeconomic and monetary policies (Kennedy 1991). In this area, the national monetary authorities still held sway, especially the German Bundesbank, which controlled the Deutschmark as a leading international currency.

The creation of the EU in 1993, followed by the accession of three new member states (Sweden, Finland, and Austria) in 1995, marked a key moment both in the internal political economy of the Union and in the development of the EU as an international economic 'power'. The growing demand for membership from the countries of Central and Eastern Europe was also a significant element in the changing internal and international political economy of European integration, reflected especially in the so-called Copenhagen criteria (see Chapter 13). These criteria spelt out the economic, judicial, and political conditions that countries had to meet in order to be considered eligible for EU candidacy status. In other words, this period signalled a potential increase in the power of the EU as a reflection of moves towards reinforced institutions, with ambitious goals (monetary integration, ever closer union, in time a common defence, and so on), and with the potential to control significantly larger parts of the GPE. To put it simply, in terms of the GPE, the EU would extend its power base through enlargement and through treaty reform it could arm itself with new powers that would be convertible into additional international economic influence.

As we have seen earlier in the chapter, this coming together of internal institutional reform and expansion of the EU must be evaluated in terms of the long-term development of the EU's role in the GPE. The EC started to have more economic clout in the international arena during the 1960s through the development of common policies in the area of agriculture and trade cooperation. Agricultural policies had been transferred to the supranational level, and prices were set centrally, with imports into the Community controlled in the cause of ensuring security of supply and the competitiveness of European production. It was only a short step from this to accusations of protectionism from major competitors such as the USA, accompanied by charges that the Community was dumping agricultural goods in world markets, often at the cost of development in Third World countries. The EC, like other developed nations (such as Australia, Canada, Japan, and the USA) was protecting its own domestic farmers at the expense of those abroad, and this meant that agricultural issues were often kept off the negotiating table when international trade agreements were being discussed. To the extent that this gave evidence of a kind of negative power in the GPE, the Community was clearly beginning to have an impact, not only on individual sectors but also on the management of the system more generally.

In a way, as we have seen, this trend continued through the 1970s and 1980s: the internal integration process advanced in a number of areas, but it was difficult for the Community to translate this into coherent and constructive international economic action. The Community in global trade negotiations appeared as more of a 'taker' than a provider of leadership—anxious to protect its interests, and increasingly able to do so, but not at all eager to take on the burden and the potential costs of reshaping not only the global system but also its own internal processes. The fact that the Community was also preoccupied during much of the period with absorbing new member states, and with solving knotty problems attending its own internal financing, increased this impression of introspection and defensiveness.

The single market programme, the creation of the EU, and the 1995 enlargement coupled with the prospect of further expansion to Central and Eastern Europe created the possibility of a genuine increase in the EU's leverage within the GPE. One way in which to conceptualize this process is in terms of the elaboration of a specifically 'European' model of international political economy, based on the creation and expansion of a 'social market economy' embodying not only liberal market practices but also the provision of high levels of welfare and state intervention to ensure social consensus. This was contrasted by some with the 'Anglo-Saxon' free market model of which the major example was the USA and was advocated as a solution to at least some of the problems of political transition after the Cold War and the insecurities created by increasing globalization. The location, proximity, and accessibility of the EU next to the countries of the former Soviet bloc that now had to reorient themselves, meant that the EU was attractive to the many countries that were no longer aligned with Moscow after the Soviet Union had disappeared. Almost all were immediately interested in finding ways to come closer to the EU. In the end, many if not all the countries around the EC gravitated towards the EU. It could be argued that this was a major demonstration of two types of power within the GPE: on the one hand 'soft' power and the power to reward conforming behaviour in the political economy, and on the other hand 'structural' power and the power to get under the skin of the former Soviet countries to reshape their institutions, their legal systems, and their modes of production.

The EU not only widened at this time, it also deepened and increased the scope of its interventions in the political economy of Europe. Through various treaty changes it expanded the scope of 'European' policy making. These processes intersected to produce a new surge of interest not only in market integration (especially through the process of regulation, both deregulation and reregulation) but also in the EU's role as a key player in the international arena. Increasingly, the EU became seen as a grouping capable both of setting credible rules for those operating inside the Union and of contributing to the generation of more effective international rules and regimes. Thus (for example) the EU has influence in the process of standard setting across the globe, indirectly because producers want to be able to produce for the EU market and thus change their patterns of compliance, but also directly when international cooperation on standard setting is discussed. US observers were quick to point out that in the International Organization for Standardization (ISO) the EU even before the 2004 enlargement had 16 votes, compared with the one possessed by the USA. Although numbers are not everything in such areas, the impression was a powerful one.

The pursuit and partial achievement of economic and monetary union within the EU, as we have seen, occupied much of the late 1990s. Although the EMU agenda was largely shaped by the desire for competitiveness and stability within the EU, it inevitably had an international dimension. In the case of the EU, the model was to institutionalize the way in which monetary and fiscal policies had been conducted in Germany on the eve of monetary union, and to modify the behaviour of eurozone member states through the development of a strong monetary discipline. Externally the EU had created a currency that, in one way or another, could measure itself with the leading currencies of the world (see, *inter alia*, Verdun 1997, 2009; Cohen 2003, 2007). Clearly, if this currency could establish itself and, for example, achieve a significant role in major countries' currency reserves and international bond markets, this would be a major addition to the EU's power in the GPE.

By the beginning of the new millennium, it appeared to many that the EU was established as a major 'power' in the GPE. It was continuing to exercise a major influence on international trade negotiations through the World Trade Organization (see Chapter 12); it had claimed a dominant position in the European political economy, which was about to be reinforced by enlargement to Central and Eastern Europe; it was a major player in international development assistance (Chapter 14); and it was playing an influential role in a number of emerging areas of the GPE, such as environment (Chapter 15). Does this mean that in the period 2000–10 the EU was able to fulfil its apparent role as a leader in the GPE?

One element of an answer to this question is to be found in the continuing 'gaps' in the EU's role as an actor within the GPE. First, the EU is not a state: although it possesses a number of 'state powers' and pursues important 'state functions', it cannot act as efficiently and effectively as a state (in the next section we will see examples in which this lack of efficiency and effectiveness can be a real problem). Second, and as a consequence, it is weak in a number of factors associated with a strong state: specifically, it is deficient in centralized economic government, has a small centralized budget, and has only limited powers of taxation. Finally, during the period 2000–10 Europe achieved only a relatively slow rate of growth. Other industrialized countries outperform the economic growth rates of EU countries, even per capita (although not necessarily in terms of output per hour worked—see Alesina and Giavazzi 2006; Blanchard 2004), and other emerging economic 'powers' such as China, Brazil, and India have increasingly outperformed the EU.

In summary, the EU's claim to be a major 'power' in the GPE is contestable. It is clear that the Union possesses the raw material in terms of economic 'weight', but it is not always clear that this weight is translated or translatable into effects within the GPE. One reason for this is the range of 'gaps' in the EU framework that reflect the uneasy institutional and other compromises that have been necessary in order to advance projects such as EMU. The claim that a 'European model' based on the social market economy is appropriate for other regions of the GPE is difficult to sustain, not least because the emergence of new economic 'powers' has provided new models on which the developing world and other areas can draw. The contest is no longer with the 'Anglo-Saxon' model of free market liberalism; indeed, significant elements of the 'social market' model in the EU have been abandoned during the past 20 years as 'neo-liberal' economic models have increased their influence in Brussels and elsewhere. Not only this, but the crisis in the world economy that became apparent in 2007 and after has created problems of governance both within and outside the EU that throw into question the adequacy of multinational solutions to problems in the GPE. It is to these that we turn in the next section of the chapter.

The EU and the governance of the global political economy: competition and crisis

As noted elsewhere in this volume, the EU is part of a multilevel governance structure in the GPE. This structure is formed in part by the very fact that the EU is one of the main actors in the international arena on policies such as trade and regulatory policy. The EU's influence on processes of global economic governance is thus dependent in large measure on its ability to govern internally as well as its capability to project its views in the global arena. But as we have already seen, the EU's capacity to govern key areas of policy making is not a constant: it fluctuates markedly between different areas of policy for a variety of political, institutional, and economic reasons. The EU (as opposed to its member states) can be said to govern policy-making areas such as agriculture, competition policy, and international trade. In other areas—including, crucially, monetary and macroeconomic policy—the EU has limited influence, because of the institutional and other 'gaps' we have identified.

Interestingly, though, in those areas in which the EU is a weaker actor, it can lay claim to a system of governance that still often works quite well at the EU level or at the international level, even if it does not make the EU as a 'conventional' actor look strong. This EU style consists of deliberation and consultation and seeking consensus. Sometimes the resulting policy is itself not a collective stance but allows multiple positions to occur at once. At times also, the EU seeks to reproduce at the global level the EU style of cooperation that it is familiar with at the EU level— deliberation and the search for consensus through the sharing of information and advice. The question is whether this style of governance is appropriate in a world where state policies and state interests still predominate and where there is a potentially very diverse constellation of participants ranging from states to private corporations and NGOs.

One area in which this question can be evaluated is the pursuit of economic competitiveness. In the late 1990s, the EU was being criticized for not being capable of establishing or enhancing its international competitiveness—a criticism not unconnected with the economic underperformance that we earlier identified as a key problem for the Union. The EU responded to these challenges by trying to develop a different way to govern EU prosperity. Whilst it was not possible to underpin competitiveness policy with the full range of budgetary and other instruments that a state might deploy, it was possible to pursue greater transparency and sharing of information among member states and to establish EU-wide benchmarks for performance—the so-called open method of coordination, incorporated in the Lisbon Agenda. This set the aim that the EU should become 'the world's most dynamic knowledge-based economy by 2010'. Most of the achievements, as noted above, would need to be reached via coordination of national policies, but this proved increasingly difficult in a period of economic turbulence; many of the Lisbon targets were missed and others looked increasingly redundant as 2010 approached.

The Lisbon Agenda was replaced in 2009 by the so-called EU 2020 strategy, in March 2010 renamed the Europe 2020 proposal (European Commission 2010). This plan combined the need to target sustainable development with a need to secure jobs and growth given the context of the financial and economic crisis. The core of the plan was to specialize and develop more of the economy based on knowledge and innovation and to enhance sustainable growth. This would mean the promotion of a more resource-efficient, greener, and more competitive economy whilst ensuring that the social dimension was safeguarded and that inclusive growth was pursued. The latter objective would be achieved by finding ways to ensure a high-employment economy but also by making sure there would not be too many discrepancies among various regions. As was the case with the Lisbon Agenda, the EU does not have many instruments to enforce compliance or spend considerable funds on the Europe 2020 programme. It has the power to persuade, and it can set the agenda on the European and (to a certain extent) the global stage. But as in other areas of the EU's international involvement, it cannot be taken for granted that the rest of the world will allow the EU to pursue its goals insulated from global economic trends or that the rest of the world will see the EU 'model' as one to emulate. Evidence for this assertion can be found in the ways in which the EU was challenged by and responded to the global financial and economic crisis after 2007.

The EU sought to respond to the financial crisis when it emerged first in 2007 in the money markets; then in autumn 2008 a new and greater challenge emerged when stock markets collapsed following the collapse of the Lehman Brothers investment bank in the USA and many other banks were threatened with bankruptcy; and finally the fallout of the financial crisis in 2010 led to Greece and other member-state governments encountering problems refinancing their sovereign debt. Significantly, Greece was a member of the eurozone, and thus its financial implosion threatened more than just the stability of financial markets; it challenged the entire system of monetary cooperation that had been established since the late 1990s and further exposed the inadequacy of specifically 'European' mechanisms to cope with disorder in international monetary affairs.

In this situation it was not surprising that EU member states and global financial institutions came to play a central role. In response to the financial crisis of 2007–8, individual EU member states had ended up bailing out their banks. Whilst initially, in late September 2008, just after the Lehman Brothers crisis, EU member-state governments sought to coordinate their response, it soon became clear that the problems were sufficiently national and large that member states would take national decisions, for example by deciding to secure bank deposits and recapitalize the banks themselves through a variety of methods. As they did so one by one, this had the effect of taking savers away from those countries that had not yet secured those deposits, or in which the banks were less clearly guaranteed, clearly causing a problem within the governance of the EU (Verdun 2009). Because the EU only had the opportunity to coordinate, and could not itself offer any guarantees, this implied that unless its power of persuasion was large enough, member states could just as well declare unilateral action. It took the Commission until well towards the end of November to coordinate and deliver an 'EU response' to the events of autumn 2008.

At the height of the financial crisis in autumn 2008 the weakness of the EU governance structure thus once again came to the fore. On the one hand the EU's supranational institutions insufficiently represent the EU in its entirety given the variety of areas of policy making that have shared competence. Thus the Commission could not represent the EU in responses to the crisis, except at the declaratory level. On the other hand, individual countries—with certain partial exceptions—are insufficiently influential to have strong political clout in the global arena. Thus in autumn 2008 a delegation of various EU spokespersons went to Washington to try to address the global financial crisis, including President Nicolas Sarkozy of France (President of the member state holding the rotating presidency of the EU that autumn) accompanied by José Manuel Barroso (President of the Commission). They sought to convince then US President Bush to attend a G20 meeting—the aim of which would be to discuss the global regulatory framework that might be able to prevent these crises from happening again in the future. Eventually two such G20 meetings were held in 2009, but it was noteworthy that among EU member states there was little coordinated policy: Britain, France, and Germany in particular were competitors rather than collective leaders in this process, with the French and the Germans coordinating at times against the British and US positions. Observers close to the meetings jokingly said that the meetings were familiar terrain for EU member states as they had the 'feel' of EU meetings—pursuing elusive multilateral agreements, producing a lot of declarations, searching for consensus, but not necessarily coming to any immediate or concrete conclusions. The European mode of governance seemed to prevail in these G20 meetings, but in many ways that was an admission of defeat or limited ambition. What is more, whilst the EU and its member states had been central to the G8, the G20 inevitably gave them a less influential position when compared with the new emerging 'powers' in the global arena (see previous section).

Finally, the Greek bailout crisis was another case in which the limitations both of internal EU governance mechanisms and of its contribution to international governance efforts were exposed. The EU treaties contain a clause that forbids the EU from bailing out a member state if it is experiencing problems with the refinancing of its public debt. Given this clause, it was inevitably unclear what the EU was to do when Greece during 2009–10 came under severe pressure in precisely this area. The EU leaders—both within 'European' institutions and at member-state level—had different views on what an appropriate response would be. If support was signalled too soon or too unconditionally, it might create a moral hazard problem, whereby Greece and other countries might get the impression that the EU would be there to help them any time they encountered market pressure on the credibility of their public finances. Germany was particularly concerned about this matter—and in Germany itself, the crisis evoked strong feelings about what had been given up when the Deutschmark had been sacrificed for the euro. Another concern was that the whole point of the no-bailout clause was to ensure discipline by member states. However, the longer the EU member states held off their support for Greece, the more costly it became for Greece to refinance its debt, and the more there was a danger of 'contagion' with the crisis spreading to other vulnerable eurozone economies. In May 2010 a package was offered to Greece consisting of contributions from eurozone member states coordinated by the EU and with support by the International Monetary Fund (IMF). The generous package of €120 billion seemed a major step towards securing support for Greece. A week later, following a tumultuous five days of nervousness on financial markets, the package was extended so that if other countries should need to draw on it, there would be funds for them too.

The turmoil in fiscal policy, government debt, and the lack of a timely collective response inevitably had an impact on the euro. Since its very inception it had appeared that the strength of the euro was an indicator, one could perhaps say a thermometer, of public and international financial market perception of the prevailing conditions in the European economy. When the euro was first introduced in financial markets in 1999, there was nervousness about the ability of the European Central Bank and the national governments to keep EMU together and achieve strong growth. The currency depreciated dramatically against the US dollar. Then over several years international confidence picked up and the currency strengthened. Over its first ten years the euro experienced an upward trend against the US dollar, until the financial market crisis hit hardest—a time when many fled into US treasury bonds and other US stocks, which, in turn, led to downward pressure on the euro exchange rate vis-à-vis the US dollar. With the Greek crisis reaching its zenith, the euro exchange rate again dropped considerably (see Figure 11.2), reaching a four-year low.

The effects of the uncertainty in financial markets on the euro led to another effect on internal EU governance. The dramatic decline in the value of the euro in 2010 put intense pressure on the member-state leaders to act in concert, even if in reality they did not agree with one another. The challenge to the euro and the instability in financial markets forced leaders to decide whether they were willing to assist ailing member states or whether they wanted to play hardball and not support them. The choice was for cooperation and support, even if this was difficult to sell domestically in countries such as Germany. The internal divisions had another consequence: they gave the impression that the EU was unable to be a strong actor in the global economy, particularly in terms of monetary and macroeconomic coordination. Thus internal difficulties undermined EU external power and the perceived capacity of the Union to contribute to broader global governance in key areas. The difficulties threatened to undermine the image of the EU, of the euro, and of economic and monetary union as a stable institutional project. Voices were heard that

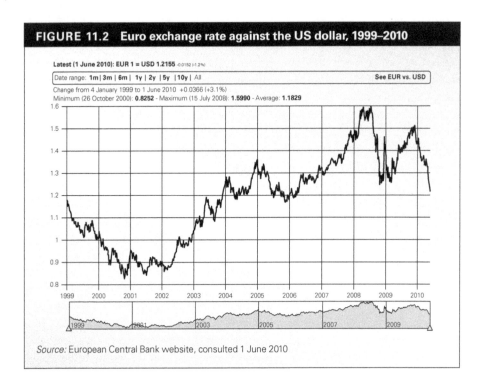

FIGURE 11.2   Euro exchange rate against the US dollar, 1999–2010

Source: European Central Bank website, consulted 1 June 2010

spoke of demise of the EU, the disintegration of EMU, and member states contemplating leaving the euro area. These internal divisions cost the EU dearly in terms of its international reputation.

These episodes in European economic governance and the turbulence in financial markets reinforce key insights from IPE, namely that in an increasingly integrated and globalized economy, the erratic effects of global forces can have a more serious impact on an economy (small economy or a region) than would be logical based on fundamentals. A similar experience had hit various other areas of the world (Argentina, Mexico, South-east Asia, and Russia). IPE literature stresses the need for clear policies to avoid a run on these countries, but in the European context these were not easy to achieve. The euro in this context seems to have had a double effect. On the one hand, the financial crisis of 2009 did not have the effect on European countries that would have been expected if all EU27 member states had different currencies—although there were clear tensions both within the eurozone and between the eurozone and other EU member states. On the other hand, as this implies, the Greek debt crisis of 2010 showed that an asymmetric EMU (a monetary union without some degree of fiscal federalism) runs the risk of being attacked when part of the union is unable to perform according to the rules, as was seen in the Greek case. Both of these dimensions contribute to continuing uncertainty about the role that the EU and the eurozone might play in the global governance of monetary and macroeconomic issues.

Conclusions

In this chapter we have evaluated the extent to which the EU is a putative economic superpower. It has strength through various channels: it has considerable influence in global economic policies, in particular trade and regulatory policies; a presence in monetary policy by virtue of having unified monetary policies of 16 member states and having a supranational institution that sets monetary policy for the euro area and issues a single currency. It boasts strength in other economic indicators such as the size of the internal market, the GDP per capita in the EU27, and its share of international trade.

Yet the EU is far from a dominant economic actor due to its weakness as a political actor and its distinctive governance structure that at times may serve as an obstacle to forceful and clear action in the global arena. The EU is an institution that on the one hand represents itself (the EU in its narrow sense) and on the other its component parts. For an outsider it is often difficult to differentiate between what the EU does as an institution and what the EU does because the EU response is the sum of its parts. Nonetheless, because its member states include various major countries, and because coordination of key policy areas adds value to purely national efforts, the EU is an actor that has helped shape the international arena and international interdependence, in particular in the economic domain.

We have seen in this chapter how the EU established its claim to power in the global arena, in particular in the economic domain, starting from its modest origins in the 1950s through to having the largest market in the world. The EU has been able to become such a leading economic power whilst not being a state in part because of the multilevel nature of EU governance. The EU has some 'state-like' capacities to negotiate and act on behalf of all member states, in particular in areas such as trade, and one can see that the EU is strong in those areas. Yet, at the same time, in other areas the EU cannot speak with one voice. In those other areas (environment, energy, banking regulation, taxation, to name but a few) it either shares competence with member states or does not have the ability at all to speak on behalf of the whole.

In this context it is easy to conclude that the financial crisis of 2008 was not addressed easily because a forceful supranational economic government is absent in the EU. The financial crisis brought to the fore the fact that many of these issues are areas of shared competence between the EU supranational actors and the member states, and that speedy decision-making is a challenge in this institutional setting. Furthermore, with a limited supranational budget, the EU could do very little directly to avert the effects of the crisis. Thus, at the height of the financial crisis Commission President Barroso could only try to lead the pack and mediate among them. This is a far cry from the kind of unified response that one would predict from national governments—but we must remember that even national governments faced considerable problems in responding to these events.

What we have seen in the case of Greece, where the demand for emergency funds required cooperation of the member states, is that in such cases the EU member-state leaders have to come together as a body of governments and coordinate amongst themselves—if necessary, with the support of global financial institutions such as the IMF. This is a challenge that can encounter difficulties in all circumstances except when a crisis is truly imminent. This weakness in the governance structure probably needs to be addressed. But the problem remains; a solution might be to federalize the EU further, something many have no appetite for; hence the challenge of EU governance.

As we noted at the beginning of this chapter, IPE literature has focused on what policy choices there are for individual nations to position themselves in the wider global economy whilst choosing a regime that works for them (be that an open or closed economy, fixed or flexible exchange rates, degree of free trade, and so on). The EU offers an institutional structure that settles a number of these issues for its member states. As a member of the EU a national government has limited room for manoeuvre left. Yet not all the space has been taken up; there remains some space for national policy. Ironically, though, when a crisis hits, a national government itself has only very limited choices and has to act very fast in order not to lose too much to financial market speculation. Thus, reflecting on the issues raised by IPE one can draw the following conclusions. By having joined the EU, a national government's room for manoeuvre has been reduced. Yet it is at once sheltered from global forces as well as exposed to a limited set of policy alternatives to choose from. This situation, in turn, affects how the EU positions itself in the global economy. In order to maximize its influence in the global political economy it would be well advised to coordinate a little better and faster when major economic challenges emerge; but thereby hangs a complex challenge of governance and collective action.

Notes

1 The European Union got its name only on 1 November 1993. However, for simplicity, I will sometimes refer back to the EU also in its past, even though that terminology is not correct.
2 Note that not all privatizations led to a decrease in prices; the UK rail privatization, for instance, did not deliver the desired results.

FURTHER READING

This chapter relies on work written by the author and reported, *inter alia*, in Verdun (2000, 2009) and Heipertz and Verdun (2010). An excellent political economy account of the creation of the single market can be found here in Jabko (2006); the atmosphere around initiation of the single market can be obtained by reading Cecchini (1988)—a work that aimed at motivating the people and businesses to get excited about completing the Single Market. The economics of EMU are explained in detail in De Grauwe (2010), whilst an overview of ten years of EMU from a political science perspective can be found in Enderlein and Verdun (2009) and a discussion of the regulatory arrangements surrounding EMU can be found in Heipertz and Verdun (2010). Further reading on the EU as a trading partner can be found in Young (2007) whereas a good book on EU and environment is Holzinger *et al.* (2008). Della Posta, Uvalic, and Verdun (2009) provides an overview of globalization including the relationship between European integration and globalization. The financial crisis is discussed in Helleiner *et al.* (2010). A discussion of the Lisbon Agenda can be found in the *EUSA Review* of autumn 2006 (which includes a number of useful references). Finally, the Greek crisis is discussed in Featherstone (2010).

Cecchini, P. (with Michael Catinat and Alexis Jacquemin) (1988), *The European Challenge, 1992: the benefits of a single market* (Aldershot; Brookfield, VT: Gower).

De Grauwe, P. (2010), *The Economics of Monetary Union*, 8th edition (Oxford: Oxford University Press).

Della Posta, P., Uvalic, M., and Verdun, A. (2009), *Globalization, Development and Integration: a European perspective* (Basingstoke: Palgrave).

Enderlein, H., and Verdun, A. (2009), 'Ten years of EMU: what have we learned in Political Science?' (Enderlein and Verdun as guest editors of a special issue of *Journal of European Public Policy*, 16:4, June: 490–639).

EUSA Review Forum (2006), 'Taking stock of the Lisbon Agenda: is Lisbon flawed, necessary, window-dressing, or all of the above?', autumn, www.eustudies.org/files/eusa_review/arialfall2006.pdf

Featherstone, K. (2010), 'The limits of Europeanization and the question of reform capacity in Greece', *Journal of Common Market Studies*, forthcoming.

Heipertz, M., and Verdun, A. (2010), *Ruling Europe: the politics of the stability and growth pact* (Cambridge: Cambridge University Press).

Helleiner, E., Pagliari, S., and Zimmerman, H. (eds) (2010), *Global Finance in Crisis: the politics of international regulatory change* (London: Routledge).

Holzinger, K., Knill, C., and Arts, B. (eds) (2008), *Environmental Policy Convergence in Europe: the impact of international institutions and trade*, (Cambridge: Cambridge University Press).

Jabko, N. (2006), *Playing the Market: a political strategy for uniting Europe*, 1985–2005 (Ithaca: Cornell University Press).

Schimmelfennig, F., and Sedelmeier, U. (eds) (2005), *The Politics of European Union Enlargement: Theoretical Approaches* (London: Routledge).

Young, A. R. (2007), 'Trade politics ain't what it used to be: the European Union in the Doha round', *Journal of Common Market Studies*, 45 (4): 789–811.

WEB LINKS

A good source of information on the EU's international economic and financial activities is the Europa website (managed by the European institutions), **http://europa.eu/**, where the main agencies and institutions post policy statements, documents, and other materials that are in the public domain. On monetary policy, see the website of the European Central Bank, **http://www.ecb.int/**. The major economic and financial newspapers have websites that offer a wide range of useful materials, for example **http://www.ft.com/** (*Financial Times*) and **http://www.theeconomist.com/** (*Economist*). On the financial crisis a useful resource is the blog by Professor Nouriel Roubini: **http://www.roubini.com/roubini-monitor**.

CHAPTER 12

The European Union as a Trade Power

Sophie Meunier and Kalypso Nicolaïdis

▍ Summary

The EU is a formidable trade power. While trade liberalization internally and externally has always been the essence of European integration, successive enlargements and the creation of the European single market have turned the EU into the world's largest trade power. The EU is responsible for making trade policy through a complex decision-making process, which has often been contested politically and was recently amended by the Lisbon Treaty but which allows it to speak on behalf of its members in international trade negotiations. This chapter argues that not only does the EU derive some inherent power from trade, but it also uses trade as the backbone of its normative power. As a result the EU is becoming a world power through trade, as one of the major actors shaping the multilateral trade agenda, and using access to its market strategically in order to obtain political concessions from its commercial partners. This role has been challenged, however, by recent changes in the relative power of global trade actors. This chapter explores the determinants of the EU's trade power (both inherent and normative) and examines the contribution of trade policy to the power of Europe in the international system, both in the context of the World Trade Organization (WTO) and in the broader framework of international relations.

Introduction

If there is any area in which the European Union (EU) has become an uncontested power in the international system, it is clearly in the field of trade policy. No wonder: trade is the EU's *raison d'être*. The objective of the 1957 Treaty of Rome was to create a customs union between the original six members of the European Community in which there would be no barriers to trade and a common external tariff would be applied to imports from third countries. From its very beginning, then, the Community became a single actor in international trade policy and almost immediately started talking on an equal footing with the USA in commercial negotiations. With its successive enlargements from six to 27 countries and the prosperous economies of its member states, the EU has become a formidable trade power and interlocutor in international trade negotiations.

Partly by design, partly by necessity, the EU entertains a very different relationship to power from that of the USA. It sees itself above all as a civilian and a normative power, apt at using non-military tools to achieve its goals in the rest of the world (Duchêne 1973; Hill 1990; Manners 2002; Nicolaïdis and Howse 2002; Laïdi 2008). Trade is at the very core of the EU's civilian power. The sheer size of the European single market, which attracts the outside world both for the possibilities it offers and from fear of being excluded, is an essential element of EU power. The collective character of European trade policy has enabled the EU to become a true rival to the USA. Yet the power of the EU in trade goes further than its capacity to defend its own interests in international commercial negotiations. It also lies in its capacity to expand its own regulatory practices to the rest of the world and to use trade to promote internationally its own values and policies according to its internal compromises. In this respect the EU constitutes neither a rival to the US nor necessarily an ally, but it can be viewed as an 'alternative' for countries seeking a power anchor when disagreeing with the USA.

In keeping with the driving themes of this volume, the present chapter explores the determinants of the EU's trade power and examines the contribution of trade policy to the power of Europe in the international system, both in the context of the World Trade Organization and in the broader framework of international relations.

In doing so we argue that it is crucial to distinguish between the inherent power derived from trade and the use of trade as the backbone of normative power. We start by recounting how the EU acquired and retained competence to represent the member states in trade policy, from Rome to Lisbon. The second section provides an overview of the EU trade policy-making process, including the changes introduced by the Lisbon Treaty, while the third section explores how enlargement is affecting the trade power of the EU. The fourth section asks whether and how the EU can still shape the global trade agenda, within and outside the WTO. We conclude by assessing the EU as a world power in trade and through trade.

The road to European competence in trade

The Common Commercial Policy is the most prominent EU policy to have been under supranational competence from the very beginning. Whether in bilateral, regional, or multilateral trade negotiations, Europe formally 'speaks with one voice' and negotiates through one agent, the European Commission. The very idea that nation states could give up such a key area of their external affairs was, and continues to be, revolutionary. But the granting of competence over trade to the supranational authority has not always been without political controversy (Meunier and Nicolaïdis 1999). This section explores the conflicts within the EU over the appropriate institutional design for trade policy making, as reflected in the balance between competences exclusive to the EU and those shared with the member states as well as the growing trade policy-making influence taken on by civil society and the European Parliament.

The Common Commercial Policy in the Treaty of Rome

As the nascent European Community's *raison d'être*, trade policy immediately came under supranational competence. In the field of trade, the Treaty of Rome was a revolutionary document. Not only did it contain unusually broad injunctions for achieving free trade internally, it also granted the new supranational entity an external personality with the authority to elaborate, negotiate, and enforce all aspects of trade relations with the rest of the world.[1] In practice, this was done through the establishment of a common commercial policy based on three principles: a common external tariff, common trade agreements with third countries, and the uniform application of trade instruments across member states.

Until the 1997 Amsterdam summit, the Treaty of Rome's original wording of Article 113,[2] which grants the Community exclusive competence in 'trade' policy (without defining the term), remained almost unchanged (Devuyst 1992; Maresceau 1993). The provisions determining the trade policy-making process delegated authority from the individual states and their parliaments to the assembly of European states, acting collectively through the Council of Ministers. This approach can be understood in classical principal–agent terms: the member states (principals) have delegated their authority to conclude trade agreements to the European Community (agent), acting on their behalf. This contrasts with areas of 'mixed' competence (such as the negotiation of association agreements), where formal authority remains with the individual member states, in particular through parliamentary ratification. In both cases, the member states represent the ultimate authority, but in the former it is as voting parties in the EU structures, while in the latter it is through their sovereign parliament. The conduct of trade policy in practice reveals a second level of delegation, this time from the Council of Ministers (principals) to the European Commission (agent), which initiates the participation of the EU in international trade negotiations and negotiates on behalf of the member states.

The challenge to exclusive competence during the 1990s

During the two decades following the Treaty of Rome, the Commission successfully negotiated on behalf of its members two major trade rounds under the General Agreement on Tariffs and Trade (GATT), as well as a host of bilateral trade agreements. Throughout the 1980s and 1990s, however, several developments challenged the clear foundations of the Community's trade competence.

The first of these challenges was the emergence of so-called 'new issues' (above all services) onto the international trade agenda in the mid 1980s. Issues such as aviation and product standards had been discussed already at the close of the Tokyo round in 1979, but most member states considered these too domestically sensitive to leave entirely to the Commission.[3] The subsequent expansion of the world trade agenda onto policies traditionally not 'at the border' (e.g. tariffs and quotas) but 'inside the state' (e.g. national laws and regulations) forced an explicit internal EU debate on the issue of competence. Several member states, reluctant to give up forever entire new sectors of their trade policy, insisted on being granted their own competences with respect to the 'new issues', arguing that these were not covered under the original Treaty of Rome.

Another challenge was the creation of the new World Trade Organization (WTO), with a broader trade agenda than GATT, which forced the issue of trade authority to the fore (Devuyst 1995). The question of membership constituted an unavoidable legal challenge for the European Community, even though the rest of the world left it up to the Europeans to decide how this would be settled. The EC had never formally substituted the member states in GATT, whose creation preceded that of the Community, but for all practical purposes, the EC—represented by the Commission—had been accepted by the other GATT partners as one of them. Moreover, formally replacing the member states by the EC could have a cost, since the individual voting rights of member states in GATT would give way to a single vote.[4]

In order to solve the competence dispute, the Commission asked the European Court of Justice for an 'advisory opinion' on the issue of competence. If member states were not going to compromise politically, perhaps their objection could be overruled legally. In November 1994, the European judges confirmed that the Community had sole competence to conclude international agreements on trade in goods.[5] In a controversial move, however, they also held that the member states and the Community shared competence in dealing with trade in the 'new issues'.[6] As we have argued elsewhere, the Court in effect had put the ball back in the politicians' court (Meunier and Nicolaïdis 1999; Nicolaïdis and Meunier 2002). To avoid future competence disputes, they would have to amend the treaty either by following the Court's opinion and enshrining this new sharing of sovereignty in the texts or by explicitly 'expanding' Community trade competence to include new issues.

From Amsterdam to Nice: a political solution to the competence dispute

The resolution of the competence dispute and the revision of Article 113 were tacked onto the broad agenda of the 1996 intergovernmental conference (IGC), which was expected to design an institutional reform that would enable the Union to function with at least 25 members in the next millennium. Yet the member states could not agree to put the competence issue in trade to rest. The IGC culminated with the signing of the Amsterdam Treaty, in which the member states eventually agreed to a simple and short amendment to Article 113 (renumbered 133) allowing for future expansion of exclusive competence to the excluded sectors through a unanimous vote of the Council.[7] In trade policy, the Amsterdam outcome was a statement that extension of Community competence should be the result of case-by-case political decisions rather than some uncontrollable spillover. In effect, this decision amounted to a European equivalent of the USA's fast-track procedures, whereby Congress grants trade negotiating authority to the White House and US Trade Representative (USTR) each time a new round of international negotiations is in sight.

Not surprisingly, it quickly became clear that the Amsterdam compromise on trade was not sustainable. Member states felt compelled to review the trade competence issue once more at Nice in December 2000 for three main reasons. First was the significant increase in trade in services which had taken place since 1997. In order to capitalize on such growth, Commission trade officials, with Frenchman Pascal Lamy at the helm since September 1999, insisted that trade in services be transferred under the exclusive competence of the Community for reasons of efficiency.

Second, trade had suddenly become a hot political issue, as globalization gave rise to a new brand of well-organized activists worldwide. The defeat of the OECD-based multilateral agreement on investment in 1998—which aimed to facilitate international investment by ensuring that host governments treat foreign and domestic firms equally favourably—was similarly interpreted by anti-globalization activists as a victory against a text that would have limited the ability of national governments to regulate the protection of their culture, environment, natural resources, and health, as well as ending the protection of their citizens from foreign investors. Trade was again highly politicized in the summer of 1999 when French sheep farmer José Bové and his companions very publicly destroyed a McDonald's in the French countryside in response to the retaliatory trade sanctions that the WTO had authorized the USA to take against the EU in the beef hormones and bananas cases (Meunier 2000a). This politicization of trade reached its peak in December 1999 when the international trade talks in Seattle, which were supposed to launch a new round of multilateral trade talks, collapsed amidst massive public demonstrations by anti-globalization protesters. All of these episodes were reflections of and further contributing factors to the increasingly contentious character of trade.[8] Specifically, anti-globalization activists focused their attention on issues such as trade in cultural, educational, and social services—issues that had been left open to further transfers of competence by the Amsterdam compromise.

Third, the prospect of the imminent enlargement of the EU to many more countries, all with disparate and even contradictory interests, lent a double sense of urgency to revisiting the trade competence issue. On the one hand, external representation—like other policy areas—risked increased inefficiency at best, stalemate at worst. An arrangement originally designed for six members would likely no longer be adequate when the 'single voice' has to represent 25 or 27 different countries. On the other hand, the current members may have had an interest in 'locking in' their preferred institutional design before the widening to new members. The prospect of new entrants eager to use their veto power to block trade liberalization in some sectors or, on the contrary, eager to favour liberalization in other areas where existing members would prefer protection may have proven enough of an incentive for the existing members of the EU to settle the institutional question in Nice.

The final agreement reflected the bargaining dynamics of the negotiation. There was a general momentum in Nice to expand qualified majority voting (QMV), and Article 133 was to be no exception. Exclusive competence became the general rule for trade in services (Article 133.5). Exceptions to exclusive competence in order to satisfy residual national sensitivities were kept to a minimum and carved out under a 'positive list' approach. First and foremost, the treaty enshrined the concept of 'mixed competence' developed by the Court in its 1994 jurisprudence as a new legal category. Particularly noteworthy is the explicit inclusion of the 'cultural exception' clause in Community law, with cultural and audiovisual services falling under mixed competence alongside education, social, and human health services. In addition, transport remained under a separate legal basis (Title V and Article 300). Finally, intellectual property was divided into two components: 'commercial aspects of intellectual property', which fall under exclusive competence, and all other aspects of intellectual property, which are shared. But the Council could decide by unanimity that the provisions relevant to exclusive competence can be extended to the latter—a last echo of the defunct Amsterdam compromise.[9] In EU parlance, the 'passerelle clause' had now been circumscribed to one last, sensitive, area of trade negotiations.

This outcome proved quite satisfactory for most member states: for France (adamant about cultural exception); for the UK (which cared more about the linkage with taxation); for Germany (which was happy about the result for air transport, and whose *Länder* were content with shared competence on culture); and for the pro-integration countries, which could claim that the original spirit of the Treaty of Rome had been, at least to some extent, restored.

Trade policy after the Lisbon Treaty

The debate over competence and representation in trade policy was not closed with the Nice Treaty. When a Convention on the Future of Europe was convened in the spring of 2002 to draft a constitution for Europe, many voices demanded a greater role for the European Parliament in trade. Indeed, these demands have increased as the reach of trade policy increased to politically sensitive issues that used to be the exclusive domain of domestic regulation, such as food safety and culture. A group of EU parliamentarians filed a constitutional amendment that would give the Parliament unprecedented powers in shaping EU trade policy, including the establishment of a right to a vote of assent in the Parliament for any significant bilateral and multilateral trade deals entered into by the EU. The Commission also pushed for a greater role for the parliament in trade policy, on the implicit grounds that a right to veto by the Parliament could provide Commission officials with greater leverage in international trade negotiations.

In the end, the Lisbon Treaty introduced several changes to trade policy making, seemingly bringing the 50-year march to total EU control over trade to its logical conclusion.

First, the Lisbon Treaty simplified trade policy making. It settled the question of competence by entrenching the principle of exclusive Community competence, ending the confusion induced by mixed competences. It also further extended the scope of trade policy, which now applies unambiguously to goods, services, and even foreign direct investment. The only exception remains transport. The use of QMV was broadened correspondingly. According to Article 207 of the Lisbon Treaty (ex-Article 133), the only exceptions to the use of QMV are trade in cultural and audiovisual services when such agreements could jeopardize the cultural and linguistic diversity of the EU (the so-called 'cultural exception'), as well as in the field of trade in social, education, and health services.

Second, the Lisbon reform opened up greater avenues for parliamentary control. According to Article 207, the 'framework for implementing the common commercial policy' now has to be adopted jointly by the Council and the Parliament 'in accordance with the ordinary legislative procedure', meaning that the Parliament shares powers with the Council when it comes to a whole variety of trade-related measures, from anti-dumping to the generalized system of preferences (GSP). Moreover, the Parliament must be kept informed of the progress of trade negotiations. Finally, according to Article 218, the Parliament needs to give its consent for the ratification of trade agreements, whether multilateral or bilateral. In the end, only the launching of new trade negotiations remains outside its remit.

It is still too early to determine whether EU trade policy will function more effectively as a result of these changes, but Article 207 appears to represent a relatively stable equilibrium after more than a decade of haggling over the precise delineation of powers between the EU and the member states. The formal involvement of the European Parliament in trade policy making will likely lead to greater emphasis on issues related to human and labour rights—e.g. 'trade and …' issues, or those related to consumer protection and safety, such as the EU ban on aircraft engine hush-kits to meet noise standards, or data privacy protection, or broadcast and motion-picture quotas. Lobbies and other non-governmental organizations might also find greater access to trade policy making through the Parliament, an issue we now turn to.

The EU trade policy-making process

How does the EU make its policy decisions in commercial policy? The key to this question is the relationship between the Commission and the member states, which can be stylized as a principal–agent relation (Nicolaïdis 2000). We outline below the precise steps and specify the actors involved during each of these steps.

We first need to distinguish between four stages in the negotiation of international agreements: 1) the design of a negotiation mandate; 2) the representation of the parties during the negotiations; 3) the ratification of the agreement once negotiated; and 4) the implementation and enforcement of the agreement once it is brought into force. Up until the entry into force of the Lisbon Treaty, it was important to compare procedures and the actors in charge at each of these stages in cases of 'exclusive' and 'mixed' competence.[10] Whether the Community is perceived to speak with 'one voice' is most relevant during the negotiations but is also affected by shared expectations about the ratification stage.

In theory, the core difference between exclusive and mixed competence comes at the ratification stage. Mixed competence in trade simply means that delegation of authority on the part of the member states is granted on an ad hoc basis for negotiation purposes rather than systematically. Individual member states retain a veto both through unanimous voting in the Council and through ratification by their own national parliament. In practice, the difference is more blurred. On the one hand, exclusive competence does not guarantee a single voice: member states might fail to find a majority behind a given policy and if so, their external front may crumble. More to the point, powerful member states still exercise an informal veto at both the mandate and the ratification stages, to the extent that the Luxembourg compromise extends to the trade area. Conversely, member states have managed to speak with one voice in areas of mixed competence or common foreign policy (as exemplified by 95 per cent of the decisions taken in common in the United Nations). The principle of unity of representation through the Commission is valid under both configurations, even if in both cases individual member states usually seek to reduce Commission autonomy to the extent tolerated by their partners. Nevertheless, the expression of dissent is dampened, the incentives for seeking compromise increased, and the role of the Commission enhanced in areas of exclusive competence.

The negotiating mandate

The European Commission has the power to propose legislation, act as the guardian of EU treaties, and ensure that EU legislation is implemented by all members. The Commission's role in the EU institutional edifice is to act in support of the collective goals and needs, independently of instructions from national governments. Therefore it is up to the Commission to elaborate proposals for the initiation and content of international trade negotiations (Johnson 1998; Meunier and Nicolaïdis 1999; Woolcock 2000; Elsig 2002; Meunier 2005). The initial proposals are made by staffers in the Trade Directorate (DG Trade), based like the rest of the Commission in Brussels. DG Trade assists, and answers to, the EU Trade Commissioner, nominated by the member states for a five-year term (Pascal Lamy 1999–2004, Peter Mandelson 2004–8; Catherine Ashton 2008–9; Karel de Gucht 2010–). DG Trade also oversees the use of trade policy instruments (see Box 12.1).

BOX 12.1   EU trade policy instruments

Trade policy instruments

The EU Commission, through DG Trade, also oversees the use of trade policy instruments, which are of the defensive and the proactive types:

- *Defensive instruments*: trade defence instruments (TDI) may be used to counter unfair trade practices by other countries, in accordance with WTO agreements. They consist of:
  - Anti-dumping measures: used to counter dumping, which occurs when manufacturers from a non-EU country sell goods in the EU below the sales price in their domestic market or below the cost of production—this is the most frequent trade-distorting practice.
  - Anti-subsidy measures: used to combat subsidies, which help to reduce production costs from abroad or cut the price of EU exports, with the consequence of distorting trade.
  - Safeguards: the WTO allows a country to temporarily restrict imports of a product if its domestic industry is seriously injured by a surge in imports.

- *Proactive instruments*: Trade barriers regulation (TBR) enables companies to lodge a complaint with the EU Commission when they feel they encounter trade barriers that restrict their access to third-country markets.

Source: http://europa.eu.int/comm/trade/issues/respectrules/tpi_en/htm

Once DG Trade has elaborated proposals for trade negotiations, the key policy discussions take place in a special advisory committee, called the Trade Policy Committee (TPC, previously named the 113 Committee and then the 133 Committee after the articles in the Treaty of Rome and Treaty of Amsterdam respectively that set out trade policy principles). It plays a key role in helping member states influence EU trade policy, even though its role is formally consultative only. The agenda of the TPC is set by the Commission, in collaboration with the rotating presidency of the EU. The TPC meets weekly at either the senior level or at the level of deputies. The senior members (titulaires), senior civil servants from the member states' national ministries, as well as the director-general of DG Trade meet once a month in Brussels. In addition they meet in Geneva whenever there are WTO plenary sessions. These senior members serve on the committee for extended periods of time and have a good sense of what actions are politically acceptable within their state of origin. They deal only with the politically sensitive problems. The TPC also meets three Fridays a month at the level of deputies, who are drawn from the member states' permanent representations in Brussels, sometimes from the national ministries, in addition to the director of the WTO unit within DG Trade, and special experts. The deputies deal with the more technical issues. Additionally, there are also subcommittees of a sectoral nature (such as '133 textiles', '133 services', '133 steel'), which prepare the work for the TPC. Matters are typically discussed until a consensus emerges, and no formal votes are recorded.[11]

The Commission almost always follows the advice of the TPC, since its members reflect the wishes of the ministers who ultimately can refuse to conclude the agreement negotiated by the Commission.[12] Once the Committee has amended Commission proposals, they are transmitted to the Committee of Permanent Representatives (Coreper)—a key group based in Brussels and composed of the member state officials who are national ambassadors to the EU, their deputies and staff. Coreper then transmits the negotiating proposal to the Council of Ministers, which has the power to establish objectives for trade negotiations (known as the 'negotiating mandate'). Composed of ministers from each government, the Council represents the national interests of the member states. The composition of the Council varies, depending on the subject matter under discussion. With respect to trade policy, the issues are often tackled by the General Affairs and External Relations Council (GAERC), where the member states are in principle represented by foreign ministers, although sometimes it is composed exclusively of trade ministers.

The Council then agrees on a negotiating mandate to hand out to the Commission. The form of the actual mandate varies depending on the negotiation: in some cases the mandate takes the form of one or several directives, while in other cases the mandate is only a very vague document.[13] 'Negotiating directives' are not legally constraining: the negotiator can depart from these directives, but then takes the risk of having to sell the negotiating package to the Council at the end of the negotiation. Court jurisprudence and treaty articles spell out the cases in which policy decisions are made according to majority or unanimity. According to the 1957 Treaty of Rome, unanimity should have been used for external trade only until January 1966, the end of the transitional period. Majority voting would have been automatically instituted after this date had France's De Gaulle not paralysed the functioning of Community institutions with the 'empty chair' crisis during the Kennedy round. The crisis resulted in the 'Luxembourg compromise', a gentleman's agreement according to which an individual member state could veto a decision otherwise taken according to qualified majority if it deemed that vital national interests were at stake. The subsequent addition of new member states increased the divergence of interests within the EC and rendered even more difficult the task of reaching a common bargaining position for international trade negotiations. The 1985 Single European Act attempted to establish the primacy of majority voting. With the exception of sensitive areas such as taxes, employee rights, and the free movement of persons, the member states agreed to use majority voting to legislate on all economic matters.[14] Since then, at least on paper, the Council agrees on a common external bargaining position for international trade negotiations on 'traditional' trade issues (exclusive of services and intellectual property) according to a 'qualified majority' system. This is a procedure under which member states are assigned different voting weights, based approximately on the size of their population, and by which roughly two-thirds of the votes are needed in order for a proposal to be accepted.[15] Nevertheless, in reaching a common bargaining position for international trade negotiations, as in reaching most other policy decisions in the Community, member states have most often attempted to find a general consensus around a given issue without resorting to a formal vote. Almost none of the cases in which Council decisions have been contested to the level at which a formal vote was needed have involved trade issues, reflecting both the more general difference in EU policy making between QMV as a legally ordained procedure and the reality, and the perceived importance of achieving unity on external policy matters.[16]

The competence over external trade negotiations has therefore long been fairly centralized at the Commission and Council levels. Until the entry into force of the Lisbon Treaty, the European Parliament had no formal say in the process. Prior treaty modifications, such as the 1986 Single European Act, the 1991 Maastricht Treaty, the 1997 Amsterdam Treaty, and the 2000 Nice Treaty, had not increased the role of the Parliament in the trade policy-making process. In practice, informal procedures existed for informing and consulting the Parliament. They have now been institutionalized and it is expected that the International Trade Committee of the Parliament (INTA) will now become an involved player in the process.

The negotiations

Following the adoption of the negotiating mandate by the Council, the actual conduct of international trade negotiations for the EU is carried out by members of the Commission, acting under the authority of the Trade Commissioner. The situation during the negotiations may seem somewhat surrealistic: member states are allowed to observe but not speak in WTO plenary sessions. In principle, as long as they remain within the limits set by the mandate, Commission negotiators are free to conduct bargaining with third countries as they wish. In practice the negotiators' latitude and flexibility vary case by case, depending on the member states' willingness to give up control over the issue being negotiated. While they remain silent in plenary, member states' ambassadors usually do not shy away from informal corridor negotiations with EU counterparts. Moreover, the TPC often meets in Geneva during the negotiations to ascertain whether the Commission remains with its mandate and to agree on changes in negotiating position. Thus if the EU Commissioner is envisaging a significant move, he needs to either call the capitals or call a meeting on the premise of the negotiations. This oversight often makes moves and concessions harder for the EU than for other trade partners, but it also gives it significant bargaining power (Meunier 2000b; Meunier 2005). From the member states' viewpoint, it is this oversight that makes it acceptable to issue vague mandates containing little indication of the actual positions to be taken in negotiation.

The ratification

At the conclusion of the negotiations, the trade agreement must be ratified. In the past, for agreements falling entirely under EU competence (such as on textiles and steel), the Council approved or rejected the final text according to qualified majority voting—with the exception of some services and intellectual property negotiations where unanimity is the rule. In most cases, however, the ratification process was complicated by the 'mixed' nature of many of the big 'packaged' trade agreements, which must be approved both by the EU as a whole and by the individual member states. EU ratification occurred through adoption in the Council. As for member states, they ratified the trade agreement according to their own internal procedures, such as a vote in parliament. Under the rules of the Lisbon Treaty, the agreements will now be ratified by the Council with the assent of the European Parliament. There should be no room for big surprises at the ratification stage of the negotiation, since member states and the Parliament will have had ample time to manifest their reservations during the course of the international negotiations.

The enlarged EU as a trade power

The EU enlarged by ten new countries in May 2004 and then two additional countries in 2007. This did not trigger any immediate disruption of trade, since the transition had been prepared for a decade. Indeed, on the eve of enlargement, over 95 per cent of the trade of the EU15 with the new entrants was already free.

Structurally, enlargement made the EU stronger in relation to its trade negotiating partners, because a larger single market is both a more attractive prize to outside economic players and a more costly opportunity loss when a threat of being cut out is carried through. Enlargement increased the size of the single market (accounting for 18 per cent of world trade and contributing to 25 per cent of the world's GDP), augmented the geographical size of the EU by 34 per cent, and boosted the total population by 105 million to a total of 450 million.[17]

By joining the EU, however, the new entrants brought in a wealth of different histories and cultures, which also means different interests, priorities, and sensibilities that had to be amalgamated in the definition of an EU trade interest. Pessimists argued that such diversity could incapacitate the EU and bog down multilateral trade liberalization while increasing EU protectionism through the mere logic of agreement over the lowest common denominator.

After only a few years' experience of enlargement, it is fair to say that these predictions have not come true. To be sure, EU negotiations have become more complex in the trade realm as elsewhere. But if anything, decision-making efficiency has increased, not decreased (Dehousse, Deloche-Gaudez, and Duhamel 2006). And enlargement generally seems to have strengthened the liberalization camp, including through an automatic drop in adjusted customs duties, with some notable exceptions in agriculture, especially for products such as wheat, beef, and dairy products, which are all important in the EU trade policy at the WTO. The further concentration of trade policy-making power in the hands of the Commission may have also helped in this regard (Van den Hoven 2002). Unsurprisingly, the new entrants have been slightly more prone than other member states to cater to US demands, although here again their material interests pull them back to the mean, in their support for anti-dumping measures for basic industrial goods such as steel, chemicals, and textiles. On the whole, the interests of the new entrants have not diverged significantly from the status quo ante, mapping onto existing cleavages and internal bargain dynamics.

The EU as champion of multilateralism?

How does the EU exercise its formidable power in trade policy? We argue that it has been by asserting its central role in the multilateral system, less to uphold the value of multilateralism as a public good than to promote the EU's own interest in this system. The EU has presented itself as a champion of multilateralism, claiming that its single market was a building block for multilateralism, using its trade power to attempt to manage globalization in its image, and often positing itself as champion of international law (by contrast to the USA, for instance). Yet can it genuinely pretend to defend developing countries in view of the amount of subsidies poured into its protectionist agricultural policy? Is the EU not trying to impose its own regulatory model as a condition for free trade instead of negotiating with world partners on an equal footing? And how can it continue to be a strong power in a world where large trading nations, such as China and India, are emerging as actors with an increasingly powerful voice?

The European single market and world trade liberalization

From its inception, the EU has played a central role in multilateral trade negotiations (Woolcock 1993; Young 2000, 2002; M. Smith 2001; Meunier 2005). In the 1960s it introduced a new radical tariff-cutting formula that greatly reduced the transaction costs of negotiations. In spite of the rising trend of 'new protectionism' in the 1970s, the Europeans led the way in attacking so-called non-tariff barriers. As the EU accelerated the pace of completion of its single market in the run-up to 1992, issues became more complicated. Quite logically, it required that firms wishing to export goods and services into the EU conform to its standards and regulations as well as to its conformity assessment procedures (Mattli and Buthe 2003). Since such requirements had not been consistently enforced before, the move initially spurred cries of 'fortress Europe'—indeed the external dimension of the single market had been dealt with a bit as an afterthought. But the EU Commission quickly sought to ensure that foreign firms be given a fair chance of access through opportunities to demonstrate their conformity to standards (Nicolaïdis and Egan 2001).

As the programme to complete the single market agreed to under the Single European Act (1987–92) coincided with the Uruguay round (1986–93), the EU progressively developed a strategy to export its approach to trade liberalization to the global level, especially in dealing with trade in services, the core new area in both settings (Drake and Nicolaïdis 1992). Along with the USA, it promoted the inclusion of 'new issues' (services, intellectual property rights, and trade-related investment measures) under the WTO, which was created at the end of the Uruguay round. Agriculture, however, has remained the glaring counter-example of liberalization. By the end of the Uruguay round in 1993, the EU did not look so good as a trade liberalizer, as the trade distortions engendered by the Common Agricultural Policy led the USA to build a coalition of GATT members against the European agricultural policy (Patterson 1997; Davis 2003). The Cairns group on its part mobilized against both US and EU farming support.[18]

But the issue is not only how much liberalization, but also what kind of liberalization and for whose benefit. During the 1990s, the developing world progressively came to question the 'grand bargain' agreed to during the Uruguay round—namely, accepting to open up their markets to services and to enforce patents in exchange for greater access for their industrial products. The cost of the former turned out to be higher than many had foreseen, while increased access for Third World exports often failed to materialize. Initially both the USA and the EU resisted their attempt to revisit this bargain, while at the same time pushing for a continued expansion of the multilateral agenda to include issues such as linkage between trade access and labour and environment standards. The tension between OECD countries—including the EU—and the developing world culminated in Seattle in 1999. But in the early years of the Doha development round, launched in November 2001, the EU managed to establish, at least partly, a new reputation as a champion of multilateralism. It promoted the adoption of a path-breaking declaration on trade and public health, which opened the way for legalizing broad exemptions from intellectual property constraints by importing generic drugs to treat diseases like AIDS (a final agreement was finally accepted by the USA in August 2003). Moreover, the EU sought to take the lead in making good on market access by launching in the run-up to the Doha round the 'everything but arms' initiative (EBA), designed to offer preferential market access to the exports of the 48 least developed countries in the world. This initiative enabled the EU to change its image in the WTO by holding the high moral ground, even though it was not able then to have its approach adopted by the entire WTO membership.

The EU also used the early years of the Doha round as an opportunity to attempt to 'manage globalization', according to the doctrine laid out by then trade commissioner Pascal Lamy (Jacoby and Meunier 2010). Promoting multilateralism was at the heart of the managed globalization agenda, based on the premise that the more members that participate in the international trading regime, the greater share of trade is subjected to rules and therefore to a less anarchic system (Abdelal and Meunier 2010). The EU gave a clear priority to multilateralism, going so far as establishing an informal moratorium on new bilateral agreements, in contrast to the policy of 'competitive liberalization' pursued by the USA at that time. But unsurprisingly, it became clear that such a policy of exclusive multilateralism not only diluted EU power and increased the power of countries with contrary interests, but also failed to provide momentum to the Doha round. As a result, Pascal Lamy's successor, Peter Mandelson, abandoned the policy in 2006 in favour of the 'Global Europe' agenda, aiming to combine a wider array of trade policy tools.

Moreover, many voices have questioned the genuineness of the EU's proclaimed commitment to putting multilateralism at the service of development. Agriculture has at last come centre stage in the Doha round, with developed countries being asked to reduce (if not eliminate) their trade-distorting farm subsidies and drastically decrease their tariffs, quotas, and non-tariff barriers. While the EU and the USA had reached a common proposal on reform of the protection of their agriculture, this was not enough. The collapse of the WTO Cancun meeting in September 2003 was due to a great extent to differences over agricultural reform, especially over the issue of cotton, between the USA, the EU, and a group of developing countries led by Brazil and India (called the G22). Perhaps more fundamentally, the meeting exposed a clash between an EU philosophy of trade liberalization based on the design and enforcement of new multilateral rules reproducing the EU's own approach (the so-called 'Singapore issues'—investment, competition policy, government procurement, and trade facilitation) and the approach of most of the rest of the world, which continues to view trade rounds as fora for the exchange of reciprocal conditions. The abrupt end of the Cancun meeting testified to this tension and left a great deal of uncertainty on how to proceed next with talks on agriculture, industrial goods, and the Singapore issues when agreements need to be reached in a consensual way in an organization with around 150 members.

In what direction is EU trade policy evolving? The EU has offered to cut agricultural tariffs by 60 per cent, reduce trade-distorting farm subsidies by 80 per cent, and eliminate agricultural export subsidies altogether, provided that others do the same and that the final agreement offers an overall balanced package on agriculture. For decades the issue of agricultural export subsidies had been a sticking point in multilateral trade negotiations, so this is close to a revolutionary proposal (even if it is easy to argue that, in the long run, the EU has little choice over giving them up). In exchange, the EU wants to obtain increased market access in the industrial goods sector. Finally, the EU expects from the round a new set of rules regarding the use of trade defence instruments and is insistent that new multilateral rules for geographical indications be approved. Negotiations over the so-called Singapore issues as well as broader governance reform issues have been left until after the round (Howse and Nicolaïdis 2008).

Settling disputes in the WTO

The WTO differs from its predecessor, the GATT, not only because it is a bona fide organization rather than a mere 'agreement' with a broader scope, but also and perhaps most importantly due to its significantly strengthened dispute-settlement mechanism, in which the EU has been an active participant. In February 2010, the EU was involved in 40 WTO disputes as both a plaintiff (16 cases) and a defendant (24 cases) with 16 of its trading partners (Argentina, Brazil, Canada, China, Colombia, Ecuador, Honduras, India, Japan, Nicaragua, Norway, Panama, Philippines, Chinese Taipei, Thailand, and the USA).[19] In the majority of these cases, the EU was paired against the USA, but the number of cases pairing the EU and China has been increasing.

Such a high level of involvement has strengthened overall the power of the EU in trade. On one hand, some of the EU's trade partners have exercised their rights to demand change in EU trade practices (such as on hormone-treated beef and bananas), which has resulted either in compliance or in the willingness by the EU to incur retaliatory sanctions. On the other hand, participation in the WTO has enabled the EU to confront other trade partners, in particular the USA, on a variety of unilateral actions (see Box 12.1). The following examples of recent and ongoing transatlantic trade disputes are evidence of the power of the EU in the multilateral trade arena.

Steel

In the spring of 2002, the Bush administration in the USA unilaterally raised steel tariffs for a three-year period by 30 per cent in order to protect the US domestic steel industry from the problem of global overcapacity during a time of restructuring. The EU (and seven other countries)[20] launched a lawsuit at the WTO, which

ruled that the tariffs were in violation of international trade rules. The WTO confirmed in November 2003 in its final ruling that the US tariffs are indeed illegal
under international trade rules. Faced with the threat that Europe would impose
100 per cent duties on $2.2 billion worth of US imports, ranging from Harley-
Davidsons to underwear to citrus juices from Florida—products chosen mainly
because of coming from swing states crucial for the 2004 US presidential election—
Washington dropped the tariffs in December 2003.

Tax breaks

In 2000 the EU asked the WTO to adjudicate on the so-called Foreign Sales Cor-
poration (FSC) dispute, because this American law was believed to confer illegal
export subsidies on many US companies by taxing exports more favourably than
production abroad. In subsequent rulings, the WTO confirmed that the FSC constituted an illegal export subsidy and gave the US administration until November
2000 to withdraw its scheme. The USA replaced the FSC law, but because the new
law did not substantially modify the export subsidy scheme, the EU challenged it
again in the WTO. In 2002 the WTO ruled again that these breaks were indeed an
illegal subsidy and authorized the EU to impose $4 billion in retaliatory sanctions
if the US law was not brought into compliance with WTO obligations. The Europeans, fearful of what the sanctions would do to their own economies given the size
of the potential disruption to transatlantic trade (more than ten times larger than
the beef and bananas sanctions combined), opted for patience and instead gave the
USA ample time to change its tax laws. In March 2004 the EU began to gradually
implement some retaliatory sanctions on US exports. The law repealing the FSC
was finally passed in October 2004 and was to be implemented as of 2005 (with a
transition period). The EU agreed to lift the sanctions when the implementation of
the new US law proved satisfactory.

Anti-dumping

In 2000 the WTO condemned the US 1916 Anti-Dumping Act for allowing sanctions against dumping not permitted under WTO agreements and gave the USA
one year to repeal the Act. In February 2004, given the non-compliance of the USA,
the WTO allowed the EU to retaliate by implementing a mirror regulation that
would be applicable only to US products.

Genetically modified organisms

Since 1998, the EU has observed a moratorium on the approval of genetically modified products, and some member states banned the import and cultivation of some
crops that had been approved prior to that date. The EU made this decision in
response to popular concern about the long-term impact of genetically modified
organisms (GMOs) on human health and the environment, although there was little scientific evidence to support these concerns but no evidence either that GMOs
are harmless (Pollack and Shaffer 2000; Vogel 2002; Rhinard 2004). This measure

led to the suspension of exports of genetically modified corn from the USA. Successive American administrations were hesitant at first to challenge at the WTO the issue of whether such public health concerns could legitimize protectionism. In May 2003, however, the Bush administration decided to finally file suit against the EU at the WTO when it was learned that the EU had warned Zambia to refuse US donations of genetically modified corn and that many poor African nations had refused to experiment with GMO crops for fear that they could not sell them in Europe. Such a lawsuit, however, was politically risky. It risked a backlash from European consumers, already quite nervous over food safety in the wake of the mad cow and foot and mouth diseases, and perhaps some consumer resistance in the USA as well.

'Open bilateralism'? The limits of transatlantic trade cooperation

In spite of these disputes, the transatlantic trade partnership is characterized by a much greater degree of cooperation than conflict, owing to the unprecedented level of interdependence between the two sides of the Atlantic. The EU and the USA are still each other's main trading partner (goods and services combined) and main investor. Trade flows across the Atlantic amount to $1.9 billion every day. While transatlantic economic cooperation is not new, the post-Cold War era has been characterized by a much greater emphasis on economic and regulatory cooperation than ever before and the growing recognition by the USA of the importance of the EU as an interlocutor over and above the member states. In the wake of the disputes surrounding the completion of the single market mentioned above, the EU and the USA signed a series of agreements to underpin their new transatlantic partnership—the Transatlantic Declaration (1990), the New Transatlantic Agenda (NTA 1995), and the Transatlantic Economic Partnership (TEP 1998). In 2007 the EU and the USA set up the Transatlantic Economic Council (TEC), a political body supposed to accelerate direct economic cooperation between the two entities and, in particular, harmonize regulations.

One of the most innovative aspects of the new transatlantic cooperation was the signing in 1997 of a series of 'mutual recognition agreements' (MRAs), from pharmaceuticals to telecoms. These agreements were certainly less ambitious than their inspirations—the mutual recognition directives enforced to complete the internal market of the EU—in that they only covered the recognition of conformity assessments rather than recognition of the standards themselves (Nicolaïdis and Egan 2001). But the difficulty of reaching such agreements should not be underestimated. US agencies like the Food and Drug Administration had to undergo a great deal of pressure before agreeing to transfer part of their regulatory authority to their EU counterparts. And accommodating the complex array of conformity assessment bodies operating in the USA for electrical standards and the like to the more coordinated system prevailing in the EU was no small feat. In fact, it has proven impossible to extend the MRA approach beyond the original six to other products or to services where the USA is notoriously plagued by regulatory fragmentation due to its federal structure. At the same time, the EU has successfully negotiated a whole array of MRAs around the world, spearheading a movement towards trade-friendly regulatory reform without deregulation. Whether its approach can serve as a laboratory for regulatory cooperation under WTO remains to be seen (Nicolaïdis and Howse 2002).

Preferential agreements, bilateralism, and regionalism: the EU's trade web

Last but not least, over the last decades the EU has built a complex web of preferential agreements that has come to encompass most of the planet—thus calling into question their 'preferential' nature. For several decades, it negotiated trade agreements only with its immediate neighbours and the former colonies with which it shared historical ties, mainly through the successive Lomé (later Cotonou) conventions. Progressively, however, the EU trade web was extended to other individual countries and regional groupings.

The EU's core set of preferential agreements remains with its neighbours and its former colonies. In 1995, it stepped up its cooperation with its Mediterranean neighbours through the 1995 Euro–Mediterranean partnership (also referred to as the 'Barcelona process'), with the goal of establishing a Euro–Mediterranean free trade area by 2010 through a combination of association agreements, between the EU and its partners, and free trade agreements between themselves. These association agreements also include respect for human rights and democratic principles as essential elements—with clauses added after 9/11 on fighting terrorism and on non-proliferation of weapons of mass destruction. In July 2008, the Barcelona process was revamped under the new label of the Union for the Mediterranean. This was a controversial development spearheaded by France under its presidency of the Union, which involved greater emphasis on project-based cooperation and an attempt to share governance with southern partners more equitably (Bechev and Nicolaïdis 2008). At the same time, the EU has developed an overarching neighbourhood policy (ENP) since 2004, which encompasses both southern and eastern partners—the latter under their own 'Eastern partnership' since 2009. The real challenge both in the east and in the south is whether it will be possible to move beyond the logic of associating more convergence with more access—above all trade access, using the trade liberalization momentum to engage in deeper polity building (Bechev and Nicolaïdis 2010).

As mentioned, the second front of core EU preferential agreements has been with ACP countries since 1963 (see also Chapter 14). However, a WTO injunction to introduce greater reciprocity or else simply to apply the GSP to these countries has led to the negotiations of Economic Partnership Agreements (EPAs) since 2003. These negotiations have been premised on the consolidation or creation of seven regions in Africa and the Caribbean, which are supposed to negotiate with the EU as a whole. The EPA negotiations, however, have been mostly stalled due to a combination of factors, including the perception of a neocolonial attitude on the part of the EU's trading partners (Collier and Nicolaïdis 2008; Jones and Marti 2009).

Beyond its neighbours and former colonies, the EU has engaged on another road, namely inter-regionalism, or region-to-region trade agreements, starting with an all-encompassing agreement with the customs union Mercosur (Argentina, Brazil, Paraguay, and Uruguay), aiming at the creation of a free trade area. While the negotiations have been going on for more than a decade, they have been stalled by a range of issues, from agriculture to standards. If the parties were to agree, however, this would be the first agreement between two customs unions. In this realm, as in others, the EU's capacity to resist using its trade stick to promote its own model is being tested.

Finally, and during the same period, the EU has negotiated trade agreements with a variety of other countries, from South Africa in 2000 to Latin America, where the EU has signed 'global agreements' (including free trade) with Mexico in 2000 and Chile in 2002 (Sbragia 2004). After the end of the informal moratorium on new bilateral agreements in 2006, it has pursued bilateralism and inter-regionalism with a vengeance, negotiating trade agreements with India, Korea, Singapore, ASEAN, Canada, Columbia, Peru, Ukraine, and Vietnam. To some extent a forced reaction to US bilateralism starting with NAFTA, it can be argued that the new policy is increasing EU power by attempting to restore a level playing field for European companies competing in the lucrative Asian and Latin American markets. It can also be argued that regionalism has enhanced the EU's normative power, as it acts as a 'globalizer' with Latin America, using inter-regional trade agreements to promote and export norms of transnational governance.

Conclusion: the EU as a power in and through trade

The EU is a formidable power *in* trade. If it is considered as one single economic unit, there is little doubt that it has become, since the last enlargement, the biggest trading block in the world. For all its manufacturing and trading might, China is still dwarfed by the EU. As a result, the EU's hegemonic economic power, based on the capacity to grant or withhold access to its internal market, has become as strong as that of the USA. Moreover, its more than 50 years of experience negotiating international trade agreements on behalf of its members have made the EU an essential player and a powerful bargainer in the multilateral trading system.

The EU is also becoming a power *through* trade. Increasingly, it uses market access as a bargaining chip to promote changes in the domestic arena of its trading partners, from labour standards to development policies. Indeed, in the last decade its policy makers have sought to 'harness globalization' and spread, through the negotiation of trade agreements, the 'European model' to the rest of the world. For many of its partners around the world such an aim smacks of neocolonialism, a kind of European hubris that is not always welcome, especially in light of its most recent setbacks around constitutional reform. At the same time, because the EU model of interstate cooperation based on free trade is widely emulated, it can still capitalize on this image without necessarily linking market access with convergence to its norms.

Will the EU be willing or able to transform its structural power into effective influence? What will be its goals in establishing itself as a global power through trade? In particular, can the EU become an important foreign policy actor through the back door, by using trade instead of more traditional diplomatic or military means? Interestingly, the Lisbon Treaty for the first time bundled trade policy under the general rubric of the EU's external action, thereby suggesting strongly that commercial policy was indeed an integral component of the EU's nascent foreign policy. But before the EU can effectively exercise power *through* trade it will need to address the conflicts and tensions between its avowed principles, between in particular its professed commitment to multilateralism and its practice of liberalism and inter-regionalism, between its commitment to non-discrimination and the proliferation of preferential agreements, between in the end a professed belief in free trade as an end in itself and the use of trade as a weapon to pursue unrelated goals (Meunier and Nicolaïdis 2006). The EU may be a trade power but it is a conflicted trade power, between its member states, between its principles, and ultimately between visions of itself.

Notes

1 The 1952 European Coal and Steel Community (ECSC) did not have external powers.

2 Article 113 was renamed Article 133 at Amsterdam.

3 At that point, they found a compromise solution whereby the Community concluded all the agreements of the round, while the ECSC tariff protocol, the standards code and the civil aircraft code were concluded jointly by the Community and the member states.

4 Since GATT operated by consensus, this had more symbolic than practical significance.

5 Including agricultural products and products covered by the ECSC and EURATOM (European Atomic Energy Community) treaties.

6 Court of Justice of the European Communities, Opinion 1/94, 15 November 1994, I-123:

    1. The Community has sole competence, pursuant to Article 113 of the EC Treaty, to conclude the multilateral agreements on trade in goods.

2. The Community and its member states are jointly competent to conclude GATS [General Agreement on Trade in Services].

3. The Community and its member states are jointly competent to conclude TRIPS [trade-related aspects of intellectual property rights].

7 The new Article 113(5) as finally adopted reads as follows: 'The Council, acting unanimously on a proposal from the Commission and after consulting the European Parliament, may extend the application of paragraph 1 to 4 to international negotiations and agreements on services and intellectual property insofar as they are not covered by these paragraphs.'

8 Meunier 2000b.

9 Article 133, para. 6:

An agreement may not be concluded by the Council if it includes provisions which would go beyond the Community's internal powers, in particular by leading to harmonization of the laws or regulations of the member states in an area for which this treaty rules out such harmonization.

In this regard, by way of derogation from the first subparagraph of paragraph 5, agreements relating to trade in cultural and audiovisual services, educational services, and social and human health services, shall fall within the shared competence of the Community and its member states. Consequently, in addition to a Community decision taken in accordance with the relevant provisions of Article 300, the negotiation of such agreements shall require the common accord of the member states.

The negotiation and conclusion of international agreements in the field of transport shall continue to be governed by the provisions of Title V and Article 300.

10 We leave out the enforcement stage, which is of less importance to our discussion.

11 The deliberations of the TPC are not published, which is a complaint often raised by anti-globalization groups like ATTAC. But with 27 delegations around the table, secrecy can only go so far.

12 See Hayes-Renshaw and Wallace 1997, 88.

13 On the formal vs. informal shapes of the negotiating mandate in trade policy, see Kerremans 2003.

14 See Moravcsik 1991 on the issue of voting in the Single European Act.

15 From 1995 to 2003, Germany, France, Italy, and the UK each had 10 votes; Spain 8; Belgium, Greece, the Netherlands, and Portugal 5; Austria and Sweden 4; Ireland, Denmark, and Finland 3; and Luxembourg 2. For a Commission proposal to be adopted, 62 votes out of a total of 87 needed to be cast in its favour. In other cases, the qualified majority remained the same but the 62 votes had to be cast by at least ten member states. The qualified majority requirements were changed by the 2001 Treaty of Nice and the 2004 Accession Treaty. A qualified majority will be obtained if the decision receives at least a specified number of votes and the decision is approved by a majority of

member states. The weighing of the votes was also changed. See, for instance, http://www.europa.eu.int/comm/ igc2000/dialogue/info/offdoc/ guidecitoyen_en.pdf for a table of the new voting weights, including those of the candidate countries.

16 In 1994 only 14 per cent of the legislation adopted by the Council was formally put to a vote and the subject of negative votes and abstentions (source: *Guide to EU Institutions*, The Council, Europa web server). Moreover, while in theory the consultation procedure (under which Commission proposals can be amended by the Council only unanimously) applies, in practice the Commission alters its proposal several times following the deliberations of the TPC in order to ensure adoption by the Council (Garrett and Tsebelis 1996 argue that the consultation procedure gives the agenda-setting Commission the possibility to act strategically in presenting its proposals to the Council). Even during the height of the crisis created by French demands for a renegotiation of the Uruguay round agricultural agreement between the EU and the US in 1993, member states insisted that the tradition of consensus be not broken. See also Devuyst 1995; Paemen and Bensch 1995; and Woolcock and Hodges 1996 on the EC negotiating process during the Uruguay round.

17 Source: Commission of the European Communities, 'Trade implications of EU enlargement: Facts and Figures.' Brussels, 4 February 2004. See http://europa.eu.int/comm/trade/issues/bilateral/regions/candidates/ff040204_en.htm.

18 The Cairns Group, founded in 1986, is a coalition of 17 agricultural exporting countries accounting for one-third of the world's agricultural exports. Its members are Argentina, Australia, Bolivia, Brazil, Canada, Chile, Colombia, Costa Rica, Guatemala, Indonesia, Malaysia, New Zealand, Paraguay, the Philippines, South Africa, Thailand, and Uruguay.

19 EU Commission, 'General overview of active WTO dispute settlement cases involving the EC as complainant or defendant', Brussels, 12 February 2010.

20 Japan, South Korea, Norway, Switzerland, China, New Zealand, and Brazil.

FURTHER READING

The following is a selection of the very substantial literature about the EU's trade policies, which reflects both the legal and the policy analysis aspects of the topic. Some historical background is provided by Devuyst (1995), Johnson (1998), Woolcock (1993), and Young (2000, 2002). The specific issues of competence and of the trade policy process (including WTO negotiations) are dealt with by Meunier (2000b, 2005), Meunier and Nicolaïdis (1999), Nicolaïdis and Meunier (2002), M. Smith (2001), and Woolcock (2000). M. Smith (2001) and Young (2002) provide analysis of the ways in which the changing nature of world trade has been reflected in EU trade policies.

Devuyst, Y. (1995), 'The European Community and the Conclusion of the Uruguay Round' in Rhodes, C. and Mazey, S. (eds), *The State of the European Union, volume 3* (Boulder, CO: Lynne Rienner).

Johnson, M. (1998), *European Community Trade Policy and the Article 113 Committee* (London: Royal Institute of International Affairs).

Meunier, S. (2000b), 'What Single Voice? European Institutions and EU–US Trade Negotiations', *International Organization* 54/1, 103–35.

Meunier, S. (2005), *Trading Voices: the European Union in International Commercial Negotiations* (Princeton, NJ: Princeton University Press).

Meunier, S., and Nicolaïdis, K. (1999), 'Who Speaks for Europe? The Delegation of Trade Authority in the EU', *Journal of Common Market Studies* 37/3, 477–501.

Meunier, S., and Nicolaïdis, K. (2006), 'The European Union as a Conflicted Trade Power', in *Journal of European Public Policy*, Vol. 13 No. 6, 2006, 906–25.

Nicolaïdis, K., and Meunier, S. (2002), 'Revisiting Trade Competence in the European Union: Amsterdam, Nice, and Beyond' in Hosli, M., van Deemen, A., and Widgren, M. (eds) *Institutional Challenges in the European Union* (London: Routledge).

Smith, M. (2001), 'The European Union's Commercial Policy: Between Coherence and Fragmentation', *Journal of European Public Policy* 8/5, 787–802.

Woolcock, S. (1993), 'The European *Acquis* and Multilateral Trade Rules: Are They Compatible?' *Journal of Common Market Studies* 31/4, 539–58.

Woolcock, S. (2000), 'European Trade Policy', in Wallace, H., and Wallace, W. (eds) *Policy-Making in the European Union*, 4th edition (Oxford: Oxford University Press), 373–400.

Young, A. (2000), 'The Adaptation of European Foreign Economic Policy: From Rome to Seattle', *Journal of Common Market Studies* 38/1, 93–116.

Young, A. (2002), *Extending European Cooperation: the European Union and the 'New' International Trade Agenda* (Manchester: Manchester University Press).

 WEB LINKS

The first port of call for all matters of EU trade policy is the website of the EU Commission, DG Trade: **http://ec.europa.eu/trade/**. Much useful information about the context for and the impact of EU trade policies can be obtained from the World Trade Organization and Organisation for Economic Co-operation and Development websites: WTO: **http://www.wto.org/**; OECD: **http://www. oecd.org/home/**. A good website providing information and analysis about trade policies and the global political economy is that of the Washington-based Institute for International Economics: **http://www.iie.com/**.

CHAPTER 13

Enlargement, the Neighbourhood, and European Order

Karen E. Smith

▮ Summary

Since the end of the Cold War, the EU has enlarged to 27 countries, ten of which are in Central and Eastern Europe. Enlargement has been the EU's principal response to the end of the Cold War: by enlarging, the EU hopes to consolidate the democratic and economic reforms in post-communist countries, and spread security and prosperity eastwards. Its enlargement policy has involved the extensive use of carrots and sticks to encourage reforms, mainly through the application of membership conditionality. But although a slew of European countries still wants to join the EU, the momentum of the enlargement project has slowed. This chapter analyses the EU's key decisions on enlargement, considers why the EU member states agreed to such a radical reshaping of the European order, and discusses the future of the enlargement project. It then analyses the EU's relations with neighbouring countries in Eastern Europe, several of whom also wish to join the EU.

Introduction

Enlargement of the European Union—or, more accurately, the prospect of enlargement—is the principal means by which the EU has tried to spread prosperity, democracy, and security to the former communist countries of Central, Eastern, and South-eastern Europe. Though largely devoid of a long-term strategic vision of Europe, the EU has thus contributed significantly to shaping the post-Cold War European order.[1] It has been actively setting the 'rules of the game', the norms of domestic and international behaviour that should guide European states, as well as shaping the institutional structure in which those states are increasingly embedded. Incorporation within the EU is seen as a way to stabilize the new democracies and foster economic growth, but the EU has also used the promise of enlargement, if certain conditions are fulfilled, to influence the domestic and foreign policies of membership aspirants and encourage political and economic reforms, which are seen as necessary to ensure security in Europe. To an impressive extent, the EU's enlargement policy has been its most successful foreign policy.[2]

The EU has been able to exercise such influence because it has exploited its enormous 'power of attraction': most post-communist governments have repeatedly declared that they want to 'return to Europe', which they consider to entail membership of the EU (and NATO). The EU has made extensive use of both carrots and sticks in its relations with other European states, turning its soft power of attraction into coercive—though still civilian—power. As a result, the EU has become an ever more significant power with considerable impact on Europe.

The factors driving such heavy EU engagement in its neighbourhood are fairly obvious ones, including the need for stability and prosperity across Europe and a shared sense of responsibility for repairing the Cold War split of Europe. What is more surprising is that the policy response to these imperatives has been enlargement of the EU itself, rather than, say, an attempt to foster another strong regional grouping with which the EU could engage in inter-regional cooperation. The former communist states are much poorer and more agricultural than the EU member states, which has important implications for EU spending, and the extension of membership could have deleterious effects on both the functioning of the EU and the integration process. Although the member states have persistently sought to reduce the negative effects of enlargement—notably through a less-than-generous extension of benefits to new members—they were eventually prepared to assume the risks of enlargement in 2004 and 2007: they shared a strong sense of responsibility for ensuring security in Europe and were convinced that enlargement was the way to do so, and they were persuaded that post-communist countries were enough like themselves that they could not reasonably be excluded from the EU. The extent to which these factors continue to drive EU decision-making on enlargement will be discussed further below.

Enlargement, in turn, has had and will have a very large impact on the EU. As has been the case with past enlargements, it increases the EU's global 'weight' and expands its international interests. The increase in the number of EU member states from six to 15 did not bring the integration process to a halt, and the prospect of further enlargement has in large part motivated four intergovernmental conferences (IGCs) on institutional reform (two led to the Amsterdam and Nice Treaties, one to the now-defunct draft Constitutional Treaty, and the last to the Lisbon Treaty). So far it would appear that the increase in the EU's membership to 27 states has not seriously hindered day-to-day decision making, but whether further integration will be possible in such a large Union must be doubtful, given the travails of the Constitutional and Lisbon treaties.

This chapter analyses the EU's enlargement policy by looking in more depth at the key decisions that it has made on enlargement. It tries to answer questions raised by the three perspectives outlined by the editors: 1) Why have the member states reached agreement on enlargement? 2) Why has the EU used enlargement as the principal policy instrument to respond to the new post-Cold War environment? 3) What has the EU's influence been on its European neighbours and on the shape of European order?

Concentric circles

The first important decision that the EU—then the European Community—took regarding enlargement was to put off the prospect by adopting a 'concentric circles' approach. Concentric circles would allow the Community to proceed with economic and political integration, while strengthening its relations with its European neighbours, short of enlarging to them.

The Community had responded relatively quickly to the collapse of communism in Europe by concluding trade and cooperation agreements with, and extending technical assistance to, the new post-communist governments. The collapse of communism in the autumn of 1989 coincided with a very dynamic period in the Community's history: it was in the midst of completing the single European market and considering plans for an economic and monetary union. As a result, there was a general expectation—both within the Community and outside it—that the Community should take the lead in responding to the astounding events.

In June 1988, the Community and the Council for Mutual Economic Assistance (CMEA), the organization for economic cooperation among communist countries, established official relations. As the 'price' for officially recognizing the CMEA, the Community insisted on developing trade relations with the CMEA member countries on a bilateral basis. 'Bilateralism' allowed the Community to differentiate between the Central and East European countries (CEECs) and apply conditionality: those countries that were further ahead in the reform process concluded trade and cooperation agreements first (see Table 13.1). In this way, the Community encouraged reforms. Bilateralism precluded the development of a regional framework for cooperation among the CEECs (the CEECs also objected to any such suggestions as attempts to 'resurrect' the CMEA). Differentiation—distinguishing between countries on the basis of how well they meet given political and economic conditions—would come to have far-reaching consequences for the EU's relations with all of its European neighbours.

In late 1989, the Community extended aid through the Phare (Pologne-Hongrie aide à la reconstruction économique) programme to help the new democracies implement economic reforms.[3] Again, aid was extended on a conditional basis, first to Poland and Hungary, then to other countries. Importantly, the Soviet Union never received Phare aid, a clear sign that relations with the Soviet Union were much more problematic than relations with those countries that had suffered under the Soviet Union's yoke.

The agreements and aid were not enough to meet the CEECs' expectations, which centred on acceding to the Community. These membership expectations sparked off a 'widening vs. deepening' debate within the Community: the external demands thus complicated policy making within the 'subsystem' of the Community. Some policy makers (notably in France) argued that the Community should enlarge only after it integrated further as a way of ensuring that a united Germany would be well secured to a more integrated European Union. Others (notably in the UK) argued that enlargement should occur first, because further integration would make it more difficult for the CEECs to join. There was little explicit discussion of *never* enlarging. This would have been difficult to justify: not only had its membership already doubled by the time of the collapse of communism (and, setting an important precedent, East Germany had been quickly incorporated into the EC in 1990 via its unification with West Germany), but the Rome Treaty also stated that any European state could apply to join the Community. Support within the EC for enlargement—though not universal—also closed off the option of never enlarging. The debate thus centred not on whether to enlarge, but when and how. Internal and external factors had to favour enlargement; in 1990–1, they did not, yet.

Instead, in 1990 the Community compromised with the concentric circles approach, championed by European Commission President Jacques Delors and German Foreign Minister Hans-Dietrich Genscher (Allen 1992, 122). An integrated European Union would be at the centre (therefore the Maastricht Treaty was negotiated); in the closest ring to the EU would be the prosperous, small members of the European Free Trade Association (EFTA) linked to the EU via the European Economic Area, which extended the single European market to the EFTA countries on 1 January 1994. The CEECs occupied the outer ring, to be connected to the EU by special association ('Europe') agreements, while the Soviet Union, off on the outer fringes of Europe, did not figure highly at all. By trying to keep everyone happy, the concentric circles approach resolved the widening vs. deepening dilemma, at least in the short run.

TABLE 13.1 The EU's agreements with its neighbours

Association agreements with Mediterranean countries (year in force)	Trade and cooperation agreements (year signed/ in force)	Europe (association) agreements (year signed/in force)	Partnership and cooperation agreements (year signed/in force)	Stabilization and association agreements (year signed/in force)
Turkey (1963) (customs union in force 1996)	Hungary (1988/1988)	Hungary (1991/1994)	Russia (1994/1997)	Former Yugoslav Republic of Macedonia (2001/2004)
Malta (1971)	Poland (1989/1989)	Poland (1991/1994)	Ukraine (1994/1998)	Croatia (2001/2005)
Republic of Cyprus (1972)	Soviet Union (1989/1990)	Czechoslovakia (1991)*	Moldova (1994/1998)	Albania (2006/2009)
	Czechoslovakia (1990/1990)	Czech Republic (1993/1995)	Armenia (1996/1999)	Montenegro (2007/not yet in force)
	Bulgaria (1990/1990)	Slovakia (1993/1995)	Azerbaijan (1996/1999)	Bosnia Herzegovina (2008/not yet in force)
	Romania (1990/1991)	Bulgaria (1993/1995)	Georgia (1996/1999)	Serbia** (2008/will be ratified only when Council decides Serbia is fully cooperating with the International Criminal Tribunal for the former Yugoslavia)
	Albania (1992/1992)	Romania (1993/1995)	In 1997, negotiations with Belarus were suspended due to violations of democracy and human rights there	
	Estonia (1992/1993)	Estonia (1995/1998)		
	Latvia (1992/1993)	Latvia (1995/1998)		
	Lithuania (1992/1993)	Lithuania (1995/1998)		
	Slovenia (1993/1993)	Slovenia (1996/1999)		

* The Community signed a Europe agreement with Czechoslovakia in December 1991, but the breakup of Czechoslovakia on 1 January 1993 complicated matters. The Community then negotiated separate agreements with the Czech Republic and Slovakia.

** The SAA with Serbia will not apply to the territory of Kosovo.

Europe agreements were to be strictly conditional: only countries clearly committed to democratic and market economic principles were eligible. The first to meet the grade were Czechoslovakia, Hungary, and Poland, in 1991 (see Table 13.1). Yugoslavia, in early 1990, was initially considered a prospective associate, but not even a year later it was clearly in deep trouble and was therefore kept outside all concentric circles (see Box 13.1).[4] Europe agreements provided for the gradual establishment of a free trade area, and for political dialogue on foreign policy matters. They also, despite resistance by several member states, made reference in the preamble to the associate's aspirations to join the EU.

At the end of 1991, the Soviet Union broke up. The Community's reaction to this was muted: it concluded partnership and cooperation agreements with the new countries emerging from the Soviet federation (see Table 13.1), but these were considerably less generous than the Europe agreements and did not include any reference to EU membership. The Community also set up a separate aid programme, TACIS (Technical Assistance for the CIS countries), further indicating that the former Soviet republics were in the most distant concentric circle. The exception to this was the three Baltic republics, which, for historical, political, and geographical reasons, were soon incorporated into the circle with the other CEECs.

The Copenhagen European Council, June 1993

The very rational concentric circles approach did not last long: few countries were content to stay out of the inner core. While the rich EFTA countries were fairly easy to embrace—and Austria, Finland, and Sweden acceded to the EU in January 1995—enlargement to the CEECs any time soon posed problems, particularly because of the need for adjustments to the EU budget and policies such as the Common Agricultural Policy and structural funds for poor areas. Who would pay for eastern enlargement? Even those member states (such as Germany and the UK) most supportive of eastern expansion seemed unwilling to do so.

But the CEECs' demands for a *promise* of eventual accession, made persistently throughout 1992, eventually became impossible to deny, especially as violence spread in the east (the former Yugoslavia, Albania, the Caucasus). A promise to enlarge would foster the reform process, by boosting reformers, and thus help ensure peace and security in Europe (see European Commission 1993, European Council 1993, 12). But the promise was made only in June 1993 because until then the Community was embroiled in internal difficulties, notably regarding the ratification of the Maastricht Treaty; once the treaty was ratified, enlargement could be agreed.

In June 1993, the Copenhagen European Council agreed that the CEECs could join the EU, if they satisfied certain conditions (see Box 13.2). The membership conditions—though not new, they had not been stated so explicitly before—helped to reassure reluctant member states that enlargement would not wreck the

BOX 13.1   The EU and the wars in the former Yugoslavia

The descent of Yugoslavia into bloodshed is the most stunning tragedy of post-Cold War Europe. The country had been the most 'Western' of what were then known as East European countries, with a mixed economy and a non-aligned foreign policy, and was a popular destination for West European tourists. But instead of blossoming after the Cold War, it collapsed.

When Yugoslavia disintegrated into war in mid 1991, the European Community publicly assumed responsibility for trying to halt the violence. But its record in the wars in Croatia and Bosnia (1991–5) is dismal. Although active in the first year of the conflicts—sponsoring a peace conference, sending monitors to negotiate local ceasefires, imposing sanctions on Serbia/Montenegro—the Community did not greatly improve the prospects for peace. And in early 1992 it controversially recognized Slovenia and Croatia after Germany broke ranks with a common position and declared that it would recognize the two republics. Even more controversially, it then recognized Bosnia Herzegovina, while Greece blocked Macedonia's recognition until after it was renamed the Former Yugoslav Republic of Macedonia (FYROM). Moreover, several member states opposed sending a Western European Union force to back up their diplomacy; instead they contributed troops to a UN peacekeeping force.

These diplomatic failures contributed to a widespread loss of confidence in the EU as an international actor. From summer 1992, it was sidelined; it first worked *alongside* the UN to gain approval of a peace plan, without success, and then stood by as the Contact Group, composed of the USA, Russia, the UK, France, and Germany, took over the diplomacy, and NATO enforced UN resolutions. In summer 1995, NATO's military activity increased in Bosnia, helping to establish the conditions for a peace agreement. In the end, the USA alone mediated the Dayton peace plan, signed in Paris in December 1995, and NATO troops policed its implementation.

Following Dayton, in 1996 the EU devised a strategy to strengthen regional stability, promising trade relations, aid, and cooperation agreements if the South-east European countries (the republics of former Yugoslavia plus Albania) met conditions such as respect for democracy and human rights, and cooperation with their neighbours (Council of the European Union 1996). But the EU's approach was long term; in the short run, it was harder to balance stability with a concern for democracy and human rights, and to deal with violence as it continued to erupt in the region. Hence, for example, Slobodan Milošević's regime in Serbia was tolerated from 1995 to 1998 in the interests of maintaining peace in Bosnia Herzegovina, while Western governments supported Sali Berisha's barely democratic government in Albania until it collapsed in 1997. The EU did not respond to the corresponding spread of disorder in Albania, even though Italy and Greece called on it to act. The large member states (above all, Germany and the UK) did not want to add new commitments to their role in Bosnia, so instead Italy assembled a 'coalition of the willing', acting under a UN mandate, to help restore calm in Albania (see Silvestri 1997). Nor did the EU play a large role in the Kosovo conflict. In 1997–8, Serbia/Montenegro's leader, Slobodan Milošević, pursued a brutal campaign to impose Belgrade's rule over Kosovo, a province of Serbia inhabited mostly by Albanian Muslims. The EU pressed Belgrade to cease offensive military actions, but was in no position to force Serbia to comply. After a peace conference failed in January 1999, NATO took the

---

BOX 13.1 **(Continued)**

military initiative, bombing Serbia until its troops withdrew from Kosovo. A NATO peace-keeping force, KFOR, is still deployed in the territory. Kosovo's declaration of independence in February 2008 has divided the EU member states, with 22 recognizing the state but five (Cyprus, Greece, Romania, Slovakia, and Spain) refusing to do so. Nonetheless, the EU agreed to deploy a rule of law mission (EULEX) to Kosovo, which took over from a UN mission in late 2008. Elsewhere, when inter-ethnic violence erupted in FYROM in early 2001, it was the EU that took the initiative, leading efforts to resolve the crisis, in close cooperation with NATO. From August 2001, a NATO force collected weapons from ethnic Albanian rebels, while the EU pressured the FYROM government to enact reforms enhancing Albanian minority rights. The EU took over the NATO mission in early 2003, replacing it with a police mission in late 2003 and withdrawing in 2006.

BOX 13.2 **The EU's membership conditions**

The Treaty of Rome stated that 'Any European state may apply to become a member of the Community' (Article 237). The 1999 Amsterdam Treaty added that any European state that respects the principles of liberty, democracy, respect for human rights and fundamental freedoms, and the rule of law may apply to become a member of the Union (Articles 5 and 49).

The Copenhagen European Council in June 1993 declared that membership candidate countries must have achieved:

- a functioning market economy with the capacity to cope with competitive pressures and market forces within the EU;
- stability of institutions guaranteeing democracy, the rule of law, human rights, and respect for and protection of minorities;
- the ability to take on the obligations of EU membership including adherence to the aims of economic and political union (the *acquis communautaire*).

In addition, the European Council stated that 'the Union's capacity to absorb new members, while maintaining the momentum of European integration, is also an important consideration in the general interest of both the Union and the candidate countries'.

By 1999, the EU had formally added 'good neighbourliness' to the list of conditions. The December 1999 Helsinki European Council stated that candidate countries must resolve outstanding border disputes peacefully, if necessary by referring them to the International Court of Justice (European Council 1999b, paragraph 4).

(apparently fragile) Union. The European Council declared: 'The Union's capacity to absorb new members, while maintaining the momentum of European integration, is also an important consideration in the general interest of both the Union and the candidate countries' (European Council 1993, 13). This was clearly designed to protect the 'club'; to ensure, as the Commission argued, that 'widening must not be at the expense of deepening' (European Commission 1992, 10). 'Absorption capacity' played little role in subsequent debates regarding the CEECs but has figured highly in debates about enlargement to Turkey and South-eastern Europe.

The Copenhagen conditions were aimed at the six countries that had concluded or were negotiating Europe agreements: Bulgaria, the Czech Republic, Hungary, Poland, Romania, and Slovakia. But events once again complicated the EU's policy. Four newly independent countries—Estonia, Latvia, Lithuania, and Slovenia—could not reasonably be kept in an outer circle, especially given that they had backers within the EU, and in December 1994, the Essen European Council affirmed that they met the conditions for Europe agreements and would thus be formally included in the membership queue (European Council 1994, point I.14). All ten CEECs then applied for membership between 1994 and 1996 (see Table 13.2). In June 1994, the Corfu European Council also extended membership invitations to Malta and, controversially, to the Republic of Cyprus (see Box 13.3). This was a response to the concerns of southern member states that the 'southern dimension' was being neglected in favour of eastern enlargement. While the six new prospective members did seem more likely candidates than other European countries, the expansion of the enlargement queue seems to reflect the exigencies of intra-EU balancing.

Thus, within a year and a half of the Copenhagen summit, an initially difficult decision on enlargement was extended—with little discussion of the implications for other European countries or European order. Admittedly, at this stage it looked unlikely that 'outsiders' were credible membership candidates, with South-eastern

---

BOX 13.3   The EU and the Republic of Cyprus

In June 1994, the European Council decided that the EU would open negotiations with the Republic of Cyprus at the same time as it opened talks with the first wave of CEECs. This was controversial because the island is divided between the internationally recognized Republic of Cyprus, where most Greek Cypriots live, and the unrecognized Turkish Republic of Northern Cyprus (TRNC), where most Turkish Cypriots live. In 1974, at a time of great ethnic violence amid attempts to unite Cyprus with Greece, Turkey invaded the island; the 'green line' (patrolled by UN peacekeepers) eventually divided the two communities. Turkish troops are still present in the TRNC, as are a large number of Turkish mainland settlers. In 1998, the EU opened negotiations only with the Republic of Cyprus, which negotiated on behalf of the entire island. The EU hoped that the promise of enlargement would push both sides towards a solution and did not threaten to exclude Cyprus if none was reached. But throughout 2002 and 2003 it also insisted that Turkey put pressure on the TRNC to accept an agreement on unification. In this sense, the EU was successful: in April 2004, a referendum in the TRNC accepted a UN plan on reunification. The Republic of Cyprus, however, rejected it, yet on 1 May it acceded to the EU. Since then, the EU has found it difficult to 'reward' the TRNC, given the latter's unusual legal situation and while the Republic of Cyprus blocks any EU move it perceives as contrary to international law. Negotiations between the two Cypriot sides began again in 2008 but have yet to result in a solution to the conflict.

TABLE 13.2 Applications for EU membership since 1987

	Date of application	Date of accession
Turkey	14 April 1987	–
Austria	17 July 1989	1 January 1995
Cyprus	3 July 1990	1 May 2004
Malta*	16 July 1990	1 May 2004
Sweden	1 July 1991	1 January 1995
Finland	18 March 1992	1 January 1995
Switzerland**	26 May 1992	–
Norway***	25 November 1992	–
Hungary	31 March 1994	1 May 2004
Poland	5 April 1994	1 May 2004
Romania	22 June 1995	1 January 2007
Slovakia	27 June 1995	1 May 2004
Latvia	13 October 1995	1 May 2004
Estonia	24 November 1995	1 May 2004
Lithuania	8 December 1995	1 May 2004
Bulgaria	14 December 1995	1 January 2007
Czech Republic	17 January 1996	1 May 2004
Slovenia	10 June 1996	1 May 2004
Croatia	21 February 2003	–
FYROM	22 March 2004	–
Montenegro	15 December 2008	–
Albania	28 April 2009	–
Iceland	23 July 2009	–

* In 1996, Malta froze its membership application after an anti-membership party won elections. It was thus excluded from Agenda 2000 and Luxembourg European Council decisions. It later reactivated its application, and negotiations opened in 2000.

** Switzerland froze its membership application, after Swiss voters rejected participation in the European Economic Area in December 1992.

*** Norway completed accession negotiations in 1994, but Norwegian voters rejected EU membership in a referendum (again, having done so in 1972).

Europe still embroiled in war, and the former Soviet republics plagued by war, instability, and a general lack of progress in economic and political reform. Yet, the question surely arose: would the EU eventually expand to include all of Europe?

Expanding the queue of applicants does mean that the EU can exercise influence over a greater number of countries, but, as will be seen below, this requires careful managing both of that queue and of the implications for the internal functioning of the EU.

Following Copenhagen, the EU launched a pre-accession strategy, primarily to help the CEECs adopt and implement the *acquis*. Another IGC was held to reform the EU treaties and thus prepare the EU for enlargement, principally by expanding the use of qualified majority voting and streamlining the EU's institutions. Although the resulting Amsterdam Treaty was disappointing in that regard (in fact, the Amsterdam 'leftovers' had to be resolved at a later IGC, which led to the Nice Treaty),[5] the European Council nonetheless declared that the enlargement process could proceed. In July 1997, one month after the Amsterdam IGC concluded, the European Commission published its opinions on the membership applications in a wide-ranging report entitled 'Agenda 2000' (European Commission 1997).

In the run-up to Agenda 2000, the EU actively used membership conditionality to influence the applicant countries. This went beyond merely encouraging them to implement the *acquis*: the EU criticized domestic political processes and outcomes, and foreign policy choices, and expressed strong preferences for particular changes. Conditionality was used to lay the basis for European security *before* enlargement. For example, during the pact for stability, a multilateral negotiating framework led by the EU between May 1994 and March 1995, the CEECs were encouraged to conclude 'good-neighbourly' agreements with each other on borders and the treatment of minorities. The EU also criticized domestic politics. During the period of Vladimír Mečiar's government in Slovakia (1992–8), for example, the EU issued numerous warnings that Slovakia must meet democratic norms before it could join the EU. The EU's demands were not always met with full compliance but the extent to which they were is still striking—and contributed to the view that membership conditionality is the EU's most powerful foreign policy instrument.

Obviously then, the pressure on the CEECs before the Commission issued its opinions in Agenda 2000 was quite high. But it was also increasingly apparent that other considerations besides conditionality would play a role in enlargement decisions, in particular the effects of those decisions on European order. There was debate within the EU over how many countries should join initially: should the EU go for a more easily manageable first enlargement and only let in a few (two or three) CEECs? Or should it go for the big-bang approach, and let in as many as feasible, thus prioritizing enlargement (and the vision of a peaceful and united Europe) over the deepening of integration among only some of Europe's states?

The Luxembourg and Helsinki European Councils

There was much concern about the impact of leaving countries outside. Each membership application would be judged on its merits; in principle, differentiation should spur progress with reforms. But the application of membership conditionality—after all, part of a strategy to spread peace and security—could actually end up destabilizing countries, as it isolates and excludes (for a time) some states from the benefits of EU membership (see Senior Nello and Smith 1998). Alienation from the EU could consequently reduce its leverage, and where relations between countries inside and those left out have been tense, enlargement could be particularly destabilizing. The inclusion/exclusion dilemma has dominated enlargement policy making ever since.

The EU tried to lessen the negative implications of differentiation in four successive ways: by taking a multilateral approach to relations with the CEECs and their neighbours; by establishing an inclusive 'accession process'; by opening negotiations with all of them; and finally by agreeing to admit ten countries in one fell swoop. First, the EU tried to encourage multilateralism, mainly by granting aid to regional cooperation initiatives such as the Central European initiative and pact for stability projects. But this did not reduce the centrality of the bilateral relationship between the EU and each CEEC, which was dominated by the accession process.

The next two ways of lessening the impact of differentiation are in practice just ways of postponing it, because they deal with the impact of exclusion from membership *negotiations*, not from membership itself. The EU initially developed an inclusive 'accession process', launched at the same time as the decisions were made in 1997 to differentiate between two groups of applicant countries and begin membership negotiations with only one of them.

In Agenda 2000, the European Commission recommended that membership negotiations be opened with five countries: the Czech Republic, Estonia, Hungary, Poland, and Slovenia (in addition to Cyprus). Although no candidate country met all of the membership conditions, these five states came closest to doing so. The other five CEECs did not, and of these, Slovakia was singled out as the only country that did not meet the political conditions. The decision to include Estonia and Slovenia, in addition to the three countries traditionally considered the front runners (the Czech Republic, Hungary, and Poland) was influenced by NATO's June 1997 decision to expand to only three countries in the first instance, viz. the Czech Republic, Hungary, and Poland.[6] In December 1997, the Luxembourg European Council agreed with the Commission's recommendation, and in March 1998 membership negotiations formally began with Cyprus, the Czech Republic, Estonia, Hungary, Poland, and Slovenia. This round of enlargement was to be larger, partly in the interests of stabilizing the Baltic and Balkan regions. But this still left the problem of stabilizing the unlucky applicants.

Although accession negotiations were opened only with the 'Luxembourg six', annual accession partnerships were drawn up for all the applicant countries, listing the objectives that the EU wanted each applicant to meet. The accession process kept up the pressure on all the applicants, since only those countries that met the membership conditions would join, while the remaining applicant countries were promised that if they made good progress in that respect, then they too could start accession talks.

However, the EU's strategy started to unravel within a year, paradoxically because it worked quickly. Latvia and Lithuania made rapid progress in meeting the conditions, while elections in Slovakia in September 1998 resulted in defeat for the Mečiar government. As Geoffrey Pridham argues (2002, 963), while EU pressure had little effect on the Mečiar government, it clearly had an impact on Slovak society. The new government under Prime Minister Mikuláš Dzurinda sought to reverse Slovakia's isolated position. Thus by late 1998, three more CEECs (plus Malta) were close to joining those already negotiating accession, leaving Bulgaria and Romania in the 'slow lane'.

Excluding Bulgaria and Romania became untenable, however, when war erupted between Serbia and NATO over the treatment of Kosovar Albanians in March 1999. The risks of further isolating Bulgaria and Romania—given the instability in their neighbourhood and the support they had given to NATO action—made it infeasible to leave them out of the next round of negotiations. In October 1999, the Commission recommended that the EU open negotiations with all of the applicant countries except Turkey: this would make a 'decisive contribution to stability and prosperity' in Europe, a political imperative for the EU (European Commission 1999, 30; see also Verheugen 1999). The Commission justified its recommendation by arguing that the six applicant countries met the *political* conditions for membership (the most important), if not the other conditions. This also provided a convenient way to handle Turkey's membership application: negotiations would not open with Turkey because it did not (yet) meet the political conditions, but Turkey would conclude an accession partnership with the EU.

The Helsinki European Council in December 1999 approved the Commission's recommendations, and opened negotiations with the six countries, because it was 'determined to lend a positive contribution to security and stability on the European continent' (European Council 1999a, paragraph 10). In February 2000, formal membership negotiations started with the 'Helsinki six'. The EU would still complete talks with each country only as it was ready. While differentiation keeps up the pressure on the candidates to meet the conditions, it further defers the basic dilemma: at some point, countries would inevitably be excluded from the first round of eastern enlargement, whatever the political implications.

How can we explain these decisions of 1997–9? A rationalist perspective, as several observers have noted, does not help much. This explains such outcomes as intergovernmental compromises among member states that are bargaining on the basis of their material interests. But for Frank Schimmelfennig, the member states had far too divergent interests regarding enlargement. Instead, with a sociological approach, the Luxembourg European Council's decision to open negotiations with only five CEECs 'can be explained as the inclusion of those countries that have come to share its liberal values and norms' (Schimmelfennig 2001, 48). Schimmelfennig maintains that since the EU professed itself to be based on such norms, the CEECs argued successfully that the credibility of the entire integration project depended on a commitment to enlarge to other liberal democracies. Since the

Luxembourg six met liberal norms, reluctant member states were shamed into fulfilling the promise of enlargement. They were trapped by their own rhetoric. Helene Sjursen emphasizes identity, and argues that the EU is motivated by a strong sense of duty to enlarge to fellow Europeans and overcome the division of Europe. This shared identity explains why the EU prioritized enlargement to the CEECs over Turkey, whose candidacy is accepted only on utility calculations (geostrategic benefits) rather than shared identity (Sjursen 2002, especially 502–9).

Undeniably, a deep sense of responsibility to enlarge to the democratizing Central and East European states was an important motivation for enlargement, and the EU really had little choice but to enlarge, given its rhetorical and treaty-based commitments. But this still does not fully explain the decisions of the Luxembourg and Helsinki European Councils. We need to add more of a 'foreign policy' perspective to explain why particular decisions were taken: political and security considerations played a major role in these decisions (which also prompted the member states to overcome disagreements based on material interests). The Luxembourg decision encompassed five CEECs and designed an accession process for all of them in a deliberate attempt to be as inclusive as possible, more so than NATO at the time, and to lessen the negative effects of differentiation.[7] The Helsinki decision included two states that patently did not meet the membership conditions, but which could not be left out for political and security reasons. In other words, the implications for European security were a determining factor in decisions on the enlargement *process*: security was not just the anticipated result of enlargement itself; steps had to be taken to avoid instability along the way. In addition, the extensive pressure placed on the candidate countries to conform to the membership conditions does not fit comfortably with sociological explanations of enlargement. The EU used membership conditionality both to limit the potential negative consequences of enlargement for itself (hence prospective members must be functioning and competitive market economies, implement most of the *acquis communautaire*, and resolve their disputes with neighbours before they join), and to create the basis for a secure Europe by demanding political reform. Although it had to respond to the CEECs' demands to make good on its promises to overcome the division of Europe, the EU retained much leverage to influence the CEECs.

Big-bang enlargement

The membership negotiations were marked by considerable haggling over the terms of entry (and particularly the financial benefits to be extended to the new member states), as well as delays caused both by slow implementation of the *acquis* by the CEECs and events such as looming elections in EU member states or the Commission's resignation in March 1999. *The* question in 2000–1, however, was how many countries would conclude negotiations by the 2002 deadline agreed by the member states for any front runners. In 2000, support for a 'big-bang' enlargement—up to ten candidate countries joining at once—grew among observers, though not yet among all the member states. Taking in ten countries together would leave fewer on the outside (and thus minimize the problem of exclusion, particularly of Poland, whose membership preparations were not as advanced as several other CEECs), and necessitate only one large-scale (though daunting) adjustment by the EU. But acceptance of a big-bang enlargement also risked disappointing the front runners (would they then have to wait for everyone else to catch up?) and could reduce the pressure on all of them (if they are all going to get in, why make much of an effort to meet the onerous conditions?).

The Commission eventually joined the big-bang bandwagon, thus tilting the debate in favour of this option. In early September 2001, Commissioner Verheugen (2001) maintained that ten countries could join in the next round of enlargement: all of the candidates except for Bulgaria and Romania. The terrorist attacks on the USA then reinforced the security rationale for the big-bang option. In November 2001, the Commission declared that '[a] strong and united Europe is more important than ever before, against the background of the terrorist attacks of 11 September and subsequent developments', and stated that ten candidate countries could conclude negotiations by the end of 2002 (European Commission 2001b, 4). By late 2001, the big-bang option was widely perceived to be a certainty. This made it all the more difficult for the EU to take any other decision, although French Foreign Minister Hubert Védrine warned of the dangers of leaving Bulgaria and Romania out. Despite the doubts, the Laeken European Council stated that all but Bulgaria and Romania could be ready to conclude negotiations within a year (European Council 2001, paragraph 8).

In October 2002, the Commission maintained that the ten countries would be able to assume the obligations of membership from 2004 (European Commission 2002, 20-1). The last two months of 2002 were a dash towards the finishing line, with brinkmanship on both sides of the negotiating table, particularly over agriculture and financial matters (and the candidate countries were unhappy with the EU's stinginess on both). But at the December 2002 Copenhagen European Council, the deal was done; the ten countries acceded to the EU on 1 May 2004.

As for Bulgaria and Romania, the Copenhagen European Council stated that 'depending on further progress in complying with the membership criteria, the objective is to welcome Bulgaria and Romania as members of the European Union in 2007' (European Council 2002a, 4). This is striking, because previous European Councils had been so hesitant to set a definite date for the accession of specific candidates. The risks of alienating Bulgaria and Romania were considered too great *not* to give a firmer indication of when those two countries might finally accede. And despite fears that neither country fully met the conditions, Bulgaria and Romania joined the EU on 1 January 2007. Concerns about corruption and organized crime, however, led to the creation of an extraordinary process to monitor both countries after their accession; in 2008, the European Commission froze several hundred million euros of funding for Bulgaria as a result of suspected corruption.[8]

So in spite of the tough bargaining, and the calculable and incalculable costs of enlargement, the EU still agreed to a very large first round of eastern enlargement. The sense of responsibility towards the candidate countries, the sense of shared European identity, the strategic imperatives favouring a big-bang enlargement, and the fact that the EU could not have backed down from its promises without a serious loss of credibility and legitimacy all helped to sustain the momentum. But the successful management of the exclusion dilemma for the candidate countries has very profound implications for the EU's relations with other European states.

Relations with South-eastern Europe

In principle, strategic imperatives also favour enlargement to the troubled Southeast European region. Since the 1995 Dayton peace agreement, the EU has assumed more and more responsibility for the reconstruction, stabilization, and integration of South-eastern Europe. Although it played little role in the Albanian and Kosovo crises (see Box 13.1), with the end of the Kosovo war the EU took the lead in constructing a post-war order in South-eastern Europe. It added a stability pact (modelled on the earlier pact for stability in Central and Eastern Europe) and stabilization and association agreements (see Table 13.1) to its previous strategy. Most importantly, it explicitly extended the promise of eventual accession to the Southeast European countries.

In April 1999, the German presidency proposed that the EU make a clear commitment that the countries in the region could eventually accede to the EU. This would encourage them to undertake political and economic reforms and to work on cooperating with each other (German presidency 1999, paragraph IV.1); a month later, the rest of the EU agreed (Council of the European Union 1999, recitals, paragraph 7). The June 2003 Thessaloniki European Council then reiterated the membership promise. The perceived success of membership conditionality elsewhere meant that it was tempting to try to repeat that success in South-eastern Europe: this would be the key to EU influence in the region. Most South-east European states have since applied for membership (see Table 13.2) and Croatia began negotiations with the EU in October 2005.

There are two important reasons why conditionality was successful in Central and Eastern Europe: first, the EU—despite a few wobbles—was basically committed to the enlargement project and therefore its promise of enlargement was credible; second, the costs to accession countries of meeting the membership conditions were high, but still acceptable. Neither of these reasons holds unreservedly in South-eastern Europe. First, the EU's commitment to further enlargement has seemed shaky in recent years, despite the geopolitical imperatives favouring enlargement to South-eastern Europe. After the French and Dutch rejected the constitutional treaty in referenda, the Copenhagen criterion of 'absorption capacity' began to appear in EU discourse. The European Commission's November 2006 annual report on enlargement included a special annex on 'the EU's capacity to integrate new members' (European Commission 2006d). And the December 2006 European Council declared that 'The pace of enlargement must take into account the capacity of the Union to absorb new members.' Opinions on applications for membership are now to include an assessment of such capacity. While the European Council affirmed that the EU would 'keep its commitments' regarding ongoing negotiations, this appeared to place in doubt enlargement to countries not yet in negotiations (European Council 2006b). It certainly indicated that enlargement was now dependent on institutional reform. And since by 2009 the EU had still not ratified the constitutional treaty's replacement, the Lisbon Treaty, the momentum behind enlargement noticeably slowed. Then came the financial crisis of 2007 followed by recession, together with numerous other foreign policy issues, all draining attention away from the region. Ratification of the Lisbon Treaty removes one potential obstacle, but the challenges of 'exporting the European order' to South-eastern Europe remain high. Croatia's accession, expected in 2011 or early 2012, could boost the credibility of the EU's membership promise, but the remaining challenges should not be underestimated.

Second, the long-term vision of an expanding European order based on EU enlargement to South-eastern Europe has been difficult because of immediate problems within South-eastern Europe, tensions between some EU member states and South-east European countries, and disagreements between EU member states over relations with the region. South-east European governments have to take unpalatable decisions to comply with the membership conditions (including handing over popular indictees to the International Criminal Tribunal for the former Yugoslavia, or ICTY). There have been positive signs of progress towards democracy throughout the region and some bilateral issues have been settled peacefully (such as the break-up of the State Union of Serbia and Montenegro in 2006). To some extent EU membership conditionality has prodded governments into taking unpopular steps: Croatia finally cooperated with ICTY and handed over an indicted general in 2005, thus paving the way for a start to its membership negotiations. But there are other serious challenges: Bosnia Herzegovina is hardly functioning as a coherent entity; Greece and the Former Yugoslav Republic of Macedonia (FYROM) continue to squabble over the latter's name (which led Greece to veto FYROM's entry into NATO, and to insist that the country can join the EU only if the name dispute is resolved); Slovenia and Croatia have been at loggerheads over a territorial dispute, as a result of which Slovenia blocked Croatia's membership negotiations for almost a year; and the question of Kosovo's independence remains an open wound in the region, as well as one that divides the EU member states (see Džihić and Kramer 2009).

Furthermore, not every country that joined in the 2004 big-bang enlargement implemented the membership conditions to the same standard (and the good-neighbourly condition was not even applied with respect to Cyprus), while question marks remain about Bulgaria's and Romania's compliance. The strategic imperatives favouring enlargement (and overcoming the exclusion dilemma) trumped the consistent application of conditionality. The experience of Bulgarian and Romanian membership could lead the EU to conclude that conditionality should be applied more strictly before a country joins the EU (Vachudova 2009)— and certainly issues of the rule of law have featured prominently in recent Commission reports on enlargement. But this will still require tough choices: the dilemmas created by differentiation and exclusion are even more pronounced in South-eastern Europe. For example, the EU has been clumsy in handling a Serbia that has still not fully complied with its commitments to ICTY (Ratko Mladić, indicted for several serious crimes, has not been captured), but whose cooperation is needed if the Kosovo issue is ever to be resolved satisfactorily.[9]

Relations with Turkey

Nothing illustrates better the loss of momentum in the enlargement project than the EU's relations with Turkey, the longest-standing membership applicant. The EU's relations with Turkey have historically been problematic and the member states have frequently been divided over how to handle the country. Turkey is a member of NATO and the Council of Europe and is located in a sensitive region (its neighbours include Syria, Iran, Iraq, and the Caucasus, which would have significant implications for European foreign and security policy in the event of accession). The Bosphorus, which cuts through Istanbul, is considered the geographical boundary between Europe and Asia; some argue this disqualifies Turkey from EU membership. Turkey is a democracy, but there have been coups d'état in the past and the military has long played a decisive role in politics. There have been human rights problems: torture has been practised; freedom of speech has not been protected; and the use of force against Kurdish guerrillas has often caused civilian casualties. Turkey is also a very large and mostly agricultural country—which alone poses plenty of problems for the EU. Although the state is secular, its population is predominantly Muslim. It is this last characteristic that has been the focus, implicitly or explicitly, of debates regarding Turkey's membership bid. To opponents of Turkish membership, Turkey lacks the requisite 'European identity'.

In 1987, Turkey applied for membership; in 1989, the Commission's opinion concluded that it would not be appropriate to open accession negotiations. Turkey then watched the EFTA countries and CEECs jump the membership queue, while various European politicians cited cultural and religious factors for its exclusion. It suspected that it would never become a member of the club even if it had a fully functioning democracy and exemplary human rights record. When the December

1997 Luxembourg European Council placed Turkey in its own separate category of applicant states, Turkey suspended its relations with the EU.

The EU's leverage over Turkey diminished, and consequently the EU altered its policy. The Helsinki European Council in December 1999 classified Turkey as an official candidate, although it made it clear that membership negotiations would only be opened once the political conditions had been met. At the Copenhagen European Council in December 2002, the EU came under intense pressure from the USA to open membership negotiations with Turkey (a crucial ally in the run-up to the war on Iraq). Instead, the EU agreed to consider opening negotiations in December 2004 if Turkey met the political conditions by then (including a resolution of the Cyprus dispute). The EU's influence increased, as the Turkish Parliament passed several laws strengthening the protection of human rights and democratic principles, and Turkey fostered the Turkish Republic of Northern Cyprus's acceptance of the UN plan for Cyprus. Formal negotiations opened in October 2005.

Since then, however, the negotiations have stagnated—with few of the 35 negotiating 'chapters' opened and only one closed. This is formally because Turkey has not complied with the demand that it normalize its relations with all EU member states, including Cyprus, and allow Cypriot vessels to enter its ports. At the same time, opposition to Turkish membership has been loudly proclaimed in Austria, France, and Germany—with politicians there suggesting that a 'privileged partnership' be negotiated instead. But it is rather late in the day to change course, without causing a serious rupture in relations with Turkey—whose geopolitical importance is arguably growing, not to mention its significance as a transit country for oil and gas from further afield. The lack of agreement on a long-term strategy for shaping the wider European order is apparent in the EU's disarray over how to handle Turkey.

Relations with the 'wider Europe'

Such disarray has also been evident in intra-EU discussions regarding relations with the remaining countries in the former Soviet sphere. The enlargement commitments discussed above leave out the former Soviet republics, several of which have also expressed a desire to join the EU. Here the EU faces a dilemma: if it does not promise further enlargement, its influence could suffer; but if it does, the promise may lack credibility, as the countries are quite far from meeting the conditions, and it is not clear at all that an enlarged EU would be capable of taking decisions on further enlargement, much less enjoy public backing for doing so. Since 2002, it has struggled to formulate a coherent strategy for the 'wider Europe' (see Dannreuther 2003). On top of that, it is now facing outright competition for influence in the region from a resurgent Russia (see Popescu and Wilson 2009). The EU's neighbourhood policy has come right up against Russia's different approach to international relations, based more on balance of power and sphere of influence considerations than institutionalized cooperation.

The member states have never had much of an agreed strategy on how to deal with Russia, partly because Russia itself has had different approaches towards the West and partly because several member states (particularly the big three of France, Germany, and the UK) consider Russia to be too important a global player to let the EU lead in relations with it. In the past, those relations have been at times very difficult, over issues such as NATO enlargement, the wars in Bosnia and Kosovo (where Western diplomacy and military action were frequently criticized by Russia), and the wars in the breakaway Russian republic of Chechnya (which prompted considerable criticism of Russia in European circles but little consistent action to back it up). More recently, Russia's war in Georgia (and subsequent recognition of the independence of the breakaway regions of Abkhazia and South Ossetia) in 2008 and its use of gas and oil supplies as leverage in its relations with its neighbours (above all Ukraine) have presented a stark challenge to the EU—but one that has also divided the 27, with the new member states much warier of Russian power than some of the older ones. Russia does not participate in the 'flagship' EU policies towards the region, the European Neighbourhood Policy (ENP) and the Eastern partnership (EaP), though arguably both policies are profoundly affected by it.

The origins of the ENP lie in a UK proposal in 2002 for a 'wider Europe' initiative, which would be aimed at Belarus, Moldova, Russia, and Ukraine, but not the South-east European countries, already involved in the stabilization and association process, or other Western ex-Soviet republics such as Armenia, Azerbaijan, and Georgia. In December 2002, the European Council agreed, but included the southern Mediterranean countries in the initiative, on the insistence of southern member states. In June 2004, after considerable lobbying by the Caucasian republics (and a peaceful 'revolution' in Georgia), the Council extended the initiative still further to Armenia, Azerbaijan, and Georgia. Russia refused an invitation to participate.

Under the ENP, neighbours are offered increased economic integration and closer political cooperation conditional on meeting benchmarks (see European Commission 2003a). But weaknesses in the ENP have been obvious: the EU is hardly offering the promised 'all but institutions'. The benchmarks are many but the benefits on offer are few. Agricultural trade liberalization is too controversial for the member states to contemplate. And visa-free access for citizens from the neighbourhood has not been offered; in fact, enlargement meant the extension of Schengen rules, so new member states had to impose visa requirements on nationals from neighbouring countries, which has caused considerable friction with, for instance, Ukraine. Above all, the ENP does not hold out the prospect of future membership for the East European countries. The lumping together of Mediterranean and East European countries was seen as unsatisfactory, particularly by EU member states keen on keeping open the option of offering membership to their European neighbours.

In 2008, Sweden and Poland proposed the EaP, partly also to balance a French move to create a Union for the Mediterranean. Under the EaP, Armenia, Azerbaijan, Belarus, Georgia, Moldova, and Ukraine will be offered association agreements, creating a 'deep free trade area', as well as mobility partnerships eventually allowing visa-free travel to the EU. Multilateral meetings of heads of state or government, ministers, and experts will be held regularly. The prospect of accession to the EU is still, however, off the table, as it is far too controversial a prospect within the EU.

Furthermore, the EU's bilateral relations with the EaP countries have been difficult—and again, there are intra-EU disagreements over those relations, as well as difficulties within the partners, that complicate relations. Ukraine poses a unique set of problems. It has repeatedly indicated that it wishes to join the EU, but its lack of progress on political and economic reforms has not helped its case for stronger relations with the EU. The hopes of the Orange Revolution of 2004 have fizzled out as the various political parties try to outmanoeuvre each other, leaving severe economic problems (and a debilitating dependence on Russian gas) to fester. The EU's response to the Orange Revolution was lacklustre, as it offered hardly any additional carrots to encourage political and economic reform. It has also had a hands-off approach to the various disputes over gas supplies between Russia and Ukraine, even when these disputes have led to reduced gas supplies to EU countries. Part of the ambivalence towards Ukraine reflects divisions within the EU over Russia: a stronger EU policy on Ukraine could have negative implications for its relations with Russia, which some member states fear.

Elsewhere in the neighbourhood the prospects for prosperity and democracy currently seem distant. Belarus has been languishing under authoritarian misrule, and has been isolated by the EU since 1997. Its nominal inclusion in the EaP was controversial, but signalled an attempt to reach out to the regime and convince it to liberalize. Moldova has at times been paralysed by a simmering ethnic conflict (evident in the breakaway region of Transnistria) and more recently by quite intense political conflict. In April 2009, following disputed elections, protesters set fire to the parliament; new elections in July 2009 resulted in continuing stalemate.

The war in Georgia in August 2008 did spark a remarkable spurt of diplomatic activity by the French President Nicholas Sarkozy, who was able to negotiate a ceasefire between Russia and Georgia. But Russian forces remain ensconced in Abkhazia and South Ossetia. The EU's reaction to this has been muted: Italy blamed the Georgian president for the war, while some Central and East European countries saw it as confirmation of their views of a belligerent and aggressive Russia. The EU's relations with the two other Caucasian states, Armenia and Azerbaijan, are even more low key. Although there is CFSP involvement in the region (principally through the activities of special representatives) as well as the ENP and now the EaP, the EU's influence pales in comparison to that of other regional actors (Russia and Turkey) and the USA.

There are two basic problems for the EU in Eastern Europe. First, unless it promises membership, it cannot overcome the dilemma of exclusion: 'No matter how frequently NATO and EU officials reiterate that they have no intention of redividing Europe, irrespective of how many "partnership" agreements they offer to non-members, the inevitable consequence of admitting some countries to full membership of the organizations and excluding others is to produce "insiders" and "outsiders"' (Light *et al.* 2000, 77). Second, the policy instruments available to the EU are inadequate, and they are being wielded with little sense of urgency by an ambivalent EU. Far too little is on offer, both to encourage democracy, economic reform, and so on from the 'bottom up' (via aid and the free movement of people), and to try to force governments to comply with political and economic conditions. Unless the EU can provide more resources to try to make up for the lack of a medium-term membership prospect, it is unlikely to exercise much influence in the former Soviet Union. But to do this it needs to find more unity and coherence in its approach. Whether the EU can agree and implement its idea of European order much beyond the borders of the current EU is a question still unanswered.

Conclusion

Since the end of the Cold War, the EU has increasingly but emphatically 'flexed its muscles' in Europe, assuming responsibility for an ever expanding geographical area—primarily through enlargement and the expansion of its 'security community'. It is certainly a power in European international relations, and has reshaped much of the European order largely in its own image.

The most significant step taken was the decision to expand to ten Central and East European countries. Although they may have disagreed over aspects of the policy (such as the potential costs), the member states were still able to agree to enlarge the EU's membership. They could not escape from the fact that the EU was the focus of European countries' demands; this necessarily overshadowed their bilateral relations with them. Furthermore, those demands—notably for accession—could *only* have arisen within the Union context and thus had to be handled in that forum. And once the member states had explicitly agreed on the prospect of eastern enlargement, there appeared to be no turning back.

Explaining why the member states agreed to enlargement—when the costs are not only large (though uncertain) but unevenly distributed—requires the use of several theoretical approaches. Approaches that emphasize shared identity certainly help, as does recognition that the member states effectively had little room for manoeuvre—they could not realistically reject enlargement as a policy option. But we need to add geopolitical and security factors to the explanation: enlargement was considered a way to ensure European stability and security. Furthermore, the member states then had to deal incrementally with the geopolitical and security consequences that each successive enlargement decision created, and these factors dominated decision-making. Geopolitics helps to explain why enlarging the EU has been accepted as an imperative, but also why there are now doubts about the enlargement project within and outside the EU.

The EU's enlargement project and its wider influence in shaping the European order face severe internal and external challenges. Enlargement fatigue appears to have set in, which damages the credibility of the promise of membership, on which so much of the EU's influence depends. The EU member states have often been divided in their views of what the EU should be doing in the wider neighbourhood, making it more difficult, if not impossible, for the EU to address some of the quite profound problems in the region. Russia is openly challenging the EU's vision of the European order and, thus far at least, the EU has not come up with a convincing response. Iceland's recent application for EU membership is one bright spot on the horizon: negotiations should be relatively easy (with the probable exception of fisheries) and providing the Icelandic population approves of EU accession (by no means certain), this could be another success story in the EU's enlargement project. However, it remains to be seen whether accepting a small and potentially prosperous country on the margins of Europe will create the momentum to tackle much more difficult applicant and prospective applicant countries in South-eastern Europe, Turkey, and beyond.

Notes

1 The definition of 'order' here follows that of William Wallace (2001, 2): 'a relatively stable pattern of shared assumptions, rules and institutions which together constitute what Hedley Bull defined as not only a "state system", but more broadly also a "society of states" '.

2 The EU's enlargement policy is rightly considered 'foreign policy'—even though its aim is the eventual incorporation of the 'targets' into the EU—primarily because of the way the EU has used the prospect of membership to influence the domestic and foreign policies of those targets. The EU's policy towards its European neighbours is cross-pillar (and often led by the first, not second, pillar)—which may blind some observers to its foreign policy characteristics.

3 Aid to help implement democratic reforms was much slower in coming, with the first programme set up only in late 1992. The Community clearly thought that the top-down pressure of conditionality would be enough to foster democratization. After Yugoslavia proved that a democratic transition can go badly wrong, democracy aid was extended to the CEECs and to TACIS (Technical Assistance for the CIS countries) aid recipients. By 2002, Phare aid was over €1.5 billion a year (and total pre-accession aid topped €3 billion).

4 In December 1989, the European Council had stated that it would strengthen its relations with Yugoslavia, the Soviet Union, and the Central and East

European countries (European Council 1989, 14–15). A year later, Yugoslavia and the Soviet Union were undoubtedly in separate categories.

5 Several member states—Belgium, France, and Italy—made it clear in a declaration attached to the Amsterdam Treaty that further reform would have to precede enlargement.

6 Estonia in particular seemed only a marginally (if at all) more suitable candidate than Latvia and Lithuania (which those two countries bitterly pointed out afterwards). The inclusion of only one Baltic country would expand the first round of enlargement but not scarily so, and would help reassure the Baltic republics that they were firmly within the EU's 'sphere of influence'.

7 On the inclusive nature of the accession process, see Friis (1998). Friis and Murphy (1999) point out that widening the first round of negotiations also ensured the support of southern and northern member states.

8 The verification mechanism is in addition to safeguard measures, included in all of the accession treaties with the Central and East European countries, which allow member states and the Commission to take protective measures against new member states if they are not implementing their membership commitments.

9 Thus the EU eventually negotiated a stabilization and association agreement with Serbia because it sought to boost pro-reformers before important elections there, but will not ratify the agreement until Serbia demonstrates full compliance with ICTY.

 FURTHER READING

All of the books below provide a good historical account of the EU's enlargement policy. Cremona (2003) includes chapters on the EU's policy towards South-eastern Europe and the effects of enlargement on the EU's external relations and its internal development. Barbé and Johannson-Nogués (2003) concentrate on the effects of enlargement on the EU's external relations. Schimmelfennig (2003) develops the theory of rhetorical entrapment. Vachudova (2005) and Grabbe (2006) analyse the EU's use of membership conditionality.

Barbé, E., and Johansson-Nogués, E. (eds) (2003), *Beyond Enlargement: the new members and new frontiers of the enlarged European Union* (Barcelona: Universitat Autonoma de Barcelona).

Cremona, M. (ed.) (2003), *The Enlargement of the European Union* (Oxford: Oxford University Press).

Grabbe, H. (2006), *The EU's Transformative Power: Europeanization through conditionality in Central and Eastern Europe* (Houndmills: Palgrave).

Mayhew, A. (1998), *Recreating Europe: the European Union's policy towards Central and Eastern Europe* (Cambridge: Cambridge University Press).

Schimmelfennig, F. (2003), *The EU, NATO and the Integration of Europe: Rules and Rhetoric* (Cambridge: Cambridge University Press).

Smith, K. E. (2004), *The Making of EU Foreign Policy: The Case of Eastern Europe*, 2nd edition (Basingstoke: Palgrave Macmillan).

Vachudova, M. (2005), *Europe Undivided: democracy, leverage, and integration after communism* (Oxford: Oxford University Press).

 ## WEB LINKS

The European Commission's Directorate General for Enlargement handles relations with countries that have applied for membership and those that are expected to do so (**http://ec.europa.eu/enlargement/index_en.htm**). Its Directorate General for External Relations is responsible for the European Neighbourhood Policy and Eastern partnership (see **http://ec.europa.eu/external_relations/enp/index_en.htm**).

Both the Centre for European Reform in London (**http://www.cer.org.uk/**) and the Centre for European Policy Studies in Brussels (**http://www.ceps.eu/index3.php**) have published studies on enlargement and the neighbourhood policy. The European Council for Foreign Relations has a research programme specifically on Russia and the wider Europe (**http://ecfr.eu/content/programmes/C9/**).

CHAPTER 14

The EU and the Developing World: Partnership, Poverty, Politicization

Maurizio Carbone

▌ Summary

This chapter reviews the evolution of development policy in the European Union since the Treaty of Rome. Between the 1950s and the 1990s, EU development policy could be characterized mainly as a post-colonial policy. The Lomé Convention, hailed as a model for north–south cooperation for its emphasis on partnership, gave the EU a distinctive role in the international arena. Since the turn of the century, EU development policy has undergone a number of transformations. On the one hand, the Cotonou Agreement combined traditional development measures with the new political objectives. On the other hand, there has been an attempt to federalize the policies of the member states around a common vision on development. More generally, the EU has used development policy as part of its wider external relations agenda in an attempt to establish itself as an influential global actor. However, there have been no signs that it has shifted away from the fight against world poverty, though the policy space for developing countries has been significantly reduced.

Introduction

Development policy in the European Union (EU) has undergone a number of substantial transformations since the beginning of the new century. This *new* era involves both the programme managed by the European Commission (EC)—which has become more poverty oriented and efficient, though at the cost of reduced developing country ownership of their development process—and the attempt to 'federalize' the policies of the member states: hence the adoption of the European Consensus on Development and the ambitious agenda on aid effectiveness.[1] This chapter, however, aims to show how the nature of EU development policy has evolved over the past five decades. In particular, between the 1950s and the 1990s, EC development policy was conceived (and also studied) as an interaction between a donor and a group of recipients. This *old* approach, exemplified by the Lomé Convention with its generous trade and aid packages and emphasis on partnership between the parties, gave the EU a distinctive place in the international arena. The erosion of the special relationship with the African, Caribbean, and Pacific (ACP) group had already started in the mid 1980s, so that by the end of the 1990s its normalization was not a surprise. Predictably, the Cotonou Agreement combined traditional development measures with new political objectives, such as trade liberalization, prevention of migratory flows, and the promotion of global security. More generally, it is argued here, the EU has used development policy as part of its wider external relations agenda, in the attempt to establish itself as an influential global actor. This search for more Europe has not necessarily meant a shift away from the fight against world poverty, but it has certainly reduced the policy space for developing countries.

The Treaty of Lisbon has confirmed these trends. Not only has development policy been kept as an autonomous policy and the framework introduced by the Treaty of Maastricht been strengthened, but for the first time sustainable development and poverty eradication have been included among the general principles of the EU's external action. The application of these new provisions, nevertheless, has preoccupied development practitioners, who have raised doubts about a potential subordination of development to foreign policy objectives. Following this introduction, the second section briefly discusses the evolution, from the 1950s to the end of the 1990s, of what was considered mainly a (post-)colonial policy. The third section focuses on the changes introduced since 2000, including the attempt to create a common vision on international development and to promote synergies between foreign aid and other policies. Particular attention in both sections is devoted to the EC–ACP relationship, which has generally been considered the hallmark of EU development policy. Finally, the conclusion summarizes the central argument of this chapter.

The rise and fall of a (post-)colonial development policy

There is often some confusion when analysts discuss EU development policy, as they tend to conflate two dimensions. One the hand, the EU is a bilateral donor transferring financial resources directly to developing countries via the European Commission—hence the use of the term 'EC development policy'. This level of resources has progressively increased both in absolute terms—since the mid 1990s the European Commission has consistently been among the top four donors in the world—and in relation to overall EU aid allocations (the EC has increased its share from 7 per cent in the early 1970s to about 22 per cent at the end of the 2000s). On the other hand, the EU is a (particular type of) multilateral donor. In fact, the largest portion of EU aid is managed by the member states, which historically have resisted any proposal to pool sovereignty in this area. Thus, it is only when these two dimensions are combined that the EU becomes the largest provider of official development assistance (ODA) in the world. The origin of this dichotomy goes back to the Treaty of Rome itself and it has since become a 'structural component' of the relations between the EU and the developing world (Grilli 1993).

The Lomé Convention

In the context of the negotiation of the Treaty of Rome, the then six member states agreed to set up a twin package for their colonies in sub-Saharan Africa: a free trade area and a small foreign aid programme, the European development fund (EDF; see Box 14.1), in addition to their own bilateral policies. These provisions were certainly driven by a clear sense of obligation and historical responsibility for Europe's colonial past, but there was also the need to ensure the supply of primary goods to Europe's markets and to open up colonies to further trade and investments from European firms. In the face of a French ultimatum, which was seeking to maintain its influential presence in Africa, Germany and the Netherlands opposed the idea of a sort of 'EurAfrica' with a more global policy, but eventually had no other choice than to accept. This division between regionalists and globalists has characterized the evolution of EC development policy since. Regionalists—initially France, Belgium, and Italy, eventually joined by Spain and Portugal—sought exclusive or privileged relations with former colonies and other areas of the developing world on a regional basis. Globalists—initially Germany and the Netherlands, eventually joined by the UK and the Nordic countries—placed more emphasis on levels of poverty and development as a whole (Shaw 1979; Grilli 1993; Mayall 2005; Carbone 2007).[2] With decolonization, the relationship evolved from unilateral 'associationism' to a contractual and negotiated arrangement (see Table 14.1). The Yaoundé Convention, signed in 1963 with 18 Associated African states and

TABLE 14.1 Evolution of EC–ACP relations

Agreement	Date	EU members	ACP members	EDF	EDF (€ million)
Rome	March 1957	6	31	1 (1958–64)	581
Yaoundé I	July 1964	6	18	2 (1964–70)	666
Yaoundé II	July 1969	6	19	3 (1970–5)	843
Lomé I	February 1975	9	46	4 (1975–80)	3,124
Lomé II	October 1979	9/10	57	5 (1980–5)	4,754
Lomé III	December 1984	10/12	66	6 (1985–90)	7,754
Lomé IV	December 1989	12	69	7 (1990–5)	10,800
Lomé IV-bis	November 1995	15	71	8 (1995–2000)	12,967
Cotonou	June 2000	15	77	9 (2000–7)	13,500
Cotonou-bis	February 2005	27	78	10 (2008–13)	22,682

Source: European Commission online database

BOX 14.1   The European Development Fund

The European Development Fund (EDF) is the main financial instrument for cooperation between the EU and the ACP group. It is not included in the EU budget but is replenished every five years by the member states. Decisions are made through a weighted system based on the financial contributions made by individual member states (see Table 14.3). Budgetization of the EDF was originally proposed by the European Parliament and eventually supported by the European Commission to ensure greater transparency on how money is allocated, but it has consistently been opposed by the member states, who wish to retain control of the aid decision-making process.

Madagascar (AASM) and then renewed in 1969, broadly confirmed the provisions of the Treaty of Rome, though it established free trade areas between the EU and each of the African states and increased the volume of aid substantially (Cosgrove Twitchett 1981; Lister 1988).

The adoption of the Lomé Convention in 1975 was hailed as the latest step in a historical process which went from colonialism towards mutual cooperation and equality (Zartman 1976). In fact, while the Yaoundé Convention was simply communicated to African countries, the newly born ACP group, acting as a united block under the leadership of Nigeria, negotiated with unexpected skills. True, the generous provisions reflected the relative power of developing countries at that time (Gibb 2000). Moreover, the diversity of the development package that was eventually agreed, which included measures for agricultural and industrial development, managed to satisfy the needs of different types of developing countries (Gruhn 1976; Shaw 1979). Various scholars have concentrated on the EU's decision-making process, some arguing that it was driven by a convergence of the interests of France and the UK, others highlighting the central role of the European Commission, particularly Commissioner Claude Cheysson, in unblocking the stalled negotiations (Frey-Wouters 1980; Lister 1988; Grilli 1993).

That Lomé represented a prime example of successful cooperation between developed and developing states, a step towards a new international economic order (NIEO), has been the object of a contentious debate. Supporters point mainly to three elements: the principle of contractuality in foreign aid and the fact that development assistance was meant to be free from any interference in the political affairs of the recipients; the introduction of a non-reciprocal trade regime, which implied that almost all ACP goods, with the exception of a small number of 'sensitive' agricultural products, could enter the EU free of any tariff or quota restrictions; the provision of compensatory schemes in case of price fluctuations for countries dependent on commodity and mineral exports, respectively Stabex and Sysmin (Gruhn 1976; Zartman 1976; Alting von Gesau 1977; Cosgrove Twitchett 1981). By contrast, more critical observers argued that, rather than transcending, Lomé perpetuated inequalities between the north and the south, establishing a new form of colonialism, with a partial modification of the principle of international capitalism. By securing sources of raw materials, a vast market for its manufacturing goods and a climate conducive to multinational investment, it represented one of the greatest achievements for Europe, but not for the developing world (Galtung 1976; Mytelka 1977; Dolan 1978). Ravenhill has maintained that both parties benefited since they valued items differently (i.e. aid and raw materials). He has, nonetheless, defined the relationship as collective clientelism, which is 'a relationship in which a group of weak states combine in an effort to exploit the special ties that link them to a more powerful state or group of states' (Ravenhill 1985, 22).

The Lomé Convention was renegotiated four times and with each revision even the more optimistic observers became disillusioned. First, the small growth of subsequent EDFs combined with fast population growth in the ACP group meant a substantial reduction of the per capita aid received by each country. Moreover, not only was aid disbursement very slow and failed to reach the poorest people, but the EU gradually attached new conditionalities, initially focusing on macroeconomic frameworks and eventually expanding into political issues (Brown 2002; Dimier 2006). Second, from an economic point of view, the ACP countries did not perform as expected. For instance, the share of ACP products over the total EU imports from third countries declined from 8.1 per cent in 1980 to 2.7 per cent in 2000. In particular only a few countries (e.g. Mauritius, Seychelles, the Caribbean region) were able to take advantage of the preferential trade regime, while the large majority even regressed (Holland 2002; Babarinde and Faber 2005). The introduction of the generalized system of preference in 1971, which diluted ACP preferential

treatment, and the barriers imposed by the EU's protectionist Common Agricultural Policy—strict rules of origin, sensitive products, and safeguard clauses—contributed to limiting access to the European market and preventing diversification in
developing countries. Some analysts even suggested that the discontinuation of the
trade preferences would benefit ACP countries by obliging them to become more
competitive (Davenport 1992).

The expiry of the Lomé Convention in 2000 offered an opportunity to rethink
the EC–ACP development model. A large consultative process, involving actors in
Europe and in the ACP group, was instigated by the 1996 Green Paper, in which
the European Commission, presenting a very critical picture, acknowledged that
'ACP–EU relations are still a key part of the Union's identity. The postcolonial era
is coming to an end but our responsibilities towards the ACP countries continue' (European Commission 1996). In light of the disappointing performance of
most ACP economies, it called for the replacement of the existing non-reciprocal trade regime with one that was no longer incompatible with WTO rules: in
fact, by offering preferences to ACP countries, the EU was discriminating against
other low-income countries. Similarly, it criticized foreign aid, which had failed to
reduce the number of the poor and had become a very bureaucratic practice (Holland 2002). In sum, what had contributed to raise the EU's international profile in
the 1970s risked jeopardizing its role as a credible development actor—hence the
need to change.

Maastricht and the three Cs

The creation of a supranational dimension in EU development policy by the Treaty
of Rome was seen by some as the first step of a process leading to the full commu-
nitization of aid. The added value of the first EDF, which was very small, was 'its
existence, not its dimension' (Grilli 1993, 50). However, in the following 30 years,
member states rejected any attempt to promote better coordination as a threat to
their national sovereignty. Some discussions occurred in the early 1970s, when a
proposal for a gradual transfer of competence to the supranational level of areas
in which the European Commission had a comparative advantage was discarded
by the Council. In the 1980s the debate continued, but the Council saw in 'voluntary *à la carte* coordination' the greatest level possible of cooperation. In the run-up
to Maastricht, the European Commission relaunched the debate, proposing even
sanctions for defiant member states. France and the UK resisted any proposal for
donor coordination, but for different reasons: the latter in line with its traditional
Euroscepticism, the former to preserve the status quo. Germany and the Netherlands did not exclude it, but preferred to concentrate respectively on improving
the effectiveness of EC aid and enhancing the synergies between development and
other policies (Faber 1982; Grilli 1993; McMahon 1998; Hoebink 2004).

The Treaty of Maastricht laid the foundations for a change of direction by introducing a new legal framework for development policy and institutionalizing three

new principles—coordination, complementarity, and coherence—which became known as the three Cs. By coordination, it meant that member states and the European Commission should consult each other and coordinate on their aid programmes, including in international organizations and international conferences, with a view to speaking with a single voice; the level of coordination was not specified, but the European Commission was given the task of taking initiatives to promote it. By complementarity, the treaty acknowledged that development policy was a shared competence and that the programme managed by the European Commission should complement those of the member states. The European Court of Justice ruled against the subordination of EC development to the bilateral policies of the member states and even established that once the EC adopts a decision, the member states cannot take any action that goes against it. By coherence, the treaty meant that the EU should take development objectives into account in all those policies likely to affect poor countries (Carbone 2007).

Throughout the 1990s, the EU held a number of debates in the Council, issued resolutions, and set up pilot projects. Yet little, if anything, was achieved. At a more general level, numerous member states considered development policy to be a key area of national sovereignty, useful to cultivate historical and/or strategic relations with third countries; other member states were hardly interested or, especially in the case of the smaller states, felt that a single development policy would simply reflect the interests of France and the UK, and penalize their recipient-led approaches. At a policy level, most aid bureaucracies opposed any attempt towards better coordination and complementarity, in some cases to preserve power and jobs, in other cases on the basis of their alleged superiority as aid agencies, particularly vis-à-vis the European Commission. A similar fate befell the initiatives on Policy Coherence for Development (PCD). The European Commission, which was paralysed by territorial and ideological clashes between various Directorates-General (DGs), failed to lead. The timid initiatives of some member states (i.e. the Netherlands and Denmark) were resisted by those who argued that the needs of developing countries were sufficiently taken care of by foreign aid. The most vocal actors were the European non-governmental organizations (NGOs), which launched a number of public campaigns against the EU's agricultural and fisheries policies, particularly in West Africa (Hoebink 2004; Carbone 2009; 2010).

Meanwhile, the end of the Cold War and the EU's attempt to create a Common Foreign and Security Policy (CFSP) had important consequences for development policy. First, the Treaty of Maastricht introduced the principle of consistency in external relations, which meant that development policy had to contribute to the general goals that the EU pursues in the international arena. In particular, the creation of the CFSP provided the legal underpinning for the insertion of political issues into relations with the developing world. Clauses on democracy and human rights started to figure in all development cooperation agreements. Moreover, the EU engaged in conflict prevention and resolution in Africa, though its record was far below expectations. Second, with the fall of the Berlin Wall, a large

TABLE 14.2 Regional distribution of ODA by the EC					
	1987–8	**1992–3**	**1997–8**	**2002–3**	**2007–8**
Sub-Saharan Africa	58.3 (32.1/48.3)	55.6 (28.4/40.6)	40.4 (29.5/41.8)	44.0 (34.5/48.4)	40.3 (33.7/41.0)
North Africa and Middle East	10.9 (18.8/15.9)	24.7 (23.2/22.7)	21.1 (12.1/13.1)	15.9 (11.7/9.7)	17.6 (21.9/22.4)
Europe	–	–	11.7 (4.5/4.9)	17.5 (7.2/8.9)	19.5 (4.2/5.3)
Latin America and Caribbean	10.2 (12.1/10.1)	8.7 (13.5/12.4)	12.7 (13.6/14.7)	8.3 (11.6/11.0)	8.9 (9.0/9.6)
South and Central Asia	11.0 (14.8/11.9)	5.6 (10.2/8.4)	8.1 (13.4/9.2)	9.3 (16.2/12.3)	9.1 (15.9/11.7)
Other Asia and Oceania	9.5 (22.2/13.7)	5.4 (24.7/15.8)	6.1 (27.1/16.2)	5.1 (18.8/9.7)	4.6 (15.3/9.9)

Data represent percentage share of total gross disbursement. Data in parentheses are respectively Development Assistance Committee (DAC) EU countries and DAC average. Data for 1987–8 and 1992–3 for North Africa and the Middle East also include Europe.

Source: DAC online database

amount of resources was allocated to Central and East European countries in view of the enlargement, as well as to new states in the former Soviet Union and later in the former Yugoslavia. Moreover, the attempt to affirm the EU as a global actor also implied an intensification of relations with the Mediterranean and, to a lesser degree, Latin America and Asia. The weight of different regions in the EU's external assistance programme significantly changed (see Table 14.2), but this evolution occurred in a piecemeal way so that the European Commission had to face significant criticism (Bretherton and Vogler 2006). Some observers, predictably, questioned the added value of the EU's supranational development policy, concluding that it increasingly had turned into 'a symbolic gesture ... primarily useful to demonstrate its breadth of commitment to, and relationship with, the south' (Arts and Dickson 2004, 3).

Development policy in the new century

At the beginning of the 21st century, a new stage began in EU development policy. These transformations should be seen against a changing international context. In September 2000, leaders signed the Millennium Declaration, which was operationalized into eight millennium development goals (MDGs), making the fight against poverty high on the global policy agenda. This implied both more aid—the EU and the US pledges in the context of the financing for development conference held in Monterrey in March 2002 were complemented by other donors—and better aid, as a new emphasis was placed on donor harmonization and alignment, which culminated in the 2005 Paris Declaration on aid effectiveness and the 2008 Accra agenda for action. Meanwhile, the terrorist attack in the USA in September 2001 was seen as a signal pointing to the increased gap between rich and poor and to the need to tackle new threats in international security. Various countries decided to boost the security–development nexus, which for some meant a strenuous fight against international terrorism and for others a new focus on 'fragile states' (Woods 2005; Bretherton and Vogler 2006).

The precondition for the new stage in EU development policy, however, was the extensive reform of all EC external assistance programmes that the European Commission carried out in an attempt to address criticisms—like, for instance, that of the British Secretary of State for International Development, Clare Short, who defined the EC as 'the worst development agency in the world' (Santiso 2002). At the policy level, a development policy statement adopted by the European Commission and Council in November 2000 clarified the principles and practice of EC development policy. In particular, it made poverty eradication the primary goal, reduced the areas of intervention to those in which the EC was deemed to have a comparative advantage, and reiterated the EU's commitment to the three Cs (Council of the European Union 2000a). At the management level, a number of measures were adopted to make sure that aid would be disbursed faster, including the creation of a new body (EuropeAid) in charge of implementing all external assistance across the various regions, the further devolution of activities to the external delegations, and the simplification of instruments for external assistance (Dearden 2003; 2008).[3] All these measures not only contributed to improving the record of EC development policy but also restored the credibility of the European Commission, which explains why some of the most sceptical member states changed their attitude when new proposals for better donor coordination were launched in the mid 2000s. But first the new century opened with the signing of a new EC–ACP convention.

The Cotonou Agreement

Following lengthy and tense negotiations, the Cotonou Partnership Agreement (CPA) was signed in June 2000, this time for 20 years, with a revision clause every five years—though it came into force only in April 2003 due to delays in the ratification process. Some characterized it as 'incremental change', in line with the idea that the Lomé Convention was an international regime (Lister 1997; Forwood 2001; Farrell 2009). For others, it represented a fundamental break with the past (Holland 2002; Babarinde and Faber 2005; Flint 2009). The negotiation process shows that, despite the renewed emphasis on partnership, a large majority of the EU's proposals, if not the totality, were agreed, so that Hadfield (2007, 46) has concluded that its interventionist stance has 'transformed the CPA into a deeply politicized development convention that was no longer comprehensively linked to its stated goal of poverty reduction'. In fact, while the most cited innovations concerned the aid and trade regimes, there were also significant changes involving the political component.

In the area of development assistance, the Cotonou Agreement replaced the principle of aid entitlements, which implied fixed allocation of aid for five years, with a system meant to secure value for money. Aid allocation would no longer be based only on an assessment of needs (i.e. population, per capita income, social indicators, indebtedness, dependence on export earnings) but also on performance (i.e. progress in institutional and macroeconomic reforms, effective use of resources, implementation of measures towards poverty eradication and sustainable development). The country strategy papers (CSPs) and national indicative programmes (NIPs), to be elaborated in collaboration with recipient governments and non-state actors (see Box 14.2), have become the tools to reward and penalize countries— although the EU has retained the sole responsibility for financing decisions. The reduction of instruments to deliver aid—one providing budgetary, sectoral, and project support, and another providing for emergencies—implied the demise of Stabex and Sysmin, to the disappointment of the ACP group (Dearden 2003; Babarinde and Faber 2005).

In the area of trade, the CPA dropped the principle of non-reciprocity and replaced it with trade liberalization. It also introduced the principle of differentiation,

---

| BOX 14.2 | **Non-state actors and development policy** |

NGOs have played an important role in EC development policy since the mid 1970s, when a co-financing budget line was established for European NGOs that implemented projects in developing countries and, later, raised public awareness on development in Europe. In the following two decades, not only did the amount of these resources keep increasing, but they also started to be involved in policy advocacy. This honeymoon came to a conclusion at the end of the 1990s, when the co-financing budget line became a victim of its own success—too many applications for too little money—and the NGO umbrella body was accused of mismanagement of funds. The adoption of a long-awaited communication on non-state actors—which included civil society, business association, and social groups—marked a change of direction, with emphasis placed on southern NGOs. In particular, the Cotonou Agreement provided a comprehensive framework for integrating civil society in the development process, by establishing that non-state actors must be involved in all phases of the development process. The practice, however, has been very different. Efforts have been made to involve as many actors as possible; nonetheless, the overall quality of participation has been far from optimal and has been characterized by ad hoc information sessions, lack of transparency in the selection of participants, and little feedback on the results (Carbone 2008a).

with divisions based both on geography—negotiations of the so-called Economic Partnership Agreements (EPAs) with six regions (four in Africa, one in the Caribbean, and one in the Pacific) were to be finalized by January 2008—and levels of development, with the group of least developed countries (LDCs) still to benefit from preferential access to the European market. This was the result of a difficult compromise within the European Union, which put the ACP countries in a 'take it or leave it' situation. Some member states (e.g. France) sought to preserve the existing trade regime together with the integrity of the ACP group; others (e.g. Germany) proposed a new grouping of the ACP countries based on continents, and wished to normalize the trade regime; yet others (e.g. the UK and the Nordics) raised concerns about the potential marginalization of the LDCs caused by free trade (Forwood 2001; Babarinde and Faber 2005). The rationale used by the European Union to introduce the EPAs—poor performance of the EC–ACP preferential trade regime, the need to comply with WTO rules, the pursuit of regional integration—was considered hypocritical and ill justified. Not only did the EU try to shrug off responsibility for its own policy when it could have tried to alter these rules (Hurt 2003), but the triumph of neo-liberalism failed to take into account transformation costs, the loss of customs revenue for developing countries, and the limited scope for trade expansion for countries that depended heavily on primary goods, to say nothing of the problems caused by the EU's Common Agricultural Policy (Holland 2002).

With Cotonou, the relationship between the EU and the ACP group became more politicized. The inclusion of new topics such as good governance, illegal migration, and anti-corruption, did tighten up the conditions for receiving aid, but for some it was a consequence of the incorporation of development policy within the CFSP: 'It was no longer possible to quarantine development policy as being purely economic in content; its association with CFSP made it undeniably political as well' (Holland 2004, 288).[4] For others, more critically, the new political dimension was strictly linked with economic liberalization: 'Market freedom and political freedom (in the shape of liberal democracy) are mutually interdependent, and essential to the achievement of developmental outcomes' (Farrell 2005, 278). The Cotonou Agreement also contributed to strengthening the link between aid and security by foreseeing the funding of activities in the area of peace building, conflict prevention, and resolution. This, for Hadfield (2007, 44), confusedly merged the objectives of the EC as a donor (i.e. promotion of development) with the EU as an actor (i.e. reduction of security threats) and ultimately 'has generated an international actor whose development policy remains separate from its explicit foreign policy perimeters but yet visibly obtains as a foreign policy platform'.

The implementation of Cotonou has raised even more controversies than its conclusion. An empirical assessment of two generations of CSPs (2002– and 2008–13) demonstrates that aid effectiveness has been enhanced, and not only because of the large use of budget support. The European Commission, however, seemed too eager to show that it was able to disburse money quickly. Hostage to its past management failure, in a majority of cases it failed to effectively engage with recipient governments and civil society (Carbone 2008b). At the same time, the geographical distribution of aid and new aid commitments demonstrates that since 2000 sub-Saharan Africa countries have received more financial assistance than they did in the 1990s, which supports the view of those who argue that poverty eradication has become the main goal for the EU's development policy (Olsen 2008b). The agreement of the 'peace facility for Africa' in 2003 sent the message that the EU is genuinely committed to promoting regional security, although the use of EDF money to fund it was criticized. The commitment to democracy and human rights proved more rhetorical than substantive, confirming the fact that the EU's lofty aspirations do not always match the reality, often resulting in significant policy evaporation on the ground (Crawford 2005). The politicization of the EC–ACP relationship was augmented with the first revision in February 2005 and the second one in June 2010, thanks to the adoption of new measures aimed to combat terrorism, control migration, and tackle climate change (Mackie 2008).

In the case of the EPA negotiations, the European Commission's emphasis on reciprocal trade liberalization over development—as a consequence of the lead role taken by DG Trade—initially attracted little public attention. The ACP group seemed acquiescent, or simply reluctant to actively engage with the EU. The agreement of the 'everything but arms' (EBA) regulation in May 2001, by granting quota and duty-free access to all goods coming from the LDCs with the exception of arms and ammunitions, had provided the poorest among the ACP countries with an alternative to regional free trade agreements.[5] Increasingly, criticism towards DG Trade mounted: some member states (i.e. the UK and Denmark, supported by the Nordics), decided to break ranks and manifested their dissent publicly, emphasizing development and social dimensions over trade liberalization; the ACP group accused the EU of simply wanting to impose its views, which was in violation of the principle of partnership enshrined in the Cotonou Agreement; the 'stop EPAs' campaign launched by Oxfam and endorsed by a large number of European NGOs received wide attention. These continuous expressions of dissatisfaction with the EPA negotiations affected the Commission's behaviour, which began to be more positive in its attitude towards development-oriented agreements. When the December 2007 deadline was reached, only the Caribbean region had signed a full EPA; 20 countries had agreed to an 'interim' EPA; 43 countries had chosen not to sign anything. The interim EPAs, which still reflected the EU's offer, focused on trade in goods, included a transition period for sugar and rice and a gradual liberalization of trade in ACP countries, as well as a range of development-supporting measures (Elgström 2009). An important consequence, nevertheless, was that one of the main aims of the EPAs—promotion of regional integration—not only failed to materialize, but some countries, both in the Pacific (i.e. Papua New Guinea, Fiji) and in Africa (i.e. Cameroon, Ghana, Côte d'Ivoire), decided to abandon their regional partners and signed interim individual EPAs (Stevens 2006; Faber and Orbie 2009a; Elgström and Frennhoff Larsén 2010).

The European Consensus on Development

A central component in the new stage in EU development policy has been the search for a more coordinated and coherent development policy. In view of the 2002 international conference on financing for development, the member states decided to make a joint commitment on volume of aid and other financing issues. The most visible outcome was the pledge to increase their collective volume of aid from 0.33 to 0.39 as a percentage of their collective gross national income (GNI) by 2006. The importance of this decision—together with the monitoring role assigned to the European Commission—was not so much linked to the actual increase of aid, as to its consequences: it reversed declining trends in foreign aid; it raised to the EU level an area in which national sensitivities had always prevailed; it showed that, by acting as a single actor and setting an example, the European Union was able to lead—in fact, a number of other donors, including the USA, boosted their foreign aid budgets (Carbone 2007). Not only was the target on volume of aid achieved before the deadline, but, in May 2005, the EU committed itself to a more ambitious target, that of reaching 0.56 per cent by 2010 and 0.7 per cent by 2015. Of course, some member states (i.e. Germany, Greece, Italy) were reluctant to accept these commitments and used budget constraints as potential obstacles. Nevertheless, they 'set in motion a process of peer pressure among European member states, making it politically costly for any single government to renege on its ODA promise' (Orbie and Versluys 2008, 76).

These commitments on the quantity of aid were supplemented by a new emphasis on the quality of aid. Following the British leading role, in December 2005 the European Union adopted two regulations, which established the full untying of all EC aid on a reciprocal basis with other international donors. Moreover, member states committed themselves to a transparent mapping and monitoring of their activities through the periodical update of an EU donor atlas, to establish joint multi-annual programming and country-based harmonization roadmaps and to increase the number of co-financed projects (Carbone 2007). Another central component of this new stage of EU development policy is the agenda on Policy Coherence for Development. In May 2005, the European Commission launched an ambitious programme for the whole EU, eventually endorsed by the Council. A large number of policy areas, 12 in total, were identified, and for each of these areas specific 'coherence for development commitments' were agreed. When this agenda was launched, it was celebrated as a major success for the EU, succeeding where other international organizations had failed (Carbone 2009).[6]

All these attempts to improve the EU's development record and image culminated in the European Consensus on Development (ECD)—signed in December 2005 by the Presidents of the European Commission, Parliament, and Council (European Commission 2006b). The ECD was celebrated by EU official discourse as a document that for the first time ever provided a policy platform setting out common objectives and principles, to be applied not only to the policy implemented by the European Commission but also to those of the member states. Reaching a final agreement, however, was complicated. The European Commission initially tried to sell it as an update of the 2000 development policy statement. In this sense, it was accepted that unlike the member states, the European Commission should be present in all developing countries but concentrate on a limited number of areas, on the basis of a dialogue with partner countries. By contrast, its role as promoter of EU-wide coordination met with the resistance of several member states. By doing so, it was argued, the European Commission was simply attempting to increase its role in development policy, transcending the shared competence issue and seeking a form of integration by stealth. On the one hand, a first group of countries (France, Belgium, and more passively the southern member states) supported the initiative for a 'European vision on development', including a more active role for the European Commission. On the other hand, a second group of member states (the UK and the Scandinavians) tried to resist any change to the status quo. In between, a third group of countries (Germany, together with Finland and the Netherlands) endorsed the idea of better coordination between European donors, but did not want to assign any privileged role to the European Commission (Carbone 2007) .

The ECD, adopted when some of the most controversial Commission proposals were eliminated from the final draft, can be interpreted in various ways.[7] First, it represented the crystallization of the EU's aspiration to a value-based identity, a sort of 'force for good', that had emerged vigorously since the early 2000s. In particular, to the traditional core and subsidiary norms identified by Manners (2002) in his analysis of 'normative power Europe' (e.g. freedom, human dignity, democracy, the rule of law, equality), we can now add some that are more closely related to development policy: ownership, political dialogue, and participation of non-state actors. Second, it confirmed the emerging new views of a multidimensional approach to poverty eradication that is more suitable to the global agenda of the EU and to its attempt to increase its global leverage (Hadfield 2007). In this sense, the ECD complemented the 2003 European Security Strategy (ESS). It did so by reiterating the fact that the EU would promote multilateralism and contribute to a system of rules, institutions, and international instruments set up and implemented by the international community. But at the same time, it rectified the subordination of development to security policy—'security is a precondition for development'— by establishing that the two are mutually reinforcing goals. Finally, while some saw it as a perpetuation of the post-Washington consensus stress on poverty reduction, democracy, and good governance, as well as an alignment with the MDGs (Hurt 2010), the ECD was an attempt to differentiate the EU's approach from that of other actors dominant in development thinking: that is, the Bretton Woods institutions and the USA—hence the initial idea for a 'Brussels consensus on development'— and increasingly the emerging donors, most notably China.

Various initiatives were taken to operationalize the European Consensus on Development. The first was the code of conduct on complementarity and division of labour, adopted by the Council in May 2007. On the one hand, member states would concentrate their activities in a number of priority countries, making sure that a balance is found between 'aid darlings' (countries that receive large quantities of aid, such as Mozambique, Tanzania, Rwanda, Ghana, or Burkina Faso) and 'aid orphans' (countries that are generally overlooked, for instance Chad, Burundi, Guinea, and the Central African Republic). On the other hand, member states would limit their activities to no more than three sectors per country and delegate in other sectors to other European donors. The novelty of the code of conduct is that member states would make decisions on their bilateral aid policies by engaging in dialogue not only with the developing countries, but also with their European peers. Moreover, the exercise of responsibility towards forgotten states could be seen as a manifestation of the fact that the EU cares about all developing countries, regardless of their colonial past or strategic importance. The second initiative concerned the agreement in October 2006 of a harmonized approach on the issue of good governance based on policy dialogue and incentives, meant to reward countries that engage in reforms and consolidate democratic practices. By using positive conditionality rather than selectivity, the EU was not only seeking to promote aid effectiveness but also raising its profile in international development, thus challenging the leadership of the World Bank and the USA (Carbone 2010).

Another important commitment was the attempt to promote a common and coherent policy towards the whole African continent. A first strategy was adopted in December 2005, resulting from two different documents, one adopted by the European Commission emphasizing poverty eradication and the achievement of the MDGs, and the other by the High Representative for the CFSP, arguing that peace and security were key not only to the EU's role in Africa but also to the CFSP. A new joint Africa–EU strategy was adopted in December 2007 since its predecessor was criticized for lack of adequate consultation of all stakeholders. The starting point was the idea of a 'new strategic partnership' based on a 'Euro-African consensus on values, common interests and common strategic objectives'. To meet these objectives, a detailed action plan for 2008–10 was adopted, including eight EU–Africa partnerships.[8] This renewed interest in Africa by the EU had some normative motivations and reflected also changes in Africa—with the agreement of NEPAD (the New Economic Partnership for Africa's Development) and the African Union, African leaders had sent a clear message that they wanted to take ownership of their own future. Nevertheless, it cannot be separated from the threats coming from China's rising profile in the region. Moreover, although the joint Africa–EU strategy was a comprehensive document, the result of an extensive dialogue between European and African actors, the EU's motives and views were still dominant, as witnessed by the disagreement over the issue of trade liberalization when the document was signed in Lisbon in December 2007 (Olsen 2008a).

The scoreboard on the achievement of the MDGs at the end of 2009 indicated that, like most international donors, the EU had lagged behind schedule and a majority of developing countries were destined not to meet most of the targets by

2015. The global economic crisis that hit the world in 2007–8 had negative consequences on developing countries in terms of worsened trade conditions, lowered remittances, and, of course, cuts in foreign aid. A number of member states were still far from meeting the 2010 EU aid target, yet the volume of aid given by the EU as a whole had more than doubled between 2000 and 2009 (see Table 14.3). The initial implementation of all the measures on aid effectiveness and policy coherence for development, moreover, showed that the EU suffered from an implementation deficit, as it so often does (see Chapter 8). In particular, empirical evidence suggested that the limited progress on joint multi-annual programming and on the code of conduct was caused in part by hesitant developing countries—which often lack capacity but also fear a potential loss of resources and the imposition of stricter conditionalities by a gigantic donor—but principally by recalcitrant member states, fearing the loss of visibility and influence. Unsurprisingly, some European aid officials spoke of 'coordination fatigue', which seemed to confirm more general trends on the global agenda on donor harmonization (Carbone 2010). In the case of policy coherence for development, progress was also much below expectations. Of course, achieving policy coherence is not an easy task due to conflicting political priorities and interests among member states, but even the European Commission (under the leadership of DG Development) in its 2007 and 2009 monitoring reports acknowledged that the EU needs to find a better balance between the promotion of its interests and the concerns of developing countries, particularly in sensitive areas such as migration and security. Nevertheless, the importance of PCD was finally recognized within the European Commission and by the member states, and this was reflected by the many mechanisms put in place to promote it (Carbone 2009).

The implications of Lisbon

The entry into force of the Treaty of Lisbon in December 2009 has substantially changed the framework for the EU's external relations, including development policy. At a more general level, in addition to the new President of the European Council, which should ensure continuity of policy priorities across the rotating presidencies, the creation of the new post of High Representative (HR) for Foreign Affairs and Security Policy, and of the European External Action Service (EEAS) should reinforce the overall consistency of the EU's action in the international arena and increase the EU's capacity to act on the world stage. Development policy was included as one of the EU's areas of external actions and for the first time sustainable development and the eradication of poverty are included among the overall objectives of the EU's external action. At a more specific level, the Treaty of Lisbon confirmed most of the existing provisions in a separate section devoted solely to development policy. It established fighting poverty as the central goal of the EU's development policy. Moreover, while the principles of policy coherence for development remained unchanged, the principles of complementarity and coordination

TABLE 14.3 Aid efforts by the EU's member states

	ODA 2009 € million	ODA 2009 % of GNI	Aid to EC 2009 % of total ODA	10th EDF € million	10th EDF % of total
Austria	823	0.30	28.53	547	2.41
Belgium	1868	0.55	22.72	801	3.53
Bulgaria	12	0.04	–	32	0.14
Cyprus	29	0.17	–	20	0.09
Czech Republic	161	0.12	53.01	116	0.51
Denmark	2017	0.88	9.63	454	2.00
Estonia	14	0.11	–	11	0.05
Finland	924	0.54	16.87	333	1.47
France	8927	0.46	23.33	4434	19.55
Germany	8605	0.35	24.12	4650	20.50
Greece	436	0.19	43.80	333	1.47
Hungary	83	0.09	64.54	125	0.55
Ireland	718	0.54	16.26	206	0.91
Italy	2380	0.16	56.17	2917	12.86
Latvia	15	0.08	–	16	0.07
Lithuania	35	0.14	–	27	0.12
Luxembourg	289	1.01	9.59	61	0.27
Malta	11	9.20	–	7	0.03
Netherlands	4614	0.82	8.97	1100	4.85
Poland	249	0.08	69.21	295	1.30
Portugal	364	0.23	37.14	261	1.15
Romania	99	0.08	–	84	0.37
Slovakia	53	0.08	–	48	0.21
Slovenia	51	0.15	–	41	0.18
Spain	4719	0.46	18.76	1781	7.85
Sweden	3267	1.12	6.54	621	2.74
UK	8267	0.52	16.31	3361	14.82
Total	49030	0.42 (weighted average)	–	22,682	100

Source: DAC, European Commission, and UK Foreign and Commonwealth Office online databases

have been strengthened: previously EC development policy had to complement national development policies, but now the two components must 'complement and reinforce each other', with the European Commission still in charge of promoting coordination.

The new institutional framework, particularly the EEAS and the issue of funding, initially generated mixed feelings among practitioners. On the one hand, some pointed to the fact that development cooperation was kept in a separate section. Further deconcentration, with new responsibilities delegated to the EU delegations, could have a positive effect on the implementation of programmes—though the heads of the development cooperation sections may need to fight to keep resources for development purposes. On the other hand, some warned against a potential sidelining of development, with funding being instrumentalized to pursue foreign policy objectives. Another fear concerned the role of the Development Commissioner vis-à-vis the High Representative. In the new Barroso Commission, interestingly, the post of Development Commissioner—now separated from humanitarian aid (see Box 14.3)—was assigned to the Latvian Andris Piebalgs, who despite coming from a member state with relatively little experience in development cooperation, performed strongly in his hearing before the European Parliament. Finally, some observers have raised concerns about the impact of the extended competence that the European Commission has acquired in trade policy, particularly in the light of its bullying tactics in the negotiations over the EPAs (Koeb 2008; European Think-Tanks Group 2010).

BOX 14.3   Humanitarian aid in the European Union

The European Union, through the Humanitarian Aid department of the European Commission (ECHO), carries out its own humanitarian aid policy, and with more than 10 per cent of the total is the world's second largest humanitarian donor (after the USA). In the 1990s, EC humanitarian aid was linked to the emergence of the EU as an international actor and was often used as a surrogate for political action or a gap-filler for development cooperation. With the new century the trend has been that of de-politicization. More importantly, the European Commission has played a major role as promoter of humanitarian coordination and harmonization, proposing the European consensus on humanitarian aid, eventually signed by the Commission, Council and Parliament in December 2007. When the EC and the bilateral efforts of the member states are combined, the EU provides around half of the overall international humanitarian assistance, making it by far the world's leading humanitarian donor. The consensus aims to promote good practices in humanitarian aid by encouraging coordination between the European institutions and by stressing the need to establish good relationships with those actors that are active on the ground, most notably the United Nations and the community of NGOs (Versluys 2008b).

Development and the EU's role in the international arena

It should be clear by now that development policy links to broader considerations of the EU's role in the international arena. In line with what is suggested by the editors of this volume in their introduction, this section first looks at the EU as a sub-system of international relations, concentrating on the interaction of member states and other relevant actors in the making of development policy. Then it examines the EU as part of the wider processes of international relations, focusing on the role it plays in setting the global agenda on development. Finally, it examines the EU as a power, looking also at how it is perceived by other actors.

The EU's role in international development has been significantly affected by the issue of competence, and the parallel existence of 27+1 development policies. The preferences of the two former colonial powers (i.e. France and the UK) and the changing membership of the EU have shaped the evolution of EC development policy, though after Cotonou this has become less of an issue. Various cleavages, however, exist on the extent to which development policy should be carried out through the EU, which reflect the way in which Member States conceive and manage their bilateral programmes. The most identifiable group is made of a number of like-minded countries (i.e. Denmark, Luxembourg, Ireland, the Netherlands, Sweden, UK), which tend to give higher percentages of foreign aid, and allocate most of their resources to poor and democratic states, making use of programme and untied aid. They consult before meetings of the Council (as well as the EDF Committee), so that their collective preferences prevail. A second set of countries (i.e. France, Belgium, Italy, Spain, Portugal, Greece), which, however, does not act as a group, has historically given a lower percentage of aid, allocated resources for strategic reasons (including to former colonies) and made more use of project and tied aid. The latter countries tend to support proposals for a 'European' approach to international development; by contrast, the former countries tend to react less enthusiastically, considering it an additional layer of bureaucracy between the national and the international (preferably the UN) level. The countries in Central and East Europe—in light of their limited tradition and low financial contribution to this sector—play a secondary role, though they welcome the idea of a common European approach (Arts and Dickson 2004; Carbone 2007; Lightfoot 2008).

Significant clashes occur also within the European Commission, which ultimately affects the EU's ability to take coherent initiatives. Unsurprisingly, the three DGs which deal mostly directly with the developing world do not necessarily share the same views: DG Development being in charge of programmes in the ACP group and general development issues; DG RELEX dealing with Asia, Latin America, and the Mediterranean and political aspects of development; DG Trade tasked with the aid–trade nexus and the EPA negotiations. Periodically, DG Development may be accused by DG RELEX of ignoring broader foreign policy goals, and DG Trade is chastised by both DG Development and DG RELEX for overlooking human rights, security, and development issues in trade agreements (Carbone 2007; Holden 2009). Nevertheless, while bureaucratic quarrels have increasingly received more attention in the literature, the European Commission may 'no longer be the key problem' (Grim 2008) and in fact its role as promoter of coordination with a view to making the EU an influential player in the global discourse on development has been acknowledged even by traditionally sceptical analysts (Farrell 2009). Some scholars, however, have preferred to see the European Commission as part of a transnational alliance, composed of some international organizations and several EU member states pushing towards the fight against world poverty (Olsen 2008b). This argument lends support to those who argue that development policy in the European Union should be seen as a product of multilevel governance (Holland 2002), in which the role of the member states and the European Commission must be complemented by other actors within Europe (e.g. civil society) as well as out-side it (e.g. states and civil society in developing countries).

This takes us to the second issue, the extent to which the EU affects the global development agenda. With the conclusion of the Lomé Convention, the EU put forward a distinctive approach to international development, based on values such as responsibility, non-interference, and partnership. This progressive approach was compromised in the 1980s, when hopes that the EU would add weight to the 'alternative development project' supported by the UN proved misplaced: the EU started to follow the dominant development paradigm set by the Bretton Woods institutions, based on neo-liberal principles and on aid conditionality (Lister 1997; Arts and Dickson 2004; Holden 2009). Since the beginning of the new century, there has been another attempt to shape the pace of international development, with a number of initiatives on volume of aid, donor coordination, and policy coherence for development. Whether the EU leads or follows is the subject of contentious debate. Some have maintained that the EU once again has simply aligned itself to an international consensus built around key international organizations. In particular, issues like aid effectiveness, ownership, participation, all found in EU agreements, resonate with the language used by the Bretton Woods institutions (Farrell 2008); the EU's emphasis on reciprocity is underpinned by the WTO consensus on the benefits of free trade for development (Hurt 2010). Others have claimed that the EU's acquisition of tasks traditionally performed by the DAC (e.g. promotion of donor coordination), and the alignment with the policies carried out by the UN (e.g. achievement of the MDGs) mean sacrificing some policy autonomy, although it is welcomed by developing countries themselves (Holland 2008; Orbie and Versluys 2008). The issue is not whether the EU is able to produce innovative ideas. In fact, even if the commitments on the quantity and quality of aid and on policy coherence for development show that the EU has imported these ideas from elsewhere, by taking firm commitments it is still able to condition the behaviour of other international actors, which in some cases have no other choice than to follow the EU's lead (Carbone 2010).

Assessing the impact of the EU in the international debate on development is linked to the issue of the EU as a power. Historically, analyses have concentrated on the evolution of EC development policy, with two competing views having emerged. On the one hand, some have considered the EU an aid superpower, arguing that Lomé favoured neocolonial exploitation and increased economic dependence between Europe and Africa (Galtung 1976; Ravenhill 1985). On the other hand, Lomé was seen as the EU's benevolent contribution to international development, a model for north–south relations (Zartman 1976; Shaw 1979; Karagiannis 2004). Similarly, in the case of the Cotonou Agreement, there are those who saw in it a 'triumph of realism over idealism', with the EU imposing its interests on weaker partners and using even the more normative aspects—democratic principles, participatory approaches, dialogue—to coerce developing countries (Hurt 2003; Farrell 2005). There are those who saw in it an indirect instrument of structural power through which the EU sought to impose development and generic liberalization rather than its specific interests (Holden 2009) or more simply explained it as a consequence of a normative shift, with old norms like partnership and obligation being replaced by such principles as liberalization and democratization (Elgström 2000). Increasingly, development policy has been included in the booming literature on normative power. The EU's attempt to construct an image of 'force for good', promoting the interest of developing countries and norms such as peace, democracy, human rights, sustainable development, and regional integration has, however, produced mixed results (Scheipers and Sicurelli 2008; Flint 2009; Farrell 2009; Söderbaum and Stålgren 2009). In fact, an increasing tension may exist between conditionality and developing country ownership, in negotiations characterized by asymmetrical relations, in spite of the rhetorical claims that the EU differs from other international actors through its emphasis on dialogue (Storey 2006; Elgström 2009; Hout 2010). Finally, another strand of literature to consider is that on outsiders' perceptions. Empirical evidence seems to suggest that expectations are high on the EU to 'champion the interests of the developing countries' and that developing countries often turn to the EU for leadership in international settings. But this is nothing new, as one of the motivations behind the adoption of Lomé was that of being seen as a benign actor, not to mention, more recently, the adoption of the EBA before the WTO round in Doha and the 'solidarity race' with the USA on volume of aid before the 2002 Monterrey conference (Lister 1997; Santiso 2002; Bretherton and Vogler 2006; Chaban et al. 2006; Lucarelli and Fioramonti 2009).

Conclusion

This chapter has reviewed the evolution of EU development policy over the past five decades. Curiously, the end point of this analysis—the negotiation of the EPAs with six regions in the ACP group—is a return to the starting point, of the agreement of a free trade area with African countries under the Treaty of Rome. In general, EC development policy until the late 1990s can be characterized as primarily post-colonial. The signing of the Lomé Convention, for many observers the most comprehensive and progressive framework for north–south cooperation, inaugurated a season of optimism and gave the EU a distinctive place in the international arena. But with time, not only were those hopes not realized, but the EU lost its identity through following trends set by other international organizations and by imposing strict conditions on developing countries. At the turn of the century, the strengthened political dimension of the Cotonou Agreement, the normalization of trade relations with developing countries, and the common strategy for Africa were symptoms of an increasingly spasmodic search for a coherent external policy. More importantly, the determination to project a 'European vision of development' through the European Consensus on Development and the new agenda on aid effectiveness was not only an attempt to make aid work better but is consistent with the EU's overall agenda in external relations, that is to establish itself as a global power.

It seems evident that the real added value of EU development policy—whatever the doubts expressed by scholars and practitioners—is not linked to its global presence but to its role in aid coordination and the promotion of policy coherence for development. In its relations with the developing world, the European Union is not only an agency disbursing development assistance, but also an international actor. While the boundaries between foreign and development policies have increasingly become blurred, there are no signs that the EU has de-prioritized the fight against world poverty. Contrary to what is generally argued, new political objectives have complemented and not replaced development goals, so that development policy has contributed to raising the profile of the EU in the international arena. The emphasis placed on efficiency and consistency in external relations, however, has inevitably resulted in a further reduction of the policy space for developing countries. The new institutional setting introduced by the Lisbon Treaty has meant for some that an autonomous development policy might be at risk, with a further politicization of development cooperation and the instrumentalization of development funds for foreign policy objectives. Still, it represents an important step forward for development cooperation by crystallizing the view that poverty eradication is the central aim of development policy, strengthening the principle of policy coherence for development and requiring that member states' and EC development policies complement and reinforce each other.

Notes

1 For the sake of clarity, the term 'EC aid' refers only to the programme managed by the European Commission, thus excluding bilateral aid from individual

member states. The term 'EU aid' includes both EC aid and the bilateral aid managed and disbursed by the 27 member states.

2   Incidentally, a similar evolution can be seen in the EU's trade policy towards developing countries, particularly the divide between liberals and protectionists. When EU trade policy becomes politicized, France forms a protectionist alliance of mainly southern member states (i.e. Italy, Spain, Portugal, and Greece, and often Austria and Belgium) that opposes trade liberalization. Germany and the UK generally lead the northern coalition of 'free traders' and are generally supported by the Netherlands, Sweden, Denmark, and Finland. The eastern enlargement in 2004 has not had a major effect on trade policy: Poland and Slovakia may be associated with the protectionist side, whereas Estonia, the Czech Republic, and Slovenia could be seen as part of the liberal camp.

3   In addition to political instruments (i.e. the instrument for stability, the European instrument for democracy and human rights initiative, the instrument for pre-accession, and the instrument for macroeconomic assistance) and to the instrument for humanitarian assistance, the development cooperation instrument is meant to support development-related projects and programmes. It can be used for activities in Latin America, Asia, and South Africa and for activities in five thematic areas: environment, migration, non-state actors, and decentralized cooperation; food security; social sectors; asylum and migration.

4   Migration and good governance proved two very contentious issues. Eventually, the EU 'persuaded' the ACP to accept the readmission of any illegal immigrant present in the EU's member states, at 'that member state's request and without further formalities' (Article 13). Good governance was included only as an essential element (rather than fundamental), whose violation would not necessarily lead to the suspension of aid.

5   From the EBA regulation three other goods were also excluded, whose liberalization was deferred: bananas (January 2006), sugar (July 2009), and rice (September 2009). In general, as largely predicted, its impact in terms of trade flows has been modest. However, when it was launched it was a showpiece of the development-friendly nature of EU trade policy towards developing countries and an element of the EU's strategy to gain approval from developing countries for the launch of the Doha development agenda (Faber and Orbie 2009b).

6   For a detailed analysis of the EU's agenda on policy coherence for development see Carbone (2009).

7   Among the most controversial proposals made by the European Commission that disappeared from the final draft we should point to: the idea that EU development policy might play a significant role to 'harness globalization', dear to France but criticized by the UK, was replaced by a stronger emphasis on poverty eradication as the primary objective of development policy; the

initial emphasis on foreign aid was complemented by a stronger reference to policy coherence for development, to satisfy the requests of the Nordic countries; the provision of a common framework to implement the common development vision was dropped as a result of the resistance of the UK and the Nordic countries (Carbone 2007).

8 These partnerships included: peace and security; democratic governance and human rights; trade and regional integration (including the implementation of the EU–Africa partnership for infrastructure, launched in 2006); millennium development goals; energy; climate change; migration, mobility, and employment; and science, information society, and space.

FURTHER READING

General overviews are offered by Grilli (1993), Lister (1997), Holland (2002), Arts and Dickson (2004), and Mayall (2005). A number of books cover wider aspects of EU development policy. Ravenhill (1985) and Babarinde and Faber (2005) focus on EC–ACP relations, respectively the Lomé Convention and the Cotonou Agreement; Carbone (2007 and 2009) discusses the politics of foreign aid and the issue of policy coherence for development; Holden (2009) looks at the use of EC aid as a global political instrument; Söderbaum and Stålgren (2009) investigate the link between development and inter-regionalism; Faber and Orbie (2009) evaluate the EPAs.

Arts, K., and Dickson, A. K. (eds) (2004), *EU Development Cooperation: From Model to Symbol* (Manchester: Manchester University Press).

Babarinde, O., and Faber, G. (eds) (2005), *The European Union and Developing Countries: the Cotonou Agreement* (Leiden: Brill).

Carbone, M. (2007), *The European Union and International Development: the Politics of Foreign Aid* (London: Routledge).

Carbone, M. (ed.) (2009), *Policy Coherence and EU Development Policy* (London: Routledge).

Faber, G., and Orbie, J. (eds) (2009a), *Beyond Market Access for Economic Development: EU–Africa Relations in Transition* (London: Routledge).

Grilli, E. (1993), *The European Community and the Developing Countries* (Cambridge: Cambridge University Press).

Holden, P. (2009), *In Search of Structural Power: EU Aid Policy as a Global Political Instrument* (Aldershot: Ashgate).

Holland, M. (2002), *The European Union and the Third World* (Basingstoke: Palgrave).

Lister, M. (1997), *The European Union and the South: Relations with Developing Countries* (London: Routledge).

Mayall, J. (2005), 'The Shadow of Empire: the EU and the Former Colonial World', in Hill, C., and Smith, M. (eds), *International Relations and the European Union* (Oxford: Oxford University Press).

Ravenhill, J. (1985), *Collective Clientelism: the Lomé Conventions and north–south relations* (New York: Columbia University Press).

Söderbaum, F., and Stålgren, P. (eds) (2009), *The European Union and the Global South* (Boulder, CO: Lynner Rienner).

 WEB LINKS

A good starting point for information on EU development policy is the European Commission website, particularly DG External Relations, DG Trade (**http://ec.europa. eu/trade/**) **http://eeas.europa.eu/index_en.html** and EuropeAid (**http://ec.europa. eu/europeaid/**). On the relations between the EU and the ACP, see the website of the ACP Secretariat (**www.acpsec.org/**). The Development Assistance Committee (DAC) of the Organisation for Economic Co-operation and Development provides data on foreign aid and publishes analyses on the development programmes of the EU and most of its member states (**www.oecd.org/dac/**). Much useful information can be obtained from the European Centre for Development Policy and Management (**www.ecdpm.org/**), the European Association of Development Institutes (**www.eadi.org/**), Europe's Forum on International Cooperation (**www.euforic.org/**), as well as two leading NGOs, Concord (**www.concordeurope.org/**) and Eurostep (**www.eurostep.org/**).

CHAPTER 15

The Challenge of the Environment, Energy, and Climate Change

John Vogler

Summary

The EU has established a pre-eminent role in the global politics of the environment. This chapter examines how EU external environmental policy was established on the basis of internal policies. Despite problems of coordination and coherence under shared competence, the EU has been able to exercise leadership in global environmental governance and most significantly in the development of the climate change regime. Because the latter concentrates on reducing greenhouse gas emissions, the EU has faced the challenge of aligning its energy and climate policies, and internal and external action has been closely interrelated, raising questions of climate and energy security. The second part of the chapter traces the way in which the Union has led attempts to create an international climate regime up until the 2009 Copenhagen conference and considers the ways in which the different energy interests of the member states have been accommodated in order to sustain European credibility. Finally, there is an analysis of the problems encountered by the Union as a climate negotiator.

Introduction

Environmental policy in general, and climate change policy in particular, represent key areas of EU involvement in the processes of global governance. A theme running through this chapter is that in this area there is a very close relationship between the internal and external policies of the Union. The acquisition of internal competences led to very extensive Community (now Union) participation in a wide range of international environmental cooperation, from the regulation of international trade in hazardous waste to the Kyoto Protocol. As will be demonstrated in the discussion of the links between external climate and internal energy policy, international requirements have also driven domestic policy formulation within the EU. Since the 1980s sustainable development has provided the *leitmotif* of global environmental politics. For the EU this highlights problems of 'coherence' between its environmental, trade, and development policies, which can limit their effectiveness and legitimacy. It also links to two of the key themes of this volume: the functioning of international relations within the EU and the links between the EU and broader processes of international relations.

Despite this, and some of the limitations of coordination and competence that will be examined in this chapter, the EU has made strong claims to international leadership. This has been of some significance for the Union's emergent international identity. Whatever the failings of the CFSP, climate leadership did provide an arena in which success might be claimed and in which the EU could be regarded as constituting a 'power' (thus providing evidence for the third of the key themes in this volume), orchestrating regime construction, mediating between the developed and developing worlds, and taking on the US government over climate and other issues. The USA in particular has provided the 'other' in this process of identity construction.

Engagement with the international regime for climate change, from its inception in the late 1980s, has required that the Union take action to limit emissions from the burning of fossil fuels. There had already been some limited connection between energy and environmental policy in the campaign to combat 'acid rain' deposited by emissions from power stations during the 1970s and 1980s, but now wholesale reform of the ways in which Europe generated and used energy became essential both to fulfilling EU obligations under the Kyoto Protocol and to maintaining the credibility of the Union's position in the search for a successor 'post 2012' agreement. However, the Union had not developed anything resembling a common energy policy and entered into the climate negotiations of the 1990s without a credible foundation (Adelle *et al.* 2009). Leadership in the developing international climate change regime required that such an internal basis be established, but climate and energy policy came to impinge upon some important member-state interests and to reveal major differences between countries at different levels of economic development with diverse 'energy mixes' and dependence upon external suppliers. Thus climate change policy is illustrative of another of the themes of this volume, highlighting the internal politics of the EU as an international system in its own right, as the Commission, member states (and latterly the European Parliament) struggled to reconcile their differing energy requirements in a way that would fulfil the Union's international obligations and ambitions.

Once energy and environmental policy had become entangled in the politics of climate change it was also clear that there were significant contradictions and complementarities between conceptions of energy and climate security. Energy policy tended to be framed in terms of security of supply, with many external policy implications of a largely orthodox kind. On the other hand, climate security involved a rather different perspective in which environmental changes potentially threatened the longer-term interests of the Union. Examining the various ways in which policies conflict or provide much-sought-after 'synergies' is a useful approach to examining the climate–energy connection. It also provides an important example of attempts to achieve sustainability through EU policy coherence, both internal and external.

After its successes in ratifying the Kyoto Protocol and initiating the world's first international emissions trading scheme (the European Emissions Trading Scheme or ETS), the Union has found it much more difficult to take the lead in attempts to develop the climate regime post 2012 and many regard the Copenhagen climate conference of 2009 as a major reverse for EU claims to leadership. This prompts an analysis, in the final section of this chapter, of the factors that determine the success or failure of the EU in climate diplomacy. Some of these relate to its coordination and competence problems that can hinder effective negotiation, but probably more significant are changes in the structure of the international system that first assisted and then served to deny the EU's aspiration to climate leadership.

Environmental policy

The environment received not a mention in the Treaty of Rome. The Treaty's focus was upon economic regeneration and expansion, and the full consequences of success in this enterprise could not be grasped by its framers. Nonetheless, activists in the Commission were able to provide creative interpretations of some of its articles such as to allow the early development of environmental policy. The first piece of environmental legislation is traceable to a 1959 directive on radiological protection under the EURATOM (European atomic energy community) Treaty, to be followed by a range of measures that used the harmonization of standards within the common market to insert environmental rules. The types of issue covered were vehicle emissions and packaging standards, which if not regulated by the Community could result in distortions to the free flow of goods and services within the market.

This 'niche' approach was necessitated by the weak legal and institutional position of environmental policy.

An upsurge of green political consciousness within the USA and many other advanced societies was evident from the late 1960s and the United Nations held its first landmark conference on the human environment (UNCHE) in Stockholm in June 1972. In October of that year the Paris summit of the six and Britain, Denmark, and Ireland issued a formal declaration that henceforth economic growth would be tempered by a concern to protect the environment (McCormick 2001, 47). A number of well-publicized accidents and environmental disasters alongside an increasing recognition of the scale of trans-boundary pollution encouraged European action to protect the environment—a process that was generally promoted by 'green leader' states, Denmark, the Netherlands, and Germany (Andersen and Liefferink 1997). In 1973 an environmental action programme was announced, the first of successive programmes under which a mass of environmental legislation was to be generated—in excess of 250 specific acts. By the 1990s action on the environment had resulted in one of the most substantial areas of European law. European Community and now Union competences (where the right to make policy passes from the member states to the Union) were acquired in a range of significant areas, including atmospheric and water quality, the disposal of hazardous waste, noise abatement, and the protection of wildlife and habitats—to the extent that upwards of 80 per cent of member-state domestic environmental legislation is initiated by EU environmental directives. Environmental policy achieved treaty recognition in the Single European Act of 1986 and is now incorporated in the Treaty of Lisbon (Treaty on the functioning of the European Union Articles 191 and 192). A 'high level of protection and improvement of the quality of the environment' is one of the objectives of the Union, which shall also 'contribute to the sustainable development of the earth' (Article 3, (3,5)). It is important to note the changes introduced by the entry into force of the Lisbon Treaty. Previously there was a distinction between the Community and the member states, with the Community having its own competences and a separate legal personality. From 2010 the Union will 'replace and succeed the European Community' (TEU Article 1) and have its own legal personality, allowing it to sign treaties in its own right or alongside the member states.

In fact, for most issues involving environmental policy, competences are shared between the Union and the member states (TFEU Article 4 (e).[1] The proportions of competence vary by issue. For example, in relation to trade in hazardous waste there is a very high degree of Union competence, while for climate change there are important areas of exclusive member state competence. For EU environmental policy under Article 191, the normal legislative procedures apply, which means the application of qualified majority voting in the Council and co-decision with the Parliament. Questions of shared competence and internal legislative procedures have significant implications for the role and effectiveness of the EU in international environmental politics, to which we shall now turn.

The international dimension

As with other areas, such as transport, it was evident that the implications of the European Community's decisions could not easily be contained within the boundaries of the common market. Member states, of course, already had a range of existing international commitments and treaty obligations. Whereas in the case of trade it had been clear from the outset that authority to negotiate on behalf of all members had to be transferred to the Commission, this was hardly the case elsewhere. Indeed, the very idea of handing over rights to conduct external policy was strongly contested by some member-state governments. It was only following a significant legal judgement of the European Court of Justice (ERTA 1970; see Box 15.1) that the relationship between internal and external European Community policy was finally established. The precise terms and circumstances are given in Box 15.1 and are significant because the ERTA judgement provided the basis upon which the Commission was able to assert its right to represent the European Community externally where internal environmental policy competence had been achieved.

The judgement provided the basis for participation of the Community alongside member states in international negotiations. Both were allowed to be signatories to international undertakings, known as 'mixed agreements'. In negotiations it is possible for either the Commission or the presidency to take the lead in representing the Union, depending upon their competences, and this has sometimes irritated and bewildered outsiders who have to interact with the EU. Furthermore, there is a need to attain agreement during a negotiation among the member states such that there is usually an internal EU negotiation being conducted within the international meeting. Much time is spent by the Commission and national officials in coordination meetings, which run alongside the official negotiations. With a rotating presidency, shared competences, and an increasing number of member states, it might have been expected that the EU would be an ineffective environmental negotiator, hamstrung by its own internal deliberations and capable only of moving at the speed of the slowest member state. However, as we shall see, the EU was able to make credible claims to leadership in environmental diplomacy, although, as will also be evident over the issue of climate change, its internal arrangements still cause difficulty. The entry into force of the Lisbon Treaty has reopened debates about the extent of Union competence and the right to represent the EU in climate and other environmental negotiations.[2]

Even if the EU was able to organize itself for the conduct of environmental diplomacy, there remained the question of external recognition. The Community and now the Union enjoy international legal personality, that is to say they have the formal right to incur international obligations in the same way as the member states. However, although the Commission may assert the Union's right to participate in international organizations, this has not always been accepted by outsiders. An example is provided by the 1973 Convention on International Trade in Endangered Species (CITES). This is an international agreement where one might expect that on the basis

> **BOX 15.1   ERTA 1970: from internal to external competence**
>
> The case at issue covered relatively mundane road transport issues. It was the intention of the Treaty of Rome that a common transport policy should be developed and that this would involve the setting up of a common framework of rules (TEC Article 71). Because road transport operated right across the European continent and involved member states and non-members alike, there was a clear logic to ensuring that common standards were maintained and that such issues as rest periods for drivers were not handled differently on either side of the Community's boundaries.
>
> The attempt to provide a set of Europe-wide regulations commenced with the signature of a European agreement concerning the work of crews and vehicles engaged in international road transport in January 1962 (ERTA). Among the signatories were five of the six EC states, but insufficient ratifications were obtained during the 1960s for the agreement to enter into force. Meanwhile the Community took the first steps towards the common transport policy, envisaged in the Treaty of Rome, when at the end of the decade it legislated on the harmonization of social legislation relating to road transport (Regulation 543/69) .The matters covered, involving driver standards and rest periods, were essentially similar to those covered in the ERTA. New negotiations to revise and ratify the latter had begun in 1967 and, aware of this, the member states agreed in a Council meeting of May 1970 to concert their national approaches to the negotiations and ensure they were in line with the new community regulation. The Commission reacted to this apparently sensible arrangement by taking legal action against the Council at the European Court of Justice (ECJ), calling for the Council's decision on the negotiations to be annulled. Thus begun the legal proceedings, known as the ERTA case, that were to define the relationship between internal and external competence and which served as the basis for much subsequent external policy development by the Community (ECJ case 22/70, 31 March 1971).
>
> The argument of the Council was that the member states were quite within their rights to continue to negotiate the ERTA on an intergovernmental basis because the Treaty did not so provide in the area of transport and that 'authority to enter into agreements with third countries cannot be assumed in the absence of an express provision in the Treaty' (ECJ 22/70). On the issue of principle, the Court disagreed and sided with the Commission. It found that the authority to negotiate externally 'arises not only from an express conferment by the Treaty but may equally flow from other provisions of the Treaty and from means adopted' (ECJ 22/70:16). Once the Community has laid down common rules in whatever form, the member states 'no longer have the right, acting individually or even collectively, to undertake obligations with third countries which affect those rules or alter their scope' (ibid.:17). Thus 'the system of internal Community measures may not be separated from that of external relations'. This doctrine of 'parallelism' between internal and external policy, and that competence for one implies the other, has been of critical importance in the development of EU external relations.

of trade and animal welfare competences, the Union would be a fully recognized participant, but this continues to be denied by other CITES members. The Union is also recognized as a full member of relatively few international organizations.

It has this status at the World Trade Organization (WTO) and at the UN Food and Agriculture Organization (FAO) but not within the United Nations Environment Programme (UNEP) or at the UN General Assembly where, since 1974, it has enjoyed only observer status. Thus an important part of the history of the EU in international environmental politics has been the struggle for recognition.

The ERTA judgement allowed environmentally minded Commission officials (in the Environment and Consumer Protection Service in DGIII—a dedicated Environment DG was set up only in 1981) to assert the external competence of the Community alongside the member states.[3] This first occurred at a regional level with the 1975 Bonn Convention for the protection of the Rhine against chemical pollution, to be followed by the Barcelona Convention of 1976 for the protection of the Mediterranean Sea. The Community could bring to the table not only its policy competences but, more persuasively, a budgetary contribution.

By the end of the decade the Community was engaged on a broader scale with international attempts to deal with trans-boundary air pollution and acid rain. The negotiations for a convention on long-range trans-boundary air pollution (LRTAP) under the auspices of the United Nations Economic Commission for Europe were themselves, in part, a consequence of the changes in East–West politics and the Helsinki process that had helped to stimulate the development of European Political Cooperation during the 1970s. Just as the EC had competence for the trade aspects of East–West relations, so it had competence for questions of atmospheric pollution and for the implementation of any agreement arrived at. Previously the Soviet Union and its allies had refused to recognize the Community, a practice that involved avoiding eye contact with Commission officials at UN meetings and leaving the room when they spoke. Now, in the hope that COMECON would achieve similar recognition, a special status of Regional Economic Integration Organization (REIO) was invented for the EC, which has ever since served to allow the participation of the Community alongside the member states. The Union remains the only extant example of an REIO but most recent global environmental conventions on biodiversity, desertification, persistent organic pollutants, climate, etc. contain an REIO clause. This allows the Union to be a full participant and signatory according to its competences and to cast the votes of all the member state parties, but not to vote in addition to them.

Internal environmental legislation gathered pace during the 1980s, and Community competence was definitively established through the treaty amendments agreed under the Single European Act of 1986, which also introduced qualified majority voting in the Council. These events coincided with a series of significant external opportunities for the development of environmental policy. From 1985 to 1987 the Montreal protocol to the Vienna Convention, to combat depletion of the stratospheric ozone layer, was negotiated. The Community was heavily involved, although not always productively, because its position was too often dominated by the interests of European chemical industries that wished to continue production of ozone-depleting chemicals (CFCs). US negotiators complained that constitutional wrangling within the European delegation hampered the conduct of negotiations (Benedick 1991). Nonetheless, agreement was achieved on what has become probably the most successful and effective international environmental regime. This was also probably the last occasion that the USA, as opposed to Europe, could lay claim to global environmental leadership.

Sustainable development

The late 1980s were a period of intense international environmental activity leading to the negotiation of global conventions on climate, biodiversity, and desertification, all of which were scheduled to be signed at the 'Earth summit', to be held in Rio in 1992, formally the United Nations Conference on Environment and Development (UNCED). In 1987, in preparation for this landmark meeting, the Brundtland Report (WCED 1987) popularized the concept of sustainable development. Sustainable development has become a very significant idea for the EU and for the wider discussion of the linkages between economic activity, development, and environmental degradation. There are many different and changing interpretations, but its political essence is that there can be no progress without a political and financial accommodation between the desire of the north to avoid ecological degradation and collapse and the urgent demands of the south for development and poverty reduction. Since Rio the Union has embraced the concept as one of its primary objectives, to be 'mainstreamed' in its policies. The extent to which sustainability can go beyond more conventional and limited ideas of environmental protection is evident from the European Council's own definition:

It is about safeguarding the Earth's capacity to support life in all its diversity and is based on the principles of democracy, gender equality, solidarity, the rule of law and respect for fundamental rights, including freedom and equal opportunities for all. It aims at the continuous improvement of the quality of life and well-being on Earth for present and future generations. To that end it promotes a dynamic economy with full employment and a high level of education, health protection, social and territorial cohesion and environmental protection in a peaceful and secure world.

(European Council 2006a)

One need not go quite this far to recognize that once environmental policy was reframed in terms of sustainability, the common commercial, agricultural, and fisheries policies of the Union and its extensive development activities could hardly be excluded. They often provided a source of embarrassment because of the ecological and developmental consequences of the Common Agricultural Policy (CAP) and the way in which fisheries policy, for example, not only served to deplete European fish stocks, but did actual damage to sustainable livelihoods elsewhere.[4] A major challenge remains in attempting to integrate external environmental policy with fisheries, trade, development, and transport policy in pursuit of the commitments to sustainability contained in the Treaty on European Union and expressed in the revisions to the Community Treaty from 1987 onwards. The problem is often described in terms of policy 'coherence', both horizontal (between the different activities of the Union) and vertical (between the priorities of the member states and the Union). Although efforts have been made to remedy some of the more damaging consequences of the southern fisheries agreements, and the Common Fisheries Policy is supposedly in a process of transformation to a regime for the sustenance rather than exploitation of fish stocks, there is still evidence of a narrow concern with the latter.[5] Trade policy has only been marginally affected by environmental concerns and negotiations continue to be conducted according to a set of zero-sum assumptions about commercial advantage, although to be fair the EU is the only major power in the WTO that has taken trade, environment, and animal welfare issues at all seriously. This also serves to highlight a key sustainability issue in the 'coherence' of the Union's policies where trade, development, and environment frequently appear to pull in opposing directions. Coherence between the Union's approaches towards energy and climate, which is discussed below, overlaps significantly with these other areas. There has, for example, been pressure for border tax adjustments to shield industries subject to the higher energy costs imposed by the EU's internal emissions trading system from external competition.

Substantial efforts have been made in the Cardiff process (launched in 1998) and elsewhere to encourage 'horizontal' policy coherence in the pursuit of sustainable development, although it is difficult to judge their success and there has been 'no significant impact' on climate and energy coherence (Adelle *et al.* 2009, 50).[6] While it is easy to be cynical about these matters, it remains, for example, the case that the EU is almost alone among WTO members in taking issues such as animal welfare, trade impact assessments, and eco-labelling seriously. Sustainability was the keynote theme of the 1992 Rio conference, and the EU has continued to be a leading player in the Commission for Sustainable Development (CSD), which it set up, and subsequent UN conferences, notably the 2002 Johannesburg World Summit on Sustainable Development (WSSD). Prior to Rio, much effort was devoted to drafting *Agenda 21*, a massive compendium of good sustainable development practice, which still has currency. It was clear that much of its content was covered by Community competence, but the Commission was burdened with the problem of its lack of status at the United Nations. The latter remained an organization of sovereign states and the EC had only been admitted by the General Assembly in 1973 as an observer without speaking or voting rights. Much effort was extended by the Commission in advance of UNCED to improve this situation, sometimes in the teeth of member-state opposition. One result was the following footnote to *Agenda 21*:

When the term Governments is used, it will be deemed to include the European Economic Community acting within its areas of competence.

In contrast to practices established by the Conventions including those signed in Rio, where the Union has the status of an REIO, the UN General Assembly, its conferences, and the CSD remain areas of difficulty in terms of the full representation of the Union alongside the member states (Vogler and Stephan 2007).

EU leadership

The 1990s were a decade of heavy EU involvement in international environmental diplomacy, despite the negotiating difficulties typically encountered where competence is shared between the Community and the member states and agreements are 'mixed'. Indeed, the European Commission has been a leading player in the Basel Convention on hazardous waste, the Rotterdam Convention on hazardous chemicals and pesticides in international trade, the Stockholm Convention on persistent organic pollutants and the Cartagena Protocol on genetically modified organisms and biosafety. The growth of internal policy has been parlayed into a major external leadership role and the Community is now an active participant in more than 60 international environmental conventions (See Box 15.2).

The significance of the Union for what is often now referred to as global environmental governance extends beyond its participation in multilateral environmental agreements to leadership (Vogler and Stephan 2007; Wurzel and Connelly 2010).

BOX 15.2	Some major international environmental agreements to which the Union is a party

Long-Range Trans-boundary Air Pollution Convention 1979 and protocols

Vienna Convention on the Protection of the Stratospheric Ozone Layer 1985 and Montreal Protocol 1987

United Nations Framework Convention on Climate Change (UNFCCC) 1992 and Kyoto Protocol 1997

United Nations Convention on Desertification 1994

United Nations Convention on Biological Diversity 1992 and Cartagena Protocol on Biosafety 2000

Basle Convention on the Control of the Trans-boundary Movement of Hazardous Wastes and their Disposal 1989

Rotterdam Convention on Prior Informed Consent Procedure (PIC) for Hazardous Chemicals and Pesticides 1998

Stockholm Convention on Persistent Organic Pollutants (POPs) 2001

United Nations Convention on the Law of the Sea 1982

Convention for the Prevention of Marine Pollution from Land Based Sources and Paris Protocol 1986

Convention on the Conservation of Antarctic Marine Living Resources 1980

Aarhus Convention on Access to Environmental Information 1998

Leadership involves both structural and normative components and may be conceptualized in terms of three categories: power-based, directional, and intellectual (Skodvin and Andresen 2006). Power-based or structural leadership involves the use of both incentives and penalties. Traditionally the EU has been able to provide incentives because of the development and other funding that it can employ, and there are numerous examples of EU-funded environmental initiatives, both bilateral and multilateral. At the same time, one of the major contributions made by the EU to the raising of environmental standards has been through the accession process, where aspiring candidates are required to accept and implement its *acquis* (Schreurs 2004). This extends to international conference diplomacy, where the accession countries and others are persuaded to follow the line laid down by the Presidency or the Commission. Directional leadership relies heavily on the demonstration effect and credibility deriving from the success of the EU's internal environmental policies, which is closely related to intellectual leadership. The latter describes the way in which the EU can determine the way that agendas are set and would include the widespread acceptance of its policy ideas such as the precautionary and 'polluter pays' principles. As we shall see, the exercise of such leadership, based on its targets and internal policies, was a key component of the Union's approach to the climate change convention.

The leadership that the EU has been able to provide has occurred within a specific political context. The ending of the Cold War and the upsurge of global environmental concern in the late 1980s provided a political space within which the EU could begin to assert its leadership based upon its internal policy achievements. However, there is also little doubt that the international prominence of EU environmental policy is in many ways the reciprocal of US abdication. It should always be remembered that the USA virtually invented modern environmental policy and was up until the late 1980s a clear leader. There is probably no other area that can rival that of climate change in terms of the profile attained by the EU at the expense of the USA (Vogler and Bretherton 2006).

The climate and energy problem

The issue of climate change emerged on to the international agenda at the end of the 1980s. For the EU it represented both a profound challenge and an opportunity. The problems associated with the enhanced greenhouse effect were very different from those that could be more narrowly classified under the heading of environmental policy, although DG Environment and the environmental formation of the Council of Ministers were to take the lead. Mitigating emissions of greenhouse gases (GHGs) and adapting to the likely consequences of increases in mean global temperatures set the most severe and varied challenges to policy and, unlike other environmental problems, such as stratospheric ozone depletion, potentially touch almost every aspect of the economy and society. The problem was compounded by lack of scientific certainty as to predicted temperature rises and associated climatic impacts. The Intergovernmental Panel on Climate Change (IPCC) was created in 1988 to provide authoritative reviews of the evidence. Over the period of the EU's involvement in climate politics, IPCC assessments have steadily narrowed the range of uncertainty at least as far as the probability of substantial rises in mean temperatures consequent on human activities are concerned. Fully mindful of this, EU ministers have been committed since 1996 to holding the mean increase in global temperature below the 'dangerous' level of 2 °C, implying an increase in atmospheric carbon of less than 450 parts per million by volume (against a current level of around 380). This in turn translates to EU and developed-world emission reductions of 20–30 per cent by 2020 and 60–80 per cent by 2050 (Council of the European Union 2005b, 10–11). Thus climate policy has been predicated upon the best available science, something that marks the EU out from some of its international competitors although, as will be discussed below, there are some solid interests involved alongside the benefits of burnishing the Union's international identity.

Climate change has been an international issue because the atmosphere may be regarded as a 'global common' and the preservation of atmospheric quality and a stable climate has the characteristic of a public good. Accordingly, concerted international action is necessary if only to prevent 'free riding', a situation where some countries might benefit from pollution controls adopted by others without bearing the costs involved. There are other requirements for cooperative international action as well—the funding of scientific investigation and, most important, the transfer of funds and technology to allow developing nations to participate in mitigating emissions and to adapt to climate change. There is also a key element of compensation here for any restrictions on their growth that may be required to restrain GHG emissions. The UN climate regime that has developed from the Climate Change Convention of 1992 attempts to cope with these problems. It has a somewhat narrow approach to the changing climate, recognizing six GHGs but prioritizing reductions in carbon dioxide.[7] With shipping and aviation excluded from the convention, this places a heavy emphasis on reducing energy-related CO_2 emissions. Thus from the beginning of EU involvement, climate policy has been related to energy policy and the EU has sought not only to abide by the agreements that it has signed but more than that, to establish credibility through leadership by example. This effort has been beset by a number of difficulties because although climate and energy policy may be seen as complementary to one another, there are also contradictions. These can be usefully explored by considering the various concepts of security that underpin the EU's approach. Security, defined as the avoidance of a range of physical threats, economic scarcities, and related politico-military dangers will, we can assume, be the ultimate end of Union policy.

Climate and energy security

In classical accounts of international relations, security typically implies the absence of, or the ability to resist, a threat of armed attack across borders. In the search for security the struggle for scarce energy resources characterized a large number of 20th century conflicts. Less well understood in the academic and policy literature was the way in which a changing climate could not only stimulate conflict over diminishing resources but also lead to various other forms of instability and war (Barnett 2001). Such an awareness of what we may call the orthodox security implications of climate change has now become part of the approach adopted in the European Security and Defence Policy. Climate change was placed on the UN Security Council agenda by a member state in April 2007 and was conceptualized as a 'threat multiplier' by the then High Representative for the CFSP, Javier Solana (2008).[8] Solana's concerns were with the way in which a changing climate could serve to exacerbate existing conflicts, with for example increasing desertification in Africa, or even create new ones such as those presaged by the melting of Arctic ice. In the short term there are evident changes in the Arctic and elsewhere that are already giving rise to new strategic competition. On the southern edge of the Union there are the migration pressures driven, in part, by climate change-related desertification in Africa. Over the longer term, the predictions of the effects of global mean temperature increases in the Fourth Assessment Report of the IPCC, including sea-level rise, forest die-back, and loss of agricultural land, have direct implications for Europe. Additionally, one may refer to climate security in terms of achieving a stable global mean temperature that minimizes dangerous change. Such a view involves a different conceptualization of the essential nature of the threats posed to societies and political systems, and would prioritize mitigation of and adaptation to climate change rather than military responses.

Energy security is a treaty objective of the Union (Article 194(1) TFEU). Confusingly—although obviously related to the other notions of security—it tends to have a rather different meaning. As Yergin (2006, 70) points out, it is defined in the developed world as 'simply the availability of sufficient supplies at affordable prices' but elsewhere it may be seen in terms of 'security of demand' for energy exports or in the Russian case 'the reassertion of state control over "strategic resources"'. The EU has been faced with a security-of-supply problem over many years. Dependence on imported energy has been recognized as a source of EU vulnerability since the oil-price shocks of the 1970s and re-emphasized by the interruption of gas supplies from Russia in the winters of 2006 and 2009. The wider context of energy policy is one of rising global demand and prices with the inevitability that at some point in the current century most fossil fuel resources will be exhausted.

The Union currently depends upon hydrocarbon imports to meet approximately 50 per cent of its needs, a proportion that is predicted to rise dramatically over the next 20–30 years.[9] A standard response to energy insecurity is to diversify sources of supply. For the EU this has proved to be a problem because it is heavily dependent upon Russia, Norway, and Algeria for vital imports of hydrocarbons. With the decline of the UK's North Sea oil reserves, all member countries share an acute dependence on imported oil mainly sourced from OPEC states in the Middle East (see Table 15.1).

To compound this problem, the levels of vulnerability of the member states differ sharply. Some are almost self-sufficient in gas and coal, others such as France have extensive nuclear power generation sectors, while still others such as Romania and Bulgaria are dangerously dependent upon a single supplier, Russia. In 2006 and then again in January 2009 this vulnerability was starkly underlined by disputes between Russia and the Ukraine over the pricing of natural gas, which led the former to shut off supplies. The knock-on effect was that EU members reliant on the same pipelines also suffered, and there was a brief crisis in EU–Russia relations involving summit-level discussions in Moscow. The Commission's responses to the crisis are revealing in that they specify the continuing lack of coordination and transparency between the member states over energy issues and the lack of a properly functioning internal energy market, both of which would be required to ensure an effective response to the kind of energy security challenge encountered in January 2009 (European Commission 2009b). There was also an obvious

TABLE 15.1 Sources of EU energy imports 2008

Crude oil		Natural gas	
Russia	32.9	Russia	40.4
Norway	15.5	Norway	23.3
Libya	9.3	Algeria	17.5
Saudi Arabia	8.3	Nigeria	4.6
Iran	6.3	Libya	2.6
Kazakhstan	4.7	Egypt	2.6
Nigeria	3.5	Qatar	2.0
Iraq	2.9	Trinidad	1.3
Algeria	2.9	Uzbekistan	1.0
Azerbaijan	2.1	Croatia	0.4
Venezuela	1.9	Turkmenistan	0.3
Others	9.2	Others	3.7

Figures are percentages of total EU energy imports.

Source: Eurostat 2010, *Energy production and imports*, Table 3, Main origins of primary energy imports, epp.eurostat.cc.europa.eu/statistics_explained/index.php

external dimension to the energy security problem, which had led the Commission to assert:

> [E]nergy must become a central part of all external EU relations: it is crucial to geo-political security, economic stability, social development and international efforts to combat climate change . The EU must therefore develop effective energy relations with all its international partners.
>
> (European Commission 2006c, 17)

A favoured approach by the Commission was to attempt to create a common regulatory space around Europe, effectively extending its own market into a 'pan-European energy community'. Unfortunately, individual member states continued to negotiate their own energy supply deals with the Russian government, which in its turn was happy to profit from divisions within the EU and to resist Brussels's calls for liberalization of its own energy industry. Under these circumstances the EU's other strategy for security of energy supply is more geopolitical in tone. It seeks to avoid dependence on a single supplier or route through support for the building of new pipelines, although once again member states have different priorities in this regard. There are additional 'north stream' and 'south stream' pipelines that will provide alternative routes for Russian gas and, most controversially, the Nabucco pipeline, which is routed via Turkey and will provide access to Caspian reserves, bypassing Russian territory. In the view of one commentator, this 'hovers ineffectively between the market and geopolitics' and what is really required is a means of '*conjoining* markets and politics as mutually conditioned parts of comprehensive energy security' (Youngs 2007, 15).

However, strategies for energy security that merely ensure that large quantities of hydrocarbons continue to be burnt, thus adding to the greenhouse effect, are in the long run self-defeating. An egregious example is provided by the exploitation of Arctic resources made accessible by the melting of the ice. In a malign positive-feedback loop the burning of these fossil fuels contributes to further warming, ice-melt and a diminished albedo effect, which in turn allows further extraction of fossil fuels. EU policy makers, since 2000, appear to have begun to understand the interconnections: 'intensifying discussions on the security of future energy supplies to Europe have lent strong support to the development of stringent climate policies' (Oberthür and Pallemaerts 2010b, 15). Also, there are clear synergies and sought-after 'win–win solutions' potentially available in the development of renewable energy sources that do not emit greenhouse gases: 'climate change and energy security are two sides of the same coin [and t]he same remedies must be applied to both problems' (Piebalgs 2009). This realization now animates EU policy, in the sense that the pursuit of renewable energy sources and demand reduction can serve not only to achieve energy and climate security objectives, but also contribute to achieving the economic objectives of the Lisbon Agenda—setting 'the pace for a new global industrial revolution' (European Commission 2007, 20). The principal conjunction between energy and climate security remains, however, 'the likely reduction in fossil fuel consumption and imports' (Adelle *et al.* 2009, 37). The elements of such an approach are now in place with the 2008 climate and energy package, which has been a critical component of the EU's attempt at international climate leadership.[10]

The EU in international climate diplomacy

As noted earlier, a distinctive characteristic of EU climate policy has been the tight coupling of the internal and external. 'Throughout their two decades of history, international and European climate policy have evolved in tandem and have fed back on each other' (Oberthür and Pallemaerts 2010a, 27). One might add, on the basis of the previous discussion, that climate policy has also become energy policy. The precise ways in which external requirements have related to internal initiatives have varied, but there is no question that the dimension of climate leadership has increasingly framed EU policy development. There are several reasons for this. Obviously, awareness of the gravity of the climate crisis has been significant, but also the fact that the EU's external activities on climate change retain a consistently high level of level of popular support across the Union (Eurobarometer 2009). Climate leadership has also provided an identity and indeed a palpable success for the Union during a difficult period of constitutional change—from the convention that drew up the constitution in 2003, through its rejection in the referendums of 2005 until the final adoption of the Treaty of Lisbon in late 2009.

The Union played a central role in the development of the United Nations Framework Convention on Climate Change (UNFCCC) and is fully recognized as an REIO alongside the member states. Before Rio and the signature of the UNFCCC, the EU first adopted the strong position on requiring 'targets and timetables' for emissions reductions that was to become the hallmark of its subsequent approach. Prior to the signature of the UNFCCC it clashed with the first Bush administration over the critical question of whether the new agreement should contain a binding target for developed world emissions reductions (to reduce emissions to 1990 levels by 2000). This commitment would have been dependent upon the implementation of a failed internal EU carbon tax (Skjaerseth 1994). In the event, US refusal led to a watered-down aspiration (Article 4.2) in a convention that imposed no obligations on its parties other than to provide national inventories and reports. The convention actually entered into force in 1995 and, at the first Conference of the Parties (CoP 1) meeting in Berlin, gave themselves a mandate to negotiate, by 1997, a protocol that would bind Annex I (developed) countries to make real cuts in their emissions. In the ensuing two years the EU set out the ambitious target of a 15 per cent reduction by developed countries against a 1990 baseline. Controversially, the fact that the EU could commit itself to this offer was based upon an internal 'burden-sharing agreement', popularly known as the EU 'bubble' (see Table 15.2).

TABLE 15.2 The 1998 burden-sharing agreement	
	% from 1990 baseline (Percentage reduction in each national total)
Austria	−13.0
Belgium	−7.5
Denmark	−21.0
Finland	0.0
France	0.0
Germany	−21.0
Ireland	+13.0
Italy	−6.5
Luxembourg	−28.0
Netherlands	−6.0
Portugal	+27.0
Spain	+15.0
Sweden	+4.0
UK	−12.5

Note: EU aggregate reduction (15 Union States) is −8.0%

Source: 2106 Council (Environment) 16/6/1998, Press Release: 205 Nr. 094021/98

This arrangement allowed some less developed member states to enjoy very large increases in their permitted emissions while at the same time delivering an overall EU reduction (first of 10 per cent and subsequently 8 per cent). It was only achievable because of the highly fortuitous circumstances attending the use of the 1990 baseline, allowing painless but large reductions by Germany through the closure of inefficient plants in the old DDR, and by the UK, through its transition from coal-based power generation to gas.[11]

Japan and other developed countries offered much less than 15 per cent, while the USA insisted upon what became known as the 'flexibility mechanisms'. These sought to provide a less painful way of reducing emissions through carbon trading and international offsets—joint implementation (JI) and the Clean Development Mechanism (CDM). JI covered deals between developed countries and the CDM dealt with developed-country activities in the developing world. The essential idea behind both was that in terms of climate stability it made no difference where cuts in emissions were achieved; thus highly developed economies could meet at least part of their own emissions targets by investing in reductions elsewhere in the world. This was likely to prove effective because investment in cleaning up a highly inefficient power plant in a developing country would result in much greater reductions than spending the same amount of money on an already efficient plant in a developed country like Japan. The other favoured mechanism was emissions trading—the creation of a market in rights to emit carbon by issuing permits, the number of which would be steadily reduced over time in a 'cap and trade' system. This was already part of US environmental policy and had been much discussed as an economically efficient way of using market forces to bring about the desired cuts in carbon emissions. Prior to Kyoto such mechanisms were opposed by the EU as being antithetical to its own regulatory tradition—usually described as one of 'command and control' where environmental targets were set for member states and they were required to comply.

The CoP at Kyoto held late in 1997 managed to produce a binding protocol to the UNFCCC. The EU, led by the Luxembourg Presidency (joined in the Troika by the new UK Environment Minister, John Prescott) was able to negotiate an agreement on targets and timetables among the developed countries. It was agreed that, using a baseline of 1990, a set of differentiated emissions targets would be achieved by the first commitment period, 2008–12. The USA agreed a national reduction target of 7 per cent, which even then seemed to represent a very poor deal in terms of the level of economic damage that would result from meeting it, Japan 6 per cent, and the Europeans 8 per cent. Separate targets were agreed for the East European 'economies in transition' that were already in accession negotiations with the Union. In return the EU accepted the US-proposed 'flexibility mechanisms', which at that time merely existed in outline form. Another important provision was that entry into force could only occur if 55 per cent of the parties ratified, with the additional condition that they must be responsible for 55 per cent of global emissions.

The ratification process was to extend over the next seven years, the protocol finally entering into force early in 2005. It was in these years that the EU was called upon to display leadership if the nascent climate regime was to survive. Even before the ink was dry on the Kyoto signatures it was clear that there would be a problem with US ratification. Not only was the target of 7 per cent difficult and costly to achieve, but the Senate had already made it clear in its 1997 Byrd-Hagel Resolution that it would not ratify an agreement that allowed the developing-world economic competitors of the USA to avoid making cuts in their own emissions. The 2000 CoP at the Hague revealed the depths of disagreement between the EU and the USA (Grubb and Yamin 2001). In March 2001 the incoming administration of George W. Bush formally denounced US signature and then proceeded to pursue a campaign of outright opposition to the protocol.

At the June 2001 Gothenburg European Council, the EU took the momentous decision to proceed without the USA. The challenge was very substantial. Could a regime, much of which only existed in draft form, work without the participation of what was then the world's largest emitter of carbon dioxide and when the 55 per cent rule applied to ratification? In the event the Union was able, in successive

CoPs, in Berlin and Marrakesh, to turn the Kyoto Protocol into an agreement capable of ratification and implementation. This was no mean achievement because of the sheer complexity and novelty of some of its provisions relating, for example, to monitoring and compliance with the rules of the CDM. Furthermore, there was the need to counter US opposition and to gather sufficient ratifications. This required a concerted diplomatic effort by the Union to ensure that Japan ratified but also to persuade the Russian government; some Russian ministers had expressed open scepticism about the validity of climate science, and a warming climate might be regarded as bringing benefits. Russian ratification was achieved in 2004, in part on the basis of promising EU support for Russian entry into the WTO (Bretherton and Vogler 2006, 109).

The year 2005 was an important one for the Union, marking both the ratification of the protocol and the initiation of the Union's key mechanism for achieving around half of its 8 per cent reduction target—the European Emissions Trading Scheme (ETS). During the Kyoto ratification process the previous discontinuity between internal energy policy and climate leadership began to erode, with the realization that strong internal measures would be required if the Union was to remain a credible leader (Oberthür and Pallemaerts 2010a). The ETS was the most important of a set of internal energy measures agreed between 2002 and 2005.[12] It was a 'cap and trade' scheme covering fossil fuel-based power generation. The intention was to create a carbon market in rights to emit but under ETS I from 2005–7 the carbon price collapsed, because most member states had overestimated their emissions in their national allocation plans. For ETS II, 2008–12, the Commission reformed the system by imposing a rigorous review and reduction of the allocation plans, which in turn led to legal challenges by a number of East European member states (Vogler 2009). ETS represented a major reversal in the EU's approach, from opponent to principal advocate of an international market-based approach to emissions reduction and one driven by external commitments (Cass 2005; Wettestad 2005). That ETS should be seen to function became essential to the EU's exemplary strategy and, in the absence of a new climate agreement, there were even hopes that a substitute could be found by extending the ETS market to individual US states and elsewhere.

By 2005 it was clear that, even if the Kyoto targets were to be achieved, which was far from certain, they fell far short of what would be required to give a reasonable chance of climate stability. Above all, the large developing countries would have to participate in restricting their projected emissions. In 2004, the International Energy Agency had released figures demonstrating that at current rates of growth, developing-country emissions would exceed those of the Annex I countries at some point in the 2020s. The differences in relation to energy use and levels of development within the EU are mirrored to a much greater extent across the rest of the world economy. Developing countries can claim that their per capita GHG emissions are a fraction of those existing among the OECD countries. Furthermore, greenhouse gases have an atmospheric lifetime of up to 100 years, so there is also the question of the historical burden imposed upon the earth by the industrial development of the advanced economies. Under these circumstances the UN framework convention would not have been negotiable without agreement on the principle of 'common but differentiated responsibilities'. This essentially meant that developed countries undertook to take the lead in making emissions reductions, as the Annex I signatories to the 1997 Kyoto Protocol did. However, it rapidly became apparent that the average 5.2 per cent cuts that were promised against a 1990 baseline were woefully inadequate when seen against the requirement to avoid a 2° C temperature increase. Effective action would require not only more cuts in developed-country emissions but major contributions from the fast-developing economies of the south. Whereas in 1992 the EU had been second only to the USA in its carbon emissions, by 2007 both had been surpassed by China in terms of current (but not cumulative) emissions (see Table 15.3).

It was equally apparent that the USA would have to be re-engaged with the climate regime, even though transatlantic relations on climate issues had descended to a new low with virtually the only point of agreement being the need to stimulate new climate-friendly technology. The UK and then the German EU presidencies in late 2005 and 2007 coincided with their respective presidencies of the G8. This provided an opportunity to broaden the search for a successor to the Kyoto agreement beyond the apparatus of regular but often unproductive UNFCCC meetings. The Blair government used the 2005 Gleneagles summit to engage major developing countries, the G8+5, in climate discussions and at an informal EU European

TABLE 15.3 Comparative CO₂ emissions 2006

	CO₂ in billion m.t.	% global emissions	m.t. per capita
China	6.1	21.5	04.62
USA	5.7	20.2	18.99
EU	3.9	13.8	08.07
Russia	1.56	05.5	10.92
India	1.51	05.3	01.31
Japan	1.29	04.6	10.11
South Africa	0.41	01.5	08.59
Australia	0.37	01.3	18.12
Brazil	0.35	01.2	01.86

m.t. = metric ton

Sources: UNFCCC (http://unfccc.int/ghg_data/ghg_data_unfccc/items/4146.php, for carbon emissions and CO₂ per capita from the UN (http://mdgs.un.org/unsd/mdg/seriesDetail.aspx?srid=751andcrid=)

Council at Hampton Court led a debate on a long-term coherent energy policy. Further impetus was provided by the first of the Ukrainian gas crises in January 2006. This effort was continued through to early 2007 and:

Energy policy successfully 'piggybacked' on the more popular climate policy, which was deliberately highlighted in the German presidency's and the Commission's communication strategy.

(Adelle *et al.* 2009, 58)

In the spring of 2007 the Environment Council and then the European Council committed to a 20 per cent emissions reduction by 2020 and a 30 per cent reduction if other developed-country parties were prepared to match the EU, plus an internal target of a 20 per cent share for renewables. This provided what had been lacking since the initiation of discussions on the future of the climate regime: a clear statement of intent that would allow the resumption of EU leadership. However, there was no consensus among the member states about precisely how these goals were to be reached. In marked contrast to the events of 1997, preceding the signature of the Kyoto Protocol, a very intense period of EU energy policy formulation ensued in preparation for a new post-2012 climate agreement.

At this point the USA was still refusing to discuss targets and timetables and was even continuing to question the scientific basis of anthropogenic climate change. The primary requirement, as seen from Brussels, was still to engage the USA while preserving the Union's investment in the Kyoto Protocol. At the Bali CoP 13 in late 2007 progress was made by dividing negotiations into two tracks: the first a working group on the future of the Kyoto Protocol without US participation; the second a working group on the future of the Convention in which the USA was persuaded to participate.[13] The Bali plan of action envisaged broad-ranging discussions to produce a new climate agreement on mitigation, adaptation, finance, and technology by CoP 15, scheduled to be held in Copenhagen at the end of 2009.

Negotiating the internal means to implement the EU's stated targets and timetables was regarded as critical to its external credibility. There were serious concerns, given the failings of ETS I, where the carbon price had dropped to almost nothing, that despite all the leadership rhetoric the Union as a whole would fail to achieve its 8 per cent Kyoto target. At the same time the legislative process to agree the climate and energy package, that would provide the means to achieve the targets set in March 2007, was prolonged and difficult with extensive lobbying throughout 2008 by industrial interests, who saw their competitiveness eroded by potential rises in energy prices and by member states aggrieved at their treatment under the new arrangements to curb emissions in the next phase of the ETS. After a great deal of horse-trading and compromise, the final amended package was piloted through the December 2008 European Council by the French Presidency (see Box 15.3).[14]

Very high expectations were soon invested in the Copenhagen CoP, not least in Brussels where EU statements continued to be prefaced by references to its

---

BOX 15.3   The EU climate and energy package

Provides the means to achieve the EU's 20–20–20 climate and energy targets and was finally agreed at a European Council held in December 2008, entering into force in June 2009. The key elements were as follows:

- A revised Emissions Trading System (ETS) to commence from 2013. National allocation plans will be replaced by a single EU-wide emissions cap. This will be progressively reduced in order to yield a 21 per cent reduction in emissions by 2020 relative to 2005. The auctioning of allowances will be introduced to replace the system of free allocation, although derogations from this rule were negotiated to assist some coal-dependent power generators and to counter the risks of 'carbon leakage' where foreign competitors might otherwise take advantage of relatively high EU energy prices. A limited use of JI and CDM credits will continue to be allowed (Directive 2009/29/EC amending Directive 2003/87/EC).

- An 'effort-sharing' decision to cover emissions from transport, agriculture, housing, and waste not controlled under the ETS (which covers power generation and from 2012, aviation). Member states have agreed to binding national targets that vary according to their level of development in much the same way as the previous burden-sharing agreement. The overall 2020 target is for a 10 per cent reduction from 2005 levels but within this new EU 'bubble' there are wide variations. Denmark is committed, for example, to a 20 per cent reduction and the UK to 16 per cent, while Bulgaria is allowed a 20 per cent increase (Decision 406/2009/EC).

- There are similar binding national targets for the introduction of renewable energy sources to achieve an EU average of 20 per cent by 2020. Again there are substantial differences reflecting national circumstances; the Finnish target is 38 per cent while that for Malta is only 10 per cent (Directive 2009/28/EC).

- The promotion of carbon capture and storage technology is the final part of the package—whereby it is hoped that the carbon dioxide released by burning coal can be prevented from adding to the greenhouse effect through capture and then storage underground. This technology is as yet unproven on a large scale and is the subject of EU collaboration with China (Directive 2009/31/EC).

---

leadership role. Such expectations were only increased by the election of US President Barack Obama who, unlike his predecessor, was prepared not only to take the climate problem seriously but to support domestic legislation for a 'cap and trade' system and to commit the USA to emissions reduction targets. This enabled a convergence of positions with the USA at the expense of the EU's previous commitment to the continuation of the Kyoto Protocol. Instead the objective was a 'comprehensive, ambitious, fair, science-based and legally binding global treaty' (European Commission 2009a). However, by the autumn of 2009 it had become clear that with preparatory negotiations in the two working groups making little or no progress on a text littered with square brackets, the best that could be achieved at Copenhagen was a comprehensive political agreement rather than a binding treaty text (ibid.). The EU set out to reassert its exemplary leadership with its uni-lateral offer (of 20 per cent emissions reductions by 2020, potentially increasing to 30 per cent conditional upon an international agreement), but this had already become less impressive because of the effects of the 2008–9 economic recession. Ever aware of the importance of ensuring adaptation and mitigation in the south, the EU also brought forward a substantial aid package that had been regarded as the price that would have to be paid for a new climate agreement within the UNFCCC framework. Finally agreed at a European Council in December, it promised €7.2 billion 'start-up funding' to be provided to least developed countries before 2013, and proved the most difficult part of the EU's Copenhagen preparations as East European members argued that they had just as much right themselves to such assistance.[15] Highly damaging to the EU's relationship with the developing coun-tries was the apparent dropping of its previous commitment to the continuation of the Kyoto Protocol in an attempt to involve the USA in a new comprehensive and legally binding climate regime.

It would be an understatement to say that for the EU the outcome of the long-awaited Copenhagen meeting was a disappointment. The Swedish Presidency characterized the conference as 'a disaster' while Chancellor Merkel put the best gloss on proceedings—'a step, albeit a small one, towards a global climate architec-ture' (Egenhofer and Georgiev, 2009, 1). That the EU was 'the biggest victim of the Copenhagen failure' (Laïdi 2010) was an opinion widely shared in press commen-tary. The 'Copenhagen Accord' was not a legally binding text and was noted rather than being adopted by the conference.[16] It formally recognizes the 2 °C thresh-old and there is a reference to 'opportunities to use markets, to enhance the cost effectiveness of, and to promote, mitigation actions'. There was also new climate funding for developing countries, for which the EU had been a major advocate and which it had been hoped would unlock the impasse that existed between north and south over participation in emissions reductions under a new climate regime.[17] However, there was no agreement on the central issue of binding targets and time-tables and no comprehensive agreement to replace Kyoto, and the EU was not able to deploy its 30 per cent reduction as an incentive for others to follow suit. Instead, parties were invited to submit a series of national pledges, which, judging by the offers that were already on the table before Copenhagen, would, if implemented, fail to ensure that a 2 °C increase in global mean temperature could be avoided.[18]

The EU as climate negotiator

In some ways the EU's leadership in the climate regime was surprising. In this area of shared competence, which involves taxation and energy policy, leadership and representation falls to the rotating presidency. The EU negotiates at 28 and the Commission at 27 member states. In the Kyoto negotiations the Troika operated, but there have been real problems in ensuring continuity across a complex range of issues in successive negotiation rounds (Van Schaik and Egenhofer 2005). In order to cope, particular member states have been allowed to lead on issues on which they have specialized and the working practice of the Council has been to involve Presidencies over an 18-month cycle (Oberthür and Roche 2008). As with other external policy areas, coordination within the negotiation is required, can take up excessive amounts of time, and irritate interlocutors of the EU. The negotiating effects are that the EU can appear cumbersome and that there has often been a lack of agility and flexibility. Climate conferences involve long negotiating sessions at official level but end with a high-level segment in which final political deals are done over outstanding issues arising from an agreed text. High-level involvement can become problematic if there are many complex issues unresolved and attempts are made to short circuit the UN process through an informal deal. Ministers and heads of government can interfere with the EU's operating procedures, attempting, for example, to circumvent them by having informal conversations with the USA and other parties. The 2009 Copenhagen CoP provides evidence of the manifold difficulties faced by the Union.[19] The Presidency was held by Sweden, but the appearance of heads of government Brown, Merkel, and Sarkozy tended to divert attention and they pursued their own lines of negotiation. When President Obama conferred with the EU it presented itself in the form of Commission President Barroso, Swedish President in Office Reinfeldt, and the UK, French, and German leaders. In these circumstances the previous ability of the EU to function as an entity, to supervise the negotiation of the terms of the Kyoto Protocol, and make a credible claim to climate leadership appear remarkable, but the Copenhagen conference appears to have placed too much strain on the Union's coordinating capabilities. As the Danish chair of the CoP and EU Climate Change Commissioner designate Connie Hedegaard remarked:

There are very important lessons from Copenhagen. In the last hours, China, India, Russia, Japan each spoke with one voice, while Europe spoke with many different voices … A lot of Europeans in the room is not a problem, but there is only an advantage if we all sing from the same hymn sheet. We need to think about this and reflect on this seriously, or we will lose our leadership role in the world.[20]

The Copenhagen negotiation coincided with the entry into force of the Lisbon Treaty on 1 December 2009 and the reorganization of the Commission. As noted above, there are renewed arguments over competence in external environmental and climate policy, and questions about who will represent the Union in future climate talks, with a role for the new External Action Service and possibly the new Presidency of the European Council. At the same time the new Commission has moved responsibility for climate policy from DG Environment to a new DG Climate Action (DG CLIMA) and created a separate DG Energy (from the previous DG Transport and Energy DG TREN).

Difficulties of internal coordination were far from being the only reason for the EU's disappointing performance in Copenhagen. Much more significant than any organizational or tactical shortcomings were profound changes in the structure of the international system that had begun to work themselves out in the political dynamics of the climate change regime. The EU's initial rise to prominence in global environmental politics depended to a great degree on the favourable international conditions that flowed from the ending of the Cold War. EU leadership was sustained by the willingness of the countries of Eastern Europe to associate themselves with its policies and by the special position that it held as the largest donor of development aid (when both EU and national programmes are counted) with a set of long-standing relationships with the African, Caribbean, and Pacific countries. Furthermore, its role in climate politics was firmly anchored to its position in the international economic structure—the Union being second only to the USA in the league of carbon emitters. The abdication of the USA from its previous role of environmental leadership left the field open for the EU to assert itself and to emphasize its identity as climate leader. As we have seen, this opportunity was seized in the EU's successful campaign to turn the Kyoto Protocol into a functioning international regime.

However, even at the point of Kyoto ratification it was becoming evident that the underlying international structure was shifting. In general terms this has been associated with the rise of the so-called BRIC countries, Brazil, Russia, India, and China, to which South Africa should also probably be added (see Chapter 17). At the WTO the kind of duopoly that had previously existed between the USA and the EU was no longer evident, reflected in the emergence of the G20. In terms of climate politics even an enlarged EU found itself in third place in terms of current carbon emissions, China having overtaken both Europe and the USA. Up until this point both China and India had been relatively quiescent in climate politics, protected by the 'common but differentiated responsibilities' formula, which did not require them to make any emissions reductions under the Kyoto Protocol. In the post-2012 discussions this was no longer a tenable assumption and the USA would, in any case, never accept it. The other critical development was the re-engagement of the USA under the Obama administration. The logic of the situation appeared to suggest that any future climate arrangements would not centre upon an extension of the Kyoto Protocol but would require a fundamental agreement between what was increasingly portrayed as the G2—the USA and China—or perhaps the broader combination of Brazil, South Africa, India, and China (the BASIC countries). This had very wide-ranging implications not least for the whole multilateral UNFCCC–Kyoto structure that had been so painstakingly created since 1992. Furthermore, although the G77 and China as non-Annex I countries had previously negotiated as a bloc (and the EU often attempted to mediate between them and the Annex I countries) there was now a clearer distinction between the least developed countries, likely to be the first victims of climate change, and fast-developing new economic powers of the south. The importance of such changed circumstances for EU leadership was driven home at the 2009 Copenhagen CoP.

Conclusions

Environment and climate change have been areas in which the Union has managed to carve out for itself a central leadership role. The foundation of this achievement was the development of the EU's internal environmental *acquis*, which allowed the attainment of external competences. Over the years the Union has been more successful than might have been predicted in the light of the problems of coordination, competence, and coherence that continue to afflict its external activities even after the entry into force of the Lisbon Treaty.

Climate change poses a very different challenge because of the high economic stakes involved if effective action is to be taken and because of the ways in which it impacts upon the security of the Union. Most particularly it conjoins environmental and energy policy. In the initial stages of involvement in the climate regime the EU was able to claim leadership without the assistance of an internal carbon tax and to agree the Kyoto Protocol under the rather favourable circumstances of the burden-sharing agreement. Kyoto implementation and the search for a post-2012 successor, however, required the serious development of internal energy policy in the ETS and subsequently the 2008 climate and energy package. The latter was only achieved with some difficulty and compromise because of the differing interests of member states. In all this, two points are worth making. First, it was the discourse of climate security and the Union's external commitments and reputation that provided much of the impetus for internal reform. Second, however much the 20–30 per cent target may be criticized for its inadequacy, the EU was in 2010 the only major player that possessed a credible and legally binding means of delivering its climate pledge in the Copenhagen Accord.

The evidence in this chapter provides strong support for the three key themes around which this volume centres. First, it is clear that the ways in which the EU has evolved as a (sub)system of international relations have played a key role in conditioning its ability to operate on a broader stage. The development of an internal regime for environmental policy making and the emergence of an embryonic energy security policy show in different ways the effects of the internal balance of interests and forces on EU external policy. Not only this, but the interaction of environmental and energy policy making with broader processes of international relations shows the ways in which the EU system is penetrated by broader forces. This leads to our second theme: that the EU has become an indispensable part of the broader processes of regime building and negotiation in climate change and has helped to shape as well as be shaped by these processes. The picture is less clear in energy, partly at least because the development of institutionalized processes in that area is less advanced than in climate change and environmental politics more generally.

Climate diplomacy has also clearly provided an arena in which the EU is a 'power'. It has proved capable of executing an exemplary strategy of 'targets and timetables' and has taken responsibility for turning the Kyoto Protocol into a functioning international agreement. This was no mean achievement when operating under shared competence and negotiating 'at 16' and after the 2004 enlargement 'at 26'. The ratification process demonstrated an ability to deploy diplomatic assets and to use trade instruments in pursuit of climate policy objectives. Unfortunately the experience of Copenhagen appears to reveal that the EU's previous climate leadership also rested upon some peculiarly favourable international circumstances— US abdication and the relative quiescence of the BASIC countries. Climate action continues to have significance for the international identity of the Union but there is an increasing realization that its longer-term security is also at stake.

Notes

1 This is also the case for energy policy (Article 4 (i)).
2 The arguments hinge upon the interpretation of articles in the Treaty. Article 216 (1) TFEU apparently gives the Union and hence the Commission the right to conduct negotiations where the conclusion of an agreement is necessary to achieve the objectives referred to in the Treaty. Combating climate change is one of these objectives under Article 191 TFEU. Subsequent to the Copenhagen Accord, parties to the conference undertook to provide details of their emissions pledges by the end of January 2010. The Commission claimed the right to do this for the EU but this was contested in Coreper by the member states. In the event both the Commission and Presidency submitted the document to the United Nations Framework Convention on Climate Change (UNFCCC) secretariat. The arguments continued over whether the Commission or Presidency would draw up the mandate for opening negotiations under the auspices of the United Nations Environment Programme (UNEP) for an international agreement on mercury (Rankin 2010).
3 This usually proved to be possible but in some instances the existing parties to an agreement failed to alter their rules to admit the Community as well as the member states. A good example is provided by the 1973 Convention on International Trade in Endangered Species (CITES) where Union competence is clear, but the parties have, at the time of writing, still not approved the Gabarone Amendment, which would admit the Union.
4 The reference here is to the notorious 'southern agreements' of the Common Fisheries Policy (CFP) where West African governments were persuaded to sell fishing rights to EU trawlers to the detriment of the sustainable development of their own coastal populations. Both the CAP and CFP have been subject to extensive reform to render them more sustainable but both continue to damage the EU's reputation.

5 See for example the evidence given by the British Antarctic Survey on the positions taken up by the Commission at meetings of the Convention on the Conservation of Antarctic Marine Living Resources in the UK Parliament (House of Lords Select Committee on Science and Technology, *Minutes of Evidence*, The Antarctic Treaty System, April 2004).

6 Initiated by a 1998 European Council, this 'horizontal' process seeks to integrate environmental protection into the definition and implementation of all Union activities and policies. Implementing the Kyoto Protocol is one of the priority areas.

7 The gases are carbon dioxide, nitrous oxide, and methane, along with three additional industrial gases. The chlorofluorocarbons are also GHGs but are separately controlled under the Montreal Protocol. The Convention also covers reduction by 'sinks', but their inclusion is controversial if it allows avoidance of actual emissions cuts. REDD (the United Nations Collaborative Programme on Reducing Emissions from Deforestation and Forest Degradation in Developing Countries), which involves funding for the preservation of forest sinks is an important part of post-2012 discussions in the climate regime.

8 The UK placed it on the agenda on 17 April 2007, although it did not result in a resolution. It was supported by the EU and its member states but opposed by China and members of the G77 on the grounds that the Council was not competent to discuss the climate issue.

9 Under business-as-usual assumptions the figure for import dependence is predicted to rise to 65 per cent of total consumption in 2030. The equivalent increase for gas is from 57 to 84 per cent and for oil from 82 to 93 per cent (European Commission 2007, 3).

10 The list of EU international energy policy priorities to be pursued in external policy is headed by the pursuit of international agreements, a post-2012 climate deal, and the extension of emissions trading. Following this are objectives involving better relations with neighbours and Russia and a 'deepening dialogue with key energy producers and transit countries' (European Commission 2007, Annex 1).

11 For the details of the internal negotiations on burden sharing which would only have achieved 10 per cent reductions rather than the EU's public offer of 15 per cent, see Ringius (1999).

12 Examples of the results of the EU's European climate action programme include directives on the energy performance of buildings, on the use of biofuels for transport, and reduction of GHG emissions from fluorinated gases.

13 The ad hoc working group on further commitments for Annex I parties under the Kyoto Protocol (AWG-KP) and the ad hoc working group on long-term cooperative action under the convention (AWG-LCA).

14 The climate and energy package was subject to co-decision procedures and the final details were negotiated at the level of the European Council with

significant concessions being granted to Poland and other East European countries. For a comparison of the internal decision making in 1997 and 2007–8, see Vogler (2009). For a detailed treatment of the changes in the ETS that have implications for Union competence, see Skjaerseth and Wettestad (2010) and for the 'effort-sharing' arrangements, Lacasta *et al.* (2010).

15 While agreeing the start-up funding which comprised around one-third of the money promised in the final Copenhagen Accord, there was no further agreement on how the much larger sums required after 2013 were to be raised. There were also differences over the 30 per cent target, with the UK arguing that it should be placed on the table against Polish objections (O'Donnell (2009).

16 UNFCCC Copenhagen Accord, draft decision CP-15.

17 The extent of the EU financial contribution was a major bone of contention within the Council in the preparations for Kyoto. In the Accord, developed-country funding is agreed at $30 billion for 2010–12 ($10 billion from the EU) with a long-term target of raising $100 billion per annum for mitigation and adaptation in developing countries by 2020. There was also agreement on REDD action to provide financing for the preservation of forests that serve as carbon sinks.

18 The pledges were, using a 1990 baseline to be achieved by 2020: EU 20 per cent (30 per cent), Japan 25 per cent conditional on others, Russia 22–25 per cent, USA 3.8 per cent. The Chinese made no pledge on actual reductions but promised to cut the carbon intensity of its economy by 40–45 per cent in the period 2005–20. A critical argument at the conference was over monitoring, reporting, and verification, with the USA and other developed world countries demanding that developed world mitigation actions that received international financial support must be internationally verified. This is part of the Accord text, while purely national action by developing countries is not subject to this requirement. The developed country parties did not succeed in escaping from the Kyoto Protocol, the maintenance of which was a key requirement of the G77. The Accord 'requests the ad hoc working group on further commitments of Annex 1 parties to continue its work'.

19 The chair of the conference was the host state Denmark, which controversially floated its own informal text (widely regarded as embodying the Union's real negotiating position), replaced its environment minister in the chair by its prime minister, who was himself removed in the final hours by a coalition of countries, including an EU member state.

20 EP Hearings 15 January 2010 reported in EU Observer.com.

FURTHER READING

There is no book-length study of EU external environmental policy, although a number of collections on climate leadership are beginning to appear—Oberthür and Pallemaerts (2010a) along with Wurzel and Connolly (2010) are good recent examples. Damro (2006) and Lightfoot and Burchill (2004) cover the EU in UN environmental politics, while Falkner (2007) considers the biotechnology negotiations and Hadfield (2008a) the EU's difficult energy relationship with Russia. International leadership is a key theme examined by Schreurs and Tiberghien (2007) and others, while Bretherton and Vogler (2006) consider this from an actor perspective. Jordan *et al.* (2010) brings together some of the latest research on EU climate policy making along with useful general and historical surveys.

Bretherton, C., and Vogler, J. (2006), *The European Union as a Global Actor*, 2nd edition, Chapter 4 (Abingdon: Routledge).

Damro, C. (2006), 'The EU and International Environmental Politics: The Challenge of Shared Competence', in Laatikainen, K. V., and Smith, K. E. (eds) *The European Union at the United Nations*, (Basingstoke: Palgrave Macmillan), 175–192.

Falkner, R. (2007), 'The Political Economy of "Normative Power" Europe: EU Environmental Leadership in International Biotechnology regulation', *Journal of European Public Policy,* 14, 4, 507–26.

Hadfield, A. (2008a), 'Energy and Foreign Policy: EU–Russia Energy Dynamics', in Smith, S., Hadfield, A., and Dunne, T. (eds) *Foreign Policy: Theories, Actors, Cases* (Oxford: Oxford University Press).

Jordan, A., Huitma, D., Van Asselt, H., Rayner, T., and Berkhout, F. (eds) (2010), *Climate Change Policy in the European Union: Confronting the Dilemmas of Mitigation and Adaptation* (Cambridge: Cambridge University Press).

Lightfoot, S., and Burchill, J. (2004), 'Green Hope or Greenwash? The Actions of the European Union at the World Summit on Sustainable Development', *Global Environmental Change,* 14, 4, 337–44.

Oberthür, S., and Pallemaerts, M., with Kelly, C. R. (eds) (2010a), *The New Climate Policies of the European Union Internal Legislation and Climate Diplomacy* (Brussels: VUB Press).

Schreurs, M., and Tiberghien, Y. (2007), 'Multilevel Reinforcement: Explaining European Union Leadership in Climate Change Mitigation', *Global Environmental Politics,* 7, 4, 113–37.

Vogler, J. (2005), 'The European Contribution to Global Environmental Governance' *International Affairs,* 81, 4, 835–49.

Wurzel, R., and Connolly, C. (eds) (forthcoming 2010), *The European Union as a Leader in International Climate Change Politics* (Abingdon Routledge).

WEB LINKS

The Europa website, **http://europa.eu**, provides the essential point of entry from where you can navigate to the relevant parts of the Commission, DGs Environment, CLIMA, and Energy, as well as the Council and Parliament. There are also useful web pages on specific topics such as climate change or the marine environment. The European Environment Agency is a mine of information at **http://www.eea.europa.eu**. EU activities and communications on climate change can be found at the official UNFCCC site, **http://unfc-cc.int**, while this and all other major environmental negotiations are reported in detail by the Earth Negotiations Bulletin, which can be found at the International Institute for Sustainable Development site **http://www.iisd.org**. For energy and environmental questions there are also two key international organizations, the International Energy Agency at **http://www.iea.org** and the UN Environment Programme at **http://www.unep.org**.

CHAPTER 16

The European Union, the BRICs, and the Emerging New World Order

Stephan Keukeleire and Hans Bruyninckx

▌ Summary

The acronym 'BRIC' was launched in 2001 by Goldman Sachs to illuminate the potential of the economies of Brazil, Russia, India, and China—not only as investment opportunities for their clients but also as transformational forces within the global economy. Less than a decade later, the BRICs have become a household name in academic and policy debates about the relative decline of the West, economic globalization, global governance, and specific areas of interest such as climate change and energy security. The BRICs have started to organize themselves and reached some first successes on the international scene by translating their economic weight into political leverage. The first two sections of this chapter assess how the EU is challenged by the BRICs, illuminate the nature of the BRIC phenomenon and provide an overview of the contractual and political relations between the EU and the four BRIC countries, to conclude with an evaluation of the EU's 'strategic partnership' with these powers. The next three sections analyse the EU–BRICs relationship on the basis of the three key perspectives that were introduced by Hill and Smith in the introductory chapter of this book: the EU as a subsystem of international relations (which assesses the EU's capacity to generate external collective action towards the BRIC countries), the EU as a power in international relations (which evaluates the EU and the BRICs from the perspective of both relational and structural power), and the EU as part of the wider processes of international relations (which assesses their relations within the context of shifts in the global governance architecture).

Introduction: the EU challenged by the BRICs

The various chapters in this book illuminate most of the basic features of the EU's role in international relations. The main foundation for its international role is its economic integration, its trade power, and its position as the strongest economic power after the USA. This allows the EU both to manage international economic interdependence and to use its trade power to gain economic and political leverage outside its borders. Despite the generally still limited impact of the CFSP and CSDP, the EU has managed to use its power to impact upon developments and structures in the surrounding countries and regions. Characteristic for the EU is also that it actively promotes inter-regional cooperation with other parts of the world as well as multilateralism on a global level. Several of these major features of the EU's international position are increasingly challenged by the BRICs and by the broader phenomenon of shifts in the global power structure towards Asia and the southern part of the world.

The challenge is clearest in the economic field. In its 2001 and 2003 reports, Goldman Sachs launched some predictions that were quite dramatic for the European countries. Whereas the BRICs' economies in 2000 represented merely 15 per cent of the size of the six strongest economies (USA, Japan, Germany, France, Italy, and the UK), China was expected to overtake the largest European economy (Germany) rather quickly and by 2050 each of the four BRICs was expected to surpass each of the four strongest European economies—implying that by then no single EU member state would figure in the top rank of economies (O'Neill 2001; Wilson and Purushothaman 2003). In practice, the economic growth of the BRICs proved to be even stronger than predicted, with the BRIC countries clearly leading the global recovery after the financial crises of 2008–9 (Goldman Sachs 2007; Yamakawa *et al.* 2009); this indicates that the economic rise of the BRICs is not only to be seen as a threat or challenge but also an opportunity as they are major trade partners for the EU (see also Leal-Arcas 2009). The tables below illustrate the mutually interdependent economic relationship. Table 16.1 shows how China, Russia, Brazil, and India now take respectively the 2nd, 3rd, 9th, and 10th positions in the ranking of the EU's major trade partners, with China already being the EU's leading partner in terms of imports. Although China and Russia are more important than Brazil and India, all four countries are important in their own

TABLE 16.1 EU trade with main partners (2008)

	The major import partners				The major export partners				The major trade partners		
Rank	Partners	Millions of euro	%	Rank	Partners	Millions of euro	%	Rank	Partners	Millions of euro	%
1	China	247,857.6	16.0	1	USA	249,595.3	19.1	1	USA	435,995.5	15.2
2	USA	186,400.3	12.0	2	Russia	105,153.1	8.0	2	China	326,325.0	11.4
3	Russia	173,617.2	11.2	3	Switzerland	97,742.1	7.5	3	Russia	278,770.2	9.7
4	Norway	92,035.6	5.9	4	China	78,467.4	6.0	4	Switzerland	177,848.3	6.2
5	Switzerland	80,106.1	5.2	5	Turkey	54,260.9	4.1	5	Norway	135,736.0	4.7
6	Japan	74,948.8	4.8	6	Norway	43,700.4	3.3	6	Japan	117,342.0	4.1
7	Turkey	45,886.6	3.0	7	Japan	42,393.3	3.2	7	Turkey	100,147.5	3.5
8	South Korea	39,406.6	2.5	8	United Arab Emirates	31,679.6	2.4	8	South Korea	65,063.6	2.3
9	Brazil	35,554.4	2.3	9	India	31,540.2	2.4	9	Brazil	61,908.2	2.2
10	Libya	34,233.1	2.2	10	Brazil	26,353.7	2.0	10	India	60,980.2	2.1
11	India	29,440.0	1.9	11	Canada	26,106.7	2.0	11	Canada	49,900.8	1.7

Source: European Commission, DG Trade; *Eurostat* September 2009

TABLE 16.2	Population, GDP, and economic interaction between the EU, the BRICs, and the USA					
	Brazil	**Russia**	**India**	**China**	**USA**	**EU**
Population in millions (2008)	191.9	142.0	1.190.5	1.327.7	304.4	497.6
Current GDP 2008 in billions of euros	1.069.4	1.139.9	822.5	2.992.7	9.698.5	12.304 (2007)
GDP per capita in euros (2008)	5.573.4	8.027.6	690.9	2.254.1	31.859.6	24.800 (2007)
EU27 import in millions of euros (2008)	35.554.4	173.617.2	29.440.0	247.857.6	186.400.3	-
EU27 export in millions of euros (2008)	26.353.7	105.153.1	31.540.2	78.467.4	249.595.3	-
EU27 inward stocks of FDI (2007) billions of euros	15.9	23.7	4.3	4.6	1.029.8	-
EU27 outward stocks of FDI (2007) billions of euros	97.5	73.0	19.1	38.4	1.043.4	-
US import in millions of euros (2008)	21.806.4	18.991.2	18.310.8	242.262.0	-	256.310.4
US export in millions of euros (2008)	22.375.6	6.347.0	12.691.3	48.583.8	-	187.170.5

Source: European Commission, DG Trade; OECD statistical extracts; *Eurostat Yearbook 2009*

way. China's role as 'factory of the world' creates large imports into the EU for a wide variety of products. Russia's main economic significance stems from energy imports (mainly natural gas). Together China and Russia account for more than 20 per cent of the EU's trade interactions. India has developed an important service sector in cities such as Mumbai and Bangalore and is regarded as a major potential market due to its rapid growth and large population. The EU is already the largest foreign investor in India. Brazil is of importance for agricultural imports and is a leading (regional) economy and institutional innovator. However, the tables also demonstrate the continuing economic dominance of the USA, both in general terms and in relationship to the EU, which also helps to put the challenge of the BRICs in a broader perspective.

Less visible are the political challenges posed by the BRIC countries. Individually, the BRIC countries are increasingly influential in their neighbourhoods and other parts of the world. The section in this chapter on the EU as a power demonstrates the shifts particularly in the structural power of the EU and the BRICs—with structural power referring to the power to influence the political, socioeconomic, legal, and other structures of third countries and third regions. The BRICs are increasingly becoming competing structural powers in various parts of the world as well as on a global stage. As is discussed in the section on the EU and the processes of international relations, the EU is not only challenged by the BRICs because of their impact on specific international agreements (for example with regard to the financial crisis or climate change) but also, and more importantly, because they promote a different approach to international policy matters and a different kind of multilateralism—and because they reflect a broader shift in the international balance of power.

Before turning to the EU's relationship with the BRIC countries and assessing in more detail the challenges outlined above, it is useful to gain some more insight into the nature of the BRICs phenomenon. To what extent is 'BRIC' more than an acronym invented by a major global financial services firm? In the late 2000s, as their economic power increased, the realization dawned upon the BRIC countries that they could exploit their economic weight by strengthening their mutual contacts. A process of political dialogue started in 2006 when, in the margins of the UN General Assembly meeting, the ministers of foreign affairs met for the first time in the BRIC format. Meetings in the BRIC format received a boost from mid 2008 onwards, when their deliberations before or in the margins of UN or G20 meetings were complemented by stand-alone meetings of the BRICs on the level of the ministers of foreign affairs or ministers of finance, in addition to diplomatic and expert meetings on lower levels and meetings of specialized agencies. And as a culmination of this process, in June 2009 the leaders of Brazil, Russia, India, and China held their first summit meeting in the Russian city of Yekaterinburg (with Brazil hosting the second BRIC summit in April 2010) (see President of Russia—official web portal 2009a and 2009b).

However, the existence of some important differences and divergences between the four countries supports the hypothesis that the potential of the BRIC dialogue being transformed into a firm and coherent bloc is rather limited. Table 16.2 provides some basic statistics to illustrate these major differences: in terms of population (with India and China having more than one billion inhabitants whereas Brazil and Russia count less than 200 million people), of GDP per capita (with still a huge gap between Russia on the one hand and India on the other: €8,028 versus €691 in 2008), and of trade and foreign direct investment (with China exporting more to the EU than the three other BRIC countries combined). The four countries not only differ substantially in terms of economic power but also in terms of political and military power, internal political and societal systems, and in terms of their regional and global interests and ambitions. And generally, both China and Brazil stand out: China because it has the greater basis to act as a world power and Brazil because it plays in a lower category with regard to most indices of power (see Armijo 2007; Goldman Sachs 2007; Lennon and Kozlowski 2008). However, as pointed out by Hurrell (2006, 1–3), the BRIC countries also have several features in common, which distinguish them from other (emerging) powers and which may bring them closer to each other—as is also mirrored in their joint statement in Yekaterinburg. They possess the capacity to contribute to the production of international order, regionally or globally; they share the belief that they are entitled to gain a more influential role in world affairs; and they all lie outside or on the margin of the US-led set of international and multilateral structures. It is this combination of factors that leads to the willingness of the BRIC countries to strengthen their mutual relations and to promote alternative or complementary international forums and linkages beyond the predominantly Western-dominated organizations.

This short assessment of the BRIC phenomenon indicates that it is not in itself a problem that the EU has no 'BRIC policy', that the BRICs as a group are rarely referred to in EU documents, and that the EU has developed a bilateral policy towards each of the BRIC countries separately (see also the overview in Grevi and de Vasconcelos 2008). This is not surprising in view of the major differences between the four BRIC countries, the absence of a BRIC bloc, and the different trajectories of developments both within these four countries and in their relations with the EU (as will be discussed in the next section). However, it is more problematic that the EU has no policy to deal with the generally changing balance of power in the 21st century—a phenomenon in which the rise of the BRICs has to be situated.

Contractual and political relations: strategic partnerships?

In the introduction to this book, Hill and Smith emphasize that the EU is a relentless generator of framework agreements and strategies, and is consistently searching for settled, stable, and predictable frameworks within which to define and pursue its international relationships and activities. This profound desire to systematize or pigeonhole its growing range of relationships is also visible in the relationship of the EU with the four BRIC countries. The EU's formal relations with the four countries follow largely the same patterns. Firstly, various kinds of long-standing 'cooperation agreements' or 'partnership and cooperation agreements' provide the legal framework for cooperation, mostly in the field of trade and various econo-my-related sectors, but increasingly also in a variety of non-economic sectors. The generally growing intensity and widening scope of this cooperation reflect the EU's own growing competences as well as the trajectory of the partner country: from large developing countries or countries in transition (with the EC/EU being in the position of an economically superior donor) to major economic powers (with the EU being forced to approach these countries on a basis of equality). Secondly, the various agreements establish the institutional frameworks for the bilateral relation-ships, including regular summit meetings, ministerial meetings, and expert-level meetings. Thirdly, more recent political agreements attempt to strengthen the polit-ical or 'strategic' dimension of the relationship and to widen and concretize the scope of cooperation and dialogue—thereby reflecting the growing importance of the partner countries as well as the increasing political character of the EU as an international actor.

The EU's relationship with Russia is the most peculiar and complex one, with the shadow of the past still looming over the current relationship. Not only is Russia the successor to the Soviet Union, which for half a century was the main antag-onist of the West but more importantly, ten of the current 27 EU member states were until the late 1980s part of the Moscow-dominated Soviet bloc or (in the case of the Baltic states) Soviet territory, leading to a residual strong suspicion and in some cases, such as in Poland, outright hostility towards Russia and Russia–EU rapprochement. On the other hand, in the late 1980s, the then European Commu-nity was among the first Western entities to support the reform processes initiated by Soviet leader Mikhail Gorbachev, which from 1990 on was also translated into financial support through the TACIS (Technical Assistance for the CIS countries) programme. This was followed by the signing of the 1994 Partnership and Cooper-ation Agreement (PCA) with the Russian Federation, which is still the formal basis of the EU's current contractual relations with Russia (including now two summit meetings a year). The wars in Chechnya in 1994–6 and 1999, however, blocked a further intensification of EU–Russia relations.

When Russia in 2003 rejected the proposed participation in the EU's European Neighbourhood Policy (ENP) (which also includes other former Soviet republics), Brussels and Moscow agreed to strengthen cooperation through the long-term cre-ation of four jointly agreed 'common spaces' in the framework of the PCA: a com-mon economic space; a common space of freedom, security, and justice; a common space of external security; and a common space of research, education, and cultural aspects. The EU also provided further financial assistance to Russia through the European Neighbourhood and Partnership Instrument (ENPI), with €120 million being allocated for the period 2007–10, in addition to support through other finan-cial instruments such as the nuclear safety instrument (see Blockmans 2008). Fol-lowing difficult negotiations, in 2005 these common spaces were translated into a detailed 'road map' (Vahl 2007). The implementation of this road map, though, proved to be problematic within a context of generally deteriorating relations. In

June 2008, after Medvedev took over from Putin as President of the Russian Federation, negotiations were launched on a 'new EU/Russia agreement', which was to replace the existing PCA and include legally binding commitments covering all main areas of the relationship. These negotiations were presented as the start of a new phase in the process of deepening the strategic partnership between the EU and Russia (Slovenian Presidency of the EU 2008). However, two months later, the conflict in the Caucasus broke out and the EU postponed further meetings in a reaction to the Russian use of military force against Georgia—with new meetings depending on the withdrawal of Russian troops from that country (Fischer 2008; Trenin 2008; Allison 2009). As is explained below, it confirmed that in Eastern Europe and the Southern Caucasus, the EU and Russia are engaged in a 'strategic competition', rather than in a 'strategic partnership'.

The EU's relationship with China reflects a similar pattern of progress as well as standstill after the use of violence by Beijing (see historical overview in Casarini 2009). The EEC and China established formal relations in 1975, which was followed in 1978 by a trade agreement and in 1985 by a trade and cooperation agreement (TCA), which also included political dialogue. The 1989 Tiananmen Square massacre, with Chinese military forces crushing the democratization movement in the country, led to the imposition of an EU arms embargo against China and to a deterioration of the political relations between the EU and China. In the mid 1990s, the EU initiated a policy of 'constructive engagement' with China, which was celebrated in 1998 with a first—from then on annual—EU–China summit of the heads of state and government. It also included support for China embedding itself within the predominant global (in fact 'Western') structures and embracing free market economy principles, with China joining the World Trade Organization (WTO) in 2001.

In 2003 the EU and China agreed to upgrade their relationship to a strategic partnership, including cooperation in strategic and security-related issues. This was reflected in, for instance, the Chinese participation in the European Galileo satellite system (the competitor to the American GPS) and in the prospect of lifting the arms embargo against China. EU–China relations rapidly gained depth and scope, with regular political, trade, and economic dialogue meetings and an extensive set of sectoral dialogues and agreements covering a wide range of sectors, from environment and energy to satellite navigation, agriculture, and regional policy (Algieri 2008). As the 25-years-old TCA still served as the main legal framework for EU–China relations, it was agreed at the 2006 summit to start negotiations on a single and overarching PCA. This was seen as providing the new legal basis for the further development of a comprehensive strategic partnership (Kerr and Fei 2007; Godement 2008; Shambaugh et al. 2008; Zhongping 2008). Anticipating the PCA, the EU had already allocated €128 million for China for the period 2007–10. However, negotiations on a new PCA turned out to be much more problematic than expected, not only as a result of divergent views on the contents of this agreement (particularly on trade issues), but also as a result of firm American opposition to a too-close

EU–China partnership (and to the lifting of the arms embargo) and the political fallout of Chinese military actions in Tibet and Xinjiang. The decision of the Chinese to postpone the yearly EU–China summit in December 2008 was a first major indication that the 'love affair' (Casarini 2009, 1) between the EU and China, which had started in 2003, was indeed short lived.

The EU's contractual relations with India and Brazil are much less complicated, are both labelled as 'strategic', but are at the same time also less developed and less essential for the EU. Both countries have in common their specific historical (colonial) relationship with one of the EU countries: the UK for India (as it was part of the British Empire until independence in 1947 and still is a major member of the Commonwealth) and Portugal for Brazil (though with Brazilian independence going back to 1822). Both former colonies also have in common that they have not been included in the EU's main cooperation and assistance scheme for developing countries: the 2000 Cotonou Agreement with now 79 African, Caribbean, and Pacific (ACP) countries, which succeeded the Lomé Conventions with the ACP countries (see Mayall 2005 and Chapter 14).

When negotiating the 1975 Lomé Convention (following Britain's accession to the EEC), France feared that the inclusion of large developing countries such as India would undermine the EEC's preferential treatment of its mainly African former colonies. The result was that 'despite the strong ties between the UK and the Indian subcontinent in particular, no Asian country was permitted to join the Lomé Convention', which was a missed opportunity that 'confined Asian–EU relations to the lowest of priorities for the next two decades' (Holland 2002, 60). In the mid 1990s, within a context of increased European attention for Asia, the EU and India in 1994 concluded a cooperation agreement, which still provides the legislative framework for current EU–India cooperation. This bilateral agreement was important for the EU's relations with India, particularly in view of India's absence or rather marginal position within respectively ASEAN (Association of South East Asian Nations) and ASEM (Asia–Europe meeting), which are the two main frameworks for inter-regional cooperation schemes between Europe and Asia. A decade later the EU and India launched the 'EU–India strategic partnership' and joint action plan, which were both further strengthened and expanded in 2008 (Jain 2007; Snyder 2007; Wagner 2008). The 2004 decision to upgrade their relations reflected the growing international profile of both the EU and India as well as the consciousness that they share common values as fully fledged democracies. In financial terms, EU funding for India was quite significant in comparison with the assistance to the other BRIC countries, with €470 million being allocated for India for the period 2007–13. As indicated in the EU's country strategy paper for India, this financial support was seen as transitional, showing a progressive shift from development assistance to new areas of mutual interest and cooperation. This also included India's participating in the EU's Galileo satellite system. However, on a political level, the 'strategic partnership' mainly remained symbolic, as shown in the diverging positions adopted by the EU and India on some fundamental issues, such as the Doha round, the reform of the UN Security Council (UNSC) or nuclear non-proliferation (Narlikar 2006; Baroowa 2007).

Latin America was also excluded from the EU's main cooperation and assistance scheme for developing countries and, just as with Asia, received much less European attention. This gradually changed after the 1986 entry of Spain and Portugal, with both countries promoting new cooperation schemes with their former colonies. In 1992, the EC and Brazil signed a bilateral framework agreement for cooperation, which still governs their current relationship, and in 1995 this was followed by the interregional framework cooperation agreement between the EU and Mercosur. For ten years, this inter-regional agreement was the main framework through which the EU developed its relations with Brazil. However, gradually the limitations of both EU–Mercosur cooperation and of Mercosur as a forum for regional integration became apparent, and in 2004 negotiations on a wide-ranging EU–Mercosur association agreement stalled (Klom 2003; Vasconcelos 2007). In July 2007, in an answer to the stalemate in EU–Mercosur relations and in recognition of the growing importance of Brazil, the first-ever EU–Brazil summit was held. Both sides also decided to launch a 'strategic partnership' in order to further deepen and upgrade their mutual ties (Garcia 2008). Central topics of the new partnership were effective multilateralism, climate change, sustainable energy, and the fight against poverty. For the period 2007–13, a total of €61mn was earmarked for Brazil in the EU's Brazil country strategy paper, which also indicated that from a budgetary perspective Brazil remained the least important partner of the four BRICs.

A common feature of the EU's relationship with the four BRIC countries is that they are all labelled as 'strategic partnerships'. However, the proliferation of 'strategic partnerships' points to what seems to have become a standard operating procedure, that is to periodically upgrade the label of the EU's relationship with other major powers—thus the status of 'strategic partner' was also granted or promised to other mid-sized powers such as Japan, Canada, Mexico, and South Africa (Renard 2009, 39). This seems to reflect the EU's inability to agree and decide which third actors are genuine strategic partners and consequently its inability to behave strategically in relation to these partners. The agreements and action plans with the EU's various 'strategic partners' indeed read more as a catalogue of policy domains that are on the agenda of their meetings, rather than as well-formulated strategies to pursue well-defined objectives through intensive and purposeful common actions. One example can illustrate this. Environmental policy is covered in each of the partnerships and the 2009 Copenhagen climate summit was prominent on the agenda of the high-level meetings with each of the four BRIC countries in the months preceding this summit. But this did not result in any meaningful common actions and could not prevent the EU in Copenhagen from being completely sidelined by its strategic partners. Box 16.1 provides a brief summary of the problems encountered by the EU in this case.

The use of the label 'strategic partnership' in fact functions as a rhetorical façade which masks the reality that the EU in fact has failed to transform the relations with the BRIC countries into strategic partnerships. The EU in the 1990s missed the

> **BOX 16.1**   **Climate change and EU–BRIC relations: losing power, losing leadership**
>
> Framework for EU–BRIC climate relations: from 1990 until 2008 the EU had positioned itself, and was perceived, as the lead actor in global climate governance under the United Nations Framework Convention on Climate Change (UNFCCC). Especially during and after the Kyoto Protocol negotiations of 1997, and given the absence of any US leadership, the EU established both relational and structural power in climate negotiations.
>
> The BRIC countries were largely absent as strong powers for most of this period because of their low CO_2 emissions, reflecting their relatively small economies and status as developing countries.
>
> Economic growth in the BRIC countries formed the basis for their growing importance in climate change politics, as they became major emitters (China has been the largest emitter of greenhouse gases since 2009). However, in political terms, this did not really translate into much influence in the UNFCCC negotiating process until 2008. During this whole period the EU remained, or continued to be perceived as, the global leader.
>
> It is important to note that the EU did not manage to develop much of a strategy towards the BRICs in terms of climate governance. Diplomatic attempts remained largely insignificant and structural efforts to understand the BRIC countries' positions did not lead to significant changes in the EU position.
>
> A major shift in power position took place in 2008–9. The BRICs started to meet as a group and the economic crisis created the necessity, if not the opportunity, to strengthen their position through the G20 (no longer the G8) as the forum for global governance, and a set of multilateral governance arrangements with BRIC membership, but not including the EU (see text).
>
> At the Copenhagen climate summit (UNFCCC, Conference of the Parties 15) in December 2009, the shift in power was demonstrated in a painful way (at least for the EU). While the EU entered the front door of the conference with a self-perception of global leadership, it left via the back door confronted with an unexpected new demonstration of BRIC power. China, India, and Brazil formed the leading trio of negotiations that ran parallel to the official agenda and which led on the last day to the so-called Copenhagen Accord. While President Obama was able to break into these talks, the EU failed to do so and had to undergo the result.
>
> Copenhagen illustrated an EU with relative power loss to the BRICs and a failure to develop a functional strategy. It also illustrated divergent (if not diametrically opposed) beliefs about multilateralism. The EU was hoping for a legally binding global convention; the BRICs managed to reach their result based on a concept of strong sovereignty and non-binding multilateralism.

historic opportunity of treating Russia as a real partner and of anchoring post-communist Russia more firmly into a process of wider European integration (Casier 2007, 86). By not lifting the weapons embargo, by scaling down common strategic endeavours (such as on Galileo), and continuing to preach in the relationship with Beijing, the EU missed the historic opportunity to opt for China as a genuine strategic partner for the 21st century (Casarini 2009). The EU was arguably never honestly interested in India and never intended to consider this largest pluralist democracy in the south as a privileged partner on the international scene (Jain 2007, 99). And perhaps most importantly, the proliferation of declaratory 'strategic partnerships' conceals the reality that for many EU countries the only genuine strategic partnership is the one with the USA—with Washington having the structural and relational power to assure that the Europeans, even if they intended to do so, do not move into strategic partner-swapping.

The EU–BRICs relationship and the EU as a subsystem of IR

What does the relationship between the EU and the BRIC countries tell us about the EU as a subsystem of international relations? The previous section indicated that the member states consider the EU as a useful setting to develop relatively stable, comprehensive, and institutionalized frameworks for their relationships with the BRIC countries. With regard to a wide spectrum of policy fields, the EU by and large manages to promote the general European interest vis-à-vis the BRIC countries and to aggregate the interests and preferences of the member states. This is as such an achievement given the member states' different views on relations with the BRICs. This divergence is particularly visible with regard to China and Russia, while relations with Brazil and India suffer from another problem: the lack of interest of the member states.

In their 'power audit' of EU–China relations, Fox and Godement (2009) demonstrate how the member states are split on both the economic and political dimension. With regard to economic relations, the question is how to manage China's impact on the European economy: in a negative sense (protecting its own economy vis-à-vis the growing Chinese economic power) or in a positive sense (making use of the trade and investment opportunities offered by the growing Chinese economy). With regard to political relations, the question is how to engage China politically: in a negative sense (adopting a critical attitude towards China in view of its stance on human rights, Tibet, Taiwan, etc.) or positive sense (prioritizing friendly or strategic political relations with China). These categories can also be used to analyse the member states' diverging interests and priorities with regard to Russia, with the economic dimension being closely linked to Russia's energy power (see Leonard and Popescu 2007). A further complication arises when we take into account that the policy positions of the member states are not always stable and that differences in interests and preferences must also be aggregated on the national level. This implies that shifts in governmental coalitions and leadership can lead to shifts in national policies and can facilitate or complicate EU policy making.

The preceding analysis points to both the strength and weakness of the EU as a subsystem of international relations with regard to its relations to the other major powers. On the one hand, the EU is able to aggregate diverging interests and preferences of member states and to translate this into external collective action. This leads to useful comprehensive frameworks for relations with the BRIC countries—common frameworks that nevertheless still allow member states to pursue their own policy objectives through their bilateral relations. On the other hand, it is not surprising that the EU cannot always be successful in overcoming the diverging interests and preferences and in generating unambiguous collective action. This is particularly the case when the politically most sensitive issues appear on the agenda and when China or Russia explicitly raises the pressure (for instance by threatening to cut down the supply of energy or to cancel a summit meeting) or when Europe's main strategic partner—the USA—becomes closely involved (cf. the non-decision on lifting the arms embargo on China) (see Stumbaum 2009).

Beyond the differences in the member states' economic and political interests, some other factors explain the problems and constraints in the EU's collective action and policy making towards the BRIC countries—with these factors further strengthening the divergence of interests and preferences. First, the challenges posed by the emerging powers show themselves in a multitude of policy sectors (trade, environmental, energy, foreign policy, security...) in which the EU has wide-ly varying legal competences and in which also the policy instruments at the EU's disposal vary considerably. Whereas the EU has exclusive competences with regard to most dimensions of trade policy, this is not the case for most other policy areas. Even more, for some aspects of external relations, the EU has no or only very limited competences. For instance, until the entry into force of the Lisbon Treaty in 2009 the EU had no clear competences to develop a policy with regard to the supply of energy resources. From this perspective, it is logical that the EU cannot function and is indeed also not seen by the EU member states as the only appropriate framework within which to move towards collective action vis-à-vis the BRIC countries.

This is related to a second factor: the existence of alternative bilateral or multilateral paths for the member states to defend their interests in relationship to the BRIC countries. In view of their greater weight in international relations, the largest member states in particular often prefer the bilateral route to deal with the challenges posed by the individual BRIC countries or to profit from the opportunities that good relations may offer. In their introductory chapter, Hill and Smith correctly emphasize that the EU as a subsystem of IR is part of an emerging system of multilevel governance in the global arena. However, this is not only true for the EU itself, but also for its member states. Instead of the EU (or as a complement to the EU), member states can also prefer other frameworks such as the UN, NATO, the WTO, or specific contact groups: if their relative weight in these forums is larger than in the EU, if the approaches generally adopted in these forums are closer to their own preferences, and if they judge that their interests will be better defended within these institutional frameworks. Moreover, within these other international settings, France, Germany, and the UK in particular often need the support or at least the tacit agreement of the two most powerful BRIC countries to achieve other major foreign policy objectives, for instance with regard to the fight against terrorism, the negotiations with Iran on its nuclear capabilities, the war in Afghanistan or the peace process in the Middle East. This also is one of the reasons why Paris, Berlin, and London regularly consider their bilateral relationships or the more restricted and exclusive multilateral settings as the appropriate venues within which to try and develop a strategic partnership with China and Russia.

A third factor is not related to the BRICs as such, but to two general features of the EU as a subsystem of international relations. The first feature is that the EU's institutional system is not always capable of generating common views on important foreign policy issues. It is difficult for the EU to engage in a sensible foreign policy dialogue with the BRIC countries and to gain their support for the EU's views if the EU, as a precondition, is not able to aggregate the interests and views of its member states on that policy issue. A clear example of this was the status of Kosovo, where the EU could not even try to convince Russia to follow its policy choices, as it was internally highly divided on the issue. The second feature is related to the EU's decision-making process: member states and institutions often have to spend so much energy and time in generating a common view on a foreign policy issue that, even if they find a common view, they often have no more time to gain support for the EU's positions. The climate conference in Copenhagen was again a case in point: at the very moment that the EU member states were negotiating to determine the EU's common position, China, India, Brazil, and the USA were brokering the final conclusions of the conference (see Chapter 15 and Box 16.1).

The EU–BRICs relationship and the EU as a power in IR

A second perspective from which to evaluate the EU–BRICs relationship is to look at the EU as a power that is able to shape its external environment. It is useful for the analysis of the EU's relationships to the BRICs in particular to analyse these from the perspective not only of relational power and hard power (with a focus on coercion, crises, and conflicts) but also from that of structural power (being the power to influence the political, economic, legal, and other structures of third countries and third regions) (Keukeleire 2008). In this section, we first focus on the structural power perspective and move subsequently to the relational hard power dimension (for a normative power perspective, see Tocci 2008).

Since the mid 1990s, the EU has used its comprehensive contractual and political relations with other regions in the world as an instrument to exert structural power vis-à-vis these regions. The EU seeks to promote structural changes in third countries and assist them in the development towards liberal economies and pluralist democracies, including through the use of positive and negative conditionality. This structural foreign policy resulted in successes in Central and Eastern Europe and recently also the Balkans, and more mixed results or outright failures in relationship to Mediterranean and African countries (Keukeleire and MacNaughtan 2008; Holden 2009). However, the EU largely failed to use its relations with the BRICs as leverage to influence the internal political and societal structures and developments in these countries. This reflected the changing balance of power as well as their emphasis on national sovereignty and non-intervention in internal affairs.

This tendency became particularly obvious in relations with Moscow and Beijing, which increasingly countered the EU's attempts to include references to human rights, minorities, and other sensitive issues in the various contractual and political agreements. When negotiating the 1994 partnership and cooperation agreements, Russia still accepted the 'didactic, smug and often patronizing language of the PCA' (Light 2001, 20). A decade later Moscow rejected the EU's demands to insert explicit and binding references to human rights, minorities, and democracy in the 'common spaces' and the 'road map'—leading to a virtual absence of political conditionality (Vahl 2007). In view of the gradual deterioration in Russia of 'Western' norms (i.e. rule of law and respect for human and civil rights) and the Russian emphasis on 'sovereign democracy' as an alternative to the Western 'pluralist democracy', the EU was clearly not successful in assuring that Russia would share the EU's fundamental choices (Averre 2007; Marsh 2008). This reluctance to insert itself into the structures promoted by the EU became also increasingly visible with regard to energy, with Moscow refusing to ratify the European energy charter and challenging the EU's views on the contents and purpose of the EU–Russia energy dialogue (Hadfield 2008b; Romanova 2008; see also Chapter 15). A similar tendency is obvious in EU–China relations. Beijing accepts the EU's (modest) support for its internal socioeconomic reforms through cooperation and assistance in various sectors of the economy (Shambaugh *et al.* 2008, 160). However, it is increasingly irritated by the EU's stated goal of supporting China's transition towards an open and pluralist society based on the rule of law and respect for human rights. For instance, whereas Beijing in 1998 agreed to start a regular human rights dialogue, the Chinese later refused to participate in this dialogue and also made sure that politically sensitive issues disappeared from the agenda of the summit meetings. Whereas the 'web of European-inspired dialogues and agreements is supposed to entangle China in rules and commitments … transforming Chinese policy along European lines', it became increasingly clear that Europe would not be able 'to mould China in its own image' (Fox and Godement 2009, 19–20). And this may point to the main problem for the Europeans, that is that they hold the illusion that Europe's tradition of legal–institutional structuring through law, governance, and markets can also function within a context of what Kerr labels as Asian organicism (2007, 296–8).

From the mid 2000s on, the EU was increasingly confronted with Russia and China—and gradually also India and Brazil—becoming competing structural powers in the world (see also Keukeleire and MacNaughtan 2008). They became competitors to the EU and the West in general by strengthening and using their growing structural power in order to gain or regain ground in other regions in the world (mainly Eastern Europe and Caucasus for Russia; Africa, Asia and Latin America for the other BRICs) and to influence the rules of the game on a global scale.

The structural power contest between Russia and the EU is most visible in the former Soviet republics in Eastern Europe (Ukraine, Belarus, Moldova) and the Southern Caucasus (Armenia, Azerbaijan, Georgia). Crushed between the EU and Russia, these countries became the object of a 'clash of integration processes' between the Brussels-steered integration process in the framework of the ENP and the Moscow-steered integration process in the framework of the Commonwealth of Independent States (CIS) (Malfliet *et al.* 2007; Casier 2007). The EU's enlargement turned Belarus, Ukraine, and Moldova into immediate neighbours and increased the pressure to pursue Western-oriented reforms—which was mirrored in the democratic revolutions in Georgia and Ukraine in 2003–4. The EU had also fuelled aspirations in these countries by actively supporting structural changes in these countries and their gradual integration into the EUs regulatory and cooperation structures: through PCAs, by launching its ENP in 2004 and 'Eastern partnership' in 2009, and by providing financial support through the ENPI (Gänzle 2009; see also Chapter 13). In combination with NATO's drive to the east, the EU's policy led to a growing resentment in Russia against Western involvement in Russia's traditional sphere of influence. Moscow used its growing economic strength to avoid further erosion of Russian influence in its immediate neighbourhood: by further promoting the CIS, by integrating some of the partner countries more firmly within its economic, monetary, and energy structures, and by exploiting the dependency of most of its neighbours on Russia. Russia complemented its use of structural power with the use of hard power, not only by disrupting the supply of gas to dissenting countries such as Ukraine but also by the use of military force against Georgia (Allison 2009).

The competing structural power of China is felt on a wider scale, although less clear cut than in Russia's case. China's rapidly growing economy and related quest for energy and raw material has been the primary driving force behind its gradual emergence as a global structural power over the last decade (Ziegler 2006). Added to this is the attractiveness of its developmental model: one in which economic liberalization and growth need not go hand in hand with political liberalization and development towards Western norms. China's model has been espoused not only by authoritarian leaders in Africa but also by former Soviet republics in Central Asia, some countries of South Asia, and policy makers in Latin America and the Middle East (Gill and Huang 2006, 20; Alden 2007; Kurlantzick 2007). China's increasingly active diplomacy in regions prioritized by the EU, including Africa and the Middle East, threatens to thwart the political, societal, and economic structures that the EU promotes through positive and negative conditionality. However, the EU is yet to develop a proper response to counter or encompass this emerging Chinese structural power worldwide, although a debate has been launched within the EU on triangular cooperation between the EU, China, and Africa (Wissenbach 2009). China has also taken an activist approach to sub-regional and regional institution building in Asia, thereby providing an alternative to the Western-dominated international organizations.

Although less visible and still on a much lower scale, India and Brazil are also increasingly active and present in other parts of the world, including Africa. Although they neither represent nor promote an opposing developmental model, they are clearly more reluctant than the EU to actively promote Western structures and values. For instance, despite being itself the largest democracy in the world, India only at a late stage pointed to declarations in democracy promotion as a possible foreign policy objective, with its contributions to democracy promotion in Afghanistan being the only example of operational support for such a policy. India traditionally has no democracy promotion policy, as its focus on national security, solidarity with developing countries, and respect for national sovereignty led to a foreign policy that basically ignores the internal orientation of the regimes it is engaging with. This implies that whereas India might seem to be a natural ally to the EU in jointly promoting democratic structures in other parts of the world, this is not at all the case in practice. This is reflected in concrete cases such as the policy towards the dictatorial regime in Burma/Myanmar, where the EU has called for strengthening sanctions whereas New Delhi, for political and strategic interests, stresses a policy of 'constructive engagement' with that country, including defence cooperation (Mohan 2007; Kumar 2008). Also Brazil, since the election of president Lula da Silva in the early 2000s, has given priority to intensifying relations with the south (including China, India, South Africa, and Africa in general) and countering Western dominance in the various international political and economic forums, rather than trying to influence the internal political and societal structures within third countries (Soares de Lima and Hirst 2006).

How does the EU relate to the BRIC countries with regard to traditional issues of foreign and security policy, where diplomatic interaction and hard relational power are more important? The EU's attempts to intensify its relations with China and Russia in particular have been regularly undermined by conflicts and crises related to the use of military power by both countries, within their own territory or in their immediate neighbourhood (cf. Tiananmen Square in 1989, Chechnya in the 1990s, Georgia in 2008, Tibet and Xinjiang in 2008 and 2009). These events clearly hampered the development of closer political relations as well as the adoption of new generations of agreements with the EU. However, on each occasion the EU internally struggled with the questions of to what extent and how long these events should be allowed to undermine the mutual relations. The EU also had problems in defining an operational policy towards these crises in order to contribute effectively to conflict resolution. One of the rare cases where the EU was seen as relatively successful was the Georgia war, in view of the useful mediating role of French President Sarkozy (who at the time held the role of President of the European Council) and the ability of the EU to quickly set up an EU monitoring mission. Yet it is clear that in general the EU has no comprehensive peace-building policy towards the Caucasus and Central Asia, where hard power is at the heart of interstate and intrastate relations (see Merlingen and Ostrauskait 2009).

A look at Asia provides an even more sobering perspective on the nature and relevance of the EU as an international actor. The EU's stance in Asia can in general be characterized by a perceived lack of European strategic interests (Shambaugh 2005, 167). This is translated into the absence of a fully-fledged policy on, and sometimes simply into lack of attention for, some of the major conflicts and sources of instability in Asia—conflicts in which India, China, and Russia are also involved. The EU has developed a very modest Afghanistan policy (including the training of Afghan soldiers and a contribution to the reconstruction efforts in that country) but hardly a policy towards the many other issues that are important for regional and global security and that affect China–India relations (cf. competition in the Indian Ocean), China–USA relations (cf. Taiwan), India–Pakistan relations (cf. Kashmir), China's relationship with other Asian powers, or the complex phenomenon of terrorism in Asia.

The EU–BRICs relationship and processes of global governance

The third perspective is on the EU as part of the wider processes of international relations, which refers to the legal, institutional, and political mechanisms through which the problems of international conflict and/or political economy are addressed. We frame this debate by referring to the term global governance. The main global governance institutions are the reflection of a US–European consensus, with the UN as the main framework to deal with global challenges. For security this is the UNSC, for economic and financial issues the World Bank (system) and the International Monetary Fund (IMF), for trade the WTO, for sustainable development the UN Commission on Sustainable Development (Weiss and Daws 2008). The G7/8 has also been framed as a sort of global governance system based on economic capacity and power (Hajnal 1999). The dominance of the US and European countries (EU members) in these institutions is well described and increasingly problematic (Mahbubani 2008). The position of the EU and its individual member states is particularly disputable given major changes in relative economic importance and the EU's stance on traditional 'hard power' solutions.

The EU's view on global governance can best be captured by the 'effective multi-lateralism' doctrine (European Commission 2003d; Wouters et al. 2008). It is based on three fundamental elements. First, the EU prefers legally binding agreements or treaties as the outcomes and instruments of global coordination; second, the EU prefers multilateralism (in essence the UN system) over more limited (in terms of number of participants) arrangements; third, the EU does not consider the two previous points as an essential assault on national sovereignty. The EU in particular and the BRICs (in addition to the USA) diverge strongly on a number of fundamental elements of global governance. The contents of the political declarations and agreements between the EU and each of the four countries could indeed give the impression that the relations with the BRIC countries were 'partnerships for effective multilateralism' (Grevi and Vasconcelos 2008). However, the EU's experience with the BRICs in multilateral settings demonstrates that these four countries have a quite different view on exactly what multilateralism means and what the policy goals are that have to be achieved through multilateralism. The BRIC countries have a preference for non-legally binding political commitments, do not have a particular preference for all-inclusive multilateralism, and generally start from a realist perspective on sovereignty (hard sovereignty).

The current position of the BRICs in global governance is closely related to two fundamental critiques of the dominant governance institutions: they are not representative of the global population and they do not reflect the fundamental changes in the world since the strong surge of globalization in the 1990s. These critiques have been voiced for over two decades regarding the UN system. Several steps have been taken to modify the current global governance institutions. The inclusion of Russia in the G7 (to form the G8) was only a modest first step to recognize the renewed importance of Russia as successor state of the Soviet Union (Bayne 1999). A more important step was the formation of the G8+5. Tony Blair, Prime Minister of the UK, in 2005 invited the leading emerging countries (China, India, Brazil, Mexico, and South Africa) to the G8 summit at Gleneagles in Scotland. In 2007, German Chancellor Angela Merkel took the initiative to further institutionalize the permanent dialogue between the G8 countries and the five greatest emerging economies through the 'Heiligendamm Process' (University of Toronto, G20 Research Group). The next step, the full integration of the five in a G13, was pushed by French President Nicolas Sarkozy in 2008, yet, this step has not so far been taken as G8 states have diverging positions on this issue. The USA and Japan oppose enlargement, the UK and France are strongly in favour, whereas Italy, Germany, Russia, and Canada are reserved. The G8+5 is the first global governance institution to include all five BRIC countries. The fact that India, Brazil, and China are 'only +5' demonstrates the hesitation of tradition-strong countries in global governance to fully adapt the institutions to the changes in relative power positions.

An important breaking point (or breakthrough, depending on the interpretation) came with the financial crisis of 2008, when the G20 became an important response mechanism to the global banking crisis. The G20, an informal group of the finance ministers and the governors of the central banks of 19 countries and the EU, was formed in 1999 to discuss policy coordination in light of the financial crisis of 1997–9 (University of Toronto, G20 Information Centre). Since then, there has been a finance ministerial meeting every autumn. In November 2008, in the aftermath of the financial crisis, US President George W. Bush hosted the first G20 summit with the leaders of the G20 countries in Washington DC, to coordinate a truly global response. It was the start of further G20 summits in London in Spring 2009 and Pittsburgh in September 2009. The idea that major global challenges needed a governance response that was more global had gained ground in a major way. The EU has been an active participant in these forums, yet has not been able to come to a common position or strategy to reform the global governance architecture. Diverging opinions between some of the largest member states, which hold strong positions in the UNSC, the G7/8, the World Bank, and the IMF, etc., and the other EU members have been the main obstacles to the EU playing a larger role. Without a strong strategic position, the EU has obviously not succeeded in setting up a significant or successful dialogue with the BRICs on this issue.

The lack of EU engagement with the BRICs on this matter has not slowed down the latters' efforts to actively set up new multilateral frameworks centred around the BRICs (see Figure 16.1). Firstly, there is the increasing dialogue and cooperation in variations on the BRIC format: bilateral meetings between BRIC countries (mainly Russia–China and India–China) (Deng 2007); trilateral 'RIC meetings' (Russia, India, China); the IBSA initiative that was formally launched in 2003 with India, Brazil, and South Africa; and potentially also the CISA trialogue with China, India, and South Africa, being the trio of Asian and African drivers in the South (Alden and Vieira 2005; Shaw, Cooper, and Antkiewicz 2007). Secondly, Russia, China, and India have also actively been promoting the multilateralization of their dialogues and trialogues, with several new international forums emerging in which Russia, China, and/or India play a particularly important role. These include the Shanghai Cooperation Organization (SCO) (including Russia, China, Kazakhstan, Uzbekistan, Tajikistan, and Kyrgyzstan, with India, Pakistan, Iran, and Mongolia having observer status); the South Asian Association for Regional Cooperation (SAARC); the ASEAN+3 process (including the ASEAN countries plus China, Japan, and Korea); and the East Asia Summit (including China, India, together with other Asian countries as well as Australia and New Zealand) (Malik 2006; Cook 2008; Bin 2009). Important for global geo-economic and geopolitical changes is also the Asia–Pacific Economic Cooperation (APEC), which links the increasingly important Asian continent with the USA as still the largest political, economic, and military power.

The BRIC countries increasingly use their new position in traditional and new global governance settings as a platform to agree on how to tackle specific international challenges and negotiations (such as on the financial crisis or on environmental issues) and to subsequently attempt to impose them or present them as a fait accompli in other international forums (such as the G20). As already noted, the—for the Europeans—most painful illustration of this phenomenon may be the final stage of the Copenhagen climate conference. The Copenhagen Accord was

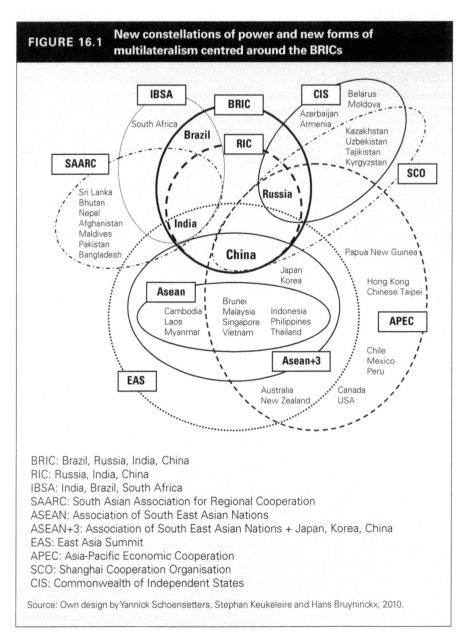

FIGURE 16.1 New constellations of power and new forms of multilateralism centred around the BRICs

BRIC: Brazil, Russia, India, China
RIC: Russia, India, China
IBSA: India, Brazil, South Africa
SAARC: South Asian Association for Regional Cooperation
ASEAN: Association of South East Asian Nations
ASEAN+3: Association of South East Asian Nations + Japan, Korea, China
EAS: East Asia Summit
APEC: Asia-Pacific Economic Cooperation
SCO: Shanghai Cooperation Organisation
CIS: Commonwealth of Independent States

Source: Own design by Yannick Schoensetters, Stephan Keukeleire and Hans Bruyninckx, 2010.

essentially discussed between China, India, Brazil, Australia, and South Africa, with the USA managing to break into the deal and the EU completely sidelined. Whereas the official negotiations ended without any result, they formulated the accord outside the negotiating dynamic, and it seemed that the fundamental option not to accept binding commitments was not taken in Copenhagen itself but at the APEC meeting of November 2009 in Singapore. It illustrates that the emerging powers' choice for multilateralism is in fact a 'choice for effective multilateralism'—but with a very different meaning from the one the Europeans have in mind—as they increasingly manage to use the various multilateral frameworks to impact upon the world order in the way they prefer.

The question for the EU is how to react to this proliferation of new governance constellations, in which it plays no role. The EU may have to complement the 'effective multilateralism' doctrine with an 'effective multiple polarity' (or 'effective multiple bilateralism') doctrine, with the latter potentially being a precondition for the first. The EU will have to start investing more time and energy in external negotiations instead of the currently predominant internal negotiations and decision-making. It has to invest in active diplomacy, taking into account the interests and perceptions of these new or emerging powers in the formulation of its own positions (and not only the interests and perceptions of its own member states and institutions), which is a far more complicated task than in the preceding context when the EU only had to take into account one power (the USA). Yet even then, the receptivity of the BRICs might be low as the EU is, in the first instance, a trade bloc and not a fully-fledged partner for the BRIC countries. Whether the EU is capable of doing this is doubtful at best. The internal divisions on the reform of the UNSC do not promise well in any case, as this issue precisely touched upon the redistribution of power to the regional powers in other continents; as a consequence, it also implied that the EU should accept a reduction or at least a dilution of the power of the member states, not only of large member states, such as in the UNSC, but also of medium-sized countries such as the Netherlands and Belgium in the IMF and World Bank. If the EU is unable to deal with such issues internally, the chances are small that it will have a major impact on the larger debates that surpass parochialisms.

Conclusions

The EU currently has no BRICs strategy, largely because of the reasons mentioned above. Whether this is problematic is debatable. The BRICs are probably too different and too much of an ad hoc group to permit the development of a coherent strategy towards them. More problematic is therefore that the EU does not have a strategy to tackle the various emerging powers and the parallel decline of its own weight in international relations and global governance. This is mirrored in the elite, media, and public perceptions in the BRIC countries, which indicate that the EU is perceived as a rather weak power, which also confirms the doubts about the importance of the 'strategic partnership' with the EU (Morini *et al.* 2010; Olivier and Fioramonti 2010). The BRICs and emerging powers not only pose a challenge to the EU and its member states but also to the scholarly community in Europe. There exists a strong need to increase knowledge about these emerging powers and, even more importantly, to overcome the often predominant Eurocentric or

Western-centric perspectives on foreign policy and global governance, and include perspectives and concepts from other parts of the world. Limited knowledge of China, India, Brazil, and other emerging powers (surely in comparison with the USA) in the EU's and member states' foreign policy structures and in European universities and think tanks is hampering the development of more comprehensive views on possible dynamics, opportunities, and consequences of the global shift towards the east and the south (see Shambaugh 2005, 161–5; Tickner and Waever 2009; Mahbubani, 2008).

FURTHER READING

Publications on the BRIC phenomenon and on overall EU–BRIC relations are rare. The main publication on these relations is the volume edited by Grevi and de Vasconcelos (2008). The EU–Russia strategic partnership is evaluated by Haukkala (2010) and Gower (2009), while Malfliet *et al.* (2007) provides an assessment of the EU and Russia in the context of the clash of integration processes. An expanding number of books is being published on EU–China relations. Casarini (2009) illuminates the evolution of this relationship, while Kerr and Liu (2007) and Shambaugh *et al.* (2008) assess various dimensions of this relationship. The comprehensive volume edited by Snyder (2009) includes the basic documents on EU–China relations from 1949 to 2008. Works on the EU and India are rare, with Jain (2007) providing the main publication, while EU–Brazil relations have not yet been the subject of a major publication in English.

Casarini, N. (2009), *Remaking Global Order: The Evolution of the European–China Relationship and its Implications* (Oxford: Oxford University Press).

Gower, J. (2009), *Russia and Europe in the Twenty-First Century. An Uneasy Partnership* (London: Anthem Press).

Grevi, G., and de Vasconcelos, A. (eds) (2008), *Partnerships for Effective Multilateralism: EU Relations with Brazil, China, India and Russia* (Paris: EU Institute for Security Studies).

Haukkala, H. (2010), *The EU–Russia Strategic Partnership: the Logic of Post-Sovereignty in International Relations* (Taylor & Francis Group).

Jain, R.K. (ed.) (2007), *India and the European Union: Building a Strategic Partnership* (New Delhi: Radiant Publishers).

Kerr, D., and Liu Fei. (eds) (2007), *The International Politics of EU–China Relations* (Oxford: Oxford University Press).

Malfliet, K., Verpoest, L., and Vinokurov, E. (eds) (2007), *The CIS, the EU and Russia: Challenges of Integration* (Basingstoke: Palgrave Macmillan).

Shambaugh, D., Sandschneider, E., and Hong, Z. (eds) (2008), *China–Europe Relations: Perceptions, Policies and Prospects* (London: Routledge).

Snyder, F. (ed.) (2009), *The European Union and China, 1949–2008: Basic Documents and Commentary* (Oxford: Hart Publishing).

WEB LINKS

Information on the EU's relations with the BRIC countries can be found on the websites of the Commission (**http://ec.europa.eu/external_relations/regions/index_en.htm, http://ec.europa.eu/trade/creating-opportunities/bilateral-relations/**) and Council of Ministers (**http://www.consilium.europa.eu**). See also the official governmental websites of the individual BRIC countries: **http://www.mre.gov.br (Brazil); http:// eng.kremlin.ru** (Russia); **http://meaindia.nic.in/** (India); **http://www.fmprc.gov. cn/eng/** (China). More links to official websites and references to academic literature can be found in the 'World powers' section of the online resource guide hosted by the University of Leuven (**http://www.exploring-europe.eu/foreignpolicy**). An economic assessment of the BRICs is conducted regularly by Goldman Sachs (**http://www2.gold-mansachs.com/ideas/brics/index.html**). Information on global governance and on the G20 can be found on the website of the World Economic Forum (**http://www.weforum. org/en/index.htm**) and the G20 Research Group of the University of Toronto (**http:// www.g20.utoronto.ca**).

CHAPTER 17

The EU and the United States

Michael Smith and Rebecca Steffenson

Summary

The United States has always been the most 'significant other' of the European integration project in the world arena. This chapter explores the implications of this factor for the international relations (IR) of the EU, first by introducing the key features of the EU–US relationship and by considering the ways in which these raise issues of analysis and policy. Second, the chapter explores the ways in which the EU–US relationship reflects and affects the workings of the EU as a system of international relations. Third, the chapter focuses on the ways in which the EU–US relationship affects the broader process of international relations. Finally, the chapter evaluates the ways in which the roles of the EU as a 'power' in international relations are shaped, and perhaps limited, by its relationship with the USA, and the ways in which this moulds the EU's role in pursuing international order.

Introduction

The European Union (and previously the European Community) has been intimately entangled with the United States since the very beginnings of European integration in the 1950s. In the areas of trade, monetary relations, and economic management this gives the USA a key role not only in the international policies of the EU, but also in the management of both the European economy and the broader global political economy. In the area of security, the European project has always been linked to and embedded in the European and world security order, whilst politically the EU and its predecessors have been a key part of the US-led group of liberal democracies. US influence stimulated the European project in two senses. On the one hand, the US federal system was an inspiration to European leaders such as Jean Monnet and to Americans who saw the European project as a means of creating a United States of Europe. On the other hand, European integration was inspired to a substantial extent by the desire to match US and Soviet superpower, or at least to create a 'third force' in international relations (DePorte 1987; Ellwood 1992: Winand 1993; Heller and Gillingham 1996). This ambivalence—the USA as a key partner and leader but also as a potential rival in world politics—has been central to EU–US relations and to the international relations of the EU ever since (Smith 1984; Smith and Woolcock 1993; Smith 1998a; McGuire and Smith 2008, Chapters 1 and 2).

These two dynamics, producing what can be called 'competitive cooperation' (Smith 1998a), are visible in all three of the core components of transatlantic life. Separate but interconnected economic, political, and security relationships define transatlantic relations and go a long way towards shaping both EU politics and the changing global order. In this context, dealing with the USA has been one of the key tests of the extent to which the EU has developed into an effective international actor with a distinct set of policy positions and instruments. Partly as a consequence, the EU–US relationship has, some would say increasingly, been a subject of political and policy debate, attracting the attention and disagreement of those involved in shaping the key questions of world order (M. Smith 2004a; Todd 2003; Kagan 2003).

This chapter aims to explore the ways in which EU–US relations enter into the international relations of the EU, and to assess the implications for key areas of the EU's growing international activity. In the first section, the focus is on the changing shape and focus of the transatlantic relationship as it enters into economic, political, and security questions. The following three sections address the key themes raised by this volume as a whole, by successively dealing with the impact of EU–US relations on the EU's system of international relations, on the EU's role in the processes of international relations, and on the EU's position as a 'power' in international relations.

The changing shape of EU–US relations

Economic interdependence has always been at the core of the EU–US relationship. European integration itself was closely connected with the economic reconstruction of Europe through the Marshall Plan in the 1940s and 1950s, and the European project has been closely linked to both the evolution of the 'Western world economy' during the Cold War and to 'globalization' in the 21st century. The destabilizing impact of the 2008–9 financial crisis, which arguably started with bank collapses in the USA, to be followed by bank runs across the UK and a succession of further crises within the eurozone, reaffirmed the extent to which globalization has prompted interdependence of economies not only across the Atlantic but around the globe. Within this general context, Box 17.1 summarizes a number of features of this relationship as it existed in the early 2000s.

BOX 17.1   The EU–US economic relationship in the 2000s

By the early 2000s, according to European Commission figures (European Commission 2003b), this deeply embedded economic relationship accounted for 37 per cent of world merchandise trade and for 45 per cent of world trade in services (2002 figures). While these figures had decreased slightly by 2007 to 33 per cent of world merchandise trade and 42 per cent of world trade in services, the EU and the USA clearly remain each other's single largest trading partner. In 2007, two-way cross-border trade in goods and services (imports and exports) between the EU and the USA amounted to more than €707 billion (€440 billion in goods and €267 billion in services). In 2002 these trade figures represented about 21 per cent of each partner's trade in goods alone and approximately 39 per cent of EU and 35 per cent of US total cross-border trade in services, and this amounted to 36 per cent of total bilateral trade in goods and services. By 2007, however, the EU was recording trade surpluses in both goods (€80 billion) and services (€11 billion), and China had replaced the USA as the number one importer into the EU. The larger value of the EU–US relationship arguably rests on Foreign Direct Investment (FDI). The EU and the USA in 2000 accounted for 54 per cent of total world inflows of FDI and for 67 per cent of total world outflows. By 2001, the USA absorbed 49 per cent of the EU's outward investment flows, and the EU 46 per cent of US outward flows; EU investment was 54 per cent of total investment in the USA, and US investment in the EU was 69 per cent of the total. Over a more extended period, nearly three-quarters of all foreign investment in the USA in the 1990s came from the EU. As a result, the total accumulated investment by the EU in the USA and the USA in the EU amounted by 2001 to €1500 billion—by far the largest investment relationship in the world. This trend continued throughout the 2000s. In 2007 EU investment flow to the USA was €112.6 billion while US investment to the EU was €144.5 billion. EU investment outflows represented 42 per cent of inflows to the USA, and the EU was the recipient of half of all private direct investment from the USA.

The very intimacy of this relationship, and the depth of its historical and institutional roots, gives rise to a number of important trends in EU–US economic relations. First, there has been a consistent growth of the economic links between the EC/EU and the USA and a continuous deepening of economic links over a more than 50-year period. These links have notably continued to deepen and widen even when transatlantic political or security relations have been troubled (for example, during the later years of the Cold War, or during the period leading up to the war in Iraq during 2002–3). A second trend concerns the ways in which the EC/EU, through processes of economic growth and enlargement, has increasingly come to be seen as an economic superpower. Both the EU and the USA are advanced industrial and service-based economies of continental size, and both are deeply entangled both with each other and with the development of the global economy. In other words, the EU–US relationship has become a partnership of equals, at least in economic terms (Peterson 1996; Guay 1999; Smith, M. 2009a).

But this evidence also raises a number of questions about the nature of EU–US economic relations. Given the continuous widening and deepening of the relationships, is it fair to see the EU and the USA as effectively 'integrated' within an Atlantic political economy? How far is it possible to see the EU and the USA as global economic rivals, given the simultaneous rise of disputes and more extensive conflicts over trade, investment, competition, and other areas of regulatory policy, and what are the implications of this? Is the EU, despite its apparent equality with the USA in quantitative terms, actually able to mobilize its economic resources to achieve equal influence with the USA, within both economic and other contexts— and how might this EU–US balance be affected by the rise of other major economies such as China and India? These and other economic issues will be addressed later in the chapter. The EU–US relationship also reflects a number of fundamental political forces (McGuire and Smith 2008, Chapter 1). In this sense, the foundations of the European project and the transatlantic relationship were as much political as they were economic. The defeat of almost all of the European states during the Second World War, the de-legitimization of governments and underlying regimes in all parts of Europe, coupled with the looming threat of Soviet political domination in Eastern Europe, played a key role in shaping the political complexion of the 'new Europe' after 1945. A fundamental US commitment to a Western market system was thus paralleled by the desire to promote the strengthening of liberal democracies in Europe. The development and consolidation of anti-communism in the 1950s, the development of European socialisms and 'Euro-communism' in the 1970s and 1980s, and the spread of free market and liberal ideas in the 1980s reflect key phases in the development of the political relationship (Ellwood 1992; Heller and Gillingham 1996). It is difficult to establish the extent to which these events affected American engagement in Europe, but it is clear that consistent and deep relationships between European and American political and diplomatic elites underpinned Cold War Europe.

The political changes initiated by the end of the Cold War promised (or threatened) to transform the character of EU–US relations. Whilst the removal of the Soviet hold over Central and Eastern Europe created new scope for the extension of liberal democracy and market ideas, it also revealed some of the fault lines and key policy questions that had been at least partly masked by the Cold War. To what extent did the EU and the USA really share common values? Was it possible for the EU to develop and export a different brand of democracy, underpinned by economic success and by the mechanisms in the Common Foreign and Security Policy (CFSP)? How would this find its expression in the economic and security challenges likely to face the 'winners' in the contest between Western democracy and communism? These were not simply analytical or academic questions: they reflected the uncertainties of political and policy-making elites on both sides of the Atlantic (Haftendorn and Tuschhoff 1993; Smith and Woolcock 1993; Peterson 1996). As Box 17.2 shows, the sheer range of areas covered by political initiatives in the immediate post-Cold War period raised important questions of transatlantic coordination, not only among foreign ministries and the EU's external relations apparatus but also in areas previously seen as 'internal' or 'domestic' in their political impact. Here, as elsewhere, the EU–US relationship demonstrated in concentrated form the questions that had to be addressed by all political leaders and foreign policy officials.

Inescapably, the economic and political factors outlined above have been linked to the security question (indeed, many of the initiatives listed in Box 17.2 are security issues in many respects, as well as indicators of political cooperation). The EU can plausibly be analysed as a 'security community', as it gathers societies together in a pluralistic yet common framework, within which war between the members is effectively unthinkable. More directly, there are two standard explanations for the origins of the European project: on the one hand, Franco–German rapprochement and the creation of a new framework for the prevention of

---

| **BOX 17.2** | **Examples of transatlantic political initiatives (post-Cold War)** |

- Declaration on combating terrorism.
- Energy research cooperation agreement.
- Statement on communicable diseases in Africa.
- EU–US Biotechnology Consultative Forum.
- Declaration on the responsibilities of states on transparency regarding arms exports.
- Declaration on common orientation of non-proliferation policy.
- Precursors chemical agreement.
- Joint initiative on trafficking in women.
- Caribbean drugs initiative.

armed conflict in Western Europe, on the other hand the creation of economic and political conditions that would buttress the West in the conduct of the Cold War. Here, of course, the EC/EU was not and is not the only game in town. American influence over its European allies was well and truly cemented with the creation of NATO in the 1950s, embodying what has been seen as a transatlantic 'security community' (Sloan 2002).

For this purpose, it is possible to see the European integration project as part of the institutional underpinning of the Cold War in general and the EC as part of the jigsaw that constituted the Western alliance. But the EC was and remained throughout the Cold War a 'civilian power', contained as well as supported by the Western alliance and subject to US security dominance, especially at the 'hard security' end of the spectrum. The security dominance of the USA extended also to the economics of military production and the development of defence industries.

The EU–US relationship in security was thus both intimate and uneven during the Cold War, and it can plausibly be argued that the trend lines of European and US strength within the relationship were far apart—in contrast to the relative and growing equality of the two parties in the economic sphere and the diversity at many levels of political organization and ideas. But here too the end of the Cold War, combined with the development of new EU capacities, raised fundamental questions. How far might and should the EU aim to duplicate, complement, or even supplement the USA in European security issues and in the broader security debate within the global arena? How far was the notion of 'civilian power' in the European project simply a reflection and rationalization of subordination and containment by the USA, and how far might that rationalization be challenged as the Cold War structures themselves were challenged? Did the EU—or could it ever—represent an alternative model of security politics as well as a possible alternative economic or political model for the organization of the post-Cold War world?

It is not surprising that the development of EU–US relations has been accompanied by debate, controversy, and the proposal of different, often strongly conflicting, models of the way the relationship could or should develop. As the European integration process gained momentum and spread into areas of foreign policy cooperation during the 1970s and 1980s, speculation about the future of the relationship became a focus of policy debate among political and economic elites on both sides of the Atlantic (Smith 1984). The end of the Cold War posed new challenges and opportunities for the economic, political, and security domains, and in many cases linked them together in new and potent ways. It affected both the composition and the conduct of the relationship, which for the purposes of this chapter raises important questions about how we interpret the transatlantic alliance and the EU's position within it:

- If we conceive of the EU as itself being a system of international relations, how exactly does this system relate to the presence of the USA, to its dominance of key areas of policy development and to the inevitable collision between the EU and the US systems of policy making and policy coordination?

- If we analyse the EU as part of the wider process of international relations, how do we factor in the ways in which the EU and the USA interact, the changes that have occurred in these interactions, and the balance sheet of advantage and disadvantage of the economic, political, and security domains?

- Finally, if we conceive of the EU as a power in international relations, how exactly does this power relate to the USA and to US power in the 21st century, and how can this relationship help us to understand key questions and disputes over the establishment of international order, both in the global political economy and in the global security arena?

EU–US relations and the EU's system of international relations

In earlier chapters, this book has presented the EU's international relations in part as expressing a system of international relations within the EU itself and in part as a subsystem of the broader international system. In other words, the EU's member states and institutions comprise a complex and multilayered system within which national policies are adjusted, 'European' policy positions are developed and revised, and actions are produced in a number of coexisting and overlapping contexts. This has important consequences for the ways in which the EU enters into and conducts international relationships, and many of the chapters in this book bear witness to the ways in which this can be demonstrated. For the purposes of this chapter, the most important focus is upon the ways in which the EU–US relationship shows the operation of the intra-EU system of international relations and, by implication, also the ways in which the United States can enter into that system both as a contextual factor but also as, in some instances, a participant in the system itself.

The multilevel governance literature provides a logical analytical starting point for a discussion about the complex relationships between EU member states, European institutions, and the USA. According to this literature the EU is characterized by shared authority and policy-making competencies across multiple levels of government—subnational, national, and supranational (see also Marks *et al.* 1996). This has important effects on EU external policies, and it is not surprising that the 'US factor' inevitably enters into the many different levels at which EU policies are made (Pollack and Shaffer 2001). In the first instance, there are formal diplomatic relations between the EU and the USA, especially via the Commission in the field of external economic policies. The member states also retain important economic relations with the USA, and in a number of areas these national interests and policies are at least as significant as those determined collectively. This is especially true in monetary and investment policy, which differs greatly depending on membership or non-membership of the eurozone. The coexisting and overlapping policy arenas allow the US administration, US state governments, and private companies to intervene in many different areas. Many large US companies are so long established in the EU that they are effectively 'European' in terms of their interests and their ability to exert pressure. This means that in terms of international economic relations, the USA can be seen almost as a direct participant in the EU's multilevel system (McGuire and Smith 2008, Chapter 2).

Interestingly, the USA too can be seen less and less as a unitary state, and more as a multilevel system of economic policy making, even if it has the federal structure that the EU still lacks. It is thus important to highlight the shared competencies between separate national as well as state institutions in US foreign policy making (Smith 1998a; Peterson and O'Toole 2001), which will not necessarily always agree among themselves about the positions to be adopted in relation to the EU. 'Cooperative federalism', in which powers and competencies are shared and treated as shared between levels, is another way of characterizing the US decision-making structure (Nicolaïdis and Howse 2001). Shared authority affects the capacity of the USA to exercise international relations, because as Peterson and O'Toole (2001, 300) argue, 'federalism usually gives rise to less formal intricate structures within which a large number of actors, each wielding a small slice of power, interact'. It is not clear how and to what extent this enables the EU collectively or through its many possible agents to intervene in US domestic economic and political processes, but it is clear that there are important respects in which the changing nature of the global political economy has led to a convergence of state forms on the two sides of the Atlantic.

Many scholars have begun to focus on multiple actors and multiple levels of influence within international relations theory more generally (see Putnam 1988; Risse-Kappen 1995; Milner 1997). The idea that domestic and international politics are not separable, and that domestic agents—be they political institutions, domestic groups, state or non-state actors—influence international negotiations, is uniting a number of emerging IR theories. In this respect, the overlapping and interpenetrating external relations systems of the EU and the USA can be seen as a key example of growing trends in the international arena as a whole. But it is clear that the most concrete examples of this phenomenon can be found in the area of political economy—dealing with the choices made and the positions adopted by the EU and the USA in respect of welfare and a widening range of social issues (M. Smith 2009a).

What happens when we look at the EU's system of international relations in the more political and security-related domains? Here we have to consider the notions that statehood and strategic action by major players still shape a large number of international patterns, including those in which the EU and the USA are increasingly engaged as part of the global security system. The relationships between the EU and its member states are very different in political and security concerns from those that have developed in the political/economic domain, as is the capacity of the USA to intervene and to exert influence in the system. More specifically, the US ability to incite defection from common EU positions, to develop 'special relationships' with member states, and to undermine the solidarity of the EU is greatly increased. This need not be a matter of conscious or explicit US policies; it can simply be a reflection of the different incentives and natural political leanings shaping the policies of the member states, as well as an indication of the more intergovernmental nature of the EU's institutional setup in the areas of CFSP and European security and defence policy (ESDP, now CSDP after the Lisbon Treaty) (Hyde-Price 2007).

There are thus effectively two parallel narratives of the EU–US relationship when we examine the EU's system of international relations (McGuire and Smith 2008, Chapter 2). On the one hand there is the political economy narrative, which stresses the ways in which the EU has developed a powerful set of institutions and resources that can be used to undertake collective action in a range of contexts. These contexts are often 'domestic' as well as 'international': thus EU–US interaction occurs via many agents at a range of levels, from the global (for example, in the World Trade Organization (WTO)) through the European and then the national to the sub-national and the local. In the political-security domain, however, the narrative is very different. Although in many respects the EU's CFSP and ESDP have been developed because of the USA—as a means of filling the gaps in US policies, or responding to the challenges of successive US administrations, especially during the 1990s and 2000s—they are also severely constrained by the dominance if not hegemony of the 'only superpower' when the questions are those of crisis and conflict, and of the commitment of real resources to the conduct of war or near-war operations. The incentives for EU member states to act collectively are very different in the two areas, with the balance between solidarity and defection or abstention only shifting slowly in the political and security area towards the 'European' level.

Examples of this contrast have been legion since the end of the Cold War, with the most important of them emerging from the 'war on terror' and the invasion of Iraq (see also Chapters 9 and 10). Whereas in both of these cases the EU could maintain solidarity in the economic sphere, with the imposition of sanctions or the implementation of reconstruction programmes, the EU's system of international relations became subject to strains if not to disintegration as soon as the issues became those of 'hard security'. The collapse of European solidarity at the height of the Iraq crisis, leading to the stand-off between 'old' and 'new' Europe and to intense frictions between Britain and France in particular, seemed to indicate that whenever the USA placed intense demands on the EU's foreign policy system there would be the likelihood of disintegration rather than a great leap forward in cooperation (Peterson and Pollack 2003; McGuire and Smith 2008, Chapters 8 and 9).

But this is not the whole story: one of the other strands of development during the 1990s and beyond has been the growing scope of areas of 'soft security' and security activity engaging the 'internal' mechanisms of both the EU and the USA (see also Chapter 10 in this volume). This picture highlights very different results from the story of EU–US security cooperation and competition. The EU's system in such areas as justice and home affairs, or environmental protection, or civil administration in the aftermath of conflict, possesses far greater resources for interaction with the USA. Indeed, some have argued that in these areas the EU has a comparative advantage over the USA bestowed by the enduring traces of 'civilian power'.

What implications does this system of shared competency, of penetrated decision-making, and of competing 'languages' of international relations carry for EU collective action? First, it is clear that the overlapping decision-making competency between the internal and external spheres of politics complicates the process of collective action. It is still difficult to gauge 'who speaks for Europe' (Allen 1998; Meunier and Nicolaïdis 1999; Meunier 2000b). Although the Commission is able to exercise strategic authority in some areas of policy making, it is clear that institutional deficits and the lack of a single EU negotiating authority mean that the EU often suffers from a 'capabilities-expectations gap' (see Hill 1993a, 1998a) (and even a simple 'capabilities' gap because there are just no instruments available), particularly in the foreign and security policy area. This gap has been visible even during many EU–US economic policy crises including those surrounding the Blair House agreement in the course of the Uruguay round (1992), the failed new transatlantic marketplace agreement negotiations (1997–8) and most EU–US trade disputes (Peterson 1996; Pollack and Shaffer 2001; Petersmann and Pollack 2003). As noted above, it is starkly apparent in areas where the issues are those of 'high politics' and 'hard security', where the stakes are different if not higher and where the USA's decisional capacity and institutional strength act as a competitive advantage. These 'gaps' in EU capacities for collective action are likely to be severely tested by EU–US relations, given the range and intensity of the encounters and their significance for 'internal' parties as well as the broader world arena (Smith 2004b, 2006).

While the USA has repeatedly expressed frustration with the EU's inability to reach decisions and thus provide real burden sharing in the hard security area, it has also made strategic attempts to use European disintegration to its advantage in other areas of foreign policy. This mixed view of European integration has led the USA to play an unintentional role as a 'regulator' of European integration (Peterson and Steffenson 2009). In their efforts to solicit internal security cooperation in tracking transnational terrorist cells, US negotiators have attempted to leverage special relationships with not only the UK but also with several newly admitted Eastern European member states. Transatlantic negotiations over passenger name records, visa waivers, money laundering, and mutual legal assistance have exposed divisions between old and new member states, prompting an invitation to the Commission to explore the possibilities of further European integration in these areas of judicial and police cooperation. Thus, US efforts to divide and rule may have inadvertently motivated the member states to close policy gaps in pillar three.

The Lisbon Treaty represented a much more significant attempt to close capability gaps and to establish a single European voice in external and internal security. When the implementation of Lisbon began in 2010 after a long and tortuous ratification battle, the debate both within Europe and across the Atlantic turned to the capacity of the new institutional structures to deliver common positions and deliver clear lines of external communication. Initially, at least, it appeared that the creation of new EU foreign policy positions exacerbated the problem of 'who speaks for Europe?' First, the decision to establish an EU President and a new High Representative for Foreign Affairs without eliminating the rotating Council Presidency and the External Trade Commissioner created additional new foreign policy voices in the EU and ambiguity regarding how the foreign policy agenda would be set. Second, even before the treaty granted it new foreign policy powers, the European Parliament had begun to exercise a louder voice in EU–US relations. One issue that repeatedly struck a chord with MEPs was the need to ensure EU data privacy rules were upheld in US attempts to negotiate counter-terrorism information-sharing initiatives between the USA and the EU. In early 2010 the European Parliament refused to give its consent to the interim agreement on banking data transfers (known as the SWIFT agreement) signed by the USA and the Council. The capacity of the European Parliament legally to make void the Council agreement exacerbated tensions with the USA; the lack of decisive legal authority in EU–US negotiations had already been established when the European Parliament initiated a European Court of Justice decision to overturn the 2004 Passenger Name Record agreement on the grounds that agreements should have been negotiated by the Council and not the Commission. This evidence of institutional contestation within the EU over matters of EU–US relations could be seen as a significant modification of the EU system.

EU–US relations and the processes of international relations

It will be evident from the argument so far that the transatlantic relationship is central to the broader processes of international relations. Despite the growing challenges from China, India, and others such as Brazil (see Chapter 16), the EU and the USA are the two dominant actors in the capitalist world economy. They are central to the institutions of the global system, and they contain many of the most powerful military powers, including the dominant military power in the post-Cold War world. Thus, the development of transatlantic relations themselves is of great importance to the process of world politics, and their engagement with the wider world is highly significant to the operation of a host of broader economic, political, and security processes. A number of key analytical dimensions connect EU–US relations and the processes of international relations.

First, it is important to look at the nature of the transatlantic relationship itself. Not all European–US relations are centred on the EU, and the persistence and evolution of NATO in particular means that the EU–US relationship is part of a 'multi-institutional' transatlantic system (Sloan 2002). Nonetheless, the EU–US relationship has been consistently at the core of this system, and has arguably become more central and more dominant as the EU has developed its foreign and security policies. During the 1990s, there was a consistent effort on both sides of the Atlantic to institutionalize EU–US relations and to provide a framework of rules and procedures, which would make them easier to manage (Pollack and Shaffer 2001; Steffenson 2005; Peterson and Steffenson 2009). At the outset came the Transatlantic Declaration (TAD) in 1990, which established some broad principles of organization. This was followed in 1995 by the New Transatlantic Agenda (NTA), which greatly expanded not only the scope of the arrangement but also included more detailed areas of joint action between the EU and the USA, and in 1998 by the Transatlantic Economic Partnership (TEP), which focused more specifically on the achievement of mutual recognition agreements and other technical agreements dealing with the management of trade and competition. One of the most significant outcomes of these transatlantic agreements was the establishment of an institutional structure to manage bilateral transatlantic relations, including an EU–US summit plus a host of transgovernmental dialogues designed to bring together a much larger range of foreign policy actors from the USA, the Commission, and the Council. As Figure 17.1 shows, the 'intergovernmental' and 'transgovernmental' arrangements were accompanied by efforts to construct non-governmental transatlantic dialogues and networks between business, environment, consumer, and labour groups (Pollack and Shaffer 2001; Steffenson 2005).

One implication of shared competency at different levels of decision-making is that it gives rise to 'intense transgovernmentalism' (see Wallace and Wallace 2000). The intra-EU process of decision-making is reflected in the way the EU forms relations with external partners, and there is no more convincing demonstration of this than in transatlantic relations. The EU–US process of institutionalization has created a dense structure of decision-making processes that mirror in many respects the competencies of the EU. For example, the TAD, the NTA, and the TEP have established three branches of governmental dialogue to accommodate the different competencies of EU external negotiators (Pollack and Shaffer 2001; Steffenson 2005). There is also a dense network of economic and political working groups, such as the NTA task force and the TEP working groups (see Figure 17.1). The TEP was revitalized and refocused during 2007, as the result of an initiative by the German EU Presidency, and a Transatlantic Economic Council was established consisting of high officials from both sides of the relationship. The creation of the TEC as well as other high-level issue-specific dialogues, such as the one established to

FIGURE 17.1 Transatlantic institutions (selected)

TAD, NTA, TEP Institutions	EU-US Summit, Ministerial Meetings, Troika Working Groups, Senior Level Group, NTA Task Force, TEP Steering Group, TEP Working Groups, The Transatlantic Legislators Dialogue
High Level Political Dialogues	Transatlantic Economic Council
	Policy Dialogue on Border and Transport Security, Dialogue on Climate Change, High Level Regulatory Cooperation Forum
Expert Level Regulatory Dialogues	Financial Markets Regulatory Dialogue, Insurance Dialogue, Task Force on Biotechnology Research, Dialogue on Innovation Exchange
Expert Level 'Global Challenges' Dialogues	Dialogue on Terrorist Financing, FBI-Europol Exchange Judicial Cooperation and Joint Investigation Teams, Transatlantic Development Dialogue, Dialogue on Customs Cooperation
People to People Dialogues	The Transatlantic Legislators Dialogue, The Transatlantic Business Dialogue, The Transatlantic Consumer Dialogue, The Transatlantic Higher Education Dialogue

manage EU–US interactions on climate change, was intended to increase the political weight behind transatlantic discussions. A range of complementary regulatory dialogues was created to include US regulatory agencies in discussions on transatlantic market-opening strategies. In this way, it could be argued that the EU–US relationship in political economy was 'deepening', with potentially far-reaching implications for the broader process of global governance and regulation. At the same time, however, the emergence of new economic powers challenged the 'privileged partnership' of the EU and the USA in new ways (Smith 2009a), and the intensification of 'competitive interdependence' in the global political economy was seen as creating new areas of EU–US rivalry (Sbragia 2010).

Transgovernmental networks are also prominent in the security relationship. However, the trajectory of development and the broader institutional context in this area are very different in some respects, which again raises questions about the extent to which the security domain, with its distinctive set of EU–US relations, power distribution, and external challenges, can be governed, especially through joint processes in which the EU and the USA act as relative equals. While a number of new political dialogues have emerged to facilitate EU–US counter-terrorism cooperation, decentralized internal security coordination on both sides of the

Atlantic has inhibited effective information sharing. Institutional reorganization after 11 September 11 2001 consolidated many US internal security agencies under the new US Department of Homeland Security, which in turn required adjustments to the membership of transatlantic institutions such as the political dialogue on border and transport security (see Pawlak 2007). The EU also sought to increase coordination between the member states, despite lacking the power to consolidate internal security agencies, through the creation of an EU Counter Terrorism Coordinator and Europol's Counter-Terrorist task force. However, these institutions have limited capacity to overcome barriers to information sharing stemming from distrust within and between the member states' decentralized law enforcement agencies (see Chapter 10).

The institutional changes introduced by the Lisbon Treaty became a wider source of uncertainty and confusion in transatlantic relations. In 2010 a diplomatic row broke out after the Spanish Prime Minister Zapatero learned via media reports that Obama was not planning on attending the spring EU–US summit, which would have been held in Madrid because it fell during the six-month Spanish Presidency. This revelation was widely reported in the media as a snub to the EU, especially after Obama's advisors were quoted as saying that the President had not found the previous summit meetings useful and that the creation of new European foreign policy actors had created confusion about the role of the new Lisbon institutions in Europe's foreign policy structure.

Beyond the transatlantic arena, the post-Cold War period has clearly introduced new dimensions into the processes of international relations. In a number of areas the EU and the USA often find themselves working in competition, rather than in some kind of strategic partnership. Take, for example, policies towards developing countries, where the EU has developed a wide-ranging and highly institutionalized set of relationships with the African, Caribbean, and Pacific countries (ACP), as detailed in Chapter 14, and where as a result there is a tendency—not least within the EU itself—to see the Union as a 'development superpower' with an advantage over the USA. With regard to global environmental management, the EU has at times acted as the leader of a broad coalition in the face of US intransigence and refusal to ratify major instruments such as the Kyoto Protocol (Bodansky 2003; see also Chapter 15).

The unpopular, often unilateral, policies of the Bush administration presented an opportunity for the EU to exercise its soft power, allowing it to engage other partners such as China and Russia in fighting transnational challenges. This trend continued after the 2008–9 global financial crisis when Obama faced a hostile EU, China, and Russia at the G20 meetings. The EU, led by France and Germany with the noted absence of UK solidarity, was joined by China and Russia in calls for a new global financial regulatory system. The USA shied away from the idea of any such system, focusing instead on the need for a strategy that would limit the role of the EU due to its lack of fiscal federalism. Significantly, however, when crisis erupted within the eurozone during early 2010 because of the problems of the Greek economy, the USA was prominent in proposing international solutions involving the IMF and other financial institutions but also major injections of liquidity through the European Central Bank.

The EU's ability to exercise leadership in the soft power arena was called into question again after the UN climate change meeting hosted in Copenhagen in December 2009. The Obama administration managed to intervene decisively at the end of the conference and upset Europe's plans for a new binding global climate change treaty when the President convinced the BASIC countries (Brazil, South Africa, India, and China) to agree to his alternative plan for a non-binding Copenhagen Accord. To add insult to injury, the European leaders felt compelled to endorse the agreement, despite their open irritation with Obama's diplomatic coup, even though it did not come close to their outlined targets. In this case the EU was left looking like a junior partner; this suggests that whilst in this and other areas of 'soft security', EU–US competition is conducted on changing terms, with the EU's strategic assets becoming increasingly visible and important, it is open to question how far the EU can mobilize those assets in any given negotiation, especially in the new international constellation of emerging powers.

Nonetheless, the terms of engagement change again, often dramatically, when the focus turns to 'hard security'. Here, in relation to the process of international relations, the EU has much less leverage. Some would argue, indeed, that US dominance in this field allows the EU to evade responsibility for international security processes, leaving it free to focus on those areas where its assets count (Kagan 2002, 2003). Bush's inability to rally the Europeans to donate more troops to Afghanistan after the dispute over Iraq was not a unique problem; getting the Europeans to contribute continued to be a source of tension for the Obama administration. In February 2010, US Secretary of Defense Robert Gates warned the Europeans that NATO's budgetary crisis was a matter of 'life or death'. He acknowledged the unprecedented level of burden sharing in Afghanistan but noted that the security organization would face long-term systemic threats if European allies failed to heavily invest in their defence budgets. When it comes to the management of international conflicts, the past decade has made it abundantly clear that the EU is unlikely to act collectively or to exercise influence when the stakes are high. Whilst the EU might be seen as the kinder, softer partner, it is not seen as a real player in many areas of 'hard security' and conflict management.

This conclusion seems to be borne out by the historical record. In successive conflicts during the 1990s, the Europeans passed up various opportunities to contribute collectively to conflict management. For example, many Americans felt, particularly in the early stages, that the conflict in former Yugoslavia was an opportunity for Europe to exercise its common foreign policy. In the end successive failures of EU collective action led the USA, with support from NATO allies and varying degrees of legitimation from the United Nations, to take decisive action (Zucconi 1996; Peterson 2003). Likewise the successive US engagements in the Gulf, leading eventually to the Iraq conflict of 2003, saw the EU left on the sidelines and hardly involved in either the military action or the post-war reconstruction and stabilization. Former NATO Secretary General Lord Robertson made repeated comments at the time blaming the EU member states for reinforcing a culture in which 'Americans fight wars and Europeans do the dishes' (Black 2002; see also Peterson 2003).

Despite their shortcomings, it can be argued that the EU's attempts to participate in international security processes are not completely ineffective. For example, Brussels is well equipped to deal with post-conflict management. The EU has led reconstruction efforts in the Balkans with the EUFOR (European Union Force) mission in Bosnia and the EULEX (European Union rule of law) mission in Kosovo. In both instances Europe demonstrated its capacity as a regional security actor through its nation-building activities and its willingness to dangle EU membership as a carrot to Serbia. The EU has played an important part in the post-conflict reconstruction of Afghanistan, and indeed there is a sense that the EU is the only actor that could do so.

There has also been significant—and increasingly EU-centred—engagement with conflicts beyond the European continent independent of the USA (see also Chapter 9). The EU peacekeeping mission in Chad and the Central African Republic form one example where the member states have been able to take advantage of historical links with local parties. The EU's commitment to provide security and humanitarian assistance, with UN approval, to nations coping with refugees spilling out of the Darfur region in Sudan demonstrated its growing legitimacy if not its capabilities as a security actor. Its legitimacy via the USA in the international system made it the only actor capable of exercising quick diplomacy when fighting broke out between Russia and Georgia in 2008. Whilst the USA was quick to condemn Russia from afar, demand the withdrawal of its forces from the region, and quickly move to publicly support Georgia's application for NATO membership, EU negotiators quickly flew to the region to broker a peace deal. Russia allowed EU observers into the region, and coincidentally announced that they would provide air support for the EU mission in Chad. The EU presence failed to eliminate hostilities in either of these conflicts, but these cases do demonstrate that the EU has an important role to play in international security. As with all external policy areas, the size of its role is predetermined by the commitment of its member states to act collectively (see Chapter 9); and the Georgia example, which showed elements of competition between the French Presidency of the EU, acting on its own behalf, and other EU institutions, shows both the advantages and the limitations of the EU's processes.

One way in which the EU can be seen as offering a different perspective on the process of international relations is through the exercise of its normative influence, which has led some to argue that the EU embodies a normative or 'civilizing' process in the broader world arena (Manners 2002; Sjursen 2007; Whitman 2010—see also Chapter 18). Many of the EU's most important disputes with the USA reflect underlying value differences—for example, the conception of risk as it relates to the precautionary principle, environmental burden sharing and consumer protection with regard to data privacy and food safety (for further examples in the trade and environment fields see Meunier and Nicolaïdis, Chapter 12; see also Chapter 15 in this volume). There are also varying views among the member states on issues of neutrality and security (focused partly on the EU's internal security policy developments but also on external policies such as those towards the Middle East and the successive US plans for a missile defence system). In a number of areas this translates into quite profound differences about the power of 'critical dialogue' or the comparative merits of sanctions, force, and diplomacy (Lindstrom 2003b, Chapters 1 and 2). For instance, in approaching the problem of relations with 'rogue states' or the so-called 'axis of evil', the EU has shown a consistent tendency to emphasize the merits of critical dialogue in contrast to the US focus on more coercive measures including ultimately the threat of force. More generally, it can be argued that the EU places more emphasis on ideas and processes of conflict prevention in international relations rather than coercion or even pre-emption as preached and sometimes practised by the USA. Iran would be an important case here—initial EU3 efforts seemed to establish a distinct role, but as tensions rose the EU was squeezed to the margins.

Furthermore, the EU's efforts to pursue international, regional, and bilateral cooperation are strongly shaped by ideas about 'best practice' within the EU (McGuire and Smith 2008, Chapter 7). There is a conscious effort to export the model (or at least some of the key principles and structures) of European integration in developing regions such as Central and Eastern Europe and Latin America. The externalization of practices used within the common market also applies to the EU's relations with major trading partners. For example, in the case of the expanding network of mutual recognition agreements for a range of products and processes, it is often the EU, not the USA, that takes a lead in the negotiations. The contrast between the discourses of EU and US policies can be found in very powerful ways when it comes to handling inter-regional issues of human rights or environmental matters (see Alecu de Flers and Regelsberger 2005). As in the case of the areas mentioned earlier, it can be argued quite strongly here that the EU possesses and can exploit a form of comparative advantage in processes of international relations, many of which have become markedly more prominent in the post-Cold War world.

A further and related set of questions about the connections between EU–US relations and the broader international arena relates to the problem of global governance and the strengthening of multilateral institutions. To what extent does the EU shape the agenda of such international institutions, and how does that bring it into collision with the United States? To what extent has the EU developed a distinctive role and identity in areas where it interacts with the USA (that is to say, in almost all areas of its activity)?

What is clear is that the capacity of the EU to act is wide-ranging but often conditional. Thus, there are some international organizations within which the Commission can speak and negotiate on behalf of the EU's members, such as the WTO and a number of global environmental organizations, but there are others where the

EU's representation is mixed and its voice is less unified or consistent as a result. Although the Lisbon Treaty has endowed the EU with 'international personality' for the first time, it has clearly not done away with this mixed system of representation. This means that on the one hand there are organizations where the EU as a whole can take a key role in agenda setting, in negotiation, in coalition building, and other aspects of international institutional life, and there are others where in order to achieve EU solidarity there has to be a continuous process of internal coalition building and management. In addition, there is often some discursive confusion about not only who speaks for Europe but about whether there is any EU message, in terms of values or of expectations, to communicate. For example, in international monetary and financial institutions, there are effectively 'three EUs' for different purposes: the EU of 'Euroland' comprising the eurozone member states, the EU of 27 member states agreed on certain economic and financial positions, and the EU's member states as independent financial and monetary authorities with voices and votes of their own. This kind of divided 'voice' was especially evident in some phases of the 2008–9 financial crisis, which prompted an internal debate between eurozone and non-eurozone states over the need to close the internal gap through EU-wide regulation of financial services. Whilst the Lisbon Treaty addresses this problem of consistency in a number of areas, it is far from clear that it will eliminate them in the short term (see Chapters 4 and 5).

It is important in the context of international institutions to evaluate in more depth how the EU as opposed to the member states operates in international relations and to identify the ways in which this tension feeds into transatlantic relations. As we will argue in the following section, the EU is primarily a soft power and an economic power. This 'power inventory', including the power of ideas and values, can be mobilized, often in juxtaposition or in opposition to the USA, in a variety of arenas, but it remains less substantial and less wide-ranging than that even of an internally divided USA. During the late 1990s and 2000s, the range over which the EU can deploy this kind of resource to affect the process of international political economy has been significantly broadened with the introduction of the euro, but as noted above, at least in the initial stages, this was subject to a number of limitations arising not only from the incomplete membership of the eurozone but also from the imperfections of macroeconomic management within the zone (see also Chapter 11). Thus the impact of the euro on the expectations of the USA and other players and on the interactions between the EU and the USA in international forums has to date been uncertain and patchy, and this picture continues in groupings such as the G20 that have become more prominent during the financial crisis of 2008 and after. When it comes to the potential capacity of the EU to play a bigger role in the 'hard' part of the spectrum, as its own security policy (centred on the CSDP) develops, the story is even less clear. Still, there is already some evidence that the EU collectively has more of a capacity to make its voice heard on international security issues within international institutions. At times this has caused significant friction with the United States. Although the USA was initially annoyed by European security organization, which seems to parallel if not duplicate NATO's functions, it soon came to realize that the EU is unlikely to rival NATO at least in the short term. In the longer term, the increasing development and institutionalization of the CSDP and of the CFSP is likely to cut increasingly across US interests and make itself felt in organizations where the USA has traditionally had a commanding role (Sloan 2002; Lindstrom 2003b). Arguably, this would constitute an important modification not only of the process of EU–US relations, but also of broader international security governance.

There is a more general question about the ways in which we can characterize the EU's participation in international organizations. Do the member states have a higher capacity for collective action given their experience with European integration? Sbragia and Damro (1999) argue that the EU is able to adjust policies over time to international cooperation because the member states already have experience of working cooperatively. Nicolaïdis and Egan (2001) argue that in terms of regulatory cooperation—a policy area where the member states have a considerable level of integration—the EU has initiated the exporting of its policies in order to benefit from 'first mover advantage'. This means that in studying the EU as a contributor to international relations it is important to examine it as a model of governance. As the most advanced international organization, it has become both a target for anti-globalization groups and an archetype of governance, given its emphasis on the participation of civil society. It has also arguably become a major player in the 'management of globalization' both on its own account and in terms of its engagement with global institutions (Jacoby and Meunier 2010).The issue here is the extent to which these kinds of assets and trends bring the EU into collision with the USA, and the ways in which these encounters are managed. What impact does EU–US discord have on the process of international relations as a whole? One set of implications relates to the EU's developing international role and the fact that in many areas of activity its international initiatives inevitably and immediately run into the positions and actions of the USA. The EU has proceeded in part by trying to rival the USA, in part by trying to contain it, and in part by trying to create new foundations for EU–US cooperation (see for example Sbragia 2010). The development of the EU's international role, and thus its contribution to the processes of international relations in a wide range of arenas, has been driven to a significant degree by this ambivalent relationship with the USA and by the EU–US encounters to which it gives rise.

In the context of this role initiation and role development, it is important to remember that in many respects the US role in the post-Cold War era has also been conditioned by the existence and the widening impact of the EU. There is a sense in which the EU takes up important elements of burden sharing that the USA is either unwilling or unable to sustain, both within the global political economy and the diplomatic or security arenas. As can be seen from Box 17.3, in the area of counter-terrorism activity, the EU has been able to enter into a wide range of activities alongside the United States and in the context of a variety of international

BOX 17.3	Areas of EU–US cooperation on combating terrorism

- Support for United Nations conventions on terrorism.
- Financial action task force on terrorist financing.
- Work towards laws and regulations enabling asset freezing.
- Strengthening regulation of financial institutions.
- Increased law enforcement cooperation and intelligence.
- EU–US agreements on extradition and mutual legal assistance.
- Increased security of international transport: container security, passenger records.
- Promote development, democracy, and good governance.

organizations. It is arguable that in key areas the EU has a greater 'capacity to coop-erate' and to play constructive roles in newly developing international processes or institutions than does the USA. The EU has gained legitimacy in a variety of inter-national contexts, not only from its internal integration process but also from its representation of an increasingly distinctive 'European' position. One could draw the conclusion that the evolution of individual EU and US discourses and prac-tices has had significant restructuring effects on the broader world arena—in other words, that the EU has begun to establish itself as an independent and influen-tial force in the definition and development of global governance systems. Equally, one might conclude that the deepening of EU–US partnership in a number of fields might lay the foundations for a strengthening of a form of joint leadership in which they could act as the core of new international regimes. But one must never for-get the problems that arise for the EU in the 'hard' end of the spectrum, or from the increasing securitization of a range of issues since the turn of the millennium. Inexorably this point leads to the consideration of EU–US relations in the context of understandings about the EU as a 'power'.

EU–US relations and the EU as a power in international relations

The evolution of the EU as a 'power' in international relations has inevita-bly become a point of tension with the USA (Kagan 2002, 2003; Kupchan 2003; Gordon and Shapiro 2004). As pointed out many times in other chapters of this book, and in the preceding section of this chapter, the development of EU power resources and the processes by which they are mobilized and deployed has followed a distinctive path, conditioned by the fact that the EU is an organization that is ultimately founded on states. This accounts for the conditional grants of foreign policy power to the EU and for the ways in which the member states have retained their own distinct national preferences, positions, and resources. In other words, it explains the fact that in many respects, the EU continues to be a 'civilian power' in the international arena and that its influence is largely confined to those areas that fall outside the realm of hard security and high politics.

As noted above, this has important implications for the ways in which the EU and the USA interact, both in areas affecting the EU's system of international relations and in areas that relate more to the broader process of international relations. In this part of the chapter, the emphasis is rather different. Here the focus is on the ways in which the EU and the USA express apparently different types or 'mixes' of power, on the ways in which this enters into EU and US discourses, and on the ways in which this affects EU–US relations. The EU–US relationship encompasses a number of profound ambiguities emerging from the internal evolution of both parties and their shifting roles in the broader world arena.

Examining the EU as a power in international relations raises fresh analytical and empirical puzzles. A first problem, and one that led to intense debate on both sides of the Atlantic in the early 2000s, is the nature of power itself. Power is a major preoccupation of IR theory, and brings with it a huge accumulated baggage of ideas about resources and capabilities, about the combination and mobilization of power, and about the management of power both at the national level and at the level of world order. It is thus not surprising that the end of the Cold War launched an obsessive examination by scholars and policy makers of the new power situation, in which the United States seemed to have an almost unqualified dominance, especially in military affairs. An intense debate followed in the early 2000s around what came to be seen as two qualitatively different types of power, one US, one European.

Key to this debate was the idea that the EU was constructed around a predominantly 'soft' notion of power, focusing and rationalizing the Union's interests as a 'trading state' with key interests in the economic and social realms. By focusing on soft power, the EU could logically focus on ways to achieve both economic gains and key welfare objectives. More negatively, it was argued by some that the EU version of power was a rationalization of the Union's essential weakness and that it had been so since the beginnings of the European integration project. Some argued that EU leaders settled for a second-best version of power, built on its comparative advantages, because they could not hope to match the major military powers in matters of 'hard security'. In any case these judgements were not just empirical: they were also essentially moral, on the one hand identifying the Europeans as more likely to compromise with bad regimes and bad leaders than those who saw the real nature of the international power game, and on the other seeing them as eschewing militarism and aggression. A phrase often quoted in the early 2000s was, 'Americans are from Mars and Europeans are from Venus,' and there was no doubt for many US commentators where virtue lay when confronted with the 'axis of evil' and other threats to the new world order (see Kagan 2002, 2003; M. Smith 2004a).

By contrast, the logic of American power was seen as essentially rooted in the 'hard' end of the spectrum. It had resources and could address problems in a way that the Europeans simply could not envisage. During the 1990s, this disparity was most apparent in the capacity to intervene on a global scale. It was also made very apparent much closer to home for the EU, when the Union had to rely on the USA to inject a large number of troops and other matériel into the former Yugoslavia at short notice (Zucconi 1996). The key here, however, is not just what happened in practical policy terms, but also what effect this had on the expectations and understandings of policy makers on both sides of the Atlantic. Quite simply, the mindset of policy makers in the USA, especially but not only during the first George W. Bush administration of 2000–4, was one that accommodated the possibility and even the probability of the use of military power (including its unilateral use), whereas such options were effectively foreclosed at the collective EU level (M. Smith 2004a, 2009b). As explained earlier, this has had a significant effect on the ways in which major EU member states have perceived the incentives to operate at the EU level and has also conditioned their readiness to defect at crucial moments of crisis and conflict management.

How far does this power disparity extend, and how far are its effects felt in the area of non-military power? It is clear that the EU is still predominantly an economic power, and that it most legitimately rivals the USA in international economic arenas. The EU's economic position makes it a viable foreign policy actor, especially where the use of economic sanctions, aid, or other inducements is in question; it has also invested considerable effort in its capacity to act as a soft power in terms of aid and development assistance and to operate in arenas where institutions and regimes are still being formed, such as in the environmental domain. As a result, it is possible to argue that the EU can exert a growing amount of 'institutional power' through international regimes and organizations, and that its capacity to construct wide-ranging international coalitions on certain issues gives it influence comparable to if not more impressive than that of the USA. The EU is less able to establish collective preferences and understandings in the security field, but there is a sense in which the EU has inserted itself into an increasing range of situations as a diplomatic actor, and in which it might develop considerably greater capacity to supplant the USA either with US agreement or with US 'absence' (cf. the situation in the Balkans).

To what extent does the USA—in the shape of its political leaders and commentators or analysts—perceive the EU as a major power? There is a sense in which the answer to this question has remained constant since Henry Kissinger pronounced it as 'civilian' and 'regional' in the early 1970s. The EU is also increasingly seen (both by its member states and by outsiders) as a 'soft security actor', with a significant role in the European order and an increasing but often frustrating role in the broader diplomacy of world order. For example, the EU has functioned as a full contributing member of the so-called 'Quartet' group on the Middle East (with the USA, the UN, and Russia), helping to produce the 'road map' for an Israeli–Palestinian peace settlement that was published in 2003—but the Quartet's diplomatic success has been distinctly limited . The creation of the High Representative for Common Foreign and Security Policy—the post first held by Javier Solana, and then developed into a key institutional aspect of 'European foreign policy' by the Lisbon Treaty—means that the EU is equipped to play a more significant role in international diplomacy (see Chapter 4). A key question, though, is whether other key actors perceive the EU as a persuasive voice in international affairs. The EU has established a role in Afghanistan that might be seen as parallel to that assumed in the later stages of the Balkans conflicts, but do diplomatic and reconstructive functions give the EU equivalent status to that enjoyed by the USA? Equally, the EU has a well-established role in the G7/G8 groups of leading industrial countries, but it is not clear whether this has reinforced or weakened the perception of the Union as a key player in Washington or indeed in the capitals of some member states who are also G7/G8 members. As noted above, the effective replacement of the G7/8 by the G20 in 2009–10 created new questions about the extent to which the EU collectively could be seen as a leading member.

This raises major questions about the EU's role in the broader international arena. Firstly, can the EU be plausibly seen as an alternative player to the USA for diplomatic or even security purposes in situations of regional or local conflict? This possibility has at least been raised by the EU's actions in a number of conflicts, for example in sub-Saharan Africa, during the early years of the new century. Or, secondly, should the EU be seen as a balancing force for the USA in a variety of institutional and other contexts, providing the 'soft cop' to balance the USA's 'hard cop'? Take for example the case of Iran's nuclear policies (see Box 17.4 and Everts 2004). This case seems to indicate that there was at least initially a tacit division of labour between the EU (especially three of its leading members) and the USA in trying to handle and to defuse the possibility of Iran obtaining nuclear capacity. Whilst this one episode cannot be seen as typical, it is important at least to raise the possibility that the EU and the USA could be more complementary than competitive in their uses of international power (Moravcsik 2003).

More likely is the third possibility apparent under George W. Bush's administration: that the EU would be ignored, and even 'disaggregated' either as the result of deliberate US policies or as the result of the inevitable tensions between different positions within the EU, for example on Iraq (Howorth 2003; Lindstrom 2003b; M. Smith 2004b). In this case, the distinction notoriously made by Secretary of Defense Donald Rumsfeld between 'old Europe' (France, Germany, and their supporters) and 'new Europe' (the UK, Spain, and many of the newly acceding states from Central and Eastern Europe) was intended to convey US opposition to apparent European feebleness, but also to detach some of the more significant prospective new member states such as Poland.

It is apparent that the EU has faced, is facing, and will always face a problem with the management of US power. It might also be argued that the USA has a growing

---

BOX 17.4   The EU, the USA, and Iran's nuclear programmes

During 2003–4, differences surfaced between the EU member states and the USA over how to handle nuclear weapons programmes in Iran. These tensions reflected a long-standing divergence of approaches, with the Europeans having emphasized the value of 'critical dialogue' with Tehran and the Americans having adopted a strategy based on containment or even 'rollback', Iran being one of the members of the so-called 'axis of evil'. The problem was also underlined by the transatlantic disagreements that had emerged during the build-up to and the conduct of the US-led attack on Iraq in 2003. In the case of Iran, however, there was a united EU position in favour of diplomacy and a multilateral solution; the UK, which had been the most loyal and substantial of the USA's allies in the Iraq action, pursued a strongly 'Europeanized' line on Iran, and played a leading role through what became known as the 'EU3' group along with France and Germany. Having secured Iranian agreement to adhere to the Nuclear Non-Proliferation Treaty during 2003, the EU3 (supported by Russia) then decided to offer Iran incentives to suspend its work with enriched uranium, and to multilateralize the process through the involvement of the International Atomic Energy Agency in monitoring and surveillance. However, the Bush administration did not endorse the package and explicitly canvassed the possibility of coercive sanctions or even a pre-emptive attack on Iran's nuclear facilities. The victory of George W. Bush in the US Presidential election of November 2004 created further tensions between the EU focus on 'soft power' and multilateral solutions, and the US emphasis on 'hard power' and the possibility of force. The EU's preference for using multilateral channels coupled by internal divisions among European foreign policy actors seemed unlikely to lead to EU–US convergence over Iran even after Obama took office. During his campaign, Obama had stressed the importance of abandoning the Bush administration's policy of isolation in favour of diplomatic engagement with states such as Iran. In early 2010, however, the EU and the USA were still divided on how to approach Tehran after Iran publicly defied the international community with a series of weapons tests. After months of going back and forth over the need for diplomacy through the UN, it was announced in March that consensus had been reached on the need for a new UN-led action. After an EU Council meeting in Helsinki, the Finnish Foreign Minister announced that the EU would back the USA and impose unilateral sanctions if Russia or China vetoed the proposed UN sanctions programme.

---

problem with the management of the EU's power and that both of these facets will profoundly affect the EU's developing international relations. The USA is clearly a major factor in the uneven development of the EU's own international power position, both structurally and as the result of successive policies emanating from Washington. The United States is also, as noted earlier, present in the EU itself, both as the result of the US stake in Europe and as the reflection of the place Washington and its power occupy in the minds of European political leaders and officials.

In consequence, when discussion turns to the 'capability-expectations gap' in EU policies (Hill 1993a, 1998a), Washington is both a major incentive for the gap to be closed and a major reason why in certain areas it may never be closed. This does not mean that the EU is not a 'power' in the international arena, but rather that its status has been, and most likely will continue to be, embedded in a US-dominated Western or global order. The President of the European Commission, José Manuel Barroso, during his first confirmation hearings in July 2004, felt the need to make two apparently conflicting points during his testimony. On the one hand, he attacked the arrogance of the USA and called for a more equal relationship between Brussels and Washington; on the other hand, he was at pains to emphasize his 'Atlanticist' credentials, his support for the US attack on Iraq and his commitment to support US policies in the 'war on terror'. To a greater or lesser degree, all EU leaders have had to reconcile these components in the attempt to pursue the EU's international role after 11 September 2001, and not just with respect to the Bush administration; with the accession of the Obama administration in January 2009, the Commission and a series of national leaders in the EU were concerned both to emphasize the EU's status as a key partner for the USA and to stress to varying degrees their separateness from the USA on key issues.

The USA has also given EU institutional actors a mixed reception in the foreign policy arena. In addition to confusing the established channels of transatlantic diplomacy, the election of Herman van Rompuy as the first EU President was met with disappointment in the USA by those who would have preferred to see a pro-US foreign policy personality such as former British Prime Minister Tony Blair take up the post. Similar criticisms surrounded both the creation of the High Representative post and its initial occupation by former Commissioner Catherine Ashton. The perceived 'failure' on the part of the EU to fill these posts with political heavyweights reflected Washington's ongoing struggle to understand the internal dynamics of the EU; from an 'internal' EU perspective, these choices could be seen as a delicate step towards further integration through quiet diplomacy inside the EU, because neither van Rompuy nor Ashton ran the risk of directly overshadowing the foreign ministers of the member states.

Additional uncertainty exists in the USA over the capacity of the Lisbon Treaty to transform the EU into a rival power. The controversy surrounding the ambiguity of the new foreign policy posts led some such as political scientist Stephen Walt to argue not only that Obama was right to absent himself from the 2010 EU–US summit in Spain but that he should also scale back on European commitments more generally; often, this kind of argument was coupled with the view that US policy should focus much more on China and other emerging powers than on the EU (see Chapter 16). Others in Washington feared that the Lisbon Treaty constituted a dramatic step taken by the European elites towards achieving their goal of a European superstate, which would rival the USA even in terms of hard power. Reports such as those made to Congress by Heritage Foundation analyst Sally McNamara did little to acknowledge what a small step the introduction of majority voting rules in the CFSP pillar was in relation to the wider capabilities gap that would need to be closed in order for Europe realistically to assume that role (Walt 2010; McNamara 2009).

Conclusion

This chapter has explored four key topics: the evolution of EU–US relations, the ways in which EU–US relations enter into the EU's system of international relations, the impact of EU–US relations on the EU's role in the process of international relations, and the ways in which the EU–US relationship feeds into the part played by the EU as an international 'power'. The key findings are as follows:

- The developing EU–US relationship has been a key force in shaping the development of the EU's international relations, but it is a force full of contradictions.

- In many respects, the USA (both as a governmental and a private actor) is 'present' in the EU's system of international relations, and the EU–US relationship has played a key (and contradictory) role in development of the EU's foreign policy mechanisms.

- The EU–US relationship has been crucial in conditioning the development of the EU's participation in international processes, and it will continue to be a key factor shaping the EU's role in many international contexts, including key global institutions. In this way also, it is a key element in the search for a new international order to reflect the emergence not only of a 'new' EU but also of other new economic and political forces.

- As a result of the factors mentioned above, the EU's role as a 'power' in international relations must be seen at least partly in the light of its relationship with the USA. This is so not only because of the dominant American position in a number of areas of international life, but also because of the way in which the USA enters into the expectations and understandings of those making policies within the EU as well as their key international partners. To put it directly, the fate of the EU as a 'power' is directly related to its success in constructing an effective partnership with the USA.

The overall conclusion from this discussion is necessarily nuanced and reflects a number of contradictory lines of development. In terms of international relations theory, it is clear that any analysis of EU–US relations raises major questions about 'power and interdependence' and the extent to which different worlds of international relations can coexist. EU–US relations also generate and crystallize key questions about the role of institutions in world politics and the ways in which they can be seen as sources of legitimacy as well as sources of information, support, and influence. More specifically, they also raise in a highly concentrated form questions about the possibilities and limits of collective action in international relations, both at the EU and at the global level. The EU and the USA exist in conditions of intense yet uneven integration, within an international context full of uncertainty, and dealing with its most 'significant other' will remain a dominating item on the EU's international agenda.

 FURTHER READING

There is a vast literature on the general area of transatlantic relations, which has been a key focus of scholarship and debate since the 1940s. The list below gives a sample of the more recent commentaries and of the literature relating EU–US relations to broader problems of international relations. Peterson (1996), Guay (1999), and McGuire and Smith (2008) provide historical reviews as well as dealing with contemporary policy issues; each of them also links EU–US relations to issues of international relations analysis. The more specific debates about the end of the Cold War, the conflicts of the 1990s and the tensions over Iraq are dealt with by Gordon and Shapiro (2004), Kagan (2003), Lundestad (2008), Peterson and Pollack (2003), Sloan (2002), and Smith and Woolcock (1993). Issues of political economy are covered by the general texts cited above and by Pollack and Shaffer (2001). The possible futures of EU–US relations are covered by many of the texts and specifically by Moravcsik (2003).

Gordon, P., and Shapiro, J. (2004), *Allies at War: America, Europe, and The Crisis Over Iraq* (Washington DC: Brookings Institution).

Guay, T. (1999), *The United States and the European Union: The Political Economy of a Relationship* (Sheffield: Sheffield Academic Press).

Kagan, R. (2003), *Paradise and Power: America and Europe in the New World Order* (London: Atlantic Books).

Lundestad, G. (ed.) (2008), *Just Another Major Crisis? The United States and Europe since 2000* (Oxford: Oxford University Press).

McGuire, S., and Smith, M. (2008), *The European Union and the United States: Competition and Convergence in the Global Arena* (Basingstoke: Palgrave/Macmillan).

Moravcsik, A. (2003), 'Striking a New Transatlantic Bargain', *Foreign Affairs*, 82/4, 74–89.

Peterson, J. (1996), *Europe and America: the Prospects for Partnership*, 2nd edition (London: Routledge).

Peterson, J., and Pollack, M. (eds) (2003), *Europe, America, Bush: Transatlantic Relations in the Twenty-First Century* (London: Routledge).

Peterson, J., and Steffenson, R. (2009), 'Transatlantic Institutions: Can Partnership Be Engineered?', *British Journal of Politics and International Relations*, vol 11/1, 25–45.

Pollack, M., and Shaffer, G. (eds) (2001), *Transatlantic Governance in the Global Economy* (Lanham, MD: Rowman and Littlefield).

Sloan, S. (2002), *NATO, the European Union and the Atlantic Community: The Transatlantic Bargain Reconsidered* (Lanham, MD: Rowman and Littlefield).

Smith, M. (2009a) 'Transatlantic Economic Relations in a Changing Global Political Economy; Achieving Togetherness but Missing the Bus?, *British Journal of Politics and International Relations*, vol 11/1, 94–107.

Smith, M., and Woolcock, S. (1993), *The United States and the European Community in a Transformed World* (London: Pinter/Royal Institute of International Affairs).

WEB LINKS

The most useful sites for information about EU–US relations in general are the Commission's Europa site (**http://ec.europa.eu**), especially the trade and CFSP pages, and the website of the Commission delegation in Washington DC (**http://www.eurunion. org**). See also the various US government websites including that of the US Mission to the EU (**http://www.useu.be/**) and that of the State Department (**http://www.state. gov**). There is of course a huge variety of both governmental and commercial sites dealing with the wide range of EU–US issues: see for example the site of the Brookings Institution Centre on the USA and Europe: **http://www.brookings.edu** or the site of the Institute for International Economics: **http://www.iie.org**.; or the site of the Johns Hopkins University Centre for Transatlantic Relations, which houses the American Consortium for European Union Studies: **http://transatlantic..sais-jhu.edu/partnerships/eu-us-partnership**.

PART IV

Evaluation and Conclusion

CHAPTER 18

A European Civilizing Process?

Andrew Linklater

▌ Summary

One of the most famous portrayals of the European Union casts it as a security community in which national governments have renounced the use of force between themselves and where mass publics are acquiring a palpable sense of 'we feeling'. Another celebrated approach depicts the EU as a civilian power committed to ending power politics between the member states and in the world at large. These reflections on the EU can be linked with what some sociologists call 'the civilizing process'—the process in which individual European societies became pacified and the members of national populations came to identify more closely with one another between the 16th century and the present day. One of the three questions discussed in this chapter is whether it is useful to regard the EU as an experiment in taking the civilizing process beyond the nation state—and not just within Europe. What specifically is the relationship between the EU's role in transforming political community on the continent and its conduct towards the rest of the world?

How the EU should behave towards other societies is the second key question raised in this chapter. What moral criteria should be used to decide whether the EU is realizing its potential as a civilian power in world affairs? What should the EU as a civilian power aim to achieve in future? Although the study of 'the civilizing process' is a sociological one, it offers some clues as to how to approach normative questions of this kind. One of its central empirical claims is that all societies must ask how their members can satisfy their basic needs without injuring, demeaning, frustrating, and in other ways *harming* each other time and time again. It is a small step from here to the question of what any society *should* do to prevent harm to its inhabitants and indeed to the members of other societies. The EU has tried to persuade neighbouring states to abolish the death penalty but should it take this moral stance? More specifically, what should the EU do to ensure that its attempt to build closer cooperation in Europe does not cause unnecessary harm to people who live elsewhere? A third question is whether a moral audit of the EU would reveal significant achievements in promoting common interests without harming the members of other societies or major deficiencies that the EU should aim to reduce in future.

Introduction

In May 2000 the German Foreign Minister, Joschka Fischer, described the EU as a regional political system based 'on the rejection of the European balance-of-power principle and the hegemonic ambitions of individual states that had emerged following the peace of Westphalia in 1648 (quoted in Kagan 2003, 56). Many observers share Fischer's view that the EU's greatest achievement has been to end the addiction to realpolitik that dominated the continent for almost four centuries. Analysts have argued that the EU demonstrates that classical realists and neorealists are wrong to insist that anarchy condemns states to compete for military power and to become embroiled in major wars. They maintain that Western Europe has been the site for an important experiment in transforming political community (Linklater 1998). The region has self-consciously broken with the 'totalizing project' in which the nation state ranked higher than other possible objects of identification. Efforts to promote respect for linguistic and cultural differences *within* Europe's nation states have been accompanied by measures to reduce the moral and political significance of national differences *between* sovereign political communities. Steps to devolve power to the domestic regions have developed in tandem with the endeavour to establish transnational political institutions and solidarities. The EU is rightly credited with promoting new forms of international cooperation that brought an end to the appalling suffering caused by modern war. One of its greatest achievements has been to end the historical antagonism between France and Germany. However, the EU has also been concerned with promoting greater respect for the linguistic and cultural differences that exist in its member states.

With the end of the bipolar era, the EU moved to the larger canvas of enlarging the organization to assist post-socialist societies that are struggling to achieve economic prosperity and political stability. To its earlier project of eliminating war between the European powers, the EU added the new challenge of encouraging democratic politics and respect for human rights across the continent. In large part because of their ties with the former colonies, EU members have been active in providing development assistance to poorer societies and in defending human rights on a global scale. It is striking that the project of transforming political community in Western Europe has become linked with that broader set of international concerns: that the values which EU members have used to develop a regional political identity have led them to reflect on the role the organization should have in world affairs. In this respect the EU is no different from all political associations in having to ask what its internal value commitments mean for its behaviour towards the rest of the world. It is no different in having to determine the moral significance of the boundaries between those on the inside and those on the outside.

Two images of the EU

It is useful to comment on two influential characterizations of the EU before considering links with the sociological analysis of the civilizing process in the next section of this chapter. The aim is to show how various portraits of the organization have focused on dimensions of social and political change that are central to empirical studies of the 'civilizing process'. It should be stressed from the outset that discussions of the civilizing process have mainly concentrated on long-term patterns of social and political life *within* modern European states: there has been less emphasis on any changes in the ways in which sovereign states behave towards one another. The following argument is that the idea of a civilizing process can be extended to include developments at the international level (Linklater 2004). The aim is to show that the EU can be regarded as a major experiment in developing an international civilizing process.

Two views of the EU are especially relevant to the analysis of it as a civilizing process. The first is Karl Deutsch's idea of the 'security community'—a community whose members prefer diplomacy to force as a way of resolving political differences (Deutsch 1957). Taylor (1996, 156–7) contributes to the discussion of the related phenomenon of 'we feeling' by noting how the EU has contributed to promoting trust between the peoples of France and Germany. He argues that the EU has made significant inroads into the 'in-group–out-group mentality' that underpinned suspicion, geopolitical competition, and violence between the two societies. He adds that the EU has had success in encouraging 'a degree of popular identification with the Community which [is] ahead of the perceived level of utilitarian reward'. In other words, support for the EU cannot be reduced to calculations of immediate self-interest (although those considerations underlie loyalty to all political associations). Support rests in part on the belief that the project of economic and political integration will benefit most of Europe's peoples over time.

A second example is Duchêne's frequently cited notion of the EU as a civilian power that introduces 'a new stage in political civilisation', one that replaces the balance of power with the attempt 'to *domesticate* relations between states, including those of its members and those with states outside its frontiers'. The civilian power aims 'to bring to international problems the sense of common responsibility and structures of contractual politics that have in the past been associated almost exclusively with "home" and not foreign, that is *alien*, affairs' (Duchêne 1973; italics in original). Manners (2002) develops Duchêne's theme in an influential discussion of 'normative power' Europe. He uses the expression to describe the EU's commitment to global moral causes such as abolishing the death penalty. His argument is that the dominant self-images of the EU have encouraged a foreign policy stance that aims to end what its members regard as the unnecessary suffering of cruel forms of punishment.

There are several parallels between those interpretations of the EU and the analysis of the civilizing process undertaken by the leading European sociologist, Norbert Elias (1897–1990). Those characterizations of the organization suggest that it is meaningful to regard the EU as evidence of a civilizing process 'beyond the nation state'—not that Elias saw the EU in these terms (also Maull 2005). Indeed Elias, who was rare amongst sociologists in reflecting on relations between states, did not see much evidence of a civilizing process in international relations. In common with exponents of the Hobbesian or realist approach, he was sceptical that the civilizing process can develop outside the state where centralized institutions monopolize control of the instruments of violence and maintain social and political order. The EU demonstrates that Elias was unduly pessimistic about what European states could achieve in their relations with each other and with the rest of the world (although he did maintain that humans have become more interdependent on each other, especially over the last few centuries, and in need of 'unions of states'

BOX 18.1   Norbert Elias

Norbert Elias was born in Breslau, Germany in 1897 and died in 1990. Initially a student of philosophy and medicine, Elias was drawn towards the new field of sociology. In 1933, shortly after Hitler's rise to power, Elias left Germany for Paris and then London where he completed his major work, *The Civilizing Process*, first published in Switzerland in 1939. Over the next quarter of a century, Elias published little although he continued to refine his thesis about the civilizing process. In 1954 at the age of 57 Elias was appointed to his first permanent academic position in the Department of Sociology at the University of Leicester. In the last 30 years of his life, Elias published prolifically, and his work has gradually been recognized as one of the most significant contributions to sociological thought in the 20th century.

that enable them to adapt their interests to each other). Here it is worth pausing to note that deep pessimism about what is possible in international politics has often led analysts to believe that moral and political philosophy are relevant to domestic politics, where there is evidence of social progress, but hardly relevant to international politics that display the same depressing regularities over many millennia. The success the EU has had in blurring the contrast between domestic and international politics invites philosophical reflections about what the EU should aim to achieve as a normative power committed to promoting community in international relations. Prior to considering these issues it is necessary to provide a brief overview of Elias's sociology of the civilizing process.

Norbert Elias on 'the civilizing process'

Elias claimed to have discovered important long-term patterns of change within modern European states between the 15th and 20th centuries. He argued that these societies were pacified in this period; their inhabitants came to enjoy levels of personal security that did not exist in the Middle Ages (Elias has been accused of exaggerating the differences between the Middle Ages and modern Europe, but we cannot consider that here). He maintained that over five centuries the citizens of modern states came to identify more closely with each other (but not with the members of other states to any discernible extent). One consequence was that Western European societies came to find public acts of cruelty such as public execution and violent punishment morally repugnant. Support for Elias's analysis of Western Europe can be found in the development of such taboos against violence and also in related concerns about cruelty to animals and children. That form of analysis raises questions about whether developments in international criminal law since the Nuremberg and Tokyo trials, and the growth of the universal human rights culture since the Universal Declaration of Human Rights in 1948, reveal the existence of a global civilizing process (in Elias's neutral use of that term, which was employed to describe how Europeans came to think of themselves as civilized—rather than with entering into normative debates about whether such images of cultural superiority were justified).

It is essential to stress that Elias did not argue that modern European societies are more civilized than other places although, admittedly, his language can easily lead to that (mis)interpretation. His primary task as a sociologist was to understand how Europeans came to see themselves as a civilization that was entitled, so they once believed, to colonize other societies and enslave other peoples. Far from endorsing that world view, Elias set out to comprehend its development. He was also keen to stress—we shall come back to this later—that all civilizing processes, and not only the one he analysed in the modern West, are accompanied by 'decivilizing processes' and tendencies. In other words, civilizing processes simultaneously check aggressive inclinations *and* create new possibilities for violence and domination.

Elias's conception of the civilizing process can be reduced to six basic points. First, from around the 1500s the modern state succeeded in monopolizing control of the instruments of violence; it was able to pacify society by bringing its physical power to bear on violent elements in society. Second, greater personal security made higher levels of social and economic interdependence possible within modern states. Third, over time, 'self-control' and 'internal' checks on aggressive inclinations grew in importance relative to the state's need to use force to maintain personal security; the necessity for greater self-control came to be 'taken for granted' as the populations of each modern society became increasingly interdependent (Elias 1996, 34). Here it is worth noting a parallel with Foucault's later account of the importance of self-monitoring as against external compulsion for the organization of modern societies (see also D. Smith 2001). Foucault believed that that this change marked the development of new forms of power rather than the progress of society. Some of Elias's observations about long-term changes in Europe seem to suggest that modern societies have progressed beyond the Middle Ages but he was keen to stress that the civilizing process was accompanied by more sinister forces.

Fourth, the trend towards greater control of aggressive tendencies was accompanied by a tendency 'to identify more readily with other people ... regardless of social origins'. In particular, attitudes to cruelty and suffering changed fundamentally over five centuries. Some examples of that long-term trend have been provided. An essential part of the civilizing process is that anything distasteful or disgusting—including the slaughter of animals—has been hidden 'behind the scenes' but not always eliminated entirely (Fletcher 1997, 21; Elias 2000, 161ff). Elias believed that practice reflected changing sensibilities towards violence and changing conceptions of disgust.

Fifth, the Europeans' belief that those developments demonstrated their 'inborn superiority' over other peoples had disastrous consequences for the continent in the 1930s and 1940s. During the 19th and 20th centuries, Europeans came to think that terrible cruelty belonged to the past or was typical of uncivilized peoples who had yet to emulate their process of social and political development. That myth of superiority left them unprepared for fascism and for the attempt to destroy European Jews. Sixth, it was too simple to regard the Nazi death camps as regression to a more barbaric past. The Nazis' genocidal project revealed that new totalitarian possibilities were made possible by the civilizing process. The attempt to exterminate the Jews employed a vast bureaucracy that administered genocide without directly involving the mass of the population in acts of violence or inciting collective anger or hatred. Complex questions exist about whether Nazi genocide was evidence of the dangerous side of the civilizing process or an example of its underdevelopment in the German society, but they cannot be discussed here. Nonetheless, enough has been said to explain why Elias (1996, 173) observed that the 'civilization of which I speak is never completed and always endangered'.

BOX 18.2   Elias on the civilizing process

If members of present-day Western civilized society were to find themselves suddenly transported into a past epoch of their own society, such as the medieval-feudal period, they would find there much that they esteem 'uncivilized' in other societies today ... They would, depending on their situation and inclinations, be either attracted by the wilder, more unrestrained and adventurous life of the upper classes in this society, or repulsed by the 'barbaric' customs, the squalor and coarseness ... encountered there.

(Elias 1992, 147)

That physical security from violence by other people is not so great in all societies as in our own is usually not clearly realized.

(Elias 2001a, 48)

We no longer regard it as a Sunday entertainment to see people hanged, quartered, broken on the wheel ... As compared with antiquity, our identification with other people, our sharing in their suffering and death, has increased.

(Elias 2001a, 2–3)

[O]ne can see [the] growing internalization of the social prohibition against violence and the advance in the threshold of revulsion against violence, especially against killing and even against seeing it done, if one considers that, in its heyday, the ritual of English fox-hunting, which prohibited any direct human participation in the killing, represented a civilizing spurt. It was an advance in people's revulsion against doing violence, while today, in accordance with the continued advance of the threshold of sensitivity, not a few people find even this representative of an earlier civilizing spurt distasteful and would like to see it abolished.

(Elias, in Elias and Dunning 1986, 163)

In ancient Greece and Rome we hear time and time again of infants thrown onto dung-heaps or in rivers...Until the late nineteenth century there was no law against infanticide. Public opinion in antiquity also regarded the killing of infants or the sale of children—if they were pretty, to brothels, otherwise as slaves—as self-evident. The threshold of sensibility among people in antiquity—like those of Europeans in the Middle Ages and the early modern period—was quite different from that of the present day, particularly in relation to the use of physical violence. People assumed that they were violent to each other, they were attuned to it. No one noticed that children required special treatment.

(Elias 1998c, 192–3)

So far, the civilizing of human beings and the standards of civilization have developed completely unplanned and in a haphazard manner. It is necessary to form a theory so that, in the future, we may be able to judge more closely what kind of restraints are required for complicated societies to function and what type of restraints have been merely built into us to bolster up the authority of certain ruling groups.

(Elias 1998b, 145)

A global civilizing process?

It is important to comment briefly about Elias's views about international relations before using his approach to reflect on the EU. A crucial point is that he did not think the civilizing process had made much impression on relations between states between the 15th and 20th centuries. His analysis was essentially realist. In the absence of a global monopoly of force, states had competed relentlessly for power and security. They had encouraged their populations to believe that relations between states and relations between citizens were governed by different moral codes: they had tolerated—and at times encouraged—the use of force in external relations while loudly proclaiming their achievement in eradicating violence in the relations between members of the same society (Elias 1996, 461). Elias did not think this 'curious split' within Western civilization was about to be healed.

'The fact that we have not yet learned how to curb wars ... lends support to the assumption that ... what we call modern times represents a very early rather than a late stage of development. I like best the suggestion that our descendants, if humanity can survive the violence of our age, might consider us as late barbarians.' (Elias 1991, 146–7).

The problem with that argument, it might be suggested, is that it is too realist. Elias did refer in passing to the development of new regional international organizations such as the EU—and others have provided ways of building on this possibly more optimistic dimension of his remarks on world politics by arguing that member states have come to be bound together by 'new standards of decency' (K. E. Smith 2001). Elias argued that emotional responses to suffering in war and genocide had changed perceptibly as part of the larger historical trend towards popular aversion against cruelty. There was some evidence of the development of a 'global conscience' in human affairs—and the development of a European public opinion in response to the war in Iraq can be regarded as an example of that trend. But Elias was convinced that the civilizing process was a precarious achievement. Repugnance towards excessive violence could be expected to crumble rapidly if individuals or societies confronted new threats to safety and security.

Sociologists and political scientists have not devoted much time to the question of whether the European Union has revealed how the civilizing process can develop beyond the nation state (an exception is Kapteyn 1996). But if we think about what Deutsch, Duchêne, and others have written about security communities, civilian power status, and normative power Europe, then similarities with Elias's type of analysis quickly become apparent.

There are parallels between Deutsch's conception of a security community that no longer regards force as a legitimate means of resolving differences between societies that share a sense of 'we feeling' and Elias's analysis of pacification and the development of mutual identification between human beings who belong to the

BOX 18.3	**Elias on international relations**

The ancient Greeks ... who are so often held up to us as models of civilized behaviour, considered it quite a matter of course to commit acts of mass destruction, not quite identical to those of the National Socialists but, nevertheless, similar to them in several respects. The Athenian popular assembly decided to wipe out the entire population of Melos, because the city did not want to join the Athenian colonial empire. There were dozens of other examples in antiquity of what we now call genocide.

(Elias 1996, 445)

The wars of the seventeenth century were cruel in a somewhat different sense to those of today. The army had, as far as possible, to feed itself when on foreign soil. Plunder and rapine were not merely permitted, but were demanded by military technique. To torment the subjugated inhabitants of occupied territories ... was, as well as a means of satisfying lust, a deliberate means of collecting war contributions and bringing to light concealed treasure. Soldiers were supposed to behave like robbers. It was a banditry exacted and organized by the army commanders.

(Elias 1998a, 22–3)

[W]e [may be] entering an era in which it will no longer be individual states but unions of states which will serve mankind as the dominant social unit.

(Elias 2001b, 164–5)

We may surmise that with continuing integration even larger units will gradually be assembled under a stable government and internally pacified, and that they in their turn will turn their weapons outwards against human aggregates of the same size until, with a further integration, a still greater reduction of distances, they too gradually grow together and world society is pacified.

(Elias 2000, 255)

We are nowadays more strongly aware than ever before that an enormously large part of humanity live their entire lives on the verge of starvation ... Many members of richer countries feel it to be almost a duty to do something about the misery of other human groups ... in actual fact relatively little is done. The feeling of responsibility which people have for each other is certainly minimal, looked at in absolute terms, but compared with before it has increased.

(Elias 1996, 26)

same nation state. Further parallels exist between Taylor's focus on how the EU has eroded the 'in-group–out-group mentality' especially in the relations between France and Germany, and Elias's analysis of the widening of the 'scope of emotional identification' between the members of modern states. Duchêne's notion of civilian power, which attempts 'to domesticate relations between states', bears comparison with Elias's account of what preceded this 'new stage in political civilisation', namely the civilizing process within Western European states. Manners's (2002) account of normative power Europe that is committed to the abolition of the death penalty

in other societies immediately brings to mind Elias's analysis of changing orientations to cruelty and suffering in Europe over the last few centuries.

All of those analyses deal with similar political and psychological phenomena:
the pacification of human affairs and the internalization of constraints on violent
behaviour. But of course, the analysis of such developments within the EU assumes
precisely what Elias tended to reject, namely the existence of a civilizing process
between states that have not submitted to institutions that have monopolized control of the instruments of force. The approaches to the EU that have been discussed
can be regarded as correcting Elias's overly pessimistic interpretation of what is
possible in relations between states; each might be said to describe how some of
the forces that Elias described (the widening of the scope of emotional identification, the growing aversion to cruelty and suffering, and the rise of internal checks
on aggressive inclinations) have become embedded in a widening European system of international relations. Studies of the EU can be usefully connected with
the approach Elias adopted in his investigation of the civilizing process. Although
he did not describe the EU as a new stage in the development of the civilizing process, that may be a profitable way to think about the organization. It can be regarded as an example of the trend in which domestic value commitments have gradually come to influence relations between the European powers and their conduct
towards the rest of the world. The conclusion of this section is that *the EU needs to
be understood against the background of institutional developments and psychological
and emotional changes that can be traced back over several centuries. It can be regarded
as an important new phase in the civilizing process—as a 'new stage in political civilisation' in Duchêne's phraseology.*

The changing nature of political community in Europe

The EU is a political experiment in taking the civilizing process beyond the nation
state. It is thus important to evaluate it in the context of wider changes in the normative structure of international society. This section considers some of these
changes and their influence on the development of the political communities of
Europe. We then turn to how the changing nature of political life within Western
Europe has come to be associated with a distinctive role for the EU in world affairs.
On this basis we can show how a 'moral audit' of the EU can be conducted.

Three recent accounts of changing global norms are directly relevant to this
part of the analysis. They are Neta Crawford's examination of growing revulsion
against notions of racial supremacy and the cruelties of colonial domination over
the last two centuries (Crawford 2002); Heather Rae's detailed historical account of
how 'ethnic cleansing' has come to be regarded as an offence against the universal

| **BOX 18.4** | **Conceptions of the EU** |

Given sufficiently widespread compliance habits and other favorable circumstances, a political community may become effectively integrated and thus come to function as a security community, so that war among its constituent populations is neither expected nor in fact probable. Integration into a security community may be, but need not be, accompanied by a formal amalgamation or merger of political institutions.

(Deutsch 1957, 42)

Europe as a whole could well become the first example in history of a major centre of the balance of power becoming in the era of its decline not a colonized victim but the exemplar of a new stage in political civilisation ... The European Community's interest as a civilian group of countries long on economic power and relatively short on armed force is as far as possible to *domesticate* relations between states, including those of its members and those with states outside its frontiers. This means trying to bring to international problems the sense of common responsibility and structures of contractual politics which have in the past been associated almost exclusively with 'home' and not foreign, that is *alien*, affairs.

(Duchêne 1973)

Europe's attainment is normative rather than empirical ... It is perhaps a paradox ... that the continent which once ruled the world through the physical impositions of imperialism is now coming to set world standards in normative terms.

(Rosecrance 1998, 22)

The concept of normative power is an attempt to suggest that not only is the EU constructed on a normative basis, but importantly that this predisposes it to act in a normative way in world politics.

(Manners 2002, 252)

The Union is founded on the principles of liberty, democracy, respect for human rights and fundamental freedoms, and the rule of law, principles which are common to the Member States.

(Article 6 (1) of the 1997 Amsterdam Treaty)

In its relations with the rest of the world, the Union shall uphold its values and interests. It shall contribute to peace, security, the sustainable development of the earth, solidarity and mutual respect among peoples, free and fair trade, eradication of poverty and protection of human rights, and in particular children's rights, as well as to strict adherence and development of international law, including respect for the principles of the United Nations Charter.

(Article 3, section 4 of the draft treaty establishing a constitution for Europe)

The [accession negotiations about enlarging the EU] are not about future relations between 'us' and 'them', but rather about relations between the 'future us'. It is this process of the external becoming internal which gives accession negotiations such extraordinary interest.

(Avery 1995, 4)

The transmission of the European miracle to the rest of the world has become Europe's new *mission civilisatrice* ... Europeans have a new mission born of their own discovery of perpetual peace.

(Kagan 2003, 61)

human rights culture, especially following the end of the Second World War (Rae 2002); and Ward Thomas's analysis of what he calls the 'bombing norm' (the *ius in bello* norm concerned with limiting unnecessary suffering to civilian populations in times of war that has won support since the end of the Second World War (Thomas 2001). Those new norms have changed the normative structure of contemporary international society; they have been among the main reasons for the project of transforming political communities across Europe.

The EU was established to eradicate unnecessary suffering in Western Europe, whether caused by interstate war or by economic collapse, as during the Depression. The Second World War was a total war that caused unprecedented civilian deaths and casualties. The epoch witnessed the revival of doctrines of racial supremacy and associated forms of slave labour in Europe itself—the very continent that had prided itself in having banished these evils. It saw the forced expulsion of peoples and systematic genocide without parallel in Europe's recent history. The founders of the EU envisaged the development of new forms of political community that would eradicate such cruelties through the establishment of new transnational structures of economic and political cooperation, which have come to be coupled with measures to devolve power to minority nations and protect human rights in Europe. Many visions of the EU have looked beyond the nation state to new forms of political community that are more internationalist (in reducing the moral and political significance of difference between citizens and foreigners in the member states) and more sensitive to linguistic and cultural differences (in encouraging devolution in an envisaged 'Europe of the regions'). Those visions have been accompanied by the idea that the EU should redistribute some wealth from the more to the less affluent regions if it is to build an international political community that is underpinned by mutual sympathy and solidarity.

The EU's first, if indirect, task was to pacify relations between France and Germany, and it has long been centrally involved in trying to abolish violence from the continent, a strategy that is encapsulated in its European neighbourhood policy, and is the basis for the argument that its external orientation should be guided by a 'human security agenda' that includes crisis management, conflict prevention, and the promotion of 'a ring of well-governed countries to the east of the European Union and on the borders of the Mediterranean' (K. Smith 2005; Kaldor, Martin, and Selchow 2007). The Council of Europe and the Organization of Security and Cooperation in Europe are important partners in this project. Some observers regard the EU's commitment to the 'rejection of force' as evidence of a growing 'moral consciousness' in global affairs in which 'self-enforced rules of behaviour' replace the age-old reliance on the external constraints imposed by the balance of military power (Cooper, quoted in Kagan 2003, 57). This stress on self-constraints raises the question of how far the EU has taken the six features of the civilizing process 'beyond the nation state'.

The first point to make is that the EU has revealed that separate states can make progress in developing a regional civilizing process without transferring all their

powers to a new sovereign authority. Admittedly, that experiment in regional political cooperation presupposes the existence of stable monopolies of power that
belong to a common civilization, have shared interests in preventing the return of a
violent past, and value close cooperation to deal with the challenge of global interconnectedness. A second point is that the establishment of that zone of peace has
permitted the development of high levels of social and economic interdependence.
The third is that 'self-control' and 'internal' checks on aggressive inclinations have
grown in importance across the territories of the European security community.
A fourth is that peoples in the EU have begun 'to identify more readily with other
people ... regardless of social origins', and to develop some shared responses to
human suffering (as in the case of violations of human rights and excessive violence to civilians in war). The fifth point is that the violence of the first half of the
20th century damaged Europe's belief in its 'inborn superiority', prompting efforts
to eradicate all forms of ethnocentrism.

The sixth point arising from this application of Elias's thought to Europe's place
in the world is that, despite evident progress, there are still persistent dangers that
the EU will generate its own decivilizing processes. We come back to this later.
Certainly, many interpretations of the EU advise against investing too much hope
in the association. Some realists have argued that the first stages of regional cooperation were largely the result of Europe's desire to harness its collective resources
in the era of superpower dominance. In any case they were underwritten by NATO.
In short, the association has been held together by common interests and external
support, and will only survive as long as do those shared objectives and common
interests—which have much to do with Europe's declining geopolitical significance
(see also Bull 1982). An assessment of Europe's troubled relationship with the United States since the terrorist attacks of 11 September 2001 restated the point that
the EU's commitment to peaceful change in world politics reflects its military and
political weakness (Kagan 2003). Adopting the moral high ground, it is argued, is
an attempt to compensate for the lack of influence in a world that is dominated by
the United States.

On that view, the European civilizing process may be little more than 'skin deep',
amplified for effect under conditions of relative military weakness, largely dependent on the nature of contemporary global economic and political challenges, and
rarely free from the charge that it conceals member states' interests and displays
an element of hypocrisy. The point can be elaborated by noting that references to
civilian power or normative power Europe do not alter the fact that the EU was
famously indecisive over how to respond to human rights violations in the former
Yugoslavia, and also divided over whether or not to support the US decision in
2003 to secure regime change in Iraq. Many argue that loyalty to the nation state is
still very much greater than emotional identification between the member states of
the EU, and that compassion for the poor in one's own political community continues to exceed sympathy for peoples in other parts of Europe. The benefits that
reforming the Common Agricultural Policy could bring to millions of the world's

poor have been emphasized in this context (see Hyde-Price 2008). For such reasons it may be necessary to be sceptical about the EU's capacity to have a civilizing role in world affairs.

Questions about the depth of a civilizing process in Europe—and about the extent to which the EU has a distinctive voice and influence in world affairs—raise old issues about the relative importance of interests and ideas or identities in political life. They have been central to recent debates between 'rationalist' and 'constructivist' theories of international relations. It is significant that sceptics do not deny that moral ideas have influenced the development of the EU; it is also worth noting that moral concerns about ethnic cleansing and human rights violations, about the use of force in world politics, and about unnecessary civilian suffering in war are now important elements in public orientations to international politics—as government and public responses to the Yugoslav wars and to the 2003 war against Iraq demonstrated. To acknowledge that the EU is influenced by such moral considerations leads to the question of which moral principles should govern its conduct towards the rest of the world (see the contributions to Aggestam 2008). What are the moral values that the EU should promote in its own region and in the wider world? What does the EU's project of transforming political community within Europe mean for its conduct towards other parts of the world? How should the EU behave as a civilian power?

Preventing harm in world politics

The idea of the civilizing process is useful in suggesting how to answer those questions. It is worth recalling that the civilizing process deals with the question of how human beings can satisfy their fundamental needs without 'destroying, frustrating, demeaning or in other ways *harming* each other' over and over again (Elias 1996, 31; my italics). All societies have to protect their members from what they (or in effect the most powerful) regard as serious forms of harm. Exactly the same question arises over relations between the members of an international society of states or security community. They too must address the problem of how to promote their interests without causing unnecessary harm to each other. Modern international law makes explicit reference to this issue. The international law of human rights, the law of war, and environmental law oblige states not to cause 'unnecessary suffering' in war, to avoid 'serious bodily and mental harm', and to avoid harming the natural environments of other states and the global commons. An important question is whether it is possible to identify various forms of harm that the EU should try to avoid if it is to fulfil its aspirations to be a civilizing force in world politics (for other comments on harm, see Dunne 2008; Manners 2008).

The argument of this section is that at least seven forms of harm exist in international politics. A global civilizing process can be said to exist if national governments are committed to avoiding some or all of them. The extent to which the EU is important in promoting a global civilizing process depends on how seriously it attempts to avoid those examples of harm.

The seven forms of harm can be usefully subdivided into two main groups. The first set includes three forms of harm where human beings deliberately set out to injure others. They are:

- Deliberate harm that governments and/or societies do to the members of other communities. Examples include: acts of aggression; attempts to maximize the suffering of combatants and non-combatants during military conflict, whether through deliberate acts of violence against civilians or cruelty to prisoners of war; deliberate attempts to cause hardship and suffering by imposing economic costs on other peoples; and racist and xenophobic portrayals of other peoples that aim to degrade and humiliate them. It need hardly be added that these forms of harm have been dominant features of international relations for millennia.

- Deliberate harm that governments do to their own citizens, as when torturing them or otherwise abusing human rights. That form of harm has become especially central to world politics since the end of the Second World War. In Europe and elsewhere, it has meant challenging the classical Westphalian principle that governments are not answerable to the international community for their behaviour towards subjects or citizens.

- Deliberate harm that non-state actors do to the members of different societies. Key examples are discussed in Chapter 10. They include the violence caused by international terrorist organizations and by transnational criminal organizations that trade illicit drugs or engage in the traffic of women and children for the purpose of 'sexual slavery'.

As noted earlier, Elias maintained that the civilizing process was largely concerned with controlling violent intentions and aggressive impulses; it was especially concerned with reducing cruelty to other human beings and to non-human animals. But reducing cruelty is not all there was to the civilizing process, as the following quotation reveals: 'the extent and depth of people's mutual identification with each other and, accordingly, the depth and extent of their ability to empathize and capacity to feel for and sympathize with other people in their relationships with them' are no less important indicators of the civilizing process (Elias 1996, 109). That observation raises the question of whether that process requires not only efforts to protect individuals and groups from deliberate physical or emotional injury *but also* positive steps to protect them from harms that can occur in other ways. The next four forms of harm look beyond deliberate attempts to cause mental and/or physical injury. They are:

- Unintended harm where, for example, a government or business enterprise unknowingly damages the physical environment of another society. (Since the Stockholm conference on the environment in June 1972 various international conventions have insisted that states have obligations to strive not to cause accidental damage to their neighbour's physical environment or to the global commons.)

- Negligence where, for example, a state or business enterprise knowingly submits others to the risk of harm. The failure to ensure that those involved in hazardous industries have adequate health and safety provision is a case in point. (Since the Bhopal incident of 1984 that question has loomed large in discussions of the extent to which transnational business enterprises work with a double standard of morality in world affairs—specifically with how far lower standards of health and safety, and a higher exposure to risk, should apply in poor societies hungry for foreign investment.)

- Harm through unjust enrichment where, for example, members of affluent societies benefit unfairly from protectionist strategies, from export subsidies, from the vulnerability of foreign producers who must sell products cheaply on the world market, and from the rules of global commerce that favour the strong and disadvantage the weak.

- Harm through acts of omission where, for example, a person or community fails to take measures to alleviate the suffering of others in circumstances where there is no, or little, cost to itself. That is the most controversial of the forms of harm described above. Legal systems take different positions on the extent to which individuals should be punished for failing to rescue others (see Feinberg 1984 on this topic and on the question of what counts as an excessive risk for potential rescuers). In world politics, there is no consensus about whether the failure to intervene to prevent genocide is an example of harm; and there are no laws that make the failure to rescue a punishable offence. But some philosophers argue that the failure to rescue can cause harm by inviting the vulnerable to conclude that the question of whether they survive or perish is of no concern to those who are able to help them. That question is hardly abstract. It confronts Italian and Spanish governments every week in summer, as boatloads of illegal immigrants attempt the trip across the Mediterranean, often in unseaworthy vessels provided by unscrupulous criminal gangs. To their credit, the EU states always decide to rescue those in peril but then have to decide whether they have further obligations of hospitality or whether to repatriate new arrivals.

It is possible to use that typology of forms of harm for two purposes: First, we can ask the empirical question of whether a regional association such as the EU is taking steps to avoid or prevent those forms of harm. Second, the typology can be used to conduct a 'moral audit' of the EU that tries to ascertain how far it is a force for good in world politics and how far it falls short of aspirations to be a civilian power. The case for combining these two modes of analysis is that it is not fruitful to assess the EU's performance in combating forms of harm in isolation from developments in other regions of the world political system or from sectors that include the non-governmental organization community. We need to ask whether the EU is lagging behind other regions and sectors in identifying and tackling forms of serious harm, or whether the evidence suggests it is in the forefront of progressive developments.

What are the most progressive developments and highest moral ideals that must be kept in mind when assessing the EU's conduct towards other societies? Arguably they include:

- efforts to tame the use of interstate violence, not least by defending the need for the multilateral authorization of military power as opposed to foreign policy unilateralism;

- attempts to minimize suffering in war and to use moral and at times physical sanctions against human rights violators;

- measures to combat transnational crime and international terrorism without dangerous encroachments on civil liberties and invasions of privacy;

- regard for ways in which industrial processes can spoil the environment of neighbouring states, create health hazards for other peoples, and place added burdens on the global commons;

- a commitment to ensuring that vulnerable peoples are not exposed to hazards that affluent populations are unprepared to tolerate in their own societies;

- a concern about forms of unjust enrichment in which powerful groups benefit from the disadvantaged position of others in the world economy;

- a sense of shame or guilt when those who are capable of releasing the most desperate from hunger, disease, and extreme poverty without significant costs to themselves, fail to do so.

Some of the most progressive concrete developments in world politics in recent times include the development of international criminal law and the establishment of the International Criminal Court, advances in global environmental law, and calls for radical measures to deal with global warming and climate change; sensitivity to the plight of the vulnerable as expressed in concerns about child labour and sweatshop industries, and in support for fair trade and for ethical investment; and the apparent development of a 'global conscience' that makes the affluent uncomfortable about remaining passive in the face of widespread suffering. Those developments are evidence of a global civilizing process—however modest and precarious—that is concerned with reducing cruelty in world affairs and with widening emotional identification to include the members of other societies, especially the most vulnerable. They are important reference points as we turn to the task of reflecting on what a preliminary moral audit of the EU reveals about the conduct of its external relations.

Auditing the EU

In their introduction the editors argue that one 'of the important tasks for academic observers ... now is to conduct an audit' of what the EU has achieved. They ask 'who and what ... the EU [is] for, in its international relations', and they call for further reflection on what it should 'be trying to achieve'. The claim that the EU has attempted to take the civilizing process beyond the nation state raises precisely the question of what the EU *should* seek to achieve. Those are some of the most interesting questions about the EU, and yet they are largely neglected because historical and empirical approaches to regional cooperation have dominated the field and because theoretical approaches have mostly been concerned with explaining institutional developments rather than with subjecting them to an ethical assessment. Many analysts will assume that disputes about ethical principles are a reminder of the arbitrary nature of moral preferences. On what grounds, they might ask, is any moral audit of the EU to be established? How are the values that underpin such an assessment to be selected? Can they be anything other than subjective?

International legal conventions that outlaw 'serious bodily and mental harm' suggest an answer to those questions. They prompt the observation that one way of conducting a moral audit is to ask whether the EU has been at the centre of global initiatives to establish commitments to reduce harm to individuals and various minorities. That is an immensely complex undertaking that must be left to specialists in EU studies. The main task of the following section is to encourage debate about its successes and failures, and to do that by drawing on the insights of the earlier chapters in this volume.

A preliminary audit might conclude that the EU has made progress with respect to the seven forms of harm mentioned earlier but that it also risks damaging its own values in other respects, such as hardening the boundaries between Europe and the rest of the world:

- The EU's successful early commitment to pacifying Western Europe has encouraged its members to extend the '*pax Europea*' by enlarging the EU to include former socialist societies (Tsoukalis 2005). As part of that project, it has insisted that states who want to join the EU should display 'good neighbourliness', for example by attempting to promote the peaceful settlement of territorial disputes (see Chapter 13). Its experience in collaboration and consultation has led to efforts to export regionalism to other areas (with limited success) and to promote multilateralism, including reliance on the UN system. The EU's support for multilateralism can be contrasted with the Bush administration's willingness (as in the end with that of the British government) to bypass the UN Security Council in the build-up to the 2003 Iraq War.

- The EU's general commitment to the global human rights culture and to the development of international criminal law (see K. Smith 2001 and Chapter 13) is evident in attempts within the region to promote respect for individual human rights, minority rights, the rule of law, and democracy on the part of those acceding to the EU (Spain, Portugal, and Greece in the 1970s and the former members of the socialist bloc in more recent times). Externally, it is present in conditionality clauses in an increasing number of trade and cooperation agreements.

- The EU's efforts to deal with international terrorism and transnational crime by creating transnational forms of policing and surveillance, and its steps 'to enhance the internal security provisions of the aspirant states prior to acceding them to the Union', represent the internationalization of the state, in that national borders are less important than the common external frontier. That can be regarded as a major extension of the civilizing process described by Elias and as a significant enhancement of states' surveillance of national populations.

- Regarding environmental harm, the EU has an important role in 'standard setting' that includes broad support for the precautionary principle, i.e. to take care not to cause unintended harm to other societies and to future generations. It has promoted the shift away from traditional notions of statecraft that insist on 'the absolute sovereignty of every nation … within its own territory'[1] to the internationalist commitment illustrated by Principle 21 of the Stockholm Agreement of 1972, which claims that states have a duty not to harm the environment of neighbouring states and the global commons.

- Regarding harm caused by negligence, the EU is committed to international environmental obligations such as those contained in the 1989 Basel Convention on the control of transboundary movements of hazardous wastes and their disposal. They establish the duty of prior notification of, and consultation with, states that may be affected by a potentially harmful activity, and the duty to cooperate to prevent the transfer to other states of any activities and substances that may cause severe environmental degradation or damage human health.

- The EU is credited with recognizing that globalization 'raises fundamental questions of governance' since together 'with its undeniable wealth-creating effects, globalization often brings along greater inequalities, social disruption, and environmental damage, the kinds of negative externalities that those benefiting from globalization prefer to ignore' (Tsoukalis 2005). It has played a leading role in promoting debt relief; it is a major aid donor, the largest in the world if national aid programmes are included. That role, in addition to its concerns about 'the rights of workers and distributional justice' (ibid.), reveals a commitment to promoting 'social democratic normative goals' in world politics that is at odds with the neo-liberal project that was central to US policy on global economic relations and to the policy agendas of the International Monetary Fund and the World Bank for almost 30 years (see Chapter 16).

- The EU was accused of weakness in responding to human rights violations in the former Yugoslavia. Precisely how it should respond to external humanitarian challenges is one of the most complex questions that faces the organization. Against the view that such an association should acquire military power precisely so as to become a 'good international citizen' with the capacity to intervene in civil conflicts, K.E. Smith (2001, 192) argues that 'the EU should remain true to its civilian power roots, and renounce the potential to use force, just as this potential has effectively been eliminated among its member states'. The point is that between indifference to suffering in other countries and military intervention lie many strategies that include measures to promote democracy and human rights and efforts to ensure economic stability. Where such policies fail, the EU can demonstrate its good international citizenship by supporting efforts to bring about the political reconstruction of what were war-torn societies. Its contribution to civilian policing in Kosovo and to peacekeeping in Macedonia are important examples of the attempt since the end of the Kosovo war to take 'the lead in constructing a post-war order in South-eastern Europe' (see Chapter 13).

One must also ask whether the EU's efforts to enlarge the boundaries of moral and political community may create new forms of social exclusion and new hierarchies between peoples. In Elias's terms, the question is whether the European civilizing process can proceed without generating decivilizing tendencies. On the deficit side of the EU's performance, it is necessary to include at least the following negatives:

- The recurrent fear that Europe will close in on itself, as the idea of 'fortress Europe' suggests (see Chapter 10). That is no longer a matter of economics alone, as during the debate over the single market. In particular, there are fears that efforts to create a European political identity could sharpen the differences between, for example, Europe and the Islamic world (see Aggestam and Hill, in Aggestam 2008 on the relationship between EU policy and multiculturalism).

- Economic assistance to 'outsiders'—as an intended consequence of the EU's expansion to the east—may come to mean that 'an increasing number of [the] young and worse-off will be turned into privileged citizens of the Union, although after long transitional periods intended to placate the fears of those already in. Immigration will remain a hot political issue, and much will depend on how the economic situation develops' (Tsoukalis 2005).

- An additional danger is that the EU will become less humane because of legitimate public fears about international terrorism and transnational crime. In particular, the extent to which the EU can sustain humane conduct towards refugees and asylum seekers, given public concerns about resource capabilities and anxieties about criminal elements and terrorism, is a crucial matter. Many fear that new political structures are being created that pose a threat to civil liberties and escape democratic accountability; they are concerned that the way in which the EU polices its borders 'inevitably involves coercion, discrimination, and sharp distinctions between citizens and non-citizens' (Peterson and Smith 2003, 213). Again, the danger is that the EU will create distinctions between responsible citizens and dangerous outsiders that are just as pernicious in their own way as the old national distinctions between insiders and outsiders that it has tried to leave behind (Merlingen 2007).

- The 'credibility' of the EU 'as the generous partner of poor countries will continue to be severely tested' as long as 'the European agricultural fortress keeps many of the exports of the less developed countries out of European markets' (Tsoukalis 2005; see also Chapter 12). Related forms of vulnerability arise from agricultural subsidies that harm competitors in other countries and from 'dumping' surplus production in overseas markets.

- There is the fear that humanitarian assistance and a tendency to intervention will lead the EU to acquire some of the features of an imperial power, replicating earlier notions of the 'mission civilisatrice' (Cooper 2002; Merlingen 2007; Zielonka 2008).

The main reason for an ethical audit is to decide how far the EU has succeeded in calling public attention to the forms of harm that befall individuals and groups in world politics, and in directing its political resources to the alleviation of that harm. It is also important to see how far the development of the EU, in terms of its membership and its actions, has changed the terms of the inclusion/exclusion relationship. The EU can point to many achievements in promoting, within its own region and beyond, a civilizing process that prefers the peaceful resolution of disputes to the use of force, privileges multilateralism over unilateralism, and entails the enlargement of sympathies to include the members of societies who are the victims of human rights violations. Of course, states and regional political organizations are no different from the individuals comprising them in falling short of the moral standards they claim to observe. As we have seen, the EU is especially vulnerable to the accusation that it erects barriers against weaker producers that wish to sell in its market, that there are dangers of a hardening of attitudes towards refugees and immigrants that may create sharp distinctions between the European heartland of secure democracies and the outer world of instability and danger, and that any efforts to create a European identity may run the risk of replicating some of the features of the 'in-group–out-group mentality' of the nation state. For many, the challenge facing the EU is one of moving beyond monopolistic states without creating centralized institutions and strong accompanying transnational loyalties that rest on the fear of, or on hostility towards, outsiders. If it succeeds in that project it may be able to avoid the decivilizing processes and tendencies that are present in all social and political arrangements.

Conclusions

Joschka Fischer's claim that European international relations have long been dominated by power politics was quoted in the introduction to this chapter. Realists have argued that a stark contrast between domestic and international politics has been a feature of European and world politics since the 1648 Peace of Westphalia. As they see it, domestic political progress that revolves around the establishment of health, welfare, and educational systems has proceeded without any parallel developments in relations between states. Struggles for power and recurrent war mean that emotional identification with the state or nation has towered over transnational loyalties. Policy makers such as Joschka Fischer have tended to agree, but in reaction against the realist narrative.

The EU now poses a clear and deliberate challenge to traditional power politics. Europe is the region where sharp divisions between domestic and international politics have declined in importance. The existence of the EU has raised intriguing questions about how far a regional civilizing process can develop without the physical constraints associated with the existence of a monopoly of force. Few could have predicted this development in 1945 when France and Germany ended their third major conflict in 70 years. We may view the development of the EU as an example of the planned extension of the civilizing process beyond the nation state—as an effort to create new forms of political community that are more internationalist in outlook, more sensitive to the existence of linguistic and cultural differences within nation states, and more willing to redistribute wealth towards the less affluent societies of the region. Those values inform the EU's relations with other parts of the world, although the precise extent of their influence is keenly debated, and not least because of what many see as 'realism' with respect to securing EU borders and antiterrorist policies. How internationalist commitments will fare in the coming years is a central question for students of the EU and its external relations.

Notes

1 This was the argument of the Harmon Doctrine, named after the US Attorney General, Hudson Harmon, who in 1895 dismissed Mexican claims that US use of the Rio Grande caused environmental damage in Mexico.

FURTHER READING

For a good short summary of Elias's study of the civilizing process, see R. Kilminster and S. Mennell, 'Norbert Elias' in G. Ritzer (ed.) (2003), *The Blackwell Companion to Major Contemporary Social Theorists*, Oxford: Blackwell. An accessible longer study is J. Fletcher (1997), *Violence and Civilisation: An Introduction to the Work of Norbert Elias*, Cambridge: Polity Press. Two books by Elias that are especially relevant to the themes discussed in this chapter are *The Civilising Process: Sociogenetic and Psychogenetic Investigations* (2000), Oxford: Blackwell; and *The Germans* (1996), Cambridge: Polity Press.

Studies of European integration that deal with themes related to Elias's study of the civilizing process include K. Deutsch (1957), *Political Community and the North Atlantic Area: International Organization in the Light of Historical Experience, vol. 1*, Princeton: Princeton University Press (see also E. Adler and M. Barnett (eds) (1998), *Security Communities*, Cambridge: Cambridge University Press); F. Duchêne (1973), 'The European Community and the Uncertainties of Interdependence', in M. Kohnstamm and W. Hager (eds), *Nation Writ Large: Foreign Policy Problems Before the European Community*, London: Macmillan; I. Manners (2002), 'Normative Power Europe: a Contradiction in Terms?', *Journal of Common Market Studies*, 40, 2, pp. 235–58 and P. Taylor, *The European Union in the 1990s* (1996), Oxford: Oxford University Press.

The January 2008 special issue of *International Affairs* (edited by L. Aggestam) contains several excellent articles on 'ethical power Europe'.

WEB LINKS

Copies of *Figurations: The newsletter of the Norbert Elias Foundation* can be found at **www.norberteliasfoundation.nl/figurations.php**. The site contains short papers on different aspects of the civilizing process and some reflections on the significance of Elias's thought for the study of international relations. Newsletters 17, 19, and 20 are useful in this regard.

The FORNET network, whose outputs are to be found at **http://www.fornet.info**, generates discussion of ethical as well as analytical aspects of EU external relations.

CHAPTER 19

Acting for Europe: Reassessing the European Union's Place in International Relations

Christopher Hill and Michael Smith

▌ Summary

This chapter presents the major common findings of the volume, while also stressing the different approaches and specialist areas covered by the contributors. It re-examines the usefulness of the major schools of International Relations theory as applied to the EU's external relations, seeing all as applicable in varying ways even if liberalism and its variants tend to generate most insights. It then moves on to the EU's substantive impact (or lack of it) on world politics, which has grown steadily in broad terms albeit with obvious gaps and setbacks. The three lenses introduced in Chapter 1, whereby the EU is analysed as a system of international relations, as a participant in wider international processes, and as a power, are then revisited to make possible the overall conclusions: that the EU can no longer be treated as a peculiar side issue in international relations and must now be fully integrated into the academic study of the subject; that the EU has significant powers as well as a wide-ranging presence in the international system, even if it may not yet be termed 'a power'; that processes of changes now under way in the international arena will pose new challenges both for the EU and for analysis.

Introduction

This is a lengthy book because the role of the European Union in international relations at the start of the 21st century amounts to a great deal, across a wide variety of issue areas. Such an extensive treatment would not have been easy to justify even two decades ago, but now there are three main reasons for it: the fact that the EU itself generates a significant quantity of international relations, with an increasing impact on third parties; the converse, namely that the international system is increasingly implicated in the development of the EU itself, in shaping its external strategies but also the everyday lives of its citizens; the increasing mutual relevance of the academic literature of International Relations, and the specialist study of EU external relations, previously connected only by a slim isthmus.

Our focus in this concluding chapter is on two overarching questions, which subsume the dimensions referred to above and the various themes and approaches outlined in the three introductory chapters. The first asks about the extent to which our analysis of the EU's international relations has added both to our general understanding of real-world international relations (lower case), and the theoretically driven academic subject of International Relations (upper case) which seeks to establish a framework for understanding how the world works. The second asks about how we should think about the place of the EU in contemporary international society, drawing on theory as well as the burgeoning amount of empirical material now being generated. What kind of actor is it, what kind of functions does it fulfil, and what is the trajectory of its development?

The EU and the perspectives of international relations

In Chapter 2 Filippo Andreatta (after looking at the classical federalist and neofunctionalist accounts) surveys the main theoretical approaches in International Relations of relevance to the EU's external behaviour. He summarizes these under the headings of realist, liberal, and constructivist/critical schools of thought.

Realism

Of these three approaches realism seems the least promising, centring as it does on unitary states and the international condition of anarchy. The EU is not a unitary state (nor about to become one) and it also transcends anarchy in its internal condition, just as it seeks to modify it in the wider international system. The studies that constitute the empirical core of this book do, however, suggest that realism can provide some insights for our purposes. It can, for instance, help to explain why the Common Foreign and Security Policy (CFSP) has so far been a relative failure—how can sovereign states be expected to renounce their national freedoms of manoeuvre in the interests of a long-term solidarity? It might also throw light on why, nonetheless, the EU has begun to develop a defence dimension. *Pace* John Mearsheimer's gloomy predictions, the Europeans have reacted to the end of the Cold War not by falling on each other's throats but by starting to huddle together for protection as the United States not only finds other interests beyond European security but even becomes a source of problems which Europeans think they need to reinsure against (Mearsheimer 1990; see also Hyde-Price 2007). Andreatta makes the point that European Political Cooperation (EPC)/CFSP might be seen as an extraordinarily enduring and special kind of alliance, designed to deal with friends as well as putative enemies. It is an alliance that has gradually expanded its scope and responsibilities, as Europe's external environment has become less stable. To splice a little constructivism onto realism, Venus may be starting to become more like Mars, or even vice versa. The gender stereotypes may be breaking down.

This reference to the views of Robert Kagan indicates that an adapted form of realism, at least, might cast light on the successes of EU foreign policy as well as its failures (Kagan 2003). Kagan himself was able to recognize this (Kagan 2004). Neorealism, given its highly systemic perspective and stress on the balance of power, seems to have relatively little to tell us about the EU's place in the world. The latter is more a 'pole' than a 'power', at least unless one qualifies the frame of reference by referring to the international political *economy* rather than the overall international system, which is generally understood in macro-political terms. Even with a concept like 'multipolarity', which Waltzians have little time for, the EU's role is difficult to define clearly, although Adrian Hyde-Price has made substantial efforts in this direction (Hyde-Price 2007). Classical realism, by contrast, has a stronger historical component and therefore stresses the particular circumstances in Western Europe that have given birth to the distinctive construction known as the CFSP/Common Security and Defence Policy (CSDP): partial, stuttering, but still indispensable. It is also more likely to make sense of the paradox that the major member states continue to play an important role alongside the evolving collective diplomacy. Britain and France have, if anything, reasserted their ambitions to be major players during the last ten years, while Germany, Italy, Spain, and now Poland have discovered the confidence to identify and assert national interests, through the very process of foreign policy cooperation.

Liberalism

It may be that a realist form of liberalism is best suited to explain these paradoxes, as with Andrew Moravcsik's theory of 'liberal intergovernmentalism', which has become so prominent in the analysis of the EU's internal politics (Moravcsik 1998). This adapts realism to take account of the 'two-level game' that decision-makers play between the two chessboards of the domestic environment and the EU institutions, and to allow for the possibility of lasting cooperation, through 'grand bargains'. Liberal intergovernmentalism has only just begun to be applied to the EU's external policies, even if it has some potential in this area (Moravcsik 2003). The CFSP and the external aspects of pillar III are evidently intergovernmental, and even the evolution of the Common Commercial Policy may be seen as subject to intermittent bargains between the bigger states (see Chapters 11 and 12). Yet here too we need to add something, taken from the broad church of liberalism.

Catherine Gegout (2002) has pointed out that the CFSP cannot be fully explained without reference to history and to the functioning of institutions—combined in the form of 'historical institutionalism'. The wider role of the EU, including its economic, development, and societal impact on the world, also requires more contextualization than simple bargaining models can provide. Yet the liberal IR perspectives that have most commonly provided such contextualization are themselves widely divergent, both in the particular focus of their interests and in their assumptions about the capacity of actors to generate lasting structures of cooperation (Carlsnaes 2004). Most contributors to this volume take a broadly liberal view of international relations (or are liberal realists), but they span the range from those who see institutions as having a transformational and socializing effect on the prospects for common action (for instance, Vanhoonacker, M. E. Smith), to those who see the EU's liberal values as significantly constrained by the logic of the international system and subject to the glacier-like progress of historical change (Howorth, Carbone). Some issues tend only to be highlighted in the first place by a liberal set of assumptions, as with accountability or interdependence (Lord, Verdun). In terms of Andreatta's three schools of liberalism—republican, commercial, and institutional—the first is only implicitly supported in this volume, in the sense that it is largely taken for granted that relations between member states represent a form of the 'democratic peace', and that by extension relations with new members, and prospective new members, are subject to the same kind of domestication (K. E. Smith). Indeed, it is clear that the EU regards its 'power of attraction' to be sufficiently strong to pull even those neighbours with only a remote chance of accession into its irenic orbit. Linklater's view that the EU represents a 'civilizing' impulse in international relations is closely related to this republican version of liberalism.

Commercial liberalism is more obviously central to the EU's external relations, and has been from the beginning, even with the evident tension between the model of free trade represented by the common market and that of protectionism embodied in the customs union. It can be argued, in the Cobdenite tradition, that the commitment to a civilian power foreign policy is rooted in a system that has privileged trade liberalization—and indeed transnational relations more generally—as an instrument of integration between states, and which assumes that the EEC model can be exported elsewhere. The fact that economics is the main instrument employed by EU foreign policy thus far complicates the matter, in that while the use of cooperation agreements and foreign aid helps to bind countries together, economic sanctions are inherently coercive, and represent realist more than liberal values.

The other element of commercial liberalism that is clearly borne out by a detailed look at the international relations of the EU is the latter's capacity to provide a site of agency in the complex and glutinous processes of interdependence. The chapters by Verdun and by Meunier and Nicolaïdis demonstrate the extent of the Union's trade power, both in terms of defending pure economic interests and as a way of promoting wider values, epitomized in the phrase 'normative power' (Manners 2002). Integration as an overall process, not just the Common Commercial Policy, is then to be seen as 'a highly developed system for the joint management of interdependence', notably dense within the region itself, but almost as important in terms of Europe's relations with North America, the Middle East, parts of Asia, and the ex-colonial states. From the macro viewpoint the EU can be seen as a vehicle of globalization, but to its citizens—current and potential—it seems to have the scale of resources and the decision-making apparatus required to tackle the dilemmas arising from globalization, for instance in the World Trade Organization (WTO), the international financial institutions, and the G7/8. In this context the fact that even these illustrious sites of global governance have a limited capacity to moderate the winds of economic change is less important than the EU's prestige within them.

A liberal economic zone like that of the European Union actively encourages free enterprise, as it has done with the single market project, the Lisbon Agenda and its successor, the 'Europe 2020' programme. This in turn creates much space for transnational enterprises, cultural and political as well as economic, to operate outside direct governmental control, and thus to cause difficulties for the member states. Such is the price for the stimulus to growth represented by the huge marketplace of the EU and EEA (European Economic Area) combined—now c. 500 million—and it is exerting pressure on the continental model of a social market economy. Most obviously, the financial and broader economic crises of 2007 and after have demonstrated dramatically the difficulties of sustaining this model in a networked and highly competitive world. With the most 'flexible' economy in the EU, and a relatively low rate of unemployment, Britain has come to congratulate itself on not having participated in the common monetary project. Yet it is therefore excluded from decision-making over the management of the eurozone, including the increasingly important external dimension of the common currency. In the context of economic crisis, this absence can be seen as a major asset, insulating Britain from the demands of stabilization in the eurozone—but it also exposes the British to risks over which they have no control, emanating from the country's heavy involvement in transnational financial markets, including those of eurozone members. By the same token, Britain also keeps out of the Schengen arrangements, in part so as to manage its influx of economic migrants, and thus compromises the notion of a single, 'hard' external border for the EU (Rees, Chapter 10). Again, the balance of costs and risks arising from this arrangement is felt at both the national and the EU level, while the resulting trade-offs are as much the result of domestic political pressure as of economic rationality.

The dictates of commercial liberalism therefore cut two ways for the EU and its member states. A further demonstration of the fact is the inevitable and regular clashes between the United States and Europe. The latter's *organized* economic power represents competition for the USA as well as a potential partnership in the management of the world economy. Accordingly Washington has always been ambivalent about encouraging European integration, even if it has usually concluded that the long-term advantages outweigh the short-term pains. But if Americans do not always take seriously the foreign policy pronouncements of the EU Presidency or (latterly) the High Representative, they always pay the closest attention to the activities of the Trade Commissioner or Ecofin. They have learned through prolonged disputes since the early 1960s (over everything from soya beans to pipelines, from bananas to Boeing and Microsoft) that the EU knows how to win. As Smith and Steffenson show in Chapter 17, despite its heterogeneity, in the area of trade the EU can stick to a policy, negotiate hard, and play the same games with transnational lobbying that the USA itself is adept at. Moreover—and this testifies to the broader common interests that underpin the transatlantic relationship—however sharp the disagreements in the economic field, they have remained compartmentalized, so as to leave the strategic alliance largely unscathed. This was particularly true during the Cold War, when 'linkage' was seen as a dangerous game, whether by the USA hinting at possible troop withdrawals if the Europeans did not fall into line on the anti-OPEC cartel in 1973–4, or the European outrage at US extra-territorial legislation leading to questions about the value of the Western alliance in the 1980s and 1990s. Such spats refocused attention on common interests and brought both sides back into line. Since 1991, however, it is arguable that a more fluid and competitive international environment has led implicit linkages to rise closer to the surface, and the Europeans have begun to define themselves and their common interests more in terms of competition with a globalization defined more readily as Americanization. Economics and politics thus inexorably converge, not least with the drive during the administration of George W. Bush to export values as well as the goods with which the Europeans are in competition (Tsoukalis 2003, 192–200; McGuire and Smith 2008).

Constructivist and other approaches

The constructivist and critical approaches that Andreatta analysed in Chapter 2 are mostly of a macro character, applicable in principle to the whole range of international actors and behaviour. But there are also various partial, or middle-range, theories that can be brought into play, notably those associated with foreign policy analysis (FPA). Indeed, FPA can hardly be avoided if one wishes to probe the complex processes of decision-making involved in the generation of Europe's 'foreign policy' (White 2001). Bureaucratic politics within the Commission and the Council Secretariat, distinctive 'domestic' constituencies for leaders to defer to, and serious problems of coherence and legitimacy all demand the attention of the middle-range theories generated within FPA. There is fertile ground here for future scholarship.

Other approaches go yet further in contesting the notion of more or less objective interests determining Europe's external behaviour. Institutionalization, or in this context 'Europeanization', suggests that states are influenced by common rules and procedures to draw ever closer together. The contributors to this volume would disagree on the extent to which this is happening, or is inexorable, but few would disagree with Wong that the EU has come to constitute an ever more powerful point of reference in international relations, both for its member states and for its neighbours. This is a minimal but useful definition of Europeanization.

A constructivist approach, as noted in Chapter 2, would emphasize the argument that shared understandings of what constitutes Europe's role and interest in the world are gradually giving *meaning* to the material position of the EU, a position that cannot speak for itself, as it were. The perceptions of the actors—including third parties—help to give Europe its international identity and thus some of its capabilities (Bretherton and Vogler 2006). This approach informs not just Wong's discussion of Europeanization, but also Linklater's argument that the EU is presenting itself as a civilizing force in international relations, and is increasingly being seen as such by outsiders. Constructivists would also argue that the notion of 'European interests' is one that reflects the construction of those interests in the process of responding to the demands both of integration and of the outside world, partly at least through a process of 'social learning'.

Robert Cooper's extension of this focus on identity and constructed interests, to the effect that the EU represents a high point of post-modernism in its breakdown of the distinction between domestic and foreign affairs, is not taken up explicitly in this book, although plenty of attention is given to the multilevel nature of its system for producing external policy (Cooper 2003). The side of his argument that deals with policy substance, however, attracts strong support. Cooper argued that the EU needed a commitment both to the multilateralism which is its own defining feature and to the possession of more of the traditional kind of hard, or military, power (ibid., 164–72). This view is developed in the chapters by Howorth and Rees, while Edwards and Verdun both show how extensive is the Union's pursuit and promotion of multilateral diplomatic or economic partners like itself. As Smith and Steffenson indicate, while the EU cannot hope to match the hard power of the United States, it has concluded that in order to deal with Washington on more equal terms it needs to go beyond cooperation towards some more state-like capabilities. In effect, it has to move from a loose to a tight form of multilateralism.

At the other end of the spectrum, neo-Marxist structuralism finds little favour these days as either an explanation of or a prescription for European policy, but we should be aware of its importance in shaping critical attitudes towards the treatment of the Third World in the 1960s and 1970s, in parts of which it still lives on, leading to complaints about the Lomé and Cotonou agreements as neo-colonialist (H. Smith 2002; see also Carbone, Chapter 14). Europeans themselves should bear in mind this tradition of thought, despite the collapse of communism. We do not like to think of ourselves as a conservative, wealthy force in international society, but that is how it appears to the poor majority. Nearly 40 years ago, in an under-rated book, Johan Galtung warned that the European Community was doomed to exercise structural power in the sense of being able to determine the life chances of the exploited Third World (Galtung 1973, 38–47, 55–86, but see Keukeleire 2003, and Chapter 16 here, for a more neutral use of the term 'structural power'). The differences between Europeans and Americans from this perspective are much less than we tend to think, especially given the reappearance in Europe during the early 2000s of confidence in a civilizing mission, or 'liberal imperialism' (Cooper 2002). If Europe has great economic power, then that implies an international hierarchy working to its advantage. This may be difficult to reconcile with its hopes to represent a new kind of order, or civility, for others to follow.

The place of the EU in the international system

Against this theoretical background, of inevitably competing interpretations, what can we say about the *substance* of the EU's place in the international system? If realism tends to scepticism over Europe's collective capabilities, liberalism has the opposite tendency. For its part constructivism, by emphasizing the generation of common understandings and responsiveness, looks more like liberalism than it does realism. Critical approaches in general highlight strengths and weaknesses in specific issue areas and/or parts of the world, while allowing for a discussion of what might be immanent—or merely just possible. Yet ideological preferences infect all perspectives, and thus shape the kinds of prescription they offer. Amidst this confusing cacophony, there are still some clear indications both about what the EU cannot do, and about the positive functions it performs in the international system.

What the EU is not

There are three things which it is clear the EU is *not*, in terms of its international role:

- It is *not* a straightforward 'pole' in a multipolar system. Such a system does not yet exist, given the huge inequalities of wealth and military power that still obtain between the USA and even states like China and India, although there is increasing discussion of whether multipolarity is now finally emerging. It is clear that despite recent developments in its institutional capacity, the EU still does not possess cumulative power across all major dimensions—although it aspires to do so. Its strength in trade is not yet matched even in the areas of finance and environmental policy (and one might argue that this weakness was cruelly exposed by the failure of the Copenhagen environment conference and the problems of the euro in 2009–10), while its strengths in diplomacy and development aid are intermittent and patchy at best. The EU is indeed a major point of reference for other states and possesses a distinct 'power of attraction' (Munuera 1994), but despite French ambitions it is as yet well short of being able even to constitute an equal pillar in the Western alliance.

• Yet equally the EU is *not* merely a subordinate subsystem of Western capitalism, and/or a province of a US world empire, as in their different ways both the anti-globalization movement and al-Qaeda believe. The United States certainly has a privileged position in terms of access to European decision-making, with some particularly 'special' relationships with member states and individuals (it should not be forgotten that Javier Solana, the first High Representative for Common Foreign and Security Policy, was an ex-Secretary General of NATO) as well as a formal transatlantic partnership with the EU. It often succeeds in dividing and ruling the Europeans, as well as overshadowing them in high politics. What it does not do, however, is to control them, or persistently manipulate the CFSP as an instrument of its global strategy. As Smith and Steffenson show, the EU very often stands up to Washington, at least in terms of taking a different line, and where it has the power—as in trade policy—it is not above forcing a showdown. The USA has twice backed away in tussles over the key politico-legal-economic issue of extra-territoriality, over the Siberian gas pipeline in 1982, and the Helms-Burton legislation over Cuba in 1996, and it has far less than a 100 per cent record in trade disputes with the EU. This is because the USA needs European support often enough not to be able to take it for granted—and also because the EU can use multilateral rules and institutions at least as effectively as Washington. The USA thus has to make concessions. Insofar as a division-of-labour approach is sometimes visible even in areas of 'hard security' (as possibly over Iran from 2003 onwards) this is as much on European as on US terms.

• The EU, and still less its international policies, is *not* a channel by which political agency is surrendering to the forces of functionalism and globalization. Although European integration has favoured international free trade rather than mercantilism, this does not mean that the EU has signed its own death warrant. Rather, it has given Brussels a more significant place in the regulation of the international economy, as growth has been achieved and the major states of Europe have embarked on more path-breaking projects, from the single market to EMU and the 'open method of coordination' (Wallace *et al.* 2010; Peterson and Shackleton 2006). Thus the EU itself has acquired more powers in international relations—even if it is still far from having all the necessary attributes of statehood—without robbing its member states of their own national identities. Alan Milward may have been right that the European Economic Community 'saved' the nation state in the 1950s and 1960s (Milward 1992; 2000). It may still be helping to do so with the ex-Soviet satellites in the post-Cold War era. But if this trend has slowed, and gradually the states are relinquishing some of their capacity to exercise sovereignty, the study of the EU's international relations could lead no one to suppose that the gates are being opened to a tidal wave of globalization. Despite the problems it experienced in the 2009–10 financial crisis, the EU is neither so economically liberal nor so powerless that it is at the mercy of wider forces. Indeed, this is precisely why so many Europeans are attempting to strengthen the EU: as a means of *managing* globalization. Thus the interplay of the international environment with the EU institutions has led to a renegotiation of the place of government, not its undermining, and to the creation of a parastatal entity alongside the traditional nation states, to handle those tasks with which they might otherwise struggle. The fact that the 2009–10 crisis itself led to calls for a greater degree of 'economic government' in the eurozone bears witness to the continuing vigour of this process.

The EU's positive contributions

Turning to the more positive side of the equation, on the basis of the analyses presented in this book we can see that the European Union fulfils certain distinctive functions in the international system, and is likely to continue to do so for the foreseeable future. Firstly, whatever the general truth of the 'democratic peace' hypothesis, the EU does represent a settled bloc of constitutional relations, and a zone of peace, in the international system. Indeed, it has created a regional form of international *society*. This might or might not represent a building block for the overall nature of international relations (M. Smith 2007), but it is acknowledged and respected across the world as a major political (as well as economic) achievement.

Secondly, and as a consequence of this achievement, the EU represents a model for other regional organizations. It is true that this has been the case for nearly 50 years, and yet nothing has come near to emulating the EU's success—perhaps the result of a certain idealism on both sides as to what the model entails (Nicolaïdis and Howse 2002). Nonetheless, many less mature groupings have sought bloc-to-bloc relations, as indicated by Edwards in Chapter 3 (see also Alecu de Flers and Regelsberger 2005; Hardacre and Smith 2009; Hardacre 2009). In doing so they have had to deepen their own internal structures, while following the EU in keeping foreign policy a purely intergovernmental process. The idea of regional integration, however, remains strong precisely because of the existence and growth of the EU.

To turn Schmitter's idea of the 'external federator' on its head, one could say that the need to deal with a rich and powerful EU draws other states into cooperative ventures, *especially* in their international relations (Schmitter 1969). This is as true of the Southern African Development Community (SADC), most of whose members feared the consequences of a bilateral deal between South Africa and the EU, as it is of the Asia–Europe Meeting (ASEM), which was set up precisely to create an inter-regional diplomacy that did not previously exist.

The third practical function fulfilled by the EU in world politics is that of a reference point inside other international organizations. With the steady increase in the number of sovereign states created since 1945, the universal institutions are now large and unwieldy, with evident spaces for leadership and caucuses to grow up—not least as an alternative to a US diplomatic hegemony. That the EU does not act as one in the UN Security Council is a huge gap in its portfolio, which damages its image as much as it undermines capabilities, but elsewhere there are signs of ever greater coordination. One scholar has recently observed both that 'representatives from other UN member states charge that nothing gets accomplished in many UN bodies unless the Europeans are on board', and that there is 'compelling evidence that European voting cohesion has grown rather dramatically in the UN General Assembly over the course of the 1990s' (Laatikainen 2004, 4; see also Laatikainen and Smith 2006). The influence of the EU is equally felt in the functional organizations such as the World Health Organization and the International Atomic Energy Agency (IAEA) (witness Iran's willingness to work with the IAEA and the EU, but not the USA, at various stages of the dispute over its nuclear programme). In the major international economic organizations, the EU presence is of great significance in the WTO and the Organisation for Economic Co-operation and Development (OECD) (in the latter case, EU member states constitute a substantial majority of the membership), but more subordinate to the USA and individual member states in the International Monetary Fund (IMF) and World Bank (where the complexities arising from the eurozone contribute to the fragmentation of European positions). This might change once the Union has got used to possessing the legal personality that is provided for in the Lisbon Treaty.

Still at the level of outsiders' perceptions, the EU clearly represents the hopes of many, from Russia and China through Canada and Japan to the Third World, for some kind of political counterbalance to the United States. Few hold illusions about the possibility—or desirability—of Europe rivalling the USA in military terms and thus balancing its power in the classical manner. What is seen as possible is an alternative articulation of Western interests, with more understanding shown of the underlying reasons for conflict than is sometimes on view in Washington—and which was particularly lacking in the George W. Bush administrations. In the poorer countries, save those irredeemably in the US orbit, there is a hope that the EU and its members might be able to restrain Washington, and also to encourage it (as to some extent has indeed happened) down the road of debt relief and overseas development aid. In a unipolar world, where the phrase 'hyperpower' is not mere hyperbole, only a grouping of the rich states stands much chance of 'balancing' the USA, and that only in a purely diplomatic sense. The EU is the prime candidate to lead such activity, and even it is significantly constrained—by internal divisions, by prudence, and by genuine identification with many US positions. The story of climate change negotiations during the past decade, as explored by Vogler, shows both the strengths and the weaknesses of the EU's positions in a complex and dynamic area of activity.

The last of the five substantive functions that the EU fulfils in international relations is that to which Linklater's chapter draws particular attention, namely the actualization of certain principles of conduct in foreign policy. This is related to our first point about Europe being a building block of constitutionalism in international order, but it refers more to the power of example. It is a Hegelian point about the realization of what might otherwise remain ideas and principles. Just as the collective action embodied in the EU has enabled European states to free themselves from the mindset and unpleasant associations of colonial overlordship, so Linklater demonstrates that the activities of the EU have raised a series of important questions about how to promote common interests in international relations without harming or unnecessarily antagonizing others.

The idea of 'civilian power' has been central to this process, in stressing the utility of benign means, and widely shared 'milieu' goals, over such matters as the environment or new forms of governance for a turbulent world. But in recent years the EU has gone beyond this somewhat sloganistic notion to more practical methods of standard setting, such as the promotion of a human rights culture, and of transnational processes of justice and criminal investigation. The latter cuts both ways, in that the scale of the EU and the cooperation it fosters can increase the power of surveillance and policing over ordinary citizens, thus tipping the balance of world politics even further in favour of the big battalions. But this is a tension that has been evident in the EU right from its birth.

System, process, and power

We began this book by arguing that no one theory, or approach, was suitable for the complex tasks of explaining, understanding, and prescribing for the international relations of the European Union. In this case, one size definitely does not fit all, given the multiplicity of policies, actors, and levels of decision-making involved in the relations between 27 member states, at least three major collective institutions, and well over 200 third states and international organizations—to say nothing of the plethora of non-governmental organizations and other outputs of civil society. We therefore suggested a three-part model as a way of coming to terms with not just multilevel governance but also manifold diplomacy: the EU as a *subsystem* of international relations; as enmeshed in the *processes of general international relations*; and as an actual and potential *power* in the world. We now take these three sets of issues in turn, as a means of auditing the Union's performance, in the light of the specialist accounts that make up the bulk of this book.

The EU as a subsystem of international relations

The politics that takes place inside the EU is that of the demi-monde, neither fully domestic nor authentically international. The trajectory may be that of 'European-ization', but we are still some distance from reaching the end point of such a process, especially in relation to foreign policy making. Nonetheless, the level of trust that has been achieved between member states is unprecedented in the history of international relations between sovereign units, and the range of instruments that the units have available to them in dealings with each other is spectacularly narrower than it would have been half a century earlier. If international relations still exist between the member states, they do so in a manner that is much transformed from the usual understanding of the term.

This quality of domestication is both what attracts outsiders to seek membership and what is called into question by them. Although it is tempting to project into the future the line of progress from the past, we cannot be wholly sure that the arrival of 12, perhaps ultimately 15–20, new members within a few decades will not have more effect on the Union than it has on them. Enlargement may turn out to have reimported some international relations to the Union's internal affairs, or at least to have complicated its internal functioning. What is more, the possibility of yet further rounds of enlargement, coupled with the intensification of 'neighbourhood policy' as explored by Karen Smith, makes the very distinction between the EU and its environment, between the internal and the external, ambiguous and contentious.

Another aspect of the EU as subsystem that has been carefully dissected here, particularly in the chapters of Part II, is that of the EU's existence as a means of coordinating the interests and preferences of member states for the purposes of collective action in world politics. Seen from outside, the EU represents a dense set of interactions, and a sophisticated decision-making process, albeit one that is too complex to be easily understood, or manipulated. Although third parties do not easily penetrate into the EU subsystem, it does happen. The United States is the main 'Trojan horse', but Iceland, Norway, and Turkey also have inside tracks. Canada and Japan have had regular high-level summits for more than ten years and other 'strategic partnerships' have been pursued towards India and China (see Keukeleire and Bruyninckx, Chapter 16). Conversely, EU policy making is not insulated from other networks and international organizations, whether the UN Security

Council or the international financial institutions. On several occasions, for example, European development policy has taken its cue from the World Bank, and the response of the EU to the financial crisis of 2009–10 was notable for its (eventual) coordination with the IMF.

The institutions of the Union clearly play an important part in making the European subsystem of international relations work. Vanhoonacker shows how 'historical institutionalism' has gradually shaped and consolidated key practices (Chapter 4). These may or may not strengthen Europeans' hands in the world, according to political viewpoint, but they are certainly now difficult to unstitch. For example, while the Commission's part in EU external relations has been weakened in recent years, with the decline in its general position, it remains a key player in the Common Commercial Policy, in conjunction with the Council and the Trade Policy (ex-Article 133) Committee. It has also made determined efforts to assert its role in the new EU system of diplomacy emerging in the wake of the Lisbon Treaty. Institutions and policies interact to produce various forms of path-dependency, but also at times to produce opportunities for innovation.

Although it is tempting to emphasize the strength and impact of the EU's institutions, there is also a considerable degree of heterogeneity. Lord shows how such accountability and legitimacy as exist in relation to external policy within the EU are the product of interplay between the European Parliament and national legislatures, while Gebhard makes explicit the wide range of 'coherence' problems that bedevil the Union in dealing with outsiders: neutral, benign, and malign (Chapter 5). As her language suggests, much of this may not matter too much. Indeed it may be a perfectly sensible way of providing actions 'fit for purpose', and of avoiding the conflicts inherent in trying for too much symmetry. On occasion it may also usefully confuse third parties. But there can be no dispute that coherence is perceived internally as causing sufficient problems to have preoccupied generations of officials, in attempts to dream up solutions for the inconsistencies evident to, and sometimes exploited by, outsiders.

In Chapter 7, Wong shows how Europeanization may render some of these problems redundant in the long run, but his focus on the Common Foreign and Security Policy makes it clear that there is still quite a distance to travel before that point is reached. It is here that problems of vertical consistency are most pronounced—surfacing to disastrous effect during the build-up to the Iraq war in 2002–3, to the point where there was a complete schism between two intra-European camps. Such dramas belie the long-term processes of convergence also observable in underlying foreign policy attitudes, and in the more effective work being done out of the spotlight, on subjects as diverse as Kosovo and money laundering. The Union may make mistakes in its foreign policy, but it has a systemic capacity to acknowledge them, and often to learn, as has been clear in the Balkans since the 1995 Dayton Agreement and in some of its involvements in sub-Saharan Africa. It is indeed a 'foreign policy system' in the broad sense, including the Commission, the Council and the External Action Service, now in theory being pulled together under the High Representative, plus the member states, all of which engage in a continuous if not always harmonious process of mutually constituting discussion, and some action (Hill 1991).

The EU and the general processes of international relations

All actors are solipsistic, but the EU is at the benign end of the spectrum and surprisingly open in most of its activities. The accusation of 'fortress Europe' has never been more than a squawk of fear from nervous outsiders. Given the commitments to free trade, enlargement, civilian power, and democratization, it would be difficult not to become interpenetrated with the wider processes of international relations. Even the worries about Schengen and the 'hard' external border of the Union are exaggerated. The arrangements to monitor the common frontiers are a consequence of free movements within the EU and in any case are no worse and no better than those implemented by any given nation state.

The EU is enmeshed with its neighbours, with other international organizations, and with the functional processes of rule and law making. To some, indeed, this process seems to have gone so far as to call into question its very actorness. The boundaries between value systems and processes of governance (if not physical frontiers) may become so fuzzy that 'Europe' and the EU blur into each other, or that the latter stands more for a set of principles than a distinctive and defendable set of interests (M. Smith 1996a; 2007; Christiansen *et al.* 2000). Furthermore, enlargement, especially if it involves too much expansion too quickly, might lead the EU to become more like the Organization for Security and Cooperation in Europe (OSCE) than its former self, more a framework than an 'action organisation' (Hill 2002, 107). Variable geometry might then mean not just inner groups pursuing 'structured' or 'enhanced' cooperation, but also limited groups that extend to outsiders—as already happens with the Schengen group, but was resisted when Turkey attempted to leap from the dying Western European Union straight into the ESDP (European Security and Defence Policy) process during the early 2000s.

A more reasonable interpretation, and one borne out in large part by the contents of this volume, is that the EU is both a key part of the multilateral structures of world politics and a player of growing resource and influence in its own right. As Michael E. Smith says in Chapter 8, it 'will continue its erratic though progressive development as a unique global actor'. Smith demonstrates how many resources the Union disposes of and the range of instruments this translates into. Not all are easily useable for political (that is, foreign policy) purposes, but they all help 'to shape not only the regional future of Europe, but also the international environment on which that future depends'. Diplomatic, economic, and now some limited military tools are all available to the EU, based on a population nearly 60 per cent bigger than that of the USA and on a far deeper involvement in international processes than that of the world's only superpower. This is not to say that the EU rivals the USA in power; on most indicators, including the perceptions of third states, it does not come close. But its wealth, history, range of contacts, and potential all mean that the fate of the Union is bound up with that of the international system as a whole—and possibly vice versa. This is why so many regional organizations continue to seek privileged relationships with the EU. Furthermore, as Smith and Steffenson argue in Chapter 17, between them the USA and the EU have dominated the agenda of international politics, in a relationship of 'competitive cooperation'. When they cooperate, they can determine many outcomes; when they disagree, the political space that then opens up defines the opportunities for other states. This situation, however, may be changing with major changes in the international constellation of power and consequent modifications to key processes (as argued by Keukeleire and Bruyninckx, Chapter 16).

To some extent it is the issue area that determines the nature of the EU's role in the wider system, with the EU being much more central to international processes in economics than in the high politics of, say, arms control or Security Council reform. Nonetheless, as the agenda of foreign policy widens, this distinction is itself being eroded (Hill 2003, 4). The result is more to heighten Europe's profile and status than to damage it, as the greater role for domestic and transnational actors favours an organization like the EU which stresses openness in politics and multilevel forms of governance. It is revealing, for example, that in policy terms (at least) the three-pillared structure of the Maastricht Treaty had broken down even before the Lisbon Treaty formally abolished it: 'Justice and Home Affairs' (JHA) increasingly involves international issues, and often cooperation with third states; the CFSP extended to defence, and could only work at all through liaison with the external economic policies of pillar I and with the 'homeland security' aspects of pillar III. On this basis it is clear that the Union has been flexible enough to allow issues to interrelate, and to accumulate, where the flow of events demanded it; in a sense Lisbon only recognized rather than initiated these processes.

There are, however, two important issues still unresolved in terms of the EU's involvement in international processes. The first is the fact that while issues have de facto begun to flow into each other, and the Lisbon Treaty has formally abolished the distinctions between the 'pillars', the differentiation of decision-making procedures remains. The Treaty attempts to make the operation of EU external relations easier (indeed, arguably this is its main thrust, despite having been conceived as a way of enabling the EU institutions to cope better with enlargement), but it will not unify procedures or make it much easier for outsiders to understand the basis on which a particular decision is taken. As Simon Nuttall said in the first edition of this book, 'as long as two bodies with overlapping responsibilities coexist, there will be a problem of institutional consistency' (2005, 103). Nuttall was referring to the Commission and Council Secretariat but the Treaty of Lisbon has produced a further tension. The new figures of the elected President of the European Council and the strengthened High Representative will still be subject to the constraints and complexities arising from intergovernmentalism in the CFSP and JHA coexisting with the Community method, and from the mixed policy-making modes evident in such areas as energy and the environment. Furthermore, in their mutual relations these two personalities may also add yet another discordant note to the policy-making process.

The geographical dimension is the second major issue outstanding. The EU still needs to take a position on whether it wishes its engagement with the international system to be largely regional, in its own neighbourhood; global, as an aspirant superpower with pretensions to be heard on all major issues and crises; or neither, in the sense that geography is not the main criterion for action, rather being supplanted by functional, political, or other concerns 'on their merits'. This is less a matter of hard-and-fast choice than of balance between competing considerations. The regional and the global cannot be mutually exclusive categories when the territory of one powerful neighbour stretches as far as Vladivostok, or when some member states still have territorial possessions in the Pacific or South Atlantic. Still, decisions have to be taken on priorities, and where European resources can be best made to count. Did the European Security Strategy (ESS) of December 2003 make a tacit judgement, for example, that the USA was no longer so committed to Europe and that the Union must now concentrate on its own immediate security, making common cause with like-minded neighbours? Or did the two statements in the strategy—on the one hand, that 'in an era of globalization, distant threats may be as much a concern as those that are near at hand', and on the other that there is a 'need to develop a strategic culture that fosters early, rapid, and where necessary, robust intervention'—reveal a new globalist ambition? (European Council 2003b). The tenor of the document was certainly globalist: 'an active and capable European Union would make an impact on a global scale'; but the failure so far to envisage anything like the resources needed to give meaning to the rhetoric leaves the position ambiguous if not contradictory. The revision of the ESS in December 2008, revealingly entitled only a 'Report by the Secretary General/High Representative on the European Security Strategy', changed nothing of note, and indeed stressed that security threats to the EU had to be 'tackled globally' (European Council 2008, Annexes 2 and 6). Yet if the theory is global, current practice is necessarily regional.

The EU as a power in the world

However much emphasis the EU places on multilateralism and interdependence, it will still be judged by many, and particularly the bigger states in the world, on the criterion of power. How capable are the Europeans, collectively, of defending—and asserting—their own interests, even against the opposition of others? Was Robert Kagan right in seeing the EU's distinctive international posture, including the idea of civilian power, as a mere rationalization of painful weakness (Kagan 2003)?

The first response to this kind of scepticism is that international power is divisible. In some policy arenas, generally insulated from others, the Union does indeed have considerable capacity to achieve its ends and to ensure that its positions are factored into the calculations of others. Indeed, it could without exaggeration be said that the EU is an economic superpower because of its weight in world trade, the increasing strength and importance of its common currency, and its sheer size and wealth. In the UN Human Development Index for 2009, EU member states occupied 11 of the top 20 places in a table of 182 countries that aggregates life expectancy, literacy, and education together with the familiar measure of GDP per capita (United Nations Development Programme 2009). This makes the EU a relatively conservative power, in the sense of having interests in the status quo. Yet, as Giuseppe di Lampedusa explained in *The Leopard*, to retain your advantages you need to move with the times, and the Europeans have been willing and able to force the United States into compromises at the WTO, to seek changes in Third World regimes through the political conditionality attaching to their development policy, and to use their leverage on those states in their orbit which wish for accession or special relationships.

It is on the dimension of 'hard power' that the EU justifies Kagan's jibe. Although strictly speaking the term should cover any attempt at coercion, including economic sanctions (where the Europeans generally have more leverage than the USA), it is mostly associated with military force. Howorth, in Chapter 9, shows how, given the zero baseline the EU started from in 1998, progress in recent years has been surprisingly rapid. But there is still a long way to go in terms of coordination, spending, and technological advance before the Union can attain a level of coordinated and autonomous military strength that is consonant with its size and wealth. The small operations in (for example) the Democratic Republic of Congo and other sub-Saharan African locations, Macedonia, and Bosnia are admirable in their way, but they would not be sufficient even to prevent the outbreak of large-scale fighting in these countries, let alone to defeat a determined national force in the way the USA did over Kosovo and in Iraq.

Since Saint-Malo in 1998, the Europeans have decided that soft power is not enough, while realizing that serious military capability will take at least a generation to achieve. They thus seek to square the circle by fostering a stable external environment in which multilateralism figures prominently, whether through stressing the importance of the UN or working with other compatible organizations such as NATO and the OSCE. Moral conviction and example are important, but they will do little in the short term in intractable conflicts or against intransigent adversaries. Moreover, they will carry little force if the EU itself appears to be behaving in a disreputable fashion.

This is the ultimate dilemma for the contemporary EU: should it attempt to develop its capabilities according to conventional definitions of power, including the military element, when this might put at risk the very (irenic) values which Europe has come to stand for in international relations? The emphasis on conflict prevention as an instrument of external action from the late 1990s is not surprising in this context, as it seems to offer an escape route from the dilemma. Yet since wishing does not make it so in international politics, conflict prevention remains a necessary but insufficient platform for external strategy. Even here, conventional power is often necessary in order to bring warring parties to the table, as the tragic stalemate over the Palestinian Territories in the absence of determined US pressure illustrates.

What about Europe's *impact*? How may we judge what kind of a power it is or might be in world politics? Naturally we may all draw our own political and moral conclusions about the desirability of various actions, and of possibilities like militarization and/or superpowerdom. But in terms of making as objective an assessment as possible of the extent to which the EU makes a difference to outcomes, we need to consider both perceptions and the actual pattern of events.

On the perceptions side, the EU's impact needs to be measured against the expectations of both insiders and outsiders (Hill 1993a; 1998a). Since the Saint-Malo initiative these two sets of views have not diverged markedly. The forging of the CSDP has been seen as a serious development by many, including a Turkey fearful over exclusion and a USA determined on the primacy of NATO. The failure to meet the headline goals in 2003 produced a corresponding disappointment, while the public splits over Iraq lowered expectations over both political and military capability as never before. European public opinion expected more of the Union in this crisis than at any previous time, and its failure strengthened the arguments of the CFSP sceptics. That said, hope springs eternal for the integrationists and for those in need, so that there have been continued calls for effective EU action in such diverse places as Darfur (the Sudan), the Congolese–Rwandan border, and the Ukraine, encouraged by the long-term EU presence in the Balkans. Looked at in historical perspective, the EU probably has more impact across more issues in world politics than it did 20 years ago, but since expectations have risen even more, it gets less credit.

The other side of this coin is overstretch. But this is only likely if the EU places too much emphasis on the exercise of power and an ability to make a difference in the great conflicts of international politics. If it accepts, for the time being, that at least it has a significant presence throughout international relations, plus a distinctive and relatively unthreatening identity, there are benefits to be had that might outweigh the obvious frustrations of a self-denying ordinance. For at the operational (that is, not just the psychological) level the EU does have a significant impact. Israel might have contemptuously destroyed buildings funded by the EU for the Palestinian Authority, but that was itself a recognition of the fact that European resources were being brought to bear to the Palestinian advantage; the persistent exercise of a carrot-and-stick policy toward Libya was probably as important as the invasion of Iraq in enabling Colonel Ghaddafi to come in from the cold; the rapid mediation provided by the EU, and in particular by the French Presidency, during the war in Georgia of 2008 served the interests of both Russia and the Georgian government in a way that the slower-moving UN, and *parti pris* USA, could not have done.

These are only three examples from recent years. They could be multiplied. What is clear is that the EU both *has* power, and *is* a power of a certain kind in international relations, even if these claims must be qualified by reference to geography and issue area. More generally, it has most external impact either in the purely trade and regulatory areas, or at the interface of economics and politics, where it has a distinct advantage. But even in matters of classical diplomacy the critical mass represented by 27 states acting in unison (when they do) can be impressive, while the small but useable military capabilities now available have given the EU a physical presence in certain key flashpoints. It need no longer be a question of handwringing from a distance.

In some respects the EU fits Stephan Keukeleire's model of 'structural power' (Keukeleire 2003; Keukeleire and MacNaughtan 2008; and Chapter 16 in this volume; but see the discussion above of Galtung's different use of the term). This stresses how an actor often seeks to shape the overall environment in which it and its peers operate (see also Wolfers 1962). The European Union does have the capacity to shape some important aspects of the structures, or milieux, affecting other states' choices. Measured by absolute standards this power will be found to be limited and inconsistent, but assessed in relative terms against the capacities of other actors, the EU looks like one of the most significant members of the international system. China and India have bigger populations, and the potential to be superpowers, which the EU may not choose, or be able, to follow. But they are still some distance from reaching that status, and their influence now is primarily regional. Russia still has more sway than it is given credit for, in the wake of the collapse of the USSR, but it is hobbled by internal problems and on the defensive geopolitically except where it can use its energy resources as a diplomatic weapon. Only the USA has more capacity to influence the shape and evolution of international politics than the EU.

Conclusions

In this chapter we have sought to do justice to the complexity of our subject, and to the detailed analysis provided by our contributors. But it is also important to take the broad view and to summarize the common findings of the book. They are fivefold:

1. *An understanding of the EU's evolution cannot be achieved without reference to the international dimension.* This apparent truism is necessary because of the neglect of international relations and foreign policy evident in most mainstream political science approaches to European integration over the last 40 years. Whether it is Haas (neo-functionalism) or Moravcsik (liberal intergovernmentalism), or even Hoffmann (liberal realism), the issue of the meaning of European foreign policy cooperation for the international system, and conversely the impact of international relations on the EU, have been of marginal concern (Haas 1964; Hoffmann 1995; Moravcsik 1998). There have been

exceptions, as with aspects of the work of the lawyer Joseph Weiler, but for the most part these issues have been pursued only by European foreign policy specialists, such as Ginsberg (Ginsberg 1989; Weiler 1999; 2001). Their work has gradually broadened out to include political economy and transnational issues but it has generally not been picked up on by those not already on the same expert circuit. Mearsheimer, for example, has taken some dramatic positions on Europe's international relations, but has based them on axiomatic realism rather than engage with the specialist literature on the EU (Mearsheimer 1990; 1994–5). The result is that much high-profile political science, especially in the United States, simplifies the EU's international activities by looking at them through the lens of comparative politics or neorealism, neither of which is fit for the purpose.

2. *The EU is a significant presence in the international system, along most dimensions.* Economically it is a major player; politically it represents an alternative voice within the West—yet also, paradoxically, the USA's most valued set of allies; militarily, it has finally entered the lists, and in only six years has made notable, practical progress; culturally Europe represents one of the greatest concentrations of artistic and scientific endeavour, and possesses a raft of internationally admired educational resources. In short, Europe counts. The EU represents a new 'quality' of international relations and to some degree a distinct subsystem. It is also deeply implicated in the wider, regulatory processes of the international system—political, institutional, legal, social, and normative.

3. *The academic subject of International Relations needs to place the EU's external activities nearer to the centre of its concerns.* This is true of both theory and empiricism and to some extent also of the EU more generally. Too often in the past the EU has been dependent on some major event or policy—such as the 1973 oil crisis, or the single market initiative, to attract wider intellectual attention, when the truth is that it is an inherently important and now an enduring experiment in international cooperation, with an accumulated capacity to shape the external environments of most other actors. On the empirical side, no student of the post-Cold War order, whether unipolar or potentially multipolar, can neglect the EU. Even those who take the view that national foreign policies still hold sway in Europe need to relate their studies of Germany or France, Spain, or Poland, to the CFSP framework in which they are played out. Specialists of other regions, equally, are increasingly likely to take Europe's activities into account as they attempt to explain the regional dynamics of international relations. This is most obviously true of the ex-CIS or the Middle East, but the EU is a notable factor also in Africa, and in parts of Asia and Latin America.

Theoretically, IR will benefit from incorporating the EU more fully into its *Weltanschauung*. Whether we are interested in the behaviour of states, international organization, political economy, the impact of domestic politics,

ethical foreign policy, human rights, conflict resolution, identity, or other central issues in the subject, the study of the EU in the world has much to teach
us. Given the range of the EU's international activity and its evident capacity
to transform a range of international relationships, the days have passed of
being able to bracket it out as a theoretical anomaly.

4. *The EU should fit distinctively, but without excessive strain, into the general
   categories of International Relations scholarship.* Realism, liberalism, and
   structuralism, or post-positivisms of various kinds may all be applied—and
   increasingly are being—to the problems of explaining and understanding
   the EU's international roles. So long as the original purpose is not forgotten,
   there will be significant gains from this encounter. Even if the EU is deemed
   sui generis, the definition still depends on comparisons with other kinds of
   actors. Comparative analysis, as generated in IR principally by foreign policy
   analysis, is indispensable in identifying those aspects of the political and decision-making processes which are to be found in the EU as well as in states,
   and those that can only be understood from the inside out.

5. *The EU is better thought of as having powers than as being 'a power'.* Its forms
   of presence vary, its impacts are not necessarily cumulative and its power is
   not therefore always fungible. But the EU is now much nearer being a coherent power than when Johan Galtung discussed its coming superpower status
   in 1973, and even realists no longer find it so inconceivable that it might
   actually reach that point during the present century. Enlargement, complexity, and 'the logic of diversity' are the major obstacles, as well as sharp
   normative disagreements among the citizens of Europe as to its desirability.
   Third states will also not stand idly by if they see their interests as threatened
   by growing European power. At the least they will play on internal divisions,
   which in an increasingly large and diverse Union is not so difficult. In any
   case whether superpower is, or should be, the *telos* of the EU will remain
   a hotly contested subject. What is not in dispute is the fact that the international relations of the Union are now a subject of immense political and
   intellectual significance.

This said, there are processes of change apparent in the international arena that
constitute a challenge to the continued expansion of the EU's international engagement and influence. It would be foolish to ignore the fact that changes to the international constellation of power have created new conditions for the conduct of the
EU's international relations. Contributors to this volume have identified a range
of such changes: the rise of the BRICs, the growing politicization of issues such as
energy and the environment, the continuing challenges of non-state forces such as
those of terrorism. Our contributors have also noted the challenges to the EU's continuing dynamism and capacity to innovate, arising from economic crisis and the
inevitable political constraints that this imposes. How fundamental these challenges

may prove to be, and how well equipped the post-Lisbon EU is to meet them, remains an open question. It is clear, however, that the beginnings of an answer to this question lie at least partly in the types of analysis conducted in this volume, and in the continued interaction of international relations (the process), International Relations (the field of study), and the European Union.

▌ REFERENCES

Abdelal, R., and Meunier, S. (2010), 'Managed Globalization: Doctrine, Practice and Promise', *Journal of European Public Policy* 17/3: 350–67.

Adelle, C., Pallemaerts, M., and Chiavari, J. (2009), *Climate Change and Energy Security in Europe: Policy Integration and its Limits*, Report No. 4 (Stockholm: Swedish Institute of European Policy Studies; available at www.sieps.se).

Adler, E. (2002), 'Constructivism and International Relations', in W. Carlsnaes, B. Simmons, and T. Risse (eds), *Sage Handbook of International Relations* (Thousand Oaks: Sage).

Adler, E., and Barnett, M. (eds) (1998), *Security Communities* (Cambridge: Cambridge University Press).

Agence Presse (2007a), 'EU wants north African countries to monitor EU borders in exchange for visa facilitation', No. 9554, 30 November.

Agence Presse (2007b), 'EU/Neighbourhood', No. 9558, 6 December.

Aggestam, L. (2004), 'Role Identity and Europeanisation of Foreign Policy: a Political-cultural approach', in B. Tonra, and T. Christiansen (eds), *Rethinking European Union Foreign Policy* (Manchester: Manchester University Press), 81–98.

Aggestam, L. (ed.) (2008), 'Ethical Power Europe?', Special Issue of *International Affairs* 84/1.

Aggestam, L., and Hill, C. (2008), 'The Challenge of Multiculturalism in European Foreign Policy', in L. Aggestam (ed.), 'Ethical Power Europe', Special Issue of *International Affairs* 84/1: 97–114.

Ágh, A. (1998), *The Politics of Central Europe* (London: Sage).

Ágh, A. (1999), 'Europeanisation of Policy-Making in East Central Europe: The Hungarian Approach to EU Accession', *Journal of European Public Policy* 6/5: 839–54.

Alden, C. (2007), *China in Africa* (New York: Zed Books Ltd).

Alden, C., and Vieira, M. (2005), 'The New Diplomacy of the South: South Africa, Brazil, India and trilateralism', *Third World Quarterly* 26/7: 1077–95.

Alecu de Flers, N., and Regelsberger, E. (2005), 'The EU and Inter-regional Cooperation', in C. Hill, and M. Smith (eds), *International Relations and the European Union* (Oxford: Oxford University Press), 317–42.

Alesina, A., and Giavazzi, F. (2006), *The Future of Europe: Reform or Decline* (Cambridge MA: MIT Press).

Algieri, F. (2008), 'It's the system that matters: Institutionalization and making of EU policy toward China', in D. Shambaugh, E. Sandschneider, and Z. Hong (eds), *China–Europe Relations: Perception, policies and prospects* (London: Routledge), 65–83.

Allen, D. (1978), 'The Euro–Arab Dialogue', *Journal of Common Market Studies* 16/4: 323–42.

Allen, D. (1992), 'West European Responses to Change in the Soviet Union and Eastern Europe', in R. Rummel (ed.), *Toward Political Union: Planning a Common Foreign and Security Policy in the European Community* (Boulder, CO: Westview Press).

Allen, D. (1998), 'Who Speaks for Europe? The Search for an Effective and Coherent External Policy', in J. Peterson, and H. Sjursen (eds), *A Common Foreign Policy for Europe? Competing Visions of the CFSP* (London: Routledge), 41–58.

Allen, D. (2004), 'So who will speak for Europe? The constitutional treaty and coherence in EU external relations', *CFSP Forum* 2/5 (September): 1–4.

Allen, D., and Oliver, T. (2006), 'Foreign Policy', in I. Bache, and A. Jordan (eds), *The Europeanization of British Politics* (Basingstoke: Palgrave Macmillan).

Allen, D., and Smith, M. (1990), 'Western Europe's Presence in the Contemporary International Arena', *Review of International Studies* 16/3: 19–38.

Allison, R. (2009), 'The Russian case for military intervention in Georgia: international laws, norms and political calculation', *European Security* 18/2: 173–200.

Alting von Geusau, F.A.M. (ed.) (1977), *The Lomé convention and a new international economic order* (Leyden: Sijthoff).

Andersen, M.S., and Liefferink, D. (eds) (1997), *European Environmental Policy: The Pioneers* (Manchester: Manchester University Press).

Anghel, S., Born, H., Dowling, A., and Fuior, T. (2008), 'National Parliamentary Oversight of EDSP missions', in D. Peters, W. Wagner, and N. Deitelhoff (eds), *The Parliamentary Control of European Security Policy*, Recon Report No. 6, 77/107 (Oslo: Recon/ARENA,), 51–76.

Antunes, J. (2007), 'Developing an Intelligence Capability: The European Union', *Studies in Intelligence* 49/4: https://www.cia.gov/library/center-for-the-study-of-intelligence/csi-publications/csi-studies/studies/vol49no4/Intelligence%20Capability_6.htm

Armijo, L.E. (ed.) (2007), 'Special Issue: The BRICs Countries (Brazil, Russia, India, and China) in the Global System', *Asian Perspective* 31/4: 7–224.

Aron, R. (1966), *Peace and War: A Theory of International Relations* (Garden City, NJ: Doubleday).

Arrighi, G. (2005), 'Hegemony Unravelling 1', *New Left Review* 32: 23–80.

Art, R. (1996), 'Why Western Europe Needs the United States and NATO', *Political Science Quarterly* 111/1: 1–37.

Arts, K., and Dickson, A.K. (eds) (2004), *EU development cooperation: from model to symbol* (Manchester: Manchester University Press).

Averre, D. (2007), '"Sovereign Democracy" and Russia's Relations with the European Union', *Demokratizatsiya* 15/2: 173–190.

Avery, G. (1995), 'The Commission's perspective on the EFTA accession negotiations', Sussex European Institute Working Paper No. 12 (Falmer: University of Sussex).

Avery, G., Howorth, J., Rijks, D., Duke, S., Adebahr, C., Lieb, J., Missiroli, A., Le Gloannec, A.-M., Whitman, R., Keukeleire, S., Grevi, G., and Maurer, A. (2007), *The EU Foreign Service: how to build a more effective common policy*, EPC Working Paper No. 28 (Brussels: European Policy Centre).

Axelrod, R., and Keohane, R. (1985), 'Achieving Cooperation under Anarchy: Strategies and Institutions', *World Politics* 38/1 (October): 226–54.

Babarinde, O., and Faber, G. (eds) (2005), *The European Union and Developing Countries: The Cotonou Agreement* (Leiden: Brill).

Barbé, E. (1996), 'Spain: The Uses of Foreign Policy Cooperation', in C. Hill (ed.) *The Actors in Europe's Foreign Policy* (London: Routledge), 108–29.

Barbé, E. (2004), 'The evolution of CFSP institutions: Where does democratic accountability stand?', *The International Spectator* 34/2: 47–60.

Barbé, E., and Herranz Surralles, A. (2008), 'The Power and Practice of the European Parliament in Security Policies', in D. Peters, W. Wagner, and N. Deitelhoff (eds), *The Parliamentary Control of European Security Policy*, Recon Report No. 6, 77/107 (Oslo: Recon/ARENA).

Barbé, E., and Izquierdo, F. (1997), 'Present and Future of the Joint Actions for the Mediterranean Region', in M. Holland (ed.), *Common Foreign and Security Policy: The Record and Reform* (London: Pinter).

Barbé, E., and Johansson-Nogués, E. (eds) (2003), *Beyond Enlargement: the new members and new frontiers of the enlarged European Union* (Barcelona: Universitat Autonoma de Barcelona).

Barker, R. (2003), 'Legitimacy, Legitimation and the European Union: What Crisis?', in P. Craig, and R. Rawlings (eds), *Law and Administration in Europe. Essays in Honour of Carol Harlow* (Oxford: Oxford University Press).

Barnett, J. (2001), *The Meaning of Environmental Security: Ecological Politics and Policy in the New Security Era* (London: Zed Books).

Baroowa, S. (2007), 'The Emerging Strategic Partnership between India and the EU: A Critical Appraisal', *European Law Journal* 13/6: 733–49.

Bayne, N. (1999), 'Continuity and leadership in an age of globalization', in M. Hodges, J. Kirton, and J. Daniels, *The G8's Role in the New Millennium* (Aldershot: Ashgate Publishing).

Beach, D. (2005), *The dynamics of European integration: Why and when EU institutions matter* (Basingstoke: Palgrave Macmillan).

Bechev, D., and Nicolaïdis, K. (2008), 'The Union for the Mediterranean: A Genuine Breakthrough or More of the Same?', *International Spectator* 43/3, September, 13–20.

Bechev, D., and Nicolaïdis, K. (2010), 'From Policy to Polity: Can the EU's special relations with its Neighbourhood be Decentred?', *Journal of Common Market Studies* 48/3 (June): 475–500.

Beetham, D. (1991), *The Legitimation of Power* (Basingstoke: Macmillan).

Bellier, I. (2000), 'A Europeanized Elite? An Anthropology of European Commission Officials', in R. Harmsen, and T. Wilson (eds), *Europeanisation: Institutions, Identities and Citizenship* (Amsterdam: Rodopi), 135–56.

Benedick, R.E. (1991), *Ozone Diplomacy: New Directions in Safeguarding the Planet* (Cambridge, MA: Harvard University Press).

Berenskoetter, F.S. (2005), 'Mapping the Mind Gap: A Comparison of US and European Security Strategies', *Security Dialogue* 36/1: 71–92.

Bertea, S. (2005), 'Looking for Coherence within the European Community', *European Law Journal* 11/2: 154–72.

Biava, A. (2008), *Vers un Quartier Général Européen?*, Cahiers du CEREM No. 7, 49–59.

Bickerton, C. (2010), 'Functionality in EU foreign policy: Towards a new research agenda?', *Journal of European Integration* 32/2: 213–27.

Bickerton, C., Irondelle, B., and Menon, A. (2010, forthcoming), 'Introduction: The European Union in International Security', *Journal of Common Market Studies* 48/4.

Biersteker, T. (2002), 'State, Sovereignty and Territory', in W. Carlsnaes, B. Simmons, and T. Risse, *Sage Handbook of International Relations* (Thousand Oaks: Sage).

Bin, Y. (2009), 'China–Russia Relations: Summitry: Between Symbolism and Substance', *Comparative Connections* 11/2 (July).

Biscop, S. (2005), *The European Security Strategy: A Global Agenda for Positive Power* (Aldershot: Ashgate).

Biscop, S. (2008), 'Permanent Structured Cooperation and the Future of the ESDP: Transformation and Integration', *European Foreign Affairs Review* 13/4: 431–48.

Biscop, S. (ed.) (2009), *The Value of Power, The Power of Values: a Call for an EU Grand Strategy*, Egmont Paper 33 (Brussels: Egmont Institute).

Biscop, S., and Andersson, J.J. (eds) (2008), *The EU and the European Security Strategy* (London: Routledge).

Biscop, S., Howorth, J., and Giegerich, B. (2009), *Europe: A Time for Strategy* Brussels, Egmont Institute, Egmont Paper 27.

Black, I. (2002), 'Europe's dreams of muscle dashed', *The Guardian*, 6 December.

Blanchard, O. J. (2004), 'The Economic Future of Europe', MIT Economics Working Paper No. 04-04.

Blockmans, S. (2008), 'EU–Russia Relations Through the Prism of the European Neighbourhood and Partnership Instrument', *European Foreign Affairs Review* 13/2: 167–87.

Blockmans, S., and Wessel, R.A. (2009), *The European Union crisis management: Will the Lisbon Treaty make the EU more effective?*, Cleer Working Papers 1.

Bobbitt, P. (2002), *The Shield of Achilles: War, Peace, and the Course of History* (London: Penguin).

Bodansky, D. (2003), 'Transatlantic Environmental Relations', in J. Peterson, and M. Pollack (eds), *Europe, America, Bush: Transatlantic Relations in the Twenty-first Century* (London: Routledge).

Bono, G. (2006), 'Challenges of Democratic Oversight of EU Security Policies', *European Security* 15/4: 431–49.

Börzel, T. (2002), 'Pace-Setting, Foot-Dragging and Fence-Sitting: Member States' Responses to Europeanization', *Journal of Common Market Studies* 40/2: 193–214.

Boswell, C. (2003), 'The "External Dimension" of EU Immigration and Asylum Policy', *International Affairs* 79/3: 619–38.

Boyes, R. (2010), 'Villa called Freedom where migrants wait in search for haven', *The Times*, 13 February, 52–3.

Bretherton, C., and Vogler, J. (1999), *The European Union as a Global Actor* (London: Routledge).

Bretherton, C., and Vogler, J. (2006), *The European Union as a Global Actor,* 2nd edn. (London: Routledge).

Brown, W. (2002), *The European Union and Africa. The Restructuring of North–South Relations* (London; New York: I.B. Tauris).

Buchan, D. (1993), *Europe: The Strange Superpower* (Aldershot: Dartmouth).

Bull, H. (1977), *The Anarchical Society: A Study of Order in World Politics* (London: Macmillan).

Bull, H. (1982), 'Civilian Power Europe: A Contradiction in Terms?', *Journal of Common Market Studies* 21/2: 149–64.

Bulmer, S., and Burch, M. (1999), *The Europeanisation of Central Government: The UK and Germany in Historical Institutionalist Perspective*, ARENA Working Paper 99/30 (Oslo: ARENA).

Bulmer, S., and Radaelli, C.M (2004), *The Europeanization of National Policy*, Queen's Papers on Europeanization, No. 1.

Buzan, B., Waever, O., and de Wilde, J. (1998), *Security: A New Framework for Analysis* (Boulder, CO: Lynne Rienner).

Cameron, F. (1999), *The Foreign and Security Policy of the European Union: Past, Present and Future* (Sheffield: Sheffield Academic Press).

Calleo, D. (2001), *Rethinking Europe's Future* (Princeton, NJ: Princeton University Press).

Caporaso, J. (1996), 'The European Union and Forms of State: Westphalian, Regulatory, or Post-Modern?', *Journal of Common Market Studies* 34/1: 29–52.

Carbone, M. (2007), *The European Union and international development: the politics of foreign aid* (London: Routledge).

Carbone, M. (2008a), 'Theory and practice of participation: Civil Society and EU development policy', *Perspectives on European Politics and Society* 9/2: 241–55.

Carbone, M. (2008b), 'Better Aid, Less Ownership: Multi-annual Programming and the EU's Development Strategies in Africa', *Journal of International Development* 20/2: 118–229.

Carbone, M. (ed.) (2009), *Policy Coherence and EU Development Policy* (London; New York: Routledge).

Carbone, M. (2010), 'The European Union, Good Governance and Aid Coordination', *Third World Quarterly* 31/1: 13–29.

Carlsnaes, W. (2004), 'Where is the analysis of European Union foreign policy going?', *European Union Politics* 5/4: 495–508.

Carlsnaes, W., and Smith, S. (eds) (1994), *European Foreign Policy: The EC and Changing Perspectives in Europe* (London: Sage).

Carlsnaes, W., Sjursen, H., and White, B. (eds) (2004), *Contemporary European Foreign Policy* (London: Sage).

Casarini, N. (2009), *Remaking Global Order: The Evolution of the European–China Relationship and its implications* (Oxford: Oxford University Press).

Casarini, N., and Musu, C. (eds) (2006), *The EU's Foreign Policy in an Evolving International System: the road to convergence* (Palgrave).

Casier, T. (2007), 'The Clash of Integration Processes? The Shadow Effect of the Enlarged EU on its Eastern Neighbours', in K. Malfliet, L. Verpoest, and E. Vinokurov (eds), *The CIS, The EU and Russia. Challenges of Integration* (Basingstoke: Palgrave Macmillan).

Cass, L. (2005), 'Norm Entrapment and Preference Change: The Evolution of the European Union Position on International Emissions Trading', *Global Environmental Politics* 5/2: 38–60.

Castle, S. (2010), 'New Treaty for EU but same jostling for power', *New York Times*, 8 January, available on www.nytimes.com.

Cecchini, P. (with Michael Catinat and Alexis Jacquemin) (1988), *The European Challenge, 1992: the benefits of a single market* (Aldershot; Brookfield, VT: Gower).

Cederman, L.E. (2001), 'Nationalism and Bounded Integration: What it Would Take to Construct a European Demos', *European Journal of International Relations* 7/2: 139–74.

Chaban, N., Elgström, O., and Holland, M. (2006), 'The European Union as Others See it', *European Foreign Affairs Review* 11/2: 245–62.

Chaillot paper number 117, compiled by Catherine Glière, Paris: European Union Institute for Security Studies (July 2009)

Chase-Dunn, C. (1999), 'Globalization: A World-Systems Perspective', *Journal of World-Systems Research* 2/2: 187–215.

Checkel, J. (1999), 'Social Construction and Integration', *Journal of European Public Policy* 6/4: 634–51.

Chivvis, C.S. (2010), *EU Civilian Crisis Management: The Record So Far* (Santa Monica: RAND).

Choi, Y., and Caporaso, J. (2002), 'Comparative Regional Integration', in W. Carlsnaes, B. Simmons, and T. Risse (eds), *Sage Handbook of International Relations* (Thousand Oaks: Sage).

Christiansen, T., and Tonra, B. (eds) (2004), *Rethinking EU Foreign Policy* (Manchester: Manchester University Press).

Christiansen, T., and Vanhoonacker, S. (2008), 'At a critical juncture? Change and continuity in the institutional development of the Council Secretariat', *Western European Politics* 31/4: 751–70.

Christiansen, T., Petito, F., and Tonra, B. (2000), 'Fuzzy Politics Around Fuzzy Borders: The European Union's 'Near Abroad'', *Cooperation and Conflict* 35/4: 389–415.

Clapham, A. (1999), 'Where is the EU's Human Rights Common Foreign Policy, and How is it Manifested in Multilateral Fora?', in P. Alston (ed.), *The European Union and Human Rights* (Oxford: Oxford University Press).

Clark, I. (2007), *International Legitimacy and World Society* (Oxford: Oxford University Press).

Cohen, B. J. (1977), *Organizing the World's Money* (New York: Basic Books).

Cohen, B. J. (1998), *The Geography of Money* (Ithaca and London: Cornell University Press).

Cohen, B. J. (2003), 'Global Currency Rivalry: Can the Euro Ever Challenge the Dollar?', *Journal of Common Market Studies*, 41/4, 575–95.

Cohen, B. J. (2007), 'Enlargement and the International Role of the Euro', *Review of International Political Economy*, 14/5, 746–73.

Coker, C. (2009), *War in an Age of Risk* (Cambridge: Polity Press).

Cole, A., and Drake, H. (2000), 'The Europeanisation of the French Polity: Continuity, Change and Adaptation', *Journal of European Public Policy* 7/1: 26–43.

Collier, P., and Nicolaïdis, K. (2008), 'Europe, Africa and EPAs: opportunity or car-crash?', *Open Democracy*, 7 January, available on www.opendemocracy.net.

Cook, M. (2008), 'The United States and the East Asia Summit: Finding the Proper Home', *Contemporary Southeast Asia* 30/2: 293–312.

Cooper, R. (2002), 'The new liberal imperialism', *The Observer*, 7 April, available on www.guardian.co.uk.

Cooper, R. (2003), *The Breaking of Nations: Order and Chaos in the Twenty-First Century* (New York: Atlantic Monthly Press, London: Atlantic Books).

Corbett, R., Shackleton, M., and Jacobs F. (2007), *The European Parliament* (London: John Harper Publishing).

Corkill, D. (1999), *The Development of the Portuguese Economy: A Case of Europeanisation* (London: Routledge).

Cornish, P., and Edwards, G. (2001), 'Beyond the EU/NATO dichotomy: the beginnings of a European strategic culture', *International Affairs* 77/3: 587–603.

Cornish, P., and Edwards, G. (2005), 'The Strategic Culture of the EU: a progress report', *International Affairs* 81/4: 801–20.

Cosgrove Twitchett, C. (1981), *Framework for Development: The EEC and the ACP* (London: Allen & Unwin).

Council Decision of 26 July 2010 establishing the organisation and functioning of the European External Action Service (2010/427/EU), *Official Journal of the EU*, L 201.

Council of the European Union (1996), 'Council conclusions on the principle of conditionality governing the development of the European Union's relations with certain countries of south-east Europe', *EU Bulletin* 4.

Council of the European Union (1999), 'Common Position of 17 May 1999 concerning the launching of the Stability Pact of the EU on south-eastern Europe (1999/345/CFSP)', OJ L133, 28 May.

Council of the European Union (2000a), *The European Community's Development Policy: Statement by the Council and the Commission*, 2304th Council meeting, Development, Brussels, 10 November 2000.

Council of the European Union (2000b), Paper given at Evian Informal Meeting of the General Affairs Council, September 2000.

Council of the European Union (2005a), 'A Strategy for the External Dimension of JHA: Global Freedom, Security and Justice', 14366/3/05, 30 November, Brussels.

Council of the European Union (2005b), Environment 2647 Session 6693/05, 10 March, Brussels.

Council Secretariat and European Commission (2002), 'Civil–Military Coordination', 24 September.

Cowles, M.G., Caporaso, J., and Risse, T. (eds) (2001), *Transforming Europe: Europeanization and Domestic Change* (Ihtaca and London: Cornell University Press).

Cox, R. (1987), *Production, Power and World Order. Social Forces in the Making of History* (Columbia: Columbia University Press).

Crawford, G. (2005), 'The European Union and Democracy Promotion in Africa: The case of Ghana', *European Journal of Development Research* 17/4: 571–600.

Crawford, N.C. (2002), *Argument and Change in World Politics: Ethics, Decolonization and Humanitarian Intervention* (Cambridge: Cambridge University Press).

Cremona, M. (1999), 'External Relations and External Competence: The Emergence of an Integrated Policy', in P. Craig, and G. De Burca (eds), *The Evolution of EU Law* (Oxford: Oxford University Press).

Cremona, M. (ed.) (2003), *The Enlargement of the European Union* (Oxford: Oxford University Press).

Cremona, M., and De Witte, B. (2008), *EU Foreign Relations Law: constitutional fundamentals* (Oxford and Portland: Hart).

Cremona, M., and Hillion, C. (2006), *L'Union fait la force? Potential and limitations of the European Neighbourhood Policy as an integrated EU Foreign and Security Policy*, EUI Law Working Papers 2006/36 (Florence: European University Institute).

Croft, S. (2000), 'The EU, NATO and Europeanisation: the Return of the Architectural Debate', *European Security* 9/3: 1–20.

Croft, S., Redmond, J., Rees, W., and Webber, M. (1999), *The Enlargement of Europe* (Manchester: Manchester University Press).

Cross, M.K.D. (2010a), *Cooperation by Committee: The EU Military Committee and the Committee for Civilian Crisis Management*, EU–ISS Occasional Paper No. 28 (Paris: European Union Institute for Security Studies).

Cross, M.K.D. (2011, forthcoming), *Security Integration in the European Union* (Ann Arbor: University of ,Michigan Press).

Crowe, B. (2008), *The European External Action Service: Roadmap for Success* (London: Royal Institute of International Affairs).

Dalgaard-Nielsen, A., and Hamilton,D. (eds) (2005), *Transatlantic Homeland Security: Protecting Society in the Age of Catastropic Terroism* (London: Routledge).

Damro, C. (2006), 'The EU and International Environmental Politics: The Challenge of Shared Competence', in Laatikainen, K. V., and Smith, K. E. (eds) *The European Union at the United Nations*, (Basingstoke: Palgrave Macmillan), 175–192.

Dannreuther, R. (ed.) (2003), *European Union Foreign and Security Policy: Towards a Neighbourhood Strategy* (London: Routledge).

Dannreuther, R., and Peterson, J. (eds) (2006), *Security Strategy and the Transatlantic Alliance* (London: Routledge).

Davenport, M. (1992), 'Africa and the Unimportance of Being Preferred', *Journal of Common Market Studies* 30/2: 233–51.

Davis, C.L. (2003), *Food Fights over Free Trade: how international institutions promote agricultural trade liberalization* (Princeton, NJ: Princeton University Press).

Dearden, S. (2003), 'The Future Role of the European Union in Europe's Development Assistance', *Cambridge Review of International Affairs* 16/1: 105–17.

Dearden, S. (2008), 'Delivering the EU's Development Policy: Policy Evolution and Administrative Reform', *Perspectives on European Politics and Society* 9/2: 114–27.

De Grauwe, P. (2010), *The Economics of Monetary Union*, 8th edition (Oxford: Oxford University Press).

Dehousse, R. (1998) *The European Court of Justice, The Politics of Judicial Integration* (Basingstoke, Macmillan).

Dehousse, R., Deloche-Gaudez, F., Duhamel, O. (2006), *Elargissement: Comment l'Europe s'adapte* (Paris: Presses de Sciences Po).

Deighton, A (ed.) (1997), *Western European Union 1954–97: Defence, Security, Integration* (Oxford: St Antony's).

Della Posta, P., Uvalic, M., and Verdun, A. (2009), *Globalization, Development and Integration: a European perspective* (Basingstoke: Palgrave).

Del Sarto, R.A., and Schumacher, T. (2005), 'From EMP to ENP: what's at stake with the European Neighbourhood Policy towards the Southern Mediterranean', *European Foreign Affairs Review* 10/17: 17–38.

Dent, C. (1999), *The European Union and East Asia: An Economic Relationship* (London: Routledge).

Deng, Y. (2007), 'Remolding Great Power Politics: China's Strategic Partnerships with Russia, the European Union, and India', *The Journal of Strategic Studies* 30/4–5: 863–903.

DePorte, A. (1987), *Europe Between the Superpowers: The Enduring Balance*, 2nd edn. (New Haven, CT: Yale University Press).

Der Derian, J. (1987), *On diplomacy: a genealogy of Western estrangement* (Oxford: Blackwell).

de Schoutheete de Tervarent, P. (1980), *La coopération politique européenne* (Brussels: F. Nathan Editions Labor).

de Schoutheete de Tervarent, P. (1986), *La coopération politique européenne*, 2nd edn. (Brussels: F. Nathan Editions Labor).

Deudney, D. (1995), 'The Philadelphian System: Sovereignty, Arms Control and Balance of Power in the American States Union, ca. 1787– 1861', *International Organization* 49/2: 191–228.

Deutsch, K. (1957), *Political Community at the International Level: Problems of Definition and Measurement* (London: Archon Books).

Deutsch, K. (1968), *The Analysis of International Relations* (Englewood Cliffs, NJ: Prentice-Hall).

Deutsch, K., *et al.* (1957), *Political Community and the North Atlantic Area: International Organization in the Light of Historical Experience* (Princeton, NJ: Princeton University Press).

De Vasconcelos, A. (ed.) (2009), *What Ambitions for European Defence in 2020?*, 2nd edition (Paris; EU-ISS).

Devuyst, Y. (1992), 'The EC's Common Commercial Policy and the Treaty on European Union: An Overview of the Negotiations', *World Competition* 16/2: 67–80.

Devuyst, Y. (1995), 'The European Community and the Conclusion of the Uruguay Round', in C. Rhodes, and S. Mazey (eds), *The State of the European Union, volume 3: Building a European Polity?* (Boulder, CO: Lynne Rienner).

de Zwaan, J., and Goudappel, R. (eds) (2006), *Freedom, Security and Justice in the European Union: implementation of the Hague programme*, (The Hague: T. M. C. Asser Press).

Dijkstra, H. (2008), 'The Council Secretariat's Role in the Common Foreign and Security Policy', *European Foreign Affairs Review* 13/2: 149–66.

Dijkstra, H. (2010), 'Explaining variation in the role of the EU Council Secretariat in first and second pillar policy-making', *Journal of European Public Policy* 17/4: 527–44.

Dimier, V. (2006), 'Constructing Conditionality: The Bureaucratization of EC Development Aid', *European Foreign Affairs Review* 11/2: 263–80.

Dobbins, J. (2008), *The European Union and Nation Building* (Santa Monica: RAND).

Dolan, M. (1978), 'The Lomé Convention and Europe's Relationship with the Third World: A Critical Analysis', *Journal of European Integration* 1/3: 369–94.

Dover, R. (2007), *Europeanization of British Defence Policy* (Aldershot: Ashgate).

Doyle, M. (1983), 'Kant, Liberal Legacies and Foreign Affairs', *Philosophy and Public Affairs* 12/3 (Summer): 205–35 and 12/4 (Autumn): 323–53.

Drake, W., and Nicolaïdis, K. (1992), 'Ideas, Interests and Institutionalization: Trade in Services and the Uruguay Round' *International Organization* 46/1: 37–100.

Duchêne, F. (1972), 'Europe's Role in World Peace', in R. Mayne (ed.), *Europe Tomorrow: Sixteen Europeans Look Ahead* (London: Fontana).

Duchêne, F. (1973), 'The European Community and the Uncertainties of Interdependence', in M. Kohnstamm, and W. Hager (eds), *Nation Writ Large? Foreign Policy Problems Before the European Community* (London: Macmillan).

Duke, S. (2006), 'Areas of Grey: Tensions in EU External Relations Competences', *EIPA-SCOPE*, 2006(1), 21–7.

Duke, S. (2008), 'The Lisbon Treaty and External Relations', *Eipascope* 1: 13–18.

Duke, S., and Ojanen, H. (2006), 'Bridging Internal and External Security: Lessons from the European Security and Defence Policy', *Journal of European Integration* 28/5: 477–94.

Duke, S, and Vanhoonacker, S. (2006), 'The Administrative Governance of CFSP: Development and Practice', *European Foreign Affairs Review* 11/2: 163–82.

Dunne, T. (2008), 'Good Citizen Europe', in L. Aggestam (ed.), 'Ethical Power Europe', Special Issue of *International Affairs* 84/1: 13–28.

Dür, A., and Zimmermann, H. (2007), 'Introduction: The EU in international trade negotiations', *Journal of Common Market Studies* 45/4: 771–87.

Džihić, V., and Kramer, H. (2009), 'Kosovo after Independence: Is the EU's EULEX Mission Delivering on its Promises', Friedrich Ebert Stiftung, International Policy Analysis.

Economides, S. (2005), 'The Europeanization of Greek Foreign Policy', *West European Politics* 28/2: 471–91.

Edwards, G. (1997), 'The Potential and Limits of the CFSP: The Yugoslav Example', in E. Regelsberger, P. de Schoutheete de Tervarent, and W. Wessels (eds), *Foreign Policy of the European Union: from EPC to CFSP and Beyond* (Boulder, CO: Lynne Rienner).

Edwards, G. (2000), *Europe's Security and Defence Policy and Enlargement: The Ghost at the Feast?*, EUI Working Papers RSC No. 2000/69 (Florence: European University Institute).

Edwards, G. (2008), 'The Construction of Ambiguity and the Limits of Attraction: Europe and its Neighbourhood Policy' *Journal of European Integration* 30/1: 45–62.

Edwards, G., and Phillipart, E. (1997), 'The Euro–Mediterranean Partnership: fragmentation and reconstruction', *European Foreign Affairs Review* 2/4: 465–89.

Edwards, G., and Regelsberger, E. (eds) (1990), *Europe's Global Links: The European Community and Inter-Regional Cooperation* (London: Pinter Publishers).

Egenhofer, C., and Georgiev, A. (2009), *The Copenhagen Accord: A first stab at deciphering the implications for the EU*, CEPS Commentary (Brussels: CEPS).

Eilstrup-Sangiovanni, M., and Verdier, D. (2005), 'European Integration as a Solution to War', *European Journal of International Relations* 11/1: 99–135.

Elgström, O. (2000), 'Lomé and Post-Lomé: Asymmetric Negotiations and the Impact of Norms', *European Foreign Affairs Review* 5/2: 175–95.

Elgström, O. (2009), 'Trade and aid? The negotiated construction of EU policy and economic partnership agreements', *International Politics* 46/4: 451–68.

Elgström, O., and Frennhoff Larsén, M. (2010), 'Free to Trade? Commission Autonomy in the Economic Partnership Agreement Negotiations', *Journal of European Public Policy* 17/2: 205–23.

Elgström, O., and Smith, M.H. (eds) (2006), *The European Union's Roles in International Politics: Concepts and Analysis* (London: Routledge/ECPR).

Elias, N. (1991), *The Symbol Theory* (London: Sage).

Elias, N. (1992), *Time: An Essay* (Oxford: Blackwell).

Elias, N. (1996), *The Germans* (Cambridge: Polity Press).

Elias, N. (1998a), 'The Expulsion of the Huguenots from France', in J. Goudsblom, and S. Mennell (eds), *The Norbert Elias Reader* (Oxford: Blackwell).

Elias, N. (1998b), 'An Interview in Amsterdam', in J. Goudsblom, and S. Mennell (eds), *The Norbert Elias Reader* (Oxford: Blackwell).

Elias, N. (1998c), 'The Civilizing of Parents', in J, Goudsblom, and S. Mennell (eds), *The Norbert Elias Reader* (Oxford: Blackwell).

Elias, N. (2000), *The Civilizing Process: Sociogenetic and Psychogenetic Investigations* (Oxford: Blackwell).

Elias, N. (2001a), *The Loneliness of Dying* (London: Continuum).

Elias, N. (2001b), *The Society of Individuals* (London: Continuum).

Elias, N., and Dunning, E. (1986), *The Quest for Excitement: Sport and Leisure in the Civilizing Process* (Oxford: Blackwell).

Ellwood, D. (1992), *Rebuilding Europe: Western Europe, America and Postwar Reconstruction* (London: Longman).

Elsig, M. (2002), *The EU's Common Commercial Policy. Institutions, Interests and Ideas* (Hampshire: Ashgate).

Enderlein, H., and Verdun, A. (2009), 'Ten years of EMU: what have we learned in Political Science?' (Enderlein and Verdun as guest editors of a special issue of *Journal of European Public Policy*, 16:4, June: 490–639).

ESDP Newsletter (2008), *Introducing CPCC*, Newsletter 6: 24–5; available on http://www.consilium.europa.eu/uedocs/cmsUpload/CEU8003ESDP6final_vers.pdf.

Eurobarometer (2007), *Eurobarometer No.67: Public Opinion in the European Union* (Brussels: European Commission), available on http://ec.europa.eu/public_opinion/archives/eb/eb67/eb67_en.pdf.

Eurobarometer (2009), *Special Public Opinion Polls 1972–2009*, available on http//ec.europa.eu/public_opinion/archives/eb_special_en.htm.

European Commission (1992), *Europe and the Challenge of Enlargement*, EC Bulletin Supplement 3/92 (Brussels: European Commission).

European Commission (1993), 'Towards a Closer Association with the Countries of Central and Eastern Europe', SEC (93) 648 final, 18 May.

European Commission (1996), *Green Paper on Relations between the European Union and the ACP Countries on the Eve of the 21st Century: Challenges and Options for a New Partnership* (Brussels: European Commission).

European Commission (1997), *Agenda 2000: For a Stronger and Wider Union*, EU Bulletin Supplement 5/97.

European Commission (1999), *Composite Paper: Reports on Progress Towards Accession by Each of the Candidate Countries*, Brussels, 13 October.

European Commission (2000b), *Reforming the Commission*, White Paper – Part 1, 5 April.

European Commission (2001b), *Making a Success of Enlargement: Strategy Paper 2001 and Report of the European Commission on the Progress Towards Accession by Each of the Candidate Countries*, Brussels, 13 November.

European Commission (2002), *Towards the Enlarged Union: Strategy Paper and Report on the Progress towards Accession by Each of the Candidate Countries*, COM (2002) 700 final, Brussels, 9 October.

European Commission (2003a), *Wider Europe—Neighbourhood: A New Framework for Relations with our Eastern and Southern Neighbours*, COM (2003) 104 final, Brussels, 11 March.

European Commission (2003b), *EU–US Bilateral Economic Relations*, European Union Factsheet published on the occasion of the EU–US Summit, Washington, 25th June 2003. Accessed at http://www.eurunion.org/.

European Commission (2003d), *Communication from the Commission to the Council and the European Parliament. The European Union and the United Nations: the choice of multilateralism*, Brussels, COM(2003) 526 final, 10 September.

European Commission (2006a), *Communication to the Council and the European Parliament on Strengthening the European Neighbourhood Policy*, COM (2006) 726 final, Brussels, 4 December.

European Commission (2006b), *The European Consensus on Development* (Luxembourg: Office for Official Publications of the European Communities).

European Commission (2006c), *A European Strategy for Sustainable, Competitive and Secure Energy*, Brussels, COM(2006) 105 final, 8 March.

European Commission (2006d), 'Enlargement Strategy and Main Challenges 2006–2007', COM (2006) 249, 8 November.

European Commission (2006e), *Europe in the World. Greater Coherence, Effectiveness and Visibility*, COM(2006) 278.

European Commission (2007), *An Energy policy for Europe,* Brussels, COM(2007)1 final, 10 January.

European Commission (2009a), *The Copenhagen climate conference: key EU objectives*, memo/09/534, Brussels, 2 December).

European Commission (2009b), *The January 2009 Gas Supply Disruption to the EU: An Assessment*, Brussels, Commission Staff Working Document Accompanying a Proposal for a Regulation concerning measures to safeguard security of gas supply and repealing Directive 2004/67/EC COM(2009) 363, 16 July.

European Commission (2010), 'Europe 2020. A Strategy for Smart, Sustainable and Inclusive Growth', Brussels, 3 March. http://ec.europa.eu/eu2020/pdf/

European Commission (2010), *General Budget of the European Union* (Luxembourg: Office for Official Publications of the European Communities).

European Commission Directorate-General for Economic and Financial Affairs (2010), Economic and Monetary Union: A Timeline. Checked online May 23, 2010. Available online at: http://ec.europa.eu/economy_finance/emu10/timeline_en.pdf

European Commission, DG Trade, available on http://ec.europa.eu/trade/

European Council (1989), Strasbourg, *Conclusions of the Presidency*, 8–9 December, EC Bulletin No. 12.

European Council (1993), Copenhagen, *Conclusions of the Presidency*, 22–23 June, document no. SN 180/93.

European Council (1994), Essen, *Conclusions of the Presidency*, 9–10 December.

European Council (1999a), Helsinki, *Presidency Conclusions*, 10–11 December.

European Council (1999b), Tampere, *Conclusions of the Presidency of the Special European Council*, 15–19 October.

European Council (2001), Laeken, *Presidency Conclusions*, 13–14 December.

European Council (2002a), Copenhagen, *Presidency Conclusions*, 12–13 December, document no. SN 400/02.

European Council (2002b), Brussels, *Seville Presidency Conclusions*, 24 October.

European Council (2003a), Brussels, *Presidency Conclusions*, 12 December.

European Council (2003b), *A Secure Europe in a Better World. European Security Strategy*, Brussels, 12 December.

European Council (2006a), *Review of the EU sustainable development strategy– renewed strategy*, Brussels, 1011706.

European Council (2006b), Brussels, *Presidency Conclusions*, 14–15 December, document 16879/1/06.

European Council (2007), Brussels, *Presidency Conclusions: Justice and Home Affairs*, 21–2 June.

European Council (2008), Brussels *Presidency Conclusions*, 11 December.

European Monitoring Centre for Drugs and Drug Addiction (2009), *Annual Report 2009: The State of the Drugs Problem in Europe* (Luxembourg: Publications Office of the European Union).

European Parliament (2000a), *Report on the General Budget for 2001* (European Parliament, Council) (Ferber Report) (Brussels: European Parliament).

European Parliament (2001b), *On the Financial Regulation Applicable to the General Budget of the European Communities* (Dell'Alba Report) (Brussels: European Parliament).

European Think-Tanks Group (2010), *New Challenges, New Beginnings: Next Steps in European Development Cooperation* (London: Overseas Development Institute).

Europol (2009), *EU Organised Crime Threat Assessment 2009*, The Hague, available on www.europol.europa.eu.

EUSA Review Forum (2006), 'Taking stock of the Lisbon Agenda: is Lisbon flawed, necessary, window-dressing, or all of the above?', autumn, www.eustudies.org/files/eusa_review/arialfall2006.pdf

EU Security and Defence: Core Documents, 2008, Chaillot Paper Number 117, compiled by Catherine Glière, Paris: European union Institute for Security Studies (July 2009)

Evans, P., Jacobson, H., and Putnam, R. (eds) (1993), *Double-Edged Diplomacy: International Bargaining and Domestic Politics* (Berkeley: University of California Press).

Everts, S. (2004), *Engaging Iran: a test case for EU foreign policy* (London: Centre for European Reform).

Faber, G. (1982), *The European Community and Development Cooperation: Integration in the Light of Development Policies of the Community and its Members States* (Assen: Van Gorcum).

Faber, G., and Orbie, J. (eds) (2009a), *Beyond Market Access for Economic Development: EU–Africa relations in transition* (London: Routledge).

Faber, G., and Orbie, J. (2009b), 'Everything But Arms: Much More than Appears at First Sight', *Journal of Common Market Studies* 47/4: 767–87.

Falkner, R. (2007), 'The Political Economy of "Normative Power" Europe: EU Environmental Leadership in International Biotechnology regulation', *Journal of European Public Policy*,14,4, 507–26.

Farrell, M. (2005), 'A Triumph of Realism over Idealism? Cooperation between the European Union and Africa', *Journal of European Integration* 27/3: 263–83.

Farrell, M. (2008), 'Internationalising EU Development Policy', *Perspectives on European Politics and Society* 9/2: 225–40.

Farrell, M. (2009), 'EU policy towards other regions: policy learning in the external promotion of regional integration', *Journal of European Public Policy* 16/8: 1165–84.

Featherstone, K. (1998), '"Europeanisation" and the Centre-Periphery: The Case of Greece in the 1990s', *South European Politics and Society* 2/1: 23–39.

Featherstone, K. (2010), 'The limits of Europeanization and the question of reform capacity in Greece', *Journal of Common Market Studies*, forthcoming.

Featherstone, K., and Papadimitriou, D (2008), *The Limits of Europeanization: Reform Capacity and Policy Conflict in Greece* (Basingstoke: Palgrave Macmillan).

Feinberg, J. (1984), *Harm to Others: The Moral Limits of the Criminal Law* (Oxford: Oxford University Press).

Fisher, S. (2008), 'The EU and Russia: a contested Partnership', in G. Grevi, and A. de Vasconcelos (eds), *Partnership for effective multilateralism: EU relations with Brazil, China, India and Russia*, Chaillot Paper 109 (Paris: European Union Institute for Security Studies).

Fletcher, J. (1997), *Violence and Civilisation: An Introduction to the Work of Norbert Elias* (Cambridge: Polity Press).

Flint, A. (2009), *Trade, poverty and the environment: the EU, Cotonou and the African–Caribbean–Pacific bloc* (Basingstoke: Palgrave).

Forster, A. (1999), 'EU and Southeast Asia Relations: A Balancing Act', *International Affairs* 75/4: 743–58.

Forster, A. (2000), 'Evaluating the EU–ASEM relationship: a negotiated order approach', Special Issue of *Journal of European Public Policy* 7/5: 787–805.

Forwood, G. (2001), 'The Road to Cotonou: Negotiating a Successor to Lomé', *Journal of Common Market Studies* 39/3: 423–42.

Fox, J., and Godement, F. (2009), *A Power Audit of EU–China Relations*, Policy Report (London: European Council on Foreign Relations).

Frey-Wouters, E. (1980), *The European Community and the Third World: The Lomé Convention and Its Impact* (New York: Praeger).

Frieden, J., and Martin, L. (2002), 'International Political Economy: Global and Domestic Interactions', in I. Katznelson, and H. Milner (eds), *Political Science: The State of the Discipline* (New York: W.W. Norton), 118–46.

Friedrich, C. (1968), *Trends in Federalism* (New York: Praeger).

Friis, L. (1998), '"The End of the Beginning" of Eastern Enlargement—Luxembourg Summit and Agenda-Setting', *European Integration Online Papers (EioP)* 2/7; available on http://eiop.or.at.

Friis, L., and Murphy, A. (1999), 'The European Union and Central and Eastern Europe: Governance and Boundaries', *Journal of Common Market Studies* 37/2: 211–32.

Galtung, J. (1971), 'A Structural Theory of Imperialism', *Journal of Peace Research* 8/2: 81–117.

Galtung, J. (1973), *The European Community: A Superpower in the Making?* (London: Allen and Unwin).

Galtung, J. (1976), 'The Lomé Convention and Neo-Capitalism', *African Review* 6/1: 33–42.

Gänzle, S. (2009), 'EU Governance and the European Neighbourhood Policy: a Framework for Analysis', *Europe–Asia Studies* 61/10: 1715–34.

Gänzle, S., and Sens, A. (eds) (2007), *The Changing Politics of European Security: Europe Alone* (London: Palgrave).

Garcia, M.A. (2008), 'The strategic partnership between Brazil and the European Union', in G. Grevi, and A. de Vasconcelos (eds), *Partnership for effective multilateralism: EU relations with Brazil, China, India and Russia*, Chaillot Paper 109 (Paris: European Union Institute for Security Studies).

Garrett, G., and Tsebelis, G. (1996), 'An Institutional Critique of Intergovernmentalism' *International Organization* 50/2: 269–99.

Gärtner, H., Hyde-Price, A., and Reiter, E. (eds) (2001), *Europe's New Security Challenges* (Boulder, CO: Lynne Reinner).

Gauttier, P. (2004), 'Horizontal Coherence and the External Competences of the European Union', *European Law Journal* 10/1: 23–41.

Gegout, C. (2002), 'The Quint', *Journal of Common Market Studies* 40/2: 331–44.

Gelpi, C. (1999), 'Alliances as Instruments of Inter-Allied Control', in H. Haftendorn, R. Keohane, and C. Wallander (eds), *Imperfect Unions: Security Institutions Over Time and Space* (Oxford: Oxford University Press).

German Presidency (1999), *A Stability Pact for South-Eastern Europe*, 12 April, available on http://www.bundesregierung.de/english/01/0103/3810/index.html.

Germond, B., and Smith, M.E. (2009), 'Re-Thinking European Security Interests and the ESDP: Explaining the EU's Anti-Piracy Operation', *Contemporary Security Policy* 30/3: 573–93.

Gibb, R. (2000), 'Post-Lomé: The European Union and the South' *Third World Quarterly* 21/3: 457–81.

Giegerich, B. (2006), *European Security and Strategic Culture* (Baden Baden: Nomos).

Giegerich, B., and Nicoll, A. (2008), *European Military Capabilities: Building Armed Forces for Modern Operations* (London: The International Institute for Strategic Studies).

Giegerich, B., and Wallace, W. (2004), 'Not Such a Soft Power: The External Deployment of European Forces', *Survival* 46/2: 163–82.

Gilbert, E., and Helleiner, E. (1999), *Nation-States and Money: The Past, Present and Future of National Currencies* (London: Routledge).

Gill, B., and Huang, Y. (2006), 'Sources and Limits of Chinese Soft Power', *Survival* 48/2: 17–36.

Gilpin, R. (1981), *War and Change in World Politics* (Princeton, NJ: Princeton University Press).

Gilpin, R. (1987), *The Political Economy of International Relations* (Princeton: Princeton University Press).

Gilpin, R. (2001), *Global Political Economy: Understanding the International Economic Order* (Princeton: Princeton University Press).

Gilroy, C.L., and Williams, C. (eds) (2007), *Service to Country: Personnel Policy and the Transformation of Western Militaries* (Cambridge, MA: MIT Press).

Gilson, J. (2005), 'New Interregionalism? The EU and East Asia', *European Integration* 27/3: 307–26.

Ginsberg, R. (1989), *Foreign Policy Actions of the European Community: The Politics of Scale* (Boulder, Co: Lynne Rienner).

Ginsberg, R. (2001), *The European Union in International Politics: Baptism by Fire* (Lanham, MD: Rowman & Littlefield).

Ginsberg, R. (2007), *Demystifying the European Union: the Enduring Logic of Regional Integration* (Lanham, MD: Rowman & Littlefield).

Glarbo, K. (1999), 'Wide-Awake Diplomacy: Reconstructing the Common Foreign and Security Policy of the European Union', *Journal of European Public Policy* 6/4: 634– 51.

Glarbo, K. (2001), 'Reconstructing a Common European Foreign Policy', in T. Christiansen, K.E. Jørgensen, and A.Wiener (eds), *The Social Construction of Europe* (London: Sage), 140–57.

Godement, F. (2008), 'The EU and China: a necessary partnership', in G. Grevi, and A. de Vasconcelos (eds), *Partnership for effective multilateralism: EU relations with Brazil, China, India and Russia*, Chaillot Paper 109 (Paris: European Union Institute for Security Studies).

Goertz, G., and Diehl, P. (1992), *Territorial Changes and International Conflict* (London: Routledge).

Goetz, K., and Hix, S. (eds) (2001), *Europeanised Politics? European Integration and National Political Systems* (London: Frank Cass).

Goldman Sachs Global Economics Group (2007), *BRICs and Beyond* (USA: Goldman Sachs & Co).

Gomez, R., and Peterson, J. (2001), 'The EU's Impossibly Busy Foreign Ministers: "No-one is in Control"', *European Foreign Affairs Review* 6/1: 53–74.

Gordon, P. (1997), 'Europe's Uncommon Foreign Policy', *International Security* 22/3: 74–100.

Gordon, P., and Shapiro, J. (2004), *Allies at War: America, Europe, and the Crisis over Iraq* (Washington DC: Brookings Institution).

Gowa, J. (1989), 'Bipolarity, Multipolarity and Free Trade', *American Political Science Review*, 83/4L: 1245–56.

Gower, J. (2009), *Russia and Europe in the Twenty-First Century. An Uneasy Partnership* (London: Anthem Press).

Grabbe, H. (2001), 'How does Europeanization affect CEE Governance? Conditionality, Diffusion and Diversity', *Journal of European Public Policy* 8/6: 1013–31.

Grabbe, H. (2006), *The EU's Transformative Power: Europeanization through conditionality in Central and Eastern Europe* (Houndmills: Palgrave).

Grant, R., and Keohane, R. (2005), 'Accountability and Abuses of Power in World Politics', *American Political Science Review* 99/1: 29–43.

Graziano, P., and Vink, M. P. (eds) (2006), *Europeanization: New Research Agendas* (Basingstoke and New York: Palgrave Macmillan), 3–20.

Grevi, G. (2007), *Pioneering foreign policy. The EU Special Representatives*, Chaillot Paper 106 (Paris: European Union Institute for Security Studies).

Grevi, G., and Vasconcelos, A. de (eds) (2008), *Partnerships for Effective Multilateralism: EU Relations with Brazil, China, India and Russia*, Chaillot Paper 109 (Paris: European Union Institute for Security Studies).

Grevi, G., Helly, D., and Keohane, D. (2009), *European Security and Defence Policy. The first 10 years (1999–2009)* (Paris: European Union Institute for Security Studies).

Grieco, J. (1995), 'The Maastricht, Treaty, Economic and Monetary Union, and the Neo-Realist Research Programme', *Review of International Studies* 21/1: 21–40.

Grieco, J. (1996), 'State Interests and International Rule Trajectories: A Neo-Realist Interpretation of the Maastricht Treaty and European Economic and Monetary Union', *Security Studies* 5/3: 261–305.

Grieco, J. (1997a), 'Systemic Sources of Variation in Regional Institutionalization in Western Europe, East Asia and the Americas', in E. Mansfield, and H. Milner (eds), *The Political Economy of Regionalism* (New York: Columbia University Press).

Grieco, J. (1997b), 'Realist International Theory and the Study of World Politics', in M. Doyle, and J. Ikenberry (eds), *New Thinking in International Relations Theory* (Boulder, CO: Westview Press).

Grilli, E. (1993), *The European Community and the Developing Countries* (Cambridge: Cambridge University Press).

Grim, S. (2008), *Reforms in the EU's Aid Architecture and Management*, Discussion Paper 11 (Bonn: German Development Institute).

Gross, E. (2009), *The Europeanization of National Foreign Policy: Continuity and Change in European Crisis Management* (Basingstoke: Palgrave Macmillan).

Grubb, M., and Yamin, F. (2001), 'Climate collapse at the Hague: what happened and where do we go from here?', *International Affairs* 77/2: 261–76.

Gruhn, I. (1976), 'The Lomé Convention: Inching Towards Interdependence', *International Organization* 30/2: 240–62.

Guay, T. (1999), *The United States and the European Union: the political economy of a relationship* (Sheffield: Sheffield Academic Press).

Guyomarch, A. (2001), 'The Europeanisation of Policy-Making', in A. Guyomarch *et al.* (eds), *Developments in French Politics* (Basingstoke: Palgrave).

Guyomarch, A., Machin, H., and Ritchie, E. (eds) (1998), *France in the European Union* (Basingstoke: Macmillan).

Haas, E. (1958), *The Uniting of Europe: Political, Economic, and Social Forces, 1950–1957* (Stanford, CA: Stanford University Press).

Haas, E. (1961), 'International Integration: The European and the Universal Process', *International Organization* 15/3: 366–92.

Haas, E. (1964), *Beyond the Nation-State: Functionalism and International Organization* (Stanford, CA: Stanford University Press).

Haas, P. (1992), 'Introduction: Epistemic Communities and International Policy Coordination', *International Organization* 46/1: 1–35.

Habermas, J. (1996), *Between Facts and Norms* (Cambridge: Polity).

Habermas, J. (2003), 'Why Europe Needs a Constitution', in E. Eriksen, J. Fossum, and A. Menendez (eds), *The Chartering of Europe: The European Charter of Fundamental Rights and its Constitutional Implications* (Baden-Baden: Nomos).

Hadfield, A. (2007), 'Janus Advances? An Analysis of EC Development Policy and the 2005 Amended Cotonou Partnership Agreement', *European Foreign Affairs Review* 12/1: 39–66.

Hadfield, A. (2008a), 'Energy and Foreign Policy: EU–Russia Energy Dynamics', in Smith, S., Hadfield, A., and Dunne, T. (eds) *Foreign Policy: Theories, Actors, Cases* (Oxford: Oxford University Press).

Hadfield, A. (2008b), 'EU–Russia Energy Relations: Aggregation and Aggravation', *Journal of Contemporary European Studies* 16/2: 231–49.

Haftel, Y. (2007), 'Designing for Peace: Regional Integration Arrangements, Institutional Variation, and Militarized Interstate Disputes', *International Organization* 61/1: 217–37.

Haftendorn, H., and Tuschhoff, C. (1993), *America and Europe in an Era of Change* (Boulder, CO: Westview Press).

Haine, J.-Y. (ed.) (2003), *From Laeken to Copenhagen: European Defence—Core Documents III.* Chaillot Paper 57 (Paris: European Union Institute for Security Studies), available at http://www.iss-eu.org

Hajnal, P. (1999), *The G7/G8 System: Evolution, Role and Documentation* (Aldershot: Ashgate).

Hall, P. (1986), *Governing the Economy: The Politics of State Intervention in Britain and France* (Ithaca: Cornell University Press).

Hall, P., and Taylor, R. (1996), 'Political Science and the Three New Institutionalisms', *Political Studies* 44/5: 936– 57.

Hanf, K., and Soetendorp, B. (eds) (1998), *Adapting to European Integration: Small States and the European Union* (London: Longman).

Hanggi, H., and Tanner, F. (2005), *Promoting Security Sector Governance in the EU's Neighborhood*, Chaillot Paper 80 (Paris: European Union Institute for Security Studies).

Hardacre, A. (2009), *The Rise and Fall of Interregionalism in EU External Relations* (Dordrecht: Republic of Letters).

Hardacre, A., and Smith, M. (2009), 'The EU and the Diplomacy of Complex Interregionalism', *The Hague Journal of Diplomacy* 4/2 (September): 167–88.

Harmsen, R., and Wilson, T. (2000), 'Introduction', in R. Harmsen, and T. Wilson (eds), *Europeanisation: Institutions, Identities and Citizenship* (Amsterdam: Rodopi).

Hasenclever, A., and Weiffen, B. (2006), 'International institutions are the key: a new perspective on the democratic peace', *Review of International Studies* 32/4: 563–85.

Hasenclever. A., Mayer, P., and Rittberger, V. (1997), *Theories of International Regimes* (Cambridge: Cambridge University Press).

Hassner, P. (1968), *Change and Security in Europe II: In Search of a System*, Adelphi Paper 49 (London: International Institute for Strategic Studies).

Haukkala, H. (2010), *The EU–Russia Strategic Partnership: the Logic of Post-Sovereignty in International Relations* (Taylor & Francis Group).

Haverland, M. (2007), 'Methodology', in P. Graziano, and M.P. Vink (eds), *Europeanization: New Research Agendas* (Basingstoke: Palgrave Macmillan), 59–70.

Hayes, J. P. (1993), *Making Trade Policy in the European Community* (London: Macmillan).

Hayes-Renshaw, F., and Wallace, H. (1997), *The Council of Ministers of the European Union* (London: Macmillan).

Heipertz, M., and Verdun, A. (2010), *Ruling Europe: the politics of the stability and growth pact* (Cambridge: Cambridge University Press).

Helleiner, E. (1994), *States and the Reemergence of Global Finance* (Ithaca: Cornell University Press).

Helleiner, E., Pagliari, S., and Zimmerman, H. (eds) (2010), *Global Finance in Crisis: the politics of international regulatory change* (London: Routledge).

Heller, F., and Gillingham, J. (eds) (1996), *The United States and the Integration of Europe: Legacies of the Postwar Era* (New York: St Martin's Press).

Henrion, C. (2010), *The European Union Battlegroups* (Brussels: GRIP), available on http://www.grip.org/en/siteweb/dev.asp?N=simple&O=736.

Hill, C. (1990), 'European Foreign Policy: Power Bloc, Civilian Model—or Flop?', in R. Rummel (ed.), *The Evolution of an International Actor: Western Europe's New Assertiveness* (Boulder, CO: Westview Press).

Hill, C. (1991), 'The Foreign Policy of the European Community', in R. Macridis (ed.), *Foreign Policy and World Politics*, 8th edition (New York: Prentice Hall).

Hill, C. (1993a), 'The Capability-Expectations Gap, or Conceptualising Europe's International Role', *Journal of Common Market Studies* 31/3: 305–28.

Hill, C. (1993b), 'Shaping a federal foreign policy for Europe', in Hocking (ed.), *Foreign Relations and Federal States* (Leicester: Leicester University Press), 268–83.

Hill, C. (ed.) (1996), *The Actors in Europe's Foreign Policy* (London: Routledge).

Hill, C. (1998a), 'Closing the Capability-Expectations Gap?', in J. Peterson, and H. Sjursen (eds), *A Common Foreign Policy for Europe? Competing Visions of the CFSP* (London: Routledge).

Hill, C. (2001), 'The EU's Capacity for Conflict Prevention', *European Foreign Affairs Review* 6/3: 315–34.

Hill, C. (2002), 'The Geopolitical Implications of Enlargement', in J. Zielonka (ed.), *Europe Unbound: Enlarging and Reshaping the Boundaries of the European Union* (London: Routledge).

Hill, C. (2003), *The Changing Politics of Foreign Policy* (Houndsmill: Palgrave).

Hill, C. (2004), 'Renationalizing or Regrouping? EU Foreign Policy Since 11 September 2001', *Journal of Common Market Studies* 42/1: 143–63.

Hill, C., and Smith, K. E. (eds) (2000), *European Foreign Policy: Key Documents* (London: Routledge).

Hill, C., and Smith, M. (eds) (2005), *International Relations and the European Union* (Oxford: Oxford University Press).

Hill, C., and Wallace, W. (1996), 'Introduction: Actors and Actions', in C. Hill (ed.), *The Actors in Europe's Foreign Policy* (London: Routledge).

Hillion, C., and Wessel, R.A. (2009), 'Competence contribution in EU external relations after ECOWAS: Clarification or continued fuzziness?', *Common Market Law Review* 46/2: 551–86.

Hilpold, P. (2002), 'EU Development Cooperation at the Crossroads', *European Foreign Affairs Review* 7/1: 53–72.

Hinsley, F. (1963), *Power and the Pursuit of Peace: Theory and Practice in the History of Relations Between States* (Cambridge: Cambridge University Press).

Hirst, P., and Thompson, G. (1999), *Globalization in Question: The International Economy and the Possibilities of Goverance*, 2nd edition (Cambridge: Polity Press).

Hix, S., Noury, A., and Roland, G. (2007), *Democratic Politics in the European Parliament* (Cambridge: Cambridge University Press).

Hocking, B., and Smith, M. (1997), *Beyond Foreign Economic Policy: The United States, the Single European Market and the Changing World Economy* (London: Cassell-Pinter).

Hocking, B., and Spence, D. (eds) (2002), *Foreign Ministries in the European Union: Integrating Diplomats* (Basingstoke: Palgrave Macmillan).

Hocking, B., and Spence, D. (2005), 'Afterword: Towards a European diplomatic system?', in B. Hocking, and D. Spence (eds), *Foreign Ministries in the European Union: Integrating diplomats* (Basingstoke: Palgrave Macmillan.

Hoebink, P. (ed.) (2004), *The Treaty of Maastricht and Europe's Development Co-operation* (Amsterdam: Aksant).

Hoffman, B. (1998), *Inside Terrorism* (New York, NY: Colombia University Press).

Hoffmann, S. (1966), 'Obstinate or Obsolete? The Fate of the Nation-State and the Case of Western Europe', *Daedalus* 95/3: 862–915.

Hoffmann, S. (1995), 'Balance, Concert, Anarchy, or None of the Above', in S. Hoffmann (ed.), *The European Sisyphus* (Boulder, CO: Westview Press).

Hoffmann, S. (2000), 'Towards a Common Foreign and Security Policy?' *Journal of Common Market Studies* 38/2: 189–98.

Hoffmeister, F. (2008), 'Inter-Pillar Coherence in the European Union's Civilian Crisis Management', in S. Blockmans (ed.), *The European Union and Crisis Management. Policy and Legal Aspects* (The Hague: T.M.C. Asser Institute), 157–80.

Holden, P. (2009), *In Search of Structural Power: EU Aid Policy as a Global Political Instrument* (Aldershot: Ashgate).

Holland, M. (ed.) (1991), *The Future of European Political Cooperation: Essays on Theory and Practice* (London: Macmillan).

Holland, M. (1995), *European Union Common Foreign Policy: From EPC to CFSP Joint Action and South Africa* (Basingstoke: Macmillan).

Holland, M. (2002), *The European Union and the Third World* (Basingstoke: Palgrave).

Holland, M. (2004), 'Development Policy: Paradigm Shifts and the "Normalization" of a Privileged Partnership?', in M.G. Cowles, and D. Dinan (eds), *Developments in the European Union 2* (Basingstoke: Palgrave).

Holland, M. (2008), 'The EU and the Global Development Agenda', *Journal of European Integration* 30/3: 343–62.

Holland, S. (1980), *UnCommon Market: Capital, Class and Power in the European Community* (London: Macmillan).

Hollis, M., and Smith, S. (1991), *Explaining and Understanding International Relations* (Oxford: Clarendon Press).

Holzinger, K., Knill, C., and Arts, B. (eds) (2008), *Environmental Policy Convergence in Europe: the impact of international institutions and trade*, (Cambridge: Cambridge University Press).

Hout, W. (2010), 'Governance and Development: changing EU policies', *Third World Quarterly* 31/2: 1–12.

Howorth, J. (2000), *European Integration and Defence: The Ultimate Challenge?*, Chaillot Paper 43 (Paris: WEU Institute for Security Studies), available on http://www.iss-eu.org

Howorth, J. (2001), 'European Defence and the Changing Politics of the European Union: Hanging Together or Hanging Separately?', *Journal of Common Market Studies* 39/4: 765–89.

Howorth, J. (2003), 'Reconcilable Differences: Europe, the US and the War in Iraq', http://www.thepolitic.org/news/2003/05/13/International/Reconcilable.Differences433176.shtml, 13 May.

Howorth, J. (2004), 'Discourse, Ideas and Epistemic Communities in European Security and Defence Policy', *West European Politics* 27/2: 29–52.

Howorth, J. (2005), 'From Security to Defence: the Evolution of the CFSP', in C. Hill, and M. Smith (eds), *International Relations and the European Union* (Oxford: Oxford University Press), 179–204.

Howorth, J. (2007), *Security and Defence Policy in the European Union* (Basingstoke: Palgrave Macmillan).

Howorth, J. (2009), 'ESDP and NATO: institutional complexities and political realities', *Politique Etrangère* 2009/4 (special issue on NATO): 95–106. Also published in the French edition of the same journal as: 'OTAN-PESD: Complexités institutionnelles et réalités politiques', 817–28.

Howorth, J. (2010), 'The Political and Security Committee: a case study in "supranational intergovernmentalism"?', *Cahiers Européens* 1/2010 (Paris: SciencesPo).

Howorth, J., and Keeler, J. (eds) (2003), *Defending Europe: The EU, NATO and the Quest for European Autonomy* (New York: Palgrave Macmillan).

Howorth, J., and Menon, A. (2009), 'Still not pushing back: why the European Union is not balancing the United States', *Journal of Conflict Resolution* 53/5 (October): 727–44.

Howse, R., and Nicolaïdis, K. (2008), 'Democracy without Sovereignty: The Global Vocation of Political Ethics', in Y. Shany, and T. Broude (eds), *The Shifting Allocation of Authority in International Law: Considering Sovereignty, Supremacy and Subsidiarity* (Oxford: Hart Publishing), 163–91.

Hughes, J. (2007), 'EU Relations with Russia: Partnership or Asymmetric Interdependency', in N. Casarini, and C. Musu (eds), *European Foreign Policy in an Evolving International System: the Road towards Convergence* (Basingstoke: Palgrave Macmillan).

Hunter, R.E. (2002), *The European Security and Defense Policy: NATO's Companion or Competitor?* (Santa Monica, CA: Rand).

Hurd, D. (1981), 'Political Cooperation', *International Affairs* 57/3: 383–93.

Hurrell, A. (2006), 'Hegemony, Liberalism and Global Order: What Space for Would-Be Great Powers?', *International Affairs* 82/1: 1–19.

Hurrell, A. (2007), *On Global Order: Power, Values and the Constitution of International Society* (Oxford: Oxford University Press).

Hurt, S. (2003), 'Co-operation and Coercion? The Cotonou Agreement between the European Union and ACP States and the End of the Lomé Convention', *Third World Quarterly* 24/1: 161–76.

Hurt, S. (2010), 'Understanding EU Development Policy: history, global context and self-interest', *Third World Quarterly* 31/2: 159–68.

Hutchings, R. (2009), 'The United States and the Emerging Global Security Agenda', in L. Peral (ed.), *Global Security in a Multi-Polar World*, Paris, Chaillot Paper 118 (European Union Institute for Security Studies), 103–20.

Huysmans, J. (2006), *The Politics of Insecurity: Fear, Migration and Asylum in the EU* (London: Routledge).

Hyde-Price, A. (2006), '"Normative" Power Europe: a Realist Critique', *Journal of European Public Policy* 13/2: 217–34.

Hyde-Price, A. (2007), *European Security in the Twenty-First Century: the Challenge of Multipolarity* (London: Routledge).

Hyde-Price, A. (2008), 'A "Tragic Actor"? A Realist Perspective on "Ethical Power Europe"', in L. Aggestam (ed.), 'Ethical Power Europe', Special Issue of *International Affairs* 84/1: 29–44.

[IISS] (2003), 'EU Operational Planning', *Strategic Comments* 9/10.

Ikenberry, G.J. (ed.) (2002), *America Unrivaled: The Future of the Balance of Power* (Ithaca, NY: Cornell University Press).

Ikenberry, G.J. (2004), 'Liberalism and Empire: Logics of Order in the American Unipolar Age', *Review of International Studies* 30/4: 609–30.

Ikenberry, G.J. (2008), 'The Rise of China and the Future of the West. Can the Liberal System Survive?', *Foreign Affairs* 87/1 (January–February).

International Institute for Strategic Studies (2008), *European Military Capabilities: Building Armed Forces for Modern Operations*, IISS Strategic Dossier (London: International Institute for Strategic Studies).

International Institute for Strategic Studies (2010), 'Deal Saves Europe's transport aircraft plans', *Strategic Comments* 16/8 (March).

Irondelle, B. (2003), 'Europeanization without the European Union: French military reforms, 1991–1996', *Journal of European Public Policy* 10/2: 208–26.

Jabko, N. (2006), *Playing the Market: a political strategy for uniting Europe*, 1985–2005 (Ithaca: Cornell University Press).

Jachtenfuchs, M. (2001), 'The Governance Approach to European Integration', *Journal of Common Market Studies* 39/2: 245–64.

Jacoby, W., and Meunier, S. (2010), 'Europe and the Management of Globalization', *Journal of European Public Policy* 17/3: 299–317.

Jain, R.K. (ed.) (2007), *India and the European Union: Building a Strategic Partnership* (New Delhi: Radiant Publishers).

Jervis, R. (1976), *Perception and Misperception in International Politics* (Princeton, NJ: Princeton University Press).

Joergensen, K.E. (2006), 'Making the CFSP Work', in J. Peterson, and M. Shackleton (eds), *The Institutions of the European Union* (Oxford: Oxford University Press).

Joffe, G. (2008), 'The European Union, Democracy and Counter-Terrorism in the Maghreb', *Journal of Common Market Studies* 46/1: 147–71.

Johnson, M. (1998), *European Community Trade Policy and the Article 113 Committee* (London: Royal Institute of International Affairs).

Jones, E., and Marti, D. (eds) (2009), *Updating Economic Partnership Agreements to Meet Today's Global Challenges* (Washington, DC: German Marshall Fund).

Jones, E., and van Genugten, S. (eds) (2009), *The Future of European Foreign Policy* (Routledge).

Jones, E., and Verdun, A. (2005), *The Political Economy of European Integration: Theory and Analysis* (Abingdon/New York: Routledge).

Jones, S.G. (2007), *The Rise of European Security Cooperation* (Cambridge: Cambridge University Press).

Jordan, A., Huitma, D., Van Asselt, H., Rayner, T., and Berkhout, F. (eds) (2010), *Climate Change Policy in the European Union: Confronting the Dilemmas of Mitigation and Adaptation* (Cambridge: Cambridge University Press).

Juncos, A.E. (2007), 'Cometh the "hour of Europe", cometh the institutions? Coherence and effectiveness of the EU's Common Foreign and Security Policy in Bosnia (1991–2006)', Ph.D. thesis, Loughborough University.

Juncos, A., and Reynolds, C. (2007), 'The Political and Security Committee: Governing in the Shadows', *European Foreign Affairs Review* 12/2: 127–47.

Jupille, J., Caporaso, J., and Checkel, J. (2003), 'Integrating Institutions: Rationalism, Constructivism, and the Study of the European Union', *Comparative Political Studies* 36/1: 7–40.

Kagan, R. (2002), 'Power and Weakness: Why the United States and Europe see the World Differently', *Policy Review* 113. Available at http://www.policyreview.org/JUN02/kagan.html

Kagan, R. (2003), *Paradise and Power: America and Europe in the New World Order* (London: Atlantic Books).

Kagan, R. (2004), 'Embraceable EU', *The Washington Post*, 5 December.

Kaiser, K. (1971), 'Transnational Relations as a Threat to the Democratic Process', *International Organisation* 25/3: 706–20. Reprinted in Keohane, R., and Nye, J. (eds) (1973), *Transnational Relations and World Politics* (Cambridge, MA: Harvard University Press).

Kaldor, M., Martin, M., and Selchow, S. (2007), 'Human Security: A New Strategic Narrative for Europe', *International Affairs* 83/2; 273–88.

Kaplan, L. (1996), 'NATO After the Cold War', in J. Wiener (ed.), *The Transatlantic Relationship* (New York: St Martin's Press).

Kapteyn, P.J.G. (1996), *The Stateless Market: The European Dilemma of Integration and Civilization* (London: Routledge).

Karagiannis, N. (2004), *Avoiding Responsibility: the Politics and Discourse of European Development Policy* (London: Pluto Press).

Kassim, H. (2003), 'The European Administration: Between Europeanisation and Domestication', in J. Hayward, and A. Menon (eds), *Governing Europe* (Oxford: Oxford University Press).

Kassim, H., Peters, B. G., and Wright, V. (eds) (2000), *The National Coordination of EU Policy* (Oxford: Oxford University Press).

Katzenstein, P. (ed.) (1996), *The Culture of National Security: Norms and Identity in World Politics* (New York: Columbia University Press).

Keating, T. (2004), *Constructing the Gaullist Consensus: a Cultural Perspective on French Policy Towards The United States in NATO 1958–2000* (Baden-Baden: Nomos).

Kelstrup, M., and Williams, M. (eds) (2000), *International Relations Theory and the Politics of European Integration: Power, Security and Community* (London: Routledge).

Kennedy, E. (1991), *The Bundesbank: Germany's Central Bank in the International Monetary System* (London: Pinter).

Keohane, R. (1983), 'The Demand for International Regimes', in S. Krasner (ed.), *International Regimes* (Ithaca: Cornell University Press).

Keohane, R. (1984), *After Hegemony: Cooperation and Discord in the World Political Economy* (Princeton, NJ: Princeton University Press).

Keohane, R. (1989), *International Institutions and State Power: Essays on International Relations* (Boulder, CO: Westview Press).

Keohane, R. (1989), 'International Institutions: Two Approaches' in *International Institutions and State Power: Essays in International Relations Theory* (Boulder, CO: Westview Press).

Keohane, R. (2002), 'Ironies of Sovereignty: The European Union and the United States', *Journal of Common Market Studies* 40/4: 743–65.

Keohane R. O., and Hoffman, S. (1990), 'Conclusions: Community Politics and Institutional Change', in W. Wallace (ed.), *The Dynamics of European Integration* (London: Royal Institute of International Affairs), 276–300.

Keohane, R., and Nye, J. (eds) (1972), *Transnationalism and World Politics* (Cambridge: Cambridge University Press).

Keohane, R., and Nye, J. (1977), *Power and Interdependence: World Politics in Transition* (Boston: Little, Brown).

Keohane, R., Nye, J., and Hoffmann, S. (eds) (1993), *After the Cold War: International Institutions and State Strategies in Europe* (Cambridge, MA: Harvard University Press).

Keridis, D. (2003), 'The Foreign Policy of Modernisation: From Confrontation to Interdependence?', in P. Tsakonas (ed.), *Contemporary Greek Foreign Policy*, vol.1, 297–325.

Kerr, D. (2007), 'Between Regionalism and World Order: Five Structural Factors in China–Europe Relations to 2025', in D. Kerr and L. Fei (eds), *The International Politics of EU–China Relations* (New York: Oxford University Press).

Kerr, D., and Fei, Liu. (ed.) (2007), *The International Politics of EU–China Relations* (Oxford: Oxford University Press).

Kerremans, B. (2003), 'Who Cares about Modalities? The European Commission and the EU Member States as Interdependent Actors in the WTO Negotiating Process', paper presented at the EUSA conference, Nashville, March.

Keukeleire, S. (2003), 'The European Union as a Diplomatic Actor: Internal, Traditional and Structural Diplomacy', *Diplomacy and Statecraft* 14/3: 31–56.

Keukeleire, S. (2008), 'The European Union as a Diplomatic Actor: Internal, Traditional and Structural Diplomacy', in W. Rees, and M. Smith (eds), *The International Relations of the European Union* (London: SAGE).

Keukeleire, S., and MacNaughtan, J. (2008), *The Foreign Policy of the European Union* (Basingstoke: Palgrave Macmillan).

Keukeleire, S., Smith, M., and Vanhoonacker, S. (2010), 'The emerging EU system of diplomacy: How fit for purpose?', available on http://dseu.lboro.ac.uk/.

Kilminster R., and Mennell S., 'Norbert Elias' in G. Ritzer (ed.) (2003), *The Blackwell Companion to Major Contemporary Social Theorists*, Oxford: Blackwell

Kindleberger, C.P. (1970), *Power and Money: The Politics of International Economics and the Economics of International Politics* (New York: Basic Books).

Kirchner, E., and Sperling, J. (2007), *EU Security Governance* (Manchester: Manchester University Press).

Kissinger, H. (1965), *The Troubled Partnership: A re-appraisal of the Atlantic alliance* (New York: McGraw-Hill Book Co.).

Klom, A. (2003), 'Mercosur and Brazil: a European perspective', *International Affairs* 79/2: 351–68.

Knill, C. (2005), 'Introduction: Cross-national policy convergence: concepts, approaches and explanatory factors', *Journal of European Public Policy* 2/5 (October): 764 – 774.

Koeb, E. (2008), 'A more political EU external action: Implications of the Treaty of Lisbon for the EU's relations with developing countries', *InBrief* 21 (June) (Maastricht: European Centre for Development Policy and Management [ECDPM]).

Koeb, E. (2009), 'The Lisbon Treaty – Implications for ACP–EU relations', *News and Resources on the Joint Africa–EU Strategy*. Available on http://europafrica.net/2009/10/30/the-lisbon-treaty-%E2%80%93-implications-for-acp-eu-relations-by-eleonora-koeb-ecdpm/

Koenig-Archibugi, M. (2000), 'La costruzione di una politica estera e di difesa commune per l'Unione Europea. Interessi nationali e scelta instituzionale', Ph.D. thesis, Università degli Studi di Firenze.

Koenig-Archibugi, M. (2002), 'The Democratic deficit of EU Foreign and Security Policy', *The International Spectator* 37/4: 61–73.

Koenig-Archibugi, M. (2004a), 'Explaining Preferences for Institutional Change in EU Foreign and Security Policy', *International Organization* 54/1: 137–74.

Koenig-Archibugi, M. (2004b), 'International Governance as New Raison d'État? the Case of the EU Common Foreign and Security Policy', *European Journal of International Relations* 10/2: 147–88.

Kohler-Koch, B. (1996), 'Catching up with change: The transformation of governance in the European Union', *Journal of European Public Policy* 3/3: 359–80.

Konig, T., and Slapin, J. (2006), 'From Unanimity to Consensus. An Analysis of the Negotiations at the EU's Constitutional Convention', *World Politics* 58/3: 413–45.

Korski, D., and Gowan, R. (2009), *Can the EU Rebuild Failing States? A Review of Europe's Civilian Capacities* (London: ECFR).

Krasner, S. D. (1976), 'State Power and the Structure of International Trade', *World Politics*, 28/3, 317–47.

Krasner, S. (1999), *Sovereignty: Organised Hypocrisy* (Princeton, NJ: Princeton University Press).

Kumar, R. (2008), 'India as a Foreign Policy Actor – Normative Redux', in N. Tocci (ed.), *Who is a Normative Foreign Policy Actor? The European Union and its Global Partners* (Brussels: CEPS).

Kupchan, C. (2003), 'The Rise of Europe, America's Changing Imperialism, and the End of US Primacy', *Political Science Quarterly* 118/2: 205–31.

Kurlantzick, J. (2007), *Charmoffensive: How China's Soft Power is Transforming the World* (New Haven: Yale University Press).

Laatikainen, K. (2004), 'Assessing the EU as an actor at the UN: Authority, Cohesion, Recognition and Autonomy', *CFSP Forum* 2/1; 4–9. http://www.fornet.info

Laatikainen, K., and Smith, K.E. (eds) (2006), *The European Union at the United Nations: Intersecting Multilateralisms* (Basingstoke: Palgrave).

Lacasta, N., Oberthür, S., Santos, E., and Barata, P. (2010), 'From Sharing the Burden to Sharing the Effort: Decision 406/2009/EC on Member State Emission Targets for non-ETS Sectors', in S. Oberthür, and M. Pallemaerts (eds), *The New Climate Policies of the European Union: Internal Legislation and Climate Diplomacy* (Brussels: VUBPRESS Brussels University Press), 93–116.

Ladrech, R. (1994), 'Europeanisation of Domestic Politics and Institutions: The Case of France', *Journal of Common Market Studies* 32/1: 69–87.

Laffan, B., and Stubb, A. (2003), 'Member States', in E. Bomberg, and A. Stubb (eds), *The European Union: How Does it Work?* (Oxford: Oxford University Press).

Laïdi, Z. (2008), *Norms Over Force: The Enigma of European Power* (Basingstoke: Palgrave Macmillan).

Laïdi, Z. (2010), 'Le messianisme européen en échec', *Le Monde*, 11 January.

Lake, D. (1996), 'Anarchy, Hierarchy and the Variety of International Relations', *International Organization* 50/1: 1–33.

Lake, D. (2007), 'Escape from the State of Nature: Authority and Hierarchy in World Politics', *International Security* 32/1: 47–79.

Larsen, H. (1997), *Foreign Policy and Discourse Analysis: France, Britain and Europe* (London: Routledge).

Laursen, F. (ed.) (2009), *The EU in the Global Political Economy* (Brussels: Peter Lang).

Lavenex, S. (2004), 'EU External Governance in a 'Wider Europe', *Journal of European Public Policy* 11/4 (August): 680–700.

Lavenex, S. (2006), 'Shifting up and out: The foreign policy of EU immigration control', *West European Politics* 29/2: 329–50.

Lavenex, S., and Wichmann, N. (2009), 'The External Governance of EU Internal Security', *European Integration* 31/1 (January): 83–102.

Lazarou, E., Edwards, G., Hill, C., and Smith, J. (2010), *The Evolving 'Doctrine' of Multilateralism in the 21st Century*, Mercury e-Paper no. 3, available on http://www.mercury-fp7.net/

Leal-Arcas, R. (2001), 'The European Community and Mixed Agreements', *European Foreign Affairs Review* 6/4: 483–513.

Leal-Arcas, R. (2009), 'The European Union and the BRIC Countries: Unilateralism, Bilateralism and Multilateralism', in F. Laursen (ed.), *The EU in the Global Political Economy* (Brussels: P.I.E. Peter Lang).

Legro, J. (2009), 'The Plasticity of Identity under Anarchy', *European Journal of International Relations* 15/1: 37–65.

Lehmann, J.-P. (1992), 'France, Japan, Europe and Industrial Competition: The Automotive Case', *International Affairs* 68/1: 37–53.

Lennon, A.T.J., and Kozlowski, A. (eds) (2008), *Global Powers in the 21st Century. Strategy and Relations* (Cambridge, MA: MIT Press).

Leonard, M. (2000), *The Future of Europe* (London: Foreign Policy Centre).

Leonard, M., and Popescu, N. (2007), *A Power Audit of EU–Russia Relations*, Policy Paper (London: European Council on Foreign Relations).

Lepgold, J. (1998), 'NATO's Post-Cold War Collective Action Problem', *International Security* 23/1: 76–106.

Lequesne, C. (1993), *Paris–Bruxelles: Comment se fait la politique européenne de la France* (Paris: Presses de la Fondation nationale des Sciences Politiques).

Lesser, I., Hoffman, B., Arquilla, J., Ronfeldt, D., Zanini, M., and Jenkins, B. (1999), *Countering the New Terrorism* (Washington, DC: RAND).

Light, M. (2001), 'The European Union's Russian Foreign Policy', in K. Malfliet, and L. Verpoest (eds), *Russia and Europe in a Changing International Environment* (Leuven: Leuven University Press).

Light, M., White, S., and Löwenhardt, J. (2000), 'A Wider Europe: The View from Moscow and Kyiv', *International Affairs* 76/1: 77–88.

Lightfoot, S. (2008), 'Enlargement and the Challenge of EU Development Policy', *Perspectives on European Politics and Society* 9/2: 128–42.

Lightfoot, S., and Burchill, J. (2004), 'Green Hope or Greenwash? The Actions of the European Union at the World Summit on Sustainable Development', *Global Environmental Change,* 14,4, 337–44.

Lindstrom, G. (ed.) (2003), *Shift or Rift: assessing US–EU relations after Iraq* (Paris: European Union Institute for Security Studies).

Lindstrom, G. (2007), *Enter the EU Battlegroups*, Chaillot Paper 97 (Paris: European Union Institute for Security Studies), available on http://www.iss.europa.eu/uploads/media/cp097.pdf.

Linklater, A. (1998), *The Transformation of Political Community: Ethical Foundations of the Post-Westphalian Era* (Cambridge: Polity).

Linklater, A. (2004), 'Norbert Elias, the "Civilizing Process" and International Relations', *International Politics* 14/1: 3–35.

Lipson, C. (2003), *Reliable Partners: How Democracies Have Made a Separate Peace* (Princeton, NJ: Princeton University Press).

Lister, M. (1988), *The European Community and the Developing World: The Role of the Lomé Convention* (Aldershot: Avebury).

Lister, M. (1997), *The European Union and the South: Relations with Developing Countries* (London: Routledge).

Lodge, J. (1984), 'European Union and the First Elected European Parliament: The Spinelli Initiative', *Journal of Common Market Studies* 22/4: 377–402.

Lodge, M. (2000), 'Isomorphism of National Policies? The "Europeanisation" of German Competition and Public Procurement Law', *West European Politics* 23/1: 89–107.

Lord, C. (2004), *A Democratic Audit of the European Union* (Basingstoke: Palgrave Macmillan).

Lord, C. (2008), *Some Indicators of the Democratic Performance of the European Union and how they may relate to the Recon Models*, Recon On-Line Working Paper 2008/11 (Oslo: Recon).

Lord, C., and Beetham, D. (2001), 'Legitimizing the EU: Is there a "Post-Parliamentary Basis" for its Legitimation?', *Journal of Common Market Studies* 39/3: 443–62.

Lord, C., and Magnette, P. (2004), 'E Pluribus Unum? Creative Disagreement About Legitimacy in the EU', *Journal of Common Market Studies* 42/1: 183–202.

Lucarelli, S., and Fioramonti, L. (eds) (2009), *External Perceptions of the European Union as a Global Actor* (London: Routledge).

Lucarelli, S., and Manners, I. (eds) (2006), *Values and Principles in European Union Foreign Policy* (London: Routledge).

Luif, P. (1998), 'Austria: Adaptation Through Anticipation', in K. Hanf, and B. Soetendorp (eds), *Adapting to European Integration* (London: Longman).

Lukes, S. (2005), *Power a Radical View* (Basingstoke: Palgrave Macmillan).

Lundestad, G. (ed.) (2008), *Just Another Major Crisis? The United States and Europe since 2000* (Oxford: Oxford University Press).

Lynn-Jones, S., and Miller, S. (eds) (1996), *Debating the Democratic Peace* (Cambridge, MA: MIT Press).

Mackie, J. (2008), 'Continuity and Change in International Co-operation: The ACP–EU Cotonou Partnership Agreement and its First Revision', *Perspectives on European Politics and Society* 9/2: 143–56.

Mahbubani, K. (2008), *The New Asian Hemisphere. The Irresistible Shift of Global Power to the East* (New York: Public Affairs).

Majone, G. (1996), *Regulating Europe* (London: Routledge).

Major, C. (2005), 'Europeanization and Foreign and Security Policy: Undermining or Rescuing the Nation State?', *Politics* 25/3: 175–90.

Major, C., and Pomorska, K. (2005), 'Europeanization: Fashion or Framework?', *Fornet CFSP Forum* 3/5.

Malfliet, K., Verpoest, L., and Vinokurov, E. (eds) (2007), *The CIS, the EU and Russia: Challenges of Integration* (Basingstoke: Palgrave Macmillan).

Malik, M. (2006), 'The East Asia Summit', *Australian Journal of International Affairs* 60/2: 207–11.

Mandelbaum, M. (1996), *The Dawn of Peace in Europe* (New York: Twentieth Century Fund Press).

Manners, I. (2002), 'Normative Power Europe: A Contradiction in Terms?' *Journal of Common Market Studies* 40/2: 235–58.

Manners, I. (2006), 'Normative Power Europe Reconsidered: Beyond the Cross-Roads', *Journal of European Public Policy* 13/2: 182–99.

Manners, I. (2008), 'The Normative Ethics of the European Union', in L. Aggestam (ed.), 'Ethical Power Europe', Special Issue of *International Affairs*, Special issue, 84/1: 45–60.

Manners, I. (2010), 'Global Europa: Mythology of the European Union in World Politics', *Journal of Common Market Studies* 48/1: 67–87.

Manners, I., and Whitman, R. (eds) (2000), *The Foreign Policies of European Union Member States* (Manchester: Manchester University Press).

Manners, I., and Whitman, R. (2002), 'Normative Power Europe, A Contradiction in Terms', *Journal of Common Market Studies* 40/2: 234–58.

Manners, I., and Whitman, R. (2003), 'The "Difference Engine": Constructing and Representing the International Identity of the European Union', *Journal of European Public Policy* 10/3: 380–404.

Mansfield, E., and Milner, H. (1999), 'The New Wave of Regionalism', *International Organization* 53/3: 589–627.

March, J., and Olsen, J. (1995), *Democratic Governance* (New York: Fress Press).

March, J., and Olsen, J. (1998), 'The Institutional Dynamics of International Political Orders', *International Organization* 52/4: 943–69.

Marcussen, M., Risse, T., Engelmann-Martin, D., Knopf, H., and Roscher, K. (1999), 'Constructing Europe? The Evolution of French, British and German Nation State Identities', *Journal of European Public Policy* 6/4: 614–33.

Maresceau, M. (ed.) (1993), *The European Community's Trade Policy after 1992: The Legal Dimension* (Dordrecht: Nijhoff).

Marks, G., Hooghe, L., and Blank, K. (1996), 'European Integration from the 1980s: State-Centric v. Multi-Level Governance', *Journal of Common Market Studies* 34/3: 341–78.

Marsh, S. (2008), 'EU–Russia Security Relations and the Survey of Russian Federation Foreign Policy: One Year On', *European Security* 17/2–3: 185–208.

Martin, L. (1992), *Coercive Cooperation: Explaining Multilateral Economic Sanctions* (Princeton, NJ: Princeton University Press).

Mattila, M., and Lane, J.-E. (2001), 'Why Unanimity in the Council? A Roll-Call Analysis of Council Voting', *European Union Politics* 2/1: 31–53.

Mattli, W., and Buthe, T. (2003), 'Setting International Standards', *World Politics* 56/1: 1–42.

Maull, H. (2005), 'Europe and the new balance of global order', *International Affairs* 81/4: 775–99.

Maulny, J.-P., and Liberti, F. (2008), *Pooling of EU Member States' Assets in the Implementation of ESDP*, European Parliament Directorate General External Policies of the Union,

March, available on http://www.isis-europe.org/pdf/2008_artrel_142_08-02epstudy-pooling.pdf.

Mayall, J. (2005), 'The Shadow of Empire: The EU and the Former Colonial World', in C. Hill, and M. Smith (eds), *International Relations and the European Union* (Oxford: Oxford University Press).

Mayes, D. (ed.) (1993), *The External Implications of European Integration* (Brighton: Harvester-Wheatsheaf).

Mayhew, A. (1998), *Recreating Europe: the European Union's policy towards Central and Eastern Europe* (Cambridge: Cambridge University Press).

Mazey, S., and Richardson, J. (1996), 'EU Policy-Making: A Garbage Can or an Anticipatory and Consensual Policy Style?', in Y. Mény, W. Müller, and J.-L. Quermonne (eds), *Adjusting to Europe: The Impact of the European Union on National Institutions and Policies* (London: Routledge).

McCormick, J. (2001), *Environmental Policy in the European Union* (Basingstoke: Palgrave).

McGuire, S., and Smith, M. (2008), *The European Union and the United States: Competition and Convergence in the Global Arena* (Basingstoke: Palgrave/Macmillan).

McMahon, J.A. (1998), *The Development Co-Operation Policy of the EC* (London; Boston: Kluwer Law International).

McNamara, S. (2009), *The Lisbon Treaty: Implication for the Future Relatons between the European Union and the United States*, testimony before the Committee on the Foreign Affairs on Europe of the United States House of Representatives, Washington, D.C., 15 December.

McNamara, K., and Meunier, S. (eds) (2007), *Making History: European Integration and Institutional Change at Fifty. The State of the European Union* (Oxford: Oxford University Press).

Mearsheimer, J. (1990), 'Back to the Future: Instability in Europe After the Cold War', *International Security* 15/1: 5–56.

Mearsheimer, J. (1994–5), 'The False Promise of International Institutions', *International Security* 19/3: 5–49.

Mearsheimer, J. (2001), *The Tragedy of Great Power Politics* (New York, Norton).

Menon, A. (2004), 'From Crisis to Catharsis: ESDP After Iraq', *International Affairs* 80/4: 631–48.

Menon, A. (2009), 'Empowering paradise? ESDP at ten', *International Affairs* 85/2: 227–46.

Menon, A. (2010), 'Life after Lisbon: Foreign and Security Policy', *EUSA Review* 23/1 (Winter): 2–4.

Mény, Y., Muller, P., and Quermonne, J.-L. (eds) (1996), *Adjusting to Europe: The Impact of the European Union on National Institutions and Policies* (London: Routledge).

Mérand, F. (2008), *European Defence Policy: Beyond the Nation State* (Oxford: Oxford University Press).

Mérand, F., Hofmann, S., and Irondelle, B. (2010, forthcoming), 'Transgovernmental networks in the European Security and Defense Policy', *EIOP* 14.

Merlingen, M. (2007), 'Everything is Dangerous: A Critique of "Normative Power Europe"', *Security Dialogue* 38/4: 435–53.

Merlingen M., and Ostrauskait, R. (2009), *EU Peacebuilding in Georgia: limits and achievements*, LCGGS Working Paper 35 (Leuven: Leuven Centre for Global Governance Studies).

Meunier, S. (2000a), 'The French Exception', *Foreign Affairs* 79/4: 104–16.

Meunier, S. (2000b), 'What Single Voice? European Institutions and EU–US Trade Negotiations', *International Organization* 54/1: 103–35.

Meunier, S. (2005), *Trading Voices: The European Union in International Commercial Negotiations* (Princeton, NJ: Princeton University Press).

Meunier, S., and Nicolaïdis, K. (1999), 'Who Speaks for Europe? The Delegation of Trade Authority in the EU', *Journal of Common Market Studies* 37/3: 477–501.

Meunier, S., and Nicolaïdis, K. (2006), 'The European Union as a Conflicted Trade Power', *Journal of European Public Policy* 13/6 (September): 906–25.

Meyer, C. (2006), *The Quest for a European Strategic Culture: Changing Norms on Security and Defence in the European Union* (London: Palgrave).

Michalski, A. (2006), 'The Enlarging European Union', in D. Dinan (ed.), *Origins and Evolution of the European* Union (Oxford: Oxford University Press), 271–93.

Miles, L. (2000), 'Sweden and Finland', in I. Manners, and R. Whitman (eds), *The Foreign Policies of European Union Member States* (Manchester: Manchester University Press).

Miller, D. (2007), *National Responsibility and Global Justice* (Oxford: Oxford University Press).

Milner, H. (1997), *Interests, Institutions and Information: Domestic Politics and International Relations* (Princeton, NJ: Princeton University Press).

Milward, A. (1984), *The Reconstruction of Western Europe* (London: Methuen).

Milward, A. (1992, 2000), *The European Rescue of the Nation-State* (London: Routledge).

Mishilani, P., Robert, A., Stevens, C., and Weston, A. (1981), 'The Pyramid of Privilege', in C. Stevens (ed.), *EEC and the Third World: A Survey I* (London: Hodder & Stoughton).

Miskimmon, A., and Paterson, W.E. (2003), 'Foreign and Security Policy: On the cusp between Transformation and Accommodation', in K. Dyson, and K.H. Goetz (eds), *Germany, Europe and the politics of constraint* (Oxford: Oxford University Press), 325–45.

Missiroli, A. (2001), 'European Security Policy: The Challenge of Coherence', *European Foreign Affairs Review* 6/2: 177–96.

Missiroli, A. (2003), *Euros for ESDP. Financing EU Operations*. EU–ISS Occasional Papers No. 45 (Paris: European Union Institute for Security Studies).

Mitrany, D. (1933), *The Progress of International Government* (London: George Allen and Unwin).

Mitrany, D. (1943), *A Working Peace System* (Chicago: Quadrangle Books).

Mitrany, D. (1975), 'The Prospect of Integration: Federal or Functional?', in A.J.R. Groom, and P. Taylor (eds), *Functionalism: Theory and Practice in International Relations* (London: University of London Press).

Mitsilegas, V., Monar, J., and Rees, W. (2003), *The European Union and Internal Security: Guardian of the People?* (Basingstoke: Palgrave Macmillan).

Mohan, R.C. (2007), 'Balancing Interests and Values: India's Struggle with Democracy Promotion', *The Washington Quarterly* 30/3: 99–115.

Monar, J. (1997a), 'The Finances of the Union's Intergovernmental Pillars: Tortuous Experiments with the Community Budget', *Journal of Common Market Studies* 35/1: 57–78.

Monar, J. (1997b), 'Political Dialogue with Third Countries and Regional Political Groupings: The Fifteen as an Attractive Interlocutor', in E. Regelsberger, P. de Schoutheete de Tervarent, and W. Wessels (eds), *Foreign Policy of the European Union: From EPC to CFSP and Beyond* (Boulder, CO/London: Lynne Rienner).

Monar, J. (ed.) (1998), *The New Transatlantic Agenda and the Future of EU–US Relations* (The Hague: Kluwer).

Morata, F. (1998), 'Spain: Modernization through integration', in K. Hanf, and B. Soetendorp (eds), *Adapting to European Integration* (London: Longman).

Moravcsik, A. (1991), 'Negotiating the Single European Act: National Interest and Conventional Statecraft in the European Community', in R. Keohane, and S. Hoffmann (eds), *The New European Community: Decisionmaking and Institutional Change* (Boulder, CO: Westview Press).

Moravcsik, A. (1993), 'Preferences and power in the European Community: a liberal intergovernmentalist approach', *Journal of Common Market Studies* 31/4: 473–524.

Moravcsik, A. (1998), *The Choice for Europe: Social Purpose and State Power from Messina to Maastricht* (Ithaca, NY: Cornell University Press and London: UCL Press).

Moravcsik, A. (1999), 'A New Statecraft? Supranational Entrepreneurs and International Cooperation', *International Organization* 53/2: 267–306.

Moravcsik, A. (2003), 'Striking a New Transatlantic Bargain', *Foreign Affairs* 82/4: 74–89.

Morgenthau, H. (1973), *Politics Among Nations: The Struggle for Power and Peace*, 5th edn. (New York: Knopf).

Morini, M., Peruzzi, R., and Poletti, A. (2010), 'The EU in the eyes of Russia and China', in S. Lucarelli, and L. Fioramonti (eds), *External Perceptions of the European Union as a Global Actor* (London: Routledge).

Moumoutzis, K. (2011, forthcoming), 'Still fashionable yet useless? Addressing problems with research on the Europeanization of foreign policy', *Journal of Common Market Studies*.

Muller-Wille, B. (2004), *For our Eyes Only? Shaping an Intelligence Community within the EU*, Occasional Paper 50 (Paris: European Union Institute for Security Studies), available on http://www.iss-eu.org.

Munuera, G. (1994), *Preventing Armed Conflict in Europe: lessons from Recent Experience*, Chaillot Paper 15/16 (Paris: Western European Union Institute for Security Studies).

Mytelka, L. (1977), 'The Lomé Convention and a New International Division of Labour', *Journal of European Integration* 1/1: 63–76.

Narlikar, A. (2006), 'Peculiar chauvinism or strategic calculation? Explaining the negotiating strategy of a rising India', *International Affairs* 82/1: 59–76.

Nelsen, B., and Stubb, A. (eds) (2004), *The European Union: Readings on the Theory and Practice of European Integration*, 3rd edition (Boulder, CO: Lynne Rienner).

Neuwahl, N. (1998), 'A partner with a troubled personality: EU Treaty-making in matters of CFSP and JHA after Amsterdam', *European Foreign Affairs Review* 3/2 (Summer): 177–96.

Niblett, R., and Wallace, W. (2001), *Rethinking European Order: West European Responses 1989–1997* (New York: St Martin's Press).

Nicolaïdis, K. (2000), 'Minimizing Agency Costs in Two-Level Games: Lessons from the Trade Authority Controversies in the United States and the European Union', in R. Mnookin, and L. Susskind (eds), *Negotiating on Behalf of Others* (Thousand Oaks, CA: Sage).

Nicolaïdis, K., and Egan, M. (2001), 'Regional Policy Externality and Market Governance: Why Recognize Foreign Standards?', *Journal of European Public Policy* 8/3: 454–74.

Nicolaïdis, K., and Howse, R. (2001), *The Federal Vision: Legitimacy and Levels of Government in the US and the EU* (Oxford: Oxford University Press).

Nicolaïdis, K., and Howse, R. (2002), '"This is my EUtopia…": Narrative as Power', *Journal of Common Market Studies* 40/4: 767–92.

Nicolaïdis, K., and Meunier, S. (2002), 'Revisiting Trade Competence in the European Union: Amsterdam, Nice and Beyond', in M. Hosli, A. van Deemen, and M. Widgren (eds), *Institutional Challenges in the European Union* (London: Routledge).

Nicoll, W., and Salmon, T.C. (2001), *Understanding the European Union* (Harlow: Longman).

Nilsson, H.G. (2006), 'The EU Action Plan on Combating Terrorism: Assessment and Perspectives', in D. Mahncke, and J. Monar (eds), *International Terrorism: A European Response to a Global Threat?*, College of Europe Studies No. 3 (Brussels: P.I.E. Peter Lang).

Nowak, A. (ed.) (2006), *Civilian Crisis Management: the European Way*, Chaillot Paper No. 90 (Paris: European Union Institute for Security Studies, available on http://www.iss-eu.org/chaillot/chai90.pdf.

Nuttall, S. (1992), *European Political Cooperation* (Oxford: Clarendon Press).

Nuttall, S. (1994), 'Keynote Article: The EC and Yugoslavia—*deus ex machina* or *machina sine deo*?', in N. Nugent (ed.), *The European Union 1993: Annual Review of Activities* (Journal of Common Market Studies, vol. 32) (Oxford: Blackwell).

Nuttall, S. (1996), 'Japan and the EU', *Survival* 38/2: 104–20.

Nuttall, S. (2000), *European Foreign Policy* (Oxford: Oxford University Press).

Nuttall, S. (2001), *"Consistency" and the CFSP: A Categorisation and its Consequences*, LSE European Foreign Policy Unit Working Paper No. 2001/3, available on http://www.lse.ac.uk/Depts/intrel/EuroFPUnit.html.

Nuttall, S. (2004), 'On Fuzzy Pillars: Criteria for the Continued Existence of Pillars in the Draft Constitution', *CFSP Forum* 2/3, available on http://www.fornet.info.

Nuttall, S. (2005), 'Coherence and Consistency', in C. Hill, and M. Smith (eds), *International Relations and the European Union* (Oxford: Oxford University Press), 91–112.

Nye, J. (1971), 'Comparing Common Markets: A Revised Neo-Functionalist Model', in L. Lindberg, and S. Scheingold (eds), *Regional Integration: Theory and Research* (Cambridge, MA: Harvard University Press).

Nye, J. (1990), *Bound to Lead: The Changing Nature of American Power* (New York: Basic Books).

Nye, J. (2004), *Soft Power: The Means To Success in World Politics* (New York: Public Affairs Press).

Oberthür, S., and Pallemaerts, M. (2010a), 'The EU's Internal and external Climate Policies: an Historical Overview', in S. Oberthür, and M. Pallemaerts (eds), *The New Climate Policies of the European Union Internal Legislation and Climate Diplomacy* (Brussels: VUB Press), 27–63.

Oberthür, S., and Pallemaerts, M. (eds) (2010b), *The New Climate Policies of the European Union Internal Legislation and Climate Diplomacy* (Brussels: VUB Press).

Oberthür, S., and Roche, K. (2008), 'EU Leadership in International Climate Policy: Achievements and Challenges', *The International Spectator* 43/3: 35–50.

O'Donnell, P. (2009), 'EU Warms to Action on Climate Change', *European Voice* 17 December: 6.

Øhrgaard, J. (1997), 'Less than Supranational, More than Intergovernmental: European Political Cooperation and the Dynamics of Intergovernmental Integration', *Millennium* 26/1: 1–29.

Ojanen, H. (2006), 'The EU & NATO: two competing models for a Common Defence Policy', *Journal of Common Market Studies* 44/1: 57–76.

Olivier, G., and Fioramonti, L. (2010), 'The emerging "global south". The EU in the eyes of India, Brazil and South Africa', in S. Lucarelli, and L. Fioramonti (eds), *External Perceptions of the European Union as a Global Actor* (London: Routledge).

Olsen, G.R. (2008a), 'Coherence, Consistency and Political Will in Foreign Policy: The European Union's Policy towards Africa', *Perspectives on European Politics and Society* 9/2: 157–71.

Olsen, G.R. (2008b), 'The Post September 11 Global Security Agenda: A comparative Analysis of United States and European Union Policies towards Africa', *International Politics* 45/4: 457–74.

Olsen, J.P. (2002), 'The Many Faces of Europeanisation', *Journal of Common Market Studies* 40/5: 921–52.

Olsen, J.P. (2003), 'Europeanisation', in M. Cini (ed.), *European Union Politics* (Oxford: Oxford University Press).

Olson, M. (1982), *The Rise and Decline of Nations* (New Haven, CT: Yale University Press).

Olson, M., and Zeckhauser, R. (1966), 'An Economic Theory of Alliances', *The Review of Economics and Statistics* 48/3: 266–79.

Oneal, J. (1990), 'The Theory of Collective Action and Burden-Sharing in NATO', *International Organization* 44/3: 379–402.

O'Neill, J. (2001), *Building Better Global Economies BRICs*, Global Economics Paper No. 66 (Goldman Sachs).

Orbie, J., and Versluys, H. (2008), 'The European Union's International Development Policy: Leading and benevolent?', in J. Orbie (ed.), *Europe's Global Role: External Policies of the European Union* (Aldershot: Ashgate), 67–90.

Paemen, H., and Bensch, A. (1995), *From the GATT to the WTO: The European Community in the Uruguay Round* (Leuven: Leuven University Press).

Parsons, C. (2002), 'Showing Ideas as Causes: The Origins of the European Union', *International Organization* 56/1: 47–84.

Pastore, F. (2006), 'How to assess the first stage of the EU's asylum policy', in S. Bertozzi, and E. Pastore (eds), *Towards a Common European Asylum Policy*, Multicultural Europe, European Policy Centre Paper No. 49 (October) (Brussels: European Policy Centre).

Patten, C. (2000a), 'The EU's Evolving Foreign Policy Dimension', speech by the External Relations Commissioner of the European Commission.

Patten, C. (2000b), 'A European Foreign Policy. Ambition and Reality', speech by the External Relations Commissioner of the European Commission at the Institute Francais des Relations Internationales, 15 June.

Patten, C. (2000c), 'Towards a Common European Foreign Policy – How Are We Doing?', Winston Churchill Memorial Lecture, Luxembourg, 10 October.

Patten, C. (2005), *Not Quite the Diplomat: Home Truths About World Affairs* (London: Allen Lane).

Patterson, L.A. (1997), 'Agricultural Policy Reform in the European Community: A Three-Level Game Analysis', *International Organization* 51/1: 135–65.

Paul, T.V. (2005), 'Soft Balancing in the Age of U.S. Primacy', *International Security* 30/1: 46–71.

Pawlak, P. (2007), 'From hierarchy to networks: Transatlantic governance of homeland security', *Journal of Global Change and Governance* 1/1 (Winter).

Pentland, C. (2003), 'Brussels, Bosnia and Beyond: The European Union's Search for a Role in South Eastern Europe', in C. Pentland (ed.), *Bridges to Peace: Ten Years of Conflict Management in Bosnia*, Special Issue of *Queens Quarterly*, 145–64.

Peral, L. (ed.) (2009), *Global Security in a Multi-Polar World*, Chaillot Paper 118 (Paris: European Union Institute for Security Studies).

Peters, B.G. (1998), *Comparative Politics: Theory and Methods* (Basingstoke: Macmillan).

Peters, D., Wagner, W., and Deitelhoff, N. (2010, forthcoming), 'Parliaments and European Security Policy: Mapping the parliamentary field', *European Integration online Papers*.

'Petersberg Declaration', *Europe Documents*, No. 1787, 23 June 1992.

Petersmann, E.-U., and Pollack, M. (eds) (2003), *Transatlantic Economic Disputes: The EU, the US, and the WTO* (Oxford: Oxford University Press).

Peterson, J. (1996), *Europe and America: The Prospects for Partnership*, 2nd edn. (London: Routledge).

Peterson, J. (1998), 'Introduction: The European Union as a global actor', in J. Peterson, and H. Sjursen (eds), *A Common Foreign Policy for Europe? Competing Visions of the CFSP* (London: Routledge).

Peterson, J. (2003), 'The US and Europe in the Balkans', in J. Peterson, and M. Pollack (eds), *Europe, America, Bush: transatlantic relations in the twenty-first century* (London: Routledge).

Peterson, J., and O'Toole, L. Jr (2001), 'Federal Governance in the United States and the European Union: A Policy Network Perspective', in K. Nicolaïdis, and R. Howse (eds), *The Federal Vision: Legitimacy and Levels of Governance in the United States and the European Union* (Oxford: Oxford University Press).

Peterson, J., and Pollack, M. (eds) (2003), *Europe, America, Bush: Transatlantic Relations in the Twenty-first Century* (London: Routledge).

Peterson, J., and Shackleton, M. (eds) (2006), *The Institutions of the European Union*, 2nd edn. (Oxford: Oxford University Press).

Peterson, J., and Sjursen, H. (1998), *A Common Foreign Policy for Europe? Competing Visions of the CFSP* (London: Routledge).

Peterson, J., and Smith, M.E. (2003), 'The EU as a Global Actor', in E. Bomberg, and A. Stubb (eds), *The European Union: How Does it Work?* (Oxford: Oxford University Press).

Peterson, J., and Steffenson, R. (2009), 'Transatlantic Institutions: Can Partnership be Engineered?', *British Journal of Politics and International Relations* 11/1: 25–45.

Pettit, P. (1997), *Republicanism: A Theory of Freedom and Government* (Oxford: Oxford University Press).

Pevehouse, J., and Russett, B. (2006), 'Democratic International Governmental Organizations Promote Peace', *International Organization* 60/4: 969–1000.

Phinnemore, D. (2000), 'Austria', in I. Manners, and R. Whitman (eds) *The Foreign Policies of European Union Member States* (Manchester: Manchester University Press).

Picarelli, J. (2008), 'Transnational Organized Crime', in P. Williams (ed.), *Security Studies: An Introduction* (London: Routledge).

Piebalgs, A. (2009), speech delivered at the 7th Doha Natural Gas Conference, Speech/09/102, Doha, 11 March.

Piening, C. (1997), *Global Europe: The European Union in World Affairs* (Boulder, CO/London: Lynne Rienner).

Pierson, P. (1996), 'The Path to European Integration: a Historical Institutionalist Analysis', *Comparative Political Studies* 29/2: 123–63.

Pierson, P. (2000), 'Increasing Returns, Path Dependence and the Study of Politics', *American Political Science Review* 94/2: 251–67.

Pinder, J. (1991), *European Community: The Building of a Union* (Oxford: Oxford University Press).

Pippan, C. (2004), 'The Rocky Road to Europe: The EU's Stabilisation and Association Process for the Western Balkans and the Principle of Conditionality', *European Foreign Affairs Review* 9/2: 219–46.

Pollack, M. (1997), 'Delegation, Agency, and Agenda Setting in the European Community', *International Organization* 51/1: 99–134.

Pollack, M. (2003), *The Engines of European Integration: Delegation, Agency and Agenda-Setting in the EU* (New York and Oxford: Oxford University Press).

Pollack, M. (2004), 'The New Institutionalisms and European Integration', in A. Wiener, and T. Diez (eds), *European Integration Theory* (Oxford: Oxford University Press), 137–56.

Pollack, M., and Shaffer, G. (2000), 'Transatlantic Conflict over Genetically Modified Organisms', *Washington Quarterly* 23/4: 41–54.

Pollack, M., and Shaffer, G. (eds) (2001), *Transatlantic Governance in the Global Economy* (Lanham, MD: Rowman and Littlefield).

Popescu, N., and Wilson, A. (2009), *The Limits of Enlargement-Lite: European and Russian Power in the Troubled Neighbourhood*, European Council on Foreign Relations Policy Report.

Posen, B. (2006), 'European Union Security and Defence Policy: Response to Unipolarity?', *Security Studies* 15/2: 149–86.

President of Russia (2009a), *First BRIC summit. Yekaterinburg, June 2009: Cooperation within BRIC*, available on http://eng.kremlin.ru.

President of Russia (2009b), 'Joint Statement of the BRIC Countries' Leaders', Yekaterinburg, 16 June, available on http://eng.kremlin.ru/text/docs/2009/06/217963.shtml

Pridham, G. (2002), 'EU Enlargement and Consolidating Democracy in Post-Communist States—Formality and Reality', *Journal of Common Market Studies* 40/3: 953–73.

Prodi, R. (2002), 'A Wider Europe—A Proximity Policy as the Key to Stability', speech to the Sixth ECSA-World Conference, Brussels, 5–6 December, SPEECH/02/619.

Putnam, R. (1988), 'Diplomacy and Domestic Politics: The Logic of Two-Level Games' *International Organization* 42/3: 427–60.

Quille, G. (2008), *The Lisbon Treaty and its Implications for CFSP/ESDP*, DGExPo/B/PolDep/Note/2008_014 (Brussels: European Parliament).

Quinlan, M. (2002), *European Defense Cooperation: Asset or Threat to NATO?* (Washington, DC: Woodrow Wilson Center Press).

Radaelli, C. (1997), 'How Does Europeanisation Produce Domestic Policy Change? Corporate Tax Policy in Italy and the United Kingdom', *Comparative Political Studies* 30/5: 553–75.

Radaelli, C. (2000), 'Policy Transfer in the European Union: Institutional Isomorphism as a Source of Legitimacy', *Governance* 13/1: 25–43.

Rae, H. (2002), *State Identities and the Homogenisation of Peoples* (Cambridge: Cambridge University Press).

Rankin, J. (2010), 'Row over who gets to take charge of 2010 environmental talks', *European Voice*, 15–21 April, 6/15: 4.

Ravenhill, J. (1985), *Collective Clientelism: The Lomé Conventions and North–South Relations* (New York: Columbia University Press).

Ravenhill, J. (ed.) (2008), *Global Political Economy*, 2nd edition (Oxford: Oxford University Press).

Rees, W. (2006), *Transatlantic counter-terrorism cooperation: the new imperative* (Abingdon: Routledge).

Rees, W. (2009), 'Securing the homelands: Transatlantic co-operation after Bush', *The British Journal of Politics and International Relations* 11/1 (February): 108–21.

Regelsberger, E., de Schoutheete de Tervarent, P., and Wessels, W. (eds) (1997), *Foreign Policy of the European Union: From EPC to CFSP and Beyond* (Boulder, CO: Lynne Rienner).

Reif, K., and Schmitt, H. (1980), 'Nine Second-Order National Elections: A Conceptual Framework for the Analysis of European Election Results', *European Journal of Political Research* 8/1: 3–45.

Renard, T. (2009), *A BRIC in the World: Emerging Powers, Europe and the Coming Order*, Brussels Egmont Paper 31 (Gent: Academia Press).

Rhein, E. (1996), 'Europe and the Mediterranean: A Newly Emerging Geographical Area', *European Foreign Affairs Review* 1/1: 79–86.

Rhinard, M. (2004), 'Negotiations and Multi-Level Games: The Role of the European Union in the 2000 Cartagena Protocol Negotiations', paper presented to the American Political Science Association Annual Meeting, Chicago, IL, September.

Rieker, P. (2006), *Europeanization of National Security Identity: The EU and the changing security identities of the Nordic states* (Abingdon and New York: Routledge).

Riker, W. (1964), *Federalism* (Boston: Little, Brown).

Riker, W. (1975), 'Federalism', in F. Greenstein, and N. Polsby (eds), *Handbook of Political Science* (Reading: Addison-Wesley).

Riker, W. (1996), 'European Federalism: The Lessons of Past Experience', in J. Hesse, and V. Wright (eds), *Federalising Europe? The Costs, Benefits and Preconditions of Federal Political Systems* (Oxford: Oxford University Press).

Ringius, L. (1999), 'Differentiation, Leaders and Fairness: Negotiating Climate Commitments in the European Community', *International Negotiation* 4/2: 133–66.

Risse, T. (2002), *Social Constructivism and European Integration*, Working Paper (Berlin: Freie Universität).

Risse, T. (2009), 'Social Constructivism and European Integration', in A. Wiener, and T. Diez (eds), *European Integration Theory* (Oxford: Oxford University Press), 144–160.

Risse, T., Engelmann-Martin, D., Knopf, H., and Roscher, K. (1999), 'To Euro or Not to Euro? The EMU and Identity Politics in the European Union', *European Journal of International Relations* 5/2: 147–87.

Risse-Kappen, T. (ed.) (1995), *Bringing Transnational Relations Back In: Non-State Actors, Domestic Structures and International Institutions* (Cambridge: Cambridge University Press).

Risse-Kappen, T. (1996), 'Exploring the Nature of the Beast: International Relations Theory and Comparative Policy Analysis meet the European Union', *Journal of Common Market Studies* 34/1: 53–80.

Rogers, J. (2009a), 'From "Civilian Power" to "Global Power": Explicating the European Union's "Grand Strategy" through the Articulation of Discourse Theory', *Journal of Common Market Studies* 47/4: 831–62.

Rogers, J. (2009b), *From Suez to Shanghai: the European Union and Eurasian Maritime Security*, Occasional Paper 77 (Paris: European Union Institute for Security Studies), available on http://www.iss.europa.eu/uploads/media/op77.pdf.

Romanova, T. (2008), 'The Russian Perspective on the Energy Dialogue', *Journal of Contemporary European Studies* 16/2: 219–30.

Rosamond, B. (2000a), *Theories of European Integration* (Basingstoke: Palgrave Macmillan).

Rosamond, B. (2000b), 'Europeanization and Globalization', in R. Harmsen, and T. Wilson (eds), *Europeanization: Institutions, Identities and Citizenship* (Amsterdam: Rodopi).

Rose, G. (1998), 'Neoclassical Realism and Theories of Foreign Policy', *World Politics* 51/1: 144–72.

Rosecrance, R. (1986), *The Rise of the Trading State: Commerce and Conquest in the Modern World* (New York: Basic Books).

Rosecrance, R. (1998), 'The European Union: a new type of international actor?', in J. Zielonka (ed.), *Parodoxes of European foreign policy* (The Hague: Kluwer Law International).

Rousseau, J.-J. (1973 [1762]), *The Social Contract or Principles of Political Right* (London: Everyman).

Ruggie, J., Katzenstein, P., Keohane, R., and Schmitter, P. (2005), 'Transformations in World Politics: The Intellectual Contributions of Ernst B. Haas', *Annual Review of Political Science* 8/1: 271–96.

Rummel, R. (ed.) (1990), *The Evolution of an International Actor: Western Europe's New Assertiveness* (Boulder, CO: Westview Press).

Rummel, R. (1996), 'Germany's Role in the CFSP: "Normalität" or "Sonderweg"?', in C. Hill (ed.) *The actors in Europe's Foreign Policy* (London: Routledge).

Russett, B., and Oneal, J. (2001), *Triangulating Peace: Democracy, Interdependence and International Organization* (New York: Norton).

Russett, B. *et al.* (1993), *Grasping the Democratic Peace* (Princeton, NJ: Princeton University Press).

Rutten, M. (dir) (2001), *From Saint-Malo to Nice: European Defence—Core Documents*, Chaillot Paper 47 (Paris: WEU Institute for Security Studies), available on http://www.iss-eu.org.

Salmon, T., and Shepherd, A. (2003), *Toward a European Army: A Military Power in the Making?* (Boulder, CO: Lynne Rienner).

Sandholtz, W. (1996), 'Membership Matters: Limits of the Functional Approach to European Institutions', *Journal of Common Market Studies* 34/3: 403–29.

Sangiovanni, M.E. (2003), 'Why a Common Security and Defence Policy is Bad for Europe', *Survival* 45/3: 193–206.

Santander, S. (2005), 'The European Partnership with Mercosur: a Relationship Based on Strategic and Neoliberal Principles', *Journal of European Integration* 27/3: 285–306.

Santiso, C. (2002), 'Reforming European Foreign Aid: Development Cooperation as an Element of Foreign Policy', *European Foreign Affairs Review* 7/4: 401–22.

Saunders, C. and Triggs, G. (eds) (2002), *Trade and Cooperation with the European Union in the New Millennium* (Alphen aan den Rijn: Kluwer Law International).

Sbragia, A. (2004), 'Competitive Regionalism, Trade Liberalization, and Globalization: The EU and the Americas', paper presented to Conference of Europeanists, Chicago, IL, March.

Sbragia, A. (2010), 'The EU, the US and Trade Policy: Competitive Interdependence in the Management of Globalization', *Journal of European Public Policy* 17/3: 368–82.

Sbragia, A., and Damro, C. (1999), 'The Changing Role of the European Union in International Environmental Politics: Institution building and the politics of climate change', *Government and Policy*, theme issue on European Union Environmental Policy at 25, 17/1: 53–68.

Scharpf, F. (1999), *Governing in Europe: Effective and Democratic?* (Oxford: Oxford University Press).

Scheipers, S., and Sicurelli, D. (2008), 'Empowering Africa: normative power in EU–Africa relations', *Journal of European Public Policy* 15/4: 607–23.

Schimmelfennig, F. (2001), 'The Community Trap: Liberal Norms, Rhetorical Actions, and the Eastern Enlargement of the European Union', *International Organization* 55/1: 47–80.

Schimmelfennig, F. (2003), *The EU, NATO and the Integration of Europe: Rules and Rhetoric* (Cambridge: Cambridge University Press).

Schimmelfennig, F., and Sedelmeier, U. (2004), 'Governance by conditionality: EU rule transfer to the candidate countries of Central and Eastern Europe', *Journal of European Public Policy* 11/4 (August): 669–87.

Schimmelfennig, F., and Sedelmeier, U. (eds) (2005), *The Politics of European Union Enlargement: Theoretical Approaches* (London: Routledge).

Schmidt, S. K. (2007), 'Mutual Recognition as a New Mode of Governance', special issue of *Journal of European Public Policy*, 14 /5, Schmidt as guest editor, 667–825.

Schmidt, V.A. (2008), 'Discursive Institutionalism: The Explanatory Power of Ideas and Discourse', *Annual Review of Political Science* 11 (June): 303–26.

Schmidt, V.A. (2010), 'Taking Ideas and Discourse Seriously: Explaining Change through Discursive Institutionalism as the Fourth New Institutionalism', *European Political Science Review* 2/1: 1–25.

Schmitt, H., and Thomassen, J. (2000), 'Dynamic Representation: The Case of European Integration', *European Union Politics* 1/3: 340–63.

Schmitter, P. (1969), 'Three Neo-Functional Hypotheses about European Integration', *International Organization* 23/1: 161–66.

Schmitter, P. (1974), 'A Revised Theory of European Integration', in L. Lindberg, and S. Scheingold (eds), *Regional Integration: Theory and Research* (Cambridge, MA: Harvard University Press).

Scholte, J. (2005), *Globalization: A Critical Introduction*, 2nd edition (Basingstoke and New York: Palgrave Macmillan).

Schreurs, M. (2004), 'Environmental protection in an expanding European Community: lessons from past accessions', *Environmental Politics* 13/1: 27–51.

Schreurs, M., and Tiberghien, Y. (2007), 'Multilevel Reinforcement: Explaining European Union Leadership in Climate Change Mitigation', *Global Environmental Politics*, 7,4, 113–37.

Schroeder, P. (1976), 'Alliances 1815– 1945: Weapons of Power and Tools of Management', in K. Knorr (ed.), *Historical Dimensions of National Security Problems* (Lawrence, KS: University Press of Kansas).

Secretary-General/High Representative (2000), 'The EU's External Projection. Improving the Efficiency of Our Collective Resources', Council Paper given at Evian, 2 September.

Senior Nello, S., and Smith, K. (1998), *The European Union and Central and Eastern Europe: The Implications of Enlargement in Stages* (Aldershot: Ashgate).

Shambaugh, D. (2005), 'The New Strategic Triangle: U.S. and European Reactions to China's Rise', in A.T.J. Lennon, and A. Kozlowski (eds), *Global Powers in the 21st Century: Strategies and Relations* (Cambridge, MA: MIT Press).

Shambaugh,D., Sandschneider, E., and Hong, Z. (eds) (2008), *China–Europe relations: perceptions, policies and prospects* (London: Routledge).

Shapiro, J., and Witney, N. (2009), *Towards a Post-American Europe: A Power Audit of EU–US Relations* (London: European Council on Foreign Relations).

Shaw, T. (1979), 'EEC–ACP Interactions and Images as Redefinitions of EurAfrica: Exemplary, Exclusive and/or Exploitative?', *Journal of Common Market Studies* 18/2: 135–58.

Shaw, T.M., Cooper, A.F., and Antkiewicz, A. (2007), 'Global and/or Regional Development at the Start of the 21st Century? China, India and (South) Africa', *Third World Quarterly* 28/7: 1255–70.

Shearer, A. (2000), 'Britain, France and the Saint-Malo Declaration', *Cambridge Review of International Affairs* XIII/2: 283–98.

Silvestri, S. (1997), 'The Albanian Test Case', *The International Spectator* 32/3–4: 87–98.

Simon, L. (2010), *Command and Control? Planning for EU Military Operations*, EU–IIS Occasional Paper no. 81 (Paris, European Union Institute for Security Studies), available on http://www.iss.europa.eu/uploads/media/Planning_for_EU_military_operations.pdf

Sjursen, H. (2001), 'The Common Foreign and Security Policy: Limits of Intergovernmentalism and the Search for a Global Role', in S. Andersen, and K. Eliassen (eds), *Making Policy in Europe*, 2nd edn. (London: Sage).

Sjursen, H. (2002), 'Why Expand? The Question of Legitimacy and Justification in the EU's Enlargement Policy', *Journal of Common Market Studies* 40/3: 491–513.

Sjursen, H. (2003), *The United States, Western Europe and the Polish Crisis: International Relations in the Second Cold War* (Basingstoke: Palgrave Macmillan).

Sjursen, H. (2006), 'What kind of power?', *Journal of European Public Policy* 13/2: 169–81.

Sjursen, H. (ed.) (2007), *Civilian or Military Power? European Foreign Policy in Perspective* (London: Routledge).

Skjaerseth, J.B. (1994), 'The Climate Policy of the EC: Too Hot to Handle?', *Journal of Common Market Studies* 32/1: 25–54.

Skjaerseth, J.B., and Wettestad, J. (2010), 'The EU Emissions Trading System Revised (Directive 2009/29/EC)', in S. Oberthür, and M. Pallemaerts (eds), *The New Climate Policies of the European Union Internal Legislation and Climate Diplomacy* (Brussels: VUB Press), 65–92.

Skodvin, T., and Andresen, S. (2006), 'Leadership revisited', *Global Environmental Politics* 6/3: 13–27.

Skogstad, G., and Verdun, A. (eds) (2009), *The Common Agricultural Policy: Policy Dynamics in a Changing Context* (London: Routledge).

Slapin, J. (2008), 'Bargaining Power at Europe's Intergovernmental Conferences: Testing Institutional and Intergovernmental Theories', *International Organization* 62/1: 131–62.

Sloan, S. (2002), *NATO, the European Union and the Atlantic Community: the Transatlantic Bargain Reconsidered* (Lanham, MD: Rowman and Littlefield).

Slovenian Presidency of the EU (2008), 'EU–Russia Summit: The Start of a New Age', 27 June, available on http://www.eu2008.si/en/News_and_Documents/Press_Releases/June/2706KPV_EU_Rusija1.html

Smith, D. (2001), *Norbert Elias and Modern Social Theory* (London: Sage).

Smith, H. (1995), *European Union Foreign Policy and Central America* (New York: St. Martin's Press).

Smith, H. (2002), *European Union Foreign Policy: What it is and What it Does* (London: Pluto Press).

Smith, K.E. (1998), 'The Instruments of European Union Foreign Policy', in J. Zielonka (ed.), *Paradoxes of European Foreign Policy* (The Hague: Kluwer Law International).

Smith, K.E. (1999), *The Making of EU Foreign Policy: The Case of Eastern Europe* (Basingstoke: Palgrave Macmillan).

Smith, K.E. (2001), 'The EU, Human Rights and Relations with Third Countries: "Foreign Policy" with an Ethical Dimension?', in K.E. Smith, and M. Light (eds), *Ethics and Foreign Policy* (Cambridge: Cambridge University Press), 185–204.

Smith, K.E. (2003), *European Union Foreign Policy in a Changing World* (Cambridge: Polity Press).

Smith, K.E. (2004), *The Making of EU Foreign Policy: The Case of Eastern Europe*, 2nd edn. (Basingstoke: Palgrave Macmillan).

Smith, K.E. (2005), 'The Outsiders: The European Neighbour Policy', *International Affairs* 81/4: 757–73.

Smith, K.E. (2008), *European Union Foreign Policy in a Changing World.* 2nd edn. (Cambridge: Polity).

Smith, M. (1984), *Western Europe and the United States: The Uncertain Alliance* (London: George Allen and Unwin).

Smith, M. (1996a), 'The European Union and a Changing Europe: Establishing the Boundaries of Order', *Journal of Common Market Studies* 34/1: 5–28.

Smith, M. (1996b), 'The EU as an International Actor', in J. Richardson (ed.), *European Union: Power and Policy-Making* (London: Routledge).

Smith, M. (1998a), 'Competitive Co-operation and EU/US Relations: Can the EU be a Strategic Partner for the US in the World Political Economy?', *Journal of European Public Policy* 5/4: 561–77.

Smith, M. (1998b), 'Does the Flag Follow Trade? "Politicisation" and the Emergence of a European Foreign Policy', in J. Peterson, and H. Sjursen (eds), *A Common Foreign Policy for Europe? Competing Visions of the CFSP* (London: Routledge).

Smith, M. (2001), 'The European Union's Commercial Policy: Between Coherence and Fragmentation', *Journal of European Public Policy* 8/5: 787–802.

Smith, M. (2004a), 'Between Two Worlds? The European Union, the United States and World Order', *International Politics* 41/1: 95–117.

Smith, M. (2004b), 'A Europe That Can Say No? Collective Action Problems in EU Responses to the George W. Bush Administration', paper presented at the American Political Science Association Annual Meeting, Chicago, September.

Smith, M. (2006), 'The Shock of the Real? Trends in European Foreign and Security Policy Since September 2001', *Studia Diplomatica* LIX/1: 27–44.

Smith, M. (2007), 'The European Union and International Order: European and Global Dimensions', *European Foreign Affairs Review* 12/4: 437–56.

Smith, M. (2009a), 'Transatlantic Economic Relations in a Changing Global Political Economy: Achieving Togetherness but Missing the Bus?', *British Journal of Politics and International Relations* 11/1: 94–107.

Smith, M. (2009b), 'Perceptions, Misperceptions and Transatlantic Relations: Past, Present and Future(s)', in N. Fernández Sola, and M. Smith (eds), *Perceptions and Policy in Transatlantic Relations: Prospective Visions from the US and Europe* (London: Routledge).

Smith, M., and Woolcock, S. (1993), *The United States and the European Community in a Transformed World* (London: Pinter/Royal Institute of International Affairs).

Smith, M.E. (2000), 'Conforming to Europe: The Domestic Impact of EU Foreign Policy Cooperation', *Journal of European Public Policy* 7/4: 613–31.

Smith, M .E. (2001), 'The quest for coherence: institutional dilemmas of external action from Maastricht to Amsterdam' in Stone Sweet, A., Sandholtz, W., and Fligstein, N. (eds) *The Institutionalization of Europe*, 171–93 (Oxford: Oxford University Press).

Smith, M.E. (2003), *Europe's Foreign and Security Policy: The Institutionalization of Cooperation* (Cambridge: Cambridge University Press).

Smith, M.E. (2004a), 'Institutionalization, Policy Adaptation and European Foreign Policy Cooperation', *European Journal of International Relations* 10/1: 95–136.

Smith, M.E. (2004b), 'Toward a Theory of EU Foreign Policy-making: Multi-level Governance, Domestic Politics, and National Adaptation to Europe's Common Foreign and Security Policy', *Journal of European Public Policy* 11/4: 740–58.

Smith, S. (2000), 'Wendt's World', *Review of International Studies* 26/1: 151–63.

Snyder, F. (ed.) (2007), 'The Fifth WISH/RIJC: The EU, India and China – Strategic Partners in a Changing World', *European Law Journal* 13/6: 692–879.

Snyder, F. (ed.) (2009), *The European Union and China, 1949–2008* (Oxford: Hart Publishing).

Snyder, G. (1997), *Alliance Politics* (Ithaca, NY: Cornell University Press).

Soares de Lima, M.R., and Hirst, M. (2006), 'Brazil as an intermediate state and regional power: action, choice and responsibilities', *International Affairs* 82/1: 21–40.

Söderbaum, F., and Stålgren, P. (eds) (2009), *The European Union and the Global South* (Boulder, CO: Lynne Rienner).

Solana, J. (2008), 'Climate Change and International Security: Paper from the High Representative to the European Commission and the European Council', S113/08, Brussels, 14 March.

Sorensen, G. (2008), 'The Case for Combining Material Forces and Ideas in the Study of IR', *European Journal of International Relations* 14/1: 5–32.

Spence, D. (ed) (2007), *The European Union and Terrorism* (London: John Harper Publishing)

Spinelli, A. (1972), 'The Growth of the European Movement Since the Second World War', in M. Hodges (ed.), *European Integration* (Harmondsworth: Penguin).

Steffenson, R. (2005), *Managing EU–US Relations: Actors, Institutions and the New Transatlantic Agenda* (Manchester: Manchester University Press).

Stevens, C. (2006), 'The EU, Africa and Economic Partnership Agreements: Unintended Consequences of Policy Leverage', *Journal of Modern African Studies* 44/3: 441–58.

Stie, A.E. (2010, forthcoming), 'Decision-making void of democratic qualities? An evaluation of the EU's second pillar decision making procedure', *European Integration online Papers*.

Stiglitz, J. E. (2002), *Globlization and Its Discontents* (New York: Norton).

Stokhof, W.A.L., van der Velde, P., and Yeo, L.H. (eds) (2004), *The Eurasian space: Far More Than Two Continents* (Leiden: International Institute for Asian Studies [IIAS]).

Stone Sweet, A., and Sandholtz, W. (eds) (1998), *Supranational Governance: The Institutionalization of the European Union* (Oxford: Oxford University Press).

Stone Sweet, A., Sandholtz, W., and Fligstein, N. (eds) (2001), *The Institutionalization of Europe* (Oxford: Oxford University Press).

Storbeck, J. (2003), 'The European Union and Enlargement: Challenge and Opportunity for Europol in the Fight Against International Crime', *European Foreign Affairs Review* 8/3: 283–8.

Storey, A. (2006), 'Normative Power Europe? Economic Partnership Agreements and Africa', *Journal of Contemporary African Studies* 24/3: 331–46.

Strange, S. (1970), 'The Politics of International Currencies', *World Politics*, 23/2, 215–31.

Strange, S. (1971), *Sterling and British Policy* (London: Oxford University Press).

Strange, S. (1976), 'International Monetary Relations, Volume 2', in A. Shonfield (ed.), *International Economic Relations of the Western World 1959–1971* (London: OUP for Royal Institute of International Affairs).

Stumbaum, M.-B. (2009), *The European Union in China. Decision-Making in EU Foreign and Security Policy towards the People's Republic of China* (Baden-Baden: Nomos).

Suganami, H. (1989), *The Domestic Analogy and World Order Proposals* (Cambridge: Cambridge University Press).

Szukala, A., and Wessels, W. (1997), 'The Franco–German Tandem', in G. Edwards, and A. Pijpers (eds), *The Politics of European Treaty Reform* (London: Cassell).

Szymanski, M., and Smith, M.E. (2005), 'Coherence and Conditionality in European Foreign Policy: Negotiating the EU–Mexico Global Agreement', *Journal of Common Market Studies* 43/1 (March): 171–92.

Tams, K. (1999), 'Functions of a European Security and Defence Identity and its institutional Form', in H. Haftendorn, R. Keohane, and C. Wallander (eds), *Imperfect Unions: Security Institutions Over Time and Space* (Oxford: Oxford University Press).

Tardy, T. (ed.) (2009), *European Security in a Global Context* (London: Routledge).

Taylor, P. (1996), *The European Union in the 1990s* (Oxford: Oxford University Press).

Telò, M. (2006), *Europe: A Civilian Power? The European Union, Global Governance, World Order* (Basingstoke: Palgrave Macmillan).

Telò, M. (ed.) (2007), *European Union and New Regionalism: Regional Actors and Global Governance in a Post-Hegemonic Era*, 2nd edn. (Aldershot: Ashgate).

Telò, M. (ed.) (2009), *The European Union and Global Governance* (London: Routledge/ Garnet).

Terriff, T. (2003), 'The CJTF Concept and the Limits of European Autonomy', in J. Howorth, and J. Keeler (eds), *Defending Europe: The EU, NATO and the Quest for European Autonomy* (New York: Palgrave Macmillan).

Tewes, H. (2002), *Germany, Civilian Power and the New Europe* (Basingstoke: Palgrave).

Terzi, Ö. (2005), 'Europeanization of Foreign Policy and Candidate Countries: A Comparative Study of Greek and Turkish Cases', *Politique européenne* 17: 113–36.

The 9/11 Commission Report (2004), *Final Report of the National Commission on Terrorist Attacks upon the United States* (New York: W.W. Norton).

The Miltary Balance 2010 (2010) (London: International Institute for Strategic Studies).

Thelen, K. (1999), 'Historical Institutionalism in Comparative Politics', *Annual Review of Political Science* 2 (June): 369–404.

Thomas, W. (2001), *The Ethics of Destruction: Norms and Violence in International Relations* (Ithaca, NY: Cornell University Press).

Tickner, A.B., and Waever, O. (eds) (2009), *International Relations Scholarship around the World* (London: Routledge).

Tietje, C. (1997), 'The Concept of Coherence in the Treaty on European Union and the Common Foreign and Security Policy', *European Foreign Affairs Review* 2/2: 211–33.

Tocci, N. (ed.) (2008), *Who is a Normative Foreign Policy Actor? The European Union and its Global Partners* (Brussels: Centre for European Policy Studies [CEPS]).

Todd, E. (2003), *After the American Empire: The Breakdown of the American Order* (New York: Columbia University Press).

Tofte, S. (2003), 'Non-EU NATO Members and the Issue of Discrimination', in J. Howorth, and J. Keeler (eds), *Defending Europe: The EU, NATO and the Quest for Autonomy* (New York: Palgrave Macmillan).

Tofte, S. (2005), 'Non-EU NATO Members and the post-Cold War European Security Structures: a Case Study of Norway', Ph.D. thesis, University of Bath.

Tommel, I., and Verdun, A. (eds) (2009), *Innovative Governance in the European Union: The Politics of Multilevel Policy-Making in the European Union* (Boulder, CO: Lynne Rienner).

Tonra, B. (2000), 'Denmark and Ireland' in Manners, I., and Whitman, R. (eds), *The Foreign Policies of European Union Member States* (Manchester: Manchester University Press).

Tonra, B. (2001a), *The Europeanisation of National Foreign Policy: Dutch, Danish and Irish Foreign Policy in the European Union* (Aldershot: Ashgate).

Tonra, B. (2001b), 'Setting the Agenda of European Crisis Management – The Challenge to Coherence', in A. Missiroli (ed.), *Coherence for European Security Policy: Debates–Cases–Assessments*, EU–ISS Occasional Papers No. 27 (Paris: European Union Institute for Security Studies).

Tonra, B. (2003), 'Constructing the Common Foreign and Security Policy: The Utility of a Cognitive Approach', *Journal of Common Market Studies* 41/4: 731–56.

Tranholm-Mikkelsen, J. (1991), 'Neofunctionalism: Obstinate or Obsolete? A Reappraisal in the Light of the New Dynamism of the EC', *Millennium* 20/1: 1–22.

Trenin, D. (2008), 'Russia and the European Union: redefining strategic partnership', in G. Grevi, and A. de Vasconcelos (eds), *Partnership for effective multilateralism: EU relations with Brazil, China, India and Russia*, Chaillot Paper 109 (Paris: European Union Institute for Security Studies).

Tsardanidis, C., and Stavridis, S. (2005), 'The Europeanization of Greek Foreign Policy: A Critical Appraisal', *European Integration* 27/2 (June): 217–39.

Tsebelis, G., and Garrett, G. (2003), 'The Institutional Foundations of Intergovernmentalism and Supranationalism in the European Union', *International Organization* 55/2: 357–90.

Tsoukalis, L. (2003), *What Kind of Europe?* (revised and updated edition, 2005) (Oxford: Oxford University Press).

Tsoukalis, L. (2005), 'Managing Interdependence: The EU in the World Economy', in C. Hill, and M. Smith (eds), *International Relations and the European Union* (Oxford: Oxford University Press), 225–46.

Twitchett, C.C. (1981), *A Framework for Development: The EEC and the ACP* (London: Allen and Unwin).

Ugland, T. (2011), *Jean Monnet and Canada: The Father of Europe and His Canadian Inspiration* (Toronto: University of Toronto Press).

United Nations Development Programme (2009), *Human Development Report 2009: Overcoming barriers: Human mobility and development* (Basingstoke, New York: Palgrave Macmillan), http://hdr.undp.org/en/statistics/.

University of Toronto, G20 Research Group: http://www.g20.utoronto.ca

Vachudova, M. (2005), *Europe Undivided: democracy, leverage, and integration after communism* (Oxford: Oxford University Press).

Vachudova, M. (2009), 'Corruption and Compliance in the EU's Post-Communist Members and Candidates', Special Issue of *Journal of Commons Market Studies* (Annual Review of the European Union in 2008) 47/s1: 43–62.

Vahl, M. (2007), 'EU–Russia Relations in EU Neighbourhood Policies', in K. Malfliet, L. Verpoest, and E. Vinokurov (eds), *The CIS, the EU and Russia* (Basingstoke: Palgrave Macmillan).

Van den Hoven, A. (2002), 'Enlargement and the EU's Common Commercial Policy', paper presented at the ECSA–Canada Conference, Toronto, May.

Vanhoonacker, S, and Jacobs, A. (2009), 'Exploring and explaining the domestic administrative change in ESDP. The case of Belgium', paper presented at the ISA Annual Convention, New York, 15–19 February.

Vanhoonacker, S., Dijkstra, H., and Maurer, H. (2010, forthcoming), 'Understanding the Role of Bureaucracy in the European Security and Defence Policy: The State of the Art', *European Integration online Papers*.

Van Oudenaren, J. (2001), 'E Pluribus Confusio: Living with the EU's Structural Incoherence', *The National Interest* 2001 (Fall)/65: 23–36.

Van Schaik, L.G., and Egenhofer, C. (2005), *Improving the Climate—Will the New Constitution Strengthen the EU's Performance in International Climate negotiations?*, CEPS Policy Brief 63 (Brussels: Centre for European Policy Studies).

Vasconcelos, A. de (1996), 'Portugal: Pressing for an Open Europe', in C. Hill (ed.) *The Actors in Europe's Foreign Policy* (London: Routledge).

Vasconcelos, A. de (2007), 'European Union and MERCOSUR', in M. Telo (ed.), *European Union and New Regionalism: Regional Actors and Global Governance in a Post-Hegemonic Era*, 2nd edn. (Aldershot: Ashgate).

Vasconcelos, A. de, and Joffe, G. (eds) (2000), *The Barcelona Process* (London: Frank Cass).

Venusberg Group (2004), *A European Defence Strategy* (Gutersloh: Bertelsmann).

Verdun, A. (1996), 'An "Asymmetrical" Economic and Monetary Union in the EU: Perceptions of monetary authorities and social partners', *Revue d'Integration Européenne/ Journal of European Integration*, 20/1, autumn, 59–81.

Verdun, A. (1997), 'The International Aspects of the EU's Exchange Rate Policy: European Integration and Dollar Dominance', in Alan Cafruny and Patrick Peters (eds), *The*

Union and the World: The Political Economy of a Common European Foreign Policy (London: Kluwer), 175–89.

Verdun, A. (2000), *European Responses to Globalization and Financial Market Integration. Perceptions of EMU in Britain, France and Germany*, International Political Economy Series (Basingstoke: Macmillan/New York: St. Martin's Press).

Verdun, A. (2009), 'The EU as a Global Actor: The Role of EMU and the Euro', in Finn Laursen (ed.) *The EU in the Global Political Economy* (Brussels: PIE/Peter Lang), 45–63.

Verheugen, G. (1999), 'Enlargement: Speed and Quality', speech given in The Hague, 4 November, Rapid document SPEECH/99/151.

Verheugen, G. (2001), 'Debate on EU Enlargement in the European Parliament', speech given in Strasbourg, 4 September, Rapid Document SPEECH/01/363.

Versluys, H. (2008a), 'European Union humanitarian aid: Lifesaver or political tool?', in J. Orbie (ed.), *Europe's Global Role. External Policies of the European Union* (Aldershot; Ashgate), 91–115.

Versluys, H. (2008b), 'Depoliticising and Europeanising Humanitarian Aid: Success or Failure?', *Perspectives on European Politics and Society* 9/2: 208–24.

Vink, M.P., and Graziano, P. (2006), 'Challenges of a New Research Agenda', in P. Graziano, and M.P. Vink (eds), *Europeanization: New Research Agendas* (Basingstoke and New York: Palgrave Macmillan), 3–20.

Vogel, D. (2002), 'The Hare and the Tortoise Revisited: The New Politics of Consumer and Environmental Regulation in Europe', *British Journal of Political Science* 33/4: 557–80.

Vogler, J. (2005), 'The European Contribution to Global Environmental Governance' *International Affairs*, 81,4, 835–49.

Vogler, J. (2009), 'Climate Change and EU Foreign Policy: the negotiation of burden-sharing', *International Politics* 46/4 (July): 469–90.

Vogler, J., and Bretherton, C. (2006), 'The European Union as a Protagonist to the United States on Climate Change', *International Studies Perspectives* 7/1 (February): 1–22.

Vogler, J., and Stephan, H. (2007), 'The European Union in global environmental governance: leadership in the making?', *International Environmental Agreements: Politics, Law and Economics* 7/4 (December): 389–413.

Wagner, C. (2008), 'The EU and India: a deepening partnership', in G. Grevi, and A. de Vasconcelos (eds), *Partnership for effective multilateralism: EU relations with Brazil, China, India and Russia*, Chaillot Paper 109 (Paris: European Union Institute for Security Studies).

Wagner, W. (2003), 'Why the EU's Common Foreign and Security Policy Will Remian Intergovernmental: A Rationalist Institutionalist Choice Analysis of European Crisis Management Policy', *Journal of European Public Policy* 10/4: 576–95.

Wagner, W. (2006a), 'The democratic control of military power Europe', *Journal of European Public Policy* 13/2: 200–16.

Wagner, W. (2006b), *Parliamentary Control of Military Actions: Accounting for Pluralism*, Occasional Paper No. 12 (Geneva: Centre for the Democratic Control of Armed Forces).

Wallace, W. (1983), 'Less than a Federation, More than a Regime: The Community as a Political System', in H. Wallace, and W. Wallace (eds), *Policy-Making in the European Community*, 2nd edn. (Chichester and New York: John Wiley).

Wallace, W. (1994), *Regional integration: The West European Experience* (Washington, DC: Brookings Institution).

Wallace, W. (2001), 'Rethinking European Order: West European Responses, 1989–97—Introduction', in R. Niblett, and W. Wallace (eds), *Rethinking European Order: West European Responses, 1989–97* (Basingstoke: Palgrave).

Wallace, H., and Wallace, W. (2000), *Policy Making in the European Union*, 4th edn. (Oxford: Oxford University Press).

Wallace, H., Pollack, M., and Young, A. (eds) (2010), *Policy-Making in the European Union*, 6th edn. (Oxford: Oxford University Press).

Wallace, W. (2005), 'Post-Sovereign Governance: the EU as a Partial Polity', in H. Wallace, W. Wallace, and M. Pollack (eds), *Policy-making in the European Union,* 5th edn. (Oxford: Oxford University Press), 483–503.

Wallerstein, I. (1979), *The Capitalist World Economy* (Cambridge: Cambridge University Press).

Walt, S. (2005), *Taming American Power: The Global Response to US Primacy* (New York: Norton).

Walt, S. (2010), *Reports of a Transatlantic Rift Greatly Exaggerated*, posted to Foreign Policy online, 3 February, available on http://walt.foreignpolicy.com/posts/2010/02/03/reports_of_a_transatlantic_rift_have_been_greatly_exaggerated.

Waltz, K. (1979), *Theory of International Politics* (London: Addison-Wesley).

Waltz, K. (1993), 'The Emerging Structure of International Politics', *International Security* 18/2: 44–79.

Waltz, K. (2000), 'Structural Realism After the Cold War', *International Security* 25/1: 5–41.

Ward, A. (1998), 'Frameworks for Cooperation Between the European Union and Third States', *European Foreign Affairs Review* 3/3: 503–56.

Wayman, F., and Diehl, P. (eds) (1994), *Reconstructing Realpolitik* (Ann Arbor, MI: University of Michigan Press).

Weber, K. (1997), 'Hierarchy Amidst Anarchy: A Transactions Cost Approach to International Security Cooperation', *International Studies Quarterly* 41/2: 321–40.

Weber, K., Smith, M.E., and Baun, M. (eds) (2007), *Governing Europe's Neighbourhood: Partners or Periphery?* (Manchester: Manchester University Press).

Weiler, J. (1999), *The Constitution of Europe: 'Do the New Clothes have an Emperor?' and Other Essays on European Integration* (Cambridge: Cambridge University Press).

Weiler, J. (ed.) (2000), *The EU, the WTO and the NAFTA* (Oxford: Oxford University Press).

Weiss, L. (1999), 'Globalization and National Governance: Antinomy or Interdependence?', *Review of International Studies* 25/5: 59–88.

Weiss, T., and Daws, S. (eds) (2008), *The Oxford Handbook on the United Nations* (Oxford: Oxford University Press)

Wendt, A. (1987), 'The Agent–Structure Problem in International Theory', *International Organization* 43/3: 335–70.

Wendt, A. (1992), 'Anarchy is What States Make of it: The Social Construction of Power Politics', *International Organization* 46/2: 391–425.

Wendt, A. (1999), *Social Theory of International Relations* (Cambridge: Cambridge University Press).

Wettestad, J. (2005), 'The Making of the 2003 EU Emissions Trading Directive: An Ultra-Quick Process due to Entrepreneurial Proficiency?', *Global Environmental Politics* 5/1: 1–23.

White, B. (2001), *Understanding European Foreign Policy* (Basingstoke: Palgrave Macmillan).

White House (2002), *The National Security Strategy of The United States*, Washington DC.

Whitman, R. (1998), *From Civilian Power to Superpower? The International Identity of the European Union* (London: Macmillan).Whitman, R. (ed.) (2010), *Normative Power Europe: Empirical and Theoretical Perspectives* (Basingstoke: Palgrave Macmillan).

Whitman, R., and Juncos, A. (2009), 'The Lisbon Treaty and the Foreign, Security and Defence Policy: Reforms, Implementation and the Consequences of (non-)Ratification', 14, *European Foreign Affairs Review* 14/1: 25–46.

Wielaard, R. (2010), 'How many presidents does it take to run the EU?', *Washington Post*, 8 January.

Wiessala, G. (2002), *The European Union and Asian Countries* (London: Sheffield Academic Press/Continuum for UACES).

Wilson, D., and Purushothaman, R. (2003), *Dreaming With BRICs: The Path to 2050*, Global Economics Paper No 99 (Goldman Sachs).

Winand, P. (1993), *Eisenhower, Kennedy and the United States of Europe* (New York: St Martin's Press).

Winer, J. (2005), 'Cops across borders. The evolution of transatlantic law enforcement and judicial cooperation', in A. Dalgaard-Nielsen, and D, Hamilton (eds), *Transatlantic Homeland Security: Protecting Society in an Age of Catastrophic Terrorism* (London: Routledge).

Wissenbach, U. (2009), 'The EU's Response to China's Africa Safari: Can Triangular Co-operation Match Needs?', *European Journal of Development Research* 21/4: 662–74.

Witney, N. (2008), *Re-Energising Europe's Security and Defence Policy*, European Council on Foreign Relations (ECFR) Report, available on http://ecfr.eu/page/-/documents/ESDP-report.pdf

Witney, N. (2010), 'Too many cooks', *Global Europe*, 1 February, available on http://www.globeurope.com/standpoint/too-many-cooks

Wolfers, A. (1962), *Discord and Collaboration: Essays on International Politics* (Baltimore, MD: Johns Hopkins University Press).

Wong, R. (2005), 'The Europeanization of Foreign Policy', in C. Hill, and M. Smith (eds), *International Relations and the European Union* (Oxford: Oxford University Press), 134–53.

Wong, R. (2006), 'Foreign Policy', in P. Graziano, and M.P. Vink (eds), *Europeanization: New Research Agendas* (Basingstoke and New York: Palgrave Macmillan), 321–34.

Wong, R. (2008), 'France in East Asia', in M. Maclean, and J. Szarka (eds), *France on the World Stage* (Basingstoke and New York: Palgrave Macmillan), 57–76.

Wong, R., and Hill, C. (eds) (forthcoming 2011), *National and European Foreign Policies Towards Europeanization*.

Woods, N. (2005), 'The shifting politics of foreign aid', *International Affairs* 81/2: 393–409.

Woolcock, S. (1993), 'The European *Acquis* and Multilateral Trade Rules: Are they Compatible?', *Journal of Common Market Studies* 31/4: 539–58.

Woolcock, S. (2000), 'European Trade Policy: Global Pressures and Domestic Constraints', in H. Wallace, and W. Wallace (eds), *Policy-Making in the European Union*, 4th edn. (Oxford: Oxford University Press), 373–400.

Woolcock, S., and Hodges, M. (1996), 'EU Policy in the Uruguay Round: The Story behind the Headlines', in H. Wallace, and W. Wallace, W. (eds), *Policy-making in the European Union* (Oxford: Oxford University Press), 301–24.

World Commission on Sustainable Development (WCED) (1987), *Our Common Future* (Oxford: Oxford University Press).

Wouters, J., Basu, S., and Schunz, S. (2008), *Meeting the Challenges of a Multilateralized World? The "Multilaterability" of the European Union*, LCGGS Working Paper 13 (Leuven: Leuven Centre for Global Governance Studies).

Wurzel, R., and Connelly, C. (eds) (2010, forthcoming), *The European Union as a Leader in International Climate Change Politics* (Abingdon: Routledge).

Yamakawa, T., Swarnali, A., and Kelston, A. (2009), 'BRICs Lead the Global Recovery', *BRICs Monthly* 09/05.

Yergin, D. (2006), 'Ensuring Energy Security', *Foreign Affairs* 85/2: 69–76.

Young, A. (2000), 'The Adaptation of European Foreign Economic Policy: From Rome to Seattle', *Journal of Common Market Studies* 38/1: 93–116.

Young, A.R. (2002), *Extending European Cooperation: The European Union and the 'New' International Trade Agenda* (Manchester: Manchester University Press).

Young, A. R. (2007), 'Trade politics ain't what it used to be: the European Union in the Doha round', *Journal of Common Market Studies*, 45 (4): 789–811.

Youngs, R. (2001), *Democracy Promotion: the Case of European Strategy*, CEPS Working Paper No. 167, October (Brussels: Centre for European Policy Studies).

Youngs, R. (2002), *The European Union and the Promotion of Democracy: Europe's Mediterranean and Asian policies* (Oxford: Oxford University Press).

Youngs, R. (2007), *Europe's External Energy Policy: Between geopolitics and the Market*, CEPS Working Document No. 278, November (Brussels: Centre for European Policy Studies).

Zartman, I.W. (1976), 'Europe and Africa: Decolonization or Dependency?', *International Affairs* 54/2: 326–43.

Zhongping, F. (2008), 'A Chinese perspective on China–European relations', in G. Grevi, and A. de Vasconcelos (eds), *Partnership for effective multilateralism: EU relations with Brazil, China, India and Russia*, Chaillot Paper 109 (Paris: European Union Institute for Security Studies).

Ziegler, C.E. (2006), 'The Energy Factor in China's Foreign Policy', *Journal of Chinese Political Science* 11/1: 1–23.

Zielonka, J. (1998a), *Explaining Euro-Paralysis: Why Europe is Unable to Act in International Politics*. (Basingstoke: Palgrave Macmillan).

Zielonka, J. (ed.) (1998b), *Paradoxes of European Foreign Policy* (The Hague: Kluwer).

Zielonka, J. (1998c), 'Policies Without Strategy: The EU's Record in Eastern Europe', in J. Zielonka (ed.), *Paradoxes of European Foreign Policy* (The Hague: Kluwer).

Zielonka, J. (2006), *Europe as Empire: the Nature of the Enlarged European Union* (Oxford: Oxford University Press).

Zielonka, J. (2008), 'Europe as a Global Actor: Empire by Example', *International Affairs* 84/3: 471–84.

Zucconi, M. (1996), 'The European Union in the Former Yugoslavia', in A. Chayes, and A. Chayes (eds), *Preventing Conflict in the Post-Communist World: Mobilizing International and Regional Organizations* (Washington, DC: Brookings Institution).

Zurn, M. (2000), 'Democratic Governance Beyond the Nation-State: The EU and Other International Institutions', *European Journal of International Relations* 6/2: 183–221.

de Zwaan, J., and Goudappel, R. (eds) (2006), *Freedom, Security and Justice in the European Union: implementation of the Hague programme*, (The Hague: T. M. C. Asser Press).

INDEX